Comparative Law

Joshua Aston · Aditya Tomer · Rupendra Singh
Editors

Comparative Law

Unraveling Global Legal Systems

Springer

Editors
Joshua Aston
School of Business and Law
Edith Cowan University
Joondalup, WA, Australia

Aditya Tomer
Amity Law School
Amity University
Noida, Uttar Pradesh, India

Rupendra Singh
Amity Law School
Amity University
Noida, Uttar Pradesh, India

ISBN 978-981-97-7814-0 ISBN 978-981-97-7815-7 (eBook)
https://doi.org/10.1007/978-981-97-7815-7

This Springer imprint is published by the registered company Springer Nature Singapore Pte Ltd.
The registered company address is: 152 Beach Road, #21-01/04 Gateway East, Singapore 189721, Singapore

Foreword by Justice Ritu Raj Awasthi

It is with great pleasure and honour that I extend my heartfelt commendation to the editors, Joshua Aston, Aditya Tomer, and Rupendra Singh, along with all the esteemed contributors, for their remarkable endeavour in compiling this insightful volume, *Comparative Law—Unravelling Global Legal Systems*.

In an epoch marked by rapid globalization, the role of law transcends geographical boundaries, permeating every aspect of our interconnected world. As we navigate the complexities of an increasingly interdependent global society, the imperative to comprehend and analyse legal systems from a comparative perspective becomes indispensable. This book serves as a beacon, guiding scholars, practitioners, policymakers, and students alike through the intricate labyrinth of global legal frameworks.

The editors have adeptly crafted a collaborative mosaic that not only illuminates the nuances of diverse legal systems but also underscores the transformative power of comparative analysis. By juxtaposing legal principles and practices from various jurisdictions, this volume offers invaluable insights into the convergence, divergence, and evolution of legal norms across different cultural and institutional contexts.

The significance of such comparative methodologies cannot be overstated, particularly in today's dynamic landscape where legal challenges transcend national borders. From constitutional law to intellectual property rights, from corporate governance to emerging fields like technology law, each chapter delves into the multifaceted assortments of legal regimes, unravelling the complexities inherent in their formulation, interpretation, and application.

Moreover, this compendium serves as a testament to the collective wisdom and scholarly rigour of its contributors. Their diverse perspectives, grounded in empirical research and practical experience, enrich our understanding of the subtle interplay between law, society, and governance. By fostering a nuanced appreciation of legal pluralism and cultural diversity, this volume paves the way for a more inclusive and equitable global legal order.

As a Judicial Member of the Lokpal of India, I am acutely aware of the pivotal role that comparative law plays in fostering transparency, accountability, and justice. Throughout my previous professional tenures as well, I have witnessed first-hand the transformative potential of comparative legal analysis in shaping progressive legal reforms and policy interventions.

Therefore, I wholeheartedly endorse this seminal work and commend it to all those engaged in the pursuit of legal scholarship, policy formulation, and judicial decision-making. May this volume serve as a catalyst for deeper dialogue, collaboration, and mutual understanding among legal practitioners and scholars across the globe.

In conclusion, I extend my sincere thanks to Springer for providing a platform for the dissemination of knowledge and ideas that transcend borders and enrich our collective understanding of law and society. May this book inspire future generations to continue the noble quest for justice, equality, and the rule of law in an ever-changing world.

Hon'ble Justice Ritu Raj Awasthi
Chairperson of 22nd Law Commission
of India, New Delhi, India

Foreword by Justice A. H. M. D. Nawaz

The treatise, *Comparative Law: Unravelling Global Legal Systems*, comes as a refreshing breeze in the rarefied promenade of invaluable works on comparative law and its significant manifestations. Compiling an anthology of the diverse scope, methods, and perspectives of this specialized field of inquiry is indeed an arduous and prodigious task. The oeuvre, written by leading scholars and practitioners, in a lucid and luminous style, addresses the similarities and differences between legal systems and traditions, articulating the truism that a pluralistic methodology strengthens comparative law as a specialized discipline. The stimulatingly provocative work breaks new ground by situating comparative law within a larger context, presenting its insights through a series of essayistic explorations that delve into various thematic areas. The expansive scope of the edition covers a wide range, including comparative constitutional law, comparative business law, intellectual property, artificial Intelligence, environmental law and criminal law. The varied content in the tome demonstrates the extensive range of principles and doctrines that shape the comparative material, making the book a rich and valuable resource.

It is pertinent to observe that despite some trite arguments against the use of comparison in public law and leaving aside their force for a moment, perhaps the most striking area of comparative law's expansion over recent decade has been in the area of public law: specifically comparative constitutional law. It is heartening to observe the robust discourses on comparative constitutionalism in the book, affirming that comparative constitutional law has now become an established doctrine. Discussions of foreign legal material frequently feature in constitutional judgments across many jurisdictions. This is particularly notable in constitutional human rights jurisprudence in South Africa, Canada, India, and the EU and is increasingly observed in the USA. A recent Sri Lankan Supreme Court decision held a former president liable for infringing the fundamental human rights of the people. The court found that, as Minister of Public Security, he failed in his duties, contributing to the country's saddest tragedy, which was triggered by terrorist attacks on churches and worshippers. Drawing from comparative jurisprudence across multiple jurisdictions, the Sri Lankan Supreme Court referred to the president's omissions as constitutional torts.

This case exemplifies the global “explosion” in the use of comparative methods in constitutional law, particularly within the judiciary.

Given that institutions responsible for framing, interpreting, and applying legal principles and provisions often resort to transnational “borrowing”, an analytical justification of the processes is *de riguer* in contemporary legal scholarship. The volume *Comparative Law: Unravelling Global Legal Systems* provides that justification. There has also been a dramatic increase in the number of scholarly books and journals dedicated to this topic, and the learned edition in our hands contributes to the surge of interest in the ongoing dialogue on comparative law.

In the realm of comparative criminal law, it is often argued that there is a paucity of comparative material on selected topics such as punishment theory, victims, jurisdiction, the principle of legality, the analysis of criminal liability for new offences, and general principles of criminal liability. The book fulfils the long-felt need.

The monumental works of Thomas Macaulay and Sir James Fitzjames Stephen are shining examples of how laws can transcend borders, influencing various jurisdictions. I am hopeful that the diverse topics covered in this volume will similarly cross our porous borders, offering methodologies and inspiration for further reform and judicial creativity. It is not irrelevant to observe that the modern discipline of comparative law has developed a strong bias towards private law, which is often traced back to the 1990 Paris International Congress on Comparative Law-widely considered the birthplace of modern comparative law as an academic discipline. The programme was heavily weighted towards private law, and the conference was dominated by lawyers who were in search of some kind of a jus commune in the fields of private law. The prevailing concerns of harmonization by using comparative methods to discover universal legal concepts and principles were the underlying threads of that conference, and it is undeniable that the key aim of comparative law cannot be achieved unless a fair amalgam of the legal discourse focused on private law issues.

Accordingly, the locus classicus, *Comparative Law: Unravelling Global Legal Systems* aims to achieve a balance by addressing multifaceted aspects of public and private law in both civil and common law jurisdictions. It will undoubtedly serve as a vade mecum and lodestar in comparative legal studies. National legislatures, academics, and the judiciary are bound to benefit from this enthralling collection of thought-provoking and insightful articles, as comparative inspiration continues to be relevant beyond passport control.

His Lordship Justice A. H. M. D. Nawaz
Judge of the Supreme Court
Colombo, Sri Lanka

Preface

In an era defined by constant change, the influence of law and policy remains a vital force intricately interwoven into the very fabric of society. As globalization, internationalism, and democratization reshape our world, the imperative to comprehend the global legal landscape through a comparative lens has never been more pronounced. Comparative law, a swiftly evolving discipline within the legal realm, broadens our horizons, beckoning us to explore diverse cultural contexts and their unique implementations of legal principles. Through this exploration, we unearth a distinct opportunity to craft a robust legal framework conducive to societal flourishing.

This book embarks on a collaborative journey to unravel the complexities, dilemmas, and potential remedies found within the diverse tapestry of global legal systems. It adopts a distinctive approach, illuminating the intersections and divergences among these systems. Moreover, it serves as a gateway to delve into legal architectures across nations, offering comparative insights into their methodologies and approaches. Today, legal professionals spanning from lawyers to academics, lawmakers, and political and economic scientists are increasingly focused on comparative understanding, fostering the creation, interpretation, and operation of civil, criminal, political, economic, and social laws.

Our aim is to explore the intricacies of comparative methodologies in law and policy, spotlighting the challenges and opportunities inherent in the convergence and divergence of legal and policy paradigms. Drawing upon the expertise of scholars and practitioners worldwide, this book covers an array of topics, including constitutional law, criminal law, intellectual property rights, corporate law, and emerging fields such as technology law, including the regulation of AI and OTT platforms. Each chapter embarks on a comparative analysis, elucidating the factors that shape these frameworks and their societal implications.

Ultimately, we aspire to cultivate a deeper appreciation for the multifaceted nature of law and policy across diverse contexts. We envision this book as an invaluable resource for students, scholars, policymakers, and practitioners, fostering a nuanced understanding of the significance of comparative methodologies in the study of law and policy.

Joondalup, Australia Joshua Aston
Noida, India Aditya Tomer
Noida, India Rupendra Singh

Acknowledgements

This publication embarks on an exploration of the diverse dimensions of comparative law, aiming to foster a comprehensive understanding across various domains, including comparative aspects of constitutional law, criminal law, business law, and technology and intellectual property laws. The fruition of this endeavour owes much to the dedicated efforts of numerous individuals who have contributed to its success.

We extend our heartfelt appreciation to our esteemed colleagues whose invaluable assistance has been instrumental in shaping this book. Our sincere gratitude goes to Prof. Maryam Omari, Associate Professor Prafula Pearce, Dr. Jane Eyre Mathew, Dr. Abhinav Tomer, Dr. Pranav Tewari, Dr. Priyanka Ghai, Mr. Pratik Agarwal, and Ms. Ria Garg for their unwavering support throughout this journey. We also express our profound gratitude to all the authors whose significant contributions have brought this book to fruition.

We would like to extend our gratitude to Springer for their unwavering support to us for the publication of this book. We are extremely indebted to Mr. Ram Prasad Chandrashekar, Ms. Mamun Mishra, and Ms. Emily Wong from Springer for their ongoing support throughout the project.

Finally, we acknowledge with appreciation the support provided by our respective universities, which has been integral to the realization of this book on comparative law.

We trust that the book adequately addresses the requirements of individuals engaged in comparative legal study.

Contents

Editors and Contributors

About the Editors

Associate Professor (Dr.) Joshua Aston is the associate dean of Law and member of the Executive in the School of Business and Law, Edith Cowan University, since 2020. Prior to joining ECU, he served as the dean (SW) and officer on Special Duty to the director/vice chancellor of Gujarat National Law University, India. He has also held the role of Deputy Director at Symbiosis Law School, Symbiosis International University, India. In 2022, he was appointed Adjunct Associate Professor of Law at Amity University, India. Dr. Aston's remarkable academic achievements include being awarded the prestigious *Deutscher Akademischer Austauschdienst* (DAAD) scholarship from Germany which led to his invitation as a research scholar by the Institute of Air, Space, and Cyber Law at the University of Cologne, Germany. He is also recognized as an Asian Law Institute Fellow of the National University of Singapore, Singapore. In addition, he was honoured with the Israeli Government Scholarship, channelled through the Ministry of Human Resource Development, Government of India, and was invited as a research scholar by the Buchmann Faculty of Law at Tel Aviv University for a duration of eight months. Dr. Aston's commitment to community service is exemplified by his involvement as Board Member of the Joondalup Business Association. In this capacity, he plays an integral role in fostering the success and sustainability of the local business community in the City of Joondalup, Western Australia. He is the author of 11 books; some of the acclaimed text are *Trafficking of Women and Children, Article 7 of the Rome Statute* (2015) and *Torture Behind Bars: Role of the Police Force in India* (2020) both published by Oxford University Press.

Professor (Dr.) Aditya Tomer currently serves as Additional Director/Joint Head of Amity Law School, Noida, at Amity University. As an academic, he possesses a diverse range of interests spanning various disciplines. With over 60 publications, including books, monographs, research papers, and articles in both academic and popular publications, he is recognized as a prolific writer. Professor Tomer is deeply committed to research and has supervised numerous Ph.D. and LL.M. candidates in their studies. His research endeavours primarily focus on empirical and multidisciplinary approaches, particularly within the realms of Right to Information, Arbitration and Mediation, Human Rights, and Business Law. Under his leadership, the quality of journals such as the *Amity International Journal of Juridical Sciences, Journal of Multi-disciplinary Studies, Journal of Legal Studies and Research*, and *Ami Code 3-Newsletter of Law* has been significantly enhanced. Moreover, Prof. Tomer has played a pivotal role in advancing the Law School through the organization of various national and international conferences, workshops, panel discussions, moot court competitions, and legal aid initiatives, all of which enjoy a strong reputation within the academic community. He has also contributed to the examination systems, having served as a paper setter and evaluator for the Tripura State Public Service Commission and the UPSSC judicial exams. Additionally, Prof. Tomer is Life Member of the All-India Law Teachers Congress, further demonstrating his commitment to the legal education community.

Mr. Rupendra Singh holds a law degree from Bharti Vidyapeeth Deemed University, Pune, and a master's degree from the National Law University, specializing in Corporate Law. He has practised law at various levels, including the Supreme Court of India and other subordinate courts and commissions in Delhi. Currently, Mr. Singh serves as Assistant Professor of Law at Amity Law School, Noida, within Amity University. Prior to this role, he was a faculty member at the School of Law, Lovely Professional University. His primary areas of expertise encompass Comparative Technology Law, Corporate Law, and Intellectual Property Law. Mr. Singh boasts a substantial portfolio with over 30 publications, including books, chapters, research papers, and articles featured in nationally and internationally recognized magazines. In addition to his academic pursuits, he actively conducts training sessions for law students, focusing on moot court competitions, start-up ventures, and enhancing legal writing skills.

Contributors

Tanzim Afroz School of Business and Law, Edith Cowan University, Joondalup, Australia

Joshua Aston School of Business and Law, Edith Cowan University, Joondalup, WA, Australia

Ishan Atrey Integrated Programme in Law, Indian Institute of Management, Rohtak, India

Siddharth Balani National Law University, Jodhpur, India

Jyotirmoy Banerjee Integrated Programme in Law, Indian Institute of Management, Rohtak, India

Niharika Sahoo Bhattacharya Rajiv Gandhi School of Intellectual Property Law, IIT Kharagpur, Kharagpur, India

Dhriti Bole Disputes and Litigation, King Stubb and Kasiva, Bengaluru, India

Cecilia Anthony Das School of Business and Law, Edith Cowan University, Joondalup, WA, Australia

Kanika Dhingra National Law University, Jodhpur, India

Phil Glover School of Business and Law, Edith Cowan University, Joondalup, WA, Australia

Kanchal Gupta School of Law, UPES, Dehradun, India

Setu Gupta Amity Institute of Advanced Legal Studies, Amity University, Noida, Uttar Pradesh, India

Rupam Jagota Guru Nanak Dev University, Regional Campus, Jalandhar, India

Biju Joseph School of Law, Christ University, Bangalore, India

Arshi Pal Kaur Guru Nanak Dev University, Regional Campus, Gurdaspur, India

Komal Department of Law, Gurugram University, Gurugram, India

Nikos Koutras Curtin Law School, Curtin University, Perth, WA, Australia

Manish Kumar MKA Legal Law Offices, New Delhi, India

Rajesh Kumar School of Law, UPES, Dehradun, India

Jane Eyre Mathew Amity Law School, Noida, India

Pearl Monteiro V. M. Salgaocar College of Law, Panaji, India

B. Muthu Kumar Government Law College, Ramanathapuram, India

Mostafa Mahmud Naser School of Business and Law, Edith Cowan University, Joondalup, WA, Australia

Megha Ojha IILM Law School, IILM University, Gurugram, Haryana, India

Sakshi Parashar Symbiosis Law School, Symbiosis International (Deemed) University, Noida, India

Prafula Pearce School of Business and Law, Edith Cowan University, Joondalup, WA, Australia

Nuha Rahman Amity Law School Noida, Noida, India

Haydn Rigby School of Business and Law, Edith Cowan University, Joondalup, WA, Australia

Anna Ruf Faculty of Business Law, Hochschule Schmalkalden University of Applied Sciences, Schmalkalden, Thuringia, Germany

M. L. Shilpa School of Law, Christ University, Bangalore, India

Mayank Shrivastava Hidayatullah National Law University, Raipur, India

Rupendra Singh Amity Law School, Noida, India

Rituraj Sinha School of Law, CHRIST (Deemed to be University), Delhi NCR Campus, Ghaziabad, India

Clare Jing Ni Tai School of Business and Law, Edith Cowan University, Joondalup, WA, Australia

Vanessa Tay School of Business and Law, Edith Cowan University, Joondalup, WA, Australia

Apoorva Thakur MKA Legal Law Offices, New Delhi, India

Anindhya Tiwari Hidayatullah National Law University, Raipur, India

Abhinav Tomer Amity Law School Noida, Noida, India

Aditya Tomer Amity Law School, Noida, India

Mahima Tripathi Rajiv Gandhi School of Intellectual Property Law, IIT Kharagpur, Kharagpur, India

Showkat Ahmad Wani Assistant Professor, School of Law, Alliance University, Bengaluru, India

Ananya Yadav Amity Law School, Amity University Uttar Pradesh, Lucknow, India

J. P. Yadav Amity Law School, Amity University Uttar Pradesh, Lucknow, India

Kenneth Yin School of Business and Law, Edith Cowan University, Joondalup, WA, Australia

Abbreviations

ABC	Australian Broadcasting Corporation
ACL	Australian Consumer Law
AFM	Australian Fused Materials
AI	Artificial Intelligence
AIADMK	All India Anna Dravida Munnetra Kazhagam
AICC	All India Congress Committee
AIR	All India Reporter
AMC	Asset Management Company
AMLA	Anti-Money Laundering Act
ANC	African National Congress
ASIC	Australian Securities and Investments Commission
ASIS	Australian Security Intelligence Service
ASX	Australian Securities Exchange
ATC	Aviation Technical Consultants
ATO	Australian Tax Office
ATS	Alien Tort Statute
AUD	Australian Dollar
BBC	British Broadcasting Corporation
BD	Biological Diversity
BGB	Bürgerliches Gesetzbuch (Civil code of Germany)
BIA	Bureau of Immigration Affairs
BJP	Bhartiya Janata Party
BOP	Board of Probation
BTC	Bitcoin
BWDB	Bangladesh Water Development Board
CAGR	Compound Annual Growth Rate
CB	Cyber Bullying
CDC	Centre for Disease Control
CDM	Comprehensive Disaster Management
CDPP	Commonwealth Director of Public Prosecutions
CEMPBD	Coastal Environmental Management Plan for Bangladesh

CEP	Coastal Embankment Project
CER	Certified Emission Reduction
CGT	Capital Gains Tax
CII	Confederation of Indian Industry
CJI	Chief Justice of India
CMI	Continental Motors Inc
COP	Conference of Parties
COVID	Corona Virus Disease
CPFTA	Consumer Protection (Fair Trading) Act
CSA	Canadian Securities Administrators
CSDS	Center For the study of developing societies
CTCN	Climate Technology Centre and Network
CTF	Counter Terrorist Financing
Cth	Commonwealth
CWOF	Continued Without a Finding
CZM	Coastal Zone Management
DABUS	Device for the Autonomous Bootstrapping of Unified Sentience
DLA	Disability Living Allowance
DLT	Distributed Ledger Technology
DMK	Dravida Munnetra Kazhagam
DPIIT	Department for Promotion of Industry and Internal Trade
DPT	Digital Payment Token
DSPV	Digital Sexual Privacy Violation
E2EE	End to End Encryption
ECI	Election Commission of India
ECtHR	European Court of Human Rights
EGTT	Expert Group on Technology Transfer
EJC	Exclusive Jurisdiction Connection
EPZs	Export Processing Zones
ESCAP	Economic and Social Commission for Asia and Pacific
ESIC	Employees State Insurance Corporation
ESTS	Environmentally Sound Technologies
ETH	Ether
EU	European Union
FATF	Financial Action Task Force
FBI	Federal Bureau of Investigation
FCA	Financial Conduct Authority
FGM	Female Genital Mutilation
FINMA	Financial Market Supervisory Authority
FSA	Financial Services Agency
FTCA	Federal Trade Commission Act
GARA	General Aviation Revitalization Act
GATT	General Agreement on Tariffs and Trade
GCGF	Global Corporate Governance Forum
GDP	Gross Domestic Product

GDPR	General Data Protection Regulation
GHG	Greenhouse Gas
GIF	Graphics Interchange Format
GPCC	Goa Pradesh Congress Committee
GST	Goods and Services Tax
HIPPA	Health Insurance Portability and Accountability Act
IAMAI	Internet and Mobile Association of India
IBSA	Image-based Sexual Abuse
ICESCR	International Covenant on Economic, Social, and Cultural Rights
ICGN	International Corporate Governance Network
ICO	Initial Coin Offering
ICZM	Integrated Coastal Zone Management
IIS	Interactive Information System
ILO	International Labour Organization
INR	Indian Rupee
IPC	Indian Penal Code
IPCC	Intergovernmental Panel on Climate Change
IPR	Intellectual Property Rights
IRAC	Issue-Rule-Application-Conclusion
IT	Information Technology
JAM	Japan Abrasive Materials
JCERDC	Joint Clean Energy Research and Development Centre
LCE&W	Law Commission of England and Wales
LGBTIQA	Lesbian, Gay, Bisexual, Transgender Intersex, Queer/Questioning, Asexual
LLP	Limited Liability Partnership
LRCWA	Law Reform Commission of Western Australia
LULUCF	Land Use, Land Use Change, and Forestry
MAS	Monetary Authority of Singapore
MLA	Member of Legislative Assembly
MNC	Multinational Corporation
MP	Member of Parliament
MPSG	Membership of a Particular Social Group
MSME	Micro, Small, and Medium Enterprises
NAMA	Nationally Appropriate Mitigation Actions
NAPA	National Adaptation Plan of Action
NAV	Net Asset Value
NBFC	Non-Banking Financial Company
NCP	Nationalist Congress Party
NCPCR	National Commission for Protection of Child Rights
NCRWC	National Commission to Review the Working of the Constitution
NFT's	Non-Fungible Tokens
NGO	Non-Government Organization
OECD	Organizations for Economic Cooperation and Development
ONS	Office for National Statistics

PCPIP	Paris Convention for the Protection of Industrial Property
PCT	Patent Cooperation Treaty
PCU	Program Co-ordination Unit
PDS	Public Distribution System
PIP	Priority Investment Programme
PMK	Pattali Makkal Katchi
POA	Probation of Offenders Act
PSA	Payment Services Act
PSG	Particular Social Group
RBI	Reserve Bank of India
RBP's	Restrictive Business Practices
REDD	Reducing Emissions from Deforestation and Degradation
REIT	Real Estate Investment Trusts
RJD	Rashtriya Janata Dal
RPF	Railway Protection Force
RRPP	Registered Recognised Political Parties
RSC	Real and Substantial Connection
RUPP	Registered Unrecognized Political Parties
SA	South Australia
SABC	South African Broadcasting Corporation
SCC	Supreme Court Cases
SEBI	Securities and Exchange Board of India
SGX	Singapore Exchange
SICLD	Semiconductor Integrated Circuits Layout-Designs
SIPP	Startup Intellectual Property Protection
SLF	Schwartz Levitsky Feldman
SRO	Self-Regulatory Organization
SSC	Sexual Self-Concept
SSI	Supplemental Security Income
STLT	Singapore Treaty on the Law of Trademarks
TFSV	Technology-Facilitated Sexual Violence
TM	Trademark
TPA	Transfer of Property Act
TRIPs	Trade-Related Aspects of Intellectual Property
TSX	Toronto Stock Exchange
TTAB	Trademark Trial Appeal Board
UDHR	Universal Declaration of Human Rights
UK	United Kingdom
UN	United Nations
UNCED	United Nations Conference Environment and Development
UNCRC	United Nations Convention on the Rights of the Child
UNCTAD	United Nations Conference on Trade and Development
UNEP	United Nations Environment Programme
UNFCCC	United Nations Framework Convention on Climate Change
UNHCR	United Nations High Commissioner for Refugees

UNICEF	United Nations International Children's Emergency Fund
UR	Uruguay Round
US	United States
USD	United States Dollar
VDA	Virtual Digital Asset
VPN	Virtual Private Networks
WA	Western Australia
WHO	World Health Organization
WIPO	World Intellectual Property Organization
WTO	World Trade Organization
YSRCP	Yuvajana Shramika Rythu Congress Party

Aristotle is Long Dead But His Wisdom Rules Us from the Grave: A Comparison of the Application of Logic in Legal Reasoning in Common Law and Civil Law Systems

Anna Ruf and Kenneth Yin

Abstract 'Logic' is a science that deals with the principles and criteria of the validity of inferences and demonstration, or the formal principles of reasoning. It is said that the specific task of logic as a branch of knowledge is to study the forms of a valid argument and it has been posited that any study of legal reasoning is an attempt to expiscate and explain the criteria as to what constitutes a good or a bad, or an acceptable or an unacceptable, type of legal argument. A syllogism is defined as 'a formal argument in logic that is formed by two statements and a conclusion which must be true if the two statements are true'. The syllogism is regarded as the logical and analytical framework for legal reasoning in the common law tradition. Aristotle's contribution to logic, in particular his theory of syllogism, has been regarded as having an unparalleled influence on Western thought. This chapter analyses the veracity of the theory of syllogism as the framework for reasoning in common law reasoning and compares these outcomes to a civil law system, adopting Germany as an exemplar of the latter.

Keywords Legal education · *Stare decisis* · Comparative law · Legal reasoning

A. Ruf
Faculty of Business Law, Hochschule Schmalkalden University of Applied Sciences, Schmalkalden, Thuringia, Germany
e-mail: ruf.a@gmx.net

K. Yin (✉)
School of Business and Law, Edith Cowan University, Joondalup, WA, Australia
e-mail: k.yin@ecu.edu.au

J. Aston et al. (eds.), *Comparative Law*, https://doi.org/10.1007/978-981-97-7815-7_1

1 Part I—Introduction

Logic has been explained as 'a science that deals with the principles and criteria of validity of inferences and demonstration: the science of the formal principles of reasoning'.[1] *MacCormick* said that '[t]he specific task of logic as a branch of knowledge … is to study the forms of a valid argument'[2] and that '[a]ny study of legal reasoning is … an attempt to expiscate and explain the criteria as to what constitutes a good or a bad, and acceptable or an unacceptable type of argument in the law'.[3]

In a common law system, syllogism is the logical and analytical framework for legal reasoning. *MacCormick*, who wrote a seminal text on the role of syllogism in common law reasoning[4] asked himself the question 'why then insist on the syllogism at all', to which he responded: 'the answer should be obvious, it provides the framework in which the other arguments make sense as legal arguments.'[5]

A lay definition of 'syllogism' is 'a formal argument in logic that is formed by two statements and a conclusion which must be true if the two statements are true'.[6] The meaning of 'syllogism', adopted in a book written for advocates,[7] is very similar: that it is 'a statement of logical relationship'[8] which 'typically has three parts', namely:[9]

- the *major premise*—usually a broad statement of general applicability;
- the *minor premise*—usually a narrower statement of particular applicability that is related in some way to the major premise; and
- the *conclusion*—the logical consequence of the major and minor premises.

The 'Socrates' syllogism, so well-known it is described eponymously,[10] illustrates the framework of a syllogism:

Major premise: All men are mortal.
Minor premise: Socrates is a man.
Conclusion: Therefore, Socrates is mortal.

---

[1] Merriam-Webster, 'Merriam-Webster') <https://www.merriam-webster.com/dictionary/syllogism>.

[2] Neil MacCormick, *Legal Reasoning and Legal Theory* (Oxford University Press, 2003) 24.

[3] Ibid 11.

[4] Neil MacCormick, *Rhetoric and the Rule of Law—A Theory of Legal Reasoning* (Oxford University Press, 2005).

[5] Ibid 42.

[6] .*The Britannica Dictionary*: <https://www.britannica.com/dictionary/syllogism#:~:text=Britannica%20Dictionary%20definition%20of%20SYLLOGISM,therefore%20all%20men%20are%20mortal.%E2%80%9D>.

[7] James Gardner, *The Structure and Language of Effective Advocacy* (LexisNexis, 2nd ed, 2007).

[8] Ibid 3.

[9] Ibid.

[10] Eg as in *Merriam Webster* <http://www.merriam-webster.com/dictionary/syllogism>.

Gardner argued that '[e]very good legal argument is cast in the form of a syllogism'.[11] This proposition will be relatively straightforward to establish in the context of the common law. The greater challenge, addressed in this chapter, is to establish the veracity of this proposition in the case of a civil law system, of which Germany has been selected as an exemplar.

2 Part 2—The Role of Case Law

Generally, both systems are shaped by their legal framework, which determines the interaction and correlation between case law and legislation.[12] In both the civil law and common law systems, statute law is the source of the law legitimately created by the state, but in a civil law system, the entirety of the law is considered to be comprised in a generalised codification.[13] This does not preclude case law from having a role in judicial decision making, although case law in a civil law system plays a different role from that in a common law system. An in-depth comparison of the common law and civil law systems cannot be covered; rather, this chapter is confined to a more nuanced comparative study of the specific role of logic in the legal reasoning process in common law and civil legal systems, respectively, and the role of case law within.

As a prelude to the more nuanced discussion of the role of 'logic' to follow, an attempt will be made to clarify the role of case law in both systems.

To start with, the legal framework in the German civil law system is *supplemented by* case law, whilst in a common law system, case law is *'ahead of'* and not *'alongside'* legislation.[14]

As a result of the constitutional struggle between the Sovereign and the House of Commons in seventeenth-century England, Parliament was accorded supremacy.[15] This is the genesis of the idea that in a common law country, statute law has paramountcy over case law in the sense that it is always open for Parliament to change laws by legislating.[16] But a lawyer in a common law country will understand that this is far from saying that case law is in any sense 'inferior' to statute law. As one author explains:[17]

[11] Gardner (n **7**) 8.

[12] Birke Häcker, 'Die Rolle der Rechtsprechung im Zivilrecht: Eine rechtsvergleichende Etüde ' [The Role of Case Law in Civil Law: A Copmarative Law Exercise]' [10] (2023) 1 *Zeitschrift für Europäisches Privatrecht [Journal of European Private Law]* 10, 40.

[13] Ugo Mattei and Luca G Pes, 'Civil Law and Common Law: Toward Convergence?' in Gregory A Caldeira, R Daniel Kelemen and Keith E Whittington (eds), *The Oxford Handbook of Law and Politics* (Oxford University Press, 2008) 267, 273.

[14] Häcker (n **12**) 41.

[15] Robin Creyke et al., *Laying Down the Law* (LexisNexis Butterworths, 10th ed, 2018) 288.

[16] Ibid.

[17] Chris Turner, Jo Boylan-Kemp and Jacqueline Martin, *Unlocking Legal Learning* (Taylor & Francis Group, 3rd ed, 2012) 118.

> Parliament is the supreme law maker and statute law takes precedence over case law, Judges...play an important role in developing and applying the law through the doctrine of precedent. They also though have a major role in relation to statute law. This is because, whereas the common law is based on individual principles arising from specific factual circumstances, statute law is essentially theoretical. Parliament states what the law is, but not necessarily how to apply it in factual circumstances. Even where statutes state the law in fairly explicit terms the law still needs to be understood before it can be applied. Since drafters of Acts are likely to engage in some fairly technical legal language the whole process of interpretation comes into play where the law in a particular case comes from statute.

Accordingly, in a common law system, the interpretation of a statute reflected in case law itself becomes an authority on that point because of the workings of the doctrine of precedent. Lawyers in common law jurisdictions will be familiar with the doctrine of *stare decisis;* fundamentally, *stare decisis* obliges common law courts, when faced with a case with similar facts and issues, to follow previous decisions made by higher courts in the same court hierarchy[18] and for lower courts to have limited discretion to depart from previous decisions if called on to apply them to the case before them.[19]

Thus, case law (precedents) is the *de facto* primary repository of the law in a common law system.[20] Despite the paramountcy of statute law, the law in a common law system is still very much *determined by* case law.[21]

Although the law in Germany, a civil law system, is codified, case law nevertheless strongly influences the legal reasoning process.[22] German legislative authority has consciously refrained from attempting an all-encompassing definition or explanation of the content of statute, with the intention that the latter should be furnished by case law.[23] When parts of a statute/code cannot be readily understood without an explanation of their workings, these explanations are comprised in relevant case law.[24] The legislature might also respond by developing legal principles which themselves are subsequently incorporated by the legislation within the existing legal framework (code).[25] Case law is thereby ultimately integrated into the legal framework of a civil law system.[26] Consequently, case law functions not only to substantiate the codified law but can also fill in any hiatus in the law.[27]

Thus far, it can be seen that case law in both common law and civil jurisdictions shares a role in explaining the nuances of statute law where need be. The judicial

---

[18] Rachel Field, James Duffy and Anna Huggins, *Lawyering and Positive Professional Identities* (LexisNexis Butterworths, 1st ed, 2014) 409.

[19] Creyke et al. (n **15**) 152.

[20] Mattei and Pes (n **13**) 273.

[21] Generally see Häcker (n **12**).

[22] Franz Reimer, *Juristische Methodenlehre [Legal Methodology]* (Nomos, 2nd ed, 2019) 31 [22].

[23] Häcker (n **12**) 22.

[24] Reimer (n **22**).

[25] Häcker (n **12**) 22.

[26] Ibid.

[27] Ibid 14.

treatment of case law nevertheless varies very significantly between the two legal systems.

It is recounted that in a common law system, common law courts, consistent with the doctrine of precedent, when faced with a case with similar facts and issues, are obliged to follow previous decisions made by higher courts in the same court hierarchy and lower courts have limited discretion to depart from previous decisions.[28]

To the contrary of a judge in a common law system, a judge in Germany is not obliged to follow precedent. In fact, their independence is guaranteed under *The Basic Law for the Federal Republic of Germany* (as translated from the German language).[29] This judicial independence remains, however 'subject only to the law'.[30] In Germany, in common with civil law jurisdictions, the code binds the legislative and executive,[31] and judicial decision making accordingly remains constrained by the parameters of the relevant code.[32] Nonetheless, judges of lower courts are *guided* by well-established decisions in case law established by higher courts as well as the leading opinions in literature and thus case law has a factual, but not necessarily a legally binding effect.[33]

Also, a statute/code cannot completely provide all necessary information to consequently bind a judge to the law.[34] Therefore, courts are generally permitted to develop the law. According to the German Federal Constitutional Court:[35]

> [t]he task of adjudication may require […] values which […] have not or only imperfectly been expressed in the texts […] of the laws, in an act of evaluative cognition, which also does not lack volitional elements, […] to be realized in decisions. The judge must refrain from arbitrariness, his decision must be based on rational argumentation. It must be made clear that the law does not fulfill its function […]. [The judge] closes this gap according to the standards of practical reason and the well-founded general ideas of justice of the community.

A judge in Germany might develop the law through: (1) *interpretation* (where the legal practitioner determines the meaning of an unclear legal provision on the basis

---

[28] Above, (nn **18 and 19**).

[29] 'Judges shall be independent and subject only to the law:': *Grundgesetz für die Bundesrepublik Deutschland [Basic Law for the Federal Republic of Germany] 1949* Art 97(1) ('*Grundgesetz für die Bundesrepublik Deutschland [Basic Law for the Federal Republic of Germany]*').

[30] Ibid.

[31] Jurgen Kuhling and Oliver Leith, 'Dogmatik als leitender Parameter der Rechtsgewinnung im Gemeinschaftsrecht' [Dogmatism as the Leading Parameter in the Creation of Precedent in the European Community Law]' [371] (2003) 3 *Europarecht* 371, 374. See also Roman Herzog et al. (eds), *Grundgesetz-Kommentar [Basic Law Commentary* (CH Beck, 2023) Vol 6, Art 97 GG[26].

[32] Häcker (n **12.**) 16.

[33] Ruth Blufarb, *Geschichte im Recht–Übertragung von 'Law as Narrative 'auf die deutsche Rechtsordnung [History in Law–Transfer of 'Law as Narrative' to the German Legal System]* (Nomos 2017) vol 3, 362.

[34] Winfried Hassemer, 'Gesetzesbindung und Methodenlehre' [The Rule of Law and Methodology]' [213] (2007) *Zeitschrift für Rechtspolitik* 213, 215.

[35] *Bundesverfassungsgericht [German Constitutional Court]* (1973) 34 BVerfGE 269, 287 ('*Bundesverfassungsgericht [German Constitutional Court]*').

of the wording, the legislative history systematic position and the intended purpose of the purpose of the norm), (2) *analogy* (where gaps in the regulations are filled by extending/comparing the reasoning in a regulated case to an unregulated case whose circumstances are comparable to the regulated case) and (3) determination of law *praeter legem* (a judge independently develops legal principles in an unregulated case by way of judgement). Particularly in labour law or administrative law such determinations are often subsequently codified.[36]

A judge might also *concretise* the law by defining hitherto undefined legal concepts such as 'good faith' or 'undue hardship' through a judgement to make them accessible for a specific case.[37]

The interrelationship between case law and statute in a common law jurisdiction and a civil law jurisdiction, respectively, is usefully distilled as follows:[38]

> [O]ne could observe as to the common law, that should all the statutes be abolished overnight there still would be a viable legal system, since all the general doctrines that can be used for principled application of the law to the multiple facts of life are all judge-made and contained in case law. To the contrary, should the case law be repealed in common law jurisdictions, statutes would not offer a coherent and principled body of law to apply. In the civil law, the opposite holds true. The abolition of codes would leave the system in total disarray, while the ban on utilizing all published case law would be all but irrelevant.

Consequently, case law does play an integral role in the legal reasoning process but within the German civil law system, a reasoned judgement only has effect between the parties to the dispute.[39] On the contrary, the doctrine of *stare decisis* demands that common law courts to follow previous decisions made by higher courts in the same court hierarchy.[40]

3 Part 3: Legal Reasoning Methodologies

The role of logic within legal reasoning was introduced at the outset[41] including the proposition that 'every good legal argument is cast in the form of a syllogism', a view expressed by a commentator in a common law jurisdiction.[42]

Part 2 comprised a discussion of the role of case law within the common law and civil law systems. As a prelude to the present discussion, it is recounted that two observations arose following that discussion, which can be broadly distilled as follows: *first,* case law plays an integral role in both common law and civil law jurisdictions. *Second,* the treatment of case law in a common law system differs to

[36] Blufarb (n **33**) 361.

[37] Ibid.

[38] Mattei and Pes (n **13**) 273–4.

[39] 'Blufarb (n **33**) 362.

[40] Above, (nn **18, 19**).

[41] Above, (nn **3, 4 and 5**).

[42] Above, (n **11**).

that in a civil law system because, as required by the doctrine of *stare decisis,* case law in a common law system is treated as having the force of precedent, whilst in a civil law system, the decision is only binding between the parties to the dispute.

Against this background, the methods for identification and interpretation of law necessarily differ in the different legal systems.[43] The methodologies of identifying and interpreting the law in the common law and the civil law system of Germany will be explained and contrasted; the substantive discussion will commence with a summary of the common law position, followed by the position in civil jurisdiction, again adopting Germany as an exemplar.

A. *Legal Reasoning in the Common Law*

Legal reasoning is often taught in law schools in common law countries using a format known as IRAC,[44] an acronym for Issue-Rule-Application-Conclusion. The terms in the acronym are:[45]

- The 'Issue' ('I') is, at its most fundamental, simply the problem to be solved.
- The 'Rule' ('R') is the principle of law relevant to the problem to be solved.
- The 'Application' ('A') is the application of the rule (or principle of law) to the facts of the legal problem.
- The 'Conclusion' ('C') is a conclusion reached as to the legal outcome of the problem.

The idea that IRAC is the legal variant of a syllogism has been often expressed.[46] Nedzel explained that the legal 'rule' (the R in the acronym) corresponds to the major premise (first premise), the application (the 'A' in the acronym) the minor premise (second premise), from which is derived the 'conclusion'[47] (the 'C' in the acronym).

Given the likely greater familiarity of the reader with IRAC rather than 'syllogism', having established that IRAC fundamentally is the legal variant of syllogism, the language of 'IRAC' rather than syllogism will be adopted for the purposes of the discussion in this part.

Since the 'issue' (the 'I' in the IRAC acronym) is the legal problem that needs to be solved,[48] it necessarily determines the course of the analysis.[49] 'An 'issue' is the type of question that establishes the parameters of an IRAC, and not just *any* kind

---

[43] Eg see Reimer (n **22**) 34[26].

[44] Nickolas James, 'Good Practice Guide (Bachelor Of Laws) Thinking Skills (Threshold Learning Outcome 3)' (Pt Australian Teaching and Learning Council) (2010), 11.

[45] Ibid.

[46] Bradley Clary and Pamela Lysaght, *Successful Legal Analysis and Writing: The Fundamentals* (Thomson/West, St. Paul, MN, 3rd ed, 2010) 84. See also Kenneth Yin and Anibeth Desierto, *Legal Problem Solving and Syllogistic Analysis: A Guide for Foundation Law Students* (LexisNexis Butterworths, 1st ed, 2016) 120 [6.9].

[47] Nadia Nedzel, *Legal Reasoning, Research And Writing for Intenational Graduate Students* (Wolters Kluwer, United States, 3 ed, 2012) 69.

[48] Clary and Lysaght (n **46**) 84. See also Yin and Desierto (n **46**) 120 [6.9].

[49] Yin and Desierto (n **46**) 120 [6.90].

of 'issue' or question'.[50] An issue is a legal issue if it can be addressed within the IRAC vessel, and not any 'problem' that might arise along the way, since within the IRAC vessel, the legal rule is applied to the facts to derive the 'conclusion'.[51]

Nedzel stated that knowledge of the applicable law is necessary to identify an issue, pointing out that:[52]

> [l]earning how to spot and state a legal issue is a complex task … Therefore, although issue is the first word in IRAC, as a practical matter an attorney must usually understand the applicable rule first, before refining her understanding of exactly how to phrase the client's issue'.

Thus, in common law reasoning, in the first place, every legal proposition sought to be relied on must be supported by an 'authority'[53] which in a common law jurisdiction must derive from primary sources of law, case law and legislation.[54]

Aristotle propounded, within his theory of syllogism, that induction is the 'argument from the particular to the universal'.[55] The major premise, the 'R' in the IRAC acronym, is the statement and explanation of the applicable law.[56] It serves as the blueprint for the analysis, performed in the 'application', the minor premise.[57]

As Aldisert explained, inductive reasoning 'undergirds the doctrine of precedent or *stare decisis* as like things must be treated like'.[58] *Boland* similarly stated that inductive generalisation was the way one could 'synthesize a number of cases to form a rule based *on the issue presented'*.[59] What both these statements mean is that the process of creating the rule is not just a statement of the law in the abstract but that it is the process of recognising the principles relevant to the issue at hand, and then formulating a general rule that would be applicable to those circumstances.

The rule accordingly must '[i]nstantiate the universals and prove events and facts that substantiate the alleged particular as instances of the universals [the general 'Rule', the 'R' in the IRAC acronym].'[60] The 'Rule' thus is not limited to the statement of a stark principle in case law but the factual grounding, reasons, and rationale for them.[61] This is needed so that the facts contained in the 'grounding' can then be explored in the process of working out similarities and differences between the

---

[50] Ibid 121 [6.10].

[51] Ibid 121 [6.12].

[52] Nedzel (n **47**) 122.

[53] Yin and Desierto (n 46) 3 [1.8].

[54] Ibid 14 [2.22].

[55] Robin Smith, 'Aristotle's Logic', *The Stanford Encyclopaedia of Philosophy (Web Page, 22. November 2022) [3.1]* <https://plato.stanford.edu/archives/win2022/entries/aristotle-logic/>.

[56] See e.g. Nedzel (n **47**) 69.

[57] Yin and Desierto (n **46**) 101 [5.25].

[58] Ruggiero Aldisert, *Logic For Lawyers: A Guide to Clear Legal Thinking* (National Institute for Trial Advocacy, 3rd ed, 1997) 89–90.

[59] James M. Boland, 'Legal Writing Programs and Professionalism: Legal Writing Professors Can Join the Academic Club' (2005) 18 *St. Thomas Law Review* 712, 723.

[60] MacCormick, *Rhetoric and the Rule of Law—A Theory of Legal Reasoning* (n **4**) 38.

[61] Gardner (n **7**) 28.

facts and circumstances of case law and those of the case at hand to determine if the findings in relevant case law (reflected in the Rule) should apply to the facts and circumstances of the case between the parties.[62]

Before proceeding, a key concept discussed at length earlier should be constantly borne in mind, that the 'rule' (the major premise in the language of syllogism) is formulated from case law, which, consistent with the doctrine of precedent, is binding;[63] this concept largely underpins common law legal reasoning methodologies.

The focus will now shift to the process of deduction, or 'application' (the 'A' in the IRAC acronym.

For the purposes of this chapter, a nuanced and restricted view is adopted of the meaning of 'deduction', within the context of 'legal reasoning', namely that 'deduction; is '[t]he application of the rule to the specific facts of the particular situation'.[64] Within the minor premise, this process takes place when the rule is 'tested' against the facts.[65]

The process of deduction is not like ticking off boxes or a laundry list.[66] Nor is it a 'fact versus fact' comparison.[67] The process of common law reasoning demands an explanation of why a case is important and how it is connected to the rule.[68] Put another way, the arguments must be created in context of the case (facts) and not by restating the legal principles.[69] Accordingly, by pointing out similarities and differences between the issue at hand and the facts of the case law from which the rule is derived from, arguments need to be made as to why the ruling of the case law should be applied or distinguished.[70] As Levi stated, 'finding similarities and differences is the key step in the legal process and the function of each judge'.[71]

Lord Goff of Chieveley explained:[72]

> [T]he historical fact that common lawyers have been reared on a diet of case law has had a profound effect on our judicial method. Common lawyers tend to proceed by analogy, moving gradually from case to case. We tend to avoid large, abstract, generalisations, preferring limited, temporary, formulations, the principles gradually emerging from concrete cases as they are decided. In other words, we tend to reason upwards from the facts of the cases before us … The result is that we tend to think of each case as having a relatively limited effect, a base for future operations as the law develops forwards from case to case …'.

---

[62] Ie as Nedzel explained, it is "developed into the analogical thinking that underlies the application portion of common law legal reasoning [the minor premise]': Nedzel (n **47**) 72.

[63] Above, (nn **20, 21**).

[64] Nedzel (n **47**) 70.

[65] Yin and Desierto (n **46**) 15 [2.26].

[66] Nedzel (n **47**) 88.

[67] Yin and Desierto (n **46**) 98 [5.14].

[68] Nedzel (n **47**) 88.

[69] Yin and Desierto (n 46) 56 [4.11].

[70] Ibid 62 [4.,33].

[71] Ibid.

[72] Lord Goff of Chieveley, 'The Future of the Common Law' (1997) 46 *The International & Comparative Law Quarterly* 745, 753. See also Häcker (n **12**) 20.

The conclusion to a syllogism is defined as '[t]he logical consequence of the major and minor premises'.[73] A syllogistic conclusion could range from a simple 'yes' or 'no'[74] to saying 'on balance I would conclude'.[75] Generally, the syllogistic conclusion 'requires looking at the context of the problem and the analysis'.[76] The conclusion, broadly, is the outcome of the legal analysis, as explained by Clary and Lysaght:[77]

> 'In the legal context, the major premise is the rule; the minor premise consists of the facts, and the resolution, the *'therefore'* is the conclusion.'

Schnee stated that the conclusion of the latest case then becomes 'one more case for future induction'.[78]

The entire legal reasoning process in a common law system is underpinned by the paramountcy of the legal principle contained in cases. The process of induction identifies the legal principle relevant to the circumstances at hand, a process reflected in the syllogistic major premise, or Rule. These are then applied, as part of the process of deduction, within the syllogistic minor premise, or the Application. The conclusion, reflecting the outcome, then becomes one more case for future induction, and the process then begins again when applied to the next case.

At this point, attention can conveniently be turned to the next part of our discussion, legal reasoning in a civil law system, keeping an eye constantly on the role of logic within this process.

B. *Legal Reasoning in Germany*

The term 'civil law' in a comparative law context is somewhat ambiguous. As *Häcker* points out, in its *literal* meaning 'civil law' in German means 'private law', which, besides *public law* is one of the two major areas of law comprising the German legal system.[79] On the other hand, besides its literal meaning, 'civil law' is commonly used instead of 'private law' to refer to the '*law tradition*' (legal system) of continental Europe.[80]

Public law is the law governing the relationship between an individual and the public authority (the government, federal states, local authorities and non-departmental public bodies) as well as between public authorities themselves.[81] This includes amongst others, administrative and criminal law, although the latter

[73] Gardner (n **7**) 3.

[74] Yin and Desierto (n **46**) 157.

[75] Ibid.

[76] Clary and Lysaght (n **46**) 91.

[77] Ibid.

[78] Anita Schnee, 'Logical Reasoning "Obviously"' (1997) 3 *Legal Writing: The Journal of the Legal Writing Institute* 105, 118.

[79] Häcker (n **12**) 11.

[80] Ibid.

[81] Horst Pötzsch, 'Horst Pötzsch, 'Rechtssystem' [legal system], Bundeszentrale für politische Bildung [Federal Agency for Civic Education]') <https://www.bpb.de/themen/politisches-system/deutsche-demokratie/39392/rechtssystem/>.

is recognised as a separate area of law.[82] To the contrary, *private law* determines the correlation between individual persons and includes labour law, commercial and corporate law, securities law and copyright law.[83]

The distinction between public law and private law has a significant effect on the focus of the analysis. Although an in-depth analysis of each area of law is beyond the focus of this chapter, a brief introduction is provided in the second half of this part after a generalised explanation.

1. *The methodology for legal reasoning in Germany*

The methodology used for legal problem-solving in Germany is termed *Gutachtenstil*, whose literal translation is 'appraisal style'.[84] A more compendious explanation of *Gutachstenstil* is 'how the legal analysis is structured' or 'a structure for the analysis'. The *Gutachten* is the German term given to the outcome of the reasoning process. Literally, *Gutachten* means 'opinion'.[85] A more compendious English explanation of the *Gutachten* is that it is 'the outcome of the legal analysis'.

The *Gutachten* (opinion/outcome) is the outcome of a process of analysis within a multi-levelled structure.[86] The analysis in each layer/level is conducted in four steps namely:

(1) **Obersatz:** What needs to be solved?
(2) **Precondition(s)/Definition(s):** What needs to be satisfied?
(3) **Subsumption:** Testing of the definitions against the facts.
(4) **Conclusion:** Answer to the question stated in the *Obersatz.*

The fundamental logical framework within the *Gutachten* can dissected as follows: Questions are expressed through an *Obersatz*, which are abstractly answered through definitions and the tangible application of the facts is conducted in the subsumption whilst the conclusion is the logical answer/outcome to the question articulated in the Obersatz.[87]

The application of the law must be thought of as a 'chain consisting of syllogisms.[88] Most fundamentally, the *Gutachtenstil* is the application of these four steps.[89] Although the analysis at each level is conducted through the four steps

---

[82] Stefan Holzer et al., *Öffentliches Recht—Staatsrecht und Europarecht [Public Law—Constitutional Law and European Law]* (Schäffer-Poeschel, 3rd Revised Ed ed, 2023) vol 18, 27.

[83] Ibid.

[84] The Cambridge German-English Online Dictionary: https://dictionary.cambridge.org/translate/.

[85] Ibid.

[86] Lothar Bunn and Gabriel Kacik, *Deutsch als Fremdsprache für Jurist:innen—Gutachtentechnik und Gutachtenstil: Lehr- und Lernmaterialien zum Zivilrecht, Strafrecht und Öffentlichen Recht [German as a foreign language for lawyers—Gutachtenstil and Gutachtentechnik: educational- and learning materials for civil law, criminal law and public law] Vol 3* (Waxmann, 2022) vol 3, 178.

[87] Tina Hildebrand, *Juristischer Gutachtenstil [Judicial Reasoning and Conclusions]* (A Franke, 3rd Rev Ed ed, 2017) 6.

[88] Ibid. Also Reimer (n **22**) 41 [40].

[89] Wolfgang Wohlers, Jan C Schuhr and Hans Kudlich, *Klausuren und Hausarbeiten im Strafrecht [Exams and academic papers in criminal law]* (Nomos, 6th ed, 2020) 17.

set out above, the structure of the analysis within each step varies from level to level and the two areas of law (public and private).

Aligned with the title of this chapter, the focal point of this part is to investigate how legal analysis is structured in a German legal system and to compare this with its treatment in a common law system.

Several variables affect the structure of the analysis, the most significant of which is the area of law. Generally, there are different basic types or 'patterns' of a *Gutachten* in civil law, criminal law and administrative law. However, these 'basic patterns' themselves attract variations that affect the structure of the analysis and thus the *Gutachten* itself. To address all variations would be beyond this chapter as each layer/level of the *Gutachten* is interconnected and would cause unnecessary complexity. However, a general introduction to the fundamentals of the structure of the *Gutachten* will be provided as a prelude to the analysis to follow:

The following figure illustrates the fundamental relationship and movement between each level of analysis on a general basis. The colour coding is to assist with identifying the level of the analysis (Fig. 1).

The *first* level (highlighted in green) establishes the overall framework for the analysis.[90]

At its broadest, the *Obersatz* generally is the hypothesis that needs to be verified/analysed, and which states what attracts the analysis,[91] and thus is broadly equivalent to the 'I' (for issue) in IRAC. Thus, an *Obersatz* might address (1) the element(s) of a provision (i.e. do the facts meet the precondition(s) of the named provision?) or (2) raises the 'question' whether the facts meet the definition, with the latter being the most used 'type' of *Obersatz* within the *Gutachten.*[92]

Within the *first* level, the *Obersatz* is also referred to as the 'introductory sentence'[93] and might be understood by a common lawyer as equivalent to the overarching question between the parties, or the broad 'issue', the 'I' in the IRAC acronym; however, the *Obsersatz* is generally expressed as a statement, not a question.[94]

As there are two different levels within the *Gutachten,* the *Obersatz* at each level too is expressed differently.[95] There are also potentially several sub-levels of the second level, represented by the red shapes within the above figure.

The *Obersatz* at the *second* level (and any subsequent *sub-levels*) identifies what needs to be analysed. Each precondition, stated at the *first* level, attracts a separate *Obersatz* at the second level, which subsequently might in turn attract analysis at different sub-levels, depicted broadly by the shapes shaded in red in the above figure.

The creation of what could broadly be characterised as the syllogistic major premise, in other words, the principles that would govern the case (the 'R' in the IRAC

[90] Bunn and Kacik (n **86**) 178.

[91] Hildebrand (n **87**) 12.

[92] Ibid 12–13.

[93] Jan Michael Salobir, 'Juristischer Gutachten und Urteilsstil [Legal opinion and judgment style]' (Pt Fakultät für Kommunikation und Umwelt, Hochschule Rhein-Waal), 2.

[94] Hildebrand (n **87**) 12.

[95] Ibid 12–13.

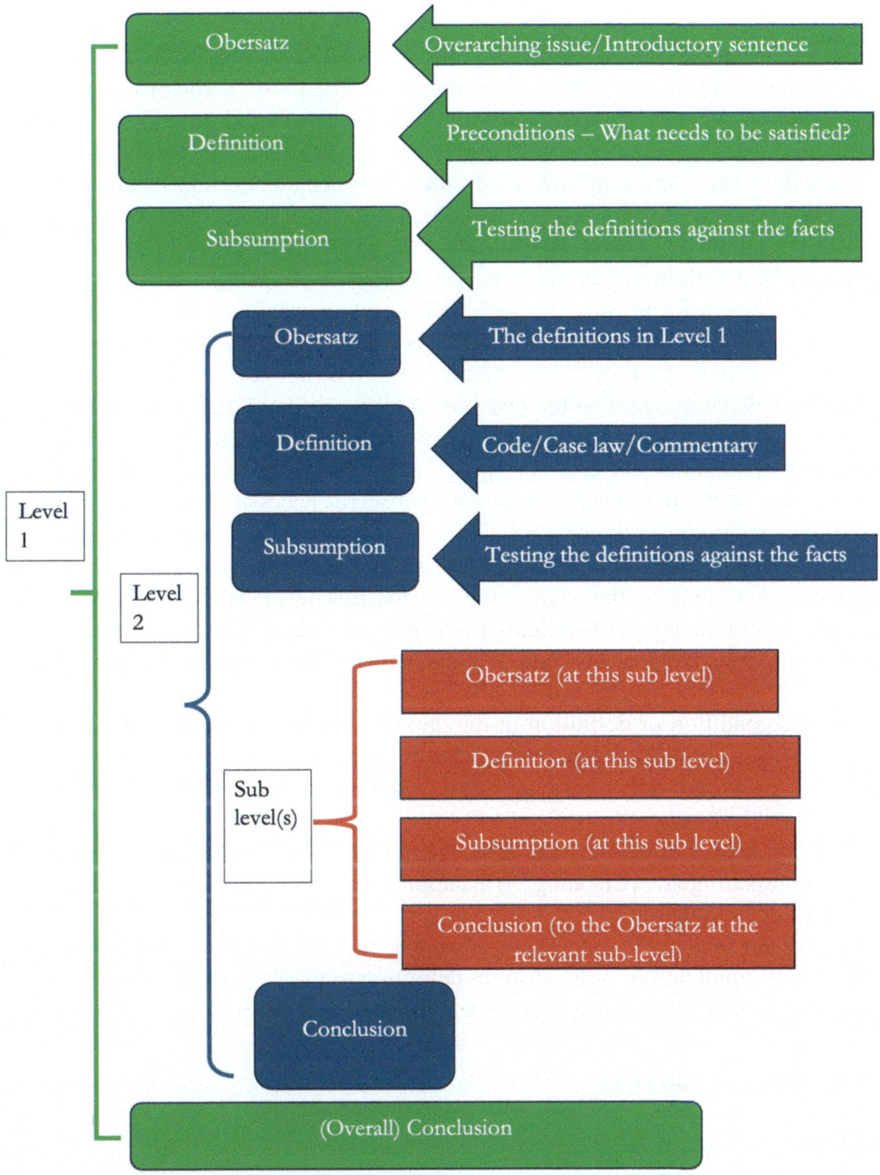

Fig. 1 The Gutachten and Gutachtenstil—the basics for legal reasoning

acronym), differs from common law reasoning.[96] The German civil law works with definitions instead of rules. Definitions generally are abstract criteria/standards.[97] As with the major premise or rule section (the 'R' in the IRAC acronym), definitions *never* contain facts of the case.[98] *Lüdeking* and *Samari* stated, relevantly: 'A definition breaks down a term into its characteristics; one could say that the definition analyses the term (similar to how a substance is broken down into its components in a chemical analysis)'.[99] By this reasoning, all the definitions (preconditions) are mandatory and must be satisfied.

Generally, a definition can either be (1) a definition/explanation of a characteristic of an element for instance through a different provision within the code or an otherwise developed definition, or (2) the preconditions of a provision (the preconditions are the 'definitions').[100] However, what is to be defined and at which level of particularity depends again on the *Obersatz* under consideration.[101]

At this first level, 'definitions' do not derive from the code but fundamentally are the overall or fundamental elements which are to be the outcomes of the analysis (the *Obersatz* at the first level). These are themselves necessarily dependent on the area of law under consideration.

It is recounted that the *Obersatz* at the *second* level is circumscribed (i.e. the issues are identified) by the 'definitions' in the first level. Within the sub-levels, these preconditions are *further* defined. Where not defined by law the definitions might be developed by case law, commentary, law professors, textbooks, or academic essays.[102]

Each precondition or definition in the law is addressed within a separate syllogism.[103] This is broadly comparable to what is termed as 'step analysis' in common law IRAC legal reasoning where 'the court or statute says first, do this; next do this; finally do this'.[104]

Attention is now directed to the minor premise, or the 'application' which is, in common law syllogistic reasoning, '[t]he application of the rule to the specific facts of the particular situation'.[105]

We recount that in German legal reasoning, the 'subsumption' broadly can be treated as the application of the abstract definition to the facts of the case.[106] Legal terms are defined to attract a certain legal consequence which occurs when the

---

[96] Yin and Desierto (n **46**) 14.

[97] Hildebrand (n **87**) 18.

[98] Ibid 23.

[99] Matthias Lüdeking and Sima Samari, "'Subsumption ohne Definition' '[Subsumption Without Definition]' (2022) 4 *Zeitschrift für die gesamte Privatrechtswissenschaft* 425, 428.

[100] Hildebrand (n **87**) 18–19.

[101] Ibid 18–19.

[102] Ibid.

[103] Ibid 5.

[104] Gardner (n **7**) 3. See also Yin and Desierto (n **46**) 148–9.

[105] Nedzel (n **47**) 70, See also Yin and Desierto (n **46**) 70.

[106] Hildebrand (n **88**) 26.

elements of a provision are met.[107] The subsumption therefore is the appraisal of whether the facts of the case fulfil a definition.[108] Thus, 'when applying the law, definitions have the task of preparing the subsumption'.[109] The minor premise/ application in common law reasoning can thus be characterised as closely equivalent to the 'subsumption' in legal reasoning in a German legal system such that within an *Obersatz,* the reasoning is essentially syllogistic, as is the case with the 'application' in common law reasoning.

That said, the differences in 'application' in common law reasoning and its equivalent in German legal reasoning, the process of 'subsumption', are significant. Mattei and Pes[110] stated that civil law lawyers tend 'to reason downwards from abstract principles embodied in a code.' Therefore, contrary to the common law, the reasoning extrapolates from the general to the particular or in other words from the general code (law) to the circumstances of the case at hand.[111] This is somewhat different to the use of case law in common law legal reasoning (where legal reasoning is performed by an explicit comparison of the similarities and differences with the facts and circumstances of case law) but rather is 'inferred', using the statute/code as the foundation of the reasoning.[112]

Reasoning in German law is based on an application of deduction.[113] To illustrate, as one author described the process, if T stands for the elements that need to be satisfied (preconditions of a provision or a definition of a legal term) and S for the facts of the case, the subsumption generally is articulated as follows:

[107] Lüdeking and Samari (n **99**) 426.

[108] Ibid.

[109] Ibid 430.

[110] Chieveley (n **72**) 653. See also Häcker (n **12**) 20, where the author cites His Lordship.

[111] Hildebrand (n **87**) 5.

[112] Ibid 37.

[113] Blufarb (n **33**) 357.

T is completely characterized by the features M_1, M_2, and M_3. [Definition/ precondition].
S has the characteristics M_1, M_2, and M_3. [Subsumption].
Therefore, S is a case of T [the 'Conclusion'].[114]

Blufarb described the application of the law as a 'search process' in which legal norms and the facts of the case influence each other.[115] It has been said to be vital to establish a concrete case reference (reference to the facts of the case) by extracting concrete facts/conditions from the scenario and show why in the concrete case the abstract definition is met.[116] In German legal reasoning, a significant error is to simply repeat the facts or substitute the subsumption through a simple statement that the condition is met.[117] The common lawyer will recognise that this would be described as committing the fallacy of 'begging the question.'[118] A missing connection to the case cannot be mended or saved by saying that a definition is 'obviously', 'clearly' or 'doubtlessly' met as strong words do not absolve the need to perform a case-oriented and content-related argumentation.[119]

In German legal reasoning, the subsumption within the *first level* (the 'application' of the content of the 'definition' at this level) does not exhaustively conclude the reasoning process. It is recounted that the *Obersatz* at the *second level* is circumscribed by the definitions in level 1 and that at the second level, the preconditions identified at level 1 are further defined. The question of whether the cause of action is satisfied is thus performed within this second level of analysis, as illustrated by the red-shaded shapes in the above figure. If necessary abstract definitions need to be further dissected (i.e. subsumed in further definitions) until they fit the case or are in disconformity with the relevant definitions or preconditions.[120] The analysis at each level nevertheless must remain in conformity with the fundamental structure of: *Obersatz*, definition, subsumption and conclusion.[121] Each element (definition) thereby can confidently be said to attract a separate syllogism.

As with common law reasoning, the structure of the analysis must be always adjusted to the concrete facts of the case at hand.[122] The judicial officer will generally focus on the relevant points, namely those which contribute to ultimate resolution of the main issue(s). Some 'steps', if considered not to be relevant or are peripheral and

---

114 Lüdeking and Samari (n **99**) 427.

115 Blufarb (n **33**) 357.

116 Wohlers, Schuhr and Kudlich (n **89**).

117 Ibid.

118 Aldisert (n **58**) 46.

119 Wohlers, Schuhr and Kudlich (n **116**) 24.

120 Hildebrand (n **87**) 29.

121 Lothan Bunn and Gabriel Kacik, *Deutsch als Fremdsprache für Jurist:innen—Gutachtentechnik und Gutachtenstil: Lehr- und Lernmaterialien zum Zivilrecht, Strafrecht und Öffentlichen Recht [German as a foreign language for lawyers—Gutachtenstil and Gutachtentechnik: educational- and learning materials for civil law, criminal law and public law]* (Waxmann) 172.

122 Ibid. 173.

which do not contribute to the resolution of the main issue, might be truncated.[123] In short, where the elements of the provision need to be shown but the facts are clear and their reasoning and conclusion therefore is evident, a de facto omission of reasoning can be made by a direct inclusion in the subsumption through a statement that an element/definition is met and a short reason(s) why.[124] On the other hand, where a longer and deeper analysis of an element is necessary or the facts are unclear, in so far as a definition might or might not apply, all four steps need to be conducted in-depth.[125]

Furthermore, where the circumstances (facts of the case) are far removed from ordinary cases, the application may not be that easy to manage. The plain wording of the law (definition) might not in such cases suffice to provide rules and guidance as to whether the term (definition) still applies.[126] As *Austin* points out '[o]rdinary language breaks down in extraordinary cases'.[127] However, there is no room for 'gut feeling'[128] so the judicial officer will reference the relevant case law and opinion(s) in the relevant literature.[129] '

However, as we recount, case law in Germany does not have precedential value as in a common law system but does nevertheless 'inform' as judges, who due to their independence, guaranteed under the *Basic Rules for the Federal Republic of Germany,* are free to make their own determinations.[130]

Attention is now directed to the 'conclusion'.

Axiomatically, the conclusion is drawn based on what has been said before.[131] Fundamentally, before the next element is analysed, the result (conclusion) of the current/prior analysis needs to be stated.[132] German legal reasoning does not countenance an indefinite answer (e.g. 'maybe') but the question raised in the *Obersatz* must be answered 'yes' or 'no'.[133] This obviously does not necessarily mean that the answer is one that is a 'positive' outcome to one side or a 'negative' to the other, merely that the outcome must be expressed as an affirmative (i.e. when the precondition is met) or a negation, when it is not.

At the second level, each precondition or definition in turn attracts its own conclusion. The overall conclusion to the analysis at the first level sets out the overall conclusion, namely the question raised in the first *Obersatz*, which, it is recounted, enlivens the overarching question.

[123] Ibid.

[124] Wohlers, Schuhr and Kudlich (n) 27.

[125] Ibid.

[126] Lüdeking and Samari (n **99**) 434,

[127] Ibid quoting J L Austin, 'The Meaning of a Word' in J O Urmson and G J Warnock (eds), Philosophical Papers (Oxford University Press, 3rd ed, 1979) 55, 68.

[128] Hildebrand (n **88.**) 18.

[129] Salobir (n **97**) 1.

[130] See above, nn (**22 - 26**).

[131] Hildebrand (n **88**) 34.

[132] Wohlers, Schuhr and Kudlich (n **116**) 26.

[133] Hildebrand (n **88**) 33.

Attention is now directed to the differences in the content and structure of the *Gutachten,* which might vary depending on whether the issue is one of public or private law.

Depending on the area of law under consideration (*public law* or *private law*) the ‘overarching issue’ or ‘question’ and thus the *Obersatz* at the first level has a different objective, and, consequently, the overall focus of the analysis might take on a different direction.

Importantly, unlike the common law, in German law, an action in civil law cases (literal meaning of ‘civil law’) is based strictly on establishing a *claim,*[134] defined as ‘[t]he right to demand that another person does or refrains from an act’.[135] Whether somebody can demand something from another person depends on the claimant having a legal basis (governed by the relevant statutory provision/code) addressing the claimed legal consequence.[136] The latter consists of (1) the preconditions that need to be met and (2) the legal consequence if they are.[137]

Accordingly, identifying the relevant legal basis for a claim within the relevant code is a crucial aspect of legal analysis in civil law cases.[138] In *public law,* the ‘overarching issue’ of the *Gutachten* depends on whether it is a criminal law or administrative law case. Importantly, in public law (here excluding criminal law) the distinction between several main areas of law (i.e. administrative law, constitutional law and European law) must be recognised as each of these attracts a different structure/’pattern’ for the analysis.[139]

The objective of an *Obersatz* at the first level in an *administrative* law case is government actions (laws, prohibitions, etc.). Here the two most asked questions (‘issues’) are 1) whether a legal remedy has a chance to succeed or 2) whether a government action was lawfully conducted.[140]

In a *criminal law* case, the usual ‘overarching issue’ is that of criminal liability under a specific criminal provision due to certain behaviour.[141] The latter is contained in the ‘*Special Part*’[142] of the German Criminal Code (§§ 80 ff.).

Focusing on the *Obersatz* within the first level for a *civil law* case (outlined in green in the above figure) enquiry *must* be directed to the question of whether the adjudication of the case could result in certain legal consequence.[143] The ‘four Ws’

---

[134] Häcker (n **12**) 39.

[135] *Bürgerliches Gesetzbuch [Civil Code]* S 194(1) (‘*Bürgerliches Gesetzbuch [Civil Code]*’).

[136] Brian Valerius, *Einführung in den Gutachtenstil: 15 Klausuren zum Bürgerlichen Recht, Strafrecht und Öffentlichen Recht [Introduction into the Report Style: 15 Exams for Civil Law, Criminal Law and Public Law]* (Springer, 2005) 2.

[137] Bunn and Kacik (n **86**) 178.

[138] Valerius (n **136**) 2.

[139] Bunn and Kacik (n 86)

[140] Hildebrand (n **87**) 117.

[141] Ibid 101. See also Wohlers, Schuhr and Kudlich (n **116**) 20.

[142] This is a term of art—see generally https://www.gesetze-im-internet.de/englisch_stgb/index.html (the official English translation).

[143] Bunn and Kacik (n **86**) 191.

(depicted by the first green arrow in the above figure) in a civil law case which must here be addressed are as follows: '*who* wants *what* from *whom* on *which* legal basis'.[144] In that context 'who' is the claimant, 'wants what' is what the clients wants to achieve (the content of the claim), 'from whom' is the person against whom the claim is asserted (defendant) and 'on which legal basis' is the provision or provisions setting out the legal consequence.

In a *criminal law* case, the 'four Ws' in the *Obersatz* are varied to contain the following elements: (1) offender, (2) act, (3) criminal offence and (4) provision.[145] The '*offender*' is the person whose act/behaviour is going to be analysed, the '*act*' is the short description of the behaviour of the person in question, as necessary including special conditions or circumstances under which it occurred, the '*criminal offence*' the offence under the criminal code, and the '*criminal provision*' the provision of the criminal code setting out the offence.[146]

The mandatory content for the *Obersatz* at level one in an *administrative law* case are: (1) which exact government action is in question, (2) who tries to enforce which remedy and (3) what is the authorisation (legal basis) that the action was based on.[147]

It is recounted that in the *Obersatz* at the first level, the definitions are somewhat predetermined. Each *Gutachten* must pay attention to the specific *Prüfungsaufbau* for the particular area of law.[148] The literal English translation of the German term '*Prüfungsaufbau*' is 'exam structure' but this does not give expression to the actual (legal) meaning of the term. A more compendious description would be that it is the 'fundamental' or 'underlaying overall structure of the analysis'. A common lawyer might think of these as 'basic elements' that need to be established.

In civil law cases, this is whether the claim was (1) '*acquired*', (2) '*not lost*' and (3) '*enforceable*'. Whether the claim was '*acquired*' applies a somewhat literal translation from the German language[149]—though a lawyer from a common law jurisdiction might better understand 'acquired' to mean 'whether the claim is successfully made out or not'.

The process of induction at the sub-level (enlivening the element of 'acquired') is determined by the set structure created by the preconditions of the legal basis of the claim.[150] Elaborating, at the sub-level the 'definition' comprises all the preconditions (written and unwritten) of the legal basis of the claim,[151] i.e. all the definitions (preconditions) are mandatory and must be satisfied. The element '*not lost*', despite its literal understanding, enlivens the question of whether the claim has been 'transferred' or 'extinguished', which is a somewhat imperfect attempt to re-express the

---

[144] Valerius (n **136**) 2.

[145] Wohlers, Schuhr and Kudlich (n **116**) 20.

[146] Ibid.

[147] Hildebrand (n **87**) 117.

[148] Bunn and Kacik (n **86**) 179.

[149] Hildebrand (n **87**) 109. See also Bunn and Kacik (n **86**) 130–131.

[150] Lars S Otto, *Gutachtenstil und juristische Methoden [Opinion and Commentary on judical methodology]* (Springer, 2012) 8.

[151] Ibid.

legal term *rechtsvernichtende Einrede* which means, literally 'defence destroying rights'. This might take place in several ways within the BGB, namely i.e.: (1) Performance (§ 362fBGB), (2) set-off (§ 389 BGB), rescission (§ 346 BGB) and (4) impossibility [Exclusion of the duty of performance] (§ 275 BGB).[152]

Where none of these cases apply, the last element—which can be widely understood as the last of a three staged test—'*enforceable*'—is where questions such as (1) limitation (§§ 194 ff.BGB) or (2) rights of retention (§§ 273, 320 BGB) could be taken into consideration.[153]

Claims in *civil law* are also structured by categories or 'hierarchy', namely: (1) contractual, (2) semi-contractual, (3) claim in rem, (4) torts and (5) unjust enrichment.[154] A detailed description cannot be conveniently explored, but the hierarchy is important as each claim (objective of the claim) must be examined separately following the above structure (hierarchy).[155]

A *criminal offence* at the first level also consists of three major elements: (1) the '*elements of the crime*', (2) '*illegality*' and (3) '*fault*'.[156] However, these might be varied in cases such as an offence of negligence, an offence of omission or an attempted offence.[157] The '*elements of the crime*' are as stated in the relevant legal provision. '*Illegality*' is the assessment of possible justification for the crime such as consent, whereas 'fault' or '*guilt*' enlivens the question whether an unlawful act on the facts of the case can be established.[158] Importantly, the elements of the crime must *all* be analysed regardless of their possible lapse due to illegality (justifications) or guilt (grounds for exemption).[159]

In a *criminal law* case, at the *second* level, the three major elements (now each enlivened in a separate *Obersatz*) are further defined although again by a set structure. The '*elements of the crime*' are sub-divided into two further elements: (1) the objective elements and (2) the subjective elements of the offence. The former is met if the offender meets all preconditions of the provision of the offence (legal basis) whilst the latter is satisfied if the offender intentionally—meaning knowingly and intentionally—incorporated the objective elements of the crime in his/her conduct.[160] Importantly, each individual offence must be examined separately for each person.[161]

---

[152] Bunn and Kacik (n **86**) 131.

[153] Hildebrand (n **87**) 98.

[154] Ibid 110. See also Bunn and Kacik (n **86**) 128.

[155] Bunn and Kacik (n **86**) 128,

[156] Wohlers, Schuhr and Kudlich (n **116**) 78; See also Bunn and Kacik (n **86**) 138–139.

[157] Bunn and Kacik (n **86**) 139, note 2, referring to p 5 of Rule 1.1.6.

[158] Karl Heinz Gössel, *Strafrecht—Mit Anleitungen zur Fallbearbeitungen und zur Subsumption [Criminal Law—With Tutorials for Case Processing and Subsumption]* (C F Muller, 8th Rev Ed ed, 2001) 16.

[159] Ibid.

[160] Bunn and Kacik (n **86**)142.

[161] Ibid 137.

In *administrative law*, the legitimacy of measures taken by the acting authority is examined.[162] These might be either an action against a citizen or another state body.[163] The legal remedy might be an objection, a constitutional complaint, or some other type of action.[164] The type of procedure (action being sought) depends on the applicant's request, i.e. the legal consequence sought by the applicant.[165] In-depth distinctions cannot be conveniently covered and this paper will explore a somewhat broader overview of the methodology of taking actions within the parameters of administrative action.

The variants that apply to the above analysis depend upon the question/action (remedy) being sought.[166]

The first consideration is whether a legal remedy has a prospect of succeeding.[167] This consideration is, for example, enlivened when an action for annulment (a type of lawsuit) is filed.[168] Here the two major elements (at level 1) are the examination of (1) the *admissibility* and (2) the *merits of the application*.[169]

The former is concerned with whether the action brought before the court is admissible based on formal criteria, i.e. the competent court or right applicant.[170] The latter is the assessment of the lawfulness of the government action.[171] The second variation applies when the question is whether a government action in form of an *administrative act*, which is defined as '… any order, decision or other sovereign measure taken by an authority to regulate an individual case in the field of public law and which is intended to have a direct external legal effect',[172] was lawfully conducted.[173] This comprises three major elements at the *first level*: (1) the 'authorisation basis', (2) the formal lawfulness and (3) material lawfulness[174] to be explored further below.

The 'authorisation basis' is the question whether there exists an authorisation for the acting authority.[175] The concept of formal lawfulness generally covers the formal process and criteria of issuing an *administrative act* whilst the concept of material

---

[162] Ibid 142.

[163] Hildebrand (n **87**) 116.

[164] Ibid 118.

[165] Ibid 119.

[166] Bunn and Kacik (n **86**) 142.

[167] Hildebrand (n **87**) 117.

[168] Ibid.

[169] Ibid 119.

[170] Ibid 116.

[171] Ibid 119.

[172] *Verwaltungsverfahresgesetz [Administrative Procedure Act] (Germany)* § 35 S. 1 ('*Verwaltungsverfahresgesetz [Administrative Procedure Act] (Germany)*').

[173] Bunn and Kacik (n **86**) 142.

[174] Ibid 143–145.

[175] Ibid 143.

lawfulness is focused on the act in issue itself.[176] Those elements are again further analysed at the second level and their sub-levels.[177]

For the purposes of enlivening the comparisons between common law and the German legal system, this is as far as the discussion concerning administrative law actions can conveniently be covered.

4 Part 4—Conclusion

Aristotle's contribution to logic was his theory of syllogism. This short chapter has probed the extent to which classical syllogistic reasoning, consisting of a major premise, minor premise and a conclusion, finds expression in the common law and German legal systems.

With the common law, the answer is explicit, as there is much commentary which supports the view that every good legal argument is in the form of a syllogism,[178] and, consistently, that IRAC, the conventional legal problem-solving structure in common law reasoning, is the legal variant of a syllogism.[179]

There are significant differences between the German style of legal reasoning and legal reasoning in the common law. These include the different roles of case law in the respective legal systems. In common law countries, case law has precedential value and the principles in case law underpin the doctrine of precedents or *stare decisis.* Germany is a civil law system and, in common with such systems, the provisions of the code underpin legal reasoning.

These differences find expression in issue identification and the treatment of the major premise. The German legal framework is defined by generalised codifications. Case law does have a role to play, as the principles contained in them might assist the judicial officer with the reasoning process where the code provisions are not clear cut, but case law does not have the precedential weight as in a common law system. In civil law, an issue of the major premise is determined by a provision (legal basis) within a code not by precedent and analogy, and this dictates the course of the analysis. The analysis follows a prescribed 'scheme' of preconditions and definitions.

The deductive process, which in syllogism finds expression in the minor premise, is the application of the facts of the case at hand to the law. In the common law, as case law has precedential weight, the judicial officer compares similarities and differences to the facts of case law.

In the German system, the minor premise or subsumption uses a chain of syllogisms. The 'preconditions' identified at the first level described above then govern the identification of the 'issue' and the resolution of the *Obersatz,* which sets out the issue at the second level. The governing code remains at the forefront of the deductive

---

176 Ibid 143–4.

177 See further eg ibid 143–5.

178 Above, (n **11**).

179 Above, (n **46**).

process as those preconditions might be further refined and defined at subsequent levels. Significantly different to the common law is that in common law the German judicial officer will reason upwards not downwards as in civil law as the enquiry is directed to the question of whether the abstract principles outlined in the code will fit the facts of the case. Principles in case law and supplementary resources might assist the judicial officer to clarify ambiguity and uncertainty, but at all times the question of the conformity or disconformity with the code is at the forefront of their reasoning process. The guaranteed independence of the judicial officer further ensures that he is not constrained by precedent in this exercise.

Although the reasoning process in the ultimate *Gutachten* is different from the methodologies in the common law, in both systems the conclusion is the logical result of major and minor premise. The conclusion to this paper reprises its title: the syllogism, which was Aristotle's contribution to logic, continues to rule the way we reason, both in ommon law and civil law.

Legal, Ethical, and Social Ramifications of the Use of Artificial Intelligence in Decision-Making: A Comparative Analysis of the European Union and Indian Law

Megha Ojha

Abstract Artificial Intelligence (AI) is one of the most essential and rapidly evolving emerging technologies. Transformational changes through AI in the future may see a significant improvement in global conditions. In contemporary legal discourse, many practical issues are intractable to address with the most powerful supercomputers, and the use of AI may give a chance to tackle such problems and challenges effectively. AI can emulate processes to develop medicine, and material design, accelerate development, and offer a new level of information security and communication. These are just a few of the advantages of AI, but AI may also be misused, and thus it may create risks. Presently, in most countries, there are no guidelines concerning the use of AI in human decision-making, so in the absence of any guidelines and/or effective laws, it would be challenging to provide appropriate relief if any dispute arises. The present research analyzes the legal, ethical, and social complications and discusses the advantages and disadvantages of the use of AI in human decision-making. The study proposes practical ways by which certain checks and balances might be incorporated into law for adjudicating matters concerning AI. The research suggests legal frameworks by comparing and analyzing Indian and European Union (EU) laws to direct governance and policy responses vis-a-vis AI.

Keywords Artificial intelligence (AI) · AI and law · AI in decision-making · Legal complications · Legal framework

1 Introduction

Since the invention of the digital computer, it has been demonstrated that computers can do highly complicated tasks with remarkable proficiency and that AI computers can be utilized in decision-making. Artificial intelligence is the simulation of human

M. Ojha (✉)
IILM Law School, IILM University, Gurugram, Haryana, India
e-mail: megha.ojha@iilm.edu

J. Aston et al. (eds.), *Comparative Law*, https://doi.org/10.1007/978-981-97-7815-7_2

intelligence processes by technology, particularly computer systems. AI applications include expert systems, natural language processing, speech recognition, and machine vision (Jake, 2022).[1] AI is widespread in our lives, from discovering proofs for mathematical theorems, playing chess, scanning emails, and receiving music, movies, and shopping recommendations. AI's primary goal is to streamline routine procedures and increase their speed and effectiveness, provided they have been implemented and supported correctly. AI approaches can provide a self-adaptive and highly reliable decision-making process in unpredictable conditions.[2] AI can appear in many different ways. The main goal of AI is to replicate and then outperform human perception and response.[3] It's quickly taking over as the foundation for innovation. AI can assist by offering more in-depth knowledge of the enormous amount of data and using predictions to automate overly complex or repetitive tasks. According to the Harvard Business Review, businesses are mainly utilizing AI to: identify and prevent security intrusions, address users' technological problems, cut back on production management tasks, and check internal compliance by hiring authorized vendors.[4] AI enables individuals to complete things more quickly, effectively, and make judgments more intelligently. The potential of AI for transformation is surprising. Moreover, with the advanced use of AI, people are expected to work together more closely and efficiently.[5] Nevertheless, several success stories have demonstrated AI's value, yet, some difficulties exist with using AI in human decision-making (Borgesius, 2018).[6]

[1] Jake Frankenfield, *Artificial Intelligence: What It Is and How It Is Used*, INVESTOPEDIA (2023), https://www.investopedia.com/terms/a/artificial-intelligence-ai.asp (last visited May 12, 2023).

[2] Amine Belhadi, Sachin Kamble, Samuel Fosso Wamba & Maciel M. Queiroz, *Building supply-chain resilience: an artificial intelligence-based technique and decision-making framework,* 60, IJPR, 4487, 4489–4490 (2021), https://www.tandfonline.com/doi/full/10.1080/00207543.2021.1950935 (last visited Feb 21, 2023).

[3] Andrej Novák, Daniel Bennett, Tomáš Kliestik, *Product Decision-Making Information Systems, Real-Time Sensor Networks, and Artificial Intelligence-driven Big Data Analytics in Sustainable Industry 4.0*, 2, EMFA, 62, 64 (2022), https://www.ceeol.com/search/article-detail?id=963242 (last visited March 27, 2023).

[4] Satyam Ramaswamy, Technology And Analytics, How Companies Are Already Using AI, HARWARD BUSINESS REVIEW (2017), https://hbr.org/2017/04/how-companies-are-already-using-ai (last visited Jan. 27, 2023).

[5] Harry Surden, *Artificial Intelligence and Law: An Overview,* 35, GSULR, 19, 21 (2019), https://heinonline.org/HOL/LandingPage?handle=hein.journals/gslr35&div=59&id=&page= (last visited Jan. 27, 2023).

[6] F.Zuiderveen Borgesius, *Discrimination, artificial intelligence, and algorithmic decision-making* (2018), https://dare.uva.nl/search?identifier=7bdabff5-c1d9-484f-81f2-e469e03e2360 (last visited Sept. 17, 2023).

2 Background

2.1 Definition of AI and Its Use in Decision-Making

A scientific field known as artificial intelligence (AI) simulates human decision-making processes. AI refers to a group of computer systems that can perceive their surroundings, reason, acquire new skills, and behave according to their goals. AI is the ability of a digital computer or computer-controlled robot to execute tasks often associated with intelligent beings.[7] The process and the ability to think with superhuman faculties are considerably more essential to AI. The term AI usually refers to constructing systems endowed with human-like cognitive functions, such as the ability to reason, discern meaning, generalize, or learn from past experience.[8] The majority of these artificial intelligence systems use machine learning, while others use deep learning, rules, and instructions. More importantly, despite significant advances in computer computational efficiency and memory capacity, there is currently a demand for initiatives that can supplement human adaptability across broader fields of study or operations.

2.2 Understanding the Use of AI in Business

Artificial intelligence has been identified as a source of business innovation. In contrast to the industrial revolution, which replaced muscles with mechanical engines and diesel-powered mechanized physical labor, the AI-powered course focuses on automating mental processes. AI streamlines business operations by lowering costs and improving consistency, speed, and scalability. AI is exaggerating almost every business and profession; however, some are being affected more quickly and deeply than others. The user experience and productivity can be significantly enhanced and increased for companies by incorporating AI into their current business processes and applications.[9] The superhuman skills of AI are transforming many occupations altogether, enhancing and, in some cases, replacing their human office co-workers by performing specific tasks. According to the PWC report, in 2030, AI might contribute

---

[7] Paolo Contardo, Emanuele Di Lorenzo, Nicola Falcionelli, Aldo Franco Dragoni, Paolo Sernani, *Analyzing the impact of police mugshots in face verification for crime investigations, IEEE International Conference on Metrology for Extended Reality, Artificial Intelligence and Neural Engineering* 236–241, *MetroXRAINE* (Nov. 17, 2022), https://ieeexplore.ieee.org/abstract/document/8821442/citations#citations (last visited Oct. 27, 2023).

[8] B. J. Copeland, *Artificial Intelligence*, BRITANNICA (2023) https://www.britannica.com/technology/artificial-intelligence (last visited Oct. 13, 2023).

[9] Anna Trunk, Hendrik Birkel & Evi Hartmann, *On the current state of combining human and artificial intelligence for strategic organizational decision making,* 13, BUSINESS RESEARCH, 875, 879 (2020), https://link.springer.com/article/10.1007/s40685-020-00133-x (last visited Oct. 13, 2023).

up to $15.7 trillion to the global economy, which would be more than China's and India's total GDP of $9.1 trillion, estimated to come from consumption-related side effects, with $6.6 trillion coming from higher productivity.[10]

Three factors are driving the spread of AI across businesses

- *Reasonably priced high-performance processing power.* Artificial intelligence (AI) is expected to boost labor productivity by fundamentally changing their proficiency for doing work, and it also confirms the relevance of humans in generating progress. AI may assist people in reaching success while also demonstrating the enormous potential of talent under constraints. AI augments human intelligence with advanced analytics and pattern prediction skills to increase decision-making quality, efficacy, and originality. More importantly, the processing capability of cloud computing facilitates access to low-cost, high-performance computing resources.
- *Readily available data sets.* AI can help detect market gaps and opportunities more quickly, as computers think differently than humans. However, AI systems require a significant amount of data to produce accurate predictions. Because of the emergence of numerous tools for labeling data, more organizations are currently designing and training AI algorithms. It is economical and easy for businesses to store and handle both structured and unstructured data.
- *Applied AI provides a competitive advantage.* AI provides competitive advantages; therefore, businesses prioritize applying AI findings to achieve business goals. AI-powered applications learn from data and deliver results. AI can be used to assess new information from several sources. AI-powered advice can speed up the decision-making process. It is possible to reduce costs, lower risks, accelerate time, and many other benefits due to several AI features and capabilities. As a result, business benefits rise with time as AI supports improving working efficiency, reducing costs, and analyzing results.

2.3 Understanding the Use of AI in Education

A research study on the artificial intelligence market in the US education sector has been released by Technavio. As per the report, between 2021 and 2026, it is anticipated that the US education sector's artificial intelligence market share will rise by USD 374.3 million, with a CAGR of 48.15%.[11] Acquisition promotes complex thinking, including imagination, feeling, and creativity. Students' digital abilities have grown due to educational innovation. Artificial intelligence-related events,

---

[10] *Sezing the price: What is the real value of AI for your business and how can you captialise?*, PWC (2017), https://www.pwc.com/gx/en/issues/analytics/assets/pwc-ai-analysis-sizing-the-prize-report.pdf (last visited Oct. 20, 2023).

[11] *Artificial Intelligence Market in the Education Sector in US by End-user and Education model,* Forecast and Analysis 2022-2026 (2022), https://www.technavio.com/report/artificial-intelligence-market-in-the-education-sector-in-us-industry-analysis (last visited Sept. 25, 2023).

including academic conferences, research projects, and technology competitions, have flourished worldwide. The use of AI in education and research has expanded and been updated quickly. Many professional courses give students multisensory instructions to help them learn, remember information, and educate them about artificial intelligence resources like digital text, videos, photos, and sounds. Most AI tools adhere to three fundamental principles: learning, which is acquiring and digesting new knowledge and developing new behavioral models; algorithm improvement to provide the most accurate outcomes through self-correction, and using specific algorithms to complete a particular task. Vision-based AI systems can assist with analysis and are being utilized in various fields. Artificial intelligence helps students understand concepts more quickly. If AI is combined with high-quality learning resources and instruction, it also helps students get back on track faster by alerting teachers.

2.4 *Understanding the Use of AI in Health Care*

AI is more likely to be used as a supplement to human doctors. Artificial intelligence technologies are effective in clinical decision-support systems ranging from pre-operative risk prediction and planning to intra-operative event detection, condition monitoring, and predictive management analytics to post-operative patient monitoring (Aven Samareh, 2019).[12] It provides support in diagnoses by offering insightful data used to learn from and improve continuously. The ongoing communication between human doctors and AI-driven diagnostics enhances the accuracy of the systems, and eventually, this gives confidence to hand off duty completely to the AI system for autonomous operation.

The three areas with the most significant potential for the use of AI in healthcare

- *Early detection of potential diseases and tracking disease incidence to aid in halting and containing the disease's spread.* Faster detection and diagnosis are possible due to the use of AI in health care, which creates possibilities for earlier intervention. With advancements in AI, more accurate diagnostics and more individualized therapy may be given, which is undoubtedly the most significant advantage of using AI in health care.[13]
- *AI aids in the diagnosis.* Slight deviations from the baseline set by the patient's personal medical history, which is used by AI-powered diagnostics, signal a potentially serious medical condition that requires additional evaluation and treatment. By spotting such slight deviations from the norm in patients' health data

[12] Aven Samareh, Xiangyu Chang, William B. Lober, Heather L. Evans, Zhangyang Wang, Xiaoning Qian and Shuai Huang, *Artificial Intelligence Methods for Surgical Site Infection: Impacts on Detection, Monitoring, and Decision Making*, 20, SURGICAL INFECTIONS, 546, 549 (2019).

[13] Ramu, Anandakumar Haldorai & Arulmurugan, *An Analysis of Artificial Intelligence Clinical Decision-Making and Patient-Centric Framework, Computational Vision and Bio-Inspired Computing. Advances in Intelligent Systems and Computing*, SPRINGER, 813, 827 (2021).

or comparing with similar patients, AI suggests effective diagnosis and aids in treatment and diagnosis.

- *Diagnostic imaging (radiology, pathology).* AI supports doctors in making diagnoses by providing insightful data. AI learns from available data and improves continuously. Ongoing communication between human doctors and AI-driven diagnostics enhances accuracy, and eventually, it gives people the confidence to hand off duty totally to the AI system for autonomous operation (artificial intelligence in health care: accountability and safety, 2020). Despite that, decision-makers and advocates for future technologies must understand the complexities of AI and the systemic issues raised by its use in healthcare institutions. Better consideration should be given to needs and added-value assessment, workplace readiness, stakeholder acceptance, technology-organization alignment assessment; financing, and investments as an essential step to ensure successful AI integration and avoid unnecessary investments and costly failures.[14]

3 Methodology and Data Source

The rapid growth of AI applications and other tremendous technological advancements have enabled computer systems to analyze and interpret data more effectively and accurately. AI has been driving decision-making based on its remarkable ability to interpret information and extract valuable insights. AI delivers reliable, consistent, and precise information to advisers and decision-makers. AI has enormous potential for evaluating information and generating critical input for strategic business decisions. More importantly, in the future, excessive use and advancement in AI will also be possible with the progression of new technology. Thus, it is required to develop new theories and practices to bring a fresh perspective to the developing ethical, social, and legal challenges surrounding the emergence of artificial intelligence in our lives due to its extensive use.[15] Here, a legal question arises due to the use of AI in decision-making about whether rights can extend to non-humans by applying philosophical and legal considerations. This question requires an answer and legal justification. While AI provides numerous benefits to people, one of the most significant issues arising from its increased use is its potential to entrench

[14] Hassane Alami, Pascale Lehoux, Jean-Louis Denis, Aude Motulsky, Cecile Petitgand, Mathilde Savoldelli, Ronan Rouquet, Marie-Pierre Gagnon, Denis Roy, Jean-Paul Fortin, *Organizational readiness for artificial intelligence in health care: insights for decision-making and practice,* 35, JHOM (2020), https://www.emerald.com/insight/content/doi/10.1108/JHOM-03-2020-0074/full/html (last visited Oct. 13, 2023).

[15] ROBERT WALTERS & MARKO NOVAK, CYBER SECURITY, ARTIFICIAL INTELLIGENCE, DATA PROTECTION AND LAW, *Artificial Intelligence and Law,* 61 (SPRINGER 2021) https://link.springer.com/chapter/10.1007/978-981-16-1665-5_3 (last visited Oct. 12, 2023).

and perpetuate bias and discrimination.[16] As new risks and challenges are associated with AI in decision-making, the present research focused on the opportunity and socio-legal difficulties linked with using AI in decision-making. The researcher studied and analyzed AI-related contemporary challenges and reinforced how the law enforcement approach is the only tactic to resolve present challenges. The research discusses a legal discourse and international framework regarding legal responsibility concerning AI. The research examines the liability of a non-human entity and a critical environmental ethic that extends moral and legal attention to non-humans. The study also compares the EU's and India's existing laws that can provide relief and remedy if harm is caused by the use of AI in human decision-making processes.

3.1 Advantages of the Use of AI in Decision-Making

Recent advances in artificial intelligence are advances in the technology of prediction.[17] AI can handle anomaly detection, data crunching, complicated analysis, and trend spotting. Artificial intelligence is crucial in decision-making as it can train itself to create data collection models.[18] These models can make appropriate judgments and provide real-time predictions, categorizations, and suggestions. As a result, better commercial decisions are possible by employing AI. AI also serves as a basis for computer learning, and it harnesses large volumes of data. Unlike humans, artificial intelligence can make optimal decisions in a few fractions of time. On various occasions, the world has already witnessed AI's game-changing impact on humans and the economy. AI acts as a hybrid capital, assisting economic and human growth. McKinsey Global Institute directed the research, and the study proposed delivering 13 trillion dollars in increased output by 2030. It is expected to increase global GDP by 1.2 percent annually (Jacques Bughin, 2018).[19] Thus, as per the research, AI will soon have a revolutionary effect on human decision-making.

Decision-making levels through the use of AI

---

[16] Zuiderveen Borgesius, F., *Discrimination, artificial intelligence, and algorithmic decision-making* (2018), https://dare.uva.nl/search?identifier=7bdabff5-c1d9-484f-81f2-e469e03e2360 (last visited Oct. 7, 2023).

[17] AJAY AGARWAL, JOSHUA GANS & AVI GOLDFARB, THE ECONOMICS OF ARTIFICIAL INTELLIGENCE: AN AGENDA 92 (University of Chicago Press 2019), https://www.nber.org/system/files/chapters/c14010/c14010 (last visited Oct. 21, 2023).

[18] Stehel, Elvira Nica & Vojtech, *Internet of Things Sensing Networks, Artificial Intelligence-based Decision-Making Algorithms, and Real-Time Process Monitoring in Sustainable Industry 4.0,* JSGME, 35, 43 (2021), https://addletonacademicpublishers.com/contents-jsme/2230-volume-9-3-2021/4065-internet-of-things-sensing-networks-artificial-intelligence-based-decision-making-algorithms-and-real-time-process-monitoring-in-sustainable-industry-4-0 (last visited Oct. 28, 2023).

[19] Jacques Bughin, Jeongmin Seong, James Manyika, Michael Chui, Raoul Joshi, *Notes from the impact of AI on the world economy,* MCKINSEY GLOBAL INSTITUTE (2018), https://www.mckinsey.com/featured-insights/artificial-intelligence/notes-from-the-ai-frontier-modeling-the-impact-of-ai-on-the-world-economy (last visited Oct. 19, 2023).

- *Assistance in decision-making*—Humans can make accurate decisions with predictive, diagnostic, or descriptive analytics. The edge comes from the combination of human intelligence with data-driven insights. When common sense and knowledge are combined, they have the potential to make the impossible possible and decrease complexity.
- *Decision enhancement*—AI uses predictive or prescriptive analytics to recommend numerous decision options. The combination of AI capabilities and human understanding allows for the speedy examination of massive amounts of data.
- *Decision-making automation*—Decision automation relies on prescriptive or predictive analytics. Humans gain from AI's scalability, speed, and consistency in decision-making.

AI and many other new digital innovations, such as the Internet of Things and distributed ledger technologies, can benefit society and the world economy. AI is known to accomplish objective functions through data-trained models. It is either machine learning or deep learning. Robust IoT connectivity, faster computer processing, and the proliferation of linked devices have increased data collection and analysis. Some industries are experimenting with AI, while others are seasoned veterans. AI decision-making becomes critical when such an AI platform manages data processing entirely or partially. The final decisions are then either totally automated or handled by a human. With no humans involved, this approach aids in quantifying data, allowing for accurate forecasts and exact decisions (Abbott, 2020).[20] Many variables contribute to the issues faced by stakeholders in AI development, including socio-economic consequences, which have significant socio-economic ramifications due to AI's new activities and services. Machines' capacity to display improved cognitive skills in natural language encoding, learning, planning, and interpretation enables innovative systems to execute further actions more efficiently than humans (Alheet, 2021).[21]

3.2 Disadvantage of the Use of AI in Decision-Making

Machines cannot create connections with living beings, which is considered necessary for teamwork. Besides that, machines can only accomplish the tasks for which they were developed or programmed; anything further causes them to crash or start producing inconclusive results, both of which can be devastating. Moreover, in any industry, adequate standards and rules for a fully autonomous system do not exist, and thus, AI can be misused and may create risks. For example, while examining two

[20] Ryan Abbott, *The Reasonable Robot: Artificial Intelligence and the Law (Excerpt)* (2020), https://www.cambridge.org/in/academic/subjects/law/e-commerce-law/reasonable-robot-artificial-intelligence-and-law?format=HB&isbn=9781108472128 (last visited Oct. 20, 2023).

[21] Alheet, Ahmad Yousef Areiqat & Ahmad Fathi, *Artificial Intelligence and Its Impact on Public Management and Decision-Making* (2021), https://link.springer.com/chapter/10.1007/978-3-030-62796-613 (last visited Sept. 15, 2023).

accidents involving Teslas that were reportedly using Autopilot, USA officials, after an investigation, highlighted the potential new risk of driving Tesla cars. Indeed, such a risk is higher compared to semi-autonomous vehicles. In the USA, teams from the National Highway Traffic Safety Administration were sent to two accidents where Teslas and motorcyclists crashed on roads, and death was caused by the use of Teslas. Also, many such accidents were reported in various countries indicating that the self-driving system is designed only to recognize cyclists, pedestrians, and other road users, and it can avoid collisions without involving humans. However, such accident cases underlined the need for more oversight of emerging technology. The main problem arises in the relationship between humans and self-driving vehicles, and thus various groups and scholars called for a ban on testing self-driving vehicles in the USA in the wake of the fatal incident, as self-driving cars may not accurately predict human behavior in all circumstances.[22] In an emergency, current vehicle safety regulations and laws in the USA assume the presence of a human driver. However, there are laws in the works for specific self-driving car functions, such as automated lane-keeping systems. There is also an international standard for autonomous systems, which includes autonomous cars.[23] The standard establishes requirements but does not address the issues of sensors, machine learning, and operational learning, though it may do so in the future.[24]

A machine can never fully replicate a human being. Machines are rational but lack emotions and moral standards. Because AI needs to understand what is ethical or legal, it lacks judgment. Machines may perform incorrectly or break down while encountering an unfamiliar environment. Furthermore, AI cannot improve through practice; it will repeat the same action if no other command has been given. Machines can store a tremendous amount of data, but in accessing and utilizing data, machines differ substantially from human intelligence. AI is incapable of adapting to changing circumstances as it has no emotions. There is no sense of belonging, community, or connection. In addition, machines can't be more creative and match the power of the human brain, as human thoughts are directed by emotions, which machines lack. No matter how powerful a machine grows, it will never be able to replace the human brain's inherent intuitive abilities; therefore, the use of AI in decision-making might be damaging and dangerous in certain circumstances.

---

[22] Jack Karsten & Darrell M. West, *The state of self-driving car laws across the U.S,* BROOKINGS (May 1, 2018) https://www.brookings.edu/articles/the-state-of-self-driving-car-laws-across-the-u-s/ (last visited Oct. 13, 2023).

[23] *Building confidence in autonomous car safety,* NOVATEL (July 28, 2020) https://blog.novatel.com/building-confidence-in-autonomous-car-safety/ (last visited Oct. 24, 2023).

[24] John McDermid, *Autonomous cars: five reasons they still aren't on our roads,* The Conversation and University of New York (July 30, 2020), https://theconversation.com/autonomous-cars-five-reasons-they-still-arent-on-our-roads-143316 (last visited Oct. 26, 2023).

4 Legal Responsibility and Artificial Intelligence

The fundamental responsibility of responsivity is crucial, not only for self-understanding but also for people and members of society. AI advancements are predicted to continue to evolve and grow in power and sophistication in the near future. AI has already delivered significant benefits, particularly in terms of increased efficiency and convenience across a wide range of social domains and activities. AI brings extraordinary promise, with the potential to deliver substantial improvements in well-being, including the capacity to exercise and enjoy rights and freedoms. However, there are valid and growing public concerns about the negative legal, ethical, and societal implications of AI.[25] New technology alters legal situations directly by creating new entities, permitting new behavior, and indirectly by modifying incentives or values.[26] Thus, while using and implementing AI in decision-making, it is imperative to include adequate safeguards to reduce the risk of harm that these technologies, such as bodily injury or other damage, may cause. More specifically, it is also well understood that a lack of political legitimacy undermines the ability to address major crises and jeopardizes the system's overall stability on various issues, including the use of AI in decision-making. The distinct characteristics of these AI applications and technologies, such as complexity, reconfiguration via new features or self-learning during operation, and poor predictability, render them unsuitable because it is difficult for an average person to understand on what basis decisions are being made employing artificial intelligence. Therefore, it is necessary to address such issues effectively; and accordingly, practical guidelines and legal frameworks are also required.

4.1 Artificial Intelligence and Legal Responsibility: European Union (EU) Law

There is currently a lack of effective legislation to address AI-related decision-making issues in the majority of countries. However, unlike other countries, the EU's position on the use of AI in decision-making is better, as European Union law requires and strives to base decision-making on sound empirical evidence through the integration of digital data into political processes.[27] In the European Union, the New Technologies Formation of the Expert Group concluded in its assessment of liability

---

[25] Karen Yeung, *Responsibility and AI*, COUNCIL OF EUROPE STUDY DGI (2019), https://rm.coe.int/responsability-and-ai-en/168097d9c5 (last visited Sept. 13, 2023).

[26] Matthijs M. Maas, *International law does not compute: Artificial intelligence and the development, displacement or destruction of the global legal order*, MJIL, 29, 51 (2019), https://search.informit.org/doi/10.3316/agisp (last visited Sept. 9, 2023).

[27] Christopher Starke & Marco Luenich, *Artificial intelligence for political decision-making in the European Union: Effects on citizens' perceptions of input, throughput, and output legitimacy*. Data & Policy (2020), https://arxiv.org/abs/2003.11320 (last visited Oct. 16, 2023).

regimes in the aftermath of emerging digital technologies that the liability regimes in place in the Member States provide at least basic protection to victims whose damage is caused by the operation of such new technologies.[28] Following extensive debate to strengthen the EU's position in terms of the use of AI in decision-making, the EU passed the General Data Protection Regulation in 2019. Under Article 22 of the General Data Protection Regulation (GDPR) of the EU, the "data subject" (identified or identifiable natural person) in Europe has the right not to be subjected to a decision based solely on automated processing, including profiling, that has legal consequences for him or her or has a similarly significant impact on him or her. Private individuals have the right under GDPR to request a human-created explanation of any AI-based algorithms used on their data. Article 82 of the GDPR states that any person who has suffered material or non-material damage as a result of a GDPR violation has the right to seek compensation from the controller or processor.[29]

4.2 Artificial Intelligence and Legal Responsibility: Indian Law

In India, if harm or damage occurs due to AI, victims can seek compensation under existing Indian law under private law liability frameworks, particularly tort law. Only the strict liability of producers for defective products, which accounts for a small portion of this type of liability regime, is harmonized by product liability in India, which may be covered under consumer protection or tort law. More importantly, according to the existing Indian legal framework, product safety standards should be strictly followed in all circumstances because protection is provided to consumers. The judiciary can protect the rights of the user/consumer in India if AI causes harm. However, concerning AI, Indian laws must be revised, as there is no way to control the damages resulting from using AI in decision-making because no legal framework and/or guidelines have been developed in India so far. Furthermore, unlike the GDPR of the EU, there is no specific regulation/law in India for data protection. Still, data is protected in India by Sections 43A and 72A of the Information Technology Act, 2000. The Act creates a restitution right for wrongful disclosure of personal information. Furthermore, the Supreme Court has declared the right to privacy fundamental under the Indian Constitution.

---

[28] European Commission, Directorate-General for Justice and Consumers, *Liability for artificial intelligence and other emerging digital technologies* (2019), https://data.europa.eu/doi/10.2838/573689 (last visited Oct. 21, 2023).

[29] *General Data Protection Regulation* (May, 2018) https://gdpr-info.eu/art-22-gdpr/ (last visited Oct. 18, 2023).

5 Conclusion and Suggestions

AI calls for significant resource investment, but it raises concerns regarding fairness, access, and the distribution of benefits and risks, particularly for underdeveloped countries and stakeholder groups. AI will undoubtedly contribute to substantial gains in computer power in the future. Still, AI has potential issues that are distinct from previous computer technologies, so discussion is required regarding the use of AI in decision-making vis-à-vis its legal, ethical, and societal realms. More importantly, it is also necessary to ascertain whether AI can impact society negatively; if yes, then to what extent. Presently, in India, there are no guidelines or laws for governance concerning the use of AI and its use in the decision-making process. Therefore, detailed work on the appropriate development and use of AI is required in India. Waiting until its commercialization may complicate catching up with governance. More importantly, it is necessary to develop effective governance concerning the use of AI to establish trust in the technology and anticipate potential risks. Critical reflection and stakeholder outreach with an inclusive stakeholder discourse ranging from technologists to industrial, political, and social leadership are required to ensure AI's coherent, cohesive, productive, and beneficial usage in human decision-making. As new social, political, and ethical issues appear with every new technology, particularly one as revolutionary as AI. Hence, the likelihood of ethical and governance difficulties relating to the usage and deployment of such technologies increases as the technology advances and its applications have broader implications. Policies and effective governance concerning AI are required to help stakeholders and the general public, as AI has a positive impact, but at the same time, potential difficulties also come with it. Thus, for all parties, from policymakers, financiers, engineers, researchers, and software developers, and also for other users who are involved in the development and use of AI, effective policies and guidelines are required to serve as a guide to get a practical solution, positive results, and clear direction for its accuracy and properness. The EU's GDPR is a good initiative, and such regulation is also required in India and various other countries.

6 Recommendations

A reasonable balance is essential for implementing governance concepts in any sector. The field of AI is intrinsically interdisciplinary, and thus a wide range of stakeholders from government, business, academia, and civil society are involved. Setting up governance principles/guidelines for the use of AI in human decision-making is crucial because AI capabilities are emerging. However, these principles/guidelines may not cover all potential future challenges. More importantly, any quantum governance program's main stakeholder is the government, and therefore, the government plays a crucial role in establishing the economic, innovation, science, and national security policies to influence the development of AI. Governments of various nations also provide funding for the development of AI, directly or indirectly; therefore, the role of governments of different countries is imperative for developing legal frameworks. As the governance system generally prioritizes higher education institutions, the role of academia in expanding AI may help ascertain AI's benefits for the public, customers, and other stakeholders. According to the principles, legal awareness is imperative while carrying out AI-related operations, even after deciding on governance systems. Additional development would be essential to utilizing AI's potential for transformational powers. In creating a robust ecosystem for AI in human decision-making, it is also required to calculate its potential benefits by enabling access to education and technology to develop the required workforce to avoid future complications. It is possible to gain additional advantages from AI by developing the workforce. However, as different social, legal, and ethical issues appear with every new technology, the likelihood of ethical, social, legal, and governance difficulties relating to the usage and deployment of such technologies increases as the technology advances, and these difficulties are connected. By keeping the pros and cons mentioned earlier in mind, it is certainly necessary to analyze the benefits and drawbacks of AI use in human decision-making. The research suggests a legal framework in India that can direct governance and policy responses for stakeholders interested in using AI in human decision-making.

Understanding the Complexity of Juvenile Delinquency Recidivism: A Comparative Analysis of Offender Persistence from Minority to Adulthood in India and USA

Ishan Atrey and Jyotirmoy Banerjee

Abstract This research paper shall undertake a comprehensive comparative analysis of recidivism in juvenile delinquency in India and the United States, with a specific emphasis on understanding the reoccurrence of offenses committed by juveniles as they transition into adulthood. The study aims to explore key facets of recidivism, including the percentage of offenders engaging in criminal activities after reaching adulthood, the causes behind juvenile offenses during their minority and into adulthood, legislative measures adopted to address this issue, and amendments in statutory provisions within both countries. The research will employ a multidimensional approach by incorporating the perspectives of key stakeholders involved in the juvenile justice system. The respondents, including police, officers of reformation homes, parents, and juveniles themselves, will contribute valuable insights to form a holistic understanding of the factors influencing recidivism. In accordance with the data collection, the research shall be facilitated through a Google survey and interview, allowing for efficient and widespread participation. The survey will be tailored to elicit responses pertaining to the aforementioned research objectives, ensuring a diverse and comprehensive dataset. The collected data will be rigorously analyzed to draw meaningful conclusions and insights. By shedding light on the factors contributing to recidivism in juvenile delinquency and assessing legislative responses, this research seeks to contribute to the ongoing discourse on effective juvenile justice systems. The findings aim to inform policy and intervention strategies to better address the complexities of juvenile recidivism in both the Indian and American contexts.

Keywords Recidivism · Juvenile delinquency · Legislative measures · Juvenile justice · Criminal offenses · Stakeholder

---

I. Atrey (✉) · J. Banerjee
Integrated Programme in Law, Indian Institute of Management, Rohtak, India
e-mail: ishan.atrey@iimrohtak.ac.in

J. Aston et al. (eds.), *Comparative Law*, https://doi.org/10.1007/978-981-97-7815-7_3

1 Introduction

Juvenile delinquency represents a complex societal challenge with far-reaching implications, encompassing the engagement of minors in criminal activities that disrupt the fabric of communities and pose intricate challenges to the criminal justice system. As scholars, policymakers, and practitioners grapple with the multifaceted nature of juvenile delinquency, the phenomenon of recidivism adds an additional layer of intricacy. Recidivism, characterized by the re-engagement in criminal behavior by individuals with a history of interaction with the legal system, underscores the complexities inherent in rehabilitation efforts. This study embarks on a comprehensive exploration, focusing on the nuanced understanding of juvenile delinquency recidivism, with a specific emphasis on minority offenders, as they navigate the intricate pathways from adolescence to adulthood within the legal frameworks of India and the United States.

The gravity of juvenile delinquency lies not only in its immediate consequences but also in its potential to shape the future trajectories of young individuals, influencing their pathways into adulthood. The stakes are particularly high for minority youth, who often face unique challenges arising from socio-economic disparities, systemic discrimination, and cultural nuances. By examining the experiences of minority juvenile offenders, this research seeks to unveil the intricacies that contribute to the persistence of criminal behavior within this demographic and to delineate the factors shaping their journeys through the justice systems of two culturally diverse nations—the vibrant tapestry of India and the constitutional framework of the United States.

Juvenile delinquency is a pervasive issue that transcends geographical and cultural boundaries, affecting societies globally. The complexities surrounding the engagement of young individuals in criminal activities necessitate a holistic and nuanced understanding of the contributing factors. The intersection of socio-economic disparities, familial dynamics, educational challenges, and systemic influences converges to create an environment where juvenile delinquency takes root. Recognizing the global scope of this challenge, it becomes imperative to scrutinize the factors that propel minors toward criminal behavior and to discern the intricate web that leads them into the legal system.

As societies grapple with the repercussions of juvenile delinquency, the phenomenon of recidivism emerges as a critical focus for researchers and policymakers alike. Understanding why some juveniles, having encountered the legal system, revert to criminal activities is essential for developing targeted and effective interventions. The pursuit of rehabilitation is a delicate balance, requiring insight into the complex interplay of individual, societal, and systemic factors that contribute to the recurrence of criminal behavior among young offenders.

2 Legal Frameworks for Juvenile Justice

In the process of determining how societies react to young people who engage in delinquent behavior, the legislative frameworks that control juvenile justice play a primary role. In these frameworks, the age at which individuals are considered to be criminally responsible is defined, punitive measures are prescribed, and the significance of rehabilitation is emphasized.[1] When these legal systems are thoroughly investigated, it is possible to gain important insights into the values, priorities, and methods that are utilized by society in order to handle the issue of juvenile delinquency. In India, the Act 2015 is the primary piece of legislation that acts as the foundation for the legislative system supporting juvenile justice. A person who has not yet reached the age of 18 is considered to be a "juvenile" or "i" in accordance with the provisions of Section 2(35)[2] of the Act of 2015. By establishing a specific age requirement, this legal provision acknowledges individuals who are younger than 18 years old as juveniles, thereby highlighting the particular vulnerabilities that these children face within the framework of the criminal justice system.

In addition, the principle of adjudication and disposal for juveniles who are in conflict with the law is further established by Section 15[3] of the Act 2015. It stipulates that the Juvenile Justice Board is required to conduct an investigation in order to ascertain the circumstances, and if it is discovered that the juvenile is in violation of the law, the board has the authority to issue orders for the juvenile's rehabilitation and social reintegration. The rehabilitative nature of the juvenile justice system in India is highlighted by this legal provision, which places an emphasis on measures that are aimed at resolving the underlying causes of delinquency and directing young people towards positive development.

Within the United States of America, the legal framework pertaining to juvenile justice is decentralized, meaning that each state is responsible for defining its own rules regarding the age of majority and juvenile punishment. The Federal Juvenile Delinquency Act 1938 (hereinafter referred to as 'Act 1938'), often known as the FJDA, is a piece of legislation that serves as a basis for federal jurisdiction. A juvenile delinquent is a kid who has violated a federal statute that would be considered a criminal if it were committed by an adult, according to the definition provided by the Act. Although the Act of 1938 serves as a framework for federal juvenile justice, the treatment of juvenile offenders is governed by legislation that is specific to each state.

There are a number of states in the United States that have different ages at which individuals are considered to be juveniles. Some states consider individuals under the age of 18 to be juveniles, while others set the age at 16 or 17.[4] It is clear that there

---

[1] Daniel P. Mears, Justin T. Pickett & Christina Mancini, *Support for Balanced Juvenile Justice: Assessing Views About Youth, Rehabilitation, and Punishment*, 31 J. Quant. Criminol. 459 (2015).

[2] Juvenile Justice (Care and Protection of Children) Act, 2015 (Act 2 of 2016), § 2(35).

[3] Juvenile Justice (Care and Protection of Children) Act, 2015 (Act 2 of 2016), § 15.

[4] Daniel P. Mears, Carter Hay, Marc Gertz and Christina Mancini, *Public Opinion and The Foundation Of The Juvenile Court* 45 Criminology 223–257 (2007).

are a wide variety of legal approaches, each of which reflects a different philosophical foundation and approach to the administration of juvenile justice. In addition, several jurisdictions in the United States use waiver mechanisms, such as judicial waiver or statutory exclusion, that enable the transfer of juveniles to adult courts based on considerations such as the gravity of the offense and the age of the criminal concerned.[5] This discretion that is allowed to the justice is an example of the intricate character of legal frameworks in the United States, where the balance between accountability and acknowledging the developmental vulnerabilities of minors is prone to variations depending on the location.[6]

The legal frameworks that govern juvenile justice contain a variety of punitive measures that are varied and reflect the changing viewpoints of this society. The notion of proportionality is enshrined in the Juvenile Justice Act, 2015, which was passed in India. This law ensures that the punishment for juvenile offenders is neither harsh nor degrading. Under the provisions of Section 18[7] of the Act 2015, the use of physical punishment is prohibited, and it is required that any form of punishment imposed on a juvenile must take into account the juvenile's age, capacity, and the circumstances surrounding the incident. A rehabilitative approach is emphasized by this provision, which discourages measures that are too punishing and encourages solutions that take into consideration the developmental stage of the juvenile as well as the circumstances surrounding the juvenile.

There has been a growing realization of the limitations of such a strategy, despite the fact that there has been a trend towards punitive measures in reaction to certain high-profile cases.[8] In recognition of the fact that punitive measures may not be sufficient to address the underlying causes of juvenile delinquency, many jurisdictions have implemented a shift towards placing a greater emphasis on rehabilitation.[9] At the same time that attempts are being made to minimize the use of juvenile confinement and promote community-based alternatives that place an emphasis on rehabilitation and support, the use of juvenile detention has come under investigation.

In accordance with the survey, the response to the question "***What is the age at which individuals are considered juveniles in both India and the U.S.A. according to their respective legal frameworks?***" which further aimed to establish the age classification for juveniles in India and the U.S., with a total of 572 responses. Figure 1 illustrates that 42% of respondents selected option c, indicating that 16 is the age for juveniles in both countries.

In both India and the United States, one of the most important themes is the emphasis placed on rehabilitation within the framework of judicial systems. According to Section 3[10] of the Act, 2015, which defines the overriding premise of

[5] Ibid.

[6] Ibid.

[7] Juvenile Justice (Care and Protection of Children) Act, 2015 (Act 2 of 2016), § 18.

[8] David P. Farrington, Rolf Loeber and James C. Howell, *Young Adult Offenders*, 11 Criminology and Public Policy 729–750 (2012).

[9] Ibid.

[10] Juvenile Justice (Care and Protection of Children) Act, 2015 (Act 2 of 2016), § 3.

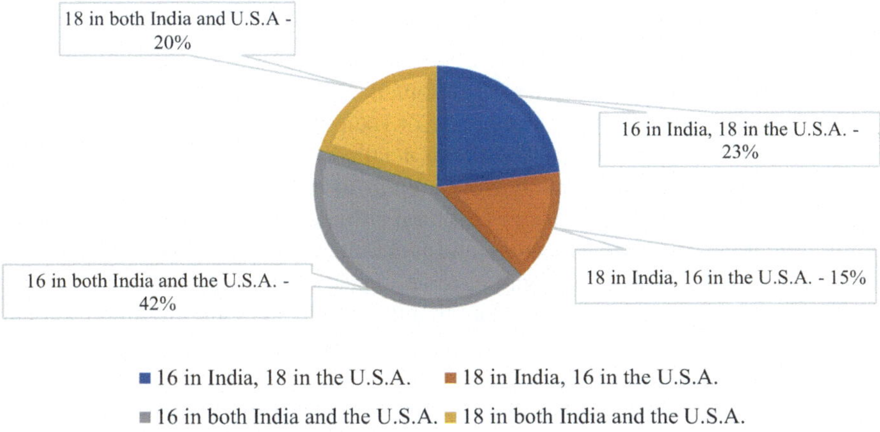

Fig. 1 Total respondents recorded 572

the best interests of the child, which serves as a guiding principle for all decisions and actions pertaining to a juvenile who is in dispute with the law. With this provision, the importance of the general well-being of juvenile offenders is brought to the forefront, highlighting the necessity of measures that are aimed at the rehabilitation and reintegration of these individuals.[11] An array of rehabilitation options, such as counseling, vocational training, and community service, are outlined in the Act. These initiatives show a holistic approach that addresses the many different components of juvenile delinquency.[12]

The legislative frameworks that govern juvenile justice serve as the foundation for the solutions that society provides to young people who participate in criminal behavior.[13] A good example of the intricate nature of these frameworks is the Act, 2015, which was passed in India, as well as the various legal approaches that are taken by different states in the United States. Some of the important factors that play a role in determining the experiences of juvenile offenders include the age at which criminal culpability begins, the effectiveness of punitive measures, and the importance placed on rehabilitation. With regard to the legal regulations, there is a careful balance between accountability and acknowledging the particular vulnerabilities that are associated with juveniles. A growing emphasis is being placed on humane treatment, rehabilitation, and the overall well-being of juvenile offenders as a result of ongoing legal changes and international standards, which contribute to the creation of these frameworks.

[11] Tony Ward, Bruce Arrigo, Mary Barnao, Anthony Beech and Deirdre A. Brown, *Urgent issues and prospects in correctional rehabilitation practice and research*, 27 Legal and Criminological Psychology 103–128 (2022).

[12] Ibid.

[13] Ibid.

3 Socio-Cultural Influences on Juvenile Delinquency

Delinquency among young people is a phenomenon that is intricately woven into the fabric of society. It is affected by a variety of socio-cultural variables that go well beyond the acts of individuals. Obtaining a detailed understanding of the paths by which young people become involved in delinquent behavior can be accomplished by analyzing the intricate interplay of cultural attitudes towards criminal behavior, family structures, educational chances, and economic inequities. This study explores the social and cultural dynamics that have an impact on the occurrence of juvenile delinquency, taking into account the fact that these influences are multidimensional and reliant on the environment in which they are experienced.

The way in which societies view and react to adolescent delinquency is largely influenced by the cultural attitudes that they now have towards criminal behavior.[14] The views that young people have towards criminal behavior are significantly influenced by the cultural norms, values, and societal expectations that come from their respective societies. When it comes to juvenile offenders, the stigma that is connected with illegal acts extends beyond the individual to the entire family in many different cultures.[15]

Educational possibilities are a significant factor in determining the paths that young offenders will take in their lives. People may be dissuaded from engaging in antisocial behavior in societies that place a high value on education and view it as a means of achieving social advancement.[16] This is because the importance of academic achievement is perceived to be of great significance. Conversely, in circumstances characterized by educational gaps and restricted access to quality schooling, young people may experience obstacles in realizing their full potential, potentially leading to frustration and an increased risk of engaging in delinquent activities. Peer pressure, bullying, and a lack of proper support systems are all examples of variables that might contribute to juvenile delinquency.

Disparities in economic conditions have a persistent impact on adolescent delinquency, and they are a reflection of larger inequalities between members of society. People who come from marginalized areas may have a more difficult time gaining access to resources, employment opportunities, and social services in societies that are characterized by severe economic disparities.[17] A situation in which people are experiencing economic difficulties might generate an atmosphere in which criminal actions are seen as legitimate alternatives for surviving or elevating their status.

Insights into the differences and similarities that shape the experiences of young offenders can be gained through the comparative analysis of socio-cultural factors affecting juvenile delinquency that is conducted between various nations. For

---

[14] J. G. Bernburg & T. Thorlindsson, *Adolescent Violence, Social Control, and the Subculture of Delinquency: Factors Related to Violent Behavior and Nonviolent Delinquency*, 30 Youth & Society 445–460 (1999).

[15] Ibid.

[16] Ibid.

[17] David F. Greenberg, *Delinquency and the age structure of society* 1 Contemp. Crises 189 (1977).

instance, the cultural views that Western societies, such as the United States, have towards authority, discipline, and individualism may be quite different from those that are held in more collectivist communities, such as many of the societies that are found in Asia. The influence of these cultural differences can be seen in the ways in which communities, legal institutions, and support structures react to the problem of adolescent delinquency.[18]

The influence of popular culture and mass media is another factor that contributes to the socio-cultural processes that are associated with adolescent delinquency.[19] Characteristics of criminal behavior that are shown in the media, which are frequently sensationalized and dramatized, have the potential to mold public perceptions and impact the attitudes of young people. In modern countries, where digital media, social networks, and rapid communication play a considerable role in forming the cultural zeitgeist, the influence of the media on shaping cultural attitudes towards criminal behavior is especially strong. However, this influence is especially pronounced in contemporary societies.

There are additional layers of complexity that are added to the socio-cultural factors that are present within the framework of minority communities. The experiences of young people living in these communities can be strongly influenced by factors such as discrimination, institutional disparities, and cultural nuances that are unique to minority groups. When attempting to comprehend the discrepancies in the rates of juvenile delinquency that exist between various demographic groups, it is essential to take into consideration the interaction of socio-cultural elements. A sense of detachment from societal standards may be a contributing factor in the alienation that minority adolescents experience in certain circumstances. This disconnection may increase the likelihood that these youth will engage in antisocial behavior.

In addition to the development of treatments and policies aimed at prevention and rehabilitation, the consequences of socio-cultural impacts on juvenile delinquency extend to the development of these policies and programs. Approaches that are culturally sensitive acknowledge the variety of factors that have an impact on the experiences of young people and acknowledge that a technique that is universally applicable may not be sufficient.[20] When it comes to tackling the underlying causes of juvenile delinquency and creating positive outcomes for young offenders, interventions that take into account cultural norms, family structures, and economic inequities have the potential to be more effective.

Further, according to the survey, the question focused on the scope of "***Which socio-cultural factor is identified as a significant contributor to juvenile delinquency in both India and the U.S.A.?***" and focused on identifying socio-cultural factors influencing juvenile delinquency in India and the U.S. Based on 572

---

[18] Ibid.

[19] Keith Roe, *'Adolescents' use of socially disvalued media: Towards a theory of media delinquency*, 24 Journal of Youth and Adolescence 617–631 (1995).

[20] Shelly Brown-Jeffy and Jewell E. Cooper, *Toward a Conceptual Framework of Culturally Relevant Pedagogy: An Overview of the Conceptual and Theoretical Literature*, 38 Teacher Education Quarterly 65–84 (2011).

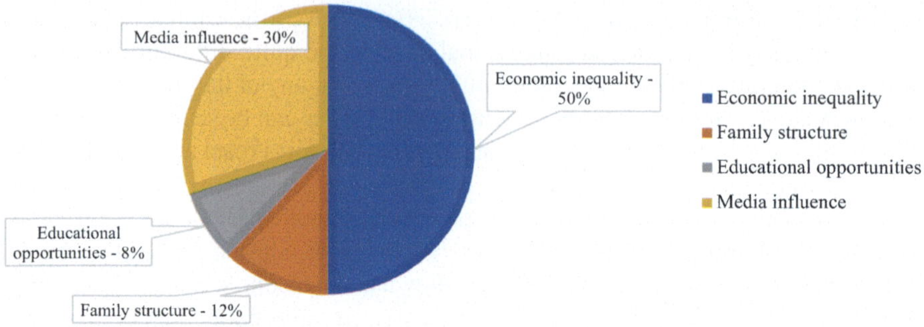

Fig. 2 Total answers recorded 572

responses, Fig. 2 reveals that 50% of respondents leaned towards option a, highlighting economic inequality as a significant contributor.

A complex web of elements that interact with one another and impact the lives of young people within a variety of cultural contexts is represented by the socio-cultural influences on juvenile delinquency.[21] There are a number of factors that contribute to the frequency of adolescent delinquency, including cultural attitudes towards criminal behavior, family structures, educational possibilities, and economic inequities. These factors all contribute collectively, with variances and similarities being visible throughout different countries.[22] For the purpose of designing comprehensive and culturally sensitive measures to prevent and address juvenile delinquency, particularly within minority populations, it is vital to have a solid understanding of these socio-cultural factors.[23] When it comes to breaking the cycle of delinquency and supporting positive outcomes for young people who are traversing complicated socio-cultural environments, the continued examination of these variables gives useful insights that may be used by policymakers, practitioners, and researchers.

4 Long-Term Trajectories

One of the most significant turning points in the life of a person who is involved with the criminal justice system is the passage from the stage of juvenile delinquency to the stage of maturity. When analyzing the long-term trajectories of juvenile offenders, it is necessary to conduct a thorough investigation of the legal provisions, societal attitudes, and systemic elements that play a role in shaping the routes that these individuals take as they negotiate the intricacies of adulthood. A legal framework that recognizes the developmental differences between juveniles and adults is provided by the Act 2015, which is applicable to the context of India. The guiding principle of the

[21] Ibid.

[22] Ibid.

[23] Ibid.

best interests of the child, which is established in Section 3[24] of the Act 2015, incorporates this recognition as an integral part of its framework. The legislation places emphasis on rehabilitation and reintegration, positioning the juvenile justice system as a vehicle for generating beneficial long-term results for these young individuals who have committed offenses.

The methods for the rehabilitation and social reintegration of adolescents who have been determined to be in conflict with the law are outlined in Section 18[25] of the Act 2015. Counseling, education, skill development, and other interventions are included in these measures. The goal of these interventions is to treat the underlying reasons for delinquency and guide juveniles towards leading a life that is in compliance with the law. In light of the fact that interventions throughout adolescence can have a substantial impact on a person's future, this law provision emphasizes the commitment to developing long-term constructive trajectories for juvenile offenders.[26]

When it comes to juvenile offenders in the United States, the long-term trajectories of these individuals are impacted by a complicated legal landscape that differs from state to state.[27] It is clear that legal rules, such as those that prevent the imposition of the death sentence or life imprisonment without parole for juvenile offenders, are a manifestation of the understanding of the developmental distinctions that exist between juveniles and adults.[28] The precedents that have been established by the decisions of the United States Supreme Court in cases such as *Roper v. Simmons (2005),*[29] *Graham v. Florida,*[30] *and Miller v. Alabama*[31] acknowledge the specific vulnerabilities that are associated with juveniles and restrict the harshness of punishments that can be handed down to them.

According to the decision in *Roper v. Simmons,*[32] the application of the death penalty to individuals who were under the age of 18 at the time of their offenses was deemed to be unconstitutional. The decision was based on the growing standards of decency that acknowledged the decreased culpability of juveniles. *Graham v. Florida*[33] was the case that established that the Eighth Amendment prohibits cruel and unusual punishment, which includes the imposition of life sentences without the possibility of release for minors who have been convicted of non-homicide offenses. This line of reasoning was extended to cases involving mandatory life imprisonment without the possibility of release for young offenders in the case of *Miller v.*

---

[24] Juvenile Justice (Care and Protection of Children) Act, 2015 (Act 2 of 2016), § 3.

[25] Juvenile Justice (Care and Protection of Children) Act, 2015 (Act 2 of 2016), § 18.

[26] Laurence Miller, *Juvenile crime and juvenile justice: Patterns, models, and implications for clinical and legal practice,* 19 Aggression and Violent Behaviour 122–137 (2014).

[27] Ibid.

[28] Ibid.

[29] 543 U.§ 551 (2005).

[30] 560 U.§ 48 (2010).

[31] 567 U.§ 460 (2012).

[32] Ibid., at 9.

[33] Ibid., at 10.

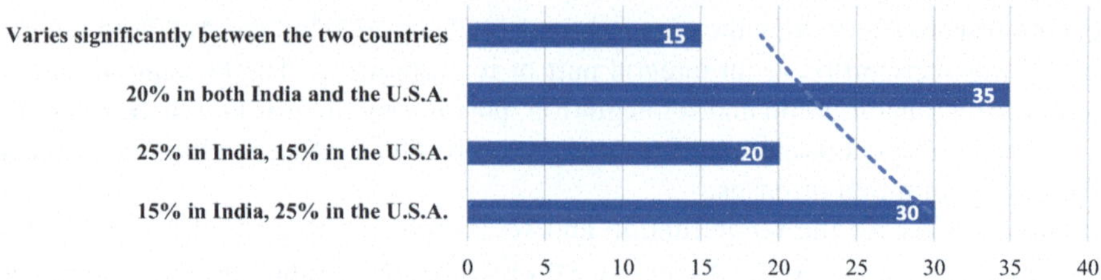

Fig. 3 Total answers recorded 572

Alabama,[34] which established that sentences of this nature ought to be subject to individual consideration.

In addition to advocating for a nuanced approach to sentencing that takes into consideration the developmental phases of juvenile offenders, these legal provisions highlight the significance of recognizing the extent to which juvenile criminals are capable of change and progress. The concept that the long-term trajectories of juvenile offenders are changeable and subject to positive change is in line with the emphasis placed on individualized consideration. This is especially true when options for rehabilitation are made available to juvenile offenders.

According to Section 39[35] of the Act 2015 in India, specifies measures for the rehabilitation and social reintegration of juvenile offenders. This section reflects the focus that is placed on education and the development of skills in India pertaining to juvenile offenders. The provision acknowledges the significance of providing young people with the knowledge and abilities that are essential for carrying out a life that is in compliance with the law. The construction of observation homes, special homes, or appropriate institutions for the purpose of rehabilitating juvenile offenders is an indication of a systematic commitment to provide a supportive environment for the long-term development of these individuals.

Similarly, in the United States, the long-term trajectories of juvenile offenders are mostly determined by systemic factors such as access to quality education and mental health treatment. These factors significantly influence the trajectory of these individuals. Legal rules that restrict punitive actions and encourage alternatives that are rehabilitative are reinforced when they are supplemented by activities that address the more comprehensive systemic difficulties that young people are confronted with.

In accordance with the survey, the question "***What percentage of juvenile offenders in India and the U.S.A. exhibit a persistent pattern of criminal behavior into adulthood?***" explores the prevalence of persistent criminal behavior among juvenile offenders in both countries. Figure 3 demonstrates that 20% of respondents selected option b, indicating that 25% of offenders in India and 15% in the U.S.A. exhibit such behavior, based on 572 responses.

It is necessary to have a full understanding of legislative provisions, societal attitudes, and systemic issues in order to investigate the long-term trajectories of

34 Ibid., at 11.

35 Juvenile Justice (Care and Protection of Children) Act, 2015 (Act 2 of 2016), § 39.

juvenile offenders. A prime example of the multifaceted nature of legal frameworks is the Act 2015, which was passed in India. In the United States of America, the many legal approaches found in different states are also examples. There is an awareness of the potential for good transformation among juvenile offenders, which is reflected in the focus placed on rehabilitation, individualized consideration, and community involvement. Addressing inequities, encouraging access to education and mental health services, and cultivating an environment that is supportive in order to facilitate the effective reintegration of juvenile offenders into society are all necessary steps in the process of achieving equitable long-term trajectories.

5 Effectiveness of Rehabilitation Strategies

The efficiency of rehabilitation programs for individuals who are involved in juvenile delinquency is an essential component of the system that governs juveniles who are involved in criminal activity.[36] By addressing the underlying causes of juvenile delinquency, guiding juveniles towards constructive behavior, and facilitating their successful reintegration into society, these solutions strive to achieve their specific goals.[37] For the purpose of determining whether or not these tactics are effective, a comprehensive analysis that takes into account the legal requirements, programmatic interventions, and the influence that these strategies have on the long-term outcomes of juvenile offenders is required.[38]

A legal framework that places an emphasis on the rehabilitation of juvenile offenders has been established in India by the Act of 2015. Measures for the rehabilitation and social reintegration of juveniles who have been in confrontation with the law under Section 19[39] under Act 1938. Some of the interventions that are included in these metrics are counseling, education, vocational training, and other interventions that are designed to address the specific requirements and circumstances of each juvenile. The Act 2015 places a strong emphasis on what is in the child's best interests, and it is in line with worldwide standards that acknowledge the specific vulnerabilities and potential for good transformation that are present in juvenile offenders.

There is a close connection between the successful application of legislative rules and the efficacy of rehabilitation techniques in India. The Act 2015 specifically describes, under Section 48,[40] the establishment of special homes, observation homes, or appropriate institutions for the purpose of rehabilitating juvenile offenders. It is anticipated that these facilities will create a supportive atmosphere that caters

[36] Malcolm W. Klein, *Deinstitutionalization and Diversion of Juvenile Offenders: A Litany of Impediments*, 52 Crime and Justice: A Review of Research 1 (1979).

[37] Ibid.

[38] Ibid.

[39] Juvenile Justice and Delinquency Prevention Act, 1974, § 19.

[40] Juvenile Justice (Care and Protection of Children) Act, 2015 (Act 2 of 2016), § 48.

to the many requirements of adolescents by providing opportunities for educational pursuits, vocational training, and leisure activities. The capacity of these institutions to cultivate an environment that is conducive to the growth and development of individuals is critical to the success of rehabilitation efforts at these institutions.[41]

A further point to consider is that Section 8[42] of the Act 2015 places an emphasis on the role that the Juvenile Justice Board plays in monitoring the correctional process. The task of conducting inquiries, determining appropriate measures for rehabilitation, and ensuring that the rehabilitation plan is in alignment with the best interests of the child has been entrusted to the Board of Directors.[43]

The nature of the interventions that are provided within the juvenile justice systems of both India and the United States is inextricably tied to the efficacy of rehabilitation programs in both countries. Within the framework of the Act 2015, Section 18[44] places emphasis on the provision of counseling, educational opportunities, and vocational training. The field of counseling, in particular, is an extremely important component in the process of comprehending and addressing the psychosocial aspects that are associated with delinquency.

It is common practice in the United States to employ a combination of community-based programs, counseling, and educational initiatives when implementing rehabilitation strategies.[45] This realization that rehabilitation goes beyond the confines of institutional settings is reflected in the focus placed on community involvement and alternatives to imprisonment within the system. When taking into consideration the fact that many juvenile offenders may have underlying mental health disorders that contribute to their delinquent behavior, the provision of mental health treatments is an essential component.

The availability of resources and the quality of those resources are two factors that determine the effectiveness of rehabilitation programs in both of these scenarios. It is not possible for legal provisions to ensure favorable outcomes on their own; rather, the influence of these provisions is mediated by the actual implementation of rehabilitation programs and the commitment of resources to support these initiatives.[46] For example, the Act of 2015, mandates the development of special homes and appropriate institutions. In order to fulfill this mandate, it is necessary to have adequate infrastructure, qualified personnel, and programs that are specifically designed to meet the multifaceted needs of juvenile offenders.

In the United States, the degree to which community-based programs are easily accessible and have adequate resources is a significant factor that determines the

---

[41] D.A. Andrews and Craig Dowden, *The Risk–Need–Responsivity Model of Assessment and Human Service in Prevention and Corrections: Crime-Prevention Jurisprudence,* 49 Canadian Journal of Criminology and Criminal Justice 439–464 (2007).

[42] Juvenile Justice (Care and Protection of Children) Act, 2015 (Act 2 of 2016), § 8.

[43] Ibid.

[44] Juvenile Justice (Care and Protection of Children) Act, 2015 (Act 2 of 2016), § 18.

[45] Juvenile Justice and Delinquency Prevention Act, 1974, § 204.

[46] Joseph Sarkis, Pilar Gonzalez-Torre and Belarmino Adenso-Diaz, *Stakeholder pressure and the adoption of environmental practices: The mediating effect of training*, 28 Journal of Operations Management 163–176 (2010).

efficacy of rehabilitation treatments.[47] It is possible for disparities in resources to contribute to unequal access to rehabilitative therapies, which in turn can have an effect on the outcomes for juvenile offenders who originate from a variety of socio-economic communities.

Education plays a crucial part in the rehabilitation measures that are being used. A provision of the Act 2015, specifically Section 18(1)(g),[48] places an emphasis on the significance of education as a form of rehabilitation. Not only can educational opportunities provide juveniles with the skills they need to succeed in life, but they also help break the cycle of delinquency by providing a path to future employment and social inclusion. In order for rehabilitation programs to be successful over the long term, it is essential to guarantee access to education of a high standard.

The United States of America recognizes the transformative power of education in reorienting the lives of juvenile offenders, and as a result, educational interventions are frequently incorporated into rehabilitation efforts. The phenomenon known as the "*School-to-Prison Pipeline*," which describes the situation in which children, particularly those who come from minority backgrounds, are at a greater risk of entering the criminal justice system as a result of harsh disciplinary practices, highlights the interdependence of the educational system and the juvenile justice system.[49] It is imperative that effective rehabilitation techniques address the systemic issues that exist within the educational system in order to prevent juvenile offenders from being directed into the criminal justice system.[50]

In furtherance to the response received on the question, "***What percentage of juvenile offenders successfully complete rehabilitation programs in India and the U.S.A.?***" It further illustrates that a notable 28% believed in the effectiveness of such programs in India, while 40% expressed confidence in the U.S. However, a considerable 20% held the opinion that both countries witness successful rehabilitation, and 12% indicated a perception of significant variability between India and the U.S. in terms of completion rates. These diverse perspectives underscore the nuanced perceptions surrounding the effectiveness of rehabilitation strategies for juvenile offenders, emphasizing the need for a comprehensive understanding of these programs in different socio-cultural contexts (Fig. 4).

As a result of the efforts that are being made within the juvenile justice system in the United States to provide therapeutic interventions and counseling, the confluence of mental health and rehabilitation is becoming increasingly apparent. Nevertheless, the efficacy of these treatments is contingent upon the accessibility of resources pertaining to mental health as well as the incorporation of mental health services within the more comprehensive framework of rehabilitation interventions. Participation from the community is yet another factor that has a substantial impact on the

---

[47] Ibid.

[48] Juvenile Justice (Care and Protection of Children) Act, 2015 (Act 2 of 2016), § 18(1)(g).

[49] Michael Rocque and Quincy Snellings, *The new disciplinology: Research, theory, and remaining puzzles on the school-to-prison pipeline*, 59 Journal of Criminal Justice 3–11 (2018).

[50] Ibid.

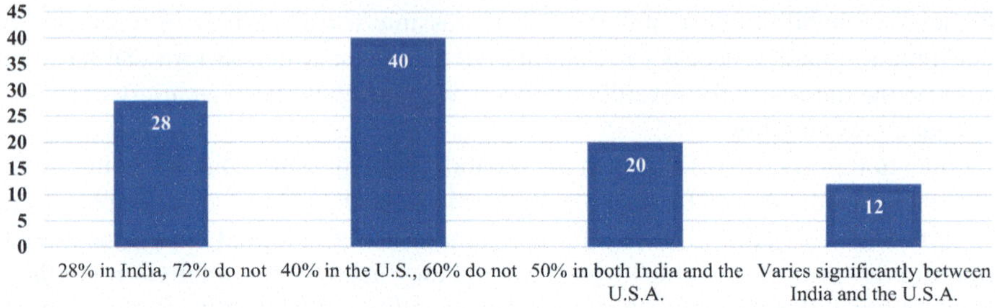

Fig. 4 Total answers recorded 572

efficiency of rehabilitation programs. The Act 2015, which describes the Section 39,[51] places an emphasis on the participation of local communities in the process of rehabilitation. When it comes to aiding the reintegration of juvenile offenders into society, community-based rehabilitation acknowledges the significance of public support, compassion, and empathy.

In the United States of America, rehabilitation plans are not complete without the inclusion of community-based programs and initiatives. The participation of local communities helps to cultivate a sense of belonging and support for young offenders, which contributes to a more holistic approach that goes beyond the confines of institutional settings. Children and adolescents who are transitioning from the juvenile justice system to adulthood might greatly benefit from the support networks that can be provided by community partnerships and mentorship programs.

In order to determine how effective rehabilitation programs are and to make adjustments based on that information, it is necessary to conduct assessments and oversee their implementation. In India, the Juvenile Justice Board is responsible for overseeing the rehabilitation process. This responsibility is defined in Section 8[52] of the Act 2015, which ensures that the procedure is continuously evaluated and scrutinized. Ongoing evaluation is reflected in the board's responsibility to conduct inquiries, decide rehabilitative methods, and protect the child's best interests. This responsibility demonstrates the board's dedication to ongoing assessment.

It is common practice in the United States to evaluate the efficacy of rehabilitation strategies by using outcome-based indicators.[53] These measures include rates of recidivism, educational achievement, and employment outcomes for juvenile offenders. Continuous evaluations of rehabilitation programs are made possible by the monitoring procedures that are part of the juvenile justice system.[54] These mechanisms include probation services and judicial oversight.

The assessment of rehabilitation solutions is also influenced by international standards and the most effective approaches there are. The United States of America and

[51] Juvenile Justice (Care and Protection of Children) Act, 2015 (Act 2 of 2016), § 39.

[52] Juvenile Justice (Care and Protection of Children) Act, 2015 (Act 2 of 2016), § 8.

[53] Juvenile Justice and Delinquency Prevention Act, 1974, § 251.

[54] Ibid.

India are both signatories to international agreements, such as the United Nations Convention on the Rights of the Child (UNCRC), which places an emphasis on the rehabilitative and restorative aspects of the juvenile justice system. When rehabilitation programs are aligned with international standards, it ensures that they are not only effective at the local level, but that they also support the values of human rights and the well-being of children.

The execution of effective rehabilitation programs for juvenile offenders is a complex endeavor that requires the incorporation of legal laws, programming interventions, and the commitment of society.[55] The Act 2015 in India and the legal framework in the United States, including rulings made by the Supreme Court, are the two pieces of legislation that establish the groundwork for programs that engage in rehabilitation. The execution of rehabilitation programs, the distribution of resources, and the ability to cater to the varied requirements of juvenile offenders are all critical factors in determining the success of these strategies. Education, mental health treatment, community involvement, and continuing assessment are all essential components that contribute to the positive outcomes that are achieved over the long term for persons who are involved in juvenile delinquency. Underscoring the need to consider juvenile offenders not merely as persons who have committed offenses but as humans who have the potential for change, growth, and successful reintegration into society is the necessity of the investigation into the efficacy of rehabilitation techniques.

6 Policy and Managerial Suggestions

It is vital for the juvenile justice system to have a harmonious integration of strong policies and competent managerial practices to effectively address the complex issue of juvenile delinquency. The purpose of these recommendations is to effectively traverse the complexities of the juvenile justice system, with a particular emphasis on the necessity of intelligent changes and proactive management in order to cultivate positive outcomes for juvenile offenders.[56]

First and foremost, there is an urgent need for a nuanced policy framework that takes into account the myriad of circumstances that contribute to the problem of juvenile delinquency.[57] The formulation and execution of interventions that are supported by evidence and that target the underlying factors that contribute to criminal behavior ought to be given top priority by policymakers. For the purpose of ensuring that the juvenile justice system functions as a facilitator of positive transformation rather

[55] Devon L.L. Polaschek, *Many sizes fit all: A preliminary framework for conceptualizing the development and provision of cognitive–behavioral rehabilitation programs for offenders*, 16 Aggression and Violent Behavior 20–35 (2011).

[56] Janay B. Sander, Jill D. Sharkey, Roger Olivarri, Diane A. Tanigawa & Tory Mauseth, *A Qualitative Study of Juvenile Offenders, Student Engagement, and Interpersonal Relationships: Implications for Research Directions and Preventionist Approaches*, 20 Journal of Education and Psychological Consultation 288–315 (2010).

[57] Ibid.

than a punishing machinery, legal rules ought to be revised so as to embrace a wider range of rehabilitative methods.[58]

Additionally, authorities must take into consideration the possibility of modifying the age criteria that the judicial system uses to differentiate between juveniles and adults. In recognition of the fact that individuals may continue to experience cognitive and emotional maturity beyond arbitrary age limitations, the criteria for adjudication of juvenile cases ought to be linked with developmental research. In order to ensure that the justice system continues to be in sync with the ever-evolving understanding of human development, it is important to have a flexible approach to age requirements.

Improvements in the training of staff involved in the administration of juvenile justice should also be a primary focus of managerial practices. A comprehensive grasp of adolescent growth, cultural sensitivity, and trauma-informed techniques is very important for everyone involved in the juvenile justice system, from law enforcement officials to members of the board representing juveniles. As an additional point of interest, there ought to be a deliberate effort made to increase the continuum of care for juvenile offenders. It is possible to guarantee that the positive momentum gained throughout rehabilitation is maintained by providing transitional support services that continue beyond the formal conclusion of a case.

It is hereby concluded that the formulation of a juvenile justice system that is in accordance with the principles of rehabilitation and individualized consideration is largely dependent on the implementation of successful policy and managerial ideas. A break from punitive measures and an emphasis on interventions that are supported by science should be emphasized in the legal provisions that are intended to reflect the changing understanding of adolescent development. In order to improve the efficacy and efficiency of rehabilitation efforts, managerial strategies should place a higher priority on interdisciplinary collaboration, training, alternative programs, and the incorporation of technology. It is hereby possible for society to develop towards a juvenile justice system that not only handles delinquency but also helps young individuals towards positive, law-abiding futures. This can be accomplished by combining sensible legislative reforms with proactive managerial techniques.

[58] Ibid.

Laws and Policies to Prevent Cyberbullying in High Schools—Lessons for India and Western Australia

Vanessa Tay and Prafula Pearce

Abstract Many countries have reported an increase of cyberbullying in their high schools. Cyberbullied children can suffer severe consequences including depression, anxiety, substance abuse and suicidal behaviour, which include suicide ideation, suicide plans and suicide attempts. Many countries are beginning to enact online safety legislation. The Australian Online Safety Act 2021 has created a new framework for online safety for all Australians and is intended to protect both adults and children, with wide powers granted to the eSafety Commissioner. Although India does not have specific anti-bullying legislation, the Indian legislation that may capture some cyberbullying offences include the Indian Penal Code (IPC) 1860, the Information Technology Act 2000, and the Protection of Children from Sexual Offences Act 2012. These legislations can be beneficial in providing some deterrence from cyberbullying offences among high school children. However, their focus is on providing a reactive response to cyberbullying, for example by seeking the removal of intimate images or videos shared online, or empowering internet service providers with powers to block access to online materials. The complaints system and take down notices provided through legislations are only helpful after the harmful content has already been posted and shared online. Prevention of cyberbullying, especially for high school children can be achieved through a culture of awareness and education in schools. Currently, the only guidance for the implementation of preventive responses for schools in Western Australia and India are through policy directives, rather than through legislation. This chapter identifies the lack of legislative compulsion in high schools in Western Australia and India to establish anti-cyberbullying culture within their school policy. However, in another Australian state, the South Australian government have implemented a state-wide community-based approach to bullying prevention, whereby the Children and Young People (Safety) Act 2017 requires prescribed organisations, including schools to provide a child safe environment. This chapter conveys Tay's research undertaken as part of her Master of Laws thesis (see https://ro.ecu.edu.au/theses/2647/), where the Western Australia approach towards bullying and cyberbullying prevention has been compared with the South

V. Tay · P. Pearce (✉)
School of Business and Law, Edith Cowan University, Joondalup, WA, Australia
e-mail: p.pearce@ecu.edu.au

J. Aston et al. (eds.), *Comparative Law*, https://doi.org/10.1007/978-981-97-7815-7_4

Australian approach, and lessons are also drawn from Ontario, Canada, where anti-cyberbullying culture is promoted through the requirement within their Education Act.

Keywords Prevention of cyberbullying · School children eSafety · Comparative policy

1 Introduction

The internet provides some of the most effective means of communication. Along with the positive aspects of the internet, cyberbullying is certainly one of the most negative aspects, especially with regard to school students. The prevalence of cyberbullying increases every year due to the advancements of digital technologies and youths' usage and attachment to social media platforms.[1]

In October 2022, Digital Around the World reported that 5.07 billion people around the world use the internet, which is equivalent to approximately 63.5% of the world's population. With social media use, they reported 4.74 billion users, which is equivalent to approximately 59.3% of the world's total population.[2]

With the increase in internet usage, most children also have to turn to cyber space for schooling as well as for socialising and communicating with others.[3] This exposure leads to attachments to social media platforms, and the exposure to cyber space increases the risk for potential cyberbullying.[4] As more children are exposed to the internet, it is important that there is awareness of the safeguards in place in order to protect them from serious harm that may flow from the internet. Governments, school authorities, teachers and parents all have a role to play in the protection of children and in the promotion of internet safety and of cyberbullying behaviours.

Victims of cyberbullying may be able to obtain legal sanctions; however, this usually occurs after the harm is done. In Australia, some states such as South Australia has recognised the need for preventive strategies by requiring schools to have an anti-bullying plan in place. Other countries, like Ontario, Canada, have implemented similar preventative strategies in their legislation.

One way to reduce cyberbullying in schools is to create an anti-bullying culture within the school. The implementation of a cyberbullying policy that promotes a positive school culture, prevention and intervention strategies, support systems, clear definitions and reporting procedures, aid in creating this culture. An effective school

---

[1] Manpreet Kaur and Munish Saini, 'Indian government initiatives on cyberbullying: A case study on cyberbullying in Indian higher education institutions' (2022) *Education and Information Technologies* 1, 2.

[2] Datareportal, 'Digital Around the World' (Web Page, 2022). https://datareportal.com/global-digital-overview.

[3] Kaur and Saini (n 1) 8.

[4] Ibid 2.

cyberbullying policy will aid in the promotion of an anti-bullying school culture and thus lead to a reduction in bullying and cyberbullying behaviours.

The message from this chapter is that both India and the State of Western Australia lack legislative compulsion for its high schools to implement transparent cyberbullying policies and could benefit from introducing legislation similar to that enacted in South Australia and Ontario.

This chapter is divided into nine parts. Following this introduction, Part 2 explores the cyberbullying and its effects. Part 3 explores the importance of establishing an anti-bullying culture in high schools and examples of how to build such a culture. Western Australia's approach to cyberbullying is explored in Part 4. South Australia's approach to cyberbullying is explored in Part 5. Part 6 provides a summary of Tay's research as part of her Master of Laws thesis by comparing the school's approaches to bullying and cyberbullying in two Australian states: Western Australia and South Australia. Part 7 explores Ontario, Canada's approach to cyberbullying. Part 8 explores India's approach to cyberbullying. Part 9 concludes the paper, reiterating the importance of legislative compulsion that require schools to establish and maintain anti-cyberbullying culture in high schools.

2 Cyberbullying and Its Effects

Cyberbullying is often referred to and considered as a subset of bullying, such as online bullying.[5] The main elements of cyberbullying include intention to harm, a power imbalance, repeated behaviour, and the harmful communication that is inflicted through the use of an electronic device.[6]

Cyberbullying is more challenging to stop when compared to traditional bullying. Cyberbullies have continuous access to the victim through the convenience of technology and hence cyberbullies can remain anonymous. Technology provides the ease of distribution of harmful materials, the potential audience that the harmful content with vast outreach, as well as the lack of oversight of online behaviour.[7] Cyberbullying has also been reported to have far more serious consequences than traditional bullying.[8]

Cyberbullying causes a range of devastating effects onto its victims. Cyberbullying puts the victims emotional and psychological wellbeing at risk, causing poor

---

[5] Karen Brown, Margaret Jackson and Wanda Cassidy, 'Cyber-Bullying- Developing Policy to Direct Responses That are Equitable and Effective in Addressing This Special Form of Bullying' (2006)(57) *Canadian Journal of Educational Administration and Policy* 1, 4.

[6] Tiffany Field, 'Cyberbullying: A narrative review' (2018) 2(1) *Journal of Addiction Therapy and Research* 10, 11.

[7] Des Butler et al., 'School Policy Responses to Cyberbullying: An Australian Legal Perspective' (2011) 16(2) *International Journal of Law and Education* 7, 8; Cyberbullying Research Center, 'What is Cyberbullying?', *Cyberbullying Research Center* (Web Page). https://cyberbullying.org/what-is-cyberbullying.

[8] Field (n 6).

self-esteem, stress, anxiety, depression, low academic performance, self-harm and suicidal behaviours.[9] This is extremely detrimental considering that the prevalence of cyberbullying mainly affects youths. Other studies have reported victims feeling sad, hopeless, and powerless, as well as being afraid to go to school, fearing for their safety, feeling embarrassed, upset and worried.[10]

Hinduja and Patchin's 2018 study explored the association between school bullying and cyberbullying, and suicide ideation and suicide attempts. Their study found that there was a stronger correlation between bullying and suicide ideation when compared to cyberbullying and suicide ideation.[11] Their research suggests that youth that experienced bullying or cyberbullying did not greatly increase suicide attempts; however, when an individual experiences both forms of bullying, it had significantly increased the likelihood of suicide ideation and suicide attempts.[12] This is due to the increase in harm and stress that is caused when an individual is affected by bullying both at school and online, and the harm becomes harder to manage.[13]

A 2014 reported Indian case in the Indian Newspaper, The Times of India, demonstrates the effect of cyberbullying on cyberbullied children. This case involved a 17-year-old student from India who committed suicide after her friends had created a fake profile of her as a form of revenge because was avoiding them.[14] The friends had uploaded a "morphed" photo of the victim on a social media platform along with her phone number, stating that she was "seeking friends" and was "open to relationships."[15] When the victim started receiving obscene calls on her phone, she felt trapped with no way of escape, leaving suicide as her only option. Her suicide note alleges that she was "forced to kill herself after being defamed on the social networking site."[16]

Another more recent reported incident in 2020 in India was an Instagram scandal known as the Bois Locker Room. It was a group chat consisting of mostly teenage boys from India that shared nude images of under-aged girls without their knowledge

---

[9] Enrique Chaux and Melisa Castellanos, 'Money and age in schools: Bullying and power imbalances' (2015) 41(3) *Aggressive Behavior* 280, 281; Ann John et al., 'Self-Harm, Suicidal Behaviours, and Cyberbullying in Children and Young People: Systematic Review' (2018) 20(4) *Journal of Medical Internet Research* 129, 129.

[10] Juliana Raskauskas and Ann D. Stoltz, 'Involvement in traditional and electronic bullying among adolescents' (2007) 43(3) *Developmental Psychology* 564, 569; Charisse L Nixon, 'Current perspectives: the impact of cyberbullying on adolescent health' (2014) 5 *Adolescent Health, Medicine and Therapeutics* 143, 145.

[11] Sameer Hinduja and Justin W Patchin, 'Connecting adolescent suicide to the severity of bullying and cyberbullying' (2018) 18(3) *Journal of school violence* 333, 341.

[12] Ibid.

[13] Ibid.

[14] Times of India, 'Girl kills self over Facebook harassment' (Web Page, 26 June 2014). https://timesofindia.indiatimes.com/city/kolkata/girl-kills-self-over-facebook-harassment/articleshow/37211521.cms?utm_source=contentofinterest&utm_medium=text&utm_campaign=cppst.

[15] Ibid.

[16] Ibid.

or consent.[17] The chat also involved offensive comments made about women, ranging from body shaming to sexual assault. When screenshots of the chats were leaked onto other social media platforms, the members of the group then threatened to leak nude photos of the people who had outed them.[18] When Delhi Women's Commission asked Instagram to investigate, they stated that they "did not allow behaviour that promotes sexual violence or exploits anyone, especially women and young people,"[19] also stating that they had taken action once they were made aware of the group. The chairman of the International Commission of Cyber Security Law stated that India is too soft on social media networks and that social media companies should be made liable.[20] A senior psychologist also stated that "these chats were typical of the kind of high-risk behaviour that children of this age indulged in."[21] This indicates the need for preventative measures for such behaviour.

As the effects of cyberbullying are vast and include suicide, schools should be required to set appropriate policies to prevent such behaviour. Importance should be placed on the schools duty towards their students as well as the negative effects of cyberbullying.

3 Importance and Requirements of Establishing Anti-Bullying Culture in High Schools

As cyberbullying mainly affects school-aged children, who spend a majority of their time at school, it is important for schools to develop policies that educate children about cyberbullying and protect them from harm. Policies are important as they provide guidance, accountability, as well as set out the standards of behaviours that are expected.

While the implementation of a school anti-bullying policy is of great importance for the protection of children, not all schools implement such a policy. Even if such policy is implemented in schools, many students and teachers are unaware that their institutions have a cyberbullying policy.[22] Schools should not assume that school staff members know how to respond when faced with the issue of bullying, even if there are procedures implemented in the schools' bullying policies that state how to handle bullying incidences.[23]

---

[17] BBC News, 'Bois Locker Room: Indian teen's lewd Instagram group cases outrage' (Web Page, 5 May 2020). https://www.bbc.com/news/world-asia-india-52541298.

[18] Ibid.

[19] Ibid.

[20] Ibid.

[21] Ibid.

[22] Julie M Luker and Barbara C. Curchack, 'International perceptions of cyberbullying within higher education' (2017) 28(4) *Adult Learning* 144, 149.

[23] Wanda Cassidy, Karen Brown and Margaret Jackson, 'Under the radar': Educators and cyberbullying in schools' (2012) 33(5) *School Psychology International* 520, 521.

When developing an effective anti-bullying and anti-cyberbullying policy in schools, an important factor to consider is a whole school approach with changes to the school's climate and culture around cyberbullying. Actively promoting the school's cyberbullying policies helps to spread awareness on cyberbullying.

Creating an anti-bullying culture and building strong and positive peer relationships is something that should be emphasised in all schools. Victims of bullying and cyberbullying need high levels of care and support as the harm that can occur from bullying can lead to interpersonal difficulties, emotional and psychological issues, as well as poor academic performance.[24] Schools should therefore focus on creating an environment of awareness and understanding of cyberbullying and the harms that come from it, and avoid punitive approaches or restricting use of the internet when cyberbullying cases occur.[25] Cyberbullying is a problem that will always be part of cyber space. It can affect anyone who uses the internet and social media. The best way to protect young people is by promoting preventative actions before they occur, rather than placing importance on only reactive remedies for the victims of bullying or cyberbullying after the harm has been done to them.

Bullying at school can create a very hostile and oppressive environment for all students.[26] Students should feel that school is a safe place to learn and grow, not to fear that they may be potential targets for bullying.[27] This shows the importance of establishing positive school climate. In order to create an anti-bullying culture at school, there must first be a positive school climate. According to Ferrer-Cascales and colleagues, school climate concerns the "quality of the interactions between students, teachers, parents, and school staff, reflecting the norm, values and goals that represent the educational and social missions of the school."[28] Research conducted by Winnaar and colleagues shows that schools with positive climate have fewer disciplinary problems, higher academic success, higher achievement scores and lower rates of bullying.[29]

To create an anti-bullying culture at school, there must also be empathy. Research by Jones and Augustine show that empathy training and empathy building programmes had decreased incidences of bullying.[30] The process of empathy building include: increased awareness and understanding of what bullying is; how

---

[24] Kaur and Saini (n 1) 6.

[25] Brian Wiseman, 'Cyberbullying in schools: A research study on school policies and procedures' (2011) *UNLV Theses, Dissertations, Professional Papers, and Capstones* 1, 50.

[26] Joseph R. Jones and Sharon Murphy Augustine, 'Creating An Anti-Bullying Culture In Secondary Schools: Characterists to Consider When Constructing Appropriate Anti-Bullying Programs' (2015) 43(3) *American Secondary Education* 73, 76.

[27] Ibid 77.

[28] Rosario Ferrer-Cascales et al., 'Effectiveness of the TEI Program for Bullying and Cyberbullying Reduction and School Climate Improvement' (2019) 16(4) *International Journal of Environmental Research and Public Health* 1, 2.

[29] Lolita Winnaar, Fabian Arends and Unathi Beku, 'Reducing bullying in schools by focusing on school climate and school socio-economic status' (2018) 38(1) *South African Journal of Education* 1, 2.

[30] Jones and Augustine (n 26) 73.

bullying behaviours can be hurtful to others; an understanding of the long-lasting impacts of bullying behaviours, and also an understanding of personal responsibility, as well as appreciating individuality.[31]

The above literature demonstrates the importance of developing a whole school approach when it comes to bullying and cyberbullying behaviours, as well as developing a positive school climate with a focus on empathy training. The next part explores why in Western Australia, there is not a big focus on preventative measures when it comes to bullying behaviours in schools when compared with the South Australian approach towards bullying and cyberbullying prevention. Unlike Western Australian, the South Australian government have implemented a state-wide preventative approach to bullying, as well as implemented legislation requiring schools to have policies and guidelines in place for the safety and protection of children and young people.

4 Western Australia's Approach to Cyberbullying

Public schools in Western Australia are governed by policies and guidelines set by the Department of Education. The West Australian Department of Education policy entitled "Student Behaviour in Public Schools Policy" applies to principals in public schools and states that they are responsible for the implementation of this policy.[32] The policy states that the school principal is required to "document a whole school plan to support positive student behaviour, implement the documented whole school plan to support positive student behaviour, and provide individual student behaviour support where the need is identified."[33] These three rules must be observed in accordance with the "Student Behaviour in Public Schools Procedures." The policy rules are lawful orders for the purposes of Section 80(a) of the *Public Sector Management Act 1994* (WA) and are therefore to be observed by all Department of Education employees, and that includes principals of public schools in the state of Western Australia.[34] The shortfall of this policy in regard to preventing cyberbullying in schools is that the focus of the policy is only on positive student behaviour, and therefore, the policy does not have a direct influence on mandating it as a preventative measure for cyberbullying.

The Department of Education's website also provides guideline intended to assist schools in their development of approaches and strategies for the prevention and

---

[31] Stacey Stanbury et al., 'The Effects of an Empathy Building Program on Bullying Behavior' (2009) 7(2) *Journal of School Counseling* 1, 21.

[32] Government of Western Australia, 'Student Behaviour in Public Schools Policy' *Department of Education* (Web Page, 2022). https://www.education.wa.edu.au/web/policies/-/student-behaviour-in-public-schools-policy?redirect=%2Fweb%2Fpolicies%2Fschool-management.

[33] Ibid.

[34] *Public Sector Management Act 1994* (WA) s 80(a).

management of bullying.[35] Cyberbullying falls under the definition of bullying in this guideline. This guideline provides for a range of effective strategies that schools can implement as part of their anti-bullying policy, such as whole school prevention strategies, targeted early intervention strategies and intervention strategies for bullying incidences.[36] However, this is only a guideline, and it is not mandatory for schools to implement guidelines, but are only persuaded to do so. The guideline serves only as a resource that schools can use and target areas that are deemed important for the successful prevention of school bullying for that school.

As the bullying guideline and its strategies are not mandatory for schools to use or implement as a part of their anti-bullying or student behaviour policy, schools can choose not to use them. As schools in Western Australia are not legally required by State legislation to implement these anti-bullying strategies within their school policies, there is a possibility that some schools may lack specific policies for the prevention or management of bullying. Schools that choose not to implement the effective strategies listed in the guideline provided may lack the required preventative measures, which ultimately affect children who are the victims of bullying and cyberbullying at school.

In comparison with Western Australia, South Australia has adopted a more legislative approach to cyberbullying as discussed next.

5 South Australia's Approach to Cyberbullying

Following the recommendations from the 2016 Child Protection Systems Royal Commission, South Australia in 2017 introduced a new child protection system that requires a collaborative effort with other non-government and government agencies to create a united community that is dedicated to protecting all children.[37] A part of reforming and reorientating the child protection system in South Australia included the enactment of the *Children and Young People (Safety) Act 2017*.

This legislation requires prescribed organisations, which include high schools, to provide a child safe environment.[38] Section 114(1)(b) highlights that certain organisations must have policies and procedures to ensure that a child safe environment is provided. The policies and procedures under this section must be "designed to ensure that safe environments for children and young people are established and maintained in respect of the services or activities provided or undertaken by the prescribed

[35] Government of Western Australia, 'Behaviour and Wellbeing', Department of Education (Web Page, 7 April 2010). http://det.wa.edu.au/studentsupport/behaviourandwellbeing/detcms/school-support-programs/behaviour-and-wellbeing/binary-files/preventing-and-managing-bullying---template-for-schools.en.

[36] Ibid.

[37] Government of South Australia, 'A fresh start' (Report, November 2016) 8. https://www.childprotection.sa.gov.au/__data/assets/pdf_file/0011/107111/a-fresh-start.pdf.

[38] *Children and Young People (Safety) Act 2017* (SA) s 114.

organisation."[39] Section 114(3) states that a prescribed organisation must provide a statement to the Chief Executive certifying that they have the child safe environment policies and procedures in place within the organisation.[40] A prescribed organisation must be able to produce for inspection, a copy of the policies and procedures they have prepared or adopted, at the request of a person to whom the prescribed organisation provides a service.[41] A prescribed organisation means a person or bodies that undertake child related work, such as education services for children.[42] This suggests that all public schools in South Australia have to certify to the Chief Executive that they have a policy that ensures a child safe environment, such as through an anti-bullying policy.

In addition, a state-wide bullying prevention strategy was introduced in 2019 by the South Australian State Government with the publication of a report aimed at strengthening the responses to children's bullying both within school grounds, as well as beyond the school gates.[43] The South Australian government approach to bullying prevention incorporates the help of the whole community, thus canvassing a community-based approach. In this community-based strategy, the State Government developed five key actions to deal with bullying in South Australia. Their bullying prevention model states that bullying is best addressed through modelling positive behaviours, challenging disrespectful behaviours, teaching conflict resolution and resilience, promoting inclusivity, and reducing power inequities in social groups.[44]

The principles underpinning bullying prevention strategy are the following:

- Having visible leadership that inspires positive environments for children where they feel respected and safe;
- Having communities that are inclusive and connected, values diversity and supports inclusion;
- Having children and young people as active participants in their own learning and wellbeing;
- Having educators, families, professionals and community members work together to support children and young people; and
- Having a community model that promotes, supports, and shares an understanding of positive and respectful behaviour.[45]

The bullying prevention initiative applies to both within and beyond the school gates. Within the school gates, the initiative states that the education sector will help strengthen school leadership by supporting schools in adopting an anti-bullying

---

[39] *Children and Young People (Safety) Act 2017*s 114(1)(b).

[40] Ibid s 114(3).

[41] Ibid.

[42] Ibid s 114(7).

[43] Government of South Australia, *Connected: A Community Approach to Bullying Prevention Within the School Gates and Beyond* (Report, 2018) 11. https://www.education.sa.gov.au/sites/default/files/connected-community-approach-bullying-prevention.pdf.

[44] Ibid.

[45] Ibid 5.

policy. This policy should include: the use of the national definition of bullying; list the steps which the school will take to prevent bullying; outline how bullying can be reported and the steps taken in response to the bullying; and how the students involved with the bullying will be supported.[46] In addition to this, the school staff and educators are required to be equipped to respond to bullying. This is achieved through training on how to recognise and effectively respond to bullying, having access to resources on the different types of bullying, access to professional development modules and access to bullying prevention resources.[47]

As regards beyond the school gates, the Department of Human Services and the Department for Child Protection have strengthened the legislative responses with regard to bullying by establishing bullying prevention guidelines as required in the *Children and Young People (Safety) Act 2017*.[48] Section 145(b)(ii) of the *Children and Young People (Safety) Act 2017* (SA) states that the Chief Executive's function is to "provide guidance on matters relating to the protection of children and young people, including how to deal with cases involving the bullying or harassment of a child or young person."[49] Other functions of the Chief Executive include "developing codes of conduct and principles of good practice for caring for, or working with children and young people"[50] as well as "defining appropriate standards of care for ensuring the safety of children and young people."[51]

The impact of the South Australian Government approach to bullying on public schools is that all public schools in South Australia are bound to have a definition of bullying, bullying prevention strategies, how the school will respond to bullying incidences, and support systems in place for people involved in bullying incidences listed under their schools bullying policy, as required by the *Children and Young People (Safety) Act 2017* and the South Australian state-wide bullying prevention strategy.

There is a clear difference of the bullying approach between Western Australia and South Australia, Western Australia through the Department of Education policy guidance, and South Australia through the *Children and Young People (Safety) Act 2017*. To determine the impact of these approaches, the author Tay, as part of her Master of Laws thesis undertook a survey of displayed policies of public high schools in Western Australia and compared them with the public high schools in South Australia. The results of her survey are discussed next.

[46] Ibid 17.

[47] Ibid.

[48] Ibid.

[49] *Children and Young People (Safety) Act 2017*s 145(b)(ii).

[50] *Children and Young People (Safety) Act 2017*s 145(a).

[51] Ibid s 145(c).

6 Tay's Survey of Western Australian and South Australian Public High School Policies Pertaining to Bullying and Cyberbullying

As part of her Master of Laws thesis, Tay conducted a survey of high school bullying and cyberbullying policies in Western Australia and South Australia. The scope of Tay's survey was to include only schools that were classed as a high school, namely those from year 7 to 12, and those which were classed as public schools. This included independent public schools and senior high schools. The public high schools also had to fall within the north and south metropolitan areas of Perth for Western Australia, and Adelaide for South Australia. Sixty-five public high schools in the Perth metropolitan area and 52 public high schools in the Adelaide metropolitan area met these criteria.

The survey criteria used by Tay included five main sections:

i. Whether the high schools publicly displayed an anti-bullying policy on their school website;
ii. Whether the policy included a definition of bullying in their policy;
iii. Whether they listed strategies for interventions, monitoring of the behaviours or prevention approaches in their policy;
iv. Whether they included the rights and responsibilities of staff, students and parents when dealing with bullying behaviours;
v. Whether there was a separate definition for cyberbullying.

The main results of her survey are summarised in the table below.

Survey results comparing Western Australian and South Australian public high school policies.

Totalsample	Have a policy on their website regarding bullying (%)	Definition of bullying (%)	Strategies for intervention (%)	Listed rights and responsibilities (%)	Mentioned cyber-bullying as a separate issue to bullying (%)	Described what bullying is, what it isn't, what it involves (%)
WA 65	51	49	37	26	5	37
SA 52	88	88	56	52	44	73

Source Tay's Master of Laws Thesis

The results of the survey on all of the five criteria that were tested demonstrate that South Australia had a much higher rate of compliance than Western Australia. While there is compulsion through the *Children and Young People (Safety) Act 2017* to implement a policy in order to provide a safe environment for children, 88% of the South Australian public high schools publicly displayed their policy. When compared to the compulsion by the Department of Education in Western Australia for public schools to implement the same type of policy to protect children, the results have shown a vast difference in policy implementation with only 51% of all Western Australia public high schools making their policy publicly available.

While some Western Australian public schools do openly display policies pertaining to bullying and cyberbullying, the percentage when compared to South Australia demonstrates that Western Australian public high schools do not openly display their bullying and cyberbullying policies to the same standard as South Australia. This also applies to the standard at which South Australian schools seek to offer support to students after the bullying has occurred. This points to a need for Western Australia to implement legislation that brings about compulsion for its high schools to put in place and then openly display their anti-bullying and anti-cyberbullying policies, like in South Australia. It is important that schools openly display their anti-bullying and anti-cyberbullying policies as it demonstrates that they do have a policy and are openly being held accountable and responsible for the protection of its students against cyberbullying. By not displaying their cyberbullying policies on their website, points to the lack of importance placed on the school's preventative strategy.

Tay's research points to a need for Western Australia to implement legislation that brings about compulsion for high schools to put in place and then openly display their anti-bullying and anti-cyberbullying policies, as seen in South Australia. While the findings from Tay's research demonstrate that legislation does not ensure perfect implementation of bullying policy, it suggests that compulsion through legislation has a better outcome compared with policy guidance.

In comparison with Western Australia and South Australia, the State of Ontario in Canada has taken a different approach to cyberbullying by incorporating cyberbullying into the *Education Act*, rather than introducing a standalone cyberbullying legislation as in South Australia, and lessons that can be drawn from Ontario is discussed next.

7 Ontario's Approach to Cyberbullying

Ontario's Bill 13, also known as the *Accepting Schools Act*, was introduced into the Legislative Assembly of Ontario in November 2011.[52] This legislation sought to amend Ontario's *Education Act* with respect to bullying and other matters. The *Accepting Schools Act* highlights the importance of having a positive school environment, feeling welcome, accepted and connected to the school, as well as having a safe, comfortable, equitable and inclusive school for all students, including LGBT students.[53]

---

[52] Legislative Assembly of Ontario, 'Bill 13, Accepting Schools Act 2012' *Legislative Assembly of Ontario* (Web Page, 2022). https://www.ola.org/en/legislative-business/bills/parliament-40/session-1/bill-13/status.

[53] *Accepting Schools Act*, 2012, S.O. 2012, c. 5.

Ontario's *Education Act* was amended to include a definition of cyberbullying. Section 169.1 states that every board shall "promote a positive school climate that is inclusive and accepting of all pupils, including pupils of any race, ancestry, place of origin, colour, ethnic origin, citizenship, creed, sex, sexual orientation, gender identity, gender expression, age, marital status, family status or disability"[54] as well as promote the prevention of bullying.[55]

Under Section 170(1)(7.1) of the *Education Act*, every school board is required to establish and provide professional development to educate school staff about bullying prevention and strategies for promoting positive school climates.[56] Under this section, every board must also provide programmes, interventions or support for victims of bullying, witnesses of the bullying, as well as for the bully themselves.[57] The support is provided by social workers, psychologists, or other professionals as determined by the school board.[58]

Ontario's *Education Act* also provides that students who engage in certain behaviours that include cyberbullying could face possible suspension.[59]

Section 301(7.1) of the *Education Act* lists strategies that must be included in a school's policy and guideline with regard to bullying prevention and intervention. These strategies are as follows:

1. Training for all teachers and other staff;
2. Resources to support pupils who have been bullied;
3. Strategies to support pupils who witness incidents of bullying;
4. Resources to support pupils who have engaged in bullying;
5. Procedures that allow pupils to report incidents of bullying safely and in a way that minimises the possibility of reprisal;
6. Procedures that allow parents and guardians and other persons to report incidents of bullying;
7. The use of disciplinary measures within the framework described in clause (6)(a) in response to bullying;
8. Procedures for responding appropriately and in a timely manner to bullying;
9. Matters to be addressed in bullying prevention and intervention plans established by boards under Section 303.3.[60]

Ontario's legislation also extends the rights of parents and guardians. At the school board level, the parents and guardians have a right to expect that the school board will establish a bullying and cyberbullying prevention and intervention plan.[61] Parents and

[54] *Education Act*, R.S.O. 1990 c. E.2 s 169.1(1)(a.1).

[55] Ibid s 169.1(1)(a.2).

[56] Ibid s 170(1)(7.1).

[57] Ibid s 170(1)(7.2).

[58] Ibid.

[59] Ibid s 306(1).

[60] Ibid s 301(7.1).

[61] Prevnet, 'For Parents' *Prevnet* (Web Page, 2019). https://www.prevnet.ca/resources/policy-and-legislation/ontario/for-parents.

guardians have a right to ask that the school board to make the bullying and cyberbullying prevention plans publicly available.[62] Parents and guardians also have the right to ensure that the school board periodically review the bullying and cyberbullying plan.[63]

At the school level, the parents and guardians have a right to remind school staff that they have to report any incidences of bullying and cyberbullying to the principal as soon as they are aware of the bullying behaviour occurring.[64] Parents and guardians also have a right to consult on matters relating to the planning of bullying and cyberbullying prevention and intervention programmes and activities for the school.[65]

The lessons that can be drawn from Ontario are that their *Education Act* portrays the awareness of the harm that can be caused by cyberbullying in schools. Sections under this Act also show that Ontario has an awareness of the importance of bullying prevention, and expects a culture within the schools that promote respect, safety, inclusivity and acceptance of others, as well as strategies for intervention and prevention. The inclusion of a Bullying Awareness and Prevention Week within the *Education Act* also demonstrates the importance of promoting safe schools and positive learning environments.

The Ontario legislators have demonstrated that promoting and creating a positive school environment is the key to reducing bullying within schools. Although there are no definitive characteristics that make a person susceptible to cyberbullying, this susceptibility has been minimised under the *Education Act* with the need to create a positive school climate that is safe, inclusive and accepting of all people, regardless of their ethnicity, race, ancestry, place of origin, ethnic origin, citizenship, creed, sex, sexual orientation, age, family status or disability. Education on these issues in schools plays an important role in shaping young people, in which they can be taught acceptance and respect for others. By promoting acceptance, inclusivity and respect in a positive school environment can prevent bullying behaviours in schools.

The next part explores India's approach to cyberbullying and whether there is a need in India to implement legislation, similar to South Australia and Ontario, Canada.

8 India's Approach to Cyberbullying

Like Western Australia, India does not have specific anti-bullying legislation. They do, however, have legislation that may capture some cyberbullying offences, including the *Indian Penal Code* (IPC) 1860, the *Information Technology Act* 2000, and the *Protection of Children from Sexual Offences Act* 2012.

---

62 Ibid.

63 Ibid.

64 Ibid.

65 Ibid.

The *Information Technology Act* 2000 was created to provide legal recognition regarding the exchange of electronic date through means of electronic communication.[66] Under this Act, there are offences that cover some acts that are classified as cyberbullying, including punishment for sending offensive messages through communication service, such as a computer resource or communication device, punishment for identity theft, punishment for violation of privacy, punishment for publishing or transmitting obscene materials in electronic form, punishment for publishing or transmitting materials containing sexually explicit acts, and punishment for publishing or transmitting materials depicting children in sexually explicit acts in electronic form.[67]

The *Indian Penal Code* (IPC) 1860 covers all criminal law in India and is the official criminal code of India. Under this Act, there are also a range of offences that cover some of the acts that are classified as cyberbullying but are not specific to cyberbullying, such as sexual harassment, stalking, defamation, criminal intimidation by anonymous communication, using words, gestures or acts intended to insult the modesty of a woman.[68] These Acts only apply after cyberbullying has been committed and the harm has already been done. It is a reactive, rather than preventative approach to cyberbullying.

In 2012, the Ministry of Home Affairs in India issued a National Advisory on Preventing and Combating Cyber Crime against Children. This advisory has created guidelines to help and collaborate with state agencies to effectively prevent and combat the increase in number of cybercrime cases involving young people.[69] This advisory also provides definitions on cyber stalking, cyberbullying, child pornography, hacking of emails or social media accounts, identity theft and unwanted exposure to sexually explicit materials.[70] Cyberbullying is defined by the advisory as "acts of harassment embarrassment, taunting, insulting or threatening behaviour towards a victim by using internet, e-mail or other electronic communication device"[71] and includes sections from the *Indian Penal Code* and the *Information Technology Act* that could apply depending on the nature of the case. Unlike the current Indian legislations that may cover the scope of some cyberbullying offences after harm has been committed, these schemes focus on preventative action to combat cyberbullying against young people. However, like Western Australia, these are only guidelines and there is no compulsion for schools and other institutions to implement them.

In 2007, the statutory body of the Commission for Protection of Child Rights in India created the National Commission for Protection of Child Rights (NCPCR).[72]

---

[66] *Information Technology Act* 2000.

[67] Ibid.

[68] *Indian Penal Code* (IPC) 1860.

[69] Ministry of Home Affairs, 'Advisory on Preventing & Combating Cyber Crime against Children' (Web Page, 2012). https://www.mha.gov.in/sites/default/files/CS-Adv-160112.pdf.

[70] Ibid.

[71] Ibid.

[72] National Commission for Protection of Child Rights, 'About NCPCR' (Web Page, 2022). http://ncpcr.gov.in/about-ncpcr.

The role of this commission is to ensure that all laws, policies, programmes and administrative systems comply with the rights of the child as stated in India's Constitution and from the United Nations Convention on the Rights of the Child.[73] One of the functions of the NCPCR is to "promote the incorporation of child rights into the school curriculum, training of teachers or personnel dealing with children."[74]

In 2017, the Central Board for School Education in India issued "Guidelines for Safe and Effective Use of the Internet and Digital Technologies in Schools and School Buses" advised all institutions affiliated to the Central Board for School Education, that schools need to promote safe and secure education environments for effective teaching and learning.[75] Included in this guideline are suggestions to educate the students on the safe and effective use of the internet, making sure teachers and parents are aware of internet safety issues, as well as drafting a school policy regarding the safe use of electronic devices, and subsequently implementing the policy.[76] Similar to the position in Western Australia, the Department of Education in India had also created guidelines to protect against cyberbullying, such as the implementation of an anti-bullying policy. While this is necessary, the implementation of these policies is not mandatory.

9 Conclusion

In conclusion, lessons can be learnt from South Australia and Ontario on how they address issues of bullying and cyberbullying within their schools. Both have enacted pieces of legislation that require schools to implement and enforce bullying and cyberbullying policies. They also focus on promoting a positive school climate and on creating communities that are inclusive, values diversity and respectful behaviours of others. In comparison, Western Australia and India lack the legislative compulsion with regard to school cyberbullying policy and the requirement for preventive cyberbullying measures for schools.

The results from Tay's survey illustrate a higher compliance when there is legislative compulsion for schools to establish anti-bullying policies. Cyberbullying school policies should include the promotion of a positive school culture, prevention and intervention strategies, support systems, clear definitions and reporting procedures, and aid in creating anti-bullying culture.

The message from this paper is that in order effectively decrease incidences of bullying and cyberbullying in high schools, policies that promote a positive school

---

[73] Ibid.

[74] National Commission for Protection of Child Rights, 'Functions and Powers' (Web Page, 2022). https://www.ncpcr.gov.in/functions-and-powers.

[75] Central Board for School Education, 'Guidelines for Safe and Effective Use of the Internet and Digital Technologies in Schools and School Buses' (Web Page, 2017). http://cbseacademic.nic.in/web_material/Circulars/2017/32_Circular_2017.pdf.

[76] Ibid.

environment and create an anti-cyberbullying culture in high schools are required in conjunction with legislative compulsion that mandate that the high school's implement those policies.

NFTS, Blockchain and Cryptocurrency: Legal Scenario Across the Globe

Manish Kumar and Apoorva Thakur

Abstract The emergence of a new technological era may be seen with the rampant visibility and broad but subtle acceptance of cryptocurrencies and blockchain technology. As a result, governments all over the globe are striving to understand and regulate these developments. Logically enough, the significance of appropriate legal solutions and services assumes huge importance at this juncture. Non-fungible tokens ("NFTs"), like cryptocurrencies, are based on blockchain and serve as proof of ownership for digital assets. Anything, ranging from an image of a painting or a GIF to a trading card or a piece of virtual real estate, falls well-within the realm of possibility for NFTs. There are numerous potential applications for cryptocurrencies in the metaverse, yet their success will resemble that of NFTs, in that it will depend on the degree to which virtual worlds evolve in a decentralized and open-source approach. Legal frameworks encouraging the worldwide usage and acceptance of cryptocurrency and blockchain technology have been established in several jurisdictions, such as Australia, Singapore, Japan, and Switzerland. However, India has not yet enacted any specific law that would regulate these emerging areas. The purpose of this doctrinal research is to explore NFT in relation to cryptocurrencies, blockchains, and related intellectual property concerns. The ultimate object of this piece of comparative study is to advance new knowledge and spread awareness about legal hazards. Depending on the motivations of various parties (or stakeholders involved) and the nature of the transaction, NFTs may be valued in myriad ways, due to their ability to facilitate decentralized consensus, streamline and verify transactions, and open whole new marketplaces and related avenues.

Keywords NFT · Blockchain · Cryptocurrency · Decentralized · Consensus · Digital assets

M. Kumar · A. Thakur (✉)
MKA Legal Law Offices, New Delhi, India
e-mail: mkalegal.llp@gmail.com

J. Aston et al. (eds.), *Comparative Law*, https://doi.org/10.1007/978-981-97-7815-7_5

1 Introduction

The new digital gold rush was sparked by cryptocurrencies and non-fungible tokens (NFTs). Due to the unprecedented growth of the market for digital products, legal professionals are compelled to take an interest in this phenomenon and have had a significant effect alongside the development of a new financial market for exchanging digital assets like cryptocurrencies (fungible tokens). Using blockchain technology to ensure its uniqueness and record its creation and future transfers, an NFT is essentially a digital asset that confers ownership on its holder. The value of an NFT originates from its rarity and scarcity. Because NFTs might reflect real-world commodities or movies, which can imply significant intellectual property (IP) difficulties, their novelty is limited to the digital realm.

Tokenized proof of title to a digital asset (e.g., picture, video, or other digital material) or physical asset (like a car) may be created using NFTs (e.g., paintings or sculptures). In the process of "minting" an NFT, a new digital copy of the work is produced in the form of a data file utilizing blockchain or similar distributed ledger technology. When first generated, NFTs have confirmed security for exclusive ownership and transaction monitoring, making them immutable and freely marketable. NFT issuances might include as little as one token or as many as several million. There is no one NFT. In contrast, the vast majority of crypto assets are fungible, meaning that any token may be exchanged for and is indistinguishable from any other token. Built into certain NFTs are "smart contracts" that specify and automate the parties' respective responsibilities and rights, such as the author of the NFT receiving a certain proportion of the revenues from each subsequent sale. Despite NFTs' current success in the digital sphere, they might one day be used to digitize otherwise inaccessible assets like actual works of art, making them much easier to buy, sell, and exchange. All real-world property might be tokenized in theory, albeit not necessarily as fungible tokens. Using NFTs, several companies have tokenized assets including event tickets, albums, entertainment and famous photos, sports highlights, sports memorabilia, artwork, memes, gaming e-sports digital content, tweets, one-of-a-kind apparel, and more.[1]

In 2021, there was a dramatic increase in the purchase of NFT. In 2021, the NFT market was estimated to be valued at around $20 billion, and by 2025, that number is projected to increase by 100%. Even though the decentralized finance (Defi) sphere and NFTs emerged in isolation, their meteoric rise caught everyone by surprise at the start of 2021, when they were used only by a small subset of digital artists and cryptocurrency aficionados. Many companies, across industries, are using NFTs to spread the word about their existence and attract new customers. The broad acceptance has helped fuel the NFTs' meteoric development in spheres as diverse as sports (as in the instance of NBA Top Shot), gaming (through the Metaverse), and

[1] "*Non-Fungible Tokens: The Global Legal Impact,*" CLIFFORD CHANCE (January 03, 2023, 9:18 PM), https://www.cliffordchance.com/non-fungible-tokens-the-global-legal-impact.pdf.

finance (as in the example of Visa's acquisition of a single, very rare CryptoPunk).[2] Regulators are worried about the unexpected and dramatic development of these digital assets because of the associated legal difficulties and inherent issues with NFTs, whether or not they are high-risk investments.

An NFT is a digital cryptographic method of verifying the ownership and validity of an underlying asset. Unique identifying codes and information are used by NFTs to prove ownership of artworks or other valuable items. Certification of ownership, intellectual property rights, academic titles, works of art, musical compositions, games, and utilities are all examples of non-fungible items. NFTs are generated or "minted" with a time stamp and then recorded in public, permissionless ledgers, much like cryptocurrencies such as Bitcoin (BTC) and Ether (ETH). The creation of NFTs takes place using smart contracts that handle the transferability and assignment of ownership.[3] One of the most potent uses for tokens is as a flexible representation of non-fungible assets on a blockchain, and this is where NFT comes in.

Their main properties are the following[4]:

Unique**:** Each non-fungible token has unique characteristics that are described in its code. Tokenized in-game things may have data that helps the game client recognize which item the player owns and its properties, just as a digital artwork may have encoded data about individual pixels.

Traceable**:** Since its inception, all transactions involving a given NFT, including each time it changed hands, have been recorded on the blockchain. The ability to verify a token's authenticity is crucial for owners and purchasers.

Rare**:** Proof of scarcity is essential for NFT to attract purchasers. Doing so will prevent an excess of assets from being produced relative to their demand.

Indivisible**:** For the most part, NFTs cannot be traded in parts. NFT cannot be subdivided into smaller values, similar to how concert tickets and trading cards cannot be purchased in halves.

Programmable**:** NFTs are completely programmable, just like any other digital asset or token based on a blockchain that can execute smart contracts. The tokens for games like CryptoKitties and Axie Infinity have built-in mechanisms for reproducing virtual pets. A higher level of functionality is feasible. So, NFTs are the pinnacle of decentralized blockchain technology and the finest features of non-fungible assets rolled

[2] Ryan Browne, "*Trading in NFTs spiked 21,000% to top $17 billion in 2021,*" CNBC (January 03, 2023, 9:31 PM), https://www.cnbc.com/2022/03/10/trading-in-nfts-spiked-21000percent-to-top-17-billion-in-2021-report.html.

[3] "*A beginner's guide on the legal risks and issues around NFTs,*" COINTELEGRAPH, (January 04, 2023, 9:47 PM) https://cointelegraph.com/learn/a-beginners-guide-on-the-legal-risks-and-issues-around-nfts#.

[4] Ibid.

into one. Normal digital assets generated and governed by centralized institutions are subject to seizure at any moment, unlike the case of NFT assets.[5]

2 General Legal Characteristics of NFTs

It has been difficult to classify and regulate NFTs under the pre-existing regulatory and legal systems around the world due to the novelty of NFT technology as well as the multiple characteristics integrated into NFTs from a commercial, legal, and regulatory perspective. Since the legal status of NFTs has not been officially interpreted, several nations are now re-evaluating the topic in light of emerging concerns. NFTs are difficult to categorize legally since they are tied to a wide variety of assets and reflect a broad dimension of rights and responsibilities. There are a number of questions that need answering, including whether or not NFTs fall within the purview of current securities laws, whether or not they are commodities, and whether or not they are virtual assets that need their own set of rules. In addition, because of their widespread adoption in cross-border trade, NFT transactions often require the evaluation of international laws and regulations.

One of the first individuals to take an NFT to court was British art collector Amir Soleymani, who sued marketplace Nifty Gateway for the sale of NFT Abundance by Beeple. When Soleymani refused to pay for an altered version of the artwork he had bid on, Smart Gateway put a hold on his finances. Even if non-fungible tokens are not yet formally regulated, the Soleymani case demonstrates that the NFT market is actively expanding alongside its legal and regulatory concerns. According to the FATF's "countering the funding of terrorism and proliferation guidelines," NFTs are defined separately from cryptocurrencies and virtual assets. On the other hand, the FATF suggests taking into account the specifics of the situation, such as the kind and purpose of the non-fungible token.[6]

3 Legal Position of NFTs and Cryptocurrency in India

NFTs may be used to prove ownership and provide a price for other digital assets, such as explicit media files. Blockchain technology and smart contracts are used to issue them on these assets, creating one-of-a-kind digital signatures and guaranteeing their validity. These assets are very risky to own because of the present state of the market, which is highly speculative and subject to sudden price drops or spikes and

[5] Kendrick Lau, "*Non-Fungible Tokens A Brief Introduction and History,*" CRYPTO, (January 04, 2023, 5:52 AM), https://assets.ctfassets.net/Crypto.com_Macro_Report_-_Non-Fungible_Tokens.pdf.

[6] "*Beginner's Guide on the Legal Risks and Issues Around NFTs.*" COINTELEGRAPH (January 04, 2023, 6:02 AM) https://cointelegraph.com/nonfungible-tokens-for-beginners/a-beginners-guide-on-the-legal-risks-and-issues-around-nfts.

cyber security risks. NFTs attempt to solve the problem of establishing ownership by using blockchain technology. As a result of the ease with which digital material may be duplicated and disseminated, the value of the original work has decreased as a result of the proliferation of this content online.

The Reserve Bank of India (RBI) published a circular instructing banks not to trade in cryptocurrencies in June 2018, sparking the first controversy concerning the legality of cryptocurrencies in India. Cryptocurrencies have been present and around in India for the past decade. The RBI's order was overturned by the Supreme Court in Internet and Mobile Association of India vs. Reserve Bank of India[7] because Article 19(1)(f) of the Indian Constitution guarantees the right to engage in commercial activity. It seems that the buying and selling of virtual currencies like Bitcoin is legal.

WazirX launched in June 2021 as India's first NFT marketplace, and its users are guaranteed complete ownership of any NFTs they purchase. Beyond Life, a line of NFTs created by Bollywood superstar Amitabh Bachchan and released in September 2021, included autographed posters from Bachchan's films and other memorabilia. In October, designer Manish Malhotra sold NFTs of digital drawings of some of his most recognizable pieces for $4000. Two minutes after the auction started, the price of the other items had already risen from $2054 to $2535 apiece, and there are many more like them there.[8]

The Confederation of Indian Industry (CII) recommended to the Government and Parliamentary Standing Committee on Finance that SEBI monitor cryptocurrencies. The CII suggests that India, like the USA, discloses cryptocurrency ownership and transactions and treats bitcoin as a capital asset for tax purposes. The research advised India to require intermediaries to declare taxes. If crypto exchanges are taxed, the government and investors may gain transparency on cryptocurrency. Thus, the crypto market's legal uncertainty would reduce volatility.

The Indian Government has stated its plan to establish a digital currency. Given its market volatility and potential for misuse, the question today is whether a ban on all private cryptocurrencies and a single regulated "official digital currency" violates the objective of cryptocurrencies or is justified. An Income Tax Act modification made VDA gains and income taxable with effect from April 1, 2022. NFTs, tokens, and other VDAs subject to the Income Tax Act have not yet been notified by the Central Government. Thus, no NFTs are now covered by the new tax system, but the definition of cryptocurrency includes tokens, so the tax authorities may choose to tax NFTs under that category. Thus, taxpayers should anticipate that NFTs they buy, trade, or otherwise engage with are taxed under the system.[9]

---

[7] Writ Petition (Civil) No.373 of 2018.

[8] "*NFT regulations in India,*" ASIA BUSINESS LAW JOURNAL, (January 04, 2023, 6:18 AM) https://law.asia/nft-regulations-india/.

[9] Justin M Bharucha and Aashika Jain, "*How Cryptocurrencies Are Taxed In India,*" FORBES, (January 04, 2023, 9:06 AM) https://www.forbes.com/advisor/in/investing/cryptocurrency/crypto currency-tax-in-india/.

4 Global NFT Financial Regulations

Creators of recent NFT issuances have made millions of dollars in the sports and digital art sectors due to the instantaneous popularity of their works. There may be legal restrictions in any given jurisdiction that prevent NFTs from being used to develop novel types of digital property, expand enterprises' and digital creators' access to customers, fans, and audiences, or facilitate the monetization of physical assets. There has been a lot of development in the law and regulation surrounding NFTs, even though their issuance has increased dramatically around the world. Our company has been counseling customers on NFTs in several different legal systems.

- **Australia**

Since Australia is seen as a safe and impartial haven for blockchain and cryptocurrency companies, the market for these goods has exploded in recent years. Businesses in the payments, crypto asset, lending, investment, and custodial services sectors have been at the forefront of this growth, which has been spurred in large part by the Government of the Commonwealth of Australia's comprehensive approach to the fintech sector and its broad support for new and creative financial products and services.[10]

The Australian Taxation Office (ATO) has made recent efforts to clarify the application of tax law, but the taxation of bitcoin in Australia remains a contentious topic. The ATO classifies cryptocurrencies as capital assets for tax reasons (rather than as money or a foreign currency). To what extent bitcoin holders are subject to taxation is very contextual. For Australian tax reasons, the information below is relevant to holders only. A profit on the sale or disposal of cryptocurrencies should be recognized as a capital gain if it was not purchased or retained in the course of carrying on a company or as part of an isolated transaction to earn a profit. According to the ATO, bitcoin is a CGT asset. As long as the taxpayer qualifies, the CGT discount rules provide for a reduction in the tax due on capital gains (the cryptocurrency is retained for a minimum of 12 months before being sold or otherwise disposed of).[11]

Transactions involving digital currency provided or received after July 1, 2017 will be treated as input taxable financial supplies and will thus not be subject to GST. As a result, exchanges and other sellers of virtual currency would not have to collect GST on their transactions, and buyers of such currencies would not be eligible for GST refunds (input tax credits). The purchase or receipt of virtual currency for goods and services is subject to the standard GST regulations on the assumption that it is a mode of payment, similar to money.

Digital money, as defined by the GST law, is a digital unit of value that has the following features:

(a) It may be used to buy anything without restriction because of its fungibility;

---

[10] "*Blockchain and Cryptocurrency Laws and Regulations 2023|Australia,*" GLOBAL LEGAL INSIGHTS, (January 06, 2023, 10:17 AM), https://www.globallegalinsights.com/practice-areas/blockchain-laws-and-regulations/australia.

[11] Ibid.

(b) It is open to the public without significant limitations;
(c) There is no national currency behind it;
(d) There is no outside source or factor that contributes to the value; and
(e) It does not provide any special rights to get additional benefits.

- **Singapore**

There are currently no regulations in place in Singapore that specifically address NFTs. Tharman Shanmugaratnam, the head of Singapore's Monetary Authority (MAS) replied to a parliamentary question on the MAS's plan to monitor NFTs on February 15, 2022. According to Shanmugaratnam, "there are currently no such intentions, which is in line with the position taken by the vast majority of other prominent jurisdictions." The provision of digital payment token (DPT) services would be considered a "payment service" and hence need a license under the Payment Services Act 2019 (PSA). However, NFTs do not meet the PSA's definition of a DPT; hence, it is very unlikely that they will be treated as such. NFTs aren't "a medium of exchange accepted by the public, or a segment of the public, as payment for goods or services or the discharge of debt" for a few reasons.[12]

The courts in Singapore now seem to recognize NFTs as a legitimate form of property. The sale of a certain "Bored Ape Yacht Club NFT" was enjoined in a recent ruling by the Singapore High Court. This decision mirrors a recent one made by the UK High Court, which ordered an injunction to halt the sale of two Boss Beauties NFTs. In its first written ruling on a matter involving an NFT, the Singapore High Court declared that such tokens may be treated as property. NFTs are digital tokens that may be traded on decentralized digital ledgers known as blockchains. Digital or real works of art, films, or musical compositions may all be represented by tokens.

Marketplaces like OpenSea, Rarible, and Mintable make it easy to buy, sell, and trade NFTs by connecting creators with buyers and sellers online. There is a common misconception that these online marketplaces are also part of the agreements to sell, buy, or transfer NFTs that their members are providing. Instead, transactions on these P2P markets are enabled via self-executing smart contracts, with the Ethereum blockchain serving as the primary location for such contracts and wallet integration.[13]

Unfortunately, it may be difficult to determine whether the Singapore court has jurisdiction to hear a claim under a specific NFT contract since most NFT transaction data is pseudonymous and parties commonly engage in smart contracts without knowing the true identities of their counterparties. In a smart contract for the acquisition and sale of NFTs, the parties should make it clear that Singaporean law will apply to the transaction and that the courts of Singapore will have jurisdiction over

---

[12] Leon Yee, Patrick Ong, and Jacob Low, "*Understanding consumer protections for NFTs in Singapore,*" IFLR, (January 06, 2023, 11:01 AM), https://www.iflr.com/understanding-consumer-protections-for-nfts-in-singapore.
[13] Ibid.

any disputes that may arise. This would ensure that everyone involved is clear on their roles and the consequences of any infractions.[14]

The buyer may have further legal protections if (a) either the buyer or the seller is a Singaporean resident at the time of the transaction or (b) the offer or acceptance relating to the transaction is made in or sent from Singapore. According to the Consumer Protection (Fair Trading) Act of 2003 (CPFTA), a buyer may seek redress from the courts if they discover that a seller has engaged in unfair business practices. If a court finds that a seller engaged in an unfair practice, the court might compel the seller to provide restitution for any losses the consumer suffered as a result of the seller's actions, or it could issue a specific performance order against the vendor. Nonetheless, the possibility of remedies under the CPFTA is realistically restricted since most sales and transactions involving NFTs on online marketplaces are undertaken between persons acting in their capacity.[15]

- **Japan**

Presently, in Japan, NFTs are not specifically governed by any legislation. In contrast, if a holder of an NFT receives cash or other property that constitutes a "distribution of profits," then the NFT is likely a "security" within the meaning of Article 2.1 of the Financial Instruments and Exchange Act. NFTs that have an economic function, such as a payment mechanism, but do not correspond to stocks may be classified as "crypto assets" or "prepaid payment instruments" under Article 2.5 or Article 3.1 of the Payment Services Act.

The lack of monetary or other asset delivery in NFT transactions suggests that NFTs have no economic purpose, other than maybe as a method of exchange, and lends credence to the notion that NFTs are not currencies in and of themselves. So, as things stand, NFTs aren't governed by the Financial Instruments and Exchange Act, the Payment Services Act, or any other Japanese legislation pertaining to finance or business. It is possible to "acquire ownership of an NFT" in certain NFT transactions. Even though Article 85 of the Japanese Civil Code establishes ownership of a thing, which is a physical item, the NFT itself, being digital information, does not acquire this status. In particular, even after paying for an NFT, the buyer does not become the legal owner of the instrument.[16]

Since Bitcoins, which are tokens on a blockchain, are not physical things, a court in Tokyo ruled on August 5, 2015, that they cannot be owned. As the buyer of digital data as described by the token, your purchase of an NFT is taken as evidence of the non-rewritable and unique technical character of that token on the blockchain. Article 45 of the Copyright Act states *"that the owner of the original work of a copyrighted piece of art may show the work publicly without the permission of the*

[14] "*NFTs can be considered property, Singapore High Court rules,*" THE STRAITS TIMES, (January 06, 2023, 01:19 PM), https://www.straitstimes.com/singapore/nfts-can-be-considered-property-singapore-high-court-rules.

[15] Ibid.

[16] "*The boom in NFTs and potential legal issues in Japan,*" LEGAL 500 IHL, (January 06, 2023, 02:17 PM), https://www.inhouselawyer.co.uk/legal-briefing/the-boom-in-nfts-and-potential-legal-issues-in-japan/.

copyright holder." Article 45 does not apply to an NFT since ownership does not come into play.

Thus, the acquirer's NFT rights and usage are governed by the copyright holder's agreement. Even though the licensing restrictions are not always clear, reselling an acquired NFT work to a third party may be considered a license. The scope of the license in the agreement may be inferred from the NFT's metadata or the platform's terms of service. While NFTs may contain untapped potential as a novel channel for content distribution, their internal workings and legal standing are as yet unclear. To build NFT enterprises responsibly in the future, all parties to a transaction must have a firm grasp on what NFTs are and for clear and appropriate standards to be developed, and these efforts are now underway.[17]

- **Switzerland**

Switzerland has a vibrant ecosystem of blockchain and crypto asset enterprises due to the country's early adoption of blockchain technology. The Swiss Financial Market Supervisory Authority's (FINMA) helpful regulations and pragmatic attitude paved the way for this growth. Switzerland has adopted a "same business, same risks, same regulations" stance, meaning that the country's existing legal and regulatory framework for commercial operations, in general, applies to the issuing and trading of crypto assets and any services given in regard to them. Additionally, FINMA applies pre-existing rules and regulations to emerging technologies without favoring any one technology.[18]

For digital assets to become a new form of capital markets instrument that may be freely issued and exchanged on trading venues, some Swiss regulations needed to be altered since the existing legal framework would have been too strained. With this in mind, on September 25, 2020, the Federal Act on the Amendment of Federal Laws took into account advancements in Distributed Ledger Technology Act (DLT Act).

Since August 2021, the DLT Act has been in full effect. Certain financial intermediation activities in connection with Initial Coin Offerings (ICOs) and tokens are governed by the Swiss Anti-Money Laundering Act (AMLA) and the Anti-Money Laundering Ordinance (AMLO):

- Payment instruments that may be used with any merchant, not only the one issuing them;
- Payment transaction services, such as money transfer and asset transfer
- Providers of services relating to the exchange of currencies.

According to the AMLA, a financial intermediary is defined as a party that is required to be connected with a recognized AML self-regulatory organization. In addition, a financial intermediary must meet the standards set out by the AMLA.

[17] Ibid.

[18] Christian Maeder and Alexandre Jann, "*Non-fungible token (NFT)—Swiss legal and regulatory considerations,*" REICHLIN HESS, (January 06, 2023, 08:45 PM), https://www.reichlinhess.ch/en/2022/02/14/non-fungible-token-nft-swiss-legal-regulatory-considerations/.

Know your Customer (KYC) and other identity requirements of the contractual party and its beneficial owner are among these duties. When money laundering or terrorist funding is suspected, financial institutions are obligated to notify the Money Laundering Reporting Office.[19]

Financial institutions subject to FINMA's supervision are, as per FINMA Guidance 02/2019 on payments on the blockchain from August 26, 2019, expected to follow the travel rule when dealing with blockchain transactions. The same anti-money-laundering requirements apply to other financial intermediaries that are members of the SRO. For this restriction to be met, the relevant Swiss financial intermediary must provide the same information that is required for fiat currency wire transfers, or send the same information as is required for cryptocurrency wire transfers.

5 NFTs and Intellectual Property Rights (IPR)

The buyer of an NFT obtains both the token and the rights to replicate and resell an exclusive digital version of the work. The scope of the purchaser's usage rights with respect to the applicable NFT will be governed by the conditions or license terms associated with the acquisition of the relevant NFT and will vary from token to token. Given this, the NFT's creator or the marketplace where it is sold may want to apply more lax licensing restrictions, allowing the NFT's buyer greater leeway in how they put their newly acquired, digitally unique copy of the work to use.

Similarly, creators should read the fine print of any marketplace's or platform's license conditions to make sure they aren't giving up more rights than necessary. Although certain crypto assets have been acknowledged as qualifying as "property" (rights "in rem") in different nations, whether a court would accept an NFT as proof of legal title to a digital version of the asset to which it is connected is still up in the air. In reality, however, all that's required for the holder of an NFT to be able to direct the transfer of that NFT to anybody of their choice is to keep a unique collection of numbers that amounts to a token in their wallet. It might be argued that this proves ownership of the linked asset. When a digital copy of the underlying work (such as an image, sound, or text) is linked to the NFT, the token ensures that the copy is an authentic reproduction of the original.[20]

It is important to understand the nature and extent of the rights represented by NFTs before making a purchase. In particular, keep in mind that the sale of an NFT does not always mean that the underlying asset's copyrights have been transferred. The copyright transfer and the NFT publisher's right to earn copyright royalties, etc.,

---

[19] Olivier Favre, Caroline Clemetson, Tarek Houdrouge, and Michael Nordin, "*Blockchain 2022,*" (January 06, 2023, 08:58 PM), https://practiceguides.chambers.com/practice-guides/blockchain-2022/switzerland/trends-and-developments.

[20] Uhthoff, Gómez Vega and Uhthoff SC, "*Relationship between NFTs and Intellectual Property,*" LEXOLOGY, (January 06, 2023, 02:05 AM), https://www.lexology.com/.

must be investigated if the NFT is accompanied by a smart contract. NFT vendors should take extra precautions to properly explain the terms and conditions of the NFTs being offered to avoid liability claims from prospective buyers. Companies sometimes engage in arrangements with creators or copyright holders to issue NFTs in exchange for the right to use the creator's or copyright holder's work. In the latter case, the issuer should talk to the creators about the essential license terms and conditions that will be a part of the sale and the appropriate NFT to ensure the least amount of legal risk possible.[21]

According to the World Intellectual Property Organization (WIPO), NFTs are still covered under the Berne Convention for the Protection of Literary and Artistic Works. The Convention specifies that permission from the copyright owners is required before any digital reproduction of a protected work may take place. Being digital works at their core, NFTs are nonetheless governed by copyright regulations. If the NFT is going to include, for instance, a logo for a corporation, the digital maker will need to get permission from the mark's owner to replicate that picture in the digital artwork.

In addition, NFT creators may benefit from the underlying creativity, design, or art by declaring royalty terms for the NFT. That way, they may continue to make money off of their ideas even if the NFT is sold several times in the future, for instance, by establishing a royalty rate. Without a physical transfer of intellectual property rights, the royalties might be programmed into the blockchain (e.g., "every time this NFT is sold and moved to a new wallet address, pay 2% to the inventors"). However, leading intellectual property consulting companies like Finnegan have been actively encouraging their customers to extend trademark registrations to encompass uses that include NFTs. For instance, in 2021, Nike registered a slew of trademarks to produce and sell fictitious shoes; this safeguards the Nike name from being inappropriately used in NFTs.[22]

As the NFT revolution continues, the mechanisms by which intellectual property laws and agreements safeguard the replication of any such protected material in these new NFTs remain unchanged. Since purchasing and selling NFTs does not include acquiring or relinquishing IP rights, there are several unsolved problems with the transferability of IP rights inside the NFT trading markets. Consequently, intellectual property (IP) rules, particularly those pertaining to the transfer of rights, will need to develop to better address these novel NFT requirements and challenges.[23]

[21] "*Digital Finance: Current Issues and Laws NFTS: Key Korean Legal Considerations,*" LEGAL 500, (January 06, 2023, 03:45 PM), https://www.legal500.com/developments/thought-leadership/digital-finance-current-issues-and-laws-nfts-key-korean-legal-considerations/.

[22] Ibid.

[23] "*Legal Implications of Non-Fungible Tokens (NFT),*" LEXOLOGY, (January 06, 2023, 11:54 PM), https://www.lexology.com/.

6 Anti-money Laundering (AML) Concerns

The Anti-Money Laundering and Countering the Financing of Terrorism and Proliferation (CFT) guidelines are established by the international organization Financial Action Task Force (FATF), which classifies NFTs as "crypto-collectables" apart from cryptocurrencies and virtual assets. When it comes to anti-money-laundering laws, NFT platforms are coming under more and more scrutiny. Concerns that nefarious actors may use NFTs to evade regulations like anti-money laundering have increased in tandem with the NFTs' rising value.

The Supreme Court of India ruled in Internet and Mobile Association of India v. Reserve Bank of India,[24] *"that the Reserve Bank of India's circular from April 6th, 2018 forbids national/organized/cooperative banks and NBFCs from dealing in virtual currency, and that the challenged circular was irrational and thus a violation of Article 19(1)(g) of the Constitution of India because it ordered all regulated companies to refrain from trading in cryptocurrencies."*

To guarantee compliance with current anti-money laundering, foreign exchange, and fighting the financing of terrorism regulations, the Reserve Bank of India (RBI) issued a circular in May 2018 demanding due diligence for transactions utilizing virtual currencies. The legality of cryptocurrencies and crypto assets is still unclear, despite repeated requests for further information from the government and other regulatory organizations. Considering that both sellers and purchasers may maintain some degree of privacy while transacting in crypto, bad actors may find NFTs to be a more convenient means of laundering funds than traditional methods. NFT markets need to be alert to these dangers, take action quickly to mitigate them, and check in often to make sure they're in line with the law.[25]

Since high-value artworks may be purchased anonymously, this has been used as a means of laundering. Physical art has its limitations in terms of its usefulness, however, since it is cumbersome and costly to move and keep. NFTs that provide a legitimate ownership interest in artwork would provide the benefits of owning tangible art without the problems of shipping and storage, which presents serious AML issues. The FATF, the worldwide AML standard setter, has noted that NFTs may enable money laundering or terrorist funding and asked for more regulation. We should anticipate international advances in this arena in the coming months. Local FATF implementations in relevant countries and the NFT's characteristics determine whether it is subject to AML regulation.

Crypto assets are defined as "a cryptographically protected digital representation of value or contractual rights that employs a form of DLT and may be transmitted, stored, or exchanged electronically" (UK Money Laundering Regulations, 2017). The regulations also detail the actions that, when taken in relation to crypto assets, necessitate registration. A registration obligation arises if an NFT meets these criteria

---

[24] Writ Petition (Civil) No.528 of 2018.

[25] *"NFT's And Its Current Scenario In India,"* LEGAL SERVICE INDIA, (January 08, 2023, 03:41 AM), https://www.legalserviceindia.com/legal/article-8895-nft-s-and-its-current-scenario-in-india.html.

and is exchanged for cash or other crypto assets, or where agreements are made for others to exchange them. If an NFT does not meet the definition of crypto assets since it does not reflect the value or contractual rights, then it is not subject to the regime.[26]

As a result of a recent revision to Taiwan's anti-money laundering laws, virtual currency platforms and trading businesses are now within the scope of the law and must comply with the same regulations as other financial institutions. In April, the Executive Yuan released the AML ruling (the cabinet), clarified the legal status of companies operating in the cryptocurrency exchange and platform industries. It was then followed by the Financial Supervisory Commission (financial regulator) promulgating rules for firms operating virtual currency platforms and trading operations with regard to anti-money laundering and combating the funding of terrorism.

According to the regulations, those in charge of running exchanges and other marketplaces for digital assets must have systems of internal control and auditing, systems for reporting suspicious transactions, and other similar measures, and KYC procedures. In July 2021, the judgment and the accompanying rules went into force. However, it is not obvious if participants in the NFT market fit under the scope indicated in the AML ruling. The crux of the matter is whether or not NFTs will be considered "virtual currencies" under the judgment. If so, all relevant market participants, including exchanges and companies offering NFT custody services, must comply with the AML Regulations and fulfill the aforementioned responsibilities.

7 Concluding Comments

Tokenized artwork sales and purchases raise questions about the legality of tokenized artwork sales and purchases, various legal considerations, including the rights of NFT holders, the responsibility of creators and holders, the applicability of numerous other overlapping regulations, and the exhaustion of copyright holders' rights after the first purchase. Since cryptocurrency and NFT use are growing rapidly in India, it is essential that the country's legal framework adequately address this phenomenon. Many analysts have expressed concerns that the current NFT craze cannot be maintained. Using ethernet for NFT transactions leads to larger energy consumption, which raises additional concerns. The longevity of NFT is uncertain since it is still a young discipline. For now, the NFT revolution seems exciting and hopeful, particularly for artists seeking to make money from their creations and protect them from unlimited digital copying.

Although NFTs and copyright will interact in the real world, most disputes will be settled on the platform itself. As it is, the market is performing the function of a gatekeeper by discouraging the creation of a place where producers may sell

---

[26] "*Quick guide to the Money Laundering Regulations 2017,*" LAW SOCIETY (January 08, 2023, 05:00 PM), https://www.lawsociety.org.uk/en/topics/anti-money-laundering/quick-guide-to-the-mlrs.

tokens they have developed, thereby eliminating the possibility of infringement. Nevertheless, the NFT field may produce a high number of copyright issues due to the structure of the market and the motivation for huge profits. It will be fascinating to see the evolution of disputes and claims of ownership in the early stages of a potentially game-changing technology.

If new applications come to more directly challenge our centralized trust systems, the differences between anarchists and speculators in how they handle risk management in the NFT market will become more evident, since national sovereignty is mainly determined by control of these mechanisms. To avoid compromising the freedom of anarchists while providing remedies to speculators, a government that desires to recover authority for its own reasons would need a growing NFT economy to operate inside a personalized experience that more readily supports governance. The anarchists and the speculators who make up the market will choose where these boundaries are drawn between freedom and accountability. The future of legal risk in the NFT industry may be predicted based on how these borders are drawn.

NFTs are the newest innovation in the world of crypto assets. NFTs may serve the purpose of securities and be exchanged on decentralized peer-to-peer exchanges if certain conditions are met. The legal and regulatory systems of countries like Singapore, Canada, Japan, and Switzerland may serve as models for India to follow. For NFT trading in India to flourish, cryptocurrency legalization is a must. Until there is a clear judgment on the derivative nature of NFT and legality of cryptocurrencies in India, NFT trading and transaction is fraught with uncertainty.

Social Security Laws: A Distinct Feature of Indian Democracy – Comparative Analysis with Existing Provisions in Various Countries

Komal

Abstract The right to social security is a fundamental human right enshrined in international law. The Universal Declaration of Human Rights (UDHR), particularly Articles 22 and 25, recognizes social security as essential for a society to function peacefully and smoothly. This right is further elaborated on in the International Covenant on Economic, Social, and Cultural Rights, specifically Articles 9, 10(2), and 10(3). These articles emphasize that social security is not just a benefit, but a right that everyone should enjoy. In recognition of this right, most countries have established social security systems that provide a safety net for their citizens. These systems come in many forms, but they typically offer various benefits, including unemployment benefits, disability benefits, healthcare, etc. This paper will delve into the details of how different countries, including the UK, USA, and others, have implemented social security systems. By analyzing the existing international conventions and legislations, the paper will explore how social security plays a crucial role in upholding human rights and fostering a stable and secure society. A welfare state is a state that provides basic economic security for its citizens by protecting them from market risks associated with old age, unemployment, accidents, and sickness. Modernization and globalization have resulted in radical socio-economic changes and given rise to new conflicts and tensions consequent upon the erosion of an age-old family and fraternal security. There are three purposes of social security: compensation, restoration, and prevention. Article 41 of the Constitution states that "the state shall, within the limits of its economic capacity and development, make effective provision for securing the right to work, to education, and to public assistance in cases of unemployment, old age, sickness and disablement, and other cases of undeserved want." While India does have social security schemes, they cover a much smaller portion of the population compared to other developed nations like the USA and the UK. If we compare the statistics, it becomes clear that India faces challenges not just in designing social security policies but also in implementing them effectively.

Komal (✉)
Department of Law, Gurugram University, Gurugram, India
e-mail: sandhukomal12@gmail.com

J. Aston et al. (eds.), *Comparative Law*, https://doi.org/10.1007/978-981-97-7815-7_6

Keywords Welfare · Social security · Unemployment

1 Introduction

> Every Indian dreamed of India with peace and harmony. Literate India, which is free of violence, terrorism, hunger, and suffering and will be filled with compassion, peace, and happiness.

Social security is a program provided by the government to ensure that individuals and households have access to health care and a guaranteed income to support them in situations such as old age, unemployment, sickness, disability, work injury, maternity, or the loss of a breadwinner. The Universal Declaration of Human Rights, under Article 22, deems the right to social security as essential. "*Everyone, as a member of society, has the right to social security and is entitled to realization, through national effort and international cooperation and by the organization and resources of each state, of the economic, social, and cultural rights indispensable for his dignity and the free development of his personality*".

Further, Article 25. of the UDHR recognizes the right of everyone to security in the event of unemployment, sickness, disability, widowhood, old age, and other lack of livelihood in circumstances beyond his or her control.[1] The International Covenant on Economic, Social, and Cultural Rights (ICESCR) has laid emphasis on securing social justice through: (a) Article 9 recognizes the right of everyone to social security; (b) Article 10(2) recognizes the right of working mothers "to adequate social security benefits". (c) Article 10(3) requires state parties to undertake special measures of protection and assistance for children and young person.[2]

Further, the International Labour Organisation defines social security as "*security that society furnishes through appropriate organizations against certain risks to which its members are exposed*".[3] Social security is a fundamental right that is recognized as a basic human right by most nations worldwide. The concept of social security was first introduced in Germany in 1883, and they became the first country to adopt an old age social insurance program in 1889. The idea was designed by Germany's Chancellor, Otto von Bismarck. Under this scheme, each member of a particular trade, such as blacksmiths, painters, weavers, etc., was required to contribute some amount from their available funds at regular intervals. The funds were used for food, lodging, hospital, and funeral expenses for elderly and disabled members of society.

The generally accepted definition of social security is the "*right to social security assistance for those unable to work due to sickness, disability, maternity, employment*

---

[1] Article 25 Universal Declaration Human Rights, 1948.

[2] Article 9, Universal Declaration Human Rights 1948.

[3] International Labour Standards on Social security available on International Labour Organisation, https://www.ilo.org/global/standards/subjects-covered-by-international-labour-standards/social-security/lang--en/index.html.

injury, unemployment, or old age." Internationally, the concept of social security as a basic human right came into play with the ILO's Declaration of Philadelphia (1944) and its Income Security Recommendation 1944 (no.67). The right to social security has been recognized and enforced by most states in the world as a human right, as reflected in various international conventions and declarations such as the Universal Declaration of Human Rights (1948) and the International Convention on Economic, Social, and Cultural Rights (1966). This paper will analyze the recognition of social security as a human right in Indian municipal laws and schemes, as well as in various international instruments. A comparison will also be made with social security features available in countries such as the UK and the USA, particularly unemployment benefits.

2 Concepts of the Modern Welfare State and Social Security

Imagine a world where you don't have to worry about going broke if you get sick or if you lose your job. That's the idea behind a welfare state. It's like a safety net that governments put in place to help people during tough times.

This concept took off after World War II, but the idea of social welfare has been around since the 1800s. Different countries approach it in different ways. Some rely more on government programs, while others depend more on the free market or families to provide support. Researchers are always studying these different approaches to see what works best.[4]

Helping those in need isn't a new idea, but the way we do it has changed dramatically. In the past, poverty relief was often like a one-time handout—a quick fix but not a long-term solution.

Modern welfare programs are different. They aim to be more comprehensive, offering a helping hand to a wider range of people facing challenges. This approach was heavily influenced by the social insurance programs developed in Germany under Bismarck. Imagine a system where everyone contributes a little bit, like putting money into a common piggy bank. Then, if someone falls on hard times, they can draw on those resources. That's the basic idea behind social insurance.

These programs weren't always run by the government directly. Sometimes, they were more like community efforts, with people coming together to support one another. However, other programs relied solely on government funding. The world has changed a lot since then. We've moved from farms to factories, and with that shift came new problems. Workers faced risks like accidents and unfair working conditions. Modern welfare programs try to address these issues too, ensuring worker safety and fair treatment. The world is a constantly changing place, and globalization

[4] M. Weir, in International Encyclopedia of the Social & Behavioral Sciences, 2001, https://www.sciencedirect.com/topics/economics-econometrics-and-finance/welfare-state.

has thrown a bunch of new challenges our way. One of the biggest impacts is on traditional family structures. In the past, families often formed a strong support system, taking care of each other during difficult times. But in today's fast-paced world, with people moving for jobs or education, those close-knit family networks are sometimes less reliable. This is where social safety nets come in. They're like a backup plan, a way to ensure everyone has a minimum level of security, no matter what life throws their way. Human development experts agree—that everyone deserves a basic level of protection.

Social security isn't just about handouts; it's an investment in people. It allows individuals and families to weather storms, like job loss or illness, without falling into poverty. This, in turn, helps people reach their full potential and contribute to society. Think of it as fertile ground. When people have their basic needs met, they're free to pursue their dreams, start businesses, and create a better future for themselves and their families. A strong social security system acts like fertilizer, enriching the soil and allowing everyone to grow and thrive.

Social security isn't just a single program; it's a three-pronged approach to ensuring everyone has a safety net during difficult times. Here's a breakdown of these three pillars:

1. **Compensation**: Imagine facing a job loss, a sudden illness, or a disability. Social security acts as a financial buffer, offering income security during these challenging periods. The idea is to prevent people from suffering a "double whammy"—losing their health or ability to work while also falling into poverty.
2. **Restoration**: Social security isn't just about financial support; it aims to get people back on their feet. This could involve rehabilitation programs for those who are injured or disabled, or job training and placement services for the unemployed. The goal is to help people regain their independence and return to a productive life.
3. **Prevention**: It's always better to prevent problems than to fix them later. Social security programs can play a proactive role by promoting health and safety measures to reduce the risk of illness or injury. Additionally, unemployment benefits can provide a temporary safety net while people search for new jobs, minimizing the disruption to their lives and careers. This focus on prevention helps maintain the overall well-being and productivity of a community.

3 Status of Social Security Benefits in India

Article 41[5] of the Constitution reads, "*The state shall, within the limits of its economic capacity and development, make effective provision for securing the right to work, to education, and to public assistance in cases of unemployment, old age, sickness, disability and other cases of undeserved want*".

---

[5] The Constitution of India,1950.

The Indian government has always prioritized social security in its plans and policies since gaining independence. The social security system in India is comprised of several schemes and programs that are regulated by the government. However, these regulations only apply to a small portion of the population. Initially, most social security programs were focused on younger generations. Healthcare and disability issues were the primary areas addressed by these schemes. Old age social security was considered a family matter, as most elderly people lived with their children. With the rapidly increasing population of older individuals and a rapidly changing socio-economic scenario, issues concerning the elderly are now being included in social security schemes. In India, government-controlled social security schemes apply to only a small portion of the population. Generally, India's social security schemes cover a few social security initiatives like pensions and gratuities, which include retirement pensions, family pensions, widow pensions, and old age pensions. Additionally, there are health insurance, medical benefits, disability benefits, and maternity benefits available to women.[6] Social security systems are like a two-legged stool, needing both sides for stability. Here's a breakdown of these two key mechanisms:

1. **Social Insurance**: Imagine a group of people putting money into a common pool—that's the basic idea behind social insurance. Everyone contributes a portion of their earnings, and those funds are used to provide benefits to those who need them. Think of it as a kind of insurance plan, but instead of paying a private company, you're contributing to a system that supports your community. Benefits are typically based on how much you've contributed over time, so there's an element of "you get out what you put in".
2. **Social Assistance**: This side of the social security system is funded directly by the government. It provides support to vulnerable groups in society, such as low-income families, the elderly, or people with disabilities. Benefits can come in the form of cash payments or in-kind support, like food stamps or subsidized housing. The goal is to ensure that everyone has access to necessities, regardless of their ability to contribute.

4 Working Together for a Stronger Society

Both social insurance and social assistance play crucial roles in creating a more secure and equitable society. Social insurance provides a safety net for those who've contributed to the system, while social assistance ensures that those who are most vulnerable don't fall through the cracks.[7] This two-pronged approach helps to foster a sense of shared responsibility and promotes the well-being of everyone in the community.

---

[6] Social Security System in India - India Guide I Doing Business in India, https://www.india-briefing.com/doing-business-guide/india/human-resources-and-payroll/social-insurance (last visited Jun 10, 2024).

[7] Social Insurance: What it is, How it Works, Investopedia, https://www.investopedia.com/social-insurance-definition-5214692 (last visited Feb 7, 2024).

This mechanism is implemented in India by way of various legislation dealing with social security benefits. Some of these are as follows:

4.1 Employees Compensation Schemes

The Employee Compensation Scheme obligates employers to pay compensation to their workers for any accidents or injuries that occur during their employment. According to Section 2(3) of the Act, the state government has the power to extend the scope of this law to include other occupations that are considered hazardous. However, the scheme does not apply to the armed forces of the Indian Union. To be eligible for compensation, an individual must be employed by the company, and their employment must be related to the employer's trade or business. Additionally, the type of work they perform must be listed in Schedule II of the Act.

Employers must provide compensation benefits to their employees for personal injury costs incurred during their employment (as per Section 3). However, if the disability doesn't last for more than 3 days (except in the case of death), the employer is not liable to pay compensation. In the event of an employee's death, the compensation amount will be equal to 50% of their monthly wages multiplied by the relevant factor or an amount of Rs. 80,000, whichever is higher. Whereas, in the case of permanent total disablement, the compensation amount will be equal to 60% of the monthly wages multiplied by the relevant factor or an amount of Rs. 90,000, whichever is higher.[8]

4.2 The Employees State Insurance Scheme

The Employee's Compensation Act provides for health care and cash benefits in cases of sickness, maternity, and employment injury. This applies to non-seasonal factories using power and employing 10 or more employees. The ESI scheme is being implemented area-wise in a phased manner. It operates in 728 centers and is administered by a statutory body called the Employees State Insurance Corp. (ESIC). The administering body comprises members representing employers, employees, central and state government, medical professionals, and Parliament. The compensation available under this scheme is financed by contributions from employers and employees. Employers contribute 4.75%, and employees contribute 1.75%. The state government shares the expenditure on providing medical care up to 12.5%. The ceiling on expenditure per insured person or family unit has been raised to Rs. 900 per

[8] The Workmen's Compensation Act 1923: A Brief Intro, cleartax, https://cleartax.in/s/workmen-compensation-act-1923 (last visited April 10, 2024).

annum.[9] The ESIC scheme provides a comprehensive range of medical facilities, from primary health care to super specialty treatment. This medical care scheme is administered by the state government. The wage ceiling for employee coverage under the ESI Act, 1948, has been increased from Rs. 7500 to Rs. 10,000 per month. Additionally, the daily rate of allowance under the vocational rehabilitation scheme has been increased from Rs. 45 to Rs. 123 per day.

4.3 Maternity Benefits

The following benefits are implemented to promote the welfare of women who work: The law disallows the employment of pregnant women for a specific period. These provisions apply to all types of establishments, including factories, mines, plantations, shops, or any establishment that employs ten or more people. Female employees are entitled to paid holidays for up to six months or 26 weeks of paid leave for their first two children. There is also a provision for free prenatal confinement and postnatal care.[10] If these services are not provided, the employer is liable to pay a medical bonus of Rs. 250. Additionally, in case of a miscarriage, leave is available for up to six weeks. The implementation of this Act is dependent on the goodwill of the employer. A woman is eligible for maternity benefits if she has worked at an establishment for at least 80 days in the preceding 12 months.

4.4 Provisions Related to the Payment of Gratuity

The provision for payment of gratuity mandates that employees engaged in factories, mines, oil fields, plantations, ports, railway companies, shops, or other establishments should receive gratuity. This applies to all employees, irrespective of their wages or designation, except for apprentices. After rendering continuous service for 5 years or more, an employee becomes entitled to receive a gratuity. Gratuity is payable at the time of termination of his services, either:

i. On superannuation
ii. Retirement or resignation
iii. On death or disablement due to accident or disease
iv. Termination of services includes retrenchment

In the event of an employee's death, a gratuity is payable to the nominee. If no nomination has been made, the gratuity will be paid to the employee's heirs.

---

[9] Employees State Insurance Act 1948, Deskera Blog (2022), https://www.deskera.com/blog/employees-state-insurance-act-1948/ (last visited Jun 10, 2024).

[10] mehul_l0125z02, Maternity Benefits in India: 1961 Act Guide, ServeHr (Mar. 11, 2024), https://servehrindia.com/maternity-benefits-in-india-1961-act-guide/ (last visited Jun 10, 2024).

The payment of gratuity is governed by both the central and state governments. Section 3 of the Act authorizes the appropriate government to appoint an officer as a controlling authority for the administration of the Act.[11] Additionally, the central and state governments are responsible for framing rules for the administration of the Act.

Pension Schemes: Other than the provisions mentioned above, there are various other pension benefits available in India.

- Haryana Pension to Widows and Destitute Women Scheme (Widow Pension)
- Old Age Samman Allowance (Pension) Scheme
- Pension to Differently Abled Persons
- Ladli Social Security Allowance Scheme
- Financial Assistance to Destitute Children Scheme
- Financial Assistance to Kashmiri Migrant Families Scheme
- Allowance to Dwarfs
- Allowance to Eunuchs.

Recently, the Code on Social Security was enacted and implemented in India, which is also comprised of the above-mentioned provisions.

5 Status of Unemployment Benefits

During the COVID-19 pandemic, unemployment in India soared to nearly 24% in April 2020. However, by January 2021, the unemployment rate had dropped to over six percent, which was a significant improvement from the previous months.[12] The total lockdown had a damaging impact on India's economy, which is one of the largest in the world. The rise in unemployment was likely due to a decrease in demand and the disruption of the workforce faced by companies.

6 Social Security in the USA

Imagine you're working hard at your job, year after year. You pay taxes into a giant piggy bank, like a social security fund. Then, when you retire, that piggy bank helps pay you back! Social Security is a program that provides financial support to people who are no longer working.

Social Security is a program run by the federal government that uses taxes paid into a trust fund to provide benefits to eligible individuals. In the event of death, the program also offers benefits to legal dependents such as spouses, children, or parents.

---

[11] The Minimum Wages Act, 1948.

[12] India: COVID-19 impact on unemployment 2022, Statista, https://www.statista.com/statistics/1111487/coronavirus-impact-on-unemployment-rate/ (last visited Jun 10, 2024).

While at work, one can pay Social Security taxes. This tax money goes into a trust fund that pays benefits to:

- Those who are currently retired
- To people with disabilities
- To the surviving spouses and children of workers who have died.

Each year, you will get credits to help you become eligible for benefits when it's time to retire.

There are four main types of benefits that the SSA offers:

- Retirement benefits
- Disability benefits
- Benefits for spouses or other survivors of a family member who's passed
- Supplemental Security Income (SSI).

Social Security was never intended to be the sole source of income for retirees. Rather, it provides a percentage of a worker's pre-retirement income based on their lifetime earnings. The amount of replacement income a retiree will receive varies based on their earnings and the age at which they choose to begin receiving benefits. If they begin benefits at their full retirement age, the percentage of replacement income ranges from 75% for low earners to about 40% for medium earners, to about 27% for high earners.[13] If they begin benefits after their full retirement age, these percentages will be higher. However, if they begin benefits earlier, these percentages will be lower.

In 2020, when a person works, 85 cents of every Social Security tax dollar goes to a trust fund that pays monthly benefits to current retirees and their families and to surviving spouses and children of workers who have died. About 15 cents goes to a trust fund that pays benefits to people with disabilities and their families. All benefits are linked to a Social Security number.

In the USA, citizens get retirement benefits not only after retirement but even while they are working. Working beyond the full retirement age can increase the benefits. SSI financing comes from general revenues, not Social Security taxes. SSI makes monthly payments to people who are 65 or older or who are blind or disabled. They don't count some of your income and some of your resources when we decide whether you're eligible for SSI. Your house and your car, for example, usually don't count as resources.

Many people think of Social Security as just a retirement program. Most of the people receiving benefits are retired, but others receive benefits because they're: • Disabled. • A spouse or child of someone getting benefits. • A divorced spouse of someone getting or eligible for Social Security. • A spouse or child of a worker who died. • A divorced spouse of a worker who died. • A dependent parent of a worker who died. Depending on your circumstances, you may be eligible for Social Security

[13] Alternate Measures of Replacement Rates for Social Security Benefits and Retirement Income, Social Security Administration Research, Statistics, and Policy Analysis, https://www.ssa.gov/policy/docs/ssb/v68n2/v68n2p1.html (last visited Jun 10, 2024).

at any age. Social Security pays more benefits to children than any other government program.

In March 2021, the United States paid out 5.36 billion U.S. dollars in unemployment benefits, which is an increase from the 3.89 billion U.S. dollars paid in March 2020. As of May 2021, the U.S. Bureau of Labor Statistics reported that the unemployment rate declined by 0.3 percentage points to 5.8%, with the number of unemployed persons falling by 496,000 to 9.3 million. For the week ending May 29, the advance figure for seasonally adjusted initial claims was 385,000, a decrease of 20,000 from the previous week's revised level.[14] This represents the lowest level for initial claims since March 14, 2020, when it was 256,000.

7 Status of Social Security Benefits in the UK

Imagine life in the UK. You might be worried about unexpected situations—what if you lose your job, get sick, or retire? The good news is that the UK has a safety net in place: social security benefits. These are like helping hands offered by the government to residents who qualify.

There's a department dedicated to managing these benefits: the Department for Work and Pensions. They handle various programs to support people in different circumstances. So, if you ever face a tough time, it's worth checking if you're eligible for some assistance.

These benefits are categorized as follows:

(a) Income Support

The department offers financial assistance to individuals over 16 years of age who belong to the low-income group. The amount of support provided is based on the individual's total earnings, capital, and savings. If an individual has savings, their payment may be reduced, and those with savings exceeding a certain amount are not eligible for the support.

(b) Jobseeker's Allowance

This category of allowance is paid to an unemployed person of more than 18 years of age who is looking for work and people under retirement age who are capable of working but out of age. It is also available to people who work 16 h or less a week. UK jobless claims jumped 70% in April as the coronavirus hit employment.[15]

According to a report published by the Office for National Statistics (ONS), the number of jobless claims in the U.K. has increased by 856,500 to 2.097 million. The report also reveals that the unemployment rate in the country rose slightly to 3.9%

[14] Total unemployment benefits paid U.S. 2024, Statista, https://www.statista.com/statistics/284857/total-unemployment-benefits-paid-in-the-us/ (last visited Jun 10, 2024).

[15] https://www.cnbc.com/2020/05/19/uk-jobless-claims-rise-by-70percent-in-april-to-2point1-million.html.

during the January–March period in 2020. However, it is important to note that this period only covered one week of the lockdown imposed in the U.K. on March 23.

In 2018/19, the government of the United Kingdom spent approximately 1.67 billion British pounds on the Jobseekers Allowance, the main benefit for unemployed people in the country. During the provided period, spending on this type of benefit peaked in 2012/13, when it reached 5.17 British pounds.[16]

(c) Child Benefit

Anyone who has a child under the age of 16 living permanently in the country is eligible to apply for Child Benefit. Additionally, parents can apply if their child is between 16 and 19 years old and in full-time education or has recently left education or training but is registered for certain work or training. Child Benefit is paid on a monthly or weekly basis to the individual who is entitled to receive it.

(d) Housing Benefit

People from low-income groups, whether employed or not, may be eligible for help in paying all or part of their rent. If the salary plus savings are below a certain level, help may be available.

(e) Council Tax Benefit

Residents, whether in a rented or privately owned property, in a flat, bungalow, or house, must pay a council tax to their local authority to pay for local services such as rubbish collection. As with Housing Benefit, for low earners or the unemployed, there is financial help available for paying Council Tax—for those who own their own home or rent it.

(f) Disability Living Allowance (DLA)

This is a tax-free benefit intended for individuals who require assistance taking care of themselves. The amount of money received varies based on the level of disability. Those who have severe difficulty walking and are between the ages of three and 65 or those between the ages of five and 65, who require assistance to move around, can be eligible to claim this benefit.

(g) Invalid Carer's Allowance

Carer's Allowance is a weekly benefit provided to those who look after someone with a disability, regardless of whether they are related to or live with them. To be eligible for this allowance, a person must be over 16 years old and spend at least 35 hours a week caring for someone who is entitled to certain benefits. However, if the claimant earns above a specific amount or is in full-time education, they may not be able to claim.[17] It's important to keep in mind that receiving a carer's allowance may affect any other benefits that are being claimed or benefits claimed by the person they are caring for.

---

[16] Expenditure on Jobseeker's Allowance in the UK 2002–2020, D. Clark, July 30, 2020 available at https://www.statista.com/statistics/283944/jsa-spending-in-the-uk/.

[17] Carer's Allowance, GOV.UK, https://www.gov.uk/carers-allowance/eligibility (last visited Jun 10, 2024).

(h) State Retirement Pension

A state retirement pension is paid to women aged 60 and over and men aged 65 and over. The eligible age for the state pension is due to rise to 66 in the future. To qualify, pensioners need to have paid enough national insurance contributions throughout their working lives. The amount they are paid depends on the contributions they have made.

We can take another example of Switzerland, the country providing these benefits to all unemployed, and it amounted to around 4.85%. Switzerland's unemployment rate increased to 5.01% in December 2020, from the previously reported number of 4.88% in November 2020. Switzerland's Unemployment Rate is updated monthly, available from January 1991 to December 2020, with an average rate of 4.10%.[18] The data reached an all-time high of 5.49% in February 2010 and a record low of 1.53% in Jan 1991. The data is reported by the Swiss Federal Statistical Office.

According to the latest reports, Switzerland's population reached 8.67 million people in December 2020. Monthly earnings in Switzerland stood at 5769.63 USD in December 2019. The country's Labour Force Participation Rate increased to 68.44% in December 2020.

8 Analysis: The Gap Between Legislation and Its Implementation

After analyzing the statistics of the USA, UK, and Switzerland, it has become apparent that India is struggling with the execution of its existing policies. Taxpayers in India are not receiving equal benefits in comparison with those provided in the USA and UK. Furthermore, there is no policy framework in place for unemployment allowances. India has not learned from the situation that arose during the pandemic, as the massive health crisis has brought to light the glaring ambiguities in social security measures aimed at reducing the suffering of marginalized sections. The COVID-19 crisis has revealed two major challenges that have crippled the effective working of social security measures in India, among other things.

Exclusionary Approach

One of the most prominent loopholes regarding the social security policy in India that was revealed during COVID-19 is that it is largely exclusionary, which keeps a considerable section of the needy population out of its purview. The prolonged lockdown and the pandemic have resulted in massive joblessness and livelihood crises for the daily wage laborers, largely in the unorganized sector. Under such circumstances, the food security schemes, although they have been expanded considerably in this crisis, still have a limited impact on completely catering to the needs of all sections

[18] George Sheldon, Unemployment in Switzerland in the Wake of the Covid-19 Pandemic: An Intertemporal Perspective, 156 Swiss J Economics Statistics 8 (2020), https://sjes.springeropen.com/articles/10.1186/s41937-020-00058-6 (last visited Jun 10, 2024).

of the population.[19] The Food Security Act of 2013 seems to have been unable to touch a major section of people who were in dire need of food for survival. The lack of adequate documentation of the people who were entitled to the social welfare benefits made it largely exclusionary and inadvertently selective.

Moreover, ground-level corruption and ineffective implementation of the Public Distribution System (PDS) have further aggravated the problem. Apart from the possibility of mass hunger, the lockdown also revealed a massive lack of proper housing facilities for migrant laborers working as daily wage laborers in various urban conglomerates in India. Though the Central Government has made concerted efforts to bring universal ration cards to the effective reach of PDS benefits and social housing schemes for laborers, these measures appeared largely to be reactive and would require a substantial amount of time for implementation.

Insufficient Implementation

The COVID-19 pandemic ripped through the world, exposing the cracks in many countries' social safety nets. In India, it became clear that some people were simply left behind by existing social welfare programs.

One reason for this gap? There is a lack of empathy in how these policies are designed. Imagine policymakers sitting in a room, far removed from the daily struggles of people who need help the most. Their programs might look good on paper, but they don't reflect the real-life challenges faced by everyday citizens.

This pandemic is a wake-up call. It's time for a fundamental shift in how India approaches social welfare. We need more inclusive policies, designed with compassion and a deep understanding of people's needs. Only then can these programs truly reach and support the most vulnerable members of society.

The pandemic served as a stark reminder: if we don't bridge the gap between rich and poor, true freedom and prosperity will remain out of reach for many Indians. We need to move toward a more cohesive society where everyone has a chance to thrive, not just a select few. By strengthening our social safety net with empathy and inclusivity at its core, we can create a brighter future for all.

In the past, the central government has implemented various programs to provide social security benefits to workers. However, these benefits were mostly limited to workers in the organized sector, and even if they were available for the unorganized sector, they were based on occupation and not universal. The social security challenges faced by workers in the unorganized sector can be divided into two categories. The first is the inability to save due to a lack of employment opportunities and low wages. This is compounded by poor health and educational status, as these workers come from economically disadvantaged backgrounds. The second challenge arises from the absence of a safety net to deal with emergencies such as illness, accidents, death, and old age.

[19] K. P. Kannan, Social Security in the Lockdown: A Time to Revisit the NCEUS Recommendations, 63 Ind. J. Labour Econ. 139 (2020), https://link.springer.com/10.1007/s41027-020-00269-8 (last visited Jun 10, 2024).

9 Conclusion

Imagine you're a worker in India. The government offers programs to help with old age, unemployment, emergencies, and even motherhood. A study in Karnataka showed that 90% of workers felt these benefits were relevant to their lives! Sounds great, right?

There's a catch, though. These programs sometimes have a limited reach, not helping everyone who needs them. Another issue is that good intentions can get stuck in red tape. By the time the money reaches people, it can feel like it costs them more in hassle than it's worth. Corruption can also play a role, diverting resources away from those who truly need them.

The government has tried to streamline things with initiatives like Aadhar, a unique identification system. The goal was to make sure aid reached the right people. However, some worry that Aadhar might infringe on individual privacy or limit people's control over their information.

So, what's the answer? India's social safety net has the potential to make a real difference in people's lives. The challenge lies in striking a balance—ensuring programs are inclusive and efficient, while still respecting individual rights.

Here's what this paper might explore further:

- **Expanding Coverage**: How can India ensure more people benefit from social welfare programs?
- **Combating Corruption**: What strategies can be implemented to ensure aid reaches those who need it most?
- **Striking a Balance**: How can India design programs that are effective and respectful of individual privacy?

We look forward to a future where the government can establish social security channels that respect the privacy of both the organized and unorganized sectors. The groups covered under social security programs in different countries depend on whether the benefits are provided through a public service, social assistance, or social insurance program.

Orphaned by Fate or Design: Navigating the Human Rights Dilemma

Joshua Aston and Cecilia Anthony Das

Abstract A growing concern has emerged concerning the exploitation of children who are trafficked under the guise of being orphans. Orphanage trafficking is a troubling trend and is particularly pronounced in least-developed countries, where institutions are used to secure high-income countries' donor funding (Kate Van Doore and Rebecca Nhep, 'Orphanage trafficking, modern slavery and the Australian response' (2019) 7(2) *Griffith Journal of Law & Human Dignity*). The proliferation of charitable organisations operating orphanages is evidence of the lucrativeness of the orphanage industry (Ibid.). To sustain this industry, it becomes necessary to maintain a specific number of children to attract funding and tourism activities. To ensure a constant supply of children to meet this demand, trafficking takes place (Ibid.). What is disheartening to note is that these institutions within these regions are often left unobserved and scrutinised by the host country. Research indicates that approximately 3.5–5.5 million children worldwide live in institutional or residential care, and 80–90% still have at least one living parent (Sonja P. Brubacher, Kathryn E. van Doore and Martine Powell, 'Responding to orphanage trafficking from an information gathering perspective' (2021) 120 *Child Abuse & Neglect* 105222). This bleak statistic underscores the unnecessary institutionalisation of many of these children. What is even more alarming is the extent to which these institutions operate under the radar, providing shelter to trafficked children without drawing significant attention. This is a pressing issue that demands immediate international scrutiny. It is crucial to monitor the flow of funds from high-income countries to these least-developed regions under the guise of charitable donations. Equally important is the need for host countries to enforce sanctions and robust monitoring mechanisms for these organisations to ensure that trafficking does not take place within their institutions. This chapter aims to delve into the prevalence of this alarming phenomenon and explore strategies that should be implemented globally to prevent its continuation. Just as international efforts are dedicated to monitoring and combating terrorism funding,

J. Aston · C. A. Das (✉)
School of Business and Law, Edith Cowan University, Joondalup, WA, Australia
e-mail: cecilia.das@ecu.edu.au

J. Aston
e-mail: j.aston@ecu.edu.au

J. Aston et al. (eds.), *Comparative Law*, https://doi.org/10.1007/978-981-97-7815-7_7

the funding funnelled through these orphanages should be subjected to scrutiny and oversight.

Keywords Trafficking · Human rights · Modern slavery · Child abuse

1 Introduction

When asked how she came to be in the orphanage, Mach [...] explained that 'a man came to my village', offering parents the opportunity for their children to go and live in an orphanage to obtain an education. Mach explained that moving to an orphanage, receiving an education, food, and learning English was a good opportunity in her village. The children all said they understood an orphanage as a home for poor children. This differs from the Western definition of an orphan as a vulnerable person who requires '... sympathy, compassion and most importantly adult intervention and care'.[1] Explaining the term 'orphan' may undoubtedly entail a nuanced examination. However, this chapter's primary objective is not to engage in such an endeavour. Instead, its principal concern lies in the legal implications of considering paper orphans as trafficked.

According to UNICEF, about 153 million children worldwide are orphans.[2] These children are orphaned due to various reasons; among those identified are poverty, natural disasters, wars, and conflicts.[3] However, it should be noted that reliable statistics are difficult to obtain to determine the number and reasons they have been orphaned. Further, it is unclear how many are genuinely orphaned, i.e. neither parent is alive and without any living relatives. Literature indicates that approximately 3.5–5.5 million children live in institutional and residential care, and about 80–90% have at least one living parent. As indicated earlier, due to inability to obtain concrete data, these figures remain an estimate.[4]

Similarly, child trafficking accounts for one-third of the detected victims of trafficking and impacts the lower income countries acutely. A notable correlation between child trafficking and forced labour has been observed, particularly in regions such as South Asia and South America.[5] The same factors may apply to children identified as 'paper orphans'. A similar correlation may be developed between paper

---

[1] Amanda Miller and Harriot Beazley, '"We have to make the tourists happy"; orphanage tourism in Siem Reap, Cambodia through the children's own voices' (2022) 20(1) *Children's Geographies* 51–63, 54.

[2] SOS, 'Children's Statistics Data on the Plight of Children') <https://www.sos-usa.org/our-impact/focus-areas/advocacy-movement-building/childrens-statistics>.

[3] Kwabena Frimpong-Manso, 'Funding orphanages on donations and gifts: Implications for orphans in Ghana' (2021) 60 *New Ideas in Psychology* 100835.

[4] Brubacher, van Doore and Powell (n 4).

[5] *Global Report on Trafficking in Persons Vienna* (United Nations, ('*Global Report on Trafficking in Persons*').

orphaning and trafficking, demanding increased concern and appropriate intervention to prevent such situations from arising.[6]

Traditionally, 'trafficking in persons involved the recruitment, transportation, transfer, harbouring, or receipt of persons, employing the threat or use of force or other forms of coercion, of abduction, of fraud, of deception, of the abuse of power or a position of vulnerability or of the giving or receiving of payments or benefits to achieve the consent of a person having control over another person, for exploitation'.[7] While traditional trafficking definitions may not perfectly align with orphanage trafficking, the recruitment, sale, and exploitation of children under the guise of shelter and care in orphanages meet the requisite elements of trafficking.[8] With an estimated 3.5 million children residing in orphanages globally, the repercussions of orphanage trafficking extend beyond the nations providing financial support and volunteers, exacerbating the separation of children from their families through trafficking.[9]

This chapter examines the concept of orphanages, scrutinises its definitional nuances, and analyses the prevalence of orphanage trafficking alongside its concomitant contributory elements. Subsequently, it discusses the global initiatives implemented to counteract exploitative practices while delineating the proactive measures embraced by states with heightened susceptibility.

2 Understanding Orphanage Trafficking: Definitions and Dynamics Revisited

The existing body of scholarly work has yet to present a cohesive and uniform argument regarding the classification of paper orphans as trafficked individuals under the purview of international law, nor has it thoroughly examined the implications of such a classification. The scarcity of literature addressing this scenario poses challenges in formulating a precise definition. Nonetheless, in the strict sense, children categorised as paper orphans do not meet the criteria outlined in Article 3(a) of the Protocol to Prevent, Suppress and Punish Trafficking in Persons.[10] The definition employed in the Article is very restrictive and does not cover situations where children are presented as orphans when their parents are still living. Van Doore argues that the lacklustre approach encourages placing more children in orphanages in the least-developed countries, attracting considerable donations channelled to these institutions by developed countries—making it a highly lucrative venture.

[6] Ibid 9.

[7] Art 3 of Palermo Protocol.

[8] Joseph M. Cheer, Leigh Matthews, et al. (2020) Modern Day Slavery and Orphanage Tourism. USA, CABI.

[9] Brubacher, van Doore and Powell (n 4).

[10] Kathryn E Van Doore, 'Paper orphans: Exploring child trafficking for the purpose of orphanages' (2016) 24(2) *The International Journal of Children's Rights* 378–407.

She believes that positive action from the States will not be forthcoming if these forms of exploitation are not recognised internationally.[11]

The literature refers to orphanage trafficking as a situation where a child has been transferred or recruited from their parents to live under false pretence as an orphan in a care institution or orphanage.[12] The process of orphanage trafficking typically begins with the falsification of a child's status as an orphan, a practice known as 'paper orphaning.[13] Thus, the child is portrayed as abandoned, facilitating their placement in residential care facilities. Here begins the dark trade, where the vulnerability of the child is exploited to garner sympathy and financial support from sympathisers, namely tourists, volunteers, and international donors.

According to the literature, four interrelated activities are identified as distinct indicators. These are (1) recruitment, (2) manipulation of gatekeeping procedures, (3) formalisation of orphanhood, and (4) maintenance.[14] Each of these activities will be explored briefly. At the recruitment stage, the traffickers manipulate the parents to access the child and place them under their care. These could be achieved through various means, from outright purchases to false promises. In the next stage, legal documents are fabricated to create a situation where the relationship between the child and biological parents is severed. Following this exercise, the orphanhood will be formalised, and new identity documents will be created to ensure the child becomes non-traceable. Finally, children are subjected to abuse, to enable them to evoke sympathy from the donors culminating into donations.[15]

Well-intentioned donors have inadvertently fuelled the expansion of orphanage trafficking, unaware of the harm inflicted upon children residing in the institutions they support. Additionally, orphanage tourism, a practice where travellers from affluent nations visit or volunteer at orphanages during vacations, exacerbates the proliferation of orphanage trafficking. Typically, these tourists are gap year students who pay to participate in programmes, contributing financially and through educational services. Both situations create a troubling cycle that endangers a child's safety and facilitates their trafficking into orphanages and care facilities. However, this chapter refrains from delving deeper into the complexities of orphanage tourism. It suffices to acknowledge its role in promoting the phenomenon of orphanage trafficking.

Although Article 3(a) of the Protocol to Prevent, Suppress, and Punish Trafficking in Persons does not explicitly address orphanage trafficking, the broader provisions concerning child trafficking under Article 3(c) may apply. Falsifying a child's status

---

[11] Ibid 383.

[12] Brubacher, van Doore and Powell (n 4).

[13] https://papers.ssrn.com/sol3/papers.cfm?abstract_id=3878544.

[14] Rebecca Nhep et al., 'Detecting orphanage trafficking and exploitation' (2024) 152 *Child Abuse & Neglect* 106813.

[15] Ibid.

to place them in an orphanage could be construed as harbouring or receiving children for exploitation. In this context, exploitation includes benefits obtained through donations from well-intentioned supporters.[16]

To date, there have not been any prosecutions globally for orphanage trafficking. The factors that could contribute to the lack of prosecution at the domestic level may stem from the fact that it is difficult to detect. According to a study of the Cambodian situation, it was observed that despite there being an enabling legal framework, the prosecution for orphanage trafficking was said to be non-existent unless it related to a child sex offence where prosecution was witnessed. The two factors that were highlighted for the lack of prosecution were poor detecting mechanisms and limited awareness of orphanage trafficking in Cambodia. Besides, there seems to be an affinity to recognise only the older forms of trafficking.[17] The issues raised here have universal applicability. States should be able to detect the offence visibly so that they can prosecute it effectively. The international platform should seek to guide on how this could be done efficiently to combat the rising dangers of orphanage trafficking before more children become displaced from their families and pushed to deplorable conditions of living contrary to the spirit and intent of Articles 7 and 8 of the Convention on the Rights of the Child where it is stated that children should grow in a family environment. They have the right to know their parents and preserve their identity, which must be ensured by the State.

3 Orphanage Trafficking—A Convoluted Web of Exploitation!

The dark waters of orphanage trafficking can be seen in the various cases highlighted in this section. A growing interest has been witnessed over the years being placed on the relationship between institutional care and human trafficking. A report submitted in 2016 by the Special Rapporteur on the Sale of Children, Child Prostitution, and Child Pornography to the Human Rights Council highlighted compelling research in this regard.[18] This research indicated that orphanages were actively involved in recruiting children and subjecting them to harmful living conditions. The main motivation behind these actions appeared to be soliciting foreign charities and donations.

In Nepal, there are believed to be over 15,000 children living in registered institutions, with likely more in unregistered or illegal ones. Shockingly, two out of three children in these institutions, often labelled as 'orphanages', are not actually orphans. Despite government policies advocating for family preservation and

[16] Van Doore (n 14).

[17] Ibid.

[18] *Report of the Special Rapporteur on the sale of children, child prostitution and child pornography*, ('*Report of the Special Rapporteur on the sale of children, child prostitution and child pornography*').

prioritising institutional care as a last resort, many children end up in institutions as a first option. Living in these institutional care often detrimentally impacts the children. Some of the impacts include impaired physical, psychological, and cognitive development, as well as diminished post-care survival skills. These issues are exacerbated in Nepal, where a young person's ties to family, community, and local culture are vital for their future prospects. Furthermore, institutionalised children are at a heightened risk of physical, verbal, and sexual abuse, with numerous cases reported. Alarmingly, only 10% of registered children's homes in Nepal meet the government's minimum standards, highlighting the widespread dangers associated with institutional upbringing.[19]

The majority of institutions in Nepal are situated in the main tourist hubs of the country, particularly in districts like Kathmandu, Lalitpur, Bhaktapur, Kaski, and Chitwan. Surprisingly, up to 90% of registered institutions are found in these areas, despite them not necessarily being the most densely populated or in greatest need. This trend suggests a deliberate strategy of establishing 'orphanages' in places frequented by tourists—'donors'. There was also evidence to indicate that 'orphanage' managers in Nepal actively sought children from traffickers, specifically requesting for those who appear impoverished, to meet the preferences of foreign donors. Additionally, there have been instances where 'orphanage' managers purposely maintain destitute or unsanitary conditions to elicit higher financial donations from volunteers and donors.[20]

Further, the case of Forget Me Not Children's Home which was founded by an Australian voluntourist in 2006 in Nepal, initially to care for what he believed were 20 female 'war orphans' is a good example to illustrate the sinister workings within the four walls of orphanages. With support from Australian donors, the girls received education, food, clothing, and other essentials. However, in 2012, the appointment of an in-country Country Director revealed a disturbing truth: the girls had been trafficked, and their families were being kept from them under threat. Despite the material care they received, their fundamental right to family was denied for profit. After legal efforts, the girls were transferred to another local NGO, allowing 15 to reunite with their families and reconnecting four more. This case highlights how the exploitation of children's rights can remain hidden behind superficial care.[21]

A similar issue is seen to happen in India. On May 27, 2014, eight individuals from Bihar, Jharkhand, and West Bengal were arrested in Palakkad for their involvement in an alleged child trafficking case. The arrests followed the detention of 589 children below the age of 12 by the Railway Protection Force (RPF) at Palakkad Railway station. The children, primarily from Bihar and Jharkhand, lacked necessary documents like birth certificates. The accused claimed the children were to be admitted to two orphanages in Kozhikode and Malappuram, namely

---

[19] Martin Punaks and Katie Feit, 'Orphanage voluntourism in Nepal and its links to the displacement and unnecessary institutionalisation of children' (2014) 1(2) *Institutionalised Children Explorations and Beyond* 179–192.

[20] Ibid.

[21] Ibid.

Mukkam Muslim Orphanage and Vettathur Anwarul Orphanage. These incidents raised concerns about the mistreatment of children in private orphanages in Kerala. Following investigations, around 60 orphanages were ordered to be closed by the State Board of Control for Orphanages due to various lapses. Many orphanages in Kerala, including Kozhikode-based Markauz Saquafathi Sunniyya, received substantial foreign aid which information was concealed from the state government. The influx of funds has led to the proliferation of orphanages, with some institutions resorting to concealing records and abandoning children to avoid scrutiny.[22]

Similar issues are observed in Uganda, where the proliferation of orphanages and residential care for children has been attributed to foreign sponsorship, donations, and voluntourism, leading to the active recruitment of children into these facilities. Despite most children in residential care having identifiable family members, the number of orphanages in Uganda has soared from 30 in the late 1990s to an estimated 800 in 2013, with the vast majority operating without proper government licencing.

4 Orphanage Trafficking—Recognition?

In 2017, the Australian Parliament released the 'Hidden in Plain Sight' report, officially recognising orphanage trafficking as a modern form of slavery. This classification aligns with contemporary understandings of slavery and encompasses various global practices. Inspired by the UK Slavery Act of 2015 and the United Nations Convention on the Rights of the Child (UNCRC) from 1989,[23] the report marked a significant step forward. In 2018, Australia furthered this commitment by formally acknowledging orphanage trafficking as a form of modern slavery in its Modern Slavery Act 2018 (Cth). Despite these efforts, there remains a need to criminalise orphanage trafficking within Australia.

Interestingly, Australia stands as one of the largest donor countries to orphanages worldwide. However, many donors are unaware of the detrimental conditions faced by children in these institutions. These conditions include inadequate nutrition, limited access to healthcare and education, and coercive practices such as performing for tourists or soliciting funds in bars. Such practices exploit children's vulnerability to evoke sympathy and generate more donations, highlighting the urgent need for increased awareness and action.

In 2015, the UK government, under Theresa May's leadership, introduced the Modern Slavery Act to combat modern slavery, appointing an Anti-Slavery Commissioner and safeguarding victims. However, the first official international framework addressing such issues was the United Nations Convention on the Rights of the

[22] Saif Rasul Khan, 'Orphanages: Omphalos for Trafficking' (2016) 3(1) *Institutionalised Children Explorations and Beyond* 55–65.

[23] Elise Degrond, 'Orphanage Trafficking: A Modern Slavery: An analysis of the impact of NGOs' advocacy in Cambodia on the Australian"Hidden in Plain Sight"report of 2017' (2022).

Child (UNCRC), signed in 1989. This landmark convention not only solidified children's rights globally but also holds the distinction of being the most widely ratified human rights treaty in history, with 196 State parties. In comparison, the Convention against Torture and Other Cruel, Inhuman or Degrading Treatment or Punishment had 173 state parties. The pivotal shift was in recognising children as individuals with inherent rights, rather than mere extensions of their parents' ownership. Consequently, parents were legally obligated to fulfil duties towards their children, legally defined as individuals under the age of eighteen. Like many UN treaties, the UNCRC aimed to inspire national implementation, backed by a commission to monitor practices related to children. Recommendations stressed the importance of a nurturing family environment, echoing UNICEF's guidelines. However, these guidelines were flouted in the Cambodian case, underscoring the limitations of global agreements.

According to the United Nations Guidelines for the Alternative Care of Children, the primary aim is to promote the Convention on the Rights of the Child by emphasising that facilities such as orphanages, residential care centres, shelters, and similar establishments should only be considered a final option for children's placement. Instead, efforts should focus on arranging community-based care whenever possible, with institutional care being temporary and reserved for situations where no other suitable alternatives are available.

5 Conclusion

The exploration of orphanage trafficking highlights the intricate nexus of socio-economic factors, legal intricacies, and humanitarian imperatives. While international law grapples with defining and addressing orphanage trafficking uniformly, it is unequivocal that the rights and welfare of children are egregiously compromised. The involvement of unwitting donors, the proliferation of orphanages in developing nations, and the exploitation of vulnerable children emphasise the pressing need for concerted global action.

Efforts to combat orphanage trafficking must embrace multifaceted strategies, including legislative enactments, awareness campaigns, and bolstering community-based care alternatives. Collaboration among governments, NGOs, and international bodies is imperative to tackle the root causes of orphanage trafficking and provide holistic support to affected children and families.

In conclusion, orphanage trafficking stands as a stark violation of children's rights and a contemporary manifestation of exploitation and enslavement. While strides have been made in acknowledging and confronting this issue at the international level, much work remains to eradicate orphanage trafficking and ensure the safety and well-being of vulnerable children worldwide. It is the collective responsibility of governments, civil society, and individuals to dismantle the structures of exploitation perpetuating orphanage trafficking, thereby enabling every child to thrive in a secure, nurturing environment conducive to their growth and flourishing.

Goa v. India: A Comparative Study of Marriage and Divorce Law

Pearl Monteiro

Abstract Personal laws regulate matters such as marriage, divorce, inheritance, maintenance, and guardianship. In India, these personal laws are based on religion, with different laws applicable to individuals based on religious affiliations. Goa, a state in India, has its own Uniform Civil Code, which it inherited from the Portuguese. This Code applies uniformly to all Goans, uniformly irrespective of religious affiliation, and is followed in substance until date with minor, negligible modifications. Marriage is viewed differently by the different laws; Hindu law regards it as a sacrament, whereas Muslim law regards it as a contract. The Civil Code also recognizes it as a special contract with a definite purpose and objective. Similarly, the divorce laws, traditionally, are varied, with diverse grounds and consequences available, which vary based on both religion and gender. Some parity has no doubt been brought about by legislation; however, the current legislative scenario is far from ideal. It is a travesty that in India, civil status, rights, and obligations that flow from purely civil situations such as marriage and divorce are still regulated directly or indirectly by religion. One's civil relations or circumstances should not depend on one's religion or gender but rather should be substantially the same depending on one's civil status. Though the Constitution of India makes equality a fundamental right and prohibits discrimination on grounds of religion and sex, the personal laws have by and large escaped the scrutiny of judicial review. It remains to be seen whether the new doctrine of constitutional morality will bring about substantial uniformity and end discrimination on extraneous grounds of religion and sex. This paper will be a comparative study of the various marriage and divorce laws as applicable to Hindus, Muslims, Christians, Parsis in the rest of India, and the Uniform Civil Code as applicable to all Goans. The paper will point out the best practices in the available laws, the changes brought about by legislation and judicial review, and critically suggest reforms.

Keywords Marriage · Divorce · Uniform civil code · Gender justice

---

P. Monteiro (✉)
V. M. Salgaocar College of Law, Panaji, India
e-mail: monteiropearl@gmail.com

J. Aston et al. (eds.), *Comparative Law*, https://doi.org/10.1007/978-981-97-7815-7_8

1 Introduction

Societal regulation is done by its legal system. Legal systems are usually categorized as civil, which places greater emphasis on codes, and common law, which places more emphasis on precedent or judicial decisions.[1] India has inherited both of these two different legal regimes, the common law tradition from the British and the civil law from the Portuguese and French. In civil law traditions, the courts have a limited role to play, they are not perceived as lawmakers.[2]

Marriage, divorce, guardianship, maintenance, inheritance, and the like are personal matters that are governed by civil codes or statutes. In India, personal matters are governed by different laws, based on the religion of the individual.

2 Legal Provisions Governing Marriages in India

Marriage, in India, is a very colorful and lavish social institution. The various personal laws define marriage either as a contract or a sacrament, and prescribe different procedures or rituals connected with it, which differ based on religion. Registration of marriage is not compulsory, except in Goa, where only registered marriage is recognized.

[1] Dainow, Joseph. "The Civil Law and the Common Law: Some Points of Comparison." The American Journal of Comparative Law, vol. 15, no. 3, 1966, pp. 419–35. JSTOR, https://doi.org/10.2307/838275. Accessed 21 Dec. 2022.

[2] Quigley, John. "Socialist Law and the Civil Law Tradition." The American Journal of Comparative Law, vol. 37, no. 4, 1989, pp. 781–808. JSTOR, https://doi.org/10.2307/840224. Accessed 21 Dec. 2022.

2.1 Hindu

Ancient Hindu law recognized eight forms of marriage: Brahma,[3] Daiva,[4] Arsha,[5] and Prajapatya[6] were the approved forms, and Asura,[7] Gandharva,[8] Rakshasa,[9] and Paishacha[10] were the unapproved forms.[11] Only the Brahma and Asura forms are prevalent today.[12] Hindu law applies by default when the parties are not Muslims, Christians, Parsis, or Jews. Hindu law is applicable when the parties are Hindu, Sikh, Jain, or Buddhist.[13] Marriage is regarded as a holy sacrament, creating a bond that lasted for seven births. Marriage was considered an imperative duty for both men and women. The importance of marriage can be evidenced by the fact that most religious rituals can only be performed by a married couple. Polygamy was permitted. The Hindu Marriage Act introduced monogamy but continued to give importance to marriage rituals.

The essentials of a Hindu marriage are[14] both parties are Hindus; neither has a previous spouse living; parties are of sound mind and capable of giving a valid

---

[3] After the student bachelor has completed his gurukulavasa, his parents approach the parents of a girl belonging to a good family and ask them to give away their daughter in marriage to their son—to make a gift of their daughter (kanyadana) to him. A marriage arranged like this is brahma. In it this girl's family does not give any dowry or jewellery to the boy's family. There is no "commercial transaction" and the goal of a brahma marriage is the dharmic advancement of two families. Of the eight forms of marriage the dharmasastras regard this as the highest. <https://www.kamakoti.org/hindudharma/part18/chap5.htm>.

[4] Marrying a girl to a rtvik (priest) during a sacrifice is called "daiva". The parents, in this type, after waiting in vain for a young man to turn up and ask for their daughter's hand, go looking for a groom for her in a place where a sacrifice is being conducted. This type of marriage is considered inferior to brahma. In the sastras, womanhood is elevated in that it is the groom's family that has to seeking bride for their son. https://www.kamakoti.org/hindudharma/part18/chap5.htm.

[5] The bride is given in exchange for two cows received from the groom https://www.kamakoti.org/hindudharma/part18/chap5.htm.

[6] In prajapatya, there is no trading and kanyadana is a part of it as in the brahma ceremony. But from the name prajapatya, it must be inferred that the bride's menarche is imminent and that a child must be begotten soon after the marriage. For this reason, the bride's father goes in search of a groom, unlike in the brahma type. The brahma type is a better type of marriage than prajapatya since, in it, the groom's people go seeking a bride who is to be the Grahalaksmi of their household. https://www.kamakoti.org/hindudharma/part18/chap5.htm.

[7] Bride's family receive money from the man who forces them to marry her to him. https://www.kamakoti.org/hindudharma/part18/chap5.htm.

[8] "love marriage" https://www.kamakoti.org/hindudharma/part18/chap5.htm.

[9] The groom battles with the girl's family, overcomes them and carries her away https://www.kamakoti.org/hindudharma/part18/chap5.htm.

[10] Paishacha is a nonrighteous form of marriage where the man rapes the woman who is asleep, intoxicated or mentally challenged. It is considered as a marriage to protect the honour of the woman. Manusmriti with the "Manubhasya" of Medhatithi. (1999). India: Motilal Banarsidass.

[11] Koppisetti Subbharao v. the State of A.P, AIR 2009 SC 2684.

[12] A. L. V. R. S. T. Veerappa Chettiar v. S. Michael 1962.

[13] S. 2. Application of Act. Hindu Marriage Act 1956.

[14] S. 5 Conditions for a Hindu marriage.

consent; parties are fit for marriage and procreation, the male is at least 21 years of age and the female is 18; the couple is not, unless permitted by custom, within the degree of a prohibited relationship[15] or sapindas.[16]

The Act recognizes the importance of religious ceremonies and permits their performance. It further says that when the Saptapadi[17] is an essential ceremony by custom of the parties, the marriage is complete on the performance of the seventh step.[18]

Hindu marriages performed in contravention of the essential conditions of monogamy, prohibited relationships, and sapindas are void.[19] Further, marriages where the consent was defective, the marriage remains unconsummated due to impotence, or the bride was enceinte by another man are voidable and may be annulled by a competent Court.[20] However, to annul the marriage, additional conditions are mentioned, such as the time period, prior ignorance of the grounds on which annulment is sought, and subsequent cessation of marital intercourse.[21]

Bigamous marriages are made void, and Bigamy may be punished under the provisions of the Indian Penal Code.[22]

Spousal property may be settled by decree of the Court during any proceeding under the Act.[23]

2.2 *Muslim*

Muslim law applies to Muslims by origin as well as converts to Islam. The Koran, Sunna, Ijma, and Kiyas are the four traditionally accepted sources of Muslim law. In addition to these, custom, equity, justice, good conscience, precedent, and legislation are applied in India.[24] The Shia and Sunni are the main Muslim sects in India, with some differences in the law. Muslim marriages are civil contracts. Polygamy, with a maximum of four wives, is permitted. However, the Koran directs the husband to treat all four wives equally, and in fact suggests marrying only one wife if equal treatment

[15] S. 3 (g) degrees of prohibited relationship.

[16] S. 3 (f) "sapinda relationship" with reference to any person extends as far as the third generation (inclusive) in the line of ascent through the mother, and the fifth (inclusive) in the line of ascent through the father, the line being traced upwards in each case from the person concerned, who is to be counted as the first generation; (ii) two persons are said to be "sapindas" of each other if one is a lineal ascendant of the other within the limits of sapinda relationship, or if they have a common lineal ascendant who is within the limits of sapinda relationship with reference to each of them.

[17] The taking of seven steps by the bridegroom and the bride jointly before the sacred fire.

[18] S. 7. Ceremonies for a Hindu marriage.

[19] S. 11. Void marriages.

[20] S. 12. Voidable marriages.

[21] S. 12 (2) Proviso for entertaining an annulment petition.

[22] S. 17. Punishment of bigamy.

[23] S. 27. Disposal of property.

[24] Diwan Paras Muslim Law in Modern India Allahabad Law Agency, Faridabad 2018.

is not possible.[25] The ceremony includes the proposal (ijab) and acceptance (qubul) in the presence of witnesses.

A concept of a temporary marriage prevails among the Ithna Asharia called Muta Marriage.

Muslim marriages may be classified as valid, void, and irregular among the Sunnis; the Shia's only recognize valid and void marriages.

2.3 *Christian*

The Christian marriage is a sacrament,[26] but the Act deems it a contract.[27] The Act governs marriage between persons, who are, or one of whom is, a Christian.[28] The age for persons intending to marry is 21 years for males and 18 years for females. Bigamous marriages are void, and witnesses are required in whose presence the parties express their intention.[29]

2.4 *Parsi*

Parsi[30] marriage is a contract with an essential religious ceremony, "Ashirwad."[31] The essentials of a valid Parsi marriage include the requirement that the parties are not consanguineous. The minimum age requirement is the same as under the Hindu Marriage Act:18 years for girls and 21 years for boys.[32] This Act also has similar provisions regarding bigamous marriages.[33]

---

[25] The Koran IV. 129.

[26] Matthew 19:6 "Wherefore they are no more twain, but one flesh. What therefore God hath joined together, let not man put asunder. 6 So they are no longer two but one flesh. What therefore God has joined together, let not man separate" Nelson, T. (2017). KJV, The King James Study Bible, Full-Color Edition: Holy Bible, King James Version. United States: Thomas Nelson.

[27] Statement of Indian Christian Marriage Act 1872.

[28] S. 4 Marriages to be solemnized according to Act.

[29] S. 60 On what conditions marriages of Indian Christians may be certified.

[30] Followers in India of the Iranian prophet Zoroaster (or Zarathustra). Britannica, The Editors of Encyclopaedia. "Parsi". Encyclopedia Britannica, 24 Aug. 2022, https://www.britannica.com/topic/Parsi. Accessed 4 December 2022.

[31] The marriage ceremony starts with affirmations and commitments from the bride and groom, in the presence of family witnesses. The priests (left) then offer advice and admonitions followed by blessings and a benediction, as they shower the couple with rice and rose petals. The ceremony ends with the bride and groom exchanging wedding rings. Then friends and family come to the stage and wish the newly-weds happiness. Kersey Antia Dr., The Wedding Ceremony—'Ashirwad' available at <http://www.avesta.org/antia/The_Wedding_Ceremony-Ashirwad.pdf> visited on 4 Dec. 2022.

[32] S. 3. Requisites to validity of Parsi marriages—The Parsi Marriage And Divorce Act, 1936.

[33] S. 5. Punishment of bigamy—The Parsi Marriage And Divorce Act, 1936.

2.5 Special Marriage Act

As most matrimonial legislation requires that both spouses profess the same religion, interreligious marriages may be legalized under the Special Marriage Act. This Act may be opted for as a matter of choice even by people who profess the same religion but wish to marry under secular law. The conditions for solemnizing a marriage under the Act include that neither party has a living spouse, parties are of sound mind and capable of giving valid consent, males have completed twenty-one years of age and females are eighteen years of age, and parties are not within prohibited degrees of relationship unless custom permits such a marriage.[34] Marriage celebrated in other forms may be registered under this Act if it fulfills the conditions laid down.[35] Marriage will be void if performed in violation of the conditions laid down[36] and voidable if not consummated if the wife is pregnant by another man and consent is defective.[37]

2.6 Goa

The personal laws in Goa are governed by the Civil Code, which is Portuguese legislation that was extended by Portugal to its colonies. The Catholic religion influences the law. The Code is patriarchal in nature, while it does not discriminate between sons and daughters in that both succeed equally to the parent's property. It is biased toward the male spouse. The husband is the head of the household, the primary guardian of the children, and the decision-maker. The right to administer the couple's assets belongs to the husbands. He may administer or maladminister the assets. The wife has to rely on the permission of the husband or approach the court for a decree permitting her to administer the assets. The Civil Code has the distinction of being the only law in India that provides for the settlement of spousal property. This concept of matrimonial regimes is governed by two principles free consent and immutability. The couple is free to choose any one of the four regimes, or may even choose a combination of regimes, before the marriage, but this regime cannot be altered after the marriage. The four matrimonial regimes are the communion of assets, the communion of acquired assets, the separation of assets, and the dotal regime. The regime comes to an end through death or divorce.

In Goa, marriage is defined as a contract with the purpose of legitimately constituting a family. There is a presumption of perpetuity in the marital contract. In Goa, there are two forms of marriage: Catholic in the church and non-Catholic before the civil registrar. In 1910, only civil marriages were valid. The requirements are that the spouses be of different sexes, ages, and consent. Further, the consent should not be

[34] S. 4 Special Marriage Act 1954.
[35] S. 15 Special Marriage Act 1954.
[36] S. 24 Special Marriage Act 1954.
[37] S. 25 Special Marriage Act 1954.

defective, and there should be no impediments. Kinship and affinity, lack of matrimonial capacity, unsoundness of mind, divorce on grounds of incurable or contagious disease, spouse murder, and subsistence of previous marriage are absolute impediments that render the marriage void. The marriage of minors and those who are not capable of giving valid consent is voidable. Marriages that violate the provisions relating to kinship, guardianship, wardship, and the inter, nuptial period, which is one year for a woman, and six months for a man, are subject to penalties. Errors and coercion make the marriage consent defective. Errors include ignorance with regard to the status of the spouse, unbailable and non-time-barred crimes committed by the spouse before the marriage, and ignorance of an irremediable physical defect. The Code also places certain duties on the spouses, including conjugal fidelity, cohabitation, and mutual support and assistance. The Code further elaborately deals with the property relations of the married couple—administration of the couple's assets, the wife's incapacity in property matters, and the matrimonial regimes. There are also provisions relating to matrimonial gifts.

3 Legal Provisions Governing Divorce in India

Traditionally, the breaking of the matrimonial tie is frowned upon and discouraged.

3.1 Hindu

The grounds for divorce available to both spouses under Hindu law include adultery, cruelty, desertion, conversion, unsoundness of mind, renunciation of the world, communicable venereal disease, and presumption of death.[38] Grounds especially available to the wife are remarriage of husband, husband guilty of rape, sodomy, or bestiality, and the option of puberty.[39] Hindu marriages may be classified as valid, void, or voidable according to the provisions of the Act. Judicial separation is also a remedy available to the parties.

3.2 Muslim

By statute, Muslim women may petition for divorce on the grounds of husbands missing, not providing maintenance, imprisonment, nonperformance of marital obligations, impotence, insanity, virulent venereal disease, the option of puberty, cruelty—assault, physical and mental cruelty, associating with immoral women,

[38] S. 13 (1) The Hindu Marriage Act, 1955.

[39] S. 13 (2) The Hindu Marriage Act, 1955.

disposing of her property or preventing her autonomy over it, preventing her from religious professions, not treating her equally to the other wives, or any other ground recognized by the shariat.[40]

The triple talaq is void and illegal.[41] A Muslim man is prohibited from the triple talaq and may be punished for the same.[42]

3.3 *Christian*

The Bible does not permit Christians to divorce.[43] Christians have been permitted divorce by law.[44] The grounds for divorce include adultery, conversion, wilful nonconsummation of the marriage, missing for seven or more years, cruelty, incurable unsoundness of mind, communicable venereal disease, noncompliance with the decree for restitution of conjugal rights, desertion, and persisting for at least two years prior to the petition, the wife has the additional grounds of rape, sodomy, and bestiality.[45] Prior to amendment, adultery was the only ground for divorce; the husband could divorce the wife on the ground of adultery, but the wife needed to prove adultery with cruelty, incest, or bigamy. In the case of adultery, there should be no collusion,[46] and the adulterer or adulteress may be required as co-respondent, unless dispensed with due to death or difficulty in identifying single persons as co-respondents, that is, multiple partners.[47] Mutual consent was not a ground for divorce, neither by statute nor by interpretation.[48] However, by amendment, mutual consent is now a ground.[49]

Marriage may also be annulled[50] on grounds of impotency, prohibited degrees of relationship, either by affinity or consanguinity, lunacy, idiocy, bigamy, or forceful or fraudulent consent.[51]

The Act also provides for judicial separation on grounds of adultery, cruelty, or desertion,[52] and the wife is deemed to be a spinster with reference to her property after

---

[40] S. 2 The Dissolution of Muslim Marriages Act 1939.

[41] S. 3 The Muslim Women Protection of Rights on Marriage Act 2019.

[42] S. 4 The Muslim Women Protection of Rights on Marriage Act 2019.

[43] But I say to you that anyone who divorces his wife, except on the ground of unchastity, causes her to commit adultery; and whoever marries a divorced woman commits adultery. Matthew 5:31–32.

[44] The Divorce Act 1869.

[45] S. 10 Grounds for dissolution of marriage.

[46] S. 12 Court to be satisfied of absence of collusion.

[47] S. 11 Adulterer to be co-respondent.

[48] Reynold Rajamani v. Union of India AIR 1982 SC 1261.

[49] S. 10 – A (Indian Divorce Amendment Act 2001)..Dissolution of marriage by mutual consent.

[50] S. 18 Petition for decree of nullity.

[51] S. 19 Grounds of decree.

[52] S. 22. Bar to decree for divorce a mensa et toro; but judicial separation obtainable by husband or. wife.

such a decree for the duration of the separation.[53] She is also considered unmarried for the purposes of contracts and suits.[54]

The Act permits divorced persons to remarry,[55] but in deference to the biblical provision, it does not compel the priest to perform the marriage ceremony[56] but is required to permit the use of his church for the same.[57]

3.4 Parsi

Parsi marriage may be annulled on the ground that consummation is impossible.[58] A Marriage may be dissolved if either party has been missing for seven or more years.[59] Divorce may be granted on grounds of wilful nonconsummation, habitual unsoundness of mind present from the time of marriage, the other party being ignorant of the fact, incurable unsoundness of mind, the bride was pregnant at the time of marriage by a person other than the groom, and the groom was ignorant of the fact, and there were no marital relations between them subsequent to disclosure of this fact, adultery, fornication, bigamy, rape, unnatural offense, cruelty, grievous hurt, communication of venereal disease, prostituting the wife, imprisonment, desertion, conversion, nonresumption of cohabitation after order of maintenance, conversion. It is pertinent to note that the Court, in its discretion may order judicial separation and not divorce on the ground of cruelty.[60] Nonresumption of cohabitation on a decree for restitution of conjugal rights is also a ground for divorce.[61] Further divorce by mutual consent is also permitted.[62] Judicial separation may be petitioned on any of the grounds of divorce.[63]

3.5 The Special Marriage Act

The grounds for divorce include adultery, desertion, imprisonment for a minimum of seven years, cruelty, unsoundness of mind or mental disorder, communicable venereal disease, and disappearance. Additional grounds available to the wife are, husband

---

[53] S. 24 Separated wife deemed spinster with respect to after-acquired property.

[54] S. 25 Separated wife deemed spinster for purposes of contract and suing.

[55] S. 57 Liberty to parties to marry again.

[56] S. 58 English clergyman not compelled to solemnize marriages of persons divorced for adultery.

[57] S. 59 English Minister refusing to perform ceremony to permit use of his Church.

[58] S. 30 Parsi Marriage and Divorce Act 1936. Suits for nullity.

[59] S. 31 Parsi Marriage and Divorce Act 1936. Suits for dissolution.

[60] S. 32 Parsi Marriage and Divorce Act 1936. Grounds for divorce.

[61] S. 32 Parsi Marriage and Divorce Act 1936. Grounds for divorce.

[62] S. 32 Parsi Marriage and Divorce Act 1936. Grounds for divorce.

[63] S. 34 Parsi Marriage and Divorce Act 1936. Suits for judicial separation.

is guilty of rape, sodomy, or bestiality, awarding maintenance to the separated wife, and nonresumption of cohabitation on a petition for restitution of conjugal rights.[64] The Act provides for judicial separation as an alternative to divorce.[65] Divorce by mutual consent is also possible.[66]

3.6 Goa

The law originally did not permit a divorce. Marriage was defined as a perpetual contract. The law was introduced by the Portuguese, who followed the Roman Catholic religion, which does not permit divorce. Later in 1910, the law was amended to include divorce. Divorce may be contested or by mutual consent. The grounds for a contested divorce are adultery, final sentencing to serious penalties under the Penal Code, serious ill-treatment or indignity, abandonment of a matrimonial home for three or more years, missing for four or more years, incurable insanity for three or more years, de facto separation for any reason, for ten or more years, addiction to gambling, incurable contagious disease, and incurable disease involving sexual aberrations.

Spouses who have been married for two or more years and are above twenty-five years of age may obtain a divorce by mutual consent.

The Code further makes provision for judicial separation. This separation may be with regard to the mere separation of assets or of separation of persons and assets without a divorce.

4 UK

Same-sex marriages are legal in the UK.[67] Prior to this, same-sex couples could enter into a civil partnership.[68] Indian divorce laws are based on The Matrimonial Causes Act of the UK. Initially, in the UK, divorce could only be granted on the ground of adultery, adultery simpliciter for males, and incestuous adultery or adultery coupled with cruelty, bestiality, rape, or sodomy for females.[69] Later amendments put both on the same footing, allowing adultery simpliciter as a ground for divorce.[70] Cruelty,

---

[64] S. 27 Special Marriage Act 1954.

[65] S. 27 A Special Marriage Act.

[66] S. 28 Special Marriage Act.

[67] In 2013, Parliament passed the Marriage (Same Sex Couples) Act which introduced civil marriage for same-sex couples in England and Wales.

[68] Civil Partnership Act 2004.

[69] Matrimonial Causes Act 1857.

[70] Matrimonial Causes Act 1923.

desertion, and incurable insanity were introduced as grounds for divorce later.[71] The irretrievable breakdown of marriage has been recognized in the UK.[72] The UK has a new divorce law that is not based on the traditional fault theory of divorce.[73] The new law does not lay down any call for proof of irretrievable breakdown of marriage as was required previously.[74]

5 Portugal

In Portugal, registration of marriage is compulsory. Same-sex marriages are legal in Portugal.[75] Marriage is a contract between two persons who intend to form a family through a full communion of life, in accordance with the provisions of this Code.[76] The requirement for a valid marriage is the absence of impediments.[77] The absolute impediments are, under sixteen years of age, notorious dementia,[78] and an undissolved previous marriage. There are also relative impediments such as relationship in the straight line or in the second degree of the collateral line,[79] affinity in the straight line,[80] parental responsibilities, previous conviction, and certain other impediments such as lack of parental permission for couples between sixteen and eighteen years of age, relationship in the third degree of the collateral line, marriage between guardian and ward, and murdering the previous spouse of the other party, which may be dispensed with by the registrar.[81] At the time of marriage registration, the prenuptial agreement may also be registered. Matrimonial regimes are the communion of assets, the communion of acquired assets, and the separation of assets. The dotal regime is no longer available in Portugal.

Divorce was introduced in Portugal and its colonies in 1910.[82] In Portugal, there have been several amendments to the law.[83]

Divorce may be by mutual consent or contentious. In cases where divorce is by mutual consent, the couple needs to produce three agreements before the Director of the Civil Registry Office, maintenance agreement, a custody agreement, family place of residence. Contentious divorce may be granted for grave and persistent breaches

[71] Matrimonial Causes Act 1937.

[72] Divorce Reform Act 1969.

[73] The Divorce, Dissolution and Separation Act 2020.

[74] S. 2 Divorce Reform Act 1969.

[75] Same-sex marriage in Portugal has been legal since 5 June 2010.

[76] Article 1577 of the Portuguese Civil Code.

[77] Article 1600 CC.

[78] Article 138 CC.

[79] Article 1578 CC.

[80] Article 1602. CC.

[81] Articles 1604 and 1609 CC.

[82] Decree of November 1910.

[83] Concordat between the Vatican and the Portuguese Republic of 7 May 1940.

of matrimonial duties,[84] de facto separation, unsoundness of mind, disappearance, or irretrievable breakdown of the marriage.[85]

6 Problems

Different laws for different individuals on the sole basis of religion are arbitrary and violate the constitutional guarantee and fundamental rights of equality and nondiscrimination enshrined in Part III. Discrimination on grounds of gender without any rational nexus to the purpose of the legislation is equally arbitrary and unconstitutional. Rights and duties are determined on the basis of religion rather than civil status. The legislation does not expressly include same-sex marriages, and similarly, transgender marriages are not adequately provided for. The existing laws do not govern tribal marriages, which are governed by custom. Matrimonial remedies include the restitution of conjugal rights, which is an outdated concept. Divorce on fault and mutual consent grounds are no longer adequate. Maintenance of cordial relationships between spouses, essential for the well-being of the children, is highly unlikely after a contested divorce.

7 Discussion and Analysis

Marriage is regarded as a sacrament under some of the laws and a contract under others; except for the Muslim law, bigamy is not permitted. Marriages may be valid, void, or voidable depending on whether a condition mentioned in the relevant law is violated or not. The law does not permit incestuous relationships and frowns on marriage between certain relations, which may be consanguine or based on affinity. The minimum age for marriage is prescribed, and free consent is emphasized.

Restitution of Conjugal rights is a remedy available under all personal laws; the court may enforce such an order by attachment of property.

A perusal of the various grounds available for divorce under the personal laws reveals certain commonalities. There are guilty grounds for divorce, including, adultery, desertion, cruelty, sentencing spouse for an offense, insanity, communicable venereal disease, impotency, disappearance of spouse, renunciation of the world, conversion, and noncompliance with a decree for restitution of conjugal rights. In addition, the wife may repudiate the marriage if the husband is guilty of rape, sodomy, and bestiality.

---

[84] Article 1779, n. 1 Portuguese Civil Code - Article 1672 (Portuguese Civil Code) refers to the duties which are incumbent upon both spouses; duties of respect, fidelity, cohabitation, co-operation, and assistance.

[85] Articles 1773 and 1781 CC.

Leprosy is no longer a ground for divorce.[86] The triple talaq is also declared unconstitutional by court and a criminal offense by legislation.

An irretrievable breakdown of marriage is not a ground for divorce under any of the statutory provisions. However, the Supreme Court has used its inherent powers and granted divorce in several cases.[87]

The laws in Goa and the rest of India were based on Portuguese and British laws, respectively; these laws have changed, but the Indian laws have not changed as substantially.

Marriage and divorce are civil status with rights, and except for the rituals, they have no rational connection with religion. The relationship with the spouse and the rights, duties, and obligations that flow from it have no legitimate connection with religion.

There are fundamental differences in the personal laws of marriage, divorce, guardianship, maintenance, and inheritance. Religion determines whether the marriage will be monogamous or polygamous, the grounds for divorce, who can claim maintenance, who will be the guardian, how much one will inherit, who will be one's heirs, and the mode of succession.

In addition to the different religion-based personal laws, within a particular religion, one's gender also determines one's rights and obligations. Legislation has tried to mitigate the matrimonial laws to a limited extent. The distinctions and injustices are more prominent in the inheritance laws.

8 Suggestions

8.1 Uniform Civil Code

The Uniform Civil Code has been discussed and debated, suggested, and recommended but never implemented.

8.2 Modernizing Marriage and Divorce Laws

Simple Procedure

The marriage and divorce laws should be updated to include a simple uniform procedure.

---

86 The Personal Laws (Amendment) Act, 2019 NO. 6 OF 2019.

87 Naveen Kohli v. Neelu Kohli AIR 2006 SC1675.

Compulsory Registration of Marriage

Registration of marriage should be compulsory.

No Compulsion to Perform Religious Ceremonies for the Validity of Marriage

The performance of the religious ceremonies connected with marriage should be optional and not the key factor in determining the validity of the marriage.

Consanguinity as a bar to Marriage

There is enough scientific evidence to show the ill effects of consanguineous marriages on children. Marriage between consanguine relatives should be legally prohibited, even if it is permitted by custom.

Permit Same-Sex Marriage

The right to marry is a fundamental right.[88] Same-sex marriage should be permitted.

Transgender to Be Included in Personal Laws

The transgender or third gender should also find a place in personal laws.

Deletion of Restitution of Conjugal Rights as a Matrimonial Relief

Restitution of conjugal rights should be deleted from the statute book.

Ground for Divorce

In addition to mutual and contentious divorce, irretrievable breakdown of marriage should be a ground.

---

[88] Lata Singh v. State of UP (2006) 5 SCC 475.

8.3 Educating Public About Procedures, Rights, and Liabilities

The new code should be widely publicized on multiple platforms. People need to be educated about their rights as well as the various legal requirements and provisions.

8.4 Rights of Children

Children should not be designated as illegitimate even if born outside of wedlock; rather, the rights of children and duties of parents should be governed by the biological tie or, in the case of adoption, by the relationship of adoption.

9 Conclusion

The existence of God cannot be proved or disproved. Religion, by its very nature, is a question of faith and belief, not empirical evidence. Belief in higher power by whatever name has several benefits, psychological relief, ethics, morals, and values are taught through religion. In India, people are more receptive to religious teachings. Personal laws continue to be based on the religion of the person. However, secular aspects of personal matters should be governed by a uniform civil code. The Uniform Civil Code should be uniform with regard to both religion and gender.

A Comparative Analysis of the Rule of Law in India and Australia and Their Adherence to Constitutionalism

J. P. Yadav and Ananya Yadav

Abstract India and Australia, both Commonwealth countries, offer a unique opportunity for comparative studies regarding the rule of law. While both nations share historical ties, their approaches to the rule of law exhibit distinctive characteristics. In India, the Dicey Concept of the Rule of Law, as espoused by Professor A.V. Dicey in the UK, is enshrined in the constitution. In contrast, Australia upholds the Rule of Law as a longstanding tradition deeply embedded in its legal system. This paper delves into the significance of the Rule of Law, a cornerstone of constitutionalism within a state. Professor Dicey, in his seminal work "An Introduction to the Law of the Constitution," expounded on the Rule of Law, attributing three interconnected meanings to it. First, it emphasizes that individuals can only be penalized through due legal process in established courts, asserting the supremacy of the law over arbitrary power. Second, it underscores the equal subjection of all to ordinary legal courts, ensuring equality before the law. Lastly, it pertains to individual rights determined and enforced by the courts, emphasizing just and reasonable laws that respect personal liberties. In India, the "procedure established by law" doctrine prevails, limiting judicial interpretation to literal compliance with laws. Australia, on the other hand, integrates the Rule of Law within its democratic and legal framework, emphasizing transparency, fairness, and the applicability of laws to all. This paper also examines relevant legal cases in both countries, demonstrating how the rule of law has shaped legal decisions and influenced constitutional principles. It highlights the crucial role of the rule of law in maintaining a balance between individual liberties and public order. The fundamental role of the Rule of Law in both India and Australia is crucial in maintaining justice, fairness, and individual freedom. This comparative analysis showcases the different approaches each nation takes to uphold this essential principle, shedding light on their distinct constitutional systems and historical backgrounds.

J. P. Yadav (✉) · A. Yadav
Amity Law School, Amity University Uttar Pradesh, Lucknow Campus, Lucknow, India
e-mail: dryadavjp@gmail.com

A. Yadav
e-mail: ananyayadav18012sectiona@gmail.com

J. Aston et al. (eds.), *Comparative Law*, https://doi.org/10.1007/978-981-97-7815-7_9

Keywords Rule of law · Comparative constitutionalism · Judicial interpretation

1 Introduction

India and Australia are both Commonwealth countries, making them natural allies for comparative studies. However, concerning the rule of law, there is a distinction in how it is approached. In the Indian Constitution, the Dicey Concept of the Rule of Law, as propounded in the UK by Professor A.V. Dicey, is adopted. In contrast, in Australia, the Rule of Law is a longstanding legal tradition within Australian society. At its core, the rule demands that laws are not only enacted but also followed and implemented.

The "Rule of Law" can form the basis of constitutionalism within a state. The doctrine was introduced by Dicey, a renowned English constitutionalist, in 1865 through his book titled "An Introduction to the Law of the Constitution," where the term "rule of law" was thoroughly explored.

Dicey attributed at least three distinct but interconnected meanings to the expression "rule of law." Firstly, it signifies that no one may be subjected to physical or property punishment unless there has been a blatant breach of the law as established by the regular legal process before the nation's regular courts. It highlights the primacy of regular law over arbitrary power, wide discretionary authority, and prerogatives.[1]

Secondly, it denotes that all social classes are equally subject to the general laws of the state, as applied by the general legal courts. This concept is known as equality before the law, and it ensures that no individuals, including officials, are exempt from their duty to obey the law or from the jurisdiction of the regular tribunals.

The third meaning attributed by Dicey is relevant to the English legal system, which lacks a written constitution and constitutionally guaranteed rights. In this context, the concept that individual rights as defined and upheld by the courts are the result of the law, not its source, is emphasized by the Rule of Law.

It signifies the predominance of the legal spirit and the idea that personal liberties are determined by judicial decisions. Implicit in this third connotation is the belief that laws must be just and reasonable, respecting individual liberties, or in modern terms, human rights.

This doctrine primarily exists in England, where there is no written constitution, serving as a higher law that can be used to assess the validity of any legislation. It underscores that every law within the state must apply universally, making the law supreme in all respects and in every sphere. It affirms the principle "No one is above the law."

---

[1] *Justice Sujata V Manohar, Former Judge of SC, awarded Ruth Bader Ginsburg Medal of Honor*, SCC Blog (July 14, 2021), https://www.scconline.com/blog/post/2021/07/14/justice-sujata-v-manohar-former-judge-of-sc-awarded-ruth-bader-ginsburg-medal-of-honour/.

Both India and Australia adhere to the concept of the rule of law. In India, the Supreme Court sits at the head of an integrated judiciary, whose rulings are binding on all other courts, and state high courts have the authority to impose their decisions on their subordinate courts. In Australia, the Constitution does not contain any such provisions, with the exception of Chapter III of the Constitution of Australia. Nonetheless, Australia adopted the US Constitution's practice of granting the courts the authority to judge whether laws approved by all governments are legitimate. As a result, the courts in Australia and India are empowered to conduct judicial reviews.

2 Rule of Law and Its Significance

This raises the question: What is the law? The answer lies in two principles:

I. Due process of law and
II. Procedure established by law

Due process is a doctrine prevalent in the USA. Judges mold it according to the particular facts and circumstances of each case, even if its scope is not precisely defined. It stands for judicial supremacy, but if the courts disregard the Constitution's bounds and abuse their power, there is a chance that judicial autocracy could occur.

The "procedure established by law" principle, which was taken from Article 21 of the Indian Constitution and is unambiguously embedded in it, is in effect in India. Because laws are made by the legislature in India, it exemplifies parliamentary sovereignty. This theory limits the authority of judges and permits only literal interpretation, rather than the creation of laws by statute.

Other components embedded in the Rule of Law include

1. The judiciary's ability to supervise the conduct of other government agencies, known as judicial review, clearly demonstrates the absence of arbitrary power on the side of the government.
2. Equality of all people before the law, which is supported by the clauses in Articles 14 to 18.
3. Constitutional law rules are not the product of regular legislation; laws passed by the legislature are required to comply with the constitution's requirements, or else they would be deemed invalid.

The legislature's sovereignty was a major factor in the rule of law in England. The plenary powers of the sovereign legislature are unrestricted by any higher law in the case of an unwritten constitution. The concepts of judicial review and a written constitution both exist in India; therefore, the Rule of Law cannot be given top priority.

2.1 Rule of Law in India

The rule of law has been crucial to the growth of Indian democracy. The two nations that the framers of the Constitution could have chosen from were the USA and England. A portion of the provisions were taken from England, while a portion came from the USA. Our founding ancestors imported the rule of law from England, and the Indian Constitution has numerous examples of this. Nobody is thought to be above the Indian Constitution, which is regarded as paramount. The concept of the rule of law is also implicitly stated in the preamble and is established in Part III of the Indian Constitution.

Articles 32 and 226 of the Indian Constitution allow one to file a complaint with the Supreme Court or a High Court in the event that their rights are violated. Justice, equality, and liberty are three legal concepts that are enhanced by the Indian Constitution. Every law passed by the federal government or any state government in India must be followed in line with the country's constitution. Any legislation passed by the legislature that is in conflict with the Constitution's provisions would be deemed invalid.

2.2 Role of Indian Judiciary

The idea of the rule of law has been brought up and explored in numerous instances. Here are a few examples of the cases.

(a) ***A.K. Gopalan V. State***[2]

The emergency detention order, also referred to as the Habeas Corpus case, was contested in this case on the grounds that it contravened the essential elements of the Indian Constitution, which uphold the rule of law. The Supreme Court was asked to rule on whether Article 21 of the Constitution constitutes the exclusive rule of law in India. Justice Khanna delivered a dissenting opinion, and the majority bench in the case reached a negative decision. He noted that the rule of law is seen as a hallmark of a free society and is acknowledged in all civilized cultures. He went on to say that the only way to strike a balance between public order and individual liberty is through the rule of law. Therefore, he believed that the state lacked the jurisdiction to take away someone's life and liberty without following the law, even in the absence of Article 21 in the Indian Constitution.

The Indian Constitution's Article 32 grants the Supreme Court the authority to grant writs of habeas corpus, mandamus, prohibition, quo warranto, and certiorari. Additionally, the Supreme Court has the authority to conduct judicial review in order to prevent any legislation that goes beyond the bounds of the "rule of law."

---

[2] A.K. Gopalan v. State, AIR 27 (SC 1950).

(b) ***A.K. Karpiak V. Union of India***[3]

The Supreme Court ruled that all state instrumentalities are subject to the Rule of Law doctrine and are obligated to carry out their duties in a just, equitable, and reasonable manner when addressing the question of whether the principle of natural justice can be applied to administrative functions. This serves as the fundamental tenet of the rule of law, without which the idea of the rule of law is meaningless. Because every governmental organ is governed by the Rule of Law, it applies to every aspect of administration.

(c) ***Indra Nehru Gandhi V. Raj Narayan***[4]

The 39th amendment to the Constitution was contested in this case, placing the Speaker of the Lok Sabha, the President, the Prime Minister, and the Vice-President unjustly in the legal system. Chief Justice Ray declared the amendment to be illegal, citing a violation of the Rule of Law, which is the fundamental framework of the Constitution. The parliament does not have the authority to enact a retroactive statute recognizing a rigged election since the Rule of Law is inimical to arbitrariness. The fundamental tenets of the Rule of Law are violated by this kind of power abuse.

The Delhi High Court said that it is the responsibility of the Court to adopt a tough approach where there is non-compliance with judicial decisions, noting that the absence of the Rule of Law or the existence of complete disregard for the Rule of Law accelerates a country toward certain disasters. Judge Subramaniam Prasad continued, saying that while dealing with such matters, the courts should not be afraid to use the harshest sanction.[5]

Chief Justice N.V. Ramana discussed the value of the Rule of Law in a democracy during a speech during which he received a Lifetime Achievement Award from the Rotary Club of Vijayawada. The CJI emphasized that the Rule of Law is essential to democracy and asked attendees, judges, and attorneys to spread awareness of its value. "When there is no rule of law in a country, anarchy takes over."[6]

(d) ***Som Raj v. State of Haryana***[7]

The ruling in this case established that the foundation of the rule of law, upon which the entire constitutional framework rests, is the lack of arbitrary power.

---

[3] A.K. Karpiak v. Union of India, AIR150 (SC 1970).

[4] Indra Nehru Gandhi v. Raj Narayan AIR 2299 (SC 1975).

[5] Live Law, Absence Of Rule Of Law Propels A Country Towards Inevitable Ruin, Duty Of Court To Take Strict View Of Non-Compliance Of Judicial Orders: Delhi HC (Apr. 26, 2022), https://www.livelaw.in/news-updates/absence-rule-of-law-non-compliance-judicial-orders-delhi-high-court-contempt-197576?infinitescroll=1,%2002.02.2023.

[6] *Ibid.*

[7] Som Raj v. State of Haryana, AIR 1176, 1990.

(e) ***Amlan Jyoti Borooah vs. State of Assam & Ors***[8]

S. B. Sinha maintained that compassion and equity are not the same thing. Equitable principles must arise from events that are peculiar and unusual in and of themselves. To guarantee that its efforts to achieve equality do not amount to judicial charity or acceptance of documented violations of fundamental rights and the rules of law, a balance must be struck, and the Court must exercise caution.

(f) ***Chief Settlement Commissioner, Punjab v. Om Prakash***[9]

The Supreme Court noted in this decision that "the concept of rule of law, which means, in the present context, the authority of law courts to test all administrative action by the standard of legality, is the central and most characteristic feature of our constitutional system." If the individual who was wronged brings the problem to notice, the administrative or executive action that does not meet the criteria will be set aside.

(g) ***Keshvananda Bharti v. State of Kerela***[10]

In this instance, the Supreme Court clarified that one of the key tenets of the basic structure theory is the rule of law.

(h) ***Gadakh Yashwantrao Kankarrao v. Balasaheb Vikhe Patil***[11]

This case involved a ration that stated, "It is the duty of the courts to appreciate the evidence and construe the law in a manner which would subserve this higher purpose and not even imperceptibly facilitate affirmation of the falling electoral standards." This is because maintaining the rule of law is essential to democracy, and maintaining the integrity of elections is a necessary concomitant. Democracy cannot thrive without the rule of law, and the best people must be selected to serve as the representatives of the people in order to properly manage the nation. The only way to do this is for men with strong moral and ethical principles to win the elections based on their own merits rather than through a process of elimination based on the candidates' relative shortcomings.

(i) ***Bilkis Yakub Rasool v. Union of India & Others***[12]

The Supreme Court emphasized that, in order to fully defend the rule of law, those involved must continue to be indifferent to the fallout from their actions, even as it set aside the concessions made to the guilty in the case. It further declared that since the rule of law must be upheld, pity and compassion have no place in society.

[8] Amlan Jyoti Borooah v. State Of Assam & Ors, 2009 (3) SCC 227, 2009.

[9] Chief Settlement Commissioner, Punjab v. Om Prakash, SC 33, AIR 1969.

[10] Keshvananda Bharti v. State of Kerela, 4 SCC 225, 1973.

[11] Gadakh Yashwantrao Kankarrao v. Balasaheb Vikhe Patil, SC 678, AIR 1994.

[12] Bilkis Yakub Rasool v. Union of India & others (CRL.) No. 491 of 2022.

(j) ***Swapnil Tripathi v. Supreme Court of India***[13]

It was held that the transcendental impact of technology is to uphold democracy and the rule of law, in addition to advancing the constitutional right to access justice.

(k) ***Association for Democratic Reforms & Anr. V. Union of India & Ors***[14]

In an attempt to gain control, the political parties spent over one thousand crore rupees on the general election (only the Parliament), yet no one is held accountable for the majority of this money or for anything else. The source of the funds is never revealed. Both the necessary accounts and the audit are missing. Nobody is aware of the source of the money. This blatant display of black money in violation of the required legal procedures is not acceptable in a democracy where the rule of law is supreme.

2.3 *Rule of Law in Australia*

Written constitutions in Australia "impose substantive and procedural limitations upon the powers of all three organs of government," as the "Commonwealth Constitution does."[15] Australian constitutional law places a special emphasis on limiting the power of the government to prevent totalitarianism. It might be countered, nevertheless, that a dictatorship can still uphold the constitution and be constitutionalist. A common British definition of constitutionalism might serve as the basis for such an argument, as it simply refers to a state that has "rules which directly or indirectly affect the distribution of the sovereign power."[16]

One important aspect of Australian democracy is the rule of law. The Australian Constitution's Covering Clause 5 declares that everyone is subject to the laws passed by the Australian Parliament, including the legislators. Australia's democracy and judicial system are fundamentally based on the rule of law.

The idea that the people and the government are subject to the same laws and are aware of them is known as the "Rule of Law." This implies that everyone is subject to the law, irrespective of their standing or situation. Laws should be simple to locate, easy to comprehend, and enforced in order to guarantee that everyone is aware of the law and their rights.

By limiting the authority of corporations, governments, and individuals, the Rule of Law shields people from the abuse of power and prevents them from making dictatorial choices that are not supported by the law.

***Role of Australian Judiciary*:** Here are a few of the cases.

[13] Swapnil Tripathi v. Supreme Court of India, 10 SCC 639 (2018).

[14] Association for Democratic Reforms & Anr. V. Union of India & ors., INSC 113, 2024.

[15] Keith Mason, The Rule of Law, in P.D. Finn (ed), Essays on Law and Government, Volume 1: Principles and Values 123 (1995).

[16] Peta Stephenson, Rebecca Ananian-Welsh, Andrew Lynch, George Williams, Sean Brennan Commentary and Materials, 8th edition p. 1 and 6.

(a) ***Lange v. Australian Broadcasting Corporation***[17]

The English common law idea of the general competence and unqualified supremacy of the legislature was superseded or rendered inapplicable by the Constitution, according to the High Court's joint ruling in the recent case that it gave the federal judiciary the authority to determine the bounds of the state and commonwealth governments' separate powers."

(b) ***Chu Kheng Lim v Minister for Immigration***[18]

The case illustrated how freedom and human rights may be safeguarded by the rule of law. In this instance, the Migration Act was modified[19] to allow for the mandatory detention of a limited number of "designated persons," who were not subject to court orders to be freed from custody.[20] The statute was overturned because it did not follow the separation of powers doctrine and Dicey's first ingredient of the rule of law. Brennan, Deane, and Dawson JJ, citing Dicey, determined that the amendment was outside the legislative authority of the Parliament to bestow upon the Executive an arbitrary power to hold citizens in custody, even though the authority was granted in a manner intended to disassociate such detention from both criminal guilt and punishment. Setting aside extraordinary circumstances, the state's forced imprisonment of a person is punishing or penal in nature and only occurs as a byproduct of the solely judicial process of determining and punishing criminal guilt. Each person is "ruled by the law and the law alone" and "may with us be punished for a breach of law, but he can be punished for nothing else".[21]

(c) ***A v. Hayden***[22]

It was observed that the rule of law functions to shield society from the potential despotism brought about by the state's unlawful acts. This case addressed the activities of Australian Security Intelligence Service (ASIS) personnel who had carried out an anti-terrorist drill at the Sheraton Hotel in Melbourne with permission from the Minister for Foreign Affairs. Prior to the practice, which included using a sledgehammer to demolish a door and guns with blank ammunition, hotel staff were unaware of it. Brennan J. said, "Neither ASIS nor the Minister nor the executive government could confer authority upon any of the plaintiffs to commit an offense or immunity from prosecution for an offense once committed," in response to the question of whether the government could permit the members of ASIS to commit illegal acts with immunity from prosecution. A parliamentary democracy is based on the executive branch's inability to exempt its employees from adhering to legislation passed by Parliament. The idea is that all ministers and officers should serve the king

[17] Lange v. Australian Broadcasting Corporation, 145 ALR 96 at 109 (1997).

[18] Chu Kheng Lim v. Minister for 176 CLR 1, Immigration (1992).

[19] Migration Act 1958 (Cth).

[20] *Ibid*, 15–19.

[21] *Ibid*, 27.

[22] A v. Hayden, 156 CL, R 532 (1984).

in accordance with the law. This is not an out-of-date regulation; rather, it is a fundamental element of our legal system that is occasionally overlooked when executive governments or their agencies are hindered or frustrated by laws that interfere with the implementation of their programs."

The significance of Dicey's second component of the rule of law,[23] the "equal subjection of all classes to the ordinary law,"[24] which includes public servants, is amply demonstrated by this ruling. People are somewhat shielded by such a premise against rogue government officials who could attempt to abuse their position of authority to behave illegally.

2.4 Elements of the Rule of Law

The Rule of Law is defined broadly, although there is disagreement over what else falls under this umbrella. Generally speaking, the following elements of Australia's legal system are part of the Rule of Law[25]:

1. Retrospective laws prohibit citizens from being held guilty of crimes for which they were not guilty at the time of the offense.
2. The presumption of innocence states that everyone is innocent unless and until proven guilty in a fair and open trial.
3. Until a court determines that a law has been broken, citizens cannot be penalized or have their rights violated.
4. The public, the media, and the legal system may all file challenges against the government for its policies.
5. Natural justice, or procedural fairness, is accorded to all citizens.

   Evaluating, amending, and repealing laws to make sure they are just and represent societal values is a crucial component of the Rule of Law. The Australian Law Reform Commission is an impartial body that advises the Australian government on legal changes.[26]
6. It produces a predictable and orderly society; it strengthens democracy because laws are enacted by representatives of the people.
7. The rights of all citizens are protected, and they are all treated fairly and legally.
8. No citizen may be arbitrarily detained, imprisoned, or tried for violating an unidentified law.
9. A transparent, neutral, and autonomous legal system.

---

[23] A.V. Dicey, Introduction to the study of the law of the Constitution (10th ed.) p. 202, 1959.

[24] *Ibid.*

[25] *Rule of law*, Parliamentary Education Office https://peo.gov.au/understand-our-parliament/how-parliament-works/system-of-government/rule-of-law/.

[26] *The Rule of Law*, Australian Constitution Centre, *available at*, http://www.australianconstitutioncentre.org.au/the-rule-of-law.html (Last visited 10/03/2024).

Governmental, corporate, and individual powers are curtailed by the Rule of Law, which also guards against the abuse of authority. Ministers of government, members of Parliament, and judges are all subject to Australian law.

Anyone needs to be able to learn about Australian laws. Until your actions are illegal, you cannot be punished by a court for them. Presumption of innocence and a fair trial are rights that you possess.

Our society is predictable and well-organized because of the rule of law. It encourages individual freedom, justice, and fairness. The Rule of Law guarantees judges' independence from the individuals and organizations whose acts they are called into question and acts as a safeguard against the arbitrary use of authority.

It is not necessary for all disagreements, or even disputes concerning legal rights and obligations, to involve every aspect of the legal system in order to uphold the Rule of Law.

It does not require that everyone disgruntled about a library fine should have a right of appeal to a court, and, if necessary, ultimately to the High Court. As a matter of fact, nobody has the ability to appeal to the High Court due to laws passed by Parliament. Special leave is necessary for all appeals and can be granted or denied for reasons specified by law.

Parliament has limited access to the courts in accordance with the Constitution, as demonstrated by the legislation that restricts appeals to the High Court. It is a way to allocate limited court resources. A parliament may choose that administrative processes, as opposed to curial ones, are more suitable for resolving disputes when they introduce new areas of possible contention, such as laws pertaining to privacy or other types of discrimination. Town planning matters can be handled politically, administratively, or legally. These matters frequently entail striking a balance between the rights of private property and the public good. Legislators possess considerable latitude in determining the best approach to handling such matters, and various Australian regions offer diverse resolutions.

As long as it complies with the Constitution, this does not conflict with the Rule of Law.

It is argued that the Constitution presupposes the rule of law. That was stated in a case that offers a potent illustration of the application of the Rule of Law and judicial review of legislative action. Commonwealth v. Australian Communist Party is the case in question.[27]

The Rule of Law is more than just a concept that the courts use to impose their will in many ways. It has authority over how courts are run.

The Rule of Law does not require the legal profession and courts to have an ever-larger role in the affairs of governments and citizens, despite what some attorneys believe. The rule of law does not imply legal authority. Parliaments have the authority to determine whether disputes are justiciable and to establish and, where necessary, restrict the mechanisms for resolving such disputes, subject to any constitutional restrictions on their authority. Parliaments frequently increase and decrease the range of topics that can be litigated. That's what creating laws mostly involves. In Australia,

[27] Commonwealth v. Australian Communist Party, 1 CLR 83 (1951).

common law actions for damages framed in the tort of negligence resulting from a motor vehicle collision are the most prevalent type of litigation, accounting for a significant portion of the backlog of courts with broad jurisdiction.[28]

3 A Comparative Approach Between the India and Australia

The US Constitution served as a source of inspiration and guidance for both the Australian and Indian constitutions, which were drafted fifty years apart. Similar to Australia, India also chose a federal system of government and established a separate judiciary from all other branches of government. Judicial review was rigorously emulated to ensure that all recipients of public power remained within the bounds of the Constitution and other relevant legislation. However, the Indian Constitution goes one step further. It embraced the republican principle, as some have proposed that the Australian Constitution presently does.[29] It also included a Bill of Rights, which was seen, until recently, to be incompatible with the idea of parliamentary sovereignty, which is fundamental to UK constitutional conceptions.[30] However, despite these significant differences between the Australian and Indian constitutions, their political and legal frameworks are essentially the same. Although the Head of State of India is referred to as the President, he functions similarly to the sovereign of the UK and the Queen and her delegates in Australia, acting at the behest of ministers who answer to the lower house of Parliament. The President's duties are comparable to those of Australia's Governor-General in this regard. Naturally, the president does not represent the monarch.[31]

As noted by Seervai,[32] in order to dispel a widespread misunderstanding, it should be clarified that the government apparatus established by our Constitution fundamentally adopts the British model rather than the American one. Neither the British Constitution nor the Indian Constitution contain the fundamental US constitutional ideas of the separation of powers and legislatures composed of representatives of the people. The British model of governance by a cabinet, that is, an executive accountable to and removable by the legislature, was adopted by our Constitution in place

[28] *Litigation and Enforcement in Australia: Overview*, Practical Law https://uk.practicallaw.thomsonreuters.com/4-5021038?contextData=(sc.Default)&transitionType=Default&firstPage=true.

[29] Indian Constitution, Preamble, first line. Note *Constitution (Forty-second Amendment) Act* 1976, s2; cf H M Seervai, *Constitutional Law of India,* vol 1, 158, 4th ed (1991).

[30] H M Seervai, *Constitutional Law of India* (4th ed, 1991), vol 1, 159; cf M Kachwaha, *The Judiciary in India,* Leiden, 15 (1998).

[31] Australian Constitution, s61 ["The executive power of the Commonwealth is vested in the Queen and is exercisable by the Governor-General as the Queen's representative and extends to the execution and maintenance of this Constitution, and of the laws of the Commonwealth"].

[32] H M Seervai, *Constitutional Law of India* (4th ed, 1991), vol 1, 159 referring to *Shamsher Singh v Punjab* [1975] 1 SCR 814; (74) ASC 2192.

of the presidential system of government, which is an executive independent of and not subject to the legislature.

In Mabo v Queensland,[33] regarding equality before the law, Wilson J. of the High Court of Australia cited rulings from the Supreme Court of India.

Wilson J. made the following observation after applying a section of Mathew J.'s reasoning in Kerala v. Thomas,[34] "Formal equality before the law does not necessarily achieve effective and true equality. A disadvantaged group's formal equality under the law may end up solidifying inequity in practice." In his ruling in Gerhardy v. Brown,[35] the Australian High Court's Brennan J. raised the same issue, citing Ray C. J.'s "pithily observed" remark that "equality of opportunity for the unequal can only mean aggravation of inequality." "The validity of these observations is manifest," said Brennan J.

4 Conclusion

An idea concerning justice, morality, and the law is known as the rule of law. It examines what ought to be and ought not to be in terms of laws, conventions, rules, processes, systems, and structures. The people and/or their competent representatives should declare norms in public. This concept is based on three realities. One is that both individuals and the government are subject to the law. Next, people need to follow the law. The third requirement is that the rules we refer to as law must be observable—not merely in the obvious, knowable, and predictable sense, but also in the most fundamental, just sense. It helps to promote stability and peace and is essential to democracy and effective administration.

The Indian Constitution, common law customs, and the judiciary's tenacious role have all contributed to the growth of the rule of law in recent decades. But occasionally, driven by sheer desire, we have retreated into government, only to ruefully and wisely return to the rule of law when the harsh realities of human nature exposed human egotism and greed, as well as the veracity of the adage that "power corrupts, and absolute power corrupts absolutely."

It can be concluded that the goal is to have supreme law, and the best means of achieving this goal is the rule of law. The court also makes some efforts in areas where people's human rights and the rule of law are intertwined. The court is developing a strategy by which it will be possible to compel the government to not only obey the law but also to foster the growth of people's capacities so that they can exercise their rights in a legitimate and significant way.

The rule of law has not produced the desired effects in Indian society. A few instances when our judiciary defended the rule of law and guaranteed justice are evident in the development of new channels for seeking remedies.

---

33 *In Mabo v Queensland*, 166 CLR 186 at 206 (1988).

34 Kerala v. Thomas 1 SCR 906 at 951 (1976).

35 Gerhardy v. Brown (1985) 159 CLR 70 at 128–129.

The discipline to which all authority is subjected and the power it withholds from individuals and governments are two aspects of the significance of the Rule of Law. The community that all government serves is the source of power in a democracy, and exercising that power requires both discipline and denial. When the public and other departments of government perceive the judiciary as upholding the discipline of the laws it enforces, judicial authority and credibility are at their peak. There is no army responsible for upholding the law. It is dependent on the public's faith in duly elected officials.

The Rule of Law embodied in the Indian Constitution is based on the Dicey Principle of the Rule of Law and became a part of the Constitution under the heading of "Right to Equality" (Article 14–18). It is also pertinent to mention that the rule is one element of constitutionalism. Similarly, the Rule of Law is also an important part of the Australian Constitution and an integral part of Constitutionalism.

It is needless to mention that both countries were British colonies at one time. Therefore, both are recognized as Commonwealth countries as well, and their comparative study with reference to the Rule of Law is very natural.

However, in order to uphold the spirit of constitutionalism, the doctrine's shadow can be found in a number of sections of both the Australian and Indian constitutions, including the foundational ideas of judicial review, natural justice, the rule of law, separation of powers, and the doctrine of check and balance.

A Legal Framework of Probation of Offenders in India: An Analysis with Special Reference to Australia and the USA

Biju Joseph and M. L. Shilpa

Abstract The criminal justice system's effectiveness against rising crime rates results in more convictions, necessitating efficient ways to reduce jail overcrowding, solutions to rising prison costs, and the finest correctional technologies. Probation is the optimal correctional response, and its comparative study is vital due to potential challenges from events like COVID-19 and extensive migration, coupled with rising cyber transactions resulting from liberalisation and globalisation. In this comparative study, researchers attempt to examine the implementation of the penal philosophy of rehabilitation of offenders under the legislation on Probation of Offenders in Australia, the USA, and India for an effective and advanced system of probation offenders in India to address the present and future challenges. Findings highlight legislative definitions, sentencing guidelines, probation conditions, and conviction-free orders focused on rehabilitation. Researchers propose adaptable sentencing guidelines for an enhanced and advanced Indian probation system to tackle present and future challenges.

Keywords Probation · Offenders · Sentencing · Rehabilitation · Community · Supervision

1 Introduction

Probation of offenders is a court-ordered disposition in corrections involving the suspension of the ultimate verdict. Rather than sending the offender to a penal or penitentiary facility, this approach allows the offender to remain within the community while receiving treatment and supervision. The offender willingly accepts specific terms and restrictions established by the Courts in exchange for being placed on probation. This method embodies the reformative theory of punishment, offering a chance for first-time offenders to rehabilitate, considering the nature of their offence

B. Joseph (✉) · M. L. Shilpa
School of Law, Christ University, Bangalore, India
e-mail: biju.joseph@res.christuniversity.in

J. Aston et al. (eds.), *Comparative Law*, https://doi.org/10.1007/978-981-97-7815-7_10

and other circumstances. It aims to prevent them from becoming repeat offenders after serving prison sentences alongside hardened criminals. In this perspective, the present study compares the legislation governing probation system in India with three jurisdictions known for their advanced probation systems in Australia and the United States. It aims to identify legislatively sound and practical guidelines for effective implementation of Probation of Offenders Act.

2 Interpretation of "Probation of Offenders"—An Overview

In India, "probation" means the conditional suspension, imposition, or execution of the Court's sentencing decisions in particular instances, notably those involving juvenile offenders who are not incarcerated but are instead granted probation, either after simple admonition pursuant to sec.3 of the Probation of Offenders Act, 1958 (POA) or on a bond, with or without sureties, to keep the peace and be of good behaviour.[1] The specific meaning and definition of probation for offenders in Australia may differ depending on the State or Territory, as each jurisdiction has its legislation and policies regarding sentencing and community-based orders. Probation is community-based sentencing or supervision imposed on offenders found guilty of a criminal offence but not sentenced to imprisonment. Probation is also known as a "community correction order,[2]" "community-based order,[3]" or "conditional order.[4]" In the United States, the term probation is defined by statutes in different states for its application within their jurisdictions. Nevertheless, it is regarded as a milder form of punishment than imprisonment while still maintaining accountability for individuals who have violated the law. It is a less expensive alternative to jail or prison, allowing people charged with or guilty of federal offences to reside with their families, work, and contribute to society.[5]

---

[1] Chena Ram v. State of Rajasthan, (2017) SCC OnLine Raj 441 (India), https://www.scconline.com/Members/SearchResult.aspx.

[2] Sentencing Act 1991(Vic), s 36.

[3] Sentencing Act, 1995(WA), s 62.

[4] Crimes Act 1914 (Cth), s 20(1)(a).

[5] United States Courts, The Federal Probation and Pretrial Services-Supervision, Administrative Office of the United States Courts, Government agency (Dec.12, 2023, 11:28 AM), https://www.uscourts.gov/services-forms/probation-and-pretrial-services/probation-and-pretrial-services-supervision

3 Legal Framework on Probation of Offenders—An Overview

It is advantageous to know the statutory sentencing options where the penal philosophy of rehabilitation and other benefits of probation of offenders are realised to improve the effectiveness of probation since the probation implementation mostly depends on court-ordered disposition. Though courts' broad discretion in probation sentencing is essential, guidance in the utilisation of discretion is all the more critical for a fair administration of criminal justice and fruitful implementation of suitable legislation. In the following paragraphs, legislative provisions providing probation for offenders in India, three states in the USA, and three jurisdictions in Australia are compared to identify more advantageous models.

3.1 Legal Framework on Probation of Offenders in India

The Probation of Offenders Act, 1958 broadly contains the law relating to probation sentencing. This Act governs the sentencing of adults over 18 years of age. The State Governments are empowered to make rules to carry out the purposes of this Act with the endorsement of the Central Government through publication in the Official Gazette. The Parliament has largely left it to Courts to decide when and how to release an offender on probation for good conduct.

The Court has authority to release certain offenders through admonition, considering the case's circumstances, including the nature of the offence and the offender's character. This applies to offences punishable by imprisonment for a maximum of two years and specific offences designated in the provision, provided the offender has no prior convictions.[6]

Additionally, the Courts are empowered to release the offenders on probation of good conduct, with or without supervision, for offences not subject to the death penalty or life imprisonment.[7] Before making the orders, the Court considers any relevant reports from the probation officer.

When the Courts find a person guilty of having committed an offence punishable with imprisonment (but not with imprisonment for life) and a person under twenty-one years of age, it should refrain from imposing a prison sentence unless it determines that, considering the specific case's circumstances, which encompass the nature of the offence and the individual's character, it would not be advisable to grant release through admonition or probation for good conduct. If the Court passes any sentence of imprisonment on such an offender, it shall record its reasons for doing so in such cases. The Court will request a report from the probation officer. It will take into account this report, if available, along with any other pertinent information about

[6] The Probation of Offenders Act, 1958, § 3, No.20, Acts of Parliament, 1958 (India).

[7] Ibid. § 4.

the offender's character and physical and mental well-being to determine whether it would not be desirable to release him after admonition or to release him on probation of good conduct.[8]

Furthermore, the Courts are empowered to mandate the released offenders to pay compensation and associated costs as part of their probation conditions.[9] Upon the probation officer's request, the Courts have the authority to modify probation terms, including bond duration and conditions, after hearing the offender and surety. The Courts that impose probation may discharge the bond if supervision is unnecessary.[10]

For bond violations, the Court can issue a warrant or summons, grant bail, or remand. After a hearing, they can face the original offence sentence or a fine up to 50 rupees. Failure to pay may lead to the sentence of original offence. If a person is found guilty and released on Probation under Sections 3 and 4, the Act prevents disqualifications linked to that conviction, except if they are re-sentenced for the original offence after release.[11]

3.2 *Legal Framework on Probation of Offenders in Australia*

Throughout Australia, the Commonwealth and the other States have established mechanisms for conditional release of offenders under the ongoing supervision of corrections officers. The statutory foundations for these supervised conditional releases differ across jurisdictions.[12] The following paragraphs examine the probation sentencing provisions of three Australian states: Northern Territory, Australian Capital Territory, and Queensland.

Australian Capital Territory

In the Australian Capital Territory, the Crimes (Sentencing) Act 2005 provides clear guidance on sentencing objectives and options, including probation. When determining the appropriateness of probation, the Court considers both the offence details and the offender's characteristics, as defined in Sections 33 and 34 of the Crimes (Sentencing) Act 2005. The Court has the authority to issue various orders[13] for rehabilitation as follows:

---

[8] Ibid. § 6.

[9] Ibid. § 5.

[10] Ibid. § 8.

[11] Ibid. §12.

[12] Honor Figgis, Probation: An Overview, NSW Parliamentary Library Research Service (15 Dec.2023, 10:01:46 AM), https://www.parliament.nsw.gov.au/researchpapers/Documents/probation-an-overview/probation.pdf.

[13] The Crimes (Sentencing) Act 2005(ACT), ss 11,12,12A,13,13(3),17,23 & 27.

The Courts are empowered to dismiss charges when imposing further punishment is deemed inappropriate or issue a good behaviour order. Notably, a non-conviction order with a good behaviour order does not include community service. Young offenders who plead guilty to eligible offences with potential imprisonment sentences ranging from one to four years may receive drug and alcohol treatment orders. Good behaviour orders are available for offenders convicted or found guilty of offences, provided they commit to fulfilling their good behaviour obligations as outlined in the Crimes (Sentence Administration) Act 2005 for a specified period.

Intensive correction orders provide an alternative sentencing option for adult offenders convicted and sentenced to imprisonment. Offenders sentenced to up to 2 years can serve their sentence in the community under an intensive correction order. For sentences ranging from 2 to 4 years, the Court may also choose to impose an intensive correction order if it considers it suitable, taking into account factors such as the impact on victims and the community, the risk posed by the offender, and the level of culpability for the offence. Suspended sentences can be imposed when offenders are sentenced to imprisonment but are also issued a good behaviour order, during which the sentence is suspended or extended as determined by the Court. These suspended sentence orders can be combined with other sentencing options. Deferred sentence orders are issued when the Court believes it is necessary to address an offender's criminal behaviour and contributing factors before the official sentencing. They are available for offenders convicted or found guilty of crimes punishable by imprisonment, provided they are not serving or liable to serve a term of imprisonment for another offence. The Courts must also be satisfied that the offender can be released on bail per the Bail Act, 1992.

The Court may issue driver licence disqualification orders in cases involving motor vehicle theft or offences specified in the Criminal Code.[14] For offences other than serious violence or sexual offences, drug and alcohol treatment orders[15]are available as a sentencing option. Reparation orders are issued when an individual (referred to as the injured person) incurs losses or expenses as a direct result of an offender's offence.[16] The Court can impose non-association orders to prohibit the offender from being in the company of specific individuals, attempting to be with them, or communicating with them in any manner, including electronic communications. Further, the courts have the authority to issue place restriction orders, which restrict the offender from entering or remaining in defined locations or areas.

For offences carrying potential imprisonment as punishment, the sentencing court may choose to impose combination sentences, including options like partial imprisonment, intensive correction, suspended sentences, good behaviour orders, fines, driver licence disqualification, reparation orders, non-association orders, place restriction orders, or other penalties under territory laws. This combination may involve penalties such as driver's licence disqualification, reparation, non-association, place restriction, or additional penalties specified in the territory's laws

[14] Ibid. s 16.

[15] Ibid. s 12A.

[16] Ibid. s 19.

for offences punishable with a fine. These comprehensive sentencing provisions allow the Court to tailor orders to more effectively address each case's unique circumstances.

Northern Territory

Key principles guide the justice system in the Northern Territory under the Sentencing Act of 1995. These principles include factors for assessing an offender's character and considering aggravating factors per sentencing guidelines. The primary goals of dismissal, discharge, and bond orders are to support offender rehabilitation, address minor infractions, and provide flexibility when a conviction or severe punishment is not appropriate. These measures consider unique circumstances deserving of leniency.[17] The Act offers various release options,[18] releasing offenders without a conviction, unconditionally dismissing those found guilty of an offence without recording a conviction, and releasing individuals on bond without a conviction, with adequate security as determined by the Court. Courts may also release offenders following a conviction, unconditionally discharge them, or allow bond release after conviction with the appropriate security.

Courts can issue community work orders in cases of a guilty verdict to enable offenders to make amends to the community through beneficial community work. These orders apply to offences excluding sexual crimes, violent offences, aggravated offences, or those specified by regulations. If a court sentences an offender to imprisonment, it can suspend the sentence, specifying the offender's residence or location for a period not exceeding 12 months.[19] Community custody orders are an option for sentences of up to 12 months, excluding sexual offences, violent crimes, aggravated offences, or specified offences.[20]

For sentences of up to five years, the Courts may suspend the sentence entirely or partially, with conditions set by the Courts. Additionally, the Court can issue a suspension order when an offender agrees to a home detention programme, provided it is deemed suitable.[21] Mental health orders are authorised when an offender exhibits signs of mental illness or disturbance, allowing the Courts to recommend admission and treatment in an approved facility upon receiving advice from the Chief Health Officer.[22]

---

[17] Sentencing Act, 1995(NT).

[18] Ibid. ss.11,12,13, Sec.33A,39A & s. 39B

[19] Ibid. s 44.

[20] Ibid. s 48A.

[21] Ibid. s 40.

[22] Ibid. s 79.

Queensland

In Queensland, the Penalties and Sentencing Act of 1992 is crucial in shaping the sentencing process and objectives. The Act encompasses probation orders and other court-issued orders, all aimed at achieving rehabilitation and ensuring justice. This legislation emphasises the importance of adhering to sentencing guidelines, evaluating an offender's character, and considering aggravating and mitigating circumstances in the sentencing process.

The Court holds the authority to release an offender without recording a conviction. This can be accomplished through unconditional release or by having the offender enter a recognisance. Various factors are considered when making this determination, including the offender's character, age, health, mental condition, the nature of the offence, past conduct, and surrounding circumstances.[23] The Court can also issue recognisances in property-related crime cases without recording a conviction.[24]

When an offender is convicted, the Court has a range of options.[25] This applies to cases where an offender is convicted on indictment,[26] released upon entering into a recognisance, or for those who are summarily convicted, with the condition of maintaining good behaviour.[27] The Court also has the discretion to release an offender on Recognizance after conviction. It can choose to record a conviction and release the offender on a probation order, which can span from six months to three years.[28] Alternatively, in cases where a conviction is recorded, the Courts may impose a prison sentence of up to one year and stipulate that the offender will be placed under a probation order upon release, which can last from nine months to three years.

The Courts can also issue community service orders, which compel the offender to engage in unpaid community service supervised by an authorised corrective services officer. This order aims to facilitate the offender's reintegration into the community, encouraging positive changes in behaviour, social connections, work-related habits, and a sense of satisfaction from aiding others. This order is applicable in specific circumstances and offences, such as affraying or wounding in public places while under the influence of intoxicating substances.[29]

A probation order and a community service order can be combined when an offender is sentenced for an offence that carries a term of imprisonment or a regulatory offence.[30] In cases of graffiti offences: whether through indictment or summary proceedings, the Courts must issue a graffiti removal order, requiring the offender to perform unpaid graffiti removal service for a specified number of hours, regardless

[23] Penalties and Sentencing Act, 1992(Qld), s 19.

[24] Ibid. s 22.

[25] Ibid. s 29.

[26] Ibid. s 30.

[27] Ibid. s 31.

[28] Ibid. ss 90 & 91.

[29] Ibid. s 108B.

[30] Ibid. s 108B.

of whether a conviction is recorded or another order is made. For sentences not exceeding one year, the Court may consider imposing an intensive correction order, which can offer an alternative to imprisonment for certain offenders.[31]

When an offender is sentenced to a prison term not exceeding five years, the Courts can issue an order wholly or partially suspending the term of imprisonment if it deems it appropriate. An operational period is specified, during which the offender must refrain from committing another imprisonable offence. This period should be no shorter than the term of imprisonment imposed and must not exceed five years. Drug and alcohol treatment orders are made to support an offender's rehabilitation by providing a judicially supervised, therapeutic, and integrated treatment programme. They are primarily designed to address severe substance use disorders, reduce related criminal activity, and mitigate associated health risks.

3.3 Legal Framework on Probation of Offenders in the USA

The USA's probation system encompasses six distinct components: juvenile probation, municipal probation, county probation, state probation, state combined probation and parole, and federal probation. In each state, a combination of these systems is operated and overseen by either a central agency, various local agencies, or a combination of both.[32] Below, we examine the sentencing provisions of three US states: Florida, Massachusetts, and California.

Florida

In Florida, the Criminal Punishment Code[33] governs sentencing guidelines, which include a chapter addressing mitigating factors.[34] "Community sanction" encompasses probation, community control, and pre-trial intervention or diversion.[35] "Community control" is closely monitored custody within the community,[36] while "probation" involves community supervision with specified conditions and regular contact with probation officers.[37] These sentencing options are available for criminal defendants, except those charged with death penalty offences. They apply to those who have received a guilty verdict from a jury, entered a guilty or nolo contendere plea, or been found guilty by the Court in a non-jury trial.

---

[31] Ibid. s 110A.

[32] Labrecque, Ryan M. "Probation in the United States: A historical and modern perspective." Routledge Handbook of Corrections in the United States (2017): 155–164.

[33] Fla. Stat. § 921.002 (2023).

[34] Ibid. § 921.0026.

[35] Ibid. § 921.0021.

[36] Ibid. § 948.001(3).

[37] Ibid. § 948.001(8).

A felony defendant may be placed on probation before the Court finds them guilty or after reserving judgement, particularly if it serves the best interests of justice or society. The department provides immediate supervision for felony offenders on probation. For misdemeanour offenders sentenced by a circuit court, supervision by the department is possible upon the Court's directive. The Court retains discretion to place defendants found guilty of non-felony offences on probation, including cases where adjudication is withheld. However, the department's supervision applies only when the circuit court is the Court of original jurisdiction.[38]

When the Court deems probation unsuitable for a felony disposition, the offender may be placed in a community control programme. The Court determines community-based sanctions, including curfews, revocation or suspension of the driver licence, community service, and more. When the law allows, the Court can impose a fine or place the defendant on probation or into community control as an alternative to imprisonment for offences punishable by both fine and imprisonment.[39] For offences where imprisonment is prescribed as a penalty (excluding capital felonies), the Courts may impose a split sentence. This means the defendant initially serves a period of imprisonment and is later placed on probation or community control. Successful compliance can lead to modifying the sentence, eliminating the remaining term of imprisonment.

"Administrative probation" is no-contact, nonreporting supervision for low-risk offenders who've completed at least half of their probation term. The Court or Department of Corrections may order this, with established department procedures.[40] In cases where a defendant is a chronic substance abuser, the Courts may stay and withhold the imposition of the sentence. Instead, the defendant may be placed on drug offender probation or enrolled in a post-adjudicatory treatment-based drug court programme, provided they meet the necessary qualifications.[41] Sex offender Probation and community control involve intensive supervision, potentially including electronic monitoring. This supervision focuses on treating and monitoring sex offenders and is administered by an officer with specialised training and a limited caseload.[42]

Massachusetts

In Massachusetts, a probation order is a formal written court order outlining the terms and conditions of probation. It is important to note that a probation order is not a contractual agreement. Probation consists of "general conditions" that apply to every probation order and "special conditions" that are specific to an individual

[38] Ibid. § 948.01.

[39] Ibid. § 948.011.

[40] Ibid. § 948.001 & §. 948.013.

[41] Ibid. § 948.001(4).

[42] Ibid. § 948.001(13).

case. Additionally, sentencing recommendations play a crucial role in determining relevant factors for sentencing.[43]

Pre-trial diversion is a mechanism to redirect offenders away from the standard trial and sentencing process, focusing on addressing the root causes of criminal behaviour to prevent reoffending.[44] Pre-trial diversion is exclusively available in the Massachusetts District Court for individuals facing charges that could result in a jail sentence within the Court's jurisdiction. Eligibility prerequisites include no prior convictions after turning 18, no outstanding warrants or appeals, and a programme recommendation indicating that participation would be beneficial.[45] Pre-trial probation, on the other hand, is a probationary status granted based on a probation order issued before a trial or before the formal submission of a guilty plea. It applies in various courts, including the superior, district, and juvenile courts.[46] Pre-trial probation does not require admitting guilt; upon completing the probationary period, the defendant's record remains free of conviction.[47]

A continuance without a finding (CWOF) occurs after an acknowledgement of guilt or admission to sufficient facts, allowing the case to be scheduled for a specific date without a formal guilty verdict. Violating the conditions in the probation order can lead to the cancellation of the continuance. If the conditions are met, the criminal case may be dismissed.[48] A nolle prosequi can be entered by the prosecuting attorney before a sentence is imposed, probation is ordered, or a CWOF is issued. It treats the matter as if charges were never filed, but it is not an acquittal and does not prevent future legal proceedings for the same conduct.[49] However, once jeopardy attaches, a nolle prosequi without the defendant's consent is treated as an acquittal for the mentioned charges, preventing further action against the defendant for the same conduct. In a "guilty filed" arrangement, a judge can delay the imposition of a defendant's sentence indefinitely if the defendant's factual guilt has been established through a guilty verdict or guilty plea, and both parties agree to this disposition.[50] The Court refrains from immediately delivering a sentence for a predetermined period, during which the defendant must remain free from new criminal charges.[51]

A straight probation (standard probation) is imposed after an admission of guilt.[52] If probation terms are violated, the Court may impose any sentence authorised by

---

43 M.G.L.c.211E §3.

44 Nate Amendola, Understanding the Massachusetts Criminal Court Process, Nate Amendola Défense (Dec.12,2023,13:43PM), https://www.amendolallc.com/blog/criminal-sentencing-in-massachusetts.

45 M.G.L.c 276A (2023).

46 Ibid. c. 276, § 87.

47 Cappetta Law Offices, Massachusetts Sentencing Options, Framingham Crime Lawyer Cappetta Law Offices, (Dec.12,2023,13: 50 PM) https://www.cappettalaw.com/massachusetts-sentencing-options.html.

48 Mass. Dist. Ct. & Mun. Ct. R. 2 (2024).

49 Mass. R. Crim. P. 16 (2022).

50 Ibid. P.28 (e).

51 Supra. note 47.

52 Ibid.

the relevant statute, including reinstating probation or ordering incarceration.[53] The advantage of straight probation is that no jail time is served, and no sentence is recorded, even in the Board of Probation (BOP) record.[54] The Court can suspend all or part of a prison sentence, except for life-or-death sentences, and place the offender on probation. This also applies when a fine and imprisonment are imposed, except for life sentences, weapon-related crimes, or felonies with prior convictions.[55] Split sentences involve a combination of incarceration and a suspended sentence with a probationary period. After serving the incarcerated portion, the defendant is released and placed on probation, with the remaining portion suspended. Violation of probation conditions can lead to the enforcement of the suspended sentence.[56] Intermediate sanctions, such as home confinement and day reporting, provide alternative sentencing options. Judges also have the authority to impose specific conditions, like mandatory substance abuse treatment or counselling, as part of the sentencing arrangement.

California

The State's Penal Code in California underscores the significance of probation services within the criminal justice system. The central objective when enforcing court-ordered probation conditions is to ensure public safety. When granting probation, critical factors considered include the nature of the offence, pursuit of justice, including aspects of punishment, offender reintegration into the community, adherence to probation conditions, victim's losses, and the defendant's needs.[57] Probation involves temporarily suspending the imposition or execution of a sentence and granting conditional, revocable release within the community under probation officer supervision. On the other hand, a conditional sentence suspends the imposition or execution of a sentence with revocable community release, subject to court-imposed conditions and without probation officer oversight. California's legislative intent is for both conditional sentences and probation to be authorised as sentencing options when permissible, particularly for infractions or misdemeanours. Sentencing guidelines and factors influencing reduced penalties guide trial court sentencing, and the 2023 California Rules of Court provide insights into circumstances that can exacerbate sentencing decisions.

In misdemeanour cases, the Court can refer the case to a probation officer for an investigation and subsequent report or immediately impose a conditional sentence.[58] However, in case of a felony conviction where probation is an option, the Court must

---

53 Mass. Dist. Ct. & Mun. Ct. R. 8(f).

54 Supra. note 44.

55 M.G.L.c. 279 §1 &1A.

56 Ibid. 279 §1 &1A.

57 CA Penal Code § 1202.7 (2023).

58 Ibid. § 1203 d.

promptly direct the case to a probation officer for investigation and report submission. This report, which outlines the crime's circumstances and the individual's prior history and record, plays a crucial role in determining appropriate punishment.[59] Notably, probation is not an option, and the suspension of sentence imposition or execution is not allowed for individuals convicted of violent or serious felonies, as explicitly outlined in the legal code. Moreover, individuals who commit a new felony offence while on probation for a prior felony are ineligible for probation. Probation is highly unlikely if the individual has caused significant bodily harm to the victim, used a deadly weapon, or engaged in actions like a prohibited drive-by shooting.[60] However, there may be rare exceptional circumstances where probation could be considered in the interests of justice. The Community-Based Punishment Act of 1994[61] focuses primarily on nonviolent offenders who would typically receive prison or jail sentences. The rationale behind this approach is that such individuals pose the lowest risk to public safety and are most responsive to personalised programming and services available through community-based initiatives. The Act introduces two key components: "community-based punishment" and "intermediate sanctions." "Community-based punishment" entails a collaborative effort between the state and a county or consortium of counties, overseeing and administering correctional services at the local government level, particularly intermediate sanctions. "Intermediate sanctions" aim to diversify responses to nonviolent offenders by providing effective alternatives to imprisonment while maintaining public safety. These intermediate sanctions encompass electronic surveillance, intensive supervision during detention, community service requirements, participation in restorative justice initiatives, job training, education, drug and alcohol treatment, literacy programmes, employment counselling, psychiatric therapy, or a combination of these interventions, among others.

California Community Corrections Performance Incentives emphasise the value of probation for offenders and facilitate funding. Probation is a court-imposed suspension of a sentence that seeks to supervise, treat, and rehabilitate offenders while they remain in the community under probation department supervision. Probation is a linchpin of the criminal justice system, closely connected with the courts and central to enhancing public safety in California's communities.[62]

3.4 Summation

The Probation of Offenders Act, 1958, in India allows courts to release certain offenders on probation based on their circumstances and the nature of their offences. The Act also permits the release of offenders who committed crimes punishable by

---

[59] Ibid. § 1203(b).

[60] Ibid. § 1203(k).

[61] Ibid. § 8050.

[62] Ibid. § 1228.

up to two years in prison and those who committed specific offences listed in the Act, considering the crime's specifics. Courts are bound to state reasons when denying probation to offenders under 21 years old. Probation conditions may include compensation and can be modified. The Act prevents disqualifications for offenders released on probation unless they are re-sentenced for the original offence after release.

In Australia, the Northern Territory sets general principles of probation sentencing and offers options for probation with or without convictions. Further, it provides community work, home detention, and mental health orders and emphasises rehabilitation and flexibility in sentencing. Australian Capital Territory provides clear sentencing objectives and offers various probation options based on nature of offence and the offender's characteristics. Further, it allows non-conviction, good behaviour orders, drug and alcohol treatment orders and employs intensive correction, suspended sentence, and combination sentences. Queensland defines probation orders, focuses on adherence to guidelines, and considers various factors. It facilitates release with or without conviction, along with various orders, prioritises rehabilitation, and offers intensive correction and drug treatment programmes. Further, it supports graffiti removal, community service, and suspended sentences and combines orders for sentencing.

In short, US legislation customises the probation system based on offence types and rehabilitation, aiming to advance public safety. Florida legislation has community sanctions such as probation offenders and other alternatives to imprisonment, which involve community supervision and specialised programmes available for criminal defendants, excluding death penalty cases. Formal probation orders with diverse options and specific conditions, pre-trial diversion without requiring guilt admission, and flexible procedures like CWOF and Guilty Field are characteristics of Massachusetts legislation. Californian legislation focuses on probation for public safety, considering conditional sentences, and probation is not available for violent or serious felonies. Community-based options, community corrections, performance incentives, etc., are specific California features.

4 Comparison Tables

To get a clear picture and identify beneficial characteristics of legal frameworks of probation of offenders of this comparative study, it is desirable to look at the comparison chart (Table 1)[63] given in the following pages.

[63] The researchers compiled a comparison table by analysing relevant provisions from the following statutes and codes: Probation of Offenders Act, 1958 (India), Crimes (Sentencing) Act 2005 (ACT), Sentencing Act, 1995 (NT), Penalties and Sentencing Act, 1992 (Qld), 2023 Florida Statutes, 2023 Massachusetts General Laws, 2024 Massachusetts District Court and Municipal Court Rules, 2022 Massachusetts Rules of Criminal Procedure, and 2023 California Penal Code.

Table 1 A comparison table of Statutory backing of judicial implementation of offenders' Probation in India, Australia, and the USA

	India	Australia			USA		
	Indian Parliament	Australian capital territory	Northern territory	Queens land	Florida	Massachusetts	California
	No definition	No definition	No definition	Defines probation order	Defines community control and probation	Definition of probation	Defines probation and declares it as an essential element, the primary goal, and Linchpin of the criminal justice system
	Probation of Offenders Act,1958	The crimes (sentencing) act 2005	The sentencingact,1995,	Penalties and Sentencing Act, 1992	The criminal punishment code	Gen laws, chapter 279	California code, penal code – pen § 2023 & California Rules of Court
1	No sentencing guidelines	Purposes of sentencing and specific sentencing options	Sentencing guidelines,	Sentencing guidelines	Sentencing guidelines	Recommended sentencing guidelines	Sentencing guidelines
2	Factors to be considered given general terms (*circumstances of the case, nature of the offence, and the character of the offender*)	Description of Relevant and Irrelevant Considerations	The particular factors to be considered in determining offenders' character and aggravating factors	Matters to be considered in determining offender's character	Mitigating circumstances	Relevant factors in sentencing	Circumstances in aggravation, aggravating, mitigating, and contributing factors
3	Admonition after conviction (found guilty)	An order to dismiss the charge after finding guilty	Release without conviction	Absolute release	Felony probation	Pre-trial diversion	Nonfelony probation

(continued)

Table 1 (continued)

	India	Australia			USA		
	Indian Parliament	Australian capital territory	Northern territory	Queens land	Florida	Massachusetts	California
4	Release offenders on probation of good conduct after conviction	Good behaviour order without conviction	Unconditional dismissal	Release on entering Recognizance before conviction	Nonfelony Probation	Pre-trial probation and post-trial probation	Summary probation
5	Power of Court to require released offenders to pay compensation and costs	Good behaviour orders after conviction on an undertaking before the Court	Release on a bond without conviction	Release of an offender convicted on indictment on entering to Recognizance	Community control programme	A continuance without a finding (CWOF)	Felony probation
6	Removal of disqualification attached to conviction	Intensive correction orders after conviction	Release on conviction	Release of an offender summarily convicted on the condition of keeping good behaviour	Probation or community control as an alternative to imprisonment	Entry of a nolle prosequi	"Community-based punishment and "intermediate sanctions

(continued)

Table 1 (continued)

	India	Australia			USA		
	Indian Parliament	Australian capital territory	Northern territory	Queens land	Florida	Massachusetts	California
7		Suspended sentences after conviction	Unconditional discharge	Probation orders by courts, whether or not a conviction is recorded	Split sentence of probation or community control and imprisonment	Guilty filed	Intensive supervision
8		Deferred sentence orders after conviction	Release on bond following conviction	Release on recognizance after conviction	Administrative probation	Straight probation/ standard probation	Home detention with electronic monitoring
9		Drug and alcohol treatment orders after conviction	Community work order	Community service order, whether or not after conviction recorded	The drug offender probation	Suspended sentence	Mandatory community service
10		Driver licence disqualification orders after conviction	Community-based orders	Mandatory community service orders	Sex offender probation" or "sex offender community control	Split sentence	Work, training, or education in a furlough

(continued)

Table 1 (continued)

	India	Australia			USA		
	Indian Parliament	Australian capital territory	Northern territory	Queens land	Florida	Massachusetts	California
11		Reparation order	Home detention order	Probation order and community service order for an offender		Intermediate sanction of home confinement,	Work in place of detention in a work release programme
12		Combination sentence after conviction	Community custody orders	Graffiti removal orders		Intermediate sanction of day reporting	Day reporting
13		Place restriction orders and non-association orders	Wholly or partly Suspended sentence of imprisonment	Intensive correction order if it records a conviction			Community-based residential programmes
14			Mental health orders	Orders of suspended imprisonment without recording a conviction			California community corrections performance incentives
15				Drug and alcohol treatment orders			

5 Judicial Dictum of "Probation of Offenders"

Probation aims to reform first-time offenders by offering a chance for rehabilitation during initial incarceration.[64] The Federal Probation Act aimed to aid rehabilitation and seize the reform opportunity.[65] Probation is a privilege, not a right, granted as an act of clemency for low-risk individuals, emphasising rehabilitation at sentencing, with trial courts exercising discretion.[66] The social stigma and harm caused by prison sentences can worsen the problem of criminal behaviour. The Probation of Offenders Act seeks to treat first-time offenders as individuals needing social help rather than punishment. It acknowledges that crimes can result from various factors, including poverty and environmental influences, and aims to reform and rehabilitate offenders instead of perpetuating a cycle of criminal behaviour.[67] The goal is to rehabilitate offenders and reintegrate them into society without exposing them to the harmful aspects of prison life.[68] Recently, the Gujarat High Court opined that the Probation of Offenders Act, 1958, is mandatory, and the Court is required to give the reason for not extending the benefit of the Probation of Offenders Act, 1958, irrespective of the offender's age.[69] The Courts must consider the offence's nature, motives, and offender's background for appropriate sentencing. This involves evaluating social standing, education, empathy, and rehabilitation potential. Considering aggravating and mitigating factors, the Courts assess the possibility of release based on good behaviour. Section 4 of the Probation of Offenders Act, 1958, guides the evaluation, considering crime details, planning, motive, conduct, weapon use, and circumstances.[70]

6 Conclusion

In India, the Probation of Offenders Act, 1958, embodies the principle of rehabilitating offenders passed by Parliament. Accordingly, the Court can either admonish and release offenders or place them on probation of good conduct. In such a release, the probationers shall not suffer any disqualification attached to their conviction. Notably, the Act does not provide a statutory definition of "probation of offenders" and lacks specific sentencing guidelines, and judges in India possess significant discretion in sentencing.

---

[64] U. S. v. MURRAY, 275 U.S. 347, (1928).

[65] Burns v. United States, 287 U. S. 216. (1932).

[66] People v. Moran, 1 Cal.5th 398(2016).

[67] Arvind Mohan Sinha v. Amulya Kumar Biswas, (1974) 4 S.C.C 222 (India).

[68] Lakhvir Singh v. State of Punjab, (2021) 2. S.C.C 763(India).

[69] Pravinbhai Babubhai Sodha Parmar v State of Gujarat, 2023 SCC OnLine Guj 3312(India). https://www.scconline.com/Members/SearchResult.aspx.

[70] Khandar Singh v. State,(2023) SCC OnLine All 70 (India), https://www.scconline.com/Members/SearchResult.aspx.

In Australia, the administration of probation falls under the purview of individual States and Territories. The Australian Capital Territory, Northern Territory, and Queensland probation systems have undergone various modifications to incorporate a range of sentencing options as part of their respective sentencing enactments. Notably, Queensland provides a specific definition of a sentencing order. Each of these jurisdictions has established sentencing guidelines that outline detailed considerations and factors to consider during sentencing. Courts in these jurisdictions can release offenders through various orders without conviction or recording convictions. Queensland, for instance, prescribes probation orders for less severe offenders. After a conviction has been recorded, other sentencing options are available for more serious offences, such as intensive correction orders, community service orders, and mandatory community service orders. Despite offering flexibility and convenience to judges, all these intend to achieve effective individualisation of sentencing. This involves tailoring sentences to address the rehabilitative needs of offenders, which can be realised through combinations of probation, community service orders, incarceration, community services, drug and alcohol treatment orders, and mental health orders.

In the USA, specifically in Florida, Massachusetts, and California, the concept and significance of probation of offenders in sentencing are underscored by legally defining probation. California, in particular, places probation of offenders at the core of its criminal justice system, considering it a pivotal and primary objective. These definitions underscore the essential role probation officers play in the probation of offenders. Legislation in these US States includes sentencing guidelines and outlines relevant mitigating and aggravating factors. Massachusetts, in particular, has distinctive features such as pre-trial diversion, pre-trial probation, continuance without finding (COWF), entry of a nolle prosequi, and guilty filed. In some instances, these features allow for the probation of offenders without a formal conviction. The Court can prescribe a community control programme in cases of unsuitability of probation or severe offences. These states provide various options, including probation or community control as alternatives to incarceration, split sentences combining probation or community control with imprisonment, administrative Probation, drug offender probation, sexual offenders' Probation, and intermediate sanctions. These measures embedded in the statutes of these States in the USA ensure an efficient approach to sentencing and the successful rehabilitation of offenders by addressing their criminogenic needs.

Australia and the USA utilise meticulously developed sentencing options grounded in evidence-based practices. This fosters both credibility and reliability in their application, thereby achieving a crucial balance between rehabilitation and public safety. The researchers identified significant benefits and advantages of probation sentencing provisions in both these countries. These various mechanisms within the sentencing options play a pivotal role in enhancing the quality of judicial decisions. They provide judges with practical tools to tailor orders that address the rehabilitative needs of offenders, ultimately ensuring a fair and consistent approach that minimises disparities in decision-making. Pre-trial, pre-conviction, or non-conviction probation sentencing orders alleviate delays in accessing justice and expedite case disposition. These orders significantly lessen the disqualifications associated with convictions, removing the Court's explicit ruling in each probation release in this regard as required in India due to the provisions of the Indian constitution on disqualification in public service still in effect. These sentencing options are practical remedies to eliminate disqualifications due to convictions that hinder released offenders from maintaining current employment and pursuing future job opportunities, often leading to stigmatisation and other limitations in their prospects. Furthermore, in Australia and the USA, probation sentencing practices have proven effective remedies for addressing prison overcrowding and have successfully reduced the cost burden associated with incarceration.[71]

The Supreme Court addressed the issue of prison overcrowding and expressed a more expansive view on releasing offenders on probation in the case of Re-Inhuman Conditions 1382(2016).[72] The situation worsened during the COVID-19 pandemic, releasing a significant number of high-risk offenders. In 2021, in the case of Lakhvir Sing v. State of Panchab[73] the Supreme Court even allowed probation in cases of offences with mandatory minimum punishment under the Indian Penal Code (IPC) and enactments predating 1958. More recently, the Gujarat High Court[74] stated that the Probation of Offenders Act, 1958, is mandatory and ruled for providing reasons for not extending the benefits of this Act when granting probation to an offender aged 58 years convicted of the offence of voluntarily causing harm using dangerous weapons or means. As a result, a broader release of probation offenders has become a necessary and practical reality. The Probation of Offenders Act, 1958 has not yet been amended or updated to keep pace with the advancements in rehabilitating offenders and the needs of the time.

Even when done by a judge, exercising unguided discretion is not advisable. Our country requires clear legal guidelines for sentencing options to reduce ambiguity in the allocation of sentences. Several factors are pertinent when determining appropriate penalties.[75] Based on the findings of this comparative study for the maximum utilisation of probation offenders, the researchers propose practical models that could be incorporated into the Probation of Offenders Act, Criminal Procedure, or enacted through a dedicated Sentencing Act. Sentencing guidelines should prioritise achieving a balance between public safety and offender rehabilitation. Alongside clear definitions of probation, its principles, and goals. These guidelines should delineate significance and applicability of probation of offenders. Additionally, they should outline factors for assessing offender character, relevant considerations during sentencing, and potential mitigating circumstances for court evaluation.

---

[71] Davis, Brandon R. "State Incarceration Policy in the US Federal System: Assessing Recent Approaches to Reducing Incarceration Rates." Publius: The Journal of Federalism (2023).

[72] (2016) 3 S.C.C 700 (India).

[73] Supra not 66 at.21.

[74] Supra. not 67 at.17.

[75] Report of the Mali math Committee on Reforms of the Criminal Justice System (2003) 170 C:/Users/Biju/OneDrive/Desktop/Dr.%20Justice%20 V.S.%20Malimath%20Report%20First%20pages.doc.pdf.

The courts should be empowered statutorily to issue pre-trial orders, orders that do not result in a conviction, or orders without recording convictions. These orders may include pre-trial diversion, pre-trial probation, continuance without a finding (CWOF), entry of a nolle prosequi, "guilty filed," orders to dismiss charges after finding guilt, good behaviour orders without conviction, and good behaviour orders following a conviction with an undertaking before the Court. Probation legislation should enable administrative probation for minor offences and specialised probation for specific offender types, such as drug and sexual offenders, ensuring risk-needs-responsivity (RNR)-based treatment programmes. The statutes shall provide probation orders with community corrections and intermediate programmes. Provisions for sentences combining probation, community service, and treatment programmes targeting criminogenic needs enable a multifaceted approach to effective offender rehabilitation. Additionally, split sentences can be incorporated to tailor the intervention to each offender's risk and specific characteristics.

Redefining Director Duties: Unveiling an Internal Benchmark for Good Faith—A Novel Comparative Approach Beyond External Standards in Corporations Act 2001 (Cth)

Clare Jing Ni Tai

Abstract This comparative legal examination navigates the complex landscape of Section 181 of the Corporations Act, delving into the challenges inherent in the duty of good faith imposed on directors and officers of corporations. In this exploration, the paper transcends current boundaries to assess the implications of interpretative uncertainties within the Corporations Act, providing a comparative perspective for redefining director duties through the lens of relational contracting theory. With the absence of explicit definitions for 'good faith' and 'best interests,' Section 181 has given rise to divergent judicial interpretations, leading to inconsistencies within the Corporations Act. Despite these divergences, the duty of good faith remains an indispensable obligation for directors, guiding the conscientious management of corporate responsibilities for the mutual benefit of the corporation and its shareholders. Acknowledging the challenges associated with assuming a 'universal' standard of reasonableness within the Corporations Act (a one-size-fits-all criterion for what is considered good faith behaviour under the Corporations Act), this study delves into the complexities arising from the lack of clear parameters for determining breaches of duty, particularly within specific managerial contexts. Drawing inspiration from lessons learned in relational contracting, the study embarks on a comparative analysis of approaches to defining and evaluating the duty of good faith. It argues for the adoption of an internal benchmark for good faith, underscoring the insights gleaned from relational contracting practices. The paper explores the distinction between externally generated and internally generated definitions of good faith. It posits that externally generated definitions, influenced by general social and cultural values, may present interpretative challenges as managerial dynamics differ from one company to another, and externally generated benchmarks may not adequately reflect specific company requirements. Much like contracting parties, a company's conventions are rooted in its relationships, and expectations regarding actions and conduct are highly dependent on their agreed relational context. Good faith, therefore, cannot exist in a vacuum. The hypothesis is introduced that internally generated definitions, grounded

C. J. N. Tai (✉)
School of Business and Law, Edith Cowan University, Joondalup, WA, Australia
e-mail: clare.tai@ecu.edu.au

J. Aston et al. (eds.), *Comparative Law*, https://doi.org/10.1007/978-981-97-7815-7_11

in the contracting relationship and practices between parties, could serve as a primary framework for deducing director behaviours, providing a more tailored expectation on directors. This, in turn, facilitates a clearer understanding for both shareholders and directors of their respective expectations. In conclusion, this comparative law analysis aims to contribute valuable insights into the complexities surrounding Section 181 of the Corporations Act. By examining various approaches to interpreting the duty of good faith, the study seeks to foster a nuanced understanding of the challenges and opportunities inherent in this critical legal provision. Additionally, it explores the potential applicability of lessons from relational contracting to enhance consistency in interpretation and promote legal practicality.

Keywords Corporate governance · Fiduciary duty · Relational contracting theory · Good faith · Director duties

1 Introduction

Directors' statutory duty to exercise their powers and discharge their duties 'in good faith and in the best interests of the corporation' can be found in s 181(1)(a) of the Corporations Act.[1] It has been recognised for hundreds of years as one of the fiduciary duties directors are expected to follow. However, it is far from clear what exactly is meant by '*good faith*' and '*best interest* of the corporation as a whole.'[2] There is no explanation of the meaning of these phrases in the legislation where this duty is contained.[3] S 181(1)(a) merely contain a set of behaviours which are permissible without indicating the criteria that the behaviour should meet in order for it to be considered good faith behaviour. It does not contain any benchmark for measuring directors' behaviours although it is deemed applicable to all directors.

This article serves as an introductory chapter for the model of relational view of s 181(1)(a)[4] of the Corporations Act as it offers a benchmark for the director to act in good faith and in the best interests of the company. In doing so, this article critically assesses the feasibility of a transplantation of the relational contracting theory into corporate law. In the light of relational contracting theory, this article considers the nature and effect of relationship within the mechanisms of corporate governance and its possible effect on the expected behaviours of the directors. Whilst there are some good accounts of the style and content of relationship,[5] few analyse its nature and effect on the behaviours of directors. By interpreting expected behaviours for

[1] *Corporations Act 2001* (Cth) s 181(1)(a).

[2] Jean Plessis, 'Directors' Duty to Act in the Best Interests of the Corporation: 'Hard Cases Make Bad Law'' (2019) 34 *Australian Journal of Corporate Law* 3, 4.

[3] *Corporations Act 2001* (Cth) s 181(1)(a).

[4] Ibid.

[5] David Rosenberg, 'Making Sense of Good Faith in Delaware Corporate Fiduciary Law: A Contractarian Approach' [2004] 29 *Delaware Journal of Corporate Law* 491, 493; Rosemary Langford,

directors to act in good faith in accordance with the internal generated standard within a corporate context (if any), this could help solve the undefined nature of good faith and the conundrum as to the extent to which directors can consider and promote the interests of stakeholders in properly carrying out their duties.[6]

The structure of this article is as follows. Section 2 traces the advance of the director duty to act in good faith and examine its underlying issue. Section 3 explores the potential for developing a benchmark to interpret director duties through the prism of relationships, drawing inspiration from relational contracting theory. It begins with an overview of the evolution of relational contracting theory and then demonstrates its applicability in corporate law by comparing its functional similarities with corporate governance.

2 S. 181(1)(a), Good Faith and Their Underlying Issues

Good faith has long been recognised as a background principle in several areas of laws,[7] including but not limited to contract law, consumer law and corporate law. However, the function of good faith is not perfectly clear, and its utility is questionable.[8] Generally, everyone understands good faith on its face, but good faith is a difficult concept to operationalise in law.[9]

In Australian corporate law, a director is required to 'exercise their powers and discharge their duties … in good faith and in the best interests of the corporations.'[10] Generally, the duty requires that directors to act in good faith in what they consider to be the company's best interests.[11] The existence of 'best interest' and 'good faith' under the same section of the Corporations Act had courts and scholars agree that the duty of good faith requires the director to act accordingly to, at least, what they

'Purpose-Based Governance: A New Paradigm' (2020) 43(3) *University of New South Wales Law Journal* 954.

[6] Rosemary Langford, 'Purpose-Based Governance: A New Paradigm' (2020) 43(3) *The University New South Wales Law Journal* 954, 955.

[7] Claire Dickerson, 'From Behind the Looking Glass: Good Faith, Fiduciary Duty and Permitted Harm' (1995) 22 *Florida State University Law Review* 955.

[8] Clare Jing Ni Tai, *The Standardised Reconciliation of Contract Practice and Good Faith: An Introduction of Relational Contracting as the Benchmark for Good Faith in Australia and CISG* (PhD thesis, University of Western Australia, 2024).

[9] Steven Burton, 'Breach of Contract and the Common Law Duty to Perform in Good Faith' (1980) 94 *Harvard Law Review* 369; David Rosenberg, 'Making Sense of Good Faith in Delaware Corporate Fiduciary Law: A Contractarian Approach' (2004) 29 *Delaware Journal of Corporate Law* 491; John Red and Matt Neiderman, '"Good Faith" and the Ability of Directors to Assert s 102(b)(7) of the Delaware General Corporation Law as a Defense to Claims Alleging Abdication, Lak of Oversight, and Similar Breaches of Fiduciary Duty' (2004) 29 *Delaware Journal of Corporate Law* 111; Jean Plessis, n x.

[10] *Corporations Act 2001* (Cth) s 181(1)(a).

[11] Rosemary Teele Langford and Ian Ramsay, 'Directors' Duty to Act in the Interests of the Company: Subjective or Objective?' [2015] 2 *Journal of Business Law* 173.

consider to be the company's interests.[12] It is contended that this duty has required the director to not pursue unauthorised conflict or profit,[13] to exercise independent judgement,[14] to look to the interests of the group rather than to the interests of the individual company, to consider the interests of creditors, etc. Other norms have also been introduced by the adjudicators as well attempting to define good faith, including but not limited to, 'reasonable,'[15] 'genuine,'[16] best interest,'[17] 'loyalty,'[18] 'state of mind,'[19] 'taking surrounding circumstances into consideration,'[20] and 'bad faith.'[21] Given the lack of meaning of the mentioned norms, the Courts normally will have to attach subjective test, objective test, or a hybrid of both on to the norms. For example,

1. Based on the reasonable objective test, what is in fact the 'best interest' of the company? Director would be assessed whether their behaviour has violated such benchmark.[22] This approach focuses on the identification of the benchmark of a company's 'best interest' in a particular situation and if the decision is one that no reasonable director would consider to be in the interests of the company, there will be a breach of duty.[23] This test is being utilised in the case of *Re Southern Countries Fresh Food Ltd.*[24]
2. Based on the reasonable objective test, has the director performed as per what a reasonable director or board would do in the given circumstances. This is comparable to the reasonable objective standard which has been developed commonly for the director duty of care, skill, and diligence to be assessed against.[25] An example of this approach is seen in the judgement of Justice Ward in the case of *Re Idylic Solutions Pty Ltd.*[26]
3. The third way of interpreting the duty of good faith is through the application of both subjective and objective tests. This combination of subjective and objective test mainly involves asking two questions.[27] First, whether directors acted bona fide in the interests of the company as a whole subjectively. This is a factual question that focuses on the state of mind of the directors. The question is whether

[12] *Shepherds Investments Ltd v Walters* [2006] EWHC 836 (Ch).

[13] *Charterbridge Coropv Lloyds Bank Ltd* [1970] Ch 62 D 74.

[14] *Walker v Winborne* (1976) 137 CLR 1.

[15] *Re Southern Countries Fresh Food Ltd* [2008] EWHC 2810; *Re Idylic Solutions Pty Ltd* [2012] NSWSC 1276.

[16] *Hutton v West Cork Railway Co* (1883) 23 Ch. D. 654.

[17] *Re Southern Countries Fresh Food Ltd* [2008] EWHC 2810; *Percival v Wright* [1902] 2 Ch 421.

[18] *Boulting v Association of Cinematograph, Television and Allied Technicians* [1963] 2 Qb 606.

[19] *Bell v Westpac (No. 9)* [2008] WASC 239.

[20] Ibid.

[21] *Japan Abrasive Materials Pty Ltd v Australian Fused Materials Pty Ltd* (1998) 16 ACLC 1172.

[22] Ibid.

[23] *Re Southern Countries Fresh Food Ltd* [2008] EWHC 2810.

[24] Ibid.

[25] *ASIC v Vines* [2005] NSWSC 738; *ASIC v Rich* (2009) 236 FLR.

[26] *Re Idylic Solutions Pty Ltd* [2012] NSWSC 1276.

[27] *Bell v Westpac (No. 9)* [2008] WASC 239.

> the directors (not the court) consider that the exercise of power is in the best interest of the company. In ascertaining this state of mind, the court is entitled to look at the surrounding circumstances and other materials that genuinely shed light upon the directors' state of mind as to whether they were honestly acting in discharge of their powers in the interests of the company.[28] The court can look, objectively, at the surrounding circumstances and at the impugned transactions or exercise of power.[29] The objective enquiry is done to assist the court in deciding whether to accept or discount the assertions that the directors make about their subjective intentions and beliefs.[30]

The prevailing tests for evaluating the duty of good faith—whether subjective, objective, or a hybrid—all share a fundamental issue: a lack of a tangible framework to define 'good faith,' 'reasonable,' and 'bad faith' conduct for directors of every Australian company and corporation.[31] This issue encompasses two subsidiary problems. First, there exists a vicious cycle of utilising open norms as substitutes, which lack concrete elements for interpreting good faith. The second issue pertains to the applicability of these norms across all Australian companies and corporations. Both of these subsidiary issues will be explored.

The arguments for other norms such as reasonable, loyalty, best interest etc. fail to realise that these open norms are mere undefined substitutes for good faith. These open norms do not contain the necessary standard and test with which director behaviour can be measured.[32] Arguments for the imposition of these open norms as *the* standard for good faith interpretation also tend to forget that open norms (reasonableness for example) itself also require a standard.[33] Therefore, the implementation of a 'reasonableness' test will only displace the issue of good faith.[34] The absence of precise criteria for what qualifies as 'reasonable' conduct poses a challenge in assessing directors' adherence to the duty of good faith. The lack of clarity associated with the term renders it challenging to assess, whether objectively, subjectively, or through a combination of both, if directors have adhered to the anticipated standard of reasonableness in their actions, particularly when the criteria for reasonableness are not clearly defined. Whether it is applied to assess the reasonable best interests of the company, or the reasonable actions expected of a director, the central issue remains—reasonableness does not possess a benchmark. Frequently, the court will then attempt to contextualise reasonableness by considering what serves the best interest of the company. Again, even when the court deems an action contrary to the 'best interest' of the company, the critical question emerges—what precisely constitutes the 'best interest' of a company, and against what benchmark should this assessment be made? The term 'best interest' introduces further complexity to

---

[28] Ibid.

[29] Ibid.

[30] Ibid.

[31] Tai (n 8) 218.

[32] Ibid.

[33] Ibid.

[34] Ibid.

the assessment of reasonableness. As argued earlier regarding 'state of mind' and 'surrounding circumstances,' without resolving the fundamental undefinable nature and identifying the fundamental benchmark or elements of 'reasonableness,' 'state of mind,' and 'surrounding circumstances,' the director's duty of good faith lacks a method to deduce directors' good faith behaviour. Introducing additional terminology such as 'reasonable,' 'genuine,' and 'state of mind' create the illusion of solving the problem whilst, in reality, it introduces another challenge for s 181(1)(a).

Second, in relation to the applicability of 'reasonable' across every Australian company and corporation, the flaw lies in the assumption that a 'universal' standard of reasonableness can be ascertained in the first place and applied. For the purpose of this paper, a 'universal' standard of reasonableness should not be interpreted as universally applicable internationally but rather as applicable universally across all Australian companies. It is not necessary to specifically search for the definition for each of norms as the determination of what truly constitutes the reasonable, best interest, etc., is a multifaceted task. This is because reasonable and best interest are not 'universal' and static concepts; it evolves based on various factors such as the company's industry, market conditions, strategic goals, and the broader economic landscape.[35] In other words, the absence of a standardised benchmark for reasonableness stems from the inherent diversity among companies in Australia.[36] Each company operates within a unique set of circumstances, business objectives, and managerial dynamics.[37] Consequently, what may be considered reasonable in one company might not be applicable or appropriate for another. This inherent subjectivity makes it challenging to establish a one-size-fits-all definition for reasonableness in corporate actions.

In fact, good faith itself is problematic as a norm. If the concept of good faith is to be treated as a norm, several inherent issues need to be addressed before it is proactively used as *the* framework that guide the directors' behaviours. First of all, good faith is not an independent duty.[38] Good faith should be a general rationale which, at most, to be a dependent concept that is attached to the corporations.[39] In normal circumstances, a company is incorporated to achieve certain objective(s), either specified in the constitution or unspecified (which in most of the case—generating profit).[40] Notably, these objectives vary from company to company, and they could be signalled via several company instruments, including but not limited to,

---

[35] Ibid 79.

[36] Paul MacMahon, 'Good Faith and Fair Dealing as an Underenforced Legal Norm' [2015] 99 *Minnesota Law Review* 2051, 2092.

[37] Langford (n 5).

[38] MacMahon, (n 36) 2092.

[39] Tai (n 8) 79.

[40] Chancellor Willian Allen, 'Ambiguity in Corporation Law' [1997] 22 *Delaware Journal of Corporate Law* 894.

constitution, ratification passed in the general meeting, shareholder agreement, oral terms, soft regulations, unspoken customs or practices, etc.[41]

Secondly, it is important to determine whether good faith as a norm itself, and whether it is a norm on which an independent duty can be based. For a rule to be stringent and manageable, it must not be a completely open norm.[42] Additionally, the effect of non-compliance with the norm should be able to be quantified.[43] If every norm is to be placed on a scale which ranges from totally open to totally closed, a norm is more open when fewer cases are excluded from its applicability.[44] The closer a norm gets to one of two extremes, the less it makes sense for such norm to become a rule.[45] A totally closed rule is one that can be applied only to one case, similar to a court order. On the other hand, a totally open rule is one that can be applied to all cases.[46] An example of this is: 'Thou shall be a good person.' Ideally, a norm should fall neatly between the two extremes. It is acknowledged that all norms should be more or less open, but it should only allow some judicial space for it to be developed, albeit the space should be a definite one. By way of examples, 'unconscionable conduct' was introduced in the *Trade Practices Act*,[47] to protect small businesses against unfair or exploitative conduct, 'unfair contract terms' in *Australian Consumer Law*.[48]

Thirdly, the necessity of having the norm of good faith within the corporate context is questionable. A few parties entering into an agreement to form a company to achieve some mutual objectives should be allowed to safely assume that, at least, the individuals (especially directors) performing this agreement are cooperating according to the terms of the agreement. Is it necessary to include the term 'good faith' if a relationship can be presumed to a presumed to be a cooperative one? Equally, can one really create trust and cooperative directors' behaviour simply by including the notion of good faith to display these characteristics?[49]

Some may then argue that good faith and best interest of the company are also statutory duties under s 181(1)(a) of the *Corporations Act*.[50] Therefore, just like the other statutory duties, this should not be interpreted through the lens of mutual objectives. For example, the duty to disclose should not only be limited to the situation in achieving mutual objectives. Directors arguably should disclose once they have

---

[41] Dimity Smith, 'Governing the Corporations: The Role of 'Soft Regulation" (2012) 35 (1) *University of New South Wales Law Journal* 378.

[42] Martin Hesselink, 'The Concept of Good Faith, in Towards a European Civil Code' [2004] *Kluwer Law International*, 623.

[43] Catherine Mitchell, 'Behavioural Standards in Contracts and English Contract Law' (2016) 33 *Journal of Contract Law* 234, 1.

[44] Hesselink (n 42) 639.

[45] Ibid.

[46] Tai (n 8) 38.

[47] *Trade Practices Act 1974* (Cth).

[48] *Competition and Consumer Act* 2010 (Cth) sch 2 ('*Australian Consumer Law*').

[49] Tai (n 8) 36.

[50] *Corporations Act 2001* (Cth) s 181(1)(a).

material personal interest in particular transaction or matter, regardless of whether the director is pursuing the company's objectives.[51] This article does not disagree with good faith and best interest in general. It would be unrealistic to assume that s 181(1)(a) good faith and best interest can be fully eliminated from the *Corporations Act* due to their longstanding history. It is also for these same reasons, the search for a framework or methodology which could be attached to good faith to deduce the required behaviour for the directors is important. Good faith and best interest have been seen as concepts without a standard.[52] Good faith merely connotes a certain type of behaviour without indicating the criteria that that behaviour must meet in order to be a good faith behaviour.[53] In other words, good faith, by itself, does not incorporate any standard by which parties' performances under sales contracts may be measured.[54] By giving good faith interpretive priority over the individual corporate context, adjudicators may unwittingly misinterpret the relationship and intention the company may have signalled.

3 The 'Internally' Generated Benchmark Via the Lens of Relationships in a Company

In order to prove the transplant-ability of the relational contracting theory into corporate law, this section will firstly briefly trace the historical development of relational contracting theory. It will then move on to demonstrate its applicability in corporate law by comparing its functional similarities with corporate governance.

A. **Relational contracting theory**

'Contract is arguably the most chatoyant legal institution—appearing in changing light when seen from a wide array of legal perspectives, but also the centre of an unmatched set of other disciplinary inroads, including political philosophy, ethics, economics, sociology, anthropology, psychology, and gender studies.'[55] The plurality approach reminds us of a contract's inherent tension between the universality of its form and the highly diverse and specific ramifications of contractual practice.[56] This tension translates into two conflicting points of departure of current contract scholarship that compete for doctrinal recognition. The normative, historical, and

[51] *Corporations Act 2001* (Cth) s 191.

[52] Steven Walt, 'The Modest Role of Good Faith in Uniform Sales Law' [2015] 33 *Boston University International Law Journal* 37, 42.

[53] Ibid 43.

[54] Ibid 44.

[55] Klass Hendrik Eller, 'Comparative Genealogies of "Contract and Society"' (2020) 21 *German Law Journal* 1393, 1393.

[56] Ibid.

ideal approaches to contracts are at one end; at the other end are the socio-legal, context-specific, and particularistic approaches.[57]

Despite the acknowledgement of novel forms of contracting and the need for new conceptualisations, the historical and philosophical origins of contract and its peculiar location between 'state' and 'society' continue to be a significant point of departure for contractual thinking.[58] This entails a steady risk of essentialising contract on the basis of its most general definition as a voluntary exchange which abstracts almost entirely from any parameter of the surrounding nation-social context.[59] Emanating from the view of contract as a voluntary exchange is an essentialising image of 'the market' as a natural order which law regulates only from the outside in order to protect its proper functioning. Ever since the realist tradition of the early twentieth century with authors like Karl Llewellyn,[60] Eugen Ehrlich,[61] Felix Cohen,[62] and Robert Hale,[63] a strong strand of contract theory scholarship has gradually moved away from classical contract theory to a more contextualised approach.[64] Here, it is acknowledged that contract creates a social relationship, a shift that produces two important consequences. First, contract is deeply embedded in a set of social and cultural norms. Second, it becomes complicated to assess the emerging contractual order from the perspective of the parties and the principle of privity alone, rather than from the perspective of society at large. A contract is no longer a set of papers which records the agreement between the contracting parties; it is a documentation device which registers the contracting practices between the contracting parties.[65]

Contracting theories which overly focus on interpreting contract as it is without taking into account the overall social interaction between the involved parties may be obsolete in the contractual context.[66] It should be noted that relational contracting theory is not a legal rule, it is a perspective/point of view where relational factors are being taken as the common denominator/equaliser for interpreting contracting behaviours. Based on the relationship of the contracting parties, what are the established expectations of contracting parties towards their respective behaviour.[67] In this way, contracting behaviours based on relational contracting theory are internally generated by the contracting relationship, practices, and custom. This could be contrasted with classical and neo-classical contract theories which externally

---

[57] Ibid.

[58] Ibid 1394.

[59] Ibid.

[60] Karl Llewellyn, 'What Price Contract? An Essay in Perspective' (1931) 40 *Yale Law Journal* 704.

[61] Eugen Ehrlich, *Grundlegung Der Soziologie Des Rechts* (Manfred Rehbinder Ed., 4th Ed. 1989).

[62] Felix Cohen, 'Transcendental Nonsense and the Functional Approach' (1935) 6 *Columbia Law Review* 809, 839.

[63] Robert Hale, 'Bargaining, Duress and Economic Liberty' (1943)43 *Columbia Law Review* 603.

[64] Ibid 1394.

[65] Tai (n 8) 116.

[66] Ibid.

[67] Eller (n 53) 1395.

generate norms including, but not limited to, fair trade and good faith. These norms do not take contracting parties' intentions into consideration when determining the actions that a contract requires; instead, the actions are influenced by a set of rules which were made based on the assumption that every contracting parties share the same contractual expectation. In fact, the meaning of an externally generated norm (e.g. good faith) varies from one person to another. Different people are very likely to draw different conclusions in regard to whether a particular conduct is in breach of good faith. If the parties have a dispute over the interpretation of a contract, it may be possible that a reasonable of the same kind as the other party could have an understanding of a written contract term under the same circumstances that are not only different from their own but also different from those of a reasonable person in their own position under the same circumstances.[68] In other words, what is reasonable for one party might not be reasonable to not only the counterparty, but also person of the same kind in the same circumstances.[69] Therefore, in order to prevent his, scholars[70] came up with relational contracting theory where trade custom or contracting practices, internally sourced the relationship of the contracting parties should be treated as the point of truth to the form the understanding and expectation of contracting parties on their respective behaviour.

To operationalise these theoretical insights in corporate law, it is crucial to compare the practical implications of relational contracting theory within the framework of corporate governance. This involves considering how relational contracting theory fits within corporate law and how internal benchmarks of good faith could be observed through governance structures.

B. The compatibility of relational contracting theory in the corporate law

[68] Donald Smythe, 'Reasonable Standard for Contract Interpretations under the CISG' (2016) 25 *Cardozo*

Journal of International and Comparative Law 1, 2.

[69] Ibid.

[70] Stewart Macaulay, 'Non-Contractual Relations in Business—a Preliminary Study' (1963) 28 *American Sociological Review* 55; Walter Powell, 'Neither Market nor Hierarchy—Network Forms of Organization' (1990) 12 *Research in Organizational Behaviour* 295; Aakko Salminen, 'Towards a Genealogy and Typology of Governance Through Contract Beyond Privity' (2020) 16 *European Review of Contract Law* 25; Stefan Grundmann and Fabrizio Cafaggi, *The Organisational Contract: From Exchange to Long-term Network Cooperation in European Contract Law* (Ashgate Publishing Limited, 2013); Ian Macneil, 'Contracts: Adjustment of Long-Term Economic Relations under Classical, Neoclassical, and Relational Contract Law' (1978) 72 *Northwestern University Law Review* 854, 901; Mika Viljanen, 'Actor-Network Theory Contract Theory' (2020) 16 *European Review of Contract Law* 74; Ian Macneil, The New Social Contract (1980); Ian Macneil, 'Contracts: Adjustment of Long-term Economic Relations Under Classical, Neoclassical, and Relational Contract Law' (1978) 72 *Northwestern University Law Review* 854; Ian Macneil, 'Efficient Breach of Contract: Circles in the Sky' (1982) 68 *Virginia Law Review* 947; Ian Macneil, 'Values in Contract: Internal and External' (1983) 78 *Northwestern University Law Review* 340; Ian Macneil, 'Restatement (Second) of Contracts and Presentation' (1974) 60 *Virginia Law Review* 589.

To elucidate the concept of 'relationship' within the corporate context, it is imperative to inspect the discourse on the contractual perspective of corporate law. Interestingly, within corporate law, scholars[71] and adjudicators[72] approach the interpretation of fiduciary duties regarding acting in good faith akin to the previously discussed externally and internally generated norm approaches. They are commonly known as the traditional view and contractarian view, respectively. Analogous to their names, the traditional view aligns with the externally generated norm approach, whilst the contractarian view predominantly adopts the internally generated norm approach, albeit to a certain extent.[73]

Traditional scholars of corporate law, view fiduciary duties as mandatory constraints which is required to curtail the possibility of abuse by directors.[74] Top-down approach does not ask what the parties understanding of their obligations was because it assumes that parties to corporate relationships all have and ought to have the same basic fiduciary obligations under the law.[75] Similar to other statutory duties such as duty to exercise care and diligence and duty to disclose, etc., the parties' understanding of their obligations is irrelevant as it assumes that directors should exercise sufficient care and skill before making a business decision[76] and disclose their material personal interest in a particular transaction or matter.[77] Thus, the use of the term good faith in the contractual sense seems misplaced in traditional corporate fiduciary jurisprudence as it assumes that good faith equally applicable to all the directors to the same standard.[78]

On the other hand, over the last few decades, many academics[79] and judges (indirectly)[80] have adopted the view that the corporation is a collection of contracts and

---

[71] Frank Easterbook and Daniel Fishcel, 'Contract and Fiduciary Duty' (1993) 36 *Journal of Law and Economics* 425; Henry Butler and Larry Ribstein, 'opting Out of Fiduciary Duties: A Response to the Anti-Contractarians' (1990) 65 *Washington Law Review* 1; David Rosenberg, 'Venture Capital Limited Partnerships: A Study in Freedom of Contract' (2002) *Columbia Business Law Review* 363; Larry Ribstein, 'Unlimited Contracting in the Delaware Limited Partnership and its implications for Corporate Law' (1991) 17 *The Journal of Corporation Law* 299.

[72] *Japan Abrasive Materials Pty Ltd v Australian Fused Materials Pty Ltd* (1998) 16 ACLC 1172; *Levin v Clark* [1962] NSWR 686.

[73] Rosenberg (n 71); Ribstein (n 71).

[74] Matthew Dore, 'The Duties and Liabilities of an Iowa Corporate Director' (2002) 50 *Drake Law Review* 207, 212.

[75] Rosenberg (n 5) 494.

[76] *Corporations Act 2001* (Cth) s 180(1).

[77] *Corporations Act 2001* (Cth) s 191.

[78] Rosenberg (n 5) 494.

[79] Henry Butler and Larry Ribstein, 'opting Out of Fiduciary Duties: A Response to the Anti-Contractarians' (1990) 65 *Washington Law Review* 1; David Rosenberg, 'Venture Capital Limited Partnerships: A Study in Freedom of Contract' (2002) *Columbia Business Law Review* 363; Larry Ribstein, 'Unlimited Contracting in the Delaware Limited Partnership and its implications for Corporate Law' (1991) 17 *The Journal of Corporation Law* 299.

[80] *Japan Abrasive Materials Pty Ltd v Australian Fused Materials Pty Ltd* (1998) 16 ACLC 1172; *Levin v Clark* [1962] NSWR 686.

that the duties imposed on the various parties in a corporation are largely indistinguishable from traditional obligations.[81] This bottom-up (similar to internally generated contracting terms approach) assumes the corporate context differs from one company to another company and interprets the director duty to act in *good faith* and modify if necessary. They contend that corporate fiduciary duties should be equally treated as other obligations to which people voluntarily agree to subject themselves through contract. Some of the academics even argued that fiduciary duties are not special duties, they have no moral footing, and they are the same sort of obligations, derived and enforced in the same way, as other contractual undertakings.[82] For contractarians, fiduciary duties are gap fillers[83] for the adjudicators to resort on as they could not possibly describe every obligation they are demanding.[84] Good faith is one of the product which academics and adjudicators thought could be the device to interpret the terms such as loyalty and care. Good faith is a flower that smells very sweet and connotes taking action that conforms to the spirit of corporate and contract law, any interpretation of the norm itself would allow for a different course of action to fall within its ambit. This method of interpretation then translates into the context of corporate director's adherence to his fiduciary duties to act in good faith by asking whether the director has violated the obligations (both explicit and implicit) conferred by the contract.[85] This is a bottom-up approach where the collection of contracts is being taken into consideration and the duty to act in good faith is to be deduced based on these contracts.

This article generally agrees with the bottom-up approach of interpreting the director duty to act in good faith and in the best interest of the company as it is functionally similar to the contractual internally generated standard approach. However, this article does not agree with the full transplantation of a contractual view into corporate law. The fiduciary duty of good faith having legislated into s 181(1)(a) is a mandatory statutory constraint which its function could be viewed equally as the other director duties,[86] the existence of which is necessary to curtail the possibility of abuse by directors.[87] Thus, the use of the term good faith in the contractual sense seems misplaced in the corporate fiduciary jurisprudence. Fiduciary duty is imposed to prevent opportunistic behaviour, and therefore, the intensity of this obligation varies accordingly to the range of opportunistic behaviour possible in each context and the potential magnitude of the harm.[88] Contract is where two contracting parties enter into a commercial arrangement to achieve a specified goal or goals collectively

---

[81] Rosenberg (n 5) 493.

[82] Easterbook and Fishcel (n 66) 426.

[83] Rosenberg (n 5) 493.

[84] Ibid.

[85] Ibid.

[86] *Corporations Act 2001* (Cth) s 180(1), 181(1)(b), 182, 183, 191, 195, 588G.

[87] Matthew Dore, 'The Duties and Liabilities of an Iowa Corporate Director' (2002) 50 *Drake Law Review* 207, 212.

[88] Gordon Smith, 'The Critical Resource Theory of Fiduciary Duty' (2003) 55 *Vanderbilt Law Review* 1399, 1409.

yet *independently* and both parties, in good faith, act accordingly to the other parties' expectation even when the contract itself may not explicitly dictate whether certain behaviour is permissible.[89] Corporate is where two or more parties enter into an arrangement to achieve a specified goal or goals collectively and *interdependently*, and these parties, in good faith, act accordingly to the other parties' expectation even when the arrangement itself may not explicitly dictate whether certain behaviour is permissible.[90] Interdependently should be viewed of having another layer of relationship where one party has more to total control over the counterparty. Arguably, the interdependent corporate relationships may impose a higher standard to act in good faith than parties to a contract. The intensity of these obligations varies according to the range of opportunistic behaviour feasible within each context. The interdependency of corporate relationship is sourced from the doctrine of separate legal entity nature of a company where the management of a company is separate from its ownership.[91] The board of directors of a company is deemed as the controller of the company whilst the shareholders holding their shares as their private assets submit the management of the company to the board of directors.[92] Such submission of control is involuntarily mainly due to the doctrine of 'the separation of ownership and control.'[93] Via this submission of control to the board of directors, the shareholders are exposed to more a higher likelihood of harm and a higher potential magnitude of harm. Both of the likelihood of harm and the potential magnitude of the harm are often less in an arm's length contract than in a corporate relationship as the allocation of control over the relevant resources in a corporate relationship provides greater opportunities for self-serving behaviour. Therefore, the s s 181(1)(a)[94] good faith and best interest is arguably stricter than the contractual duty of good faith, prima facie. Being a director of a company, it requires he or she to accept of certain responsibilities as well as the abandonment of the right to engage in a large number of other permissible opportunities, which otherwise contracting parties in arm's length contract could, because they would implicate the director's duty of loyalty. As such, people who enter into corporate relationships demand that directors have an obligation towards them to act with undivided loyalty according to his/her understanding of what the company charter, in addition to the existing law (statutory duties) demand from him/her.[95]

---

[89] Steve Burton, 'Breach of Contract and the Common Law Duty to Perform in Good Faith' (1980) 94 *Harvard Law Review* 369, 371.

[90] Tai (n 8) 209.

[91] *Salomon v Salomon and Co* [1897] AC 22.

[92] *Corporations Act 2001* (Cth) s 119 and s 124.

[93] *Corporations Act 2001* (Cth) s 119; Adolf Berle and Gardiner Means, *The Modern Corporation and Private Property* (Transaction Publishers, 1932) 352–3; Lynn Stout, *The Shareholder Value Myth: How Putting Shareholders First Harms Investors, Corporations, and the Public* (Berrett-Koehler Publishers, 2012) 17; David G Yosifon, 'The Law of Corporate Purpose' (2013) 10 *Berkeley Business Law Journal* 181, 219–22; David Millon, 'Radical Shareholder Primacy' (2013) 10 *University of St Thomas Law Journal* 1013, 1021.

[94] *Corporations Act 2001* (Cth) s 181(1)(a).

[95] Rosenberg (n 5) 511.

The subsequent question arises: If directors are anticipated to exhibit a heightened level of loyalty, how can we ascertain the appropriate degree of effort and loyalty expected from directors and managers? The key answer towards this lies within the corporate governance mechanisms. Generally, corporate governance is referred to as the system by which companies are directed and controlled.[96] Corporate governance is 'the relationship among various participants in determining the direction and performance of corporations. The primary participants are (1) the shareholders, (2) the management led by the chief executive officer, and (3) the board of directors ... Other participants include the employees, customers, suppliers, creditors and the community.'[97] Core duties are connected to, informed and shaped by the company's purposes-based loyalty.[98] Rather than a series of separate duties aimed at ensuring high standards of conduct (or at ensuring that those who govern entities act in the interests of the entity), the duties emanate from, and support, the furtherance of an entity's purposes.[99]

Corporate governance is a collection of relationships involved in a company. It could be viewed as the 'master' relationship/manual in running a company where a series of arrangements, in which some could be contractual such as shareholders agreement, should accord with its provisions. These arrangements pertain to shareholder agreement, constitution clauses, resolution passed in the general meeting, soft regulations, unspoken rules, company customs and practices, etc. The commercial reality of company relationship and in fact a contractual one was further recognised via the enforcement of statutory contract under s 140(1) of the Corporations Act.[100] S 140(1) reads:

A company's constitution (if any) and any replaceable rules that apply to the company have effect as a contract:

(a) Between the company and each member; and
(b) Between the company and each director and company secretary; and
(c) Between a member and each other member.[101]

In other words, if a company has a constitution (if not, replaceable rules), the behaviours of the director could be varied and modified depending on a company's constitution and these modifications have a contractual effect on the directors in the name of statutory contract.[102] Failure to fulfil these obligations by the directors may

---

[96] Robert Monks and Nell Minow, *Watching the Watchers: Corporate Governance for the 21st Century* (1996 Wiley), 2; Committee on the Financial Aspects of Corporate Governance (chaired by Sir Adrian Cadbury), Report (1992) at para 2.5; Working Group on Corporate Practices and Conduct (chaired by Henry Bosch AO), Corporate Practices and Conduct (3rd ed, 1995) at 7.

[97] Robert Monks and Nell Minow, *Watching the Watchers: Corporate Governance for the 21st Century* (1996 Wiley), 3.

[98] Langford (n 5).

[99] Ibid.

[100] *Corporations Act 2001* (Cth) s 140(1).

[101] Ibid.

[102] Ibid.

result in a breach of the statutory contract, potentially leading to an injunction under s 1324 of the Corporations Act.[103]

The stakeholders in a company form their own 'mini society,' abstracting themselves from their original socio-corporate context in order to collectively organise economic activity as a *separate* legal entity to achieve economic efficiency whilst achieving other societal objectives related to equity, fairness, freedom, and social responsibilities.[104] A multilayered relationship is formed within one 'master' relationship because a company often includes not only the two main organs of board of directors and shareholders but also other parties such as employees and creditors. With all these multilayered relationships in the corporate context, these parties form their own 'mini society,' and this 'mini society' is deemed to have its own understanding and their own expectation of the duties and obligations associated with their own relationship.[105] These expectations should be removed almost entirely from any parameters of other company-social context. To fully understand what a director should do in a particular company, the Corporations Act s 181(1)(a) should be interpreted 'immunely' to other company context. Hence, the basic requirement for a framework to be developed as an accurate interpretative tool to deduce the director duty to act in good faith is that it be capable of viewing company relationships as a governance mechanism and backbone of companies of various types in which is enable through the reach of autonomy. The relationships within a company should be treated as the common denominator/primary source of interpretative tool for s s 181(1)(a).

Corporate governance should be recognised and treated as the equaliser to deduce what is required for the director to act in good faith accordingly to the appropriate degree of effort and loyalty expected from them. Without doing so, the other arrangements will totally lose their functional value. The top-down interpretative method is an example as such. By assuming directors in every company are expected to act to the same degree of effort and loyalty without taking corporate governance mechanisms into consideration, the constitution clause will lose its value.

For example, assume Company A and Company B where Company A has explicitly outlined in its constitution that directors must inform shareholders of any transaction exceeding AUD 100,000. In contrast, Company B has no such predetermined agreement to this effect in its constitution. This constitution clause could establish a different benchmark for 'common understanding' of shareholders towards the director's 'reasonable' behaviour within each company. The presence of this explicit clause in Company A's constitution creates a specific standard for transparency and disclosure, indicating a clear 'common understanding' that directors will notify shareholders of transactions surpassing AUD 100,000. Further assume a director of Company A enters into a contract with a value of AUD 99,999, falling just below the specified threshold. Notably, technically speaking, the directors from

[103] *Corporations Act 2001* (Cth) s 1324.

[104] Andrei Shleifer and Robert Vishney, A Survey of Corporate Governance, National Bureau of Economic Research Working Paper No 5554, 1996.

[105] Tai (n 8) 27.

Company A are not breaching their statutory contract under s 140(1) falling just below the specified threshold. However, the director's failure to inform shareholders may still be interpreted as a breach of good faith or intentional dishonesty, as the reasonableness standard in this scenario may not solely determined by the transaction amount but also influenced by the 'common understanding' created via Company A's constitution. Constitution, forming as part of the corporate governance mechanisms, is a rule agreed in Company's A 'mini society,' and this is the appropriate degree of effort and loyalty which is expected from directors and managers.

Contrastingly, Company B, without a constitution clause on spending limits, operates under a different benchmark of 'common understanding' of reasonable director's behaviour. In Company B, the director may not be considered in breach of the director duty of good faith as there is no 'common understanding' among the shareholders that the director will perform as such.

Further assume top-down approach is utilised in this scenario—by considering that directors across various company have the same standard of effort and loyalty, without taking the contextual elements of a company into consideration, it would create a paradoxical scenario for Company A's director to be free from liability for deliberately failing to honour his/her obligations as a director just by tweaking the transaction amount to be $1 lower than the disclosure amount.[106]

> After all, a corporate director's duty of good faith is the obligation to try to perform his/her duties according to his/her understanding of what the corporate charter and existing law demand from him/her.[107]

From the above example, it can be further observed that each of the corporate governance mechanism is crafted according to the parties' own understanding and expectation towards each other. Below are several examples of relational aspects commonly affect in corporate governance mechanisms and may require further research. Corporate governance frameworks are established to define the expectations of stakeholders' roles and to mitigate potential conflicts.[108] Each aspect may vary in its influence depending on the specific company context as could be seen below as companies do not share the same context.[109] These mechanisms can be seen as relational instruments that signal the relationships among the relevant parties, thereby shaping expectations and understanding of their respective roles within the corporate structure and hence so does the director duty.

- **Institutional investors**—One obvious example illustrating how the company's context influences what is deemed reasonable within that specific company is evident in the case of *Japan Abrasive Materials Pty Ltd v Australian Fused Materials Pty Ltd*.[110] In this case, Australian Fused Materials (AFM) is a joint venture

---

[106] Rosenberg (n 5) 510.

[107] Ibid.

[108] Ian Ramsay, *Corporate Governance and the Duties of Company Directors* (1997 The Centre for Corporate Law and Securities Regulations).

[109] Ibid.

[110] *Japan Abrasive Materials Pty Ltd v Australian Fused Materials Pty Ltd* (1998) 16 ACLC 1172.

company which was established by three shareholder companies. Each shareholder company held a one-third share and had the right to appoint two nominee directors. It was proposed that AFM plant should be expanded and under Clause 4.10 of the Shareholders Agreement governing AFM, this proposal required unanimous approval of the shareholders.[111] Japan Abrasive Materials (JAM), one of the shareholders, had not approved the resolution for the proposed project at a board meeting. Therefore, JAM suggested that it was not bound to pursue the arrangement.[112] The defendants (the two remaining shareholder companies) pleaded, inter alia, that by asserting this, JAM is I breach of certain provisions of the Shareholders Agreement and was motivated in bad faith. In the Supreme Court of Western Australia, Justice Templeman, emphasising the influence of the shareholder agreement on defining fiduciary duty, concluded that JAM had not violated its obligations under the Shareholders Agreement. Furthermore, it was determined that JAM had not acted in bad faith, and the ruling held that:

> It is always open to shareholders by unanimous agreement to attenuate the fiduciary duties which the directors of their company would otherwise owe to it.[113]

Levin v Clark[114] also underscores the idea that the director's duty is not one-size-fits-all and can vary based on specific circumstances and arrangements within a company. In this case, the nominee directors appointed to the board by a mortgagee were deemed to be entitled to act primarily in the interests of the mortgagee. Justice Jacobs further held that:

> The breadth of the fiduciary duty has been narrowed, by agreement amongst the body of the shareholders.[115]

- **Disclosure of information by companies**—Such disclosure (which can be mandatory or voluntary) may be important to form a 'common understanding' and 'legitimate expectation' for shareholders in a particular company and so bear upon the issue of whether such 'legitimate expectations' are being met or are being compromised. For example, a public-listed company director could have different disclosure requirement than proprietary company as Australian Stock Exchange Listing Rule may impose another layer of disclosure requirement.[116]
- **Executive remuneration**—Specifically, whether it is incentive-based. If a director's remuneration is incentive-based, could the standard for them to exercise good faith behaviour arguably be higher?

---

[111] Ibid.

[112] Ibid.

[113] Ibid at 1178.

[114] *Levin v Clark* [1962] NSWR 686.

[115] Ibid 700.

[116] Ian Ramsay and Richard Hoad, "Disclosure of Corporate Governance Practices by Australian Companies" (1997) 15 *Company and Securities Law Journal* 454.

- **Shareholdings by managers/directors**—Other commentators suggest that high levels of such share ownership may entrench managers and directors, potentially influencing disclosure obligations and loyalty standards.[117]
- **Ownership concentration**—Does more concentrated share ownership provide greater incentives for those shareholders who have more at risk because of their significant holding to monitor managers and directors?[118]
- **Corporate financial policy**—In particular, the level of debt. Debt incurred by a company can serve as a device which bonds managers to shareholders. Are directors in such company allowed to reinvest profits unwisely? Should they expand their empire too much, could they be found to be in bad faith?

4 Conclusion

In conclusion, relational contracting theory is compatible with, and could be transplanted into the corporate law. Corporation is a collection of contractual relationships.[119] Forming their own 'min-society,' these relationships craft the parties' own understanding of how their company runs. Hence, the one-size-fits-all interpretative approach for determining good faith director behaviour 'universally' applicable to all Australian companies challenging and less than ideal, and by adopting the relational contracting theory, it provides a method to not only take contextual elements into account, but also identify the sources which could form the common understanding the expectation on the directors' duties.

The relational contracting theory could become a practical guideline used to overcome the shortcomings of the good faith concept. However, it is assumed that good faith will still be expected to be used extensively at some points due to the courts' familiarity with it. It would be unrealistic to assume that the use of good faith can be fully eliminated by the introduction of relational contracting. Generally, good faith fits with the overall nature of the Corporations Act in reminding directors to act justly. The paper argues for the attachment of relational contracting theory into good faith as a framework for good faith. A complete interpretative framework is still yet to be researched on. Unlike the indefinite nature of good faith which merely implies a set of behaviours that are permissible in all kinds of companies without indicating the criteria that the behaviour should meet in order for it to be a good faith behaviour within a specific context, relational contracting theory could afford a tangible interpretative backbone to inform 'reasonableness,' 'state of mind,' 'genuine,' etc., sourcing internally from the relationship within the company.

---

[117] Alan Craswell et al, 'Ownership Structure and Corporate Performance: Australian Evidence' (1997), *Pacific-Basin Finance Journal*.

[118] Ronald Daniels and Paul Halpern, 'Too Close for Comfort: The Role of the Closely Held Public Corporation in the Canadian Economy and the Implications for Public Policy' (1995-96) 26 *Canadian Business Law Journal* 11.

[119] Mark Roe, 'Can Culture Constrain the Economic Model of Corporate Law?' (2002) 69 *University of Chicago Law Review* 1251.

An Analysis of Legal Frameworks for the Transfer of Environmentally Sound Technologies—Challenges and the Way Forward

Mahima Tripathi and Niharika Sahoo Bhattacharya

Abstract Environmentally sound technologies (ESTs) are technologies that have the potential for significantly improved environmental performance relative to other technologies. United Nations Agenda 21, developed by the United Nations Conference on Environmental Development (UNCED), following the Rio Conference in 1992, defined ESTs as capable of mitigating climate change. These technologies protect the environment, are less polluting in nature, use resources in a more sustainable manner, recycle their wastes and products, and handle all residual waste in a more environmentally acceptable way than the technologies for which they are substituted. They are defined as a total of systems, including know-how, procedures, goods and services, and equipment, as well as organizational and managerial procedures for promoting environmental sustainability. The transfer of ESTs stands at the core of global efforts to combat climate change and promote sustainable development. The development and diffusion of ESTs are particularly complex and comprises a wide range of technologies. ESTs are considered "global public goods" but are "rational technologies"; therefore, their modes of production and exploitation vary significantly. In the present context, the authors in this paper aim to understand the evolution and recent developments in the legal context of ESTs. The paper will examine the role of various existing international environmental instruments, like the United Nations Framework Conference on Climate Change (UNFCCC), the Kyoto Protocol, the Paris Agreement, and the TRIPs Agreement, in developing an effective framework for ESTs and their transfer. Various transfer mechanisms employed for the dissemination of ESTs across borders are also discussed in the paper.

Keywords Environmentally sound technologies · Sustainable development · Technology transfer · TRIPs · Global public goods

---

M. Tripathi · N. S. Bhattacharya (✉)
Rajiv Gandhi School of Intellectual Property Law, IIT Kharagpur, Kharagpur, India
e-mail: niharika@rgsoipl.iitkgp.ac.in

J. Aston et al. (eds.), *Comparative Law*, https://doi.org/10.1007/978-981-97-7815-7_12

1 Introduction

Climate change mitigation and its impact on the ecosystem are major concerns for the present generation. Various organizations and most of the nations are proactively trying to work toward climate mitigation through sustainable development. The best way to reduce or regulate the depletion of natural resources and environmental pollution is to develop advanced technologies that can substitute for the use of natural resources and minimize environmental deterioration. The adoption of technologies utilizing advanced techniques in terms of energy generation is highly emphasized. It is good to adopt these technologies because they use renewable natural resources, which never diminish.[1] The use of renewable energy to develop new technologies or upgrade existing technologies that can help mitigate environmental issues is always encouraged.

Technologies that are developed with environmental concerns in mind cause less or no pollution, use renewable resources, and can be renewed easily are called environmentally sound technologies (ESTs), abbreviated as ESTs.[2] The terms green technology, clean technology, environmentally sound technologies, or climate-friendly technologies can be used as synonyms or interchangeably.[3] The World Trade Organization (WTO) uses the term *"environmentally rational technologies"* to denote such technologies. These technologies can mitigate or reverse the impact of human activity on the environment.[4] In this paper, the author will use these terms interchangeably.

The significance of ESTs was first mooted during the 1992 Rio Earth Summit, and since then, it has been a key element of international environmental cooperation.[5] These technologies have the ability *"to improve environmental performance in relation to other technologies."*[6] Chapter 34, Agenda 21, of the United Nations Conference Environment and Development (UNCED), 1992, titled *"Transfer of Environmentally Sound Technology, Cooperation, and Capacity Building"* defined ESTs.[7] It is UNCED's key product, as it reflects a blueprint for environmental and development strategies for the world in the twenty-first century.[8] Though Agenda 21 is not legally

---

[1] Bolfaze Iravani, 'et al.', *"Advantages and Disadvantages of Green technology; Goals, Challenges and strengths"*, Vol. 6 Issue 09, 2017, ISSN 2319-7560, International Journal of Science and Engineering Applications.

[2] Chapter 34 of AGENDA 21, United Nations Conference on Environment & Development Rio de Janerio, Brazil, 3 to 14 June 1992.

[3] Kenton W, *"What is green tech? How it works, types, adoption and examples,"* Investopedia. Available at https://www.investopedia.com/terms/g/green_tech.asp last visited 23 September 2021.

[4] Supra no. 3.

[5] United Nations Environment Program, *"Environmentally Sound Technologies."* Available at: https://www.unenvironment.org/regions/asia-and-pacific/regional-initiatives/supporting-resource-efficiency/environmentally-sound, visited on 6 April 6, 20201.

[6] Ibid.

[7] Adenda 21 Chapter 34, United Nations Sustainable Development, United Nations Conference on Environment and Development, Rio de janerio, Brazil 3–14 June 1992.

[8] Report by Director General, United Nations Conference on Environment and Development, Forty sixth world health assembly, World health organization, A46/INF.DOC./3, 11 March 1993.

binding, it echoes a global accord and political commitment at the highest level.[9] It defines ESTs as *"technologies protecting the environment, less polluting, sustainably using resources, recycling more of their wastes and products, and handling all residual wastes in a more environmentally acceptable way than the technologies for which they are substituted."*[10] ESTs cannot be perceived as individual technology. They are defined as *"total systems that include know-how, procedures, goods and services, and equipment, as well as organizational and managerial procedures for promoting environmental sustainability."*[11] ESTs in the context of pollution include *"process and product technologies" generating "low or no waste, for the prevention of pollution, and covering end-of-pipe technologies for the treatment of pollution after it has been generated."*[12]

Agenda 21 comprises imperative provisions to guide the interpretation of the definition of ESTs, with a key emphasis on accelerating availability and technology transfer, with a primary focus on developing countries, as well as the crucial role of capacity-building and technology cooperation in promoting sustainable development.[13] Novel, efficient technologies are necessary *"to increase the capabilities, of developing countries, achieve sustainable development, sustain the world's economy, and protect the environment."*[14] The importance and significance of ESTs have been acknowledged by many international instruments, and individual countries have also acknowledged their importance and have incorporated provisions for the development and dissemination of ESTs. The countries have also tried to adopt and recognize its relevance in their national legislation.

In the present context, the authors in this paper aim to understand the evolution and recent developments in the legal context of ESTs. The paper will examine the role of various existing international instruments, like the UNFCCC, the Kyoto Protocol, the Paris Agreement, and the TRIPs Agreement, in developing an effective framework for ESTs and their transfer. Various transfer mechanisms employed for the dissemination of ESTs across borders are also discussed in the paper.

2 International Agreements for ESTs

The significance of ESTs in mitigating climate change concerns has been acknowledged globally. Almost all countries are working on these technologies. The United Nations, along with its other machinery organs, started discussing its importance long ago and are still continuously working toward the goal by laying down various

[9] Ibid.

[10] Agenda 21 chapter 34.1, United Nations Sustainable Development, United Nations Conference on Environment and Development, Rio de Janeiro, Brazil, 3–14 June 1992.

[11] Ibid.

[12] Ibid.

[13] Ibid.

[14] Ibid.

frameworks for ESTs development and diffusion. Various international agreements or frameworks discuss its development and diffusion globally. These frameworks not only dialog about ESTs but also emphasize and encourage their transfer among the nations, so that all nations can adopt these frameworks in their national policies and benefit from climate change mitigating technologies. The major international agreements discussing the ESTs and their transfer are the United Nations Conference on Environment and Development (UNCED), in 1992; the United Nations Framework Conference on Climate Change (UNFCCC), in 1992, the Kyoto Protocol, in 2005; and the Paris Agreement, 2015.

a. ***United Nations Conference on Environment and Development (UNCED), 1992***

UNCED was held in Rio de Janeiro, Brazil, from June 3 to 14, 1992. The principal aim of the Rio Earth Summit was *"to create a broader agenda with a new blueprint for international action on environmental and development issues that would help and guide international cooperation and development policy in the 21st century."*[15] Its concluding remarks were an assurance that *"the concept of sustainable development is a realistic goal for the world, irrespective of the fact that they were at the local, national, regional, or international level."* UNCED was issued in 3 volumes. The resolution was adopted in Volume 1, Proceedings in Volume II, and Volume III had the Statements by state heads at the summit segment.[16]

Resolution I have adopted texts on "*environment and development*" with three annexes. Its Annex (ii) is Agenda 21. Chapter 34 of Agenda 21 deals with the *"transfer of ESTs, cooperation, and capacity building."*[17] With the objective to—*"improve the condition and processing of information, access to, and technology transfer, as well as capacity building, cooperative arrangements and partnerships, and to promote sustainable development, especially in developing countries."*[18] It emphasizes the need *"to address the improvement of technology currently used and its replacement when needed with more ESTs."* This complete chapter talks about the ESTs, their definition, objectives, commitments, and how they can be promoted, protected, and disseminated; the role of developed as well as other countries in ESTs; the importance of IPRs in ESTs, etc., which made the document very significant in the context of ESTs.

---

[15] Agenda 21, United Nations Conference on Environment & Development Rio de Janeiro, Brazil, 3 to 14 June 1992. Available at https://sustainabledevelopment.un.org/content/documents/Agenda21.pdf.

[16] Report of the United Nations Conference on Environment and Development, Rio de Janeiro, 3–14 June 1992.

[17] Volume I, Resolutions Adopted by the Conference, Report of the United Nations Conference on Environment and Development, Rio de Janeiro, 3–14 June 1992. Available at https://www.un.org/esa/dsd/agenda21/Agenda%2021.pdf.

[18] Id.

b. ***United Nations Framework Conference on Climate Change, 1992***

UNFCCC, signed at UNCED in 1992 and entered into force on March 21, 1994, acknowledged that the core cause behind climate change and the rise in greenhouse gas (GHG) emissions are various human activities; which will, have adverse effects on the common concern of humankind.[19] This conference determined that the climate system has to be protected for all generations. Its objective is *"stabilization of greenhouse gas concentrations in the atmosphere at a level that would prevent dangerous anthropogenic interference with the climate system."*[20] It focuses on the "*Principle of Common but Differentiated Responsibility*," wherein all nations are accountable for addressing environmental destruction issues globally, but with different capabilities and different responsibilities, respectively.[21] In this, developed countries should take the lead accordingly. It provides for *"promotion and cooperation in the development, application, and diffusion, including technology transfer in all sectors, including energy, transport, industry, agriculture, forestry, and waste management sectors."*[22] The conference focused on strengthening technical research with international and intergovernmental efforts.[23] In 2001, member countries of the conference consented to the formation of a technology transfer framework to speed up the enactment of, paragraph 5, Article 4, of the Convention. An expert group on technology transfer (EGTT) was formed with the aim of *"studying technology development and transfer-related issues."* For the regular review of the implementation of the conference and the related legal instruments, a supreme decision-making body called the "*Conference of Parties (COP)*" was established, *"to meet annually and review and assess the implementation of the Convention and any other legal instruments to take decisions necessary to promote the effective implementation of the Convention, including institutional and administrative arrangements."*[24] In COP, various initiatives have been taken for climate change mitigation. In 1995, the first COP was held in Berlin, Germany. In 1997, COP 3 was concluded in Kyoto, Japan, binding developed nations to emission reduction targets. In 2006 Clean Development Mechanism (CDM), a key mechanism under the Kyoto Protocol, was adopted: "that provides for emission reduction projects that generate certified emission reduction units (CERs) that may be traded in emission trading schemes."

---

[19] United Nations Framework Conference on Climate Change, 1992. Available at https://unfccc.int/resource/docs/convkp/conveng.pdf.

[20] Article 2, United Nations Framework Conference on Climate Change, 1992. Available at https://unfccc.int/resource/docs/convkp/conveng.pdf.

[21] Article 3 (1) (2), United Nations Framework Conference on Climate Change, 1992. Available at https://unfccc.int/resource/docs/convkp/conveng.pdf.

[22] Article 4, United Nations Framework Conference on Climate Change, 1992. Available at https://unfccc.int/resource/docs/convkp/conveng.pdf.

[23] Article 5, United Nations Framework Conference on Climate Change, 1992. Available at https://unfccc.int/resource/docs/convkp/conveng.pdf.

[24] Article 7 (2), United Nations Framework Conference on Climate Change, 1992. Available at https://unfccc.int/resource/docs/convkp/conveng.pdf.

c. ***Kyoto Protocol, 1997***

The Kyoto Protocol was adopted on December 11, 1997, and came into force on February 16, 2005. "It operationalizes the UNFCCC by committing industrialized countries to restrict and cut greenhouse gas (GHG) emissions following the agreed goals."[25] It places a substantial burden on developed countries under the principle of "common but differentiated responsibility and respective capabilities," as it identifies that developed nations are mainly accountable for the present high levels of GHG emissions in the atmosphere.[26] It asks the countries "to implement the guidelines and methods on mitigation and to report it periodically."[27]

Following the Kyoto Protocol, another important international agreement was signed following the UNFCCC mandate. The Marrakesh Agreement was signed in 2001 as *"a framework for meaningful and effective actions to enhance the implementation of Article 4.5 of the Convention."*[28] It is recognized that each country's requirements and strengths are unique, and their demand and need for technology also vary; therefore, a balanced approach should be adopted on this account. EGTT was set up and tasked with monitoring the technology needs assessments. In 2007, the Bali Action Plan was adopted to include an improved and modified mitigation program with special emphasis on technology, supported by the provision of financial resources and investment.[29] In 2009, the Copenhagen Accord established the basis for the technology mechanisms provided under UNFCCC.[30] Further, at many of the COP's climate change issues, actions to be taken and mechanisms for transfer of ESTs were set.

d. ***Paris Agreement, 2015***

The parties to the UNFCCC reached a landmark agreement on December 12, 2015, which came into force on November 4, 2016, with the aim *"to reduce climate change and to step up and strengthen the measures and investments needed for a sustainable low-carbon future."*[31] The Agreement was the first of its kind that brought all nations

[25] Kyoto Protocol to The United Nations Framework Convention on Climate Change, United Nations 1998. Available at https://unfccc.int/resource/docs/convkp/kpeng.pdf.

[26] Article 13 (c), Kyoto Protocol to The United Nations Framework Convention on Climate Change, United Nations 1998. Available at https://unfccc.int/resource/docs/convkp/kpeng.pdf.

[27] Article 10 (b), Kyoto Protocol to The United Nations Framework Convention on Climate Change, United Nations, 1998. Available at https://unfccc.int/resource/docs/convkp/kpeng.pdf.

[28] UNFCCC, Marrakesh, Morocco, Oct. 29–Nov. 1, 2001, The Marrakesh Ministerial Declaration, U.N. Doc. FCCC/CP/2001/13/Add.1, Decision 2/CP.7 (Jan. 21, 2002).

[29] Para 1 (b) & (e), Decision 1/CP.13, Bali Climate Change Conference, Report of the Conference of the Parties on its thirteenth session December 2007 UNFCCC. Available at https://unfccc.int/resource/docs/2007/cop13/eng/06a01.pdf.

[30] Conference of the Parties, Report of the Conference of the Parties on its fifteenth session, held in Copenhagen 2009. Available at https://unfccc.int/resource/docs/2009/cop15/eng/11a01.pdf.

[31] Article 2 (1) Paris Agreement, United Nations 2015. Available at https://unfccc.int/sites/default/files/english_paris_agreement.pdf.

together for a common cause and *"to undertake determined efforts to combat climate change and acclimate to its effects, with greater support to assist developing countries in doing so. It charted a new course in the global climate effort."*[32] Its central aim is to *"strengthen the global response to the threat of climate change by keeping a global temperature rise well below 2 degrees Celsius above pre-industrial levels and to pursue efforts to limit the temperature increase even further to 1.5 degrees Celsius."*[33] It also intends *"to strengthen the capability of countries to deal with the effects of climate change."*

The agreement established a technology framework to provide central guidance to the *"Technology Mechanism."* It demanded additional effort on R&D on technologies, endogenous capacities, and technologies to strengthen the technology mechanism.[34] Following this, the member countries will try *"to enhance their technology efforts. Together, the technology mechanism and the technology framework will support countries to limit the rise in global temperature and adapt to climate change."*[35] The Agreement defines a long-term vision of climate change technologies and sets the forum for urgently needed climate change technologies their development and transfer.

Table 1 summarizes the COP meeting by the UN and the commitments adopted till date.

The above-mentioned instruments discuss technology transfer and the need to diffuse existing sustainable technologies simultaneously while building new technologies that benefit the environment. The agreements focus on the impact of climate change on humankind and the several ways and mechanisms to be adopted by developing and least-developed countries, particularly with the help of developed countries.

3 Importance of Technology Transfer of ESTs

Technology plays a substantial part in innovation. In ESTs, innovation and technology transfer go hand in hand. Technology transfer of ESTs plays a significant part in enhancing the efficacy of the resources; it helps in the reduction of pollutants and waste from different industrial and other sectors. Access to green technology plays a vital role in the country's growth and helps to achieve the Nationally Determined Contribution (NDC) targets set at COP meetings.

---

[32] https://unfccc.int/process-and-meetings/the-paris-agreement/what-is-the-paris-agreement.

[33] Article 2 (1) (a) Paris Agreement, United Nations 2015. Available at https://unfccc.int/sites/default/files/english_paris_agreement.pdf.

[34] Article 10 Paris Agreement, United Nations 2015. Available at https://unfccc.int/sites/default/files/english_paris_agreement.pdf.

[35] Article 10 (4) Paris Agreement, United Nations 2015. Available at https://unfccc.int/sites/default/files/english_paris_agreement.pdf.

Table 1 COP meetings

S. No.	COP	Commitments
1	Rio Summit, 1992	Article 4—Technology development and diffusion
2	COP 1, Berlin, 1995	Technology transfer projects inventory, discussion on financing, establishment of technology centers
3	COP 3, Kyoto, 1997	Consultation with Global Environmental Facility; support to work of international technology information centers by international organizations
4	COP 4, Buenos, 1998	A list of publicly owned green-tech developing countries were asked from developed nations and to report their technological need
5	COP 5, Bonn, 1999	Basis to enhance the implementation of Article 4.5 of the Convention
6	COP 7, Marrakesh,2001	Adoption of EGTT for technology framework
7	COP 8, New Delhi, 2002	Capacity-building and technology transfer and efforts to be made by SBST under the Convention for their work programs on cross-cutting problems
8	COP 10, Buenos Aires, 2004	Encouraged development projects, programs, and research among Annex II parties
9	COP 12, Nairobi, 2006	EGTT was extended for one year
10	COP 13, Bali, 2007	Encouragement to collaborative R&D as technology was identified as the major driver for climate change post 2012
11	COP 14, Poznan, 2008	Global Environment Funding for ESTs; transfer activities and adoption of strategic programs on technology transfer
12	COP 16, Cancun, 2010	Establishment of TEC and CTCN; EGTT's role was concluded
13	COP 17, Durban, 2011	Arrangements for technology mechanisms to be fully operational in 2012
14	COP 18, Doha, 2012	Provisions to fully operationalize the CTCN; increased action on financial resources and investment to assist prevention, adaptation, and technology sharing
15	COP 19, Warsaw, 2013	Modalities & procedures of CTCN were adopted
16	COP 21, Paris, 2015	Link between technology and the convention's finance mechanism, to boost ESTs development and transfer through the technology framework
17	COP 23, Bonn, 2017	Review of effective execution of CTCN; renewal of the MoU on the Climate Technology Centre's hosting between the COP and the UNEP
18	COP 24, Katowice, 2018	Draft to enhance financial, technology linkages for consideration and adoption at COP 26
19	COP 26, Glasgow, 2021	Glasgow Climate Pact adopted for mitigation and adaptation of climate

(continued)

Table 1 (continued)

S. No.	COP	Commitments
20	COP 27, Egypt, 2022	Focus to implement, just, equitable, and climate-resilient development in consonance of earlier Agreements
21	COP 28, UAE, 2023	Fast-tracking the energy transition and slashing emissions before 2030 along with fulfillment of prior commitments

Technology developed should also be transferred to benefit both parties, i.e., the developers who develop the technology and the recipients who receive it. Before discussing the intricacies involved in the technology transfer of ESTs, it is important to understand what the transfer of technology means. In an elementary sense, technology transfer can be defined as "*the process of transferring the technology from one who owns or holds it to another person.*" The technology transfer may be done through selling, licensing, trade, etc. ESTs are considered "*global public goods,*" *and* therefore, to meet the need of the hour, their transfer is very vital. Documents such as the United Nations Conference on Trade and Development (UNCTAD), UNFCCC, UNCED, and World Intellectual Property Organization (WIPO) have defined technology transfer. However, there is still no consensus on any particular definition. The definition may vary as the requirements of technology also vary as per the technology developers and recipient requirements.

UNCTAD's draft International Code on the Transfer of Technology, in its definition of "*technology transfer,*" *describes* "*technology*" *as* "*systematic knowledge for the manufacture of a product, for the application of a process, or for the rendering of a service.*"[36] This definition eliminates "*goods that are sold or hired from the ambit of technology.*"[37] The objective of the International Code on the Transfer of Technology is "*to establish general and equitable standards on which to base the relationships among parties to the transfer of technology transactions and governments concerned, taking into consideration their legitimate interests and giving due recognition to the special needs of developing countries for the fulfillment of their economic and social development objectives.*"[38] To boost technology transfer transactions, especially those concerning developing countries, under circumstances where "*negotiating positions of the parties to the transactions are fair in such a way as to avert exploits of a stronger position and thereby to achieve mutually satisfactory agreements.*"[39]

The International Code of Conduct is applicable to all countries. States can adopt "*all appropriate measures for facilitating and regulating the technology transfer, in a manner consistent with their international obligations, taking into consideration the*

[36] UNCTAD Series on issues in international investment agreements, UNITED NATIONS New York and Geneva, 2001.

[37] Ibid.

[38] Draft International Code on the Transfer of Technology. Available at https://unctad.org/en/docs/psiteiitd28.en last visited 3 July 2020.

[39] Ibid.

legitimate interests of all parties concerned, and encouraging the transfer of technology under mutually agreed-upon, fair, and reasonable terms and conditions."[40] The Code also provides for "*special treatment to the developing countries and the least developed countries by the developed countries.*"[41]

Restrictive business practices (RBPs) also contribute to the growth of international instruments in technology transfer agreements. It has listed out practices that are highly restricted. Provisions like "*exclusive grant back, exclusive dealing, restrictions on research or personal use, price fixing, tying arrangements, export restrictions, patent pool or cross-licensing agreements, and other arrangements are restricted under the Code.*"[42] These practices are associated with the transfer of ESTs, too.

The World Intellectual Property Organization (WIPO) defined the transfer of technology as "a series of processes enabling and facilitating flows of skills, knowledge, ideas, know-how, and technology among different stakeholders, such as universities and research institutions, as well as international organizations, NGOs, private sector entities, and individuals, as well as international technology transfer among countries."[43]

The ESTs transfer is crucial to the global response to climate change. At the highest international levels, the transfer of ESTs has been acknowledged as a means of promoting sustainable development. States in the Rio Declaration announced to cooperate "*by enhancing the development, adaptation, diffusion, and transfer of technologies, including new and innovative technologies.*"[44] Agenda 21 of UNCED has an entire chapter for the transfer of ESTs and related technologies, and measures were taken to simplify and encourage the cooperation and transfer of ESTs among countries, especially between developed and developing countries.

The Intergovernmental Panel on Climate Change (IPCC), an organization conducting scientific assessments of human induced climate change, in its special report on technology transfer, defines technology transfer in the context of climate change as: "*the broad set of processes covering the flows of knowledge, experience, and equipment amongst different stakeholders such as governments, private sector entities, financial institutions, NGOs, and research or educational institutions. It comprises the process of learning to understand, utilize, and replicate the technology, including the capacity to choose it and adapt it to local conditions.*"[45]

Many developing countries perceive technology transfer as a major condition for an international agreement on environmental policy. However, developed investing nations consider it as a time taking and expensive process with possible threat to

[40] Ibid.

[41] Ibid.

[42] Ibid.

[43] Project on Intellectual Property and technology: Common Challenges-Building Solutions (Recommendations 19, 25, 26 and 28) WIPO doc., CDIP/6/4/Rev., 26 November 2010, Geneva, Switzerland, p. 3.

[44] Rio Declaration on Environment and Development, 1992.

[45] IPCC (2000), IPCC Special Report: methodological and Technological Issues in Technology Transfer, Cambridge University Press, p.55.

intellectual property rights risks.[46] Agreement on Trade-Related Aspects of Intellectual Property (TRIPs) is a multilateral treaty entered by the member countries of a WTO adopted in the year 1995, with the purpose to codify the standards of IP protection internationally and afford a mechanism for dispute settlement between WTO members.

The TRIPs Agreement has not used the term ESTs in general, and no specific mention regarding ESTs is provided. TRIPs provide that all fields of technology be equally protected by IPRs, and all the member countries of the WTO have incorporated minimum standards into their national legal system. TRIPs do not specify any particular treatment of ESTs. But ESTs can be covered under the wide category of "*development in all fields of technology*."

TRIPs have incorporated various provisions concerning the promotion, protection, and diffusion of inventions and technologies. All the member countries of the agreement are obliged to follow and incorporate these provisions into their respective IP legislation.

TRIPs preamble provides to "*reduce and impediments to international trade and to address the need to promote development and technology transfer.*" Its objective states that "*IPRs should contribute to the transfer and dissemination of technology, to the mutual advantage of producers and users of technological knowledge, in a manner conducive to social and economic welfare and a balance of rights and obligations.*"[47] As incorporated under Article 8, TRIPs Principles provide that "*countries may wish to prevent practices that unreasonably restrain trade or adversely affect international technology transfer.*"[48] Environmental protection, including climate change, falls within the scope of the public interest under Article 7,8 of the TRIPs Agreement.

Apart from incorporating the duties and obligations of member countries (developed and developing) between and among themselves, it also entails a special place for the least-developed country members. It provides that "*developed countries need to help promote and encourage technology transfer to least-developed country members to enable them to create a sound and viable technological base.*"[49] But the effectiveness of Article 66.2 is a big question. Adopting and practicing such provisions in policy, leading to change in the technical situations of developing countries, has proved challenging and difficult.

Even though various articles incorporated under TRIPs talk about the promotion, development, and dissemination of technologies and their transfer among the member countries, to achieve economic growth and the development of the member countries, it is observed that most of the member countries do not abide by these principles or objectives entirely, as they are not bound to adopt any policy or practice that

---

[46] Climate change investment and technology transfer in Southeast Asia Tim Forsyth http://personal.lse.ac.uk/FORSYTHT/Harr-ch13.pdf.

[47] Article 7 of Agreement on Trade Related Aspects of Intellectual Property, 1995. Available at https://www.wto.org/english/docs_e/legal_e/27-trips.pdf.

[48] Article 8 of Agreement on Trade Related Aspects of Intellectual Property, 1995. Available at https://www.wto.org/english/docs_e/legal_e/27-trips.pdf.

[49] Article 66.2 of Agreement on Trade Related Aspects of Intellectual Property, 1995. Available at https://www.wto.org/english/docs_e/legal_e/27-trips.pdf.

promotes the sharing or transfer of technologies among member countries. As a result, developing member countries and least-developed countries do not have access to most of the technologies that can be needed or adopted by them for their subsistence or growth.

4 Trade and Transfer of ESTs Globally

It is important to adopt green technologies to help mitigate climate change. ESTs are a very relative and normative concept because what technologies are sound or friendly today for climate change mitigation may not be appropriate or needed after some years. Also, the same ESTs cannot be required everywhere because the environmental degradation or emission of GHG is not the same worldwide. The need for ESTs depends upon the conditions or reasons that contribute to the degradation or pollution of the environment or mitigate the climate.

If we see the development of ESTs globally, it is evident that most of the inventions have been primarily developed in industrial countries. They are mainly concentrated in twelve countries, out of which nine are Organizations for Economic Cooperation and Development (OECD) countries like Japan, the United States, Germany, South Korea, Australia, France, the UK, Canada, and the Netherland; and three are emerging countries such as China, Brazil, and Russia.[50] Data between 2000 and 2005 shows that Japan, the USA, and Germany were the top three inventor countries of ESTs.[51] Developing countries like India, China, and Brazil are also trying to make their presence in the EST trade, and now they too are doing well. However, the maximum market is under the control of developed countries, and the performance of the emerging economies except China is comparatively low.[52] It is evident through data and studies that the international transfer of ESTs-related technologies occurs mostly between developed countries. They are rarely transferred to developing countries; even if they are transferred, they generally go to only a handful of emerging developing countries.

Based on the OECD patent database,[53] the distribution of ESTs and emerging technologies from G20 countries can be identified, which is shown in Fig. 1. Most EST patents have been listed in the US at 23 percent, followed by Korea (20 percent) and Japan (14 percent). There is a clear difference in patenting activity among developed

[50] Invention and Transfer of Climate Change Mitigation Technologies: A Global Analysis, Review of Environmental Economics and Policy, vo. l.5 no. 1.

[51] Ibid.

[52] Ibid.

[53] OECD Patent Database: https://stats.oecd.org/Index.aspx?DataSetCode=PATS_IPC accessed on March 3, 2022.

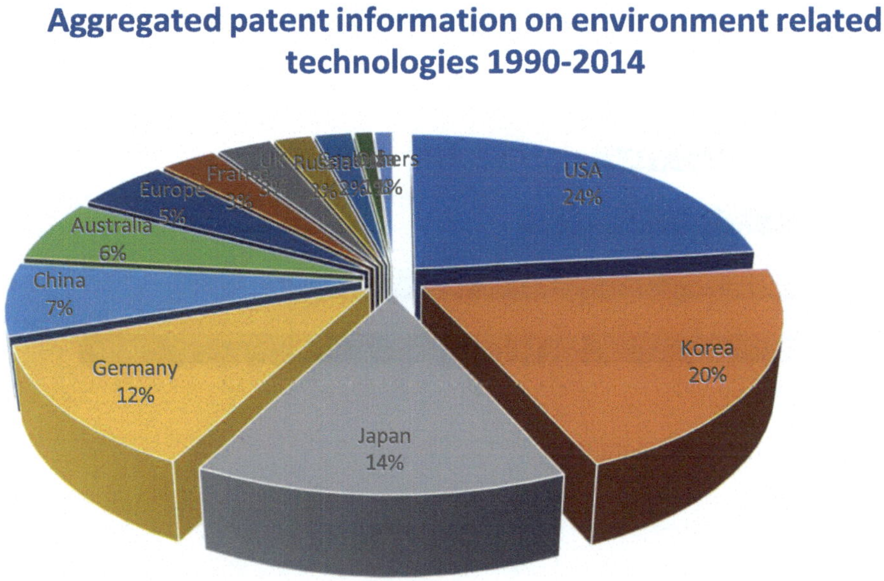

Fig. 1 G20 countries ESTs—OECD patent database

and developing countries, with China being a noteworthy exception. This difference indicates the lack of in-house capabilities of developing countries to innovate and produce ESTs, thereby depending on transfers from developed countries to developing countries.

In green patent inventions worldwide from 2007 to 2009, again, it is the developed countries that have the major share. Developed nations are the major contributors to it. China is the only emerging economy in the top 10. The total share of the top-10 countries is 78.6%. Other major transition countries, such as India, Brazil, and Russia, account for less than 1% of world innovation.[54]

From 2010 to 2019, a report from the WIPO analyzed that Japan tops the leaderboard with respect to the total number of patent applications for ESTs. The US ranked second highest, followed by Germany, China, and UK (Fig. 2).

Trade plays a very vital role in a country's development, not only from an economic point of view but also for its technological advancement and export diversification. The same is true in the trade of ESTs. It provides "*economic growth, export diversification, technological development, and environmental protection, especially for developing countries.*"[55] It has a role in the dissemination of ESTs. Significant developers of ESTs are in the fields of solar energy, solar photovoltaic cells, wind energy, biofuels and biohydrogen energy, and renewable energy.

[54] Ibid.

[55] United Nations Environment Program (2018). Trade in environmentally sound technologies: Implications for Developing Countries.

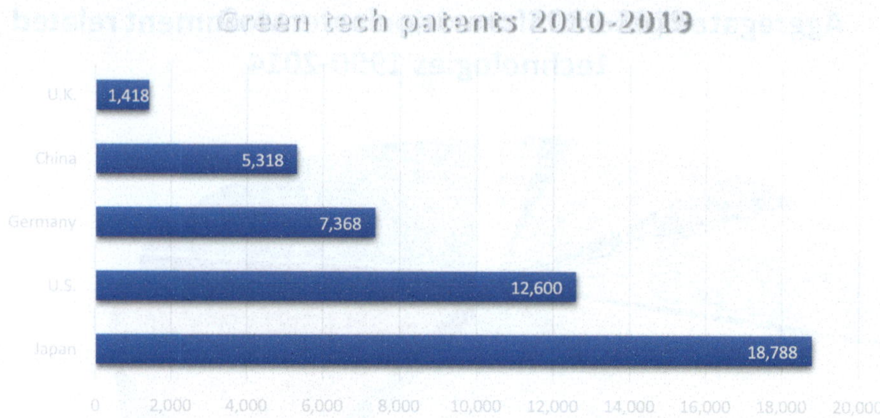

Fig. 2 Green tech patents 2010–2019

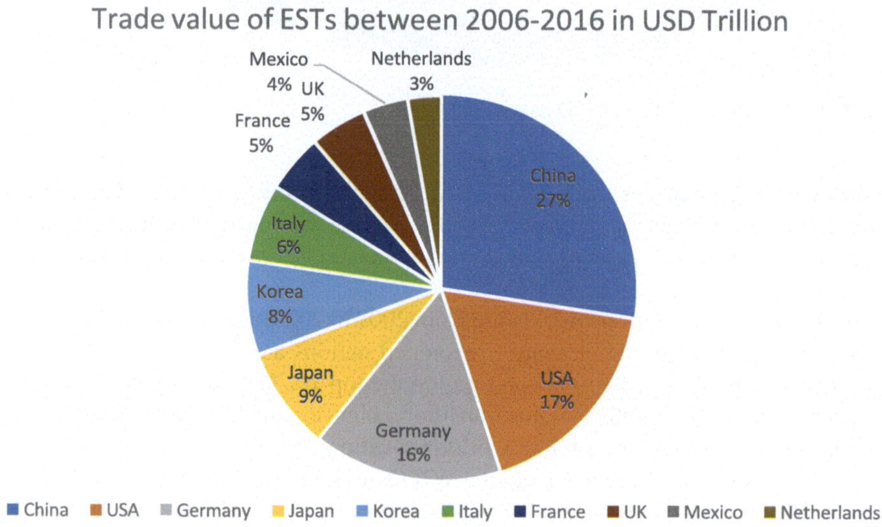

Fig. 3 Total value of top-10 countries in trade of ESTEGs, over 2006–2016[56]

Figure 3 shows the top-10 countries in terms of the trade value of the ESTs from the period between 2006 and 2016. China has become a leading exporter among developing economies over the past decades.[57]

---

[56] Ibid.

[57] United Nations Environment Program (2018). Trade in environmentally sound technologies: Implications for Developing Countries. Page 37.

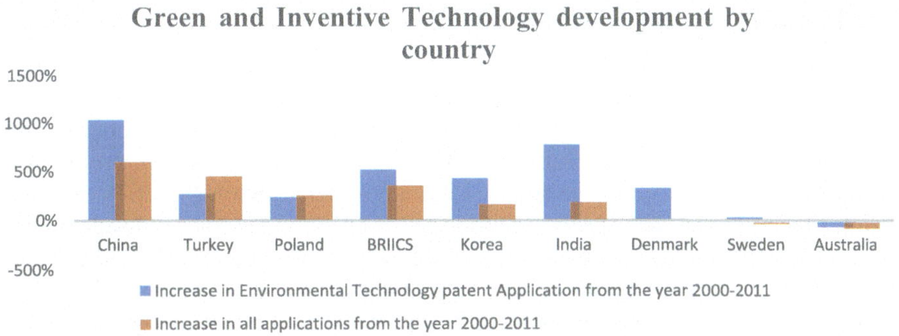

Fig. 4 Data from OECD Green Growth Indicator

Innovation is vital to establishing new patterns of production and consumption. It creates markets and opportunities for the players, keeps transformation cost-effective, and allows new ways to address environmental risk. Statistics taken from the OECD Green Growth Indicator in Fig. 4 prove that in some countries, the growth in environment related patents is faster than the growth in overall innovation.[58]

Globalization and trade liberalization, to some extent, have enabled the creation and development of ESTs market and generated prospects for companies, mainly in developing countries. In the same light, countries from all over the world have come forward to promote ESTs. Say, for example, that India, which is one of the major emerging economies, is a party to almost all the agreements and treaties concerning environmental and climate change issues. Under the Paris Agreement 2015, India has committed "*to cut GHG emission intensity to its GDP by 33–35%, increase non-fossil fuel power capacity to 40% from 28% by 2030, and is continuously trying to achieve it.*"[59] Also recently at the 26th session of the COP 26 to the UNFCCC, held in Glasgow, India presented to the world "*five nectar elements (Panchamrit) of India's climate action.*"[60] It updated India's existing NDC, marking a step toward achieving India's long-term goal of reaching net-zero by 2070.[61] To achieve these commitments internationally, India also needs to come up with more technologies, so that it can also be a technological hub for ESTs. There are many requirements and challenges to overcome in order to achieve a remarkable position in the EST domain of ESTs not for India alone but for many countries like India.

---

58 OECD, Green Patents. Available at http://www.oecd.org/environment/indicators-modelling-outlooks/green-patents.htm last visited 11 June 2021.

59 India's Intended Nationally Determined Contribution: Working Towards Climate Justice, available at, https://www4.unfccc.int/sites/submissions/INDC/Published%20Documents/India/1/INDIA%20INDC%20TO%20UNFCCC.pdf last visited 23 September 2021.

60 India's Stand at COP-26, Ministry of Environment, Forest and Climate Change 03 FEB 2022. Available at https://pib.gov.in/PressReleasePage.aspx?PRID=1795071.

61 Ministry of External Affairs, Government of India, "*National Statement by Prime Minister at COP26 Summit in Glasgow.*" Available at https://www.mea.gov.in/Speeches-Statements.htm?dtl/34466/National+Statement+by+Prime+Minister+Shri+Narendra+Modi+at+COP26+Summit+in+Glasgow. Last visited 21 December 2021.

5 Mechanisms for Transfer ESTs

The demand and market of ESTs are increasing at a high rate because of commitment by all countries at international platform. They are one of the most important and crucial technologies of the present time. Their development, adoption, promotion, and transfers are also very significant. Like any other technology, ESTs are also complex technologies and of relative nature too. Once a technology is developed by the developer, the main concern is how it will reach to its recipients. The right to use, sell, resell, license, assign, transfer, etc., vests in the developer of the technology. For the transfer of ESTs, the normal procedure applies, where the technology developer can license or assign his technology to the receipts. But as discussed earlier, since most of the technologies are vested in the hands of developed countries, the transfer to recipients mainly from developing or least-developed countries has to suffer, as the developer does not intend to transfer their technologies to developing countries due to various factors. But, as the significance of ESTs has now been acknowledged worldwide, the idea of their dissemination globally is also considered by all countries. Various initiatives have been encouraged by the public as well as the private players developing ESTs worldwide.

i. *Technology Transfer Facilitated by International Instruments*

It is believed that environmental issues are mainly generated and aggravated by industrialized developed nations; therefore, duty has been shifted to them. Many international agreements on the environment have laid a duty on developed countries to help developing countries and least-developed countries fight against climate change. Transferring the desired technology to the developing countries and financially aiding them to fight against climate change and the increase in GHG emissions is provided under the UNFCCC Kyoto Protocol and was encouraged in all other COP meetings. Also, technology transfer centers and bodies were established for the proper transfer of ESTs among countries, especially developed countries.

ii. *Technology Transfer Through National Policies*

Considering the importance and need of ESTs, countries all over the world are trying to increase their transfer. Countries are facilitating the development, dissemination, and transfer of ESTs, by incorporating various provisions in their respective national laws. Nations are actively participating in the development and transfer of ESTs through multilateral and regional agreements among the countries. More bilateral agreements are taking place between countries on reasonable terms, and technologies are shared between them. For instance, in 2009, the Clean Energy Research Centre was initiated by the United States and China to allow cooperation, R&D of sustainable energy technology.[62] The US-China Renewable Energy Forum has also been created to enhance collaboration on intellectual property issues connected to

[62] U.S.-China Clean Energy Cooperation A Progress Report by the U.S. Department of Energy, US Department of Energy, 2011. Available at https://www.energy.gov/node/266881.

renewable energy.[63] Similarly, in 2009, the "*Joint Clean Energy Research and Development Centre (JCERDC)*" was started by the United States and India to enhance clean energy and address global energy and environmental sustainability concerns.[64] India and US formally signed an agreement in 2010, to collaborate on a joint Clean Energy Research Development Centre. In 2017, expanding JCERDC has taken the lead in sponsoring innovative research in two areas crucial to enhancing the dependability, flexibility, and efficiency of the energy distribution system, i.e., smart grids and energy storage. As ESTs are generally developed by private firms, independence is provided to them to enter into any bona-fide agreement with the technology providers for the transfer of technology. These technology transfer agreements are between the companies only, and they are governed accordingly.

iii. *Technology Transfer Through Other Instruments*

Many initiatives have been taken by providing an international platform to ESTs for their promotion and transfer. This is a very important area that has to be looked upon very diligently for mitigating climate change concerns. ESTs and their importance cannot be overlooked in the present world. Access to these technologies is a priority for many countries confronting the challenges of climate change. Its transfer is one of the most important and needed objects that must be considered by all countries. There is a lack of information on the development of ESTs. There is no direct medium or source that can be accessed to get information on the development of ESTs. Keeping this problem in mind, various initiatives have been taken to solve the problem of want of information on ESTs. Several online platforms, websites, or portals have been introduced where information regarding the development of green technologies is being reported, for the promotion and dissemination, or transfer of ESTs. These websites comprehend a cross-domain database to provide empirical indication and evidence about the growth as well as the distribution of the ESTs globally. In this line, WIPO Green,[65] Green Tech Database,[66] WIPO Match,[67] etc., are very prominent names. They act as the information center for the growth and expansion of ESTs, providing information and act as the marketplace for the developed ESTs.

---

[63] US-China Renewable Energy Forum, Available at https://www.energy.gov/ia/us-china-renewable-energy-forum.

[64] Indo-US Joint Clean Energy Research and Development Centre. Available at https://iusstf.org/indo-u-s-joint-clean-energy-research-development-centre-phase-i.

[65] WIPO GREEN Strategic Plan 2019–2023, "*Accelerating the transition to a greener global economy.*" Available at https://www.wipo.int/edocs/pubdocs/en/wipo_pub_greenstrpl1923.pdf last visited 6 April 2021.

[66] Bottone G, "*Green Tech DB: Visualising sustainable innovation*." Available at https://innovationorigins.com/green-tech-db-visualising-sustainable-innovation/ 3 April 2022.

[67] World Intellectual Property Organization, "*WIPO Match Leveraging IP for Development.*" Available at https://www.wipo.int/edocs/pubdocs/en/wipo_match_flyer.pdf last visited 24 April 2021.

6 Conclusion and Suggestion

ESTs are considered global public goods that are the need of the hour, and to survive on this planet, it is important to adopt those technologies that can help in climate change mitigation. ESTs are a very relative and normative concept because what technologies are sound or friendly today for combating climate change mitigation may not be appropriate or needed after some years. Also, the same ESTs cannot be needed everywhere because the environmental degradation or emission of GHG is not the same all over the world. The need for ESTs depends upon the conditions or reasons that contribute to the degradation or pollution of the environment or mitigate the climate. So, it is not at all universal or a common rule that all countries will have the same problem; therefore, all countries should initiate to put forward their hands at least to countries that share the same gravity of the problem or are in the same situation.

Internationally, there are many frameworks or agreements that talk about the transfer of technology among the nations, that is, from developed to developing or the least-developed countries, but the non-binding nature of these agreements is the biggest hurdle in the implementation of the transfer of technology among countries. It will not be wrong to say that decision-makers or the government lack the ability to prioritize the ESTs and their categories. The government needs to come up with policies lowering costs and thereby increasing demand for ESTs. Robust and clear environmental regulation can encourage firms to acquire new technologies, whereas inadequate environmental laws, regulations, and their weak enforcement can be the main hindrances for effective diffusion of technologies. The active role of the government should be encouraged for technology transfer. Various national and international initiatives and measures by way of policies to promote the transfer of ESTs to the private sector should be encouraged. It must be adopted by all nations. Government procurement policies can also can boost EST transfer.

Moreover, governments at all levels, are the key purchasers of environmental-related services. Information networks, organizational development, and human skills are imperative for effective transfer of technology. Therefore, capacity building, i.e., adequate training to improve the capacity to capture new technologies, is also required in environmental legislation and IPR regimes. Governments, the private sector, corporations, and even citizens should try to coordinate their activities about the adoption of ESTs. The financing organs or institutions should also be ready for cooperation and investments. When capacity-building efforts accompany technology transfer, the result is generally satisfactory. Insufficient resources to acquire and adopt technologies is also another barrier to the transfer of such technologies. The adoption of ESTs must be encouraged by a voluntary approach or by the regulatory framework, thereby allowing organizations to innovate and develop the technology.

The role of academia plays a very vital role in the diffusion and dissemination of technologies. Therefore, various academic institutions should collaborate and can come forward with their work, which not only benefits for India but can be transferred worldwide as it is capable of dealing with large numbers of environmental problems.

Academia should not only help in innovation, but it can also play a significant role in discussing and analyzing the lacunas and the features of frameworks that can be drafted and adopted worldwide, resolve many major environmental issues, and mitigate climate change-related concerns.

Dated Interpretations of Gender, Sexual Orientation, and Gender Identity Within the Paradigm of the International Refugee Law: An Argument for Amending the Definition of the Refugee Convention, 1951

Setu Gupta and Sakshi Parashar

Abstract Since the time the Refugee Convention of 1951 was negotiated, asylum, when claimed on the basis of gender, sexual orientation, or gender identity, has been considered under the expressly mentioned ground of membership in a particular social group contained within the definition of refugee. These unwritten grounds of gender, sexual orientation, and gender identity have been a constant source of obfuscation for lawmakers and judges alike, leading to inconsistent interpretations across jurisdictions and even laying down bizarre tests for asylum seekers to prove the genuineness of their claims. Lack of necessary knowledge or access to experts who can assist in making psychological assessments has been a roadblock in the decision-making process as well. This has resulted in inefficacious remedies or complete denial of a remedy for asylum seekers, pushing them back to the hands of their persecutors threatening their life or liberty. The present chapter argues against the status quo and proposes that gender, sexual orientation, and gender identity must be added as separate grounds by way of amending the existing Convention definition of a refugee.

Keywords Gender · Sexual orientation · Gender identity · Refugee · Status determination

---

S. Gupta (✉)
Amity Institute of Advanced Legal Studies, Amity University, Noida, Uttar Pradesh, India
e-mail: setugupta@hotmail.com

S. Parashar
Symbiosis Law School, Symbiosis International (Deemed) University, Noida, India

J. Aston et al. (eds.), *Comparative Law*, https://doi.org/10.1007/978-981-97-7815-7_13

1 Introduction

The ultimate theme behind all five grounds has been understood to be "fundamental socio-political disenfranchisement"[1] and while grounds such as race, religion, political opinion, and nationality are straightforward and seldom create any problem for the decision-makers, over the years one specific ground, i.e., 'membership of a particular social group' (MPSG), has evolved to include factors of potential discrimination such as gender, sexual orientation, and gender identity, age and family, and has been pressed into service to provide protection to some asylum seekers.[2] However, since this is an interpretation at play, the results have been inconsistent, with some asylum seekers receiving protection while others getting rejected. Therefore, MPSG has often been referred to by scholars as the 'ground with the least clarity.'[3]

Two main approaches, i.e., the *ejusdem generis* approach[4] (protected characteristics approach) and the social perception (sociological approach),[5] have been applied by the courts in order to decide whether the claim can be allowed or not. The reason why this ground tends to face greater scrutiny is that there is an apprehension in the minds of decision-makers that it might become an all-encompassing ground with all sorts of asylum claims being filed under it, rendering the other grounds as well as the nexus clause, which bridges persecution to the grounds, superfluous.[6]

According to the *ejusdem generis* approach, the persecution should be aimed at an "immutable characteristic," in that it should be beyond the power of the individual to change it, or the characteristic should be so fundamental to the individual's identity that they cannot be expected to change it.[7] The Bureau of Immigration Affairs (BIA) further said that the "shared characteristic might be an innate one such as sex, color, or kinship ties, or in some circumstances it might be a shared past experience such as former military leadership or land ownership."[8] The reasoning of the BIA in *Re Acosta* was followed by the Supreme Court of Canada in *Canada (Attorney General) v. Ward*,[9] as well as the House of Lords in *Ex Parte Shah*,[10]

---

[1] James C. Hathaway & Michelle Foster, The Law of Refugee Status 390–391 (Cambridge University Press 2014).

[2] *Id.* at 363.

[3] Michelle Foster, The Ground with the Least Clarity: A Comparative Study of Jurisprudential Developments relating to 'Membership of a Particular Social Group' (UNHCR 2012).

[4] Originated in US Board of Immigration Appeals (BIA) decision of Re Acosta 9 I. & N. Dec. 211 (BIA, 1985).

[5] Believed to have originated in Australian jurisprudence. See Foster, *supra* note 3, at 9.

[6] Applicant A v. Minister for Immigration and Ethnic Affairs, [1997] HCA 4 (Australia: High Court, 1997).

[7] *Re* Acosta, at 233.

[8] *Id.*

[9] [1993] 2 S.C.R. 689.

[10] Islam (A.P.) v. Secretary of State for the Home Department; R v. Immigration Appeal Tribunal and Another, *Ex Parte* Shah (A.P.), Session 1998–1999, United Kingdom: House of Lords (Judicial Committee) [1999].

which endorsed the position that the grounds mentioned in the Convention definition have non-discrimination moorings. The advantage of this approach has been explained to be that it interprets social groups in a "principled framework," i.e., non-discrimination norms that have universal applicability.[11] Therefore, it brings some objectivity in refugee status determinations.

In *Applicant A v. Minister for Immigration and Ethnic Affairs*,[12] the Australian High Court adopted a "social perception" approach. It observed:

> A particular social group ... is a collection of persons who share a certain characteristic or element that unites them and enables them to be set apart from society at large. That is to say, not only must such persons exhibit some common element, the element must unite them, making those who share it a cognisable group within their society. However, one important limitation is that the characteristic or element that unites the group cannot be a common fear of persecution.

The social perception approach dictates that *firstly*, the group must be identifiable by attributes that is shared by all the members of the group; *secondly*, this characteristic cannot be the shared fear of persecution; *and thirdly*, the attribute must make the group distinguishable from the society at large.[13] Additionally, the social perception of the group can be relevant evidence in this regard.[14] Hathaway points out that the only meaningful criterion is the third one, as the first suffers from redundancy and the second merely stipulates what the group is not.[15] However, the challenge remains as to how to determine whether the group is distinguishable from society at large. The Australian High Court in *Applicant S*[16] iterated that while the fact that the group is perceived by the home society as a social group may be relevant, the general principle is that the group must be distinguishable from the rest of the society.

The French jurisprudence also adopts the social perception test, but with a slightly different requirement. Here, the applicant must display some external behavior or overt act of social transgression.[17] As has been discussed later, this is problematic since it would be asking, for example, a homosexual individual to exhibit such behavior in their society, which might incur criminal prosecution or worse consequences for the individual.

---

[11] Hathaway & Foster, *supra* note 1, at 427.

[12] [1997] HCA 4.

[13] Applicant S v. Minister for Immigration and Multicultural Affairs, (2004) 217 CLR 387.

[14] *Id.*

[15] Hathaway & Foster, *supra* note 1, at 428.

[16] (2004) 217 CLR 387.

[17] See Jean-Yvues Carlier, *Droit d'Asile et des Réfugiés: de la Protection aux Droits* in Recueil des Cours: Collected Courses of the Hague Academy of International Law 213 (Adrienne Anderson trans., Hague Academy of International Law, Martinus Nijhoff Publishers, 2008). *See also* D. Alland and C. Teitgen-Colly, Traite du droit de l'asile 427–428 (Adrienne Anderson trans., Presses Universitaires de France 2002).

The UNHCR suggested an alternative path where it recommended that it would be appropriate to "adopt a single standard" that would incorporate both the dominant approaches.[18] Consequently, it said:

> A particular social group is a group of people who share a common characteristic other than their risk of being persecuted or who are perceived as a group by society. The characteristic will often be one that is innate, unchangeable, or which is otherwise fundamental to identity, conscience, or the exercise of one's human rights.[19]

This suggestion has since then been mistakenly adopted as a cumulative standard in many jurisdictions where the interpretation has been that both the ingredients of both, instead of either, the approaches be fulfilled for a claim to proceed under the MPSG ground.[20] Having this high a threshold to succeed for the MPSG claim appears to be a great ask that runs contrary to the protection objective of the Refugee Convention, even as the UNHCR itself maintains that the cumulative approach is a misunderstanding of its guidelines.[21]

The social perception test has proven to be disadvantageous for claims based on gender, homosexuality, family, and age, as even when they satisfy the immutable characteristic of the ejusdem generis approach, they still often fail to satisfy the "social visibility" question.[22]

The next part of this paper is going to discuss 'gender' and 'sexual orientation and gender identity' to evaluate whether these should be considered to be included as independent grounds by introducing an amendment in the Convention definition in order to meet the challenges posed by inconsistent interpretations across different jurisdictions.

(a) *'Gender' as an Independent Ground for Protection*

By and large, both the jurisdictions that favor the *ejusdem generis* approach as well as those who favor the social perception approach have recognized that women can constitute a particular social group.[23] In the EU and the Netherlands, owing to the

[18] UNHCR, Guidelines on International Protection: "Membership of a particular social group" within the context of Article 1A(2) of the 1951 Convention and/or its 1967 Protocol relating to the Status of Refugees. UN Doc. HCR/GIP/02/02.

[19] *Id.*

[20] EU Qualification Directive 2004 is one example and consequently, several courts across the EU follow this dual requirement approach. *See* X, Y, Z v. Minister voor Immigratie en Asiel, C-199/12 - C-201/12, European Union: Court of Justice of the European Union, 7 November 2013 (July 19, 2023, 6:30 AM), https://www.refworld.org/cases,ECJ,527b94b14.html. For the United States, *see e.g.*, *Re* AT, (2007) 24 I & N Dec. 296, Perkeci v. US Attorney General, (2011) 446 Fed. Appx. 236.

[21] See UNHCR intervention before the United States Court of Appeals for the Tenth Circuit in the case of Rivera-Barrientos v. Holder, Attorney General, No. 10–9527, (July 19, 2023, 7:23 AM), https://www.refworld.org/docid/4c6cdb512.html at 12–13.

[22] *Re* AT, (2007) 24 I & N Dec. 296; Da Silva v. U.S. Attorney General, No. 11–12,842 (USCA, 11th Cir., 2012).

[23] *Ex Parte* Shah, (1999); K v. Secretary of State for the Home Department, [2007] 1 AC 412; Minister for Immigration and Multicultural Affairs v. Khawar, [2002] HCA 14.

restrictive approach of the Qualification Directive, the position is that "women in general do not form a social group."[24] Other jurisdictions, such as Spain, Germany, Austria, Belgium, and Switzerland, have, recognized women as a social group.[25] Overall, it has been observed that there are several hindrances to successful recognition of gender-based claims under the MPSG category.[26] The reluctance of decision-makers, for example, to regard the relevant social group as simply 'women' despite the view adopted in cases like *Minister for Immigration and Multicultural Affairs v. Khawar*[27] and *R v. Immigration Appeal Tribunal and Another Ex Parte Shah*[28] that women who form a particular social group could be characterized simply as 'women' on the basis that in any society they are distinct and recognizable as a group. The Supreme Court of Canada has ruled that gender is an 'innate characteristic.'[29] Additionally, New Zealand and the United States Circuit Courts of Appeal, applying the immutability characteristic (*ejusdem generis* approach), regard gender as a PSG.[30]

Despite this, courts have often shown reluctance in considering women as a PSG, stressing the construction of a narrower formulation based on the "floodgates concern," i.e., if a formulation is too broad, then it might suggest that all those who are part of the group are at risk.[31] The danger of this approach is that the group might be so narrowly formulated that it becomes identifiable by the threat of persecution alone, which is impermissible as an established principle.[32] However, there is no need to reduce the group to those at risk, as it is also established that not all the members of the group need to be at risk.[33] Hence, the women can be at risk by virtue of being 'women' or 'women from Pakistan' or 'women from Bangladesh,' and no further filters need to be applied.[34] It has been observed that the lack of any authoritative interpretation by the ICJ on the matter of a gender-sensitive interpretation due to the non-invocation of its jurisdiction has added to the problem, and this has led to inconsistent interpretations by judicial and administrative authorities.[35]

---

24 Foster, *supra* note 3, at 41.

25 *Id.*

26 *Id.*

27 [2002] HCA 14.

28 (1999) 2 AC 629.

29 Canada (Attorney General) v. Ward, [1992] 2 SCR 689, 739.

30 Foster, *supra* note 3, at 43.

31 *Id.* at 44. E.g., a narrower formulation might be 'young single women in Sierra Leone who are at risk of circumcision' as in Fornah v. Secretary of State for the Home Department, [2007] 1 AC 439.

32 Baroness Hale in *Fornah* pointed that the perversity of this logic since if not all members of the group are at risk, then persecution would not be due to membership of the group and if the group is reduced to those of are at not risk then it is said to be affected by the malady of being defined by persecution alone. See *Fornah* at 466.

33 Fornah v. Secretary of State for the Home Department at 466–467.

34 Foster, *supra* note 3, at 46.

35 Christel Querton, *Gender and the boundaries of international refugee law: Beyond the category of 'gender-related asylum claims'* 37(4) Netherlands Q. Human Rights 380 (2019).

Now, gender-based persecution may be understood in two different ways, i.e., "women being persecuted *as* women and women being persecuted *because* they are women."[36] The first category (gender-specific persecution) would address cases of rape, female genital mutilation (FGM), other forms of sexual violence, forced abortion, or sterilization.[37] The second category, i.e., women being persecuted *because* they are women (gender-related persecution), speaks to the "causal relationship between gender and persecution."[38] It may include persecuting a woman because she transgressed the established social mores that define how a woman is supposed to behave or act in that society or culture. For example, it might be acceptable in certain societies for men to have sexual relations outside of marriage, but strict punishments may be prescribed for women who do the same. Additionally, there may also be cases where women are persecuted *as* women and also *because* they are women, such as the cases of FGM.[39]

Gender-*specific* persecution may be understood as serious harm, while gender-*related* persecution would be the grounds of persecution and the basis of the application for asylum.[40] Gender-*related* persecution, i.e., persecution *because* of being women, is considered a part of the MPSG discourse.[41]

Scholars argue that by maintaining the focus on violations of direct rights by states, the Convention definition fails to recognize the "abuse of women as a human rights problem," insinuating that the abuse faced by women is a domestic matter better dealt with by the local community.[42] This would indicate that the identifiers of refugees in the Convention definition are drawn from activities in the public sphere primarily associated with men.[43]

The polarity of adopting a gender-sensitive interpretation of the refugee definition and adding gender as a specific ground in the Convention definition has been palpable since the 1980s.[44] Adopting a gender-sensitive interpretation has been an ask of the Executive Committee for a long time,[45] and despite this, it can be inferred from the above discussion that the call has not been answered on many occasions. Heaven

---

[36] Refugee Women's Legal Group, Gender Guidelines for the Determination of Asylum Claims in the UK (1998) (July 21, 2023, 8:35 PM), https://www.researchgate.net/publication/318859520_Gender_Guidelines_for_the_Determination_of_Asylum_Claims_in_the_UK/link/5981dfc94585150575c041a4/download.

[37] *Id.* para 1.12.

[38] *Id.*

[39] *Id.* para 1.14.

[40] *Id.*

[41] Andrea Binder, *Gender and the Membership in a Particular Social Group Category of the 1951 Refugee Convention*, 10 Columbia J. Gender & L. 168 (2001).

[42] Doreen Indra, *Gender: A Key Dimension of the Refugee Experience*, 6 Canada J on Refugees 3 (1987).

[43] *Id.*

[44] Querton, *supra* note 35, at 381–382.

[45] ExCom General Conclusion No. 73 (XLIV) – 1993 Refugee Protection and Sexual Violence, para (d) and (j); ExCom General Conclusion on International Protection No. 77 (XLVI) – 1995, para (g); ExCom General Conclusion on International Protection No. 79 (XLVII) – 1996, para (o);

Crawley argues that women can not only be considered as part of a particular social group but also provided protection under the political opinion ground since opposition to legislated discrimination or expression of views that portray independence from social or cultural dominance of men could be considered political opinion.[46] Deborah Anker argues that simply adding gender or sex to the protection grounds would not solve the problem of the ill-conceived relationship of women with the State.[47] The opposition to adding gender as a separate protection ground is also moored in the view that most of these calls are to recognize the violence faced by women in the private sphere, which meant accepting a bifurcated version of society where the lives of women were rooted in domesticity and ignoring the oppression faced by them in non-private circumstances.[48] Other scholars have preferred a gender-sensitive interpretation because opening the Convention for amendment was considered a more perilous task and seeking alteration to municipal laws was a more preferable approach.[49] It is rooted in the "pragmatic awareness" that attempts for advances might dilute the standards of protection instead.[50] Dummett opines that renegotiation might be dangerous as many states already think that the present terms of the Convention are too generous.[51]

In the 1980s, there were feminist demands in Western refugee receiving states that refugee law should recognize persecution faced by women that was specific to women. It was argued that the most effective way to extend equal protection for women and men would be to add sex or gender to the list of protection grounds.[52] The UNCHR published Guidelines on the Protection of Refugee Women in 1991, following the general framework outlined in the UNHCR Policy on Refugee Women, adopted by the forty-first session of the Executive Committee.[53] The underlying principle of the policy was "to integrate the resources and needs of refugee women into all aspects of programming to ensure equitable protection and assistance activities." It was recognized that problems faced specifically by women would require special efforts to resolve.[54]

ExCom General Conclusion on International Protection No. 81 (XLVIII) – 1997, para (t); ExCom General Conclusion on International Protection No. 87 (L) – 1999, para (n).

[46] Heaven Crawley, *Gender, Persecution and the Concept of Politics in the Asylum Determination Process*, Forced Migration Rev. 19 (2000).

[47] Deborah E. Anker, *Refugee Law, Gender, and the Human Rights Paradigm*, 15 Harv. HR. J. 139 (2002).

[48] Jacqueline Greatbatch, *The Gender Difference: Feminist Critiques of Refugee Discourse*, 1 IJRL 520 (1989).

[49] Luara Ferracioli, *The Appeal and Danger of a New Refugee Convention*, 40(1) Social Theory and Practice 126 (2014).

[50] Joan Fitzpatrick, *Revitalizing the 1951 Refugee Convention*, 9 Harv. HR. J. 234 (1996).

[51] Michael Dummett, On Immigration and Refugees 37 (Routledge 2001).

[52] Efrat Arbel et al., *Introduction: Gender in Refugee Law: From the Margins to the Centre* in Efrat Arbel et al. (eds.) Gender in Refugee Law: From the Margins to the Centre 6 (Routledge 2014).

[53] UNHCR, *Guidelines on the Protection of Refugee Women* (July 1991), https://www.unhcr.org/media/guidelines-protection-refugee-women.

[54] *Id.*

In the same year, the Second Circuit Court of the U.S. in *Gomez v. INS*,[55] upheld the rejection of political asylum by the BIA to a Salvadoran woman who sought asylum as a member of the PSG of women who had been previously battered or raped by Salvadoran guerrilla forces. Ms. Gomez had been subjected to this treatment by guerrilla members on several occasions while she was between the ages of twelve and fourteen. Every time, she was either beaten or raped, and her life was threatened. She finally managed to leave El Salvador at the age of eighteen. In her asylum claim, she argued that, by virtue of her prior attacks, she should be considered a member of the particular social group of women who had been previously battered and raped by Salvadoran guerrillas. The BIA rejected her plea, finding that she had failed to demonstrate that the guerrillas would seek to harm her based on her association with a particular social group or any other nexus ground in the refugee definition. The Second Circuit Court upheld the BIA's decision, finding that she had failed to offer evidence that the group for which she sought recognition possessed any common characteristics other than gender and youth that would identify them as a group in the eyes of the persecutor, and that there was no proof available on the record that the applicant would be subjected to further brutalization based on her membership in the purported group.[56]

In 2002, UNHCR published the guidelines for gender-related persecution,[57] so that the refugee definition could have gender-sensitive information, but still, evidence suggests that the guidelines have not been followed by the States in a consistent manner.[58]

Nancy Kelly argues that even though the definition of a Convention refugee is gender-neutral, women are much less likely to succeed in their claim due to the absence of gender as a specific protection ground in the definition.[59] Women asylum seekers are compelled to fit their claim into the MPSG category, and due to the non-existence of a universal definition, courts routinely set varying standards, resulting in the dichotomy.[60] Moreover, courts have time and again applied the social visibility approach in addition to or in lieu of the immutable characteristic approach,[61] which is very difficult to prove for victims of human trafficking or domestic violence due to

---

[55] 947 F.2d 660 (2d Cir. 1991).

[56] *Id.*

[57] UNHCR, *Guidelines on Gender-Related Persecution within the context of Article 1A(2) of the 1951 Convention and/or its 1967 Protocol relating to the Status of Refugees*, UN Doc. HCR/GIP/02/01.

[58] Heaven Crawley and Trine Lester, Comparative Analysis of Gender- Related Persecution in National Asylum Legislation and Practice in Europe (EPAU/2004/05). *See also* Valerie L. Oosterveld, *The Canadian Guidelines on Gender-Related Persecution: An Evaluation*, 8 IJRL 569, 582–583 (1996).

[59] Nancy Kelly, *Gender-Related Persecution: Assessing the Asylum Claims of Women*, 26(3) Cornell Int'l L. J. 626–627 (1993).

[60] Valerie Plant, *Honor Killings and the Asylum Gender Gap*, 15 J. Transnat'l L. & Pol'y 120 (2005) cited in Joanna J. Kallinosis, *Refugee Roulette: A Comparative Analysis of Gender-Related Persecution in Asylum Law* 6 Depaul J. Women Gender & L. 59 (2017).

[61] *E.g.*, Benitez Ramos v. Holder, 589 F.3d 426, 430 (7th Cir. 2009).

the stigma, and therefore, the asylum claims of such female victims inevitably fail.[62] Ramji-Nogales et al. argue that the fate of an asylum claim may depend on the fact that a court or official presides over the matter, as much as it may depend on the facts and law applicable to the case.[63]

(b) ***Sexual Orientation and Gender Identity as Grounds of Protection***

Sexual orientation connotes the "emotional, affectional, and sexual attraction to individuals of a different gender, the same gender, or more than one gender."[64] Sexual orientation categories have typically included attraction to members of one's own sex (gay men or lesbians), attraction to members of the opposite sex (heterosexuals), and attraction to members of both sexes (bisexuals). Some people may identify as pansexual or queer in terms of their sexual orientation, which means they define their sexual orientation outside the male and female binaries.[65]

Gender identity, on the other hand, "consists of the meanings ascribed to male and female social categories within a culture."[66] When these cultural meanings are imbibed by people into their own psyches, then gender takes on a role in their identities. By way of these gender identities, individuals comprehend themselves *vis-à-vis* culturally feminine and masculine meanings, and they may conduct themselves according to these gendered notions of male or female.[67] Some individuals may identify with a non-binary gender or even no gender at all.[68] A person's gender identity can be the same or different from the sex that they were assigned at birth.[69]

---

[62] Kallinosis, *supra* note 60, at 79.

[63] Jaya Ramji-Nogales et al., *Refugee Roulette: Disparities in Asylum Adjudication*, 60 Stan. L. Rev. 295–296 (2007). Their study revealed that "Columbian asylum applicants whose cases were adjudicated in the federal immigration court in Miami had a 5% chance of prevailing with one of that court's judges and an 88% chance of prevailing before another judge in the same building." Similarly, "a Chinese asylum seeker unlucky enough to have her case heard before the Atlanta Immigration Court had a 7% chance of success on her claim, as compared to 47% nationwide." *See also* the decision in the case of Lazo-Majano v. INS, 813 F.2d 1432 (9th Cir. 1987) where the Immigration Court as well as the BIA rejected the asylum claim on the basis of gender-related persecution filed by a Salvadoran woman who was sexually abused by an army officer for whom she performed domestic work. He even accused her of subversive activities in front of the police in order to keep her in a state of constant threat. The Circuit Court reversed the decision, on the same facts, and granted her political asylum.

[64] The Yogyakarta Principles on the Application of International Human Rights Law in relation to Sexual Orientation and Gender Identity (March 2007), https://data.unaids.org/pub/manual/2007/070517_yogyakarta_principles_en.pdf.

[65] Definitions Related to Sexual Orientation and Gender Diversity in APA Documents, (Aug. 9, 2023, 12:05 PM), https://www.apa.org/pi/lgbt/resources/sexuality-definitions.pdf.

[66] Wendy Wood & Alice H. Eagly, *Two Traditions of Research on Gender Identity*, Sex Roles 461 (2015).

[67] *Id.*

[68] Sexual orientation and gender identity (Aug. 9, 2023, 1:15 PM), https://ijrcenter.org/thematic-research-guides/sexual-orientation-gender-identity/#Defining_Sexual_Orientation_Gender_Identity.

[69] Sexual orientation and gender identity definitions (Aug. 9, 2023, 1:45 PM), https://www.hrc.org/resources/sexual-orientation-and-gender-identity-terminology-and-definitions.

Human rights of sexual minorities[70] around the world continue to be brazenly violated. Severe criminal penalties, including capital punishment, are imposed by many countries on consensual sex between persons of the same sex.[71] Additionally, sexual minorities are frequent targets of hate crimes, their freedoms of expression and association are curbed, and overall, any non-conformity with established sexual and gender norms of society is simply considered unacceptable.[72]

These human rights violations of sexual minorities by the active participation of the state or the inability or unwillingness of the state to protect them compel them to seek refuge in countries with better human rights protection. This migration has led the international community to interpret refugee protection norms, which do not explicitly mention sexual orientation or gender identity, to provide asylum to those fleeing persecution based on these grounds under the MPSG category.[73]

Sexual orientation and gender identity have long been two grounds under the main MPSG ground that have met the same fickle fate as gender, which has been discussed above. In the past, many states as diverse as Ireland,[74] United States,[75] Canada,[76] New Zealand,[77] United Kingdom,[78] Germany,[79] Belgium,[80] and South Africa[81] have granted refugee status to those fearing persecution based on sexual orientation or gender identity, some by way of codification in their domestic legislation and others by way of case law. Most of these jurisdictions follow the *ejusdem generis* approach and have found that sexual orientation and gender identity are protected and/or immutable characteristics.[82] Additionally, the decision-makers in

---

[70] The term sexual minority used here refers to the members of LGBTQ community and covers gender identity as well.

[71] See Lucas Paoli Itaborahy, State sponsored Homophobia - A world survey of laws criminalising same-sex sexual acts between consenting adults, The International Lesbian, Gay, Bisexual, Trans and Intersex Association (IGLA 2012) (Aug. 9, 2023), https://www.refworld.org/docid/50ae380e2.html.

[72] Nicole LaViolette, *UNHCR Guidance Note on Refugee Claims Relating to Sexual Orientation and Gender Identity: A Critical Commentary* 22 IJRL 173–174 (2010).

[73] *Id.*

[74] Section 1, Refugee Act, 1996 (Ireland).

[75] Karouni v. Gonzales, 399 F. 3d 1163 (9th Cir., 2005); Boer-Sedano v. Gonzales, (2005) 418 F.3d 1082 (USCA, 9th Cir., Aug. 12, 2005).

[76] Okoli v. Canada (Minister of Citizenship and Immigration), [2009] FC 332.

[77] *Re* GJ, [1998] INLR 387; Refugee Appeal No 74665/03 (7 July 2004).

[78] HJ and HT, [2010] 3 WLR 386, 394; SB (Uganda) v. Secretary of State for the Home Department, [2010] EWHC 338 (24 February 2010).

[79] 4K 772/10.A (Ger. VG Frankfurt (Oder) [German Administrative Court, Frankfurt an der Oder], Nov. 11, 2010); 13 A 1013/09.A (Ger. OVG Nordrhein-Westfalen [German Higher Administrative Court, North Rhine-Westphalia], Nov. 23, 2010).

[80] CCE No 35, 247 (Dec. 2, 2009), CCE No 36, 527 (Dec. 22, 2009) and CCE No 37, 316 (Jan. 21, 2010).

[81] Section 1 (xxi), Refugees Act 1998 (South Africa).

[82] Foster, *supra* note 3, at 49.

the case of sexual minorities (in contrast with gender) have not shown any inclination to further narrow the ground or import other elements of the definition.[83]

In one of the earlier cases, *Sanchez-Trujillo v. Immigration and Naturalization Service*,[84] the court observed that an associational and cohesive test was required for PSG, since the terms 'particular' and 'social' imply that the PSG "cannot encompass every broadly defined segment of the population." However, this view was expressly rejected by senior courts in other jurisdictions, most notably, in *Applicant A*[85] and *Islam and Shah*.[86] Lord Steyn in *Islam and Shah* used the example of gay people in order to reject the cohesiveness standard:

> In some countries, homosexuals are subjected to severe punishments, including the death sentence. In *Re G.J.*,the New Zealand Refugee Status Authority faced this question [and] concluded in an impressive judgment that depending on the evidence, homosexuals are capable of constituting a particular social group with the meaning of Art. 1(A)2 Subject to the qualification that everything depends on evidence in regard to the position of homosexuals in a particular country, I would in principle accept the reasoning in *Re G.J.* as correct. But homosexuals are, of course, not a cohesive group. This is a telling point against the restrictive view in *Sanchez-Trujillo's* case.

This means that sexual minorities do not have to know each other or even associate with each other to fall into the PSG category.[87] In fact, the US Court of Appeals in *Karouni v. Gonzales*[88] declared that "to the extent that our case-law has been unclear, we affirm that all *alien* homosexuals are members of a 'particular social group.'" Despite this, interpretational ambiguity across jurisdictions still persists, as will be seen in the following paragraphs.

It has been observed that in jurisdictions that have followed the *ejusdem generis* approach, claims of sexual minorities have succeeded, and where the social perception/social visibility approach has been followed, asylum claims have failed. Since sexual orientation and gender identity are phenomena that manifest in a person's behavior and are not as immediately visible as a person's race.[89] It has led some decision-makers to reject the asylum claims where, in their opinion, the sexual minority person could avoid persecution by concealing their sexuality or gender identity, i.e., the requirement of being 'discreet.' It has even been considered by courts and tribunals in some jurisdictions that since, unlike political opinion or religion, sexual orientation and gender identity can be concealed, it is the *duty* of the person concerned to be discreet in order to avoid persecution.[90] This is an inexplicable notion given that religion as well as political opinion can very well be concealed

---

[83] *Id.*

[84] 801 F.2d 1571 (United States Court of Appeals 9th Cir., 1986).

[85] [1997] HCA 4.

[86] Session 1998–1999, United Kingdom: House of Lords (Judicial Committee) [1999].

[87] Janna Wessels, Sexual Orientation in Refugee Status Determination, Working Paper Series No. 73, (Refugee Studies Center, University of Oxford 2011).

[88] 399 F. 3d 1163 (9th Cir., 2005).

[89] HJ (Iran) v. Secretary of State for the Home Department, [2010] UKSC 31.

[90] Catherine Dauvergne & Jenni Millbank, *Burdened by Proof: How the Australian Refugee Review Tribunal Has Failed Lesbian and Gay Asylum Seekers*, 31 Fed. L. Rev. 299 (2003).

to avert persecution and are well-known to be done so by many in various intolerant regimes. Some senior courts, on the other hand, have held that this approach is flawed and that expecting the sexual minority to repress an immutable characteristic would be to deny their fundamental right to be who they are.[91]

France has been a peculiar case in what one might call the 'requirement of openness,' i.e., the reversal of discretion. French courts have required sexual minority asylum seekers to have openly expressed their sexuality, and there must be a law prohibiting that conduct in their home country. In other words, unless the behavior of the claimant has been considered by society to have transgressed the social order, their asylum request is liable to be denied.[92] Expecting a sexual minority in a homophobic or conservative society that has outlawed any sexual behavior that is deemed violative of their social and cultural mores to openly express their sexuality is a very bizarre requirement. After all, it would be reasonable to assume that a homosexual, for example, would try to pass off as heterosexual in such a society to avoid persecution.[93]

It has been observed that decision-makers in Germany have accepted the requirement of the social perception test by a simple demonstration that homosexuals have been considered different in a country by the majority society, and therefore, they could be considered a group with a distinct identity.[94] However, an inconsistency was observed when the application of a bisexual person from Iran was rejected as homosexuality; there was not "identity defining enough."[95]

An odd condition imposed by the EU Qualification Directive sought to delimit the scope of interpretation and consequent consideration of grant of asylum by the decision-makers by stating that "[s]exual orientation cannot be understood to include acts considered to be criminal in accordance with national law of the Member States."[96] This is a lamentable point of divergence for law and human rights and has added to the lack of clarity in asylum decisions within the EU. In 2016, the EU Commission proposed a regulation on the standards for qualification, and an amendment was proposed wherein under this article it was stated that "determining authority cannot reasonably expect an applicant to behave discreetly or abstain from

---

[91] *See* HJ (Iran) v. Secretary of State for the Home Department, [2010] UKSC 31; Appellant S395/ 2002 v. Minister for Immigration & Multicultural Affairs (S395), (2003) 216 CLR 473 (Austl.); Karouni v. Gonzales, 399 F. 3d 1163 (9th Cir., 2005) (U.S.).

[92] Conseil d'Etat, 10/7 SSR, du 23 juin 1997, 171858, publié au recueil Lebon (Nov. 11, 2022, 11:15 AM) https://www.legifrance.gouv.fr/ceta/id/CETATEXT000007972727/.

[93] *See* the opinion of Posner J. in *Gatimi* v. *Holder* 578 F. 3d 611, 615 (7th Cir., 2009) (U.S.).

[94] Verwaltungsgericht (VG) Frankfurt (Oder) [Frankfurt (Oder) Administrative Court], VG4K 772/ 10.A, 11 Nov. 11, 2010), Adrienne Anderson (trans.) cited in Foster, *supra* note 3, at 53.

[95] Verwaltungsgericht (VG) Ansbach [Ansbach Administrative Court], AN 18K 08.30201, (Aug. 28, 2008), Adrienne Anderson (trans.) cited in Foster, *supra* note 3, at 53.

[96] Article 10(1)(d), The EU Qualification Directive (2011).

certain practices, where such behavior or practices are inherent to his or her identity, to avoid the risk of persecution in his or her country of origin."[97] Though this proposed regulation had not been adopted at the time of writing this paper, it is still a step in the direction of upholding the human rights of sexual minorities. It does not remedy the criminal law delimitation but does demystify the requirement, or lack thereof, of expecting discretion from sexual minorities in order to avoid persecution.

In 2012, the UNHCR issued Guidelines on International Protection for claims relating to sexual orientation and/or gender identity. It notes that:

> Discrimination is a common element in the experiences of many LGBTI individuals. As in other refugee claims, discrimination will amount to persecution where measures of discrimination, individually or cumulatively, lead to consequences of a substantially prejudicial nature for the person concerned. Assessing whether the cumulative effect of such discrimination rises to the level of persecution is to be made with reference to reliable, relevant, and up-to-date country of origin information.[98]

Additionally, the UNHCR Guidelines also state that "even if irregularly, rarely, or ever enforced, criminal laws prohibiting same-sex relations could lead to an intolerable predicament for an LGB person rising to the level of persecution."[99] This suggestion by the UNHCR addresses the criminal law limitation introduced by the EU Qualification Directive discussed above and acknowledges that such criminal laws may lead to a sexual minority's persecution. UNHCR also adds that in countries where homosexual conduct is neither criminalized nor is there any enforcement of such laws, other laws, such as those relating to public morality, may tangentially suppress a sexual minority's choice in a discriminatory manner, making life intolerable for them and therefore amounting to persecution.[100] In the case of *AT (Zimbabwe)*,[101] the Immigration and Protection Tribunal of New Zealand noted that even though Zimbabwe's criminal laws did not penalize homosexual relations between women, they did criminalize the same between men. As a result, the general atmosphere of the country considered homosexual relations, be they between men or women, as condemnable and full of social stigma. The police, too, conducted widespread arrests and detentions of not just homosexual males but also other LGBTI persons. It was apparent to the Tribunal that if the applicant were to be returned to Zimbabwe, she would face persecution due to her gender identity. The Tribunal followed the protected characteristics approach and considered the applicant's bisexuality as a protection Convention ground for refugee status.[102]

---

[97] European Commission, Doc. COM (2016) 466 (final) (Aug. 13, 2023, 10:24 AM), https://www.europarl.europa.eu/RegData/docs_autres_institutions/commission_europeenne/com/2016/0466/COM_COM(2016)0466_EN.pdf.

[98] UNHCR, *Guidelines on International Protection No. 9, Claims to Refugee Status based on Sexual Orientation and/or Gender Identity within the context of article 1A(2) of the 1951 Convention and/or its 1967 Protocol relating to the Status of Refugees* (2012), para. 17, UN Doc. HCR/GIP/12/09.

[99] *Id.* at para 27.

[100] *Id.* at para 29.

[101] [2015] NZIPT 800,798.

[102] *Id. see* paras 61–62, 71–72 and 74.

On the other hand, asylum was denied to a man who sought it on the ground that he would be persecuted in Pakistan as he was a bisexual Christian. The decision-makers ruled that he was bisexual only due to his circumstances, i.e., locked up with other men.[103] Similarly, in 2019, an asylum claim by a man from a country where homosexuality was illegal was rejected by a UK immigration judge on the grounds that the "demeanor" of the applicant was gay. A witness present in the courtroom who wore lipstick and had an "effeminate" manner was considered gay by the judge.[104] It has also been reported that LGBTQ people are being denied asylum in UK, and the authorities are demanding excessive proof of their sexual orientation and gender identity, are being disbelieved as a matter of routine, and face humiliating questioning due to flawed assumptions about the concepts of sexual orientation and gender identity.[105]

2 Conclusion

Other sub-categories under the broader MPSG ground that have been used to file asylum claims include family/kinship ties, age, disability, prior occupation, economic and social class, etc. Analysis of these sub-grounds has been deemed out of the scope of the present discussion, as it was identified during the research that these claims have faced rejection mainly due to the social visibility test in certain jurisdictions, mainly the US and Australia. As such, the need for an independent ground was felt to be desirable, specifically for gender, sexual orientation, and sexual identity. It can be safely said that decisions based on the *ejusdem generis* approach have resulted in more principled and consistent decisions. Such decisions are rooted in human rights and the principle of non-discrimination. The social-visibility approach has done nothing but confuse the decision-makers on issues that would otherwise have been quite straightforward and unnecessarily complicate the MPSG jurisprudence. Recommending abandonment of the social perception test and adherence to the immutable characteristics test will remedy inconsistencies across most jurisdictions. 'Gender' and 'sexual orientation and gender identity' are two sub-grounds where the complexities are deeper than meriting a mere change in interpretational approach, hence the recommendation of incorporating independent grounds in the Convention definition.

[103] Erik Jensen, *Bisexuality a result of detention, detainee told* (Aug. 8, 2023) https://www.smh.com.au/national/bisexuality-a-result-of-detention-detainee-told-20070509-gdq3f0.html.

[104] Robert Booth, *Judge rejected asylum seeker who did not have gay 'demeanour'* (Aug. 16, 2022, 9:38 AM), https://www.theguardian.com/uk-news/2019/aug/21/judge-rejected-asylum-seeker-who-did-not-have-gay-demeanour.

[105] Sonia Elks, *LGBT asylum seekers denied refuge in UK due to unfair demands—charity* (Aug. 16, 2022, 9:40 AM), https://www.reuters.com/article/britain-gay-asylum-idUSL8N1U855Q.

Global Class Actions: Forum Shopping Just Ain't What It Used to Be

Mostafa Mahmud Naser and Haydn Rigby

Abstract Class actions, or representative proceedings as they are known in some jurisdictions, have many obvious benefits including resolving cases of similarly situated people equitably, avoiding burdening the judicial system with a multiplicity of actions, and facilitating access to justice and redress to individuals who might not have otherwise had the resources to fund an action themselves. However, global class actions present a unique set of challenges with plaintiffs residing in different jurisdictions to each other or to the defendants, giving rise to such issues as: lack of fairness for one of the litigants arising out of the judicial forum selected; concerns about procedural fairness for absent class members residing in different jurisdictions; and comity or the extent that one nation will recognise the legislative, executive or judicial acts of another nation. In this context, this Chapter will examine the approaches that courts in various jurisdictions have taken to manage these issues: first, the tests for assumption of jurisdiction, or jurisdiction simpliciter, including the 'real and substantial connection test' ('the RSC test') using various recognised presumptive factors such as the defendant's domicile, the location of the defendant's business practices, lex loci delicti (for torts) and lex loci contractus (for contract disputes); and, second, once jurisdiction is assumed by a court, the tests employed by the courts such as forum non conveniens and modified versions of that test, with particular focus on individual connecting factors surrounding the case such as the locations of parties and witnesses, the costs and impact on the proceedings of transferring the case to another court, problems with conflicting judgments or recognition or lack of enforceability of judgments in courts in other jurisdictions, as well as the strength of the parties' connections to the different fora. After reviewing three common law jurisdictions (Australia, Canada and the US) the authors submit that, although courts in different jurisdictions in the emerging global scene have been guided by private international law rules such as presence in the jurisdiction, consent and submission to jurisdiction as determinants of the choice of judicial forum, the case law indicates that there is

M. M. Naser (✉) · H. Rigby
School of Business and Law, Edith Cowan University, Joondalup, WA, Australia
e-mail: m.naser@ecu.edu.au

H. Rigby
e-mail: h.rigby@ecu.edu.au

J. Aston et al. (eds.), *Comparative Law*, https://doi.org/10.1007/978-981-97-7815-7_14

an emerging consensus that the requirements of fairness, justice, order and comity are paramount considerations to be taken into account and may even trump some of these rules where there is a clash between such rules and these considerations. Indeed, these considerations inform the courts' more nuanced approach to determining the forum non conveniens rule and its variants than just a mechanical application of the rules of international law, particularly in the case of class actions where all of the litigants of an action are not necessarily parties and have not consented to the choice of forum. Embracing this trend, the authors endorse this holistic approach particularly the version of the forum non conveniens rule ('the clearly inappropriate forum test') adopted in their home jurisdiction of Australia as a basis for international rules resolving conflict of laws issues in global class actions and conclude with suggestions of some practical measures as to how this test may be adopted in practice.

Keywords Class actions · Globalisation · Jurisdictional challenges · Conflict of laws · Forum shopping

1 Introduction

Superior Courts have always had an inherent jurisdiction to manage their case-loads in such a way that is necessary to properly keep their houses in order. Even inferior courts possess an implied (even if not strictly an inherent) jurisdiction to manage the cases that become before them in order to do justice to the objects of their constituting acts that confer jurisdiction upon them in order to dispose of the business that comes before them in a timely, just and efficient manner. The management of the conduct of litigation is now typically contained in rules and practice directions, but as Bernard Cairns notes, in addition to these, 'the court has an inherent or implied jurisdiction to control its own processes.'[1] The rules and practice directions will never be the full story. This is particularly so for class actions which require special vigilance and nuanced thinking by a court from the point of view of case management in such complex actions, especially where the suit crosses state and national boundaries and jurisdictional issues come into play. In the sphere of private law, mechanisms abound such as choice of forum clauses in agreements by parties that confer exclusive or non-exclusive jurisdiction on a selected judicial forum which may be either symmetrical, giving both parties the option or mandate to use such jurisdiction, or asymmetrical with only one party getting to choose a jurisdiction favourable to them or being mandated to use a particular jurisdiction favourable to the other party.

However, when one bears in mind that a court has inherent or implied jurisdiction to resolve conflict of law issues, then it is clearly the court who ultimately makes the call, private mechanisms notwithstanding. This Chapter discusses how the courts have perhaps more so than ever been mindful of their inherent jurisdiction in recent years and have not been afraid to use it which the authors submit is a positive

[1] Bernard Cairns, *Australian Civil Procedure* (Thomson Reuters, Lawbook Co, 12th ed., 2020), 60.

development and should be reflected in practice when putting in place the private mechanisms to address choice of jurisdiction issues to ensure there is harmony with the courts' inherent and implied jurisdiction rather than a conflict with it.

This chapter commences with a discussion of the nature of class actions and class actions in the global context and their perceived benefits to litigants before turning to particular challenges faced in global class actions such as: concerns regarding order and fairness, procedural fairness for absent class members, and comity, and how such concerns play out depending on whether class action is an opt-in or opt-out class action. The discussion then turns to how courts in the selected jurisdictions (Australia, Canada and the US) have attempted to address some of these concerns and a comparison of their respective approaches. Noting that there does not appear to be a cohesive approach adopted in the various jurisdictions to resolve the issues that beset global class actions, the authors then, after evaluating the different approaches, submit what they believe is the best approach, particularly in relation to conflict of laws with a modified *non conveniens forum* test as adopted in their home jurisdiction of Australia ('the clearly inappropriate forum test'). The authors note that although such a test preferences the courts' inherent and implied jurisdiction to private mechanisms, private mechanisms are nevertheless included in the court's decision matrix in the proper exercise of their inherent and implied jurisdiction but are given their proper weight rather than seen as determinative of the issue.

A. *Overview of Class Actions and Associated Issues*

The underlying objective for development of class action suits is resolving cases involving many similarly situated people equitably.[2] Class action has become a common form of litigation in recent years. The class action at a national level has many complexities, such as identifying potential plaintiffs and the consistencies across their claims, obtaining consistent instructions, procuring plaintiffs' consent, and legal funding issues.

In response to this situation, settlement of class actions (also referred to as representative proceedings or group proceedings) is a common and popular way of resolving disputes where large number of people are involved in a case. There are some inherent benefits in such settlements, namely: (1) it can resolve cases involving similarly situated people equitably, (2) it can avoid multiplicity of suits by reducing the burden on the judicial system, and (3) it facilitates seeking redress by an individual who is not able financially to initiate the suit on their own.

The advent of globalisation raises at least three important scenarios:

(1) There is increased tendency of interaction in the forms of trade and businesses with people living in different jurisdictions;
(2) A larger number of people may face similar situations than in just one nation alone; and
(3) In this situation, the plaintiffs may file a representative suit (a 'global class action').

[2] Diane Wood Hutchinson, 'Class Actions: Joinder or Representational Device?' (1983) 1983 *The Supreme Court Review* 459, 460.

Unsurprisingly, then, there are some additional complexities attending global class actions involving transnational plaintiffs and/or defendants that are not usually present in national class actions brought in a single jurisdiction. For example, (1) plaintiffs and defendants are located in different countries that have very different jurisdictions; (2) choices have to be made about which jurisdiction to commence proceedings in; and (3) various factors such as private treaties or those relating to justice and fairness are considered by a court in deciding whether a class action should end up being heard in the court which proceedings have been issued in, or some court in a different jurisdiction.

To fully appreciate the challenges faced in global class actions, it is necessary to understand the global context in which this litigation takes place and to look at some high-profile global class actions that have issues typical of those that beset class actions.

B. *An Increasingly Global World*

Globalisation promotes connectivity. In the current age of globalisation, the advent of communication technologies and speedy transport facilitates increased interaction between people, businesses and organisations both within and across borders. While it brings benefits, quite often the transactions/activity may cause harm to people and businesses beyond the borders.[3] Injuries, for instance, sometimes occur on a large-scale crossing state and national boundaries triggering cross-border litigation involving multiple parties. Indeed, injury and other harms such as damage to one's private and commercial interests and rights have no respect for jurisdictional boundaries, as the following cases illustrate.

The case of Thorne v. Hudson Estate[4] involved an interesting scenario. In May 2007, two pilots and a passenger were killed in a plane crash which was flying from Oshawa, Ontario, Canada to Wilmington, Delaware, USA. The accident was caused because of power failure in left engine of the twin-engine Beech aircraft. The plane crashed shortly after aborting an attempted emergency landing at an airfield in Dunkirk, New York. The two pilots and the passenger were killed. A suit was initiated by the estates of the deceased against the companies that inspected and maintained the engine—the respondents, 1205055 Ontario Limited c.o.b. Aviation Technical Consultants ('ATC') and Corporate Aircraft Restorations Inc., together with its employee, Maurice Nesbitt (collectively 'CAR'). The deceased's estates also sued the engine's manufacturer, the appellant Continental Motors, Inc. ('CMI', formerly known as Teledyne Continental Motors Inc. and Teledyne Technologies Incorporated). ATC and CAR brought third-party and cross-claims against CMI alleging (i) the design and manufacture of the engine and replacement parts, (ii) instructions for engine repair were misleading, and (iii) there was a failure to warn about engine failures that could arise in certain circumstances. Following the conclusion of inspections following discovery, CMI moved for summary judgment on the

[3] Debra Lyn Bassett, 'U.S. Class Actions Go Global: Transnational Class Actions and Personal Jurisdiction' (2003-04) 72 *Fordham Law Review* 41, 42.

[4] (2017) ONCA 208 (CanLII).

basis that the claims made against it were time-barred by the United States federal *General Aviation Revitalization Act of 1994* ('GARA'), Pub.L. No. 103 298, 108 Stat. 1552 (codified at 49 U.S.C. § 40101 notes). In general terms, GARA bars a civil action for damages against an aircraft manufacturer in respect of deaths arising out of an accident involving an aircraft which is instituted more than 18 years after the date of delivery of the aircraft to its first purchaser. In the present case, there was no factual dispute regarding CMI originally delivering the aircraft in early 1968. CMI argued, however, that since the aircraft crashed in New York State, GARA applied and barred the various claims against it.

The summary judgment application was unsuccessful, the court finding that proceedings were correctly instituted in Ontario which was found to be not an inappropriate forum to hear the case given the main grounds for complaint (defective engine maintenance and repair and negligent misrepresentation in issuing faulty repair instructions) occurred there as opposed to negligent manufacture of the engine (manufactured in Pennsylvania) which was not the crux of the claim.

Das v. George Weston et al.[5] ('*Rana Plaza* case') was a global class action that was instituted following the collapse of the Rana Plaza building in Bangladesh. In this historic mass tort action, the estates of 1136 deceased workers and 2500 plus surviving workers sued Loblaws and Bureau Veritas, the firm retained by Loblaws to audit the Rana Plaza factories that produced Joe Fresh apparel. The Plaintiffs alleged that Loblaws assumed responsibility for the Rana Plaza garment workers to ensure that they worked in safe and legally operated factories. They alleged that Loblaws voluntarily adopted Corporate Social Responsibility standards, which required that its suppliers comply with local safety laws and regulations. They further alleged that Loblaws failed to require—and Bureau Veritas failed to recommend and perform—adequate and reasonable audits that would have detected the serious safety hazards that resulted in the collapse of the Rana Plaza. The class action was filed in Ontario, Canada, the home of Loblaws. The defendants challenged the Canadian Court's jurisdiction over the putative class members who were not present in Canada or who did not submit to the jurisdiction of the Canadian court. The defendants also argued that the substantive law governing the tort would be that of Bangladesh and as a result, Bangladesh's limitation law applied, which, the defendants argued, barred the proposed class action in Canada. The Plaintiffs argued that Ontario's conflict rules provided for the jurisdiction of an Ontario court over the action and that the substantive law of Ontario applied. The court held that Bangladesh law applied, and this was upheld on appeal.[6]

However, by way of contrast, the Ontario Court of Appeal, in *Excalibur Special Opportunities LP v. Schwartz Levitsky Feldman LLP*,[7] reversed two lower court decisions, certifying a securities fraud class action against a Canadian auditor. The majority of the class members, 98%, were non-Canadian. The class action alleged negligence and negligent misrepresentation in an audit report prepared by Schwartz

[5] (2017) ONSC 4129.

[6] [2018] ONCA 1053.

[7] [2016] ONCA 916.

Levitsky Feldman LLP ('SLF'). Excalibur, a Toronto-based fund, was one of 57 'accredited investors' that collectively invested $7.5 million in Southern China Livestock International Inc. ('Southern China'), a Nevada-based company operating hog farms in China. One other investor was a Canadian resident, while 50 were American, and the rest were residents of the Cayman Islands, Samoa, Malaysia, and the United Kingdom. In 2010, SLF prepared a one-page audit report on Southern China's financial statements, which was attached to a private placement memorandum. The crux of the claim was that, given the true state of Southern China's all-cash business, SLF could not have issued a clean audit report in line with generally accepted accounting principles, as it purported to have done.

The initial dismissal of Excalibur's certification motion was attributed to two obstacles: the 'identifiable class' and 'preferable procedure' criteria stipulated by the Ontario Class Proceedings Act. Justice Perell, at first instance, determined that there was no identifiable class due to the lack of a substantial connection to Ontario, as the vast majority of class members were non-Canadian and the transactions were subject to American law. Additionally, he determined that a joinder was a more suitable mechanism to resolve the dispute.

Justice Perell's decision, upheld by the Divisional Court, was overturned by a split Court of Appeal. The majority decision, authored by Justice MacFarland, aligned with Justice Blair's dissent in the Divisional Court and issued an order certifying the class action. The majority emphasised that the elements to consider in the certification of a 'global class', previously set out in *Currie*,[8] are:

(a) whether the Ontario court has jurisdiction *simpliciter* over the defendant;
(b) whether the Ontario court can assume jurisdiction over a non-resident class member, which largely depends on whether Ontario has a real and substantial connection with the subject matter of the action and on principles of order, fairness and comity between courts;
(c) whether it would be reasonable for the non-resident class members to expect that their rights would be determined by what to them would be a foreign court; and
(d) whether the non-resident plaintiffs can be accorded procedural fairness, including adequate notice and a meaningful opportunity to opt-out.

The first two of the above cases illuminate typical problems found in class actions. The case of *Thorne v Hudson Estate* is an example of a common scenario where the damage arising from a tort occurs in a different jurisdiction to the tortious acts themselves. The *Rana Plaza* case illustrates another common scenario where proceedings are commenced in the defendant's home jurisdiction where the defendant is situated but the class members and act complained are situated in another jurisdiction. *Excalibur* is different in the sense that it is not a case that reflects a common class action type scenario and the Court of Appeal, unable to reach for easy solutions to resolve the jurisdictional issues such as applying the *lex delicti* rule (ie jurisdiction follows

[8] *Currie v. McDonald's Restaurants of Canada Ltd.*, (2005) CanLII 3360 (ON CA). ('*Currie*').

where the wrong occurred), took a more nuanced approach to resolve the jurisdiction issue than the courts below them who seemed to place undue emphasis on the small number of investors situated in the jurisdiction selected, effectively reducing the question of jurisdiction to a numbers game which was clearly inappropriate in this case. The authors note this more nuanced multi-factorial approach reflects the current judicial trend in resolving conflict of law issues as will be seen in many of the other cases discussed in the rest of this Chapter.

C. *Class Actions in Selected Jurisdictions*

The selected jurisdictions that form the basis of the authors' present enquiry for the purpose of this Chapter are Australia (the authors' home jurisdiction), Canada, and the US. Although evident in all of these jurisdictions is a multi-factorial approach adopted by the judiciary in resolving conflict of law issues in global class actions, these various approaches as will be seen are far from uniform and can lead to inconsistencies and unpredictability of outcomes.

1. *Class action trends in Australia*

Australia's class action regime started its journey in March 1992 with the introduction of Federal Court grouped proceedings legislation (See Pt IVA *Federal Court of Australia Act* 1976 *(Cth)* ('Federal Court Act') which first introduced a statutory class action regime. Since then, it has become a significant feature of the Australian litigation landscape.[9] Initially, there was a low level of uptake by litigants. Bernard Murphy and Camille Cameron have suggested that this was 'the product of unfamiliarity with the nature, purpose and potential of the new type of action'.[10] However, these authors note that this has 'gradually given way to increased use'.[11] However, they also opine that '[n]otwithstanding this evolution, class action litigation in Australia is still young and the case law is still developing'.[12] Although, regarding class action in Australia, Murphy and Cameron observe some developments have been positive, they note 'significant obstacles remain for class action applicants'.[13]

As will be seen in the discussion below, the Australian courts have developed a conservative approach in resolving choice of forum issues based on removing a court from a clearly inappropriate forum where proceedings have been issued there but letting the matter remain in the issuing court if it is an appropriate forum rather than engaging in a far more radical course of engaging in potentially a more extensive enquiry of what is the most appropriate jurisdiction which are arguably the implications of the 'more appropriate forum' test adopted in the UK referred to

---

[9] Herbert Smith Freehills, *From little things, big things grow—Herbert Smith Freehills launches 25 years of class actions in Australia,* (Herbert Smith Freehills) https://www.herbertsmithfreehills.com/news/from-little-things-big-things-grow-%E2%80%93-herbert-smith-freehills-launches-25-years-of-class-actions.

[10] Bernard Murphy and Camille Cameron, 'Access to Justice and the Evolution of Class Action Litigation in Australia' (2006) 30 *Melbourne University Law Review,* 399, 400.

[11] Ibid.

[12] Ibid.

[13] Ibid.

below. There are similarities with Canada's real and substantial connecting factors test (the 'RSC test') when Australian courts consider factors to determine whether the relevant court is an inappropriate jurisdiction or not, but these are certainly not elevated to a constitutional imperative as we shall see is the case in Canada with its RSC test.

2. *Class Action Trends in Canada*

Canada has witnessed a dramatic increase in the number of class actions. High-profile class actions have been commenced for damages attributable to tainted blood, faulty pacemakers, defective breast implants, aboriginal residential schools, price-fixing, prospectus misrepresentation, e-coli in the water, unlawful rates of interest charged by utility companies and banks, improper bank charges and the list goes on.[14] The prospect for inter-jurisdictional conflict in class actions involving claims that spread across provincial or territorial borders is therefore a significant one in Canada.

As will be discussed, the Canadian experience shares a number of similarities with the Australian one. The main feature of the Canadian approach is the RSC test as noted above features of which we find in the Australian approach in determining the inappropriateness of a particular forum but not quite as well defined a test as in Canada and certainly not seen as something going to the structure of the federation and a constitutional imperative as it is in that country.

3. *Class Action Trends in the US*

The US is briefly discussed in this Chapter as a model similar in many respects to the Canadian and Australian jurisdictions where notions of fairness and justice are prioritised over private mechanisms in deference to the courts' inherent and implied jurisdiction. For all that, however, there lingers a preference to adopt a mechanical application of a rule developed in their jurisprudence known as the 'at home rule', which arguably to a significant extent arbitrarily fetters the exercise of the court's discretion in its inherent and implied jurisdiction, as is discussed below.

D. *Increasing Popularity of Class Actions as a Tool to Promote Access to Justice, Judicial Economy and Behaviour Modification*

Ensuring access to justice is unquestionably a fundamental objective of class action laws.[15] In the past two decades, the world has witnessed a dramatic increase in the number of jurisdictions providing framework for class proceedings. More than 35 jurisdictions, along with Australia, Canada, and the United States, allow class actions for various legal claims, encompassing 21 of the world's 25 largest economies.[16] The number of class actions or 'representative actions' initiated each year in countries like

---

[14] The Canadian Bar Association, *Class Action Database* https://www.cba.org/Publications-Resources/Class-Action-Database.

[15] Murphy and Cameron (n 10) 439.

[16] Deborah R. Hensler, 'From Sea to Shining Sea: How and Why Class Actions Are Spreading Globally' (2017) 65 *Kansas Law Review* 965, 966.

Canada, China, Germany, Israel, the Netherlands, and Japan is evidently increasing.[17] As noted above, Canada has witnessed a dramatic increase in the number of class actions in a wide range of areas, significantly increasing access to justice.

In Australia, the policy and purposes underlying Part IVA of the *Federal Court Act* were identified in the second reading speech for the Bill which confirms that improving access to justice is a fundamental goal of the class action system.[18] It provides a mechanism for individual citizens to seek legal recourse through the courts for civil wrongs committed by powerful entities such as governments and corporations, often beyond the means of an individual claimant.[19] Additionally, the judiciary has acknowledged that class action procedures facilitate the pursuit of legitimate claims stemming from widespread injustices that would likely remain unaddressed if individuals were solely responsible for seeking redress.[20]

The Law Reform Commission has acknowledged the role of class actions in increasing access to justice:

> Enabling people to have increased access to legal remedies in court proceedings could render the substantive law more enforceable and thus encourage a greater degree of compliance with laws the purpose of which is to prevent or discourage activities which cause loss or injury to others. This is an important consequence of any change in procedural remedies. Respect for the law should be enhanced if access to remedies is facilitated.[21]

As will be discussed, the initial uptake of class action litigation was originally quite modest in Australia but has increased over time with such initiatives as litigation funding.

In the US, as mentioned above, adherence to a particular rule mentioned, the 'at home' rule, has constrained plaintiff's choice of forum in initiating class actions, although in a country with an already high rate of class action litigation, it is difficult to assess how this might have reduced class action litigation in that country, if at all. The 'at home' rule is discussed in more detail below.

2 Global Class Actions Pose a Unique Set of Problems

The transnational class action faces a number of challenges. Most prominent among them is the complexity in respect to jurisdictional issues. Since multiple fora are available to the parties there is the possibility of parallel litigation involving the

---

[17] Jay P Lefkowitz, *Securities Class Action: American Phenomenon Goes Global* (Law360, 2016) https://www.law360.com/articles/793211/securities-class-actions-american-phenomenon-goes-global.

[18] Murphy and Cameron (n 10) 402.

[19] Ibid.

[20] Ibid., 403.

[21] Law Reform Commission, *Grouped Proceedings in the Federal Court*, Report No 46 (1988) 404.

same dispute in two or more countries.[22] Even if it is the suit is pending in only one court, any of the litigants or the court itself may consider that the court does not have authority to provide an optimal or adequate remedy.[23] Often it is delayed because of lengthy arguments challenging jurisdiction. Since two or more jurisdictions are involved, it is not unlikely that there is an overlap or gap between the jurisdictions of multiple countries.[24]

To cater for these problems, a diverse range of rules and approaches have been developed, including the doctrines of *forum non conveniens, lis alibi pendens*, and anti-suit injunctions.[25] In addition, *ex ante*, parties to a transaction may also opt to include a forum selection clause.[26]

A. *Concerns Regarding Order and Fairness*

The concerns of order and fairness are critical in determining jurisdiction. The Canadian case of *Excalibur Special Opportunities LP v. Schwartz Levitsky Feldman LLP*[27] considered the significance of these factors in jurisdiction analysis. In that case, as mentioned above, an investor sought to certify a class action in Ontario against a defendant accounting firm for negligence and negligent misrepresentation in an audit report. The defendants argued that a global class should not be certified due to the small number of investors from Canada.

The Court of Appeal took a more holistic approach to find that the issue of the small number of investors was not determinative of jurisdiction, but rather looked to a range of factors including those considered in the *Currie* decision referred to above ('the Currie factors').[28]

B. *Concerns About Procedural Fairness for Absent Class Members*

The class action litigation is usually resolved through settlement. Since class action is initiated by a representative party on behalf of a group of usually large number of

---

[22] See, Wendy Collins Perdue, *Procedure and Private International Law*, (Edward Elgar Publishing, 2017).

[23] Ibid.

[24] Australian Law Reform Commission (ALRC), *International Litigation* (Legal Rights in International Transactions, ALRC Report 80) < http://www.alrc.gov.au/publications/alrc-80-legal-risk-international-transactions/6-international-litigation >

[25] See Perdue (n 22).

[26] Ibid.

[27] *Excalibur Special Opportunities LP v. Schwartz Levitsky Feldman LLP*, [2014] ONSC 4118. (*'Excalibur')*.

[28] Ibid at paras [107] and [111] affirmed in [2015] ONSC 1634 (Div. Ct.), reversed, [2016] ONCA 916 *('Excalibur Appeal Judgment")*.

For ease of reference these are repeated here and include: (a) whether the Ontario court has jurisdiction *simpliciter* over the defendant; (b) whether the Ontario court can assume jurisdiction over a non-resident Class Member, which assumption of jurisdiction largely depends upon whether Ontario has a real and substantial connection with the subject matter of the jurisdiction and on principles of order and fairness and comity between courts; (c) whether it would be reasonable for the non-resident Class Member to expect that his or her rights would be determined by what to him or her would be a foreign court; and (d) whether the non-resident plaintiff can be accorded procedural fairness including adequate notice and a meaningful opportunity to opt-out.

group members having similar situations. There is a concern that the group members may be included in the proceedings without their consent withstanding the fact that there is provision for opt-out notice to ensure procedural fairness. A most concerning matter is that while settlement is in the interest of the group members which are likely to be affected by the outcome of the proceedings, they have very little participation in the court proceedings. The proceedings are mostly guided by the lawyers often in consultation with the litigation funders who will receive a potential monetary reward depending upon the outcome of the proceedings. Therefore, the settlement reached by the lawyers has to be endorsed by the court upon hearing the parties in regards to its fairness and reasonableness.[29]

In *Currie v. McDonald's Restaurants of Canada Ltd.*, the class members who were residents in Ontario had done nothing to invoke or submit to the class action litigation pending in the Illinois court.

However, Sharpe J.A. recognised that 'unnamed, non-resident class plaintiffs' were in a unique position, having not directly invoked the court's jurisdiction by bringing suit in Illinois and yet still being bound by the Illinois judgment, and his Lordship also argued that it would be justified to attach jurisdictional consequences to an unnamed plaintiff's failure to opt-out provided non-resident class members are accorded procedural fairness including adequate notice.[30] However, Sharpe J.A. ultimately concluded that the notice regime for Ontario residents in that case had been inadequate to provide the procedural fairness necessary to bind Ontario residents to an Illinois judgment.

A similar argument to that advanced by the defendants in *Currie* was rejected by Strathy J. (as he then was) in *Ramdath v. George Brown College of Applied Arts & Technology ('Ramdath').*[31] In that case, former students sued George Brown College for alleged misrepresentations it made regarding a college certificate. As many as 78 of the total 119 students were international students from 10 different countries. The defendant tendered foreign law evidence that a Canadian class action judgment would not likely be given preclusive effect in India and would certainly not be given preclusive effect in China. The defendants argued that order and fairness required the Ontario court to decline jurisdiction.[32]

Strathy J. considered *Currie* and *Morguard*[33] (among other cases) and concluded:

> I do not accept the proposition that procedural fairness in this case requires satisfying myself beyond any doubt that each member of the Class will receive actual notice of the action and of his or her right to opt-out. This is \not a requisite of a purely provincial or interprovincial class action and it could make effective international class actions a practical impossibility. Nor do I accept the proposition that the court should not exercise jurisdiction over non-resident class members where there is evidence that a particular foreign jurisdiction might

---

[29] Michael Legg, 'Class action Settlements in Australia—The Need for Greater Scrutiny' (2014) 38 *Melbourne University Law Review*, 590, 591.

[30] *Currie* (n8) [30].

[31] *Ramdath v. George Brown College of Applied Arts & Technology* [2010] ONSC 2019. (*'Ramdath'*).

[32] *Ramdath* (n 31) [52]-[61].

[33] *Morguard* Investments Ltd v De Savoye (1990) 3 SCR 1077. (*'Morguard'*).

not recognize a class action judgment either altogether (as is said to be the case in China) or in the absence of actual notice (as is said to be the case in India). The hypothetical failure of another state to observe the generally accepted principles of private international law in connection with the assumption of jurisdiction and the recognition of foreign judgments should not preclude an Ontario court from taking jurisdiction in a class action involving its residents, provided the conditions set out in Currie are met.[34]

C. *Comity*

In *Morguard*, La Forest J. has summarised the principle of comity:

For my part, I much prefer the more complete formulation of the idea of comity adopted by the Supreme Court of the United States in *Hilton v. Guyot*, 159 U.S. 113 [...] as follows:

> 'Comity' in the legal sense, is neither a matter of absolute obligation, on the one hand, nor of mere courtesy and good will, upon the other. But it is the recognition which one nation allows within its territory to the legislative, executive or judicial acts of another nation, having due regard both to international duty and convenience, and to the rights of its own citizens or of other persons who are under the protection of its laws...[35]

According to this line of authority, comity does not necessitate that Ontario courts abstain from asserting jurisdiction over cases that have a real and substantial connection, simply due to the potential non-enforcement of its judgments by a foreign court. Such a course of action would constitute a relinquishment of the Ontario court's responsibility to protect the rights of its citizens and others under its legal protection.

In *Van Breda*[36] and *Tolofson v. Jensen*,[37] the Supreme Court of Canada explicitly warned against employing principles foundational to a conflict of laws, such as fairness, efficiency, or comity, as connecting factors. While these principles contribute to the context of the test, they are not the test itself and cannot be used to entirely discard the RSC test.[38]

D. *These Concerns are Varied Depending on whether the Class Action is an Opt-in or an Opt-out Class Action*

The Court of Appeal of British Columbia in *Harrington* has recognised that non-residents can indicate their involvement through an opt-in process that they '...accept the jurisdiction of the court such that they would be precluded by the doctrine of *res judicata* from later suing or benefitting from a suit brought in another jurisdiction'.[39]

---

[34] Ramdath (n 31) [72].
Three conditions relevant here set out in Currie are: (a) there is a real and substantial connection linking the cause of action to the foreign jurisdiction, (b) the rights of non-resident class members are adequately represented, and (c) non-resident class members are accorded procedural fairness including adequate notice, it may be appropriate to attach jurisdictional consequences to an unnamed plaintiff s failure to opt-out.

[35] Morguard (n 33) [29]-[31].

[36] *Club Resorts Ltd v Van Breda* (2012) SCC 17. ('*Van Breda*').

[37] *Tolofson v Jensen* (1994) 3 S.C.R. 1022. ('*Tolofson*').

[38] *Van Breda* (n 36) [73] and [82]; *Tolofson* (n 35) [36].

[39] *Harrington* v. *Dow Corning Cmp.* (2000) BCCA 605 [74].

It is worth noting that in *Airia Brands*, subsequent to deciding that the court did not have jurisdiction over non-resident claimants, Justice Leitch issued an attornment order that delineated the procedures through which non-resident claimants could provide their consent to the jurisdiction of the Ontario court.

The court ordered that non-resident claimants '...may attorn to the jurisdiction of the Ontario court by indicating that they "expressly consent to the jurisdiction of the Ontario Court"'.[40] Justice Leitch ordered that such consent may be achieved by:

(a) Filing a claim to apply for settlement funds, if the claim indicates that the Person "expressly consents to the jurisdiction of the Ontario Court";
(b) Indicating on Class Counsel's or the claims administrator's website that the Person "expressly consents to the jurisdiction of the Ontario Court"; or
(c) Otherwise providing written notice to Class Counsel or the claims administrator that the Person "expressly consents to the jurisdiction of the Ontario Court".[41]

E. *Concerns regarding "Choice of Law"*

Canadian choice of law principles, as interpreted and applied in jurisprudence, exhibit a contextual approach to determining the lex loci in cases concerning multi-jurisdictional and transnational torts. Choice of law rules which govern breach of fiduciary duties has been scarcely applied in Canada. In *Minera Aquiline Argentina SA v. IMA Exploration Inc and Inversiones Mineras Argentina SA*,[42] in determining the law governing unjust enrichment, the Supreme Court of British Columbia adopted the principles set out in *Dicey, Morris and Collins on the Conflict of Laws.*[43] Dicey, Morris and Collins stipulate that the appropriate choice of law rule on the owing of an obligation is the 'proper law of the obligation'.[44] The 'proper law of the obligation' is determined pursuant to Rule 230 of the 14th edition of *Dicey, Morris and Collins on the Conflict of Laws*:

(a) If the obligation arises in connection with a contract, its proper law is the law applicable to the contract;
(b) If it arises in connection with a transaction concerning an immovable (land) its proper law is the law of the country where the immovable is situated *(lex situs)*; and
(c) If it arises in any other circumstances, its proper law is the law of the country where the enrichment occurs.[45]

In *Tolofson*, Justice La Forest argued that while a fixed rule based on *lex loci* is generally preferred for interprovincial and domestic torts due to its promotion

---

[40] Order (Attornment) in *Airia Brands* v. *Air Canada* [2017] ONCA 792 [2]. ('*Airia Brands*').

[41] Ibid.

[42] *Minera Aquiline Argentina SA v. IMA Exploration Inc and Inversiones Mineras Argentina SA*, (2006) BCSC 1102 [185]. (*'Minera Aquiline Argentina SA')*.

[43] See Lord Collins of Mapesbury and Jonathan Harris, *Dicey, Morris and Collins on The Conflict of Laws* (Sweet & Maxwell, 15th ed., 2012).

[44] Ibid at 2291-2292.

[45] Ibid at 2292.

of predictability, order, and respect for territoriality, it is important to note that the application of *lex loci* to multi-jurisdictional torts may be subject to the injustice exception.[46] However, Justice La Forest acknowledged that applying a strict rule in instances involving international or transnational torts could lead to unjust outcomes. Consequently, he proposed an exception to the *lex loci* rule, allowing judges to use their discretion to refrain from applying *lex loci* if doing so would lead to an unjust outcome.

Justice La Forest reasoned:

> [B]ecause a rigid rule on the international level could give rise to injustice, in certain circumstances, I am not averse to retaining a discretion in the court to apply our own law to deal with such circumstances. I can, however, imagine few cases where this would be necessary.[47]

In the case of *Tolofson*, Justice La Forest emphasised the importance of predictability, order, and territoriality, supporting the adoption of the *lex loci* principle. This principle dictates that the law of the jurisdiction where the wrongful activity occurred determines the nature and repercussions of the tort.[48] However, La Forest also acknowledged the complexities arising from determining the location of the tort, particularly in transnational cases where the wrongful act occurs in one place but the effects are felt elsewhere.[49]

The Supreme Court decision in *Tolofson* did not prescribe a specific methodology for reconciling different aspects of multi-jurisdictional torts when determining the location of the wrongful activity, particularly in international tort cases. Nevertheless, courts have consistently warned against adopting an arbitrary or inflexible approach that would lead to the automatic application of the law of the jurisdiction where the injury occurred or where the legal duty was breached.[50]

Canadian courts will decline to recognise or enforce a foreign law or judgment if it conflicts with fundamental public policy, 'essential public or moral interests', or the 'conception of essential justice and morality' within the jurisdiction.[51] For a foreign law to be disregarded on public policy grounds, it must contravene fundamental principles of justice, offend international norms, or conflict with prevalent conceptions of moral integrity or deeply rooted traditions within the forum.[52]

---

[46] *Tolofson* (n 37) 1022.

[47] Ibid [30].

[48] Ibid.

[49] Ibid.

[50] *Van Breda* (n 36) [89]; *Moran v. Pyle National (Canada) Ltd.* (1975) 1 S.C.R. 393; *Gulevich v. Miller* (2015) ABCA 411.

[51] Janet Walker, *Canadian Conflict of Laws* (Lexis Nexis Canada, 6th ed., vol. 2, 2005) Sect. 8.6, 8-10.

[52] Ibid.

3 Divided Approaches to the Jurisdiction Issue

1. *Canada*

Canadian courts draw a distinction between the existence and the exercise of jurisdiction.[53] In the first step, the court determines the existence of jurisdiction over the subject matter of a class action. Determining whether a court can assume jurisdiction over a certain claim is the first step. The preferred approach in Canada has been to rely on a set of specific factors which are given presumptive effect, as opposed to a regime based on an exercise of almost pure and individualised judicial discretion.[54] Coined as the 'real and substantial connection' ('RSC') test is Canada's chosen conflicts rule for the assumption of jurisdiction.

The Supreme Court of Canada's landmark decision in *Morguard*, along with its underlying policy rationale, has served as a cornerstone in Canadian jurisprudence for the past 35 years. Initially addressing the recognition and enforcement of judgments between Canadian provinces, the *Morguard* framework has since been extended to various actions and applications, including those within the international arena. Notably, it has been recognised as the decisive test for jurisdictional assumptions in both common law and constitutional contexts, involving both foreign plaintiffs and defendants. In *Hunt v. T & N plc*, a case examining the jurisdiction of the Supreme Court of British Columbia to adjudicate the constitutional validity of a Quebec 'blocking statute', the Supreme Court of Canada affirmed the constitutional necessity of the *Morguard* framework, emphasising its foundational role in legal proceedings.[55]

To satisfy the common law's real and substantial connection test, the party advocating for the court's jurisdiction bears the burden of identifying a presumptive connecting factor linking the subject matter of the litigation to the forum. Jurisdiction must primarily rely on objective factors that tie the legal circumstances or the subject matter of the litigation to the forum. Abstract considerations for order, efficiency, or fairness within the legal system cannot replace connecting factors that genuinely establish a 'real and substantial' connection according to the law of conflicts. Presumptive connecting factors 'connect the legal situation or the subject matter of the litigation with the forum', indicating a real and substantial connection necessary to establish *jurisdiction simpliciter*.[56]

In *Ven Breda*, Morgan Van Breda had suffered catastrophic injuries on a beach in Cuba and brought action in Ontario against numerous parties, including the appellant, Club Resorts Ltd, a company incorporated in the Cayman Islands that managed the two hotels where the accidents occurred, who argued unsuccessfully that the Ontario courts lacked jurisdiction and, in the alternative, a Cuban court would be a more appropriate forum on the basis of the doctrine of *forum non conveniens*. The Supreme

53 *Van Breda* (n 36).

54 Ibid.

55 *Hunt v. T & N plc*. (1993) 4 S.C.R. 289 [55]-[63]. *("Hunt').*

56 *Van Breda* (n 36) [90].

Court of Canada outlined the test to be applied for a court to assume jurisdiction over a multi-jurisdictional claim and adopted the following four presumptive connecting factors that, *prima facie*, entitle a court to assume jurisdiction over a dispute:

(a) the defendant is domiciled or resident in the province—on this factor the court states, "...a defendant may always be sued in the court of the jurisdiction in which he or she is domiciled or resident"[57];
(b) the defendant carries on business in the province;
(c) the tort was committed in the province; and
(d) a contract connected with the dispute was made in the province.

However, the list of recognised factors is not exhaustive, and new presumptive connecting factors may be introduced over time. When a court assesses whether a new connecting factor should be given presumptive effect, values such as order, fairness, and comity can serve as valuable analytical tools for evaluating the strength of the relationship with the forum indicated by the factor in question. These values underlie all presumptive connecting factors, whether enumerated or new. When identifying new presumptive factors, a court should seek connections that establish a relationship with the forum akin to those resulting from the listed factors.

Relevant considerations identified in *Van Breda* include:

(a) Similarity of the connecting factor with the recognised presumptive connecting factors;
(b) Treatment of the connecting factor in the case law;
(c) Treatment of the connecting factor in statute law; and
(d) Treatment of the connecting factor in the private international law of other legal systems with a shared commitment to order, fairness and comity.[58]

As illustrated in *Van Breda*, the location of the plaintiff in the jurisdiction is irrelevant for establishing *jurisdiction simpliciter*. Rather than the plaintiff's presence, it is the connection of the plaintiff's claim with the jurisdiction that establishes a connection with the forum. The presumptive connecting factors articulated by the Supreme Court of Canada do not make any reference to the plaintiffs or whether their place of residence is outside of the jurisdiction. *Van Breda* underscores that a court must assert jurisdiction when at least one presumptive connecting factor is satisfied.[59]

Once jurisdiction is established and no further objections are raised by the defendant, the litigation proceeds before the court of the forum. However, the court can only decline to exercise its jurisdiction if the defendant invokes *forum non conveniens*. The decision to invoke this doctrine lies with the parties involved, not with the court handling the claim. If the defendant raises the issue of *forum non conveniens*, they must demonstrate why the court should decline jurisdiction and choose a different forum. This entails showing that the alternative forum is significantly more

[57] Ibid [86].

[58] *Van Breda* (n 36) [91].

[59] Ibid.

appropriate and that selecting it would result in a fairer and more efficient resolution, despite denying the plaintiff the benefits of their chosen forum. When *forum non conveniens* is invoked, the court must look beyond the standard jurisdictional test and consider the overall fairness and efficiency of the dispute resolution process. This doctrine recognises that a common law court has the discretion to decline jurisdiction in limited circumstances to ensure fairness and efficiency. In cases where a stay of proceedings is sought, the court must determine if an alternative forum exists that is better equipped to handle the litigation in a fair and efficient manner.

On the other hand, a court must refrain from leaning too instinctively in favour of its own jurisdiction. The doctrine focuses on the contexts of individual cases and the factors that a court may consider in deciding whether to apply *forum non conveniens* may vary depending on the context. Such factors might include:

(a) the locations of parties and witnesses;
(b) the cost of transferring the case to another jurisdiction or of declining the stay;
(c) the impact of a transfer on the conduct of the litigation or on related or parallel proceedings;
(d) the possibility of conflicting judgments;
(e) problems related to the recognition and enforcement of judgments; and
(f) the relative strengths of the connections of the two parties.[60]

Ultimately, the decision falls within the reasoned discretion of the primary court. This exercise of discretion will be entitled to deference from higher courts, absent an error of law or a clear and serious error in the determination of relevant facts which takes place at an interlocutory or preliminary stage.

Canadian courts generally approach the issue of taking jurisdiction over class actions involving foreign plaintiffs liberally. *Excalibur Special Opportunities LP v Schwartz Levitsky Feldman LLP*[61] is a recent appellate-level decision from the Court of Appeal for Ontario, in which the Court of Appeal certified a 'global' class action even though most of the proposed class members had little or no connection to Ontario. *Excalibur* clarifies that '[t]he test to determine whether to take jurisdiction over foreign class members begins with an inquiry into jurisdiction *simpliciter* based on the principles described in *Van Breda*'.[62] The Court of Appeal for Ontario held that jurisdiction will depend on the connection between the defendant or the claim and Ontario, not the reasonable expectations of absent class members or the class members' connections with Ontario.

The framework for a Canadian court's assumption of jurisdiction over a global class had been laid out in *Currie*.[63] As has been noted, the *Currie* factors were relied upon in *Excalibur Special Opportunities LP*.[64] Furthermore, Canadian courts have consistently ruled that claims asserting international, novel, or 'unusual but arguable'

---

60 Ibid [110].

61 *Excalibur* (n 27) [34].

62 Ibid.

63 *Currie* (n 8).

64 *Excalibur* (n 27) [34].

causes of action should not be dismissed if they satisfy the necessary elements of a duty of care. In *Araya v. Nevsun Resources Ltd.*,[65] the Eritrean plaintiffs, who were non-residents of Canada, filed a lawsuit in British Columbia alleging human rights violations that took place in Eritrea. They asserted that the defendant had entered into an agreement with the Eritrean government to establish a mine, and that the government had compelled them to work in the mine under the threat of torture. The plaintiffs' claims were centred around four newly identified torts rooted in breaches of customary international law, including torture, slavery, forced labour, and crimes against humanity.

The British Columbia Supreme Court rejected the defendant's preliminary motion to strike, finding that the current state of the law was still unclear and, assuming the allegations in the claim were accurate, the defendant had not proven that the plaintiffs' claims were unlikely to succeed.[66] Moreover, the court determined that the case should proceed to allow for the contextual examination necessary to determine whether the common law, particularly the law of tort, should evolve in the manner sought by the plaintiffs.[67]

In *Choc v Hudbay Minerals Inc*, in refusing to strike the pleadings, Justice C. Brown underscored the core principles which guide the application of the plain and obvious test alleging novel causes of action as follows:

> the novelty or complexity of a cause of action does not require that the claim be struck on a summary basis. On the contrary, it is preferable that difficult and important points of law be examined within a full factual context, which can only take place at trial.[68]

The approach in these cases is more consistent with an approach that is informed by considerations of justice and fairness rather than a more technical approach relying on rigid rules, even if it perhaps comes at a price of eschewing the extra efficiency and costs-saving dividends that the latter approach might bring in otherwise allowing motions to strike hard or novel cases that take up court time and resources.

2. *USA*

Despite the apparent difference in the specific terms used, the US approach to jurisdiction is not too dissimilar to the Canadian approach. In both countries, the traditional rule was '*actor forum rei sequitur*' (the plaintiff must pursue the defendant in his forum). Accordingly, in both countries' traditional bases of jurisdiction—'*in personam*', '*quasi in rem*', and '*in rem*'—predicated adjudicatory authority on the sovereign's physical power over the defendant or their property, expecting the plaintiff to come to sue where one or the other could be found.

From there, however, things begin to differ. *Daimler AG v. Bauman*[69] is the leading case in which Justice Ginsburg of the United States Supreme Court appears to have

[65] *Araya v. Nevsun Resources Ltd* (2016) BCSC 1856. ('*Araya*').

[66] Ibid [427-429].

[67] Ibid [476-477].

[68] *Choc v Hudbay Minerals Inc* [2013] ONSC 1414 [41]-[42].

[69] *Daimler AG v. Bauman* [2014]134 S. Ct. 746. ('*Daimler AG*').

taken an approach to jurisdiction in class action context that focuses on due process and personal jurisdiction in the class action context. Many scholars and courts have resisted the implications of Justice Ginsburg's 'at home' test for general jurisdiction in *Daimler AG v. Bauman,*[70] conceiving of such a 'rigid' and 'categorical' approach as unduly straitening general jurisdiction to the disadvantage of plaintiffs.[71]

The law of personal jurisdiction, often regarded as 'rather muddled',[72] had been clarified with respect to general jurisdiction by Justice Ginsburg's groundbreaking decision in *Goodyear Dunlop Tires Operations, S.A. v. Brown.*[73] That decision declared that a court may only assert general jurisdiction over out-of-state corporations where 'their affiliations with the [forum] State are so "continuous and systematic" as to render them essentially at home' there.[74] In *Daimler AG v. Bauman,*[75] the Supreme Court provided further clarification to the principles outlined in *Goodyear* by ruling that Daimler AG, a German publicly traded company, could not be subjected to California's general jurisdiction in a lawsuit brought by Argentine plaintiffs concerning events that occurred in Argentina. This decision was based on the premise that Daimler did not have a substantial presence or significant connections in California, even when considering the activities of its subsidiary in the United States. While some have interpreted the *Daimler* case as part of a trend restricting plaintiffs' access to courts, a closer examination reveals that Justice Ginsburg applied a theory of personal jurisdiction influenced by the foundational work of Professors Arthur von Mehren and Donald Trautman[76] and initially introduced in *Goodyear* and her dissent in *J. McIntyre Machinery, Ltd. v. Nicastro*[77] that focuses fundamentally on fairness to both litigants.

Professor Mullenix noted that personal jurisdiction jurisprudence primarily addresses due process concerns regarding defendants, particularly in two-party lawsuits where jurisdiction issues typically centre on the defendant; notably, the Supreme Court applies the same due process standards to defendants from other states and foreign countries.[78]

(a) *Minimum Contacts Doctrine*

The concept of minimum contacts was initially articulated by the Supreme Court nearly eight decades ago in *International Shoe Co. v. Washington.*[79] In this case, the

---

[70] Ibid.

[71] Ibid.

[72] *Bauman v. DaimlerChrysler Corp.* [2009] 579 F.3d 1088, 1098 (9th Cir. 2009) (Reinhardt, J., dissenting).

[73] *Goodyear Dunlop Tires Operations, S.A. v. Brown* [2011] 131 S. Ct. 2846 ('*Goodyear Dunlop Tyres, SA*').

[74] Ibid.

[75] *Daimler AG* (n 69).

[76] *See* Arthur T. von Mehren and Donald T. Trautman, 'Jurisdiction to Adjudicate: A Suggested Analysis' (1966) 79 (6) *Harvard Law Review* 1121.

[77] *J. McIntyre Machinery, Ltd. v. Nicastro* [2011] 131 S. Ct. 2780. ('*J. McIntyre Machinery, Ltd.*').

[78] Bassett (n3) 50.

[79] 326 U.S. 310 (1945).

Court stated that due process requires that, to subject a defendant to a judgment *in personam*, they must have certain minimum contacts with the forum state, ensuring that the lawsuit's pursuit aligns with traditional notions of fair play and substantial justice.[80]

Regarding defendants, the U.S. Supreme Court has applied a minimum contacts analysis, focusing on the connection between the defendant, the forum state, and the litigation.[81] This analysis considers factors such as purposeful availment, reasonableness, and fairness.[82] Additionally, the relevance of the defendant's contacts with the forum state to the plaintiff's claim is also taken into account in the minimum contacts assessment.[83]

In personal jurisdiction, consent is another factor to consider. Even without minimum contacts, a court may establish personal jurisdiction if the defendant explicitly or implicitly agrees to be sued in the forum state.[84] However, the minimum contacts doctrine lacks clear definition, and there is no consistent or comprehensive method for analysing its existence. Instead, the Supreme Court has approached each case individually, often providing explanations that are too vague to offer meaningful guidance.[85]

(b) *Plaintiffs and Personal Jurisdiction*

Regarding plaintiffs, the minimum contacts test is not required in a traditional individual lawsuit. By initiating the lawsuit, as mentioned previously, the plaintiff essentially agrees to the court's assertion of personal jurisdiction over them. This ability to agree to personal jurisdiction means that plaintiffs, like defendants, can consent to jurisdiction even without minimum contacts with the forum.[86]

However, in the more complex realm of class action litigation, personal jurisdiction issues become more challenging.[87] While it is acceptable to say that a court can bind named plaintiffs who are personally involved in the lawsuit, it is a different matter to assert jurisdiction over individuals who have no direct contact with the forum state.

In traditional individual lawsuits, all plaintiffs are identified and actively participate in the legal proceedings, justifying the assumption that they consent to the court's jurisdiction. However, in class action lawsuits, where the majority of plaintiffs are unnamed and do not actively participate, the rationale for implying consent is weakened. Since absent class members do not make a deliberate choice to file in a specific court, it cannot be assumed that they automatically consent to the court's

---

[80] Ibid 316.

[81] Bassett (n3) 50.

[82] Ibid.

[83] Ibid.

[84] Bassett (n 3) 51.

[85] Ibid.

[86] Ibid.

[87] Ibid.

jurisdiction. This raises questions about how personal jurisdiction is established in class action cases.[88]

Furthermore, the presence of non-U.S. claimants in class litigation requires additional due process protections.[89] First, ascertaining personal jurisdiction involves not only an inquiry into the sovereign's territorial power, but must also protect an individual's constitutional due process rights which might be impinged upon by unduly burdensome litigation conducted in some distant forum. Second, the procedural aspects are also crucial; for instance, if service of process is ineffective, the court cannot establish personal jurisdiction over the defendant. These concepts can intersect, as seen in 'tag' jurisdiction, where serving process within the forum state fulfills the procedural requirement and grants personal jurisdiction, even if the defendant's connections with the forum would not independently meet the minimum contacts criterion.[90]

Several rulings by the US Supreme Court are widely perceived as significantly curbing access to US courts, either by constraining the extraterritorial application of US law or by imposing stricter criteria for establishing personal jurisdiction over defendants.[91] These cases include *Kiobel v Royal Dutch Petroleum Co.*,[92] *Goodyear Dunlop Titres Ops., S.A. v Brown*,[93] *J. McIntyre Mach. Ltd. v. Nicastro*,[94] *Daimler AG v. Bauman*, and *Walden v. Fiore*.[95]

However, the limitations on foreign claimants seeking to sue defendants domiciled in the US for actions primarily occurring outside US territorial limits remain ambiguous.[96]

The Alien Tort Statute (ATS) has served as a significant avenue for foreign claimants to bring forward claims in the US federal courts. The ATS, a part of the *Judiciary Act* of 1789, grants original jurisdiction to federal district courts to hear 'any civil action [brought] by an alien, for tort only, committed in violation of the law of nations or a treaty of the United States'.[97]

In the 1978 case of *Filartiga v. Pena-Irala*, the Second Circuit Court permitted litigation of disputes with purely extraterritorial aspects, thus offering a platform for resolving conflicts between aliens concerning conduct occurring outside the United States.[98]

---

[88] Ibid.

[89] Bassett (n 3) 44.

[90] Bassett (n 3) 48.

[91] James L. Stengel and Kristina P Trautmann, 'Determining United States Jurisdiction over Transnational Litigation' (2016) *The Review of Litigation*, 1, 3.

[92] *Kiobel v Royal Dutch Petroleum Co.* (2013) 569 U.S. 108. ('*Kiobel*').

[93] *Goodyear Dunlop Titres Ops., S.A.* (n 73).

[94] *J. McIntyre Mach. Ltd.* (n 77).

[95] *Daimler AG* (n 69).

[96] Ibid 4.

[97] Alien Tort Claims Act, 28 USC § 1350 (2007) ('ATCA').

[98] *Filartiga v. Pena-Irala*, [1980] 630 F.2d 876 (2d Cir. 1980).

Further, the case *Sosa v. Alvarez-Machain*, while limiting the types of claims eligible for ATS jurisdiction, implicitly acknowledged the concept of 'universal jurisdiction', affirming the appropriateness of allowing aliens to litigate against each other in US courts for actions taking place outside the United States.[99]

In *Kiobel I*, the Second Circuit Court dismissed the entire case, citing that under customary international law, only natural persons, not judicial entities like corporations, could be held liable under the ATS.[100] Therefore, the case failed for want of subject matter jurisdiction.

However, the Court's 2013 decision (*Kiobel II*) held that the ATS did not apply extraterritorially and did not address the issue of corporate liability.[101] Additionally, the court explicitly rejected the concept of universal jurisdiction.[102]

Still, it is maintained that corporations may not be found liable under the ATS.[103]

In *Al Shimari*, for instance, it was held:

> Upon applying the fact-based inquiry articulated by the Supreme Court in *Kiobel*, we hold that the plaintiff's claims 'touch and concern' the territory of the US has sufficient force to displace the presumption against extraterritorial application of the *Alien Tort Statute*.[104]

Al Shimari demonstrates that the ATS has survived *Kiobel II* and may still be applied with some vigour to these cases involving parties or claims which 'touch and concern' the United States.[105] It illuminates the complexity of the "touch and concern" test and, critically, leaves open the issue of corporate liability.[106]

In *Mastafa v Chevron Corp*,[107] the Second Circuit Court echoed the Supreme Court's assertion in *Kiobel II* that merely having a corporate presence in the United States is insufficient to override the presumption of extraterritoriality and found that 'precedents make it clear that neither the U.S. citizenship of defendants, nor their presence in the United States, is of relevance for jurisdictional purposes'.[108]

In *Ellul v Congregation of Christian Bros* 774 F.3d 791, 798 (2d Cir. 2014), the Second Circuit Court reasoned that a defendant's US citizenship is immaterial in determining jurisdiction under the ATS.[109]

The Supreme Court's deliberation on matters of personal jurisdiction intertwined with its ATS jurisprudence in *Daimler AG v. Bauman*.[110] In response to the question 'whether, consistent with the Due Process Clause courts for claims involving

---

[99] *Sosa v. Alvarez-Machain*, [2004] 542 U.S. 692.

[100] *Kiobel* (n 92).

[101] *Kiobel v. Royal Dutch Petroleum Co.* [2013] 569 U.S. 108. ('*Kiobel II*').

[102] Ibid.

[103] *Balintulo v Ford Motor Co,* [2015] 796 F 3d 160.

[104] *Al shimari v CACI Premier Tech., Inc.*, [2014] 758 F.3d 516, 520 (4th Ctr. 2014).

[105] Stengel and Trautmann (n 91) 24.

[106] Ibid.

[107] *Mastafa v Chevron Corp* [2014] 770 F.3d 170, 170 (2d Cir. 2014).

[108] Ibid 189.

[109] *Ellul v Congregation of Christian Bros* [2014] 774 F.3d 791, 798 (2d Cir. 2014).

[110] *Daimler AG* (n 69).

only foreign plaintiffs and conduct occurring entirely abroad', the Court determined that 'considerations of international rapport thus reinforce our determination that subjecting Daimler to the general jurisdiction of courts in California would not accord with the "fair play and substantial justice" due process demands.[111]

Stengel and Tautmann note that 'The decision and reasoning of *Daimler* are consistent with *Kiobel II* and reinforce the determination that United States courts should exercise caution in bringing international disputes and actors into the United States'.[112]

3 *Australia*

(a) *Personal jurisdiction and plaintiff*

An Australian court must be convinced by the claimant that it is not an 'obviously unsuitable forum' before it will assume jurisdiction.[113] *The Federal Court Act* s 33N(1) provides that the Federal Court may, on its own motion or upon application by the respondent, order that a proceeding no longer continue as a class action if:

(a) the costs that would be incurred if the proceeding were to continue as a representative proceeding are likely to exceed the costs that would be incurred if each group member conducted a separate proceeding; or
(b) all the relief sought can be obtained by means of a proceeding other than a representative proceeding under this Part; or
(c) the representative proceeding will not provide an efficient and effective means of dealing with the claims of group members; or
(d) it is otherwise inappropriate that the claims be pursued by means of a representative proceeding.

According to Murphy and Cameron, this Section has become a significant battleground for contesting class action proceedings.[114] This type of test embodies a discretionary principle that permits the court to evaluate various factors before deciding whether to exercise jurisdiction, including the location of evidence and parties, the governing law, the significance of the subject matter to the foreign state, and whether the plaintiff would receive a fair trial in the courts of the foreign state.[115]

(b) *Personal jurisdiction and foreign defendant*

When a defendant outside Australia first becomes aware of the Australian proceedings against them, at the defendant at that stage has several options:

- the defendant could choose not to come to Australia to defend the proceedings;

---

[111] Ibid 763.

[112] Stengel and Trautmann (n 91) 39.

[113] Richard Garnett, 'Foreign States in Australian Courts' (2005) 29 *Melbourne University Law Review* 704, 706.

[114] Murphy and Cameron (n 10) 416.

[115] *Spiliada Maritime Corp v Consulex Ltd* [1987] 1 AC 460 ('*Spiliada*'); *Lubbe v Cape plc* [2000] 4 All ER 268; Regie *Nationale des Usines Renault SA v Zhang* (2002) 210 CLR 491.

- the defendant could make a conditional appearance in the Australian court, submitting to the court only for the purpose of challenging its jurisdiction;
- the defendant could appear in the Australian court to defend themselves on both jurisdictional and substantive grounds;
- the defendant could initiate counter proceedings in the foreign jurisdiction which the defendant believes is the appropriate forum in which the case should be heard.

If the defendant opts not to appear in the Australian proceedings, their assets within Australia and their future ability to conduct business or travel there may be jeopardised. However, for the plaintiff seeking remedy, the absence of the defendant does not guarantee a straightforward path. The plaintiff would need to pursue legal action in the defendant's home jurisdiction, either by initiating new proceedings or seeking recognition of the Australian judgment there. Even if the Australian judgment is acknowledged, the foreign court might not exercise its discretion to provide equivalent relief.

If the defendant opts to challenge the jurisdiction of the Australian court, they can argue that the matter falls outside the court's jurisdiction or, alternatively, that the court should exercise discretion to decline jurisdiction on the basis that the Australian forum is clearly inappropriate (*forum non conveniens*). Additionally, depending on the laws of their home jurisdiction, the defendant may initiate proceedings in their home jurisdiction to seek a remedy against the plaintiff. This could involve seeking an order from their home court to prohibit the plaintiff from initiating or continuing proceedings in Australia (referred to as an anti-suit injunction), or obtaining a favourable declaration that would negate any rights sought by the plaintiff in Australia based on the principle of *res judicata.* In response, the plaintiff may seek an anti-anti-suit injunction in Australia.

Despite these legal strategies, there is a general presumption in Australian jurisdictions that legislation and laws do not extend extraterritorially, and court jurisdiction is similarly limited. Therefore, unless a statute explicitly grants extraterritorial jurisdiction while requiring a connection with the state, courts do not have jurisdiction over matters occurring beyond their territorial limits. However, this presumption against extraterritorial jurisdiction may be rebutted if it would render ineffective the operation of the relevant statute.

Certain Australian legislation has extraterritorial application. In cases where an Australian court adjudicates a claim arising from such legislation, it holds jurisdiction to make determinations regarding events and circumstances occurring outside of Australia and to issue remedies concerning those events or circumstances. However, the enforceability of its orders is confined to the territorial jurisdiction of the court. Therefore, while the legislation's extraterritorial scope broadens the range of evidence and issues considered by the court, it does not expand the territorial reach of the remedies available from the court.

In essence, the extraterritorial application of Australian laws introduces a heightened possibility of overlapping jurisdiction between Australian courts and those outside Australia. Additionally, there may be a discrepancy between the claims adjudicated by the Australian court and the remedies it can prescribe concerning those claims.

The Australian doctrine of *forum non conveniens* requires a demonstration that a court is 'clearly inappropriate' for adjudicating the dispute.[116] In such instances, the burden lies on the defendant to prove to the court that it is not a suitable forum for resolving the matter.[117] The case *Voth v Manildra Flour Mills Pty Ltd* sets forth that this is accomplished by evaluating 'connecting factors' based on the balance of convenience.[118] These factors include considerations of convenience or expense, such as the availability of witnesses, the applicable law, and the parties' residences or business locations.[119] Moreover, when a motion to stay proceedings is filed, non-exclusive jurisdiction connections (EJC) are considered as one among several connecting factors, rather than a decisive one.[120] Additionally, the court examines any legitimate juridical advantages for the plaintiff to ascertain whether justice will be served or substantial injustice will be suffered in the foreign forum.[121]

The *Voth* decision was a firm refutation of the UK position set out in the case of *Spiliada Maritime Corp v Cansulex Ltd*[122] where the courts had adopted 'the more appropriate forum test'. It is easier for a court to determine whether a court is an inappropriate forum than to determine if another court is a more appropriate forum which potentially could involve the court in their own form of 'forum shopping' having to decide which court is best to decide the matter if not itself (and raises the question of better for *whom* which introduces an element of partiality if the court is deciding this question from the perspective of one of the parties only). Can class action rights be contracted away? In Australia, the answer would appear to be no, unlike the other jurisdictions discussed. The question of whether a waiver of class action clauses can be enforced was addressed in the recent and very public '*Ruby Princess*' case.[123] In that case, Ms Karpik commenced a class action against the Respondent who was a cruise operator on behalf of a number of passengers who contracted COVID-19 in 2020 whilst aboard the 'Ruby Princess' after passengers had boarded at Sydney where the virus was contracted by some of the passengers. The Respondent brought a stay application regarding Mr Ho who was one of a number of class members who had made his passage contract outside of Australia which included terms limiting court action to the District Court of California and waiving

[116] Rosehana Amin, 'International Jurisdiction Agreements and the Recognition and Enforcement of Judgments in Australian Litigation: Is There a Need for the Hague Convention on Choice of Court Agreements?' (2010) 17 *Australian International Law Journal* 113, 118.

[117] Garnett (n 113) 30.

[118] *Voth v Manildra Flour Mills Pty Ltd* [1990] HCA 55. The factors to be considered in the *Voth* test include those enumerated by Lord Goff in *Spiliada* (n 115) 482-84.

[119] See *Spiliada* (n 115), 556-57.

[120] Amin (n 116) 118.

[121] Ibid.

[122] Spiliada (n 115).

[123] *Karpik v. Carnival PLC & Anor* [2023] HCA 39.

class action. The Federal Court at first instance enforced the exclusive jurisdiction and waiver of class action clauses which was upheld on appeal to the Full Federal Court. However, the High Court allowed the appeal and found that the waiver of the class action clause was an unfair contract term in breach of s23 of the *Australian Consumer Law* (ACL) which by virtue of s5(1) and (g) of the *Competition and Consumer Act 2010 (Cth)* had extended operation to bodies incorporated outside of Australia but carrying on business in Australia which the Respondent was. The High Court found that since the class waiver clause was void, the Respondent could not rely on it to support their stay application. In deciding whether to exercise their discretion to enforce the exclusive jurisdiction clause, the High Court decided not to as that would deprive Mr. Ho of a strong juridical advantage in remaining with the representative proceedings in the Federal Court of Australia as he would not be able to participate in a class action in the US due to the class waiver clause which would be valid there. Further, the court found that to enforce the exclusive jurisdiction clause would have the effect of *fracturing* the litigation with some class action members pursuing their claim in the Federal Court and others in the US in individual actions due to the operation of the class waiver clause.

4 Evaluation of the Different Approaches

The RSC test does not supplant the traditional grounds for jurisdiction in private international law, such as physical presence, consent, or submission. In Canada, rather than adhering to rigid and mechanical private international law rules, the courts have recognised that the nature of Canada's federal constitution and the realities of an increasingly integrated Canadian and international community necessitate a more flexible, accommodating, and generous approach to jurisdiction. La Forest J. has stated that, '…what must underlie a modern system of private international law are principles of order and fairness, principles that ensure security of transactions with justice'.[124]

The RSC test has been consistently upheld by the Supreme Court of Canada as the governing rule for resolving both private international law issues and the constitutional jurisdiction of provincial superior courts since 1993. This stance was reaffirmed by the Supreme Court in *Van Breda* and *Chevron*, as well as by the Court of Appeal for Ontario in *Excalibur*. The Court submits that the RSC test strikes an appropriate balance between: (1) the constitutionally mandated constraints on the exercise of jurisdiction by provincial superior courts; and (2) the acknowledgment that, within a federal state operating within a global economy, there will inevitably be cases and circumstances where a court's jurisdiction will have ancillary effects beyond its province.

In Australia, the 'flavour' of the RSC test can be detected in the courts' approach, following *Voth*, where the courts decide whether a court selected by a party to issue

[124] *Morguard* (n 33) [8],[28]-[39].

proceedings is an inappropriate forum provided that the party who challenges the jurisdiction of the selected court can demonstrate this and that there is an alternate appropriate forum (which does not have to be a *more* appropriate forum) to determine the matter. Further, the *Ruby Princess* case has shown that measures to protect class actions such as unfair contract terms in the case of class action waivers can have extra-territorial operation.

However, the 'clearly inappropriate forum' approach in *Voth* appears to adopt a more pragmatic approach than its cousins in Canada and the US. Rather than chasing juristic ideological notions such as a 'constitutional imperative' (Canada) or rigid constructs such as the 'at home' rule (the US), the typically Antipodean pragmatic attitude of 'if-it-aint-broke-why-fix-it' evident in the clearly inappropriate forum test appears to strike the right balance between respecting the plaintiff's choice of jurisdiction and the defendant's rights if the defendant is able to demonstrate that selected jurisdiction is a clearly inappropriate forum and that an alternative jurisdiction is appropriate to hear the matter (but not necessarily the *most* appropriate forum). Moreover, such an approach arguably comports better than any other approach with the notion of the court's inherent or implied jurisdiction in this space which is simply to manage its caseload, not to pontificate about constitutional issues as the courts do in Canada or embark on some sort of quixotic quest for some perfect jurisdictional algorithm as they do in the US.

5 Conclusion

It is widely agreed that class actions serve a crucial role in improving access to justice, and this aspect is often considered a factor favouring certification. On the other hand, there is a view that this might be too much of a good thing if parties have untrammelled rights to choose their jurisdiction or suppress or limit the rights of the other party with such mechanisms as exclusive jurisdiction clauses and class waiver clauses irrespective of considerations of fairness and justice. It would appear that the courts in jurisdictions such as Canada and Australia have used their inherent jurisdiction in a manner that preferences such considerations of fairness and justice while balancing it with considerations of efficiency and responsible use of court resources that may be advanced by private mechanisms although not those that are themselves unfair such as class action waiver clauses (in Australia at least) and asymmetrical choice of forum clauses that limits the choice of jurisdiction of one of the parties. The adoption of the clearly inappropriate forum test in Australia following *Voth* instead of the more appropriate forum test is a striking example of this in that while freedom to choose one's jurisdiction with choice of forum and exclusive jurisdiction clauses are part of the matrix of factors a court will take into account in deciding what is an inappropriate forum. The courts' inherent or implied jurisdiction to preference interests such as fairness and justice means that they will not give too much deference to private considerations nor treat them as determinative of the issue (as they usually might where the issue is purely a private law matter such as a contract dispute between the parties) or to go forum shopping themselves by engaging in what would be an exhausting enquiry on what would be the most appropriate court to hear a matter which involves the courts in what could be a partisan exercise since one jurisdiction is usually likely to be more favourable to one party than the other.

The writers submit that the *Voth* approach is the preferred stance courts of all jurisdictions should take as its pragmatic stance of 'if-it-aint-broke-don't-fix-it' best reflects the objects of inherent jurisdiction in this space which is all about case management or a court keeping its house in order. While both the Australian and Canadian approaches preference inherent jurisdiction and do not simply yield to a mechanistic approach with too much deference to private mechanisms such as exclusive jurisdiction clauses, it is heartening to see that the court still takes these mechanisms into account in resolving conflict of law issues as part of the overall factual matrix.

Indeed, while drafting their choice of forum clauses, it would behoove parties to an international agreement to bear this factor in mind rather than just include clauses in their agreement as standard boilerplate which is how these clauses are mostly treated at the drafting stage. Not only can such careless drafting lead to confusion as to whether the choice of forum clause is an exclusive jurisdiction clause or a non-exclusive jurisdiction clause which is an issue that commonly arises in this space, but whether such clause has the effect of the parties submitting to the jurisdiction of a court which might clearly be an inappropriate forum notwithstanding the significant advantage such choice might confer on a particular party.

Indeed, there could be standard form clauses for commercial agreements which reflect the clearly inappropriate forum test. Objects clauses in the agreement could also outline that the goal of the agreement, among others, is to give effect to the wishes of the party while acknowledging the paramountcy of the court's inherent or implied jurisdiction to exclude litigation from inappropriate forums and that an object of the agreement itself is to ensure the parties avoid selecting an inappropriate forum of jurisdiction. Perhaps it would be going too far to have the parties certify that they had received legal advice in respect to the drafting and effect of choice of forum clauses in their agreement or even that a lawyer certifies on the agreement that they have provided advice and that a selected forum is not in their reasonable opinion inappropriate. Obviously, prevention is better than cure and the more front-end work that can be done in agreements to prevent parties from making bad choices due to a carelessly written bit of boilerplate, the better.

There is a reason such jurisdiction is 'inherent' (in the case of superior courts) or 'implied' (in the case of inferior courts)—it goes without saying that courts must accord justice and fairness in resolving conflict issues in class actions rather than kowtow to private mechanisms at the behest of the parties. Simply put, the court's inherent and implied jurisdiction trumps contractual freedom. To those parties who believe that the court will simply rubber stamp their agreed choice of forum, will have a nasty shock and might say to themselves 'forum shopping just ain't what it used to be!'.

Convergence of Trademarks and Trade Names: Resolving the Conflict Between Trade Names and Trademark Rights Under Trademark Law vis-à-vis Company Law

Kanika Dhingra and Siddharth Balani

Abstract Protection of trademarks through registration under the Trademark Act, 1999, provides a registered proprietor with exclusive rights to use the mark in respect of goods and services for which the mark is registered. The Act provides rights to the registered proprietor of a trademark as well as identifies instances of infringement for which remedy may be sought by an action of infringement. Section 29(5) of the Act identifies a unique form of infringement whereby a registered trademark may be infringed by the use of such trademark as a trade name or business concern in respect of the same classes of goods or services. The authors attempt to examine the implications of the provision as well as its limitations in identifying certain acts as cases of infringement. It is highlighted that the provision does not provide relief in circumstances where a registered trademark is used by another person as his trade name, name of business concern, or a part thereof, in respect of dissimilar classes of goods or services. Further, the authors also explore the possible overlap between the application of Section 29(5) and Section 29(4), if any. An analysis of the judicial response in cases of infringement arising out of the use of trademarks as trade names highlights the limitations emerging due to the literal and narrow interpretation of the provision drawn by the courts. The remedy available under the Companies Act, 2013 with respect to change or rectification in the name of the company has been identified as an appropriate remedy in such cases.

Keywords Trademark · Trade names · Infringement · Rectification · Companies Act

K. Dhingra (✉) · S. Balani
National Law University, Jodhpur, India
e-mail: kanika.dhingra@nlujodhpur.ac.in

S. Balani
e-mail: siddharth.balani@nlujodhpur.ac.in

J. Aston et al. (eds.), *Comparative Law*, https://doi.org/10.1007/978-981-97-7815-7_15

1 Protection of Trademarks: An Introduction

'Any sign, or any combination of signs, capable of distinguishing the goods or services of one undertaking from those of other undertakings, shall be capable of constituting a trademark'.[1] A trademark refers to a specific type of intellectual property that includes marks/signs that are capable of distinguishing the goods or services of one enterprise from those of other enterprises.[2] These marks are essential for serving the function of identification and association of the product with the seller, manufacturer, or provider. Thus, it helps consumers identify the product and its origin and allows a buyer to easily discern items, products, or services in the market and make an informed purchase choice.[3] It is through these marks that consumers not only identify the products in the marketplace but are also able to distinguish them from the products of competitors. The trademarks are used by a person in the course of trade to identify their goods. These trademarks may either be unregistered or registered with the appropriate authorities (generally referred to as the trademark office) of respective territories.

They are a valuable strategic asset for organizations competing on product differentiation and customer loyalty since they provide added benefits of visibility and reputation.[4] Their ownership and protection have become relevant in modern times due to the increased international trade and movement of goods across borders.[5]

Enjoyment of exclusivity over trademarks is generally acquired by getting a mark registered as a trademark in respect of identified classes of goods and/or services to which the mark shall be applied or is being applied. As per the WTO Agreement on Trade-Related Aspects of Intellectual Property, *'the owner of a registered trademark shall have the exclusive right to prevent all third parties not having the owner's consent from using in the course of trade identical or similar signs for goods or services that are identical or similar to those in respect of which the trademark is registered where such use would result in a likelihood of confusion'*.[6]

Thus, obtaining a registration over a trademark grants the proprietor the exclusive right to restrict others from using 'identical' or 'similar' marks in respect of 'identical' or 'similar' goods or services such that a likelihood of confusion is avoided. A significant feature of trademarks lies in the fact that trademark rights, like other

---

[1] Art. 15.1: Protectable Subject Matter, WTO Agreement on Trade Related Aspects of Intellectual Property Rights, 1995, https://www.wto.org/english/docs_e/legal_e/27-trips.pdf [***hereinafter* TRIPs Agreement**].

[2] World Intellectual Property Organization, *Trademarks: What is a Trademark?*, https://www.wipo.int/trademarks/en/.

[3] US Patent & Trademark Office, *What is a Trademark*, https://www.uspto.gov/trademarks/basics/what-trademark.

[4] Sourabh Batar, *A Review on Importance of Trademark*, IJFANS 2543–2549 (2012), https://www.ijfans.org/uploads/paper/f4ea752430097792d349fb5f1f66b13d.pdf.

[5] Ibid.

[6] Art. 16.1 of TRIPs Agreement.

intellectual properties, are territorial in nature.[7] In principle, they are valid only within the territorial limits of the jurisdiction in which they have been registered or acquired. In order to seek protection in different jurisdictions, the proprietor shall seek registration in each such jurisdiction.[8] To enable convenience in filing and cooperation among nations, several international agreements and treaties have been concluded under the aegis of the World Intellectual Property Organization.[9]

However, some countries allow unregistered trademarks to be used and protect them through common law remedies. Owners or users of such unregistered trademarks are not entitled to seek enforcement of statutory rights under trademark legislation and remedies that are available to registered proprietors of marks. In addition to the registered and unregistered trademarks, there is also the concept of 'well-known' trademarks. These marks may be unregistered or registered, but they are widely recognized by a significant section of the public who uses or receives such goods and services under the mark and are associated with popular entities or market players.[10] Unlike other trademarks, whose goodwill and reputation are limited to a certain geographical reach and a specific class of products or services, well-known trademarks have their goodwill and reputation protected across the nation and across all categories of goods and services. Thus, well-known trademarks enjoy a greater degree of protection than registered or unregistered marks.[11] For instance, Bata, Google, Rolex, Benz, Kit Kat, Hamdard, Pizza Hut, Nestle, Canon, Microsoft, etc., have all been recognized as well-known trademarks in India.[12]

A pertinent-related concern that emerges in relation to trademarks is the use and protection of trade names that are identical or similar to trademarks or include trademarks. Existing jurisprudence and literature available vary on the meaning and definition of the concept of 'trade name'. The notion of trade name is inferred in different ways, such as 'business name', 'company name', 'firm name', etc., identified with 'trading as', 'operating as', or 'doing business as'.[13] However, in general, the term 'trade name' can be defined as the name identifying an enterprise or legal

---

[7] World Trade Organisation, *Trademarks: Module III*, p. 51, https://www.wto.org/english/tratop_e/trips_e/ta_docs_e/modules3_e.pdf.

[8] Ibid.

[9] *See* Trademark Law Treaty of 1994, Singapore Treaty on Law of Trademarks of 2006, Madrid Agreement of 1891 and Madrid Protocol of 1989, Nice Agreement concerning International Classification of Goods and Services for the Purposes of Registration of Marks of 1957 and Vienna Agreement establishing an International Classification of the Figurative Elements of Marks of 1973.

[10] Sonal Sodhani, *All You need to Know about Well-Known Trademarks*, Mondaq (May 22, 2019), https://www.mondaq.com/india/trademark/808148/all-you-need-to-know-about-well-known-trademarks.

[11] Ibid.

[12] *See* IP India, *List of Well-Known Trademarks*, https://ipindia.gov.in/writereaddata/Portal/Images/pdf/well-known-trademaks-updated-newone.pdf.

[13] Intepat, *Trade Name v. Trade Mark*, (June 9, 2016), https://www.intepat.com/blog/trade-name-vs-trademark/.

person.[14] For example, while 'Bata' is the trademark under which products such as shoes are sold, 'Bata India Ltd.', may be identified as the trade name of the enterprise. A company may have various types of trademarks for its various products, but trade names are used to distinguish themselves from other companies or enterprises.[15] However, the trade name, often known as the corporation or business name, is the firm's official and legal name. A trade name is important because it creates a relationship between the company and its general audience. One uses the company name to file taxes, pay employees, build websites and other online presences, market, and packages.[16] The trademark, on the other hand, is the mark used to identify products or services. Thus, a trade name is the name under which an individual or company conducts its business. While such use may not necessarily raise any alarming issues, as in the above illustration, the problem arises when the registered proprietor of a trademark and the owner/user of the trade name are two distinct market players. This chapter aims to address this convergence and its implications under trademark law.

2 Protection of Trademarks Under India's Trademark Act, 1999

By virtue of Section 2(1)(m) of the Trademark Act, 1999, a '*mark includes a device, brand, heading, label, ticket,* ***name****, signature, word, letter, numeral, shape of goods, packaging, or combination of colors, or any combination thereof*'.[17] This provision implies that any name, including the name of an individual, a corporate name, a trade name, a company name, or any fictitious name, may be identified as a 'mark' for the purposes of this section.[18] Also, as a general matter of practice, a number of companies, firms, and enterprises use their trade names as their trademarks and even as domain names. For instance, the trademark 'Apple' emanates from the trade name 'Apple Inc.'; the trademark 'Nike' is a component part of 'Nike, Inc.'; or 'Starbucks' from 'Tata Starbucks Pvt. Ltd.', 'Pepsi' from 'PepsiCo, Inc.', etc.[19] Thereby, some trade names may be adopted as trademarks. The requirements provided for a mark to be registered under the Act include the capability of the mark to be represented

---

[14] Ruchi Singh & Paramita Nandy Gupta, *Trademark Infringement under the Garb of Trade Name/ Company Name,* Mondaq (Apr. 20, 2023), https://www.mondaq.com/india/trademark/1299398/trademark-infringement-under-the-garb-of-trade-name--company-name.

[15] *Supra* note 4.

[16] Sakshi, *Trademarks and Trade Names: What's the Connection?* Manupatra (Feb. 11, 2022), https://articles.manupatra.com/article-details/Trademarks-and-trade-names-What-s-the-Connection.

[17] Section 2(1)(m) of Trade Mark Act, 1999.

[18] *Supra* note 14.

[19] *See* USPTO, *How Trademarks and Trade Names Differ*, https://www.uspto.gov/sites/default/files/documents/TM-Trademark-or-Trade-Name-flyer.pdf.

graphically and the capability to distinguish the goods and services of one person from those of another.[20]

Furthermore, upon obtaining registration for trademarks, the trademark proprietor acquires the '*exclusive right to the use of the trade mark in relation to the goods or services in respect of which the trade mark is registered and to obtain relief in respect of infringement of the trade mark*'.[21] This entitles the proprietor to be the sole user of the trademark and to seek reliefs such as injunctions and damages in respect of the infringement of a registered trademark.[22] The acts that amount to infringement of a registered trademark have also been listed under Section 29 of the Act.[23] These include acts such as use of identical or deceptively similar mark as a trade mark; use of identical or similar mark such as to cause confusion or likely to have an association with registered mark; use of identical or similar mark for dissimilar goods and services, where the registered mark is a reputed mark in India and its use without due cause takes unfair advantage of or is detrimental to, the distinctive character or repute of the registered trade mark; use of registered trademark in advertisements that is detrimental to its distinctive character, etc.[24] An important provision that requires pertinent mention is Section 29(5). This subsection deals with instances of infringement of registered trademarks by use of such trademark as a trade name or business concern in respect of the same class of goods and services. In such circumstances, the criterion for evaluating an infringement action entails identifying the component of the trade name containing the registered trademark, as well as that the infringer is dealing in the same products or services that the mark is registered for.[25] The issues arising out of such acts of infringement are significant. The same has been addressed in the next section.

3 Protecting Trademarks Against Use as Trade Names

Trademark law does not restrict the usage of trade names, company names, or fictitious names as trademarks in cases where the trade name and trademark are used by the same person or proprietor. Under the Trademark Act, 1999, however, the law protects registered trademarks against their potential use as trade names by another person. The Trademark Act, 1999, identifies such use of trademarks as infringement of registered trademarks under Section 29, prescribing that '*a registered trade mark*

[20] *See* Section 2(1)(zb) of the Trade Mark Act, 1999.

[21] Section 28(1) of the Trade Mark Act, 1999.

[22] Section 135 of the Trade Mark Act, 1999.

[23] Manzoor Elahi Laskar, *Passing Off and Infringement of Trademarks—India,* SSRN Electronic J. https://www.researchgate.net/publication/261181560_Passing_Off_and_Infringement_of_Trademarks_-_India.

[24] Section 29 of the Trade Mark Act, 1999.

[25] Rohan Joshua Jacob, A convergence of Trade Names and Trade Marks: A Case Comment, Mondaq (Jun. 29, 2021), https://www.mondaq.com/india/trademark/1085382/a-convergence-of-trade-names-and-trade-marks-a-case-comment.

is infringed by a person if he uses such registered trade mark, as his trade name or part of his trade name, or name of his business concern or part of the name, of his business concern dealing in goods or services in respect of which the trade mark is registered'.[26] Where a trademark owner seeks to obtain relief for use of his trademark as a trade name under this provision, he must establish:

a. the existence of a registered trademark,
b. use of such registered trademark as a trade name (or part thereof), or as a business name (or part thereof), and
c. the alleged business concern deals with the same class of goods or services for which the trademark is registered.[27]

However, these three essentials suggest that a trademark proprietor would not find any relief in cases of trademarks being used as a trade name or name of a business concern or part thereof for 'dissimilar' classes of goods and services.[28] The Act is silent on the concern of 'dissimilar' or 'non-competitive' goods or services.[29] This would leave enough scope for an interested market player to use registered marks as part of their trade names and thereby benefit from the reputation of such marks unduly.[30] This raises questions about the nature of relief that would be available to a trademark proprietor when another person uses his trademark as a part of the trade name and provides dissimilar goods and services.

The issue of unauthorized 'use' of a registered trademark 'in the course of trade' in respect of 'dissimilar goods and services' has been addressed under Section 29(4) of the Trade Mark Act, 1999. For the provision to apply and for a trademark proprietor to obtain relief for infringement, the following conditions must be met:

a. use of mark in the course of trade is made by a person who is neither a registered proprietor nor a permitted user,
b. the mark is identical or similar to a registered trademark,
c. mark is used in respect of dissimilar class/classes of goods and services,
d. registered trademark has a reputation in India, and
e. use of such mark without due cause takes unfair advantage of or is detrimental to, the distinctive character or repute of the registered trade mark.[31]

It is pertinent to note that this provision does not refer to the use of the mark as a trade name (or part thereof) or as a business name (or part thereof). Rather, the provision relates to the use of a registered trademark as a 'mark' in the course of trade. In several disputes, the Courts have clarified the scope of this provision

---

[26] Section 29(5) of the Trade Mark Act, 1999.

[27] Ibid.

[28] *See* Cipla Ltd v. Cipla Industries Pvt. Ltd., AIR 2017 Bombay 75.

[29] *Supra* note 16.

[30] Lucy Rana &. Amal Nair, *Cipla Limited vs. Cipla Industries Private Limited: Was the Court's interpretation too Literal?*, Mondaq (May 5, 2017), https://www.mondaq.com/india/trademark/591634/cipla-limited-vs-cipla-industries-private-limited-was-the-courts-interpretation-too-literal.

[31] Section 29(4) of the Trade Marks Act, 1999.

and have interpreted it to mean a dispute of 'registered trademark' v. 'mark', and not of 'registered trademark' v. 'trade name/business name'.[32] This provision could be used by registered proprietors of marks wherein the marks enjoy a considerable degree of reputation so as to prevent third parties from taking unfair advantage of the distinctive character of repute of marks.[33]

4 Judicial Response to Infringement of Trademarks by Use as Trade Names

The implications and limitations of Section 29(5) have been brought to light by several judicial pronouncements. In addition to claiming infringement under Section 29(5), such scope of infringement is also attempted to be brought within the ambit of Section 29(4) in some special circumstances.[34] However, the courts have generally interpreted the provisions literally.

The principal understanding of Section 29(5) is implicit in the judgment of the Bombay High Court in the matter of *Raymond Ltd. v. Raymond Pharmaceutical Ltd.*[35] The plaintiffs were registered proprietors of the trademark 'Raymond' in respect of textile goods including shirting, suiting and saris, dress materials, blankets, shawls, satin, bed and table covers, bedspreads, bed sheets, tissues, felts, curtains, flannel, handkerchiefs, linen, cloth linings, towels, woolen pieces of goods, etc. The defendants adopted the trade name 'Raymond Pharmaceuticals Ltd.' in respect of the product 'pharmaceuticals'. The court denied the application and fulfillment of the requirements of Section 29(5). The court held that the provisions deal with the situation where '*the defendant is not using the registered trade-mark as a trade-mark, but is using the registered trade-mark as a part of its trade name. Use of such a registered trade-mark as a part of a trade name by the defendant also amounts to infringement, but subject to one condition namely that the defendant must be dealing in goods in relation to which the trade-mark is registered*'. Thus, if the defendant uses the trademark as a trade name but does not deal with the same goods for which the mark is registered, there is no infringement under the Trademarks Act.

An important observation made by the Court highlights the legislative wisdom applied in the structure of Section 29(5). The Court highlights that '*the Legislature has not used the phrase goods similar or goods identical to the goods in respect of which the trade mark is registered*'.[36] Thus, it specifically requires that the goods of

---

[32] *See* RPG Enterprises Ltd. v. Riju Ghoshal Trading as RPG Optical & Anr. 2022 SCC OnLine Bom 626; Atlas Cycles (Haryana) Ltd. vs. Atlas. Products. Pvt. Ltd. (2008(36)PTC269(Del); Mankind Pharma Ltd vs Chandra Mani Tiwari & Anr (2018(75)PTC8(Del)).

[33] RPG Enterprises Ltd. v. Riju Ghoshal Trading as RPG Optical & Anr. 2022 SCC OnLine Bom 626.

[34] Ibid.

[35] Raymond Ltd. v. Raymond Pharmaceutical Ltd., 2010 (44) PTC 25 (Bom.).

[36] Ibid at Para 14.

the alleged infringer be the same as those of the trademark proprietor. Moreover, the other clauses in Section 29 have used clear expressions such as 'similar', 'identical' or 'dissimilar'. The same is not the case with Section 29(5).

In the case of *Bloomberg Finance LP v. Prafull Saklecha & Ors.*,[37] the Court granted an injunction against the defendant on the basis of the conditions of Section 29(4) being met. However, while refusing the relief under Section 29(5), the Court enumerated the following principles for the application of Section 29(5):

(a) the infringer must have used the registered trademark as a trade name or a part thereof and must be dealing with the same goods or services for which the mark is registered.
(b) In case one element is exiting and the second is not, there can be no case of infringement under Section 29(5).
(c) For Section 29(5) to apply, there is no requirement to establish the distinctiveness of the mark or a likelihood of confusion.

Further, in *Cipla Ltd. v. Cipla Industries Pvt. Ltd.*,[38] the Bombay High Court examined the question of infringement of the plaintiff's registered trademark 'CIPLA' that was used by the proprietor in relation to pharmaceutical products. The defendants were alleged to have adopted the trademark as a part of their corporate or trade name. However, the defendants claimed to be manufacturers of household items, such as soap dishes, photo frames, ladders, and so on. The Court held that in order to claim that use of a registered trademark as part of a trade name by the defendants amounts to infringement, the plaintiffs must establish that the defendants were dealing in the goods in respect of which the mark is registered. Finding a case of non-infringement under Section 29(5), the Court observed that Section 29(5) is in the '*nature of a per se or a 'no-fault' provision that offers a higher degree of protection where both the above elements are shown to exist. If the owner/proprietor of the registered trade mark is able to show that both of the above elements exist, then an injunction order restraining order the infringer should straightaway follow. For the purpose of Section 29(5) of the TM Act 1999, there is no requirement to show that the mark has a distinctive character or that any confusion is likely to result from the use by the infringer of the registered mark as part of its trade name or name of the business concern*'.[39] However, the Court also observed that the object of Section 29(5) was not to close the doors for a registered proprietor to seek relief in respect of a reputed trademark being used as a trade name for dissimilar goods or services. A plaintiff may resort to Section 29(4), provided the qualifications of the provision are met. Additionally, a passing off action is maintainable in the case of a well-known mark, even if the goods and services being dealt with by the parties are not similar.

[37] Bloomberg Finance LP v. Prafull Saklecha & Ors. [2013 (56) PTC 243 (Del)].

[38] Cipla Ltd v. Cipla Industries Pvt. Ltd., AIR 2017 BOMBAY 75.

[39] The Court relied on the decision of Delhi High Court in the case of Bloomberg Finance LP v. Prafull Saklecha & Ors. [2013 (56) PTC 243 (Del)].

In the case of *RPG Enterprises Ltd. v. Riju Ghoshal*,[40] the Bombay High Court examined the application of Section 29(5). The plaintiff brought an action of infringement against the defendants in respect of the use of its registered trademark 'RPG', alleging the use of the trademark by the defendants for their 'RPG Opticals' and 'RPG Pharmacy'. The plaintiff used the mark 'RPG' in connection with businesses such as tires, infrastructure, information technology, pharmaceuticals, energy, senior care, e-commerce, and plantations. The Court found a case of infringement under Section 29(4), holding that the defendants had used the identical trademark for dissimilar goods and the Plaintiff had existing reputation in the market. However, a case under Section 29(5) was not made out as the Court held that '*the Defendants are using their marks "RPG Opticals" and "RPG Pharmacy" only as a trade name, and they are not selling any goods under the mark RPG. The use by the defendants of the expression "RPG" is found only in the trading name, and hence the plaintiff has to prove infringement, if any, under Section 29(5) of the Trade Marks Act, 1999. That, for infringement of a registered trade mark by use as a trade name, the goods in which the defendant is dealing have to be "same or identical" and not "similar", which is not the case herein*'. Thus, Section 29(5) is not applicable in the case of similar or dissimilar goods. The goods must be identical to those for which the claimed trademark is registered.

Thus, the situation envisaged under Section 29(5) is restricted exclusively to the use of a registered trademark as a trade or business name dealing with the same class of goods or services in respect of which the mark is registered.[41] The problem that emerges from such interpretation of the provision is the absence of a remedy for a registered proprietor or the proprietor of even a well-known trademark, whose registered or well-known trademark is used by another person as a trade name for dissimilar goods or services. While reputed and well-known marks may still find some remedy in an action of 'passing off', the registered marks that do not have a reputation will find no relief when their registered mark is adopted as a trade name by another person for dissimilar goods and services.

5 Remedy Available Under Companies Act, 2013

On the action of infringement under Section 29(5), a perusal of the statutory provision and the interpretation of the same drawn by the courts in several decisions indicate a lack of necessary remedy for trademark proprietors in some cases. In particular, a registered trademark proprietor cannot find relief under Section 29(5) where his registered trademark is adopted as a trade name or business name for similar or dissimilar classes of goods or services. However, the only remedy available on such occasions is the remedy provided under Section 16(1)(b) of the Companies Act, 2013.

---

40 *Supra* note 33.

41 *See* Bharadwaj Jaishankar & Mohit Goel, *Section 29(4) v. Section 29(5)—Disputed Territory*, https://www.simandsan.com/intellect_sections_29_4_v_29_5.html.

The Companies Act, 2013 provides that where a company has been registered by a name that is identical with or too nearly resembles a registered trademark under the Trade Marks Act, 1999, the Central Government may direct such name to be changed or rectified on the basis of an application filed to the Central Government by the registered proprietor of the trademark.[42] The Act requires such an application to be filed by the registered proprietor within a period of three years of the incorporation, registration, or change of name of the Company.[43] If the aforementioned limitation is fulfilled, the holder of a registered trademark may take action under Section 16(1)(b) of the Companies Act, even if the company's business aim differs from the products or services covered by the registered trademark.[44] In addition to the three-year limitation set out under the section, the only consideration for the provision to be invoked is whether the name of the company is identical with or too nearly resembles a registered trademark.[45]

Furthermore, by virtue of Rule 8 of the Companies (Incorporation) Rules, 2014, some names have been identified as 'undesirable names' for the purposes of incorporation of companies under the Companies Act, 2013. The rules also suggest that 'undesirable names' also include '*the name of a registered trade mark or a trade mark which is subject of an application for registration, unless the consent of the owner or applicant for registration, of the trade mark, as the case may be, has been obtained and produced by the promoters*'.[46] Thus, a trademark that is registered under the Trademark Act, 1999, and a trademark that is the subject of an application for trademark registration are deemed to be 'undesirable' names for companies. However, if the consent of the trademark proprietor or trademark applicant has been obtained, then the mark shall not be deemed undesirable.

6 Conclusion

The Trademark Act, 1999 covers a wide scope of acts that amount to infringement of trademark proprietor's rights. Section 29 of the Act provides for different circumstances where a third party may be held liable for an act of infringement. However, the concern of using trademark as a trade name has been specifically dealt with under Section 29(5). The provision holds a third party accountable and liable for infringement for meeting two requirements:

a. use a registered trademark as a trade name by an alleged infringer, and
b. use to be made in respect of goods or services for which the trademark is registered.

---

[42] Section 16(1)(b) of the Companies Act, 2013.

[43] Ibid.

[44] *Supra* note 14.

[45] Ibid.

[46] Rule 8 (2)(a)(ii) of the Companies (Incorporation) Rules, 2014.

Various judicial pronouncements clarify that the scope and limits of Section 29(5) are unique and distinct from those provided under Sections 29(1) to (4). However, due to the limitation of Section 29(5) upon including use of the trademark as a trade name for similar or dissimilar classes of goods and services, several disputes highlight the possibility of applying Section 29(4). The analysis of the judicial decisions highlight that the courts have established a clear principle on the use of the two provisions. As per the literal interpretation of the courts, the use of trademarks as trade names falls within the absolute domain of Section 29(5). The cases of use of a trademark as a mark are covered under Section 29(4) and the cases of use of trademark as a trade name are covered under Section 29(5).

This interpretation denies the possibility for registered proprietors to claim any remedy where their registered trademark is adopted by an entity as a trade name, dealing in similar or dissimilar goods. The Trademark Act, 1999 does not afford a possible remedy in such circumstances. However, Section 16(1)(b) of the Companies Act, 2013 provides an opportunity to a registered proprietor of a trademark to seek rectification in the company name in case the name is identical with or too nearly resembles a registered trade mark. For the same reason, similarity, dissimilarity, or identity with the nature of goods and services is irrelevant. Also, precautionary safeguards are maintained under the Companies (Incorporation) Rules, 2014 as well.

However, an important perspective that remains ignored is the consumer confusion that may result from the adoption of some trademarks as trade names. For instance, in the case of *RPG Enterprises Ltd. v. Riju Ghoshal*,[47] the plaintiff was involved in the manufacturing of pharmaceutical product ingredients, among others. On the other hand, the defendant was operating a pharmacy under the name 'RPG Pharmacy'. For the purposes of establishing infringement under other clauses of Section 29, the consumer perspective may have some relevance. However, the court's decision did not consider the consumer's perspective while applying Section 29(5).

The authors recommend that the interpretation of Section 29(5) be widened. The provision shall also provide an opportunity for reputed or well-known trademark proprietors to seek remedy for infringement where their trademark is adopted as a trade name for similar and dissimilar classes of goods or services, taking into consideration the 'likelihood of confusion' or 'likelihood of association' on the part of consumers.

[47] *Supra* note 33.

Child Offender Under Juvenile Justice Act, 2022: A Comparative Study to Evolve Restorative Justice

Rupam Jagota and Arshi Pal Kaur

Abstract Children are the future citizens of the nation, the pillars of progressive growth and development, a national asset perhaps God's greatest gift to humanity. In International and national laws, the framers of the constitution declared that the state would direct its policy to ensure that children are provided with opportunities and facilities against exploitation, moral degradation, abandonment, and crime. Juveniles in conflict with the law are multiplying worldwide due to the mad race for family order, organization, and supremacy, where they become easy victims of crime. This paper is a humble attempt to analyze the Juvenile Justice Amendment Act, 2022, in the background of the Juvenile Justice Act, 2015 (hereinafter JJA Act, 2015), in which a child-friendly approach is adopted to provide care, protection, development, treatment, and social reintegration to them. The focus is on addressing the basic needs of adjudication and disposition of cases in the best interest of children. It also focuses on the rehabilitation of children and provides measures for their adoption so that they can join the mainstream of society and live their lives in the social fabric under the rule of law. The Act focuses on rules and guidelines. Adoption by a recognized agency and a regulatory framework supported by rules so that children in need of care and protection are entitled to protection. The researcher has evaluated the Juvenile Act as well as child victims of crimes and their involvement in crime. A comparative study has been done between India and the USA to arrive at an adequate analysis of how far away the future threats are. Some suggestions are put forward to reduce crime and ensure a better future for young offenders.

Keywords Child · Delinquency · Justice · Protection · Rights · Care

R. Jagota (✉)
Guru Nanak Dev University, Regional Campus, Jalandhar, India
e-mail: rupamjagota@yahoo.com

A. P. Kaur
Guru Nanak Dev University, Regional Campus, Gurdaspur, India

J. Aston et al. (eds.), *Comparative Law*, https://doi.org/10.1007/978-981-97-7815-7_16

1 Introduction

The juvenile justice system basically deals with juvenile delinquents and neglected children. This system, in its formal sense, was started in 1899 when the USA established the world's first juvenile court in Cook County, Illinois. Since then, the journey began and continues today. In the USA, the juvenile justice system began to be adopted by other western countries. With the intervention of the United Nations Organization, the issue of juvenile justice became an international agenda. In the international arena, the United Nations has been working in the direction of recognizing child rights in general and laying down minimum standards, rules, and guidelines to be followed in dealing with juveniles in particular.

The Constitution of India has also intended to secure the basic needs of the children. There are many provisions in Indian Constitution that provide for the protection of some basic rights of children. The Center and States are empowered to enact provisions for the well-being of children. Particularly after independence, the Indian government, both at the center and state levels, has strived hard to ensure a constitutional mandate regarding the protection of children. The constitutional provisions like Art. 15(3), Art. 23, Art. 24, Art. 39(e) and Art. 45 contain specific with respect to children. There provisions have also inspired the development in the field of juvenile justice." Art. 15(3), Art. 23, Art. 24, Art. 39(e), Art. 45, "contain some specific provision with respect to children. The judiciary in India plays a very important role and has passed many significant judgments in favor of child rights." In *Sheela Barse v. Union of India*,[1] "the Supreme Court issued directions to the state government to set up necessary observation homes where children accused of an offense could be lodged and to set up dedicated juvenile courts." The juvenile justice (care and protection of children) Act "brings a child found in conditions of economic and social deprivation within its protective jurisdiction. The Act also makes provision for the greater participation of the community in the operations of the juvenile justice system."

Special mention is needed for the Children Act of 1960. States and union territories had their own legislation. No uniformity was there. The Hon'ble Supreme Court took serious note of the lack of a central law on juvenile justice. After 25 years, the Indian Parliament took a historic step by enacting the Juvenile Justice Act, 1986. A common framework for juvenile justice was provided. Then, in 1992, after ratifying the Convention on the Rights of Child, the government enacted a new piece of legislation, the, Juvenile Justice Act, 2000. This law replaced the Act of 1986. Many positive changes were introduced by this Act. However, it was in December 2012 that another debate started related to the inefficacy of the Act of 2000. The demand was that juveniles should be punished for heinous offenses like rape, murder, etc. After many deliberations, finally a new law, the Juvenile Justice Act, was passed in 2015. Now almost six years have elapsed since the enactment of the Act of 2015,

[1] AIR 1986 SC 1773.

but the issue of juvenile justice is still a matter of concern among experts.[2] "After the 2012 Delhi gang rape, the government felt the need to bring a new juvenile law, and a bill was introduced in Parliament by Maneka Gandhi on August 12 2014. The Juvenile Justice (Care and Protection of Children) Bill, 2015 was passed by Lok Sabha on May 7, 2015. It was passed by the Rajya Sabha on December 22 2015. It got the assent of president on December 31, 2015 and was enforced on January 15, 2016. Juvenile Justice" (Care and Protection of Children) Act, 2015, has come into force from 15 January 2016, and repeals the Juvenile Justice (Care and Protection of Children) Act, 2000. The main feature of this act is treating juveniles in the 16–18 age group as adults in heinous offenses. The JJ Act, 2015 provides for strengthened provisions for both children in need of care and protection and children in conflict with the law. Some of the key provisions include such as change in nomenclature from *juvenile* to *child* or *child in conflict with law*, across the Act to remove the negative connotation associated with the word *juvenile*, inclusion of several new definitions such as orphaned, abandoned and surrendered children; and petty, serious and heinous offenses committed by children, clarity in powers, function, and responsibilities of Juvenile Justice Board and Child Welfare Committee, clear timelines for inquiry by Juvenile Justice Board, special provisions for heinous offenses committed by children above the age of sixteen year; separate new chapter on Adoption to streamline adoption of orphan, abandoned and surrendered children; inclusion of new offenses committed against children; and mandatory registration of Child Care Institutions."[3] "Recently, the JJ Act, 2015, was amended in 2021 to introduce multiple changes. The child rights bodies pointed out an amendment in Section 86(2) of the JJ Act, 2015, which changed the nature of certain serious crimes from *cognizable* to *non-cognizable*. The crucial amendment will prevent the police from arresting the accused without a warrant and start an investigation without the permission of the court.[4]

The term juvenile justice is therefore used to refer to social as well as juridical justice. India seeks to provide social and juridical justice to neglected and delinquent children through the use of code, constables, courts, and residential institutions for both categories of children those committing an offense and others living in circumstances likely to lead them into the life of crime. The legislation incorporating the juvenile justice system has made provisions for the care, protection, treatment, development, and rehabilitation of neglected or delinquent juveniles and for the adjudication of certain matters relating to the disposition of delinquent juveniles. Their provisions govern the relationship between children and the police, adjudicatory

[2] R. N. Chaudhary, Law Relating To Juvenile Justice in India 1708 (Orient Publishing Company 2015 (4th ed. 2015).

[3] S. P. Srivastava, Juvenile Justice in India Programmes and Perspectives 4 (Ajanta Publications, (1989).

[4] Ajoy Ashirwad Mahaprashasta, *Amendment in Juvenile Justice Act 'Shields Perpetrators': Child Rights Bodies of 4 States, The Wire, Apr. 29, 2022,* https://thewire.in/rights/juvenile-justice-act-amendment-child-rights, (Dec. 3, 2023, 10.30 PM).

bodies, correctional homes, probation services, community participation, and after-care programmes."[5] Each of its three main components; law enforcement, adjudication, and correction, frequently operate haphazardly with little knowledge of what the other segments are doing. This noncoordination leads to an inefficient utilization of resources and retards the process of justice.[6]

2 Concept of Juvenile Delinquency

The term *juvenile delinquency* has been differently interpreted, but, generally speaking, it refers to a large variety of behaviors of children and adolescents that society does not approve and for which some kind of admonishment, punishment, or preventive and corrective measures are justified in the public interest. The use of the word juvenile should be clearly understood to refer to a legal classification that is established within the parameters of culture and social custom."[7]

Ruth Cavan describes delinquency as "a delinquent child who, by habitually refusing to obey reasonable and lawful authority, is deemed to be habitually uncontrolled, habitually disobedient, or habitually a truant from home or school, or who habitually so deports himself as to injure or endanger the moral, health, or welfare of himself or others."[8]

The second United Nations Congress on the prevention of crime and the treatment of offenders, held in London in 1960, considered the scope of the problem of juvenile delinquency. Without attempting to formulate a standard definition of what should be considered to be juvenile delinquency in each country, the Congress recommended":

(a) "That the meaning of the term juvenile delinquency, should be restricted as for as possible to violation of criminal law" and
(b) "That even for protection, specific offences which would penal is small irregularities or maladjusted behaviour of minoveds but for which adults would not be prosecuted should not be created."

The need was also felt in the USA for narrowing the extent of juvenile delinquency, and the Standard Juvenile Court Act avoided most of the items of delinquency cited in the list of Rubin. The standard Act included in its provisions what corresponds to the usual delinquency definition; only two items in addition to violations of law or ordinance. These items are a child "who deserts his home or who is habitually disobedient or is beyond the control of his parents or other custodian; and who, being required by law to attend school, wilfully violates rules thereof or absents himself

[5] Ved Kumari, The Juvenile Justice System in India From Welfare to Rights 4 (Oxford University Press 2010) (2d ed., 2010).

[6] *Id.*

[7] Gus Martin, Juvenile Justice Process and System 6 (Sage Publications, 2005).

[8] R. S. Cavan, Delinquency and Crime Cross-Cultural Perspective 87 (J. B. Lippincott Co. Philadelphia, 1968).

there from. *Walker* has stated that delinquency refers to acts that violate state law or municipal ordinance by youth of juvenile court age or to conduct so seriously anti-social as to interfere with the rights of others or to menace the welfare of the delinquent himself or for the community. Criminality can lead to arrest, conviction, or incarceration for adults, while delinquency is related to juveniles committing unlawful acts."[9]

In India, the definition of juvenile delinquency presents no such problems as are faced in the "USA" and some other countries. The concept is confined to the violation of ordinary penal law of the country so far as the jurisdiction of the juveniles who are in conflict with the law and children who are in need of care and protection is called the Juvenile Justice (Care and Protection of Children) Act, 2000. This law has replaced the earlier law governing juveniles, which was known as the Juvenile Justice Act, 1986, and was in conformity with the UN Standard Minimum Rules for the Administration of Juvenile Justice (also known as the Beijing Rules 1985). However, the Juvenile Justice (Care and Protection of Children) Act, 2000, which replaces the Juvenile Justice Act, 1986 is primarily designed to give effect to the provisions of the UN Convention on the Rights of the Child, 1989 (ratified by Indian December, 1992). The Convention laid stress on the social reintegration of child victims, to the extent possible, without resorting to judicial proceedings.[10]

3 Juvenile Justice System in the USA and India

The origin of juvenile court in the United States can be traced back to the system of appointment of state agents in Massachusetts (Boston) in 1869. These state agents were to take protective care of juveniles. In 1878, the work of the state agents was transferred to the probation officer, who took care of the juvenile placed under his charge. Today, there is a juvenile court in each state of the USA. The workings of a juvenile court in the USA are relatively simple and more or less informal. As, the police first take custody of the juvenile offender, the police officer has the diction either to keep the child in custody or to immediately release him, admonish him or her, or to do both and allow parents to take custody of the child. Next, the police contact the juvenile court for notification of parents, and the person notified by the court assumes responsibility for the custody of the delinquent. The police also interrogate the offender and take his fingerprints or photographs. The record provides an important clause for tracing the juvenile. In the Kent case, US Supreme Court observed that juveniles might be receiving both less legal protection and less treatment.[11]

---

[9] Umesh Kumar, Applied Criminology 154 (Anmol Publications Pvt. Ltd. 2012).

[10] N.V. Pranjape, Criminology and Penology With Victimology 633 (Central Law Publication 2015) 16th ed. (2015).

[11] Steven M. Cox, Juvenile Justice, a Guide to Theory, Policy, and Practice 10 (Sage Publications 2014, 8th ed. 2014).

Many scholars stress the importance of reforming the juvenile justice system to increase its effectiveness and avoid discrimination. Finley argues for early intervention in juvenile delinquency and advocates for the development of programs that are more centered on rehabilitation than punishment. James C. Howell et al. argue that zero-tolerance policies overwhelm the juvenile justice system with low-risk offenders and should be eliminated. They also argue that the most effective ways to reform the juvenile justice system would be to reduce the overrepresentation of minorities and eliminate the transfer of juveniles to the criminal justice system. *Zimring and Tannenhaus* also discuss the future of the juvenile justice system in the United States. They argue that educational re-entry programs should be developed and given high importance alongside policies of dropout prevention. Re-entry programs focus on providing care and support to juveniles after being released from detention facilities, and encouraging family support to help adolescents during this adjustment period. They also argue for the elimination of juvenile sex offender registration requirements, and the reform of criminal record information for juvenile offenders.[12]

Restorative justice is an approach to justice that focuses on the needs of the victims, the offenders, and the involved community, rather than punishing the offender. Victims and offenders both take an active role in the process, with the latter being encouraged to take responsibility for their actions. Doing so is an attempt by offenders to repair the harm they have done and also provides help for the offender in order to prevent future offenses. Restorative justice is based on a theory of justice that views crime as an offense against an individual and/or a community, versus the state. Programs that promote dialog between victim and offender demonstrate the highest rates of victim satisfaction and offender accountability. In March 2005, in the case of *Roper v. Simmons* the US Supreme Court struck down the death penalty for crimes committed by people under the age of 18.[13]

Many advocates argue that the juvenile system should extend to include youth older than 18 years. Research in neurobiology and developmental psychology shows that young adults' brains do not finish developing until their mid-20s, well beyond the age of criminal responsibility in most states. New York and North Carolina remain the only states to prosecute all youth as adults when they turn 16 years of age. *Connecticut Governor, Danell Mallor* just proposed raising the age in his state to 20 years. It is very clear from the study that all the Countries have made special legislation to deal with juvenile delinquency. Age of the juvenile is maximum eighteen years in all countries. All juvenile justice system is aimed to protect the interest of the Children and for this specific provision for care protection and rehabilitation of the Children are made. United Nation also recognized the need for the care and protection of the Children. There is consensus among different countries that juveniles should be specially treated and protected because they are the future of the world.[14]

---

[12] Gus Martin, Juvenile Justice System Process and System 202 (Sage Publications, 2005).

[13] Steven M. Cox, Juvenile Justice, a Guide to Theory, Policy, and Practice, Eight Edition 10 (Sage Publications, Los Angels, 2014).

[14] See footnote 14.

The USA, similar to other nations, earlier had laws that were lenient toward juvenile offenders. However, this approach to the treatment of offenders changed over time. Refugee and reform homes were established in big cities such as New York and Chicago in the 1800s. This approach was resorted to in order to cater to the special and other private requirements of juveniles and to separate them from the associations of other adult criminals. This method also paved the way for reforming juveniles and possibly deterring future crime. The penal reformists of the USA too had the view that juveniles had to be reformed and rehabilitation was the primary motive of the laws rather than awarding criminal liability and punishment to juveniles. They were initially against the imposition of penal liability as well; this was due to the belief that these juvenile offenders were immature and reformative measures could potentially correct them and bring them back to society. Further, the point of their being impulsive in nature and having relatively impressionable minds came into play, which could lead to kids becoming delinquents. Such malleable minds in children make them extremely susceptible to unnecessary influences. To add on to such a factor, the impulsive nature of juveniles thwarts their capacity to assess and effectively comprehend the ramifications of their actions. Due to such views, which were prevalent in society, policies that spoke of deinstitutionalization and decriminalizing children were established. But their establishment was momentary. Soon, this perception transitioned in the 1900s, after looking at some of the more heinous crimes undertaken, the increase in the extent of violence and magnitude of deviance, these policies were overruled and new laws replaced the old. Under these laws, juveniles were also criminalized for the horrific acts performed. The slogan "adult crime adult time" became a popular belief and spread like wildfire throughout the nation. In a short duration, these laws were accepted and implemented by 38 states in the USA. In certain states like South Dakota and Indiana, juvenile aged 10 are also tried as adults. However, the degree of punishment varies. A child aged 12 may be awarded life imprisonment if found that he/she committed extremely gruesome and appalling crimes.[15] These serious juvenile offenders are maintained in a separate facility with a controlled environment and are given therapy and other rehabilitative programs in an attempt to turn them around. In cases where the crimes are somber and inexorable are performed by 13–15 year children, the jurisdiction of the juvenile court comes to an end and the case is moved to the adult court considering the nature of the crime.[16]

The nineteenth century witnessed a drastic change as far as the treatment of juveniles in the USA was concerned. Big cities like New York and Chicago opened the New York House of Refuge in 1825 and the Chicago Reform School in the year 1855, respectively, for juveniles to separate them from adult hardened criminals.

[15] Dr. Shivani Goswami and Dr. Neelu Mehra, *Juvenile Justice Systems in United States and India: Modern Scenario and Much Needed Modifications*, 256, Journal of Law and Criminal Justice (2014).

[16] Sumedha Sainat, *A Critical Analysis: Juxtaposing the Juvenile Justice Systems in the United Kingdom, India, and the United States of America*, International Journal of Legal Science and Innovation (Dec. 12, 2003, 10.00 PM). https://www.ijlsi.com/wp-content/uploads/A-Critical-Analysis-Juxtaposing-the-Juvenile-Justice-Systems-in-the-United-Kingdom-India-and-the-United-States-of-America.pdf.

Not only this, opportunities of rehabilitation were also provided to deter them from committing future and prospective crimes. The first juvenile Court in the USA came into existence in the year 1899 in Cook County, Illinois. After this within a span of 25 years most states in the USA had established juvenile court system. As far as these early juvenile court systems were concerned their main aim was to rehabilitate and reform the offender rather than impose punitive and penal measures on them.[17] In the rehabilitative model of juvenile system, the immaturity of young offenders played an important role."[18] "The Juveniles require different treatment to rectify them and therefore their correctional methods should also be different from adults. Both of these cannot be treated equally. The protagonist of this also believed that the criminal acts committed by young offenders reflect their immaturity, and thus similar procedures and punishment should not be meted out to the juveniles as is inflicted on the adults.[19] Not only this, some people also believed that juveniles should be less accountable because sometimes, due to the impulsiveness or malleability of youth, a crime may be committed. Impulsiveness presumably contributes to incapacity because it impedes the ability to weigh the consequences of behavior, while malleability might make juveniles vulnerable to bad influences, particularly from peers.[20]

During the 1970s and 1985, all the states adopted juvenile policies relating to decriminalization and deinstitutionalization. However, such policies were not long-lived and in the mid-1980s due to changes in the nature of crime by young offenders, increase in violence, etc., criminalization of delinquents were revived. During the early 1990s, several states in the USA had called for special legislative session to deal with youth crime. Presently, in the USA, slogan "adult crime adult time" is being adopted. In 38 states of USA, upper age of juveniles is seventeen years while in other three states it is fifteen years. There is unanimity in almost all US states on the point of trying juveniles at par with adults on juvenile attaining the age of fourteen years in certain circumstances barring states like Vermont, Indiana, South Dakota where a child of even ten years can be tried as adult. As far as punishment part is concerned there are various forms of penalties that are given to the juveniles. In heinous crimes, even life imprisonment can be granted to child aged twelve years which is considered to be the maximum punishment. Juveniles who have the potential to try serious offenses are detained in secured and tenable environment and are made to take part in rehabilitative program. All this is done to control young juveniles. Additionally rigorous punishments relating to drugs and gang-related offenses, stringent treatment such as boot camps and blended sentence have also been introduced to put them right.

---

[17] Julian Mack, *The Juvenile Court*, 1201, Harvard Law Review (1909) (Dec. 14, 2023 11.00AM), https://www.jstor.org/stable/1325042.

[18] Elizabeth S. Scotland & Thomas Grisso, *The evolution of Adolescence: A Developmental Perspective on Juvenile Justice Reform, 141–143.* The Journal of Criminal Law and Criminology (1973).

[19] Martin R Gardner, *The right of Juvenile Offenders to be Punished: Some Implications of Treating kids as Persons*, 182–191 NEB.L.REV (1989).

[20] Elizabeth S Scott & Thomas Grisso, *The Evolution of Adolescence: A Developmental Perspective on Juvenile Justice Reform*, 144 The Journal of Criminal Law and Criminology (1973).

As far as the jurisdiction part is concerned if a child usually 13 or 15 commits a grave and grim crime then their case is automatically shifted to adult court. Jurisdiction of juvenile courts is automatically waived in such cases. Position in India As far as position of Juveniles in India is concerned, since ages there has been a trend of providing different treatment for juvenile offenders. In the year 1843, i.e., during colonial regime, Lord Cornwalis established Ragged School for such children. The Apprentice Act,[21] which talked about juvenile legislation came in the year 1850. After a decade, Indian Penal Code (IPC) was enacted. Though the Code does not specifically talked about Juvenile offenders nevertheless there are certain provisions in the Code which deals with underage criminals.[22]

According to Section 82 of the IPC, children who are less than seven years of age are doliincapax, i.e., they are incapable of committing crime. They do not have mens rea or the intent to commit a crime. Section 83 basically talks about children between seven and twelve years of age. These children, while committing crime, if they can understand the nature of crime, they are punishable. Additionally, Sections 27 and 360[23,24] of the Code of Criminal Procedure, 1973, also talk about young offenders. Then came the Reformatory School Act of 1876[25] After this, the reformatory school Act of 1876 and 1897 were the next milestones for the treatment of juveniles in India, and with it, there was a shift of penal philosophy from punitive to reformatory measures, i.e., now the main aim was to reform the juveniles rather than imposing punitive measures on them.

The present juvenile justice system is governed according to several international covenants. For example: UN Conventions on the Rights of the Child (CRC), UN Standard Minimum Rules for administration of Justice (Beijing Rules). Also in India

---

[21] According to the Act, children in the age group of ten to eighteen years who committed crime were placed in apprenticeship in a trade.

[22] The talked about provisions dealing with underage criminals are Sections 82 and 83, IPC SECTION 82, IPC: Act of a child under seven years of age-Nothing is an offence which is done by a child under seven years of age. Section 83, IPC: Act of a child above seven and under twelve of immature understanding—nNothing is an offence which is done by a child above seven years of age and under twelve, who has not attained sufficient maturity of understanding to judge of the nature and consequences of his conduct on that occasion.

[23] Section 27, Cr.P.C.: If a person below sixteen years of age commits an offence other than the one punishable with death or imprisonment for life, he should be awarded a lenient punishment depending upon his previous history, character and circumstances which led him to commit the crime. His sentence can further be commuted for good behavior during the term of his imprisonment.

[24] Section 360, Cr.P.C: Any person below twenty one years of age or any woman, is convicted of an offence not being punishable with death or imprisonment for life, and no previous conviction is proved against such person, the Court may having regard to the age, character, and antecedents of the offender, and to the circumstances in which the offence was committed, order release of the offender on probation of good conduct for a period not exceeding three years on entering into a bond with or without sureties, instead of sentencing him to punishment.

[25] According to this the government was empowered to establish reformatory schools and to habitat criminals till suitable job was found for them 16Article 15(3) Constitution, India: Nothing in this article shall prevent the State from making any special provision for woman and children.

Article 15(3)[26] of the Constitution talks special provisions for children. This article has been specifically framed in the constitution for protection of children. Not only this, Article 21,[27] 23,[28] and 24,[29] of the Constitution of India deals with fundamental rights available to children. Additionally Article 39(e)[30] and Article 39(f[31]) and Article 45[32] also talks about children. Also National Policy for Children which talked about training and rehabilitation, destitution, neglected and exploited children came in the year 1974.[33] A comprehensive legislation on juvenile known as Juvenile justice Act was passed in the year 1986.[34] In the year 2000, the Juvenile Justice (Care and Protection of Children) Act was enacted. The Act provides that a child who has not completed the age of 18 years is a juvenile.[35] This 2000 Act has been amended

---

[26] INDIA CONST. art 15(3): Nothing in this article shall prevent the State from making any special provision for woman and children.

[27] INDIA CONST. art. 21: No person shall be deprived of his life or personal liberty except according to procedure established by law.

[28] INDIA CONST. art. 23: Prohibition of traffic in human beings and forced labour: (1) traffic in human beings and beggar and other similar forms of forced labour are prohibited and any contravention of this provision shall be an offence punishable in accordance with law. (2) Nothing in this article shall prevent the state from imposing compulsory service for public purposes, and in imposing such services the State shall not make any discrimination on grounds only of religion, race, caste or class or any of them.

[29] INDIA CONST. art. 24: Prohibition of employment of children in factories, etc.: No child below the age of fourteen years shall be employed to work in any factory or mine or engaged in any other hazardous employment.

[30] INDIA CONST. art 39(e): Certain principles of policy to be followed by the state: that the health and strength of workers, man and women, and the tender age of children are not abused and that citizens are not forced by economic necessity to enter avocations unsuited to their age or strength.

[31] INDIA CONST. art. 39(f): that children are given opportunities and facilities to develop in a healthy manner and in conditions of freedom and dignity and that childhood and youth are protected against exploitation and against moral and material abandonment.

[32] INDIA CONST. art. 45: Provisions for early childhood care and education to children below the age of six years. The State shall endeavour to provide early childhood care and education for all children until they complete the age of six years.

[33] Hansaria V, Jose, Juvenile Justice System 17 (Universal Law Publishing Company Pvt Ltd, 2011).

[34] Under the Act, the juvenile age for boys and girls is 16 and 18 years, respectively.

[35] In 1992, India became a signatory and ratified Child Rights Convention, 1989. Juvenile Justice Act, 1986 got repealed. The Juvenile Justice (Care and Protection of Children) Act, 2000 has made a departure from juvenile justice Act, 1986 as now under the Act uniformity of age, i.e., 18 years is made both for boys and girls. The Act basically talks about two types of children one, who are in conflict with law (an individual under the age of 18 years who is accused of committing an offence) and second those who are in need of care and protection (children from deprived and marginalized sections of the society as well as those with different needs and vulnerabilities). Under the Act, Juvenile Justice Boards were established to deal with children in conflict with law. Juvenile Justice Board consist of three members First Class Judicial Magistrate (who should be well versed in child psychology or child welfare) and two honorary social workers (who should be actively involved in welfare activities of children for minimum period of seven years). One of these two members has to be a woman. Provision is also made for termination of the members if they misuse the power vested by the Act, they have been convicted of an offence involving moral principles, failure to attend proceedings of the board for three consecutive months or is absent for three fourth of the sitting in the year. When the Board is not sitting, the child can be produced before any member

several times in the years 2006, 2010, and 2011, i.e., in the years 2006, 2010, and 2011 amendments have been made. The 2006 Amendment Act included 26 amendments. The Act provides for legal system for care, protection, treatment, and rehabilitation of both the categories of children, i.e., children in conflict with law and children in need of care and protection. Presently also the Government of India is further contemplating for various amendments and a draft bill is pending before ministry of Law and Justice for scrutiny. There is no doubt about a fact that India hails in comprehensive legislations and in spite of the fact that a detailed, comprehensive and several times amended legislation is prevalent in India, the crimes committed by juveniles are swelling and mounting up every day. Is not the liberal and open minded approach on juveniles one of the reasons why such crimes are elevating and escalating every day.[36] The total number of crimes in different years committed by juveniles clearly endorse this view.[37] How can one forget ever burning case of Nirbhaya. In the said case, a 23-year-old woman was gang raped by six men, one of whom was a minor, in the moving bus. The woman was dragged to the rear of bus and was beaten with rod and simultaneously raped in the moving bus. According to medical reports she suffered serious injuries in her abdomen, intestines, and genitals. The doctors stated that some blunt object (may be an iron rod) was used for penetration. According to the International Bureau Times, a police spokesman said, the minor in the said case was the nastiest, brutal, fierce attacker and had sexually abused his victim twice and had ripped out her intestines with bare hands. The woman struggled for so many days to beat death but unfortunately she succumbed to injuries on December 29, 2012 after suffering from brain damage, pneumonia, abdominal infection etc." "Nirbhaya is one of those cases where innocent people are tormented, anguished and persecuted by juveniles for no fault of theirs. In the said case minor was described as the most vicious, unruly and fierce attacker who was actively involved in the crime. He was the one who had sexually abused woman twice and had ripped out her intestines with bare hands. Now the question is does not he know the nature of crime and what act he is committing? The answer is probably "Yes" he knows everything. Is he really innocent? Perhaps No. Nirbhaya is not the only case. These juveniles are involved into heinous and odious crimes like murder, rape, theft, robbery, etc. and the worst part is they are taking advantage of the protection of the Act accorded to them."

---

of the Board. As far as the decision of the Board is concerned, it is the majority rule that prevails, and if no majority is there, then the opinion expressed by Principal Magistrate is final. For such children, more legal protection assured detention to be the last resort.

[36] The child apprehended by the police under juvenile justice Act is brought within a period of 24 h before JJB. The child is sent to the observation home for safe custody. The child can be set free on bail if the parents are present on certain terms and conditions. If bail not given the child continues to stay in observation home and is presented before JJB after every 15 days. After the charge sheet is filed by the police the child is told about the charges brought against them by the JJB. If the child admits his guilt, final order is passed and the child is admonished/ counselled/fine imposed or is told to remain in special home till he attains the age of eighteen years. If the child does not admit his guilt the trial continues and the orders are passed under section 15 of the juvenile Justice Act.

[37] The Hindu (Dec. 12, 2023) http://www.thehindu.com/news/national/35465-juveniles-arrested-under-ipc-in2012/article4869193.ece.

4 Child Offender Under Juvenile Justice Act, 2022: A Comparative Analysis

The Children Act, 1960, was the most important piece of juvenile justice legislation. It was applicable to Delhi and other Union Territories. The primary gap in this Act, though, was the scope of its application. Only Delhi and the Union Territories were subject to it. It was not applied consistently across the nation. The Juvenile Justice Act, 1986, which replaced the earlier Children Act, 1960, aimed at giving effect to the guidelines contained in the Standard Minimum Rule for the Administration of Juvenile Justice adopted by the UN countries in November, 1985. The Juvenile Justice Act, 1986, was one of the first central laws on juvenile justice enacted by the Indian Parliament under Article 253 of the Constitution. The JJA, 1986 gave rise to a system for uniformly defining delinquency and neglect across the nation. It gave court processes, decision-making, and corrections a unified framework. States were given flexibility in how to execute this framework at the same time. A decentralized standardization of juvenile justice was established by the law in India."[38] "Without a doubt, this legislation was the catalyst for the issue of neglected and abused children being a top priority at the center level. Lack of a formalized separation between the two kinds of children was the primary flaw.[39] Further, this law was written before the existence of international conventions and instruments on child rights, and therefore, it was found not in consonance with them. There was also a lack of rehabilitation provisions also."[40]

Thereafter, the Juvenile Justice (Care and Protection of Children) Act, 2000, "is an improvement over the law that was replaced by passing this act. The object of the legislation is to amend the law relating to juveniles in conflict with the law and children in need of care and protection, by providing for proper care, protection, and treatment and by addressing to their developmental needs. This is being done by adopting a child-friendly approach in the adjudication and disposition of matter in the best interest of children and for their ultimate rehabilitation through various institutions established under this law."[41] "This new Act was enacted particularly in consonance with the UNCRC, as India ratified it in 1992 and other important international instruments. The Act had been amended twice i.e., in 2006 and 2011. Under the Act the state Government is empowered on constitute a Board for a district or a group of districts which state may specify by a notification. These boards exercise

---

[38] Clayton A Hartjen, *Legal Change and Juvenile Justice in India*, 25 International Criminal Justice Review (1995).

[39] Suman Kakar, Juvenile Justice and Juvenile Delinquency in India, 52 (The Handbook of Juvenile Delinquency and Juvenile Justice, 2005).

[40] Erika Rickard & Jason M. Szanyi, *Bringing Justice to India's Children: Three Reforms to Bridge Practices with Promises in India's Juvenile Justice System*, 108–109 UC Davis Journal of Juvenile Law and Policy (2010).

[41] R. N. Chaudhary, Law Relating to Juvenile Justice in India, 21 (Orient Publishing Company, New Delhi, 4th ed. 2015).

the powers and discharge all such duties which are conferred upon them."[42] "Section 8 of Juvenile Justice Act provides establishment of Observation homes for keeping the juvenile."

5 Apprehensions of Juvenile in Conflict with Law

When any juvenile is apprehended by the police, he is to be handed over to a special juvenile police unit that has been designated to keep them in their custody and immediately a report is to be made to the member of the Board. The state Government has been empowered to make rule which is in consistency with this act to provide for person through whom any juvenile in conflict with law may be produced before the board these may include registered voluntary organizations. This section further provides that state will make the rule providing the manner in which such juvenile may be sent to an observation home.[43] Any person in whose charge a juvenile is placed in pursuance of this Act shall, while the order is in force have the control over the juvenile as he would have if he were his parents, and shall be responsible for his maintenance, and the juvenile shall continue is his charge for the period stated by competent authority, notwithstanding that he is claimed by his parents or any other person."[44] "Where a juvenile is arrested, the officer in charge of the police station or the special juvenile police unit to which the juvenile is brought shall, as soon as may be after their arrest, inform the probation officer of such arrest to enable him to obtain information regarding the antecedents and family background of the juvenile and other material circumstances likely to be of assistance to the Board in making the inquiry."[45]

5.1 Adoption

Section 41 of the Juvenile Justice (Care and Protection of Children) Act, 2000 read with Rule 33(1) of Central Rules expresses the following aspects of adoption: The primary aim of adoption is to provide a child who can't be cared for by his biological parents with a permanent substitute family. The family of a child has the primary responsibility to provide him care and protection".[46] "Section 42 of the act deals with Foster care of children the foster care may be used for temporary placement of those infants who are to be given for adoption."

---

[42] Section 4(1) Juvenile Justice (Care and Protection of Children) Act, 2000.

[43] Section 10(2) of Juvenile Justice (Care and Protection of Children) Act, 2000.

[44] Section 11 of Juvenile Justice (Care and Protection of Children) Act, 2000.

[45] Section 13 of Juvenile Justice (Care and Protection of Children) Act, 2000.

[46] Section 41(1) of Juvenile Justice (Care and Protection of Children) Act, 2000.

The legislation regarding the juvenile justice system is aimed at protecting the interests of juveniles. All the statute passed since the independence mainly focused on the care and rehabilitation of juveniles. Age factor of the juvenile has been contentious issue. Age of juvenile was changed in juvenile justice Act 1986, and again in Juvenile Justice Care and Protection of Children Act, 2000. And it was again amended by juvenile justice care and protection of children Act, 2015. We have very good juvenile justice laws, but main problem is effective implementation of these laws. Therefore, the main focus of the Government should be implementation of these laws."

5.2 Juvenile Justice (Care and Protection of Children) Amendment Act, 2015

The JJA, 2015, introduced many changes to the existing law based on the requirements of the day in terms of reforming the laws and making the juvenile justice system more responsive to the changing circumstances of society. The Act seeks to hold the child accused of a crime accountable, not through punishments, but through counseling. The Act amended in 2015 changed the nomenclature of *juvenile* to *child,* which is *in conflict with the law*. The Act defines orphaned, surrendered, and abandoned children. It also gives definitions for petty, serious, and heinous crimes by children. A heinous offense is one that attracts a maximum punishment of 7 years imprisonment under any existing law. A serious offense is one that attracts imprisonment of 3 to 7 years. A petty offense is one that attracts a maximum of 3 years imprisonment. The Act gives more clarity on the functions and powers of the Juvenile Justice Board and the Child Welfare Commission. The **Juvenile Justice Board** is a judicial body before which children detained or accused of a crime are brought. This acts as a separate court for juveniles since they are not to be taken to a regular criminal court. The Board consists of a judicial magistrate of the first class and two social workers, one of whom at least should be a woman. The board is meant to be a child-friendly place and not intimidating for the child. The state governments set up **child welfare committees** in districts in accordance with the provisions of the Act. The Committees have the power to dispose of cases for the care, protection, treatment, development, and rehabilitation of the children in need of care and protection, as well as to provide for their basic needs and protection. The Act provides for an efficient and organized system for the adoption of orphaned, surrendered, and abandoned children. It also makes it compulsory for all childcare institutions to be registered. The Act also **offered provisions regarding adoption**. The Act replaced the **Hindu Adoptions and Maintenance Act, 1956,** and the Guardians of the Ward Act, **1890** with a more universally accessible adoption law. The Act enabled the smooth functioning of **adoption procedures for orphans, surrendered,** and abandoned children while making the **Central Adoption Resource Authority" (CARA)** the statutory body for adoption-related matters.[47]

An important provision of the amended Act is that it provides for minors in the age group 16–18 years to be treated as adults in the case of heinous crimes. The Act also gives the Central Adoption Resource Authority" (CARA) statutory status. "**The Act distinguishes between children in conflict with the law and children in need of care and protection.** Under the previous Act, any minor, regardless of the crime committed, could be convicted only to a maximum of 3 years. Under no circumstances could the minor be tried in an adult court, sent to an adult jail, or given a penalty longer than 3 years. However, this changed with the 2015 amendment."[48] "All children below the age of 18 would be treated equally except for one departure from the norm. That is, in the case of heinous crimes. Any minor of the age group 16 to 18 and who has been accused of committing a heinous crime can be tried like an adult. For this, the Juvenile Justice Board would assess the child's physical and mental capacities, his or her ability to comprehend the consequences of the crime, etc., and determine whether the child can be treated as an adult."[49]

As per law, a juvenile is any individual below the age of 18. According to laws in India, any child below the age of 7 cannot be convicted under any law for any crime. Under earlier laws, the distinction between children in conflict with the law and children in need of care and protection was vague, as both were termed juveniles. In the amended 2015 Act, the terms are *children in conflict with the law* and children in need of care and protection, so that the distinction is clear."[50]

Juvenile Justice Act, 2015—A Critical Analysis

There are many positive outcomes in the 2015 JJA. It was enacted to correct the deficiencies in the previous legislation. There is a clear distinction between children in conflict with the law and children in need of protection and care. It makes the registration of all children's homes mandatory, bringing in more transparency and efficiency to the system. It seeks to reduce crimes committed by children between the ages of 16 and 18. By including the provision for 16–18 years olds to be tried like adults in cases of heinous crimes, it provides justice to the victims of such crimes."

On the other hand, the amended JJA also has certain negatives associated with it. Many psychological studies point out the vulnerability of the 16–18 age group of children because of hormonal and physical changes. Considering offenses committed

---

[47] Aayushi Swaroop, Adoption' Under The Juvenile Justice Amendment Bill, 2021—An Analysis, MANUPATRA (Dec. 3, 2023, 12.30 pm) https://articles.manupatra.com/article-details/Adoption-under-the-Juvenile-Justice-Amendment-Bill-2021-An-Analysis.

[48] Ibid.

[49] Pranjal Singh & Vaibhav Sangam Mishra, The Juvenile Justice Amendment Bill, 2021: to reinforce the provisions for the protection and adoption of children (Dec. 4, 2023, 9.30 PM) https://blog.ipleaders.in/the-juvenile-justice-amendment-bill-2021-to-reinforce-the-provisions-for-the-protection-and-adoption-of-children/.

[50] See footnote 50.

in this age as crimes and putting them in adult jails can cause further damage. In such environments, the minor will come into close contact with professional criminals, which can hamper their rehabilitation. Some opine that treating of minors between the ages of 16 and 18 differently is a violation of Article 14 of the Constitution, which guarantees every citizen the right to equality. India ratified the UN Convention on the Rights of the Child in 1992. According to this convention, any individual below the age of 18 is to be treated like a child. This is in contravention to the amended law that gives provisions for treating 16- to 18-year-olds like adults. A psychological assessment is to be made to assess whether the minor can be treated as an adult or not. However, this can be subjective and not entirely scientific." The argument to include 16–18-year-old minors in a special bracket was based on the data from the National Crime Records Bureau (NCRB). "This data is itself questioned by many, and also, many of the cases were in the FIR stage and under preliminary proceedings only. Most children who commit crimes are from the economically weaker sections of society. In order to reduce crime among children, there is a need to provide a better environment for the nurturing of children who grow up in slum areas. Also, there is a need to foster a culture of open communication between parents and children among all classes."

Juvenile Justice Amendment Act, 2021

The **Juvenile Justice (Care and Protection of Children) Amendment Act, 2021,** was passed **to amend various provisions of the Juvenile Justice Act, 2015**. The Amendment Act, 2021, prescribes that crimes against children, which are mentioned in the chapter "Other Offenses Against Children" of the JJ Act, 2015 that allow an imprisonment between three and seven years will be deemed "non-cognisable." The amendment provides strength to the provision of protection and adoption of children. There are many adoption cases pending before the court and **to make proceedings of the court faster now the power is transferred to the district magistrate**. The amendment provides that the **district magistrate has the authority to issue such adoption orders**."

However, there are so many concerns associated with the Juvenile Justice Amendment Act, 2021. Specifically, the **amendment under challenge is Section 86 of the JJ Act,** according to which **crimes under the special law,** with punishment between three to seven years, have been **reclassified as non-cognizable**. While the **victims themselves are unable to directly report them due to the imbalance in power,** most such crimes are **reported to the police by either parents or child rights bodies and Child Welfare Committees"** (CWC).**Parents of these Children** are mostly daily wage laborers, are either unaware of how to, or not inclined to report the crimes to the police. They **do not want to engage with the legal process** because that **would force them to take time off from work, resulting in a loss of wages. Child Welfare Committees (CWC)** first instinct in most cases is to **"talk and arrive at a settlement"** without having to escalate the matter to the police. **Making these**

crimes non-cognizable, along with several other serious crimes under the special law **would make reporting an offense to the police even more difficult**."[51]

6 Juvenile Justice (Care and Protection of Children) Model Amendment Rules, 2022 and Its Impact on the Adoption Process

The revised Juvenile Justice Care and Protection Model Amendment Rules 2022 that came into effect on September 1, 2022 immediately drew concern from lawyers, activists, parents, and numerous adoption agencies since cases already pending before the courts from the past few months will now have to be transferred and the entire process will have to be started anew. Once a parent registers for adoption, a petition for adoption orders is filed. The prospective parent is then meticulously assessed through a home study report, referred a child, and, in due course, allowed to take a child into pre-adoption foster care.[52] The fundamental issue here is that such a delay in such an order means that the child cannot get admission into a school because the parents do not have the necessary documents yet."[53]

Certain stakeholders also expressed their worry over the fact that neither judges nor the district magistrates have been made aware of these prominent changes, leading to a situation of utter chaos and disarray. It would be inconsiderate to expect district magistrates, who are already tasked with overseeing the functioning of an entire district, to take on these duties without first having undergone specialized training in juvenile matters. This has only been exacerbated by the recently introduced bill, which prevents the judicial review of adoptions even at the appellate stage."[54] "Furthermore, the vesting of judicial powers with these officers also results in blurring the lines between the executive and the judiciary with regard to the separation of powers."

The Central Adoption Resource Authority (CARA) "has claimed that at present, there are nearly 1000 adoption cases pending before the courts in the nation. A major problem with the adoption system at CARA is that it has a mere 2188 children in its official registry, whereas, a recent figure shows that there are approximately 31,000 parents eagerly waiting to adopt a child. These loopholes have given rise to illegal adoption and trafficking.[55]

---

[51] (Dec. 2, 2023, 12.45 PM) https://www.drishtiias.com/daily-news-analysis/issue-with-the-juvenile-justice-amendment-act-2021.

[52] Jagriti Chandra, *The tedious process of adoption*, The Hindu Sept.12, 2022.

[53] (Dec. 4, 2023, 10.00 AM) https://theamikusqriae.com/a-critical-review-of-the-juvenile-justice-amendment-act-2021/.

[54] Harsh Mahaseth and Nishtha Gupta, *A critique of amendments to the Juvenile Justice Act in India, (Dec. 12, 2023, 10.00 PM)* pure.jgu.edu.in.

[55] Jagriti Chandra, *The tedious process of adoption*, The Hindu, Sept. 2, 2022.

6.1 *Juvenile Justice Amendment Act, 2021: A Critical Analysis*

The Amendment Act of 2021 included multiple modifications in some essential areas of the legislation, including adoption, categorization of offenses, designated courts, and eligibility criteria for members of Child Welfare Committees" (CWCs). "The Amendment Act was overwhelmingly supported by both ruling and opposition parties. However, some of the changes made can have disastrous consequences for the welfare and best interests of children, which was the original legislation's goal."[56]

One such problematic change concerns the amendment to Section 86″(2) of the JJ Act 2015, through which some serious offenses are converted from being cognizable to non-cognizable. The amended Section 86″(2) "of the JJ Act 2015 states that where an offense under this Act is punishable with imprisonment for a term of three years and above, but not more than seven years, then such offense shall be non-cognizable and non-bailable. Recently, the Amendment Act 2021 has been challenged by the Delhi Commission for Protection of Child Rights" (DCPCR) "in the Supreme Court of India for making categories of offenses non cognisable."[57]

Section 155(2) of the CrPC "states that no police officer shall investigate a non-cognizable case without the order of a magistrate having the power to try such case or commit the case for trial."[58]

Chapter IX of the JJ Act 2015 addresses multiple offenses against children, including cruelty to a child, sale and procurement of children, child employment for begging, the penalty for giving intoxicated liquor, narcotic drug, or psychotropic substance to a child, and exploitation of child employees, etc. With the prevalence of different forms of child abuse in our country, a few additional offenses were introduced to this chapter in 2015, including the sale and procurement of children, as well as the use of children by militant groups or other adults, which became one of the defining elements of the JJ Act 2015. However, with this amendment, the following previously cognizable offenses have become non-cognizable such as cruelty to children by CCI staff" (Section 75), employing children for begging (Section 76), giving intoxicating liquor, narcotic drug, or psychotropic substance to a child (Section 77), using a child for vending, peddling, carrying, supplying, or smuggling any intoxicating liquor, narcotic drug, or psychotropic substance (Section 78), exploitation of a child employee (Section 79), sale and procurement of children for any purpose (Section 81), and use of children by militant groups or other adults (Section 83).[59]

> Making these offenses non-cognisable prevents the police from arresting the accused without a warrant and initiating an investigation without the permission of the court. Besides, the

---

[56] (Dec. 2, 2023, 4 .00 PM) https://i-probono.com/articles/juvenile-justice-amendment-act-2021-a-critical-view/.

[57] *Id.*

[58] *Id.*

[59] *Id.*

delay in investigation can provide the accused in each case with more opportunities to tamper with the evidence and influence witnesses.[60]

7 Juvenile Justice System and Judicial Trends

The judiciary has played a vital role in the development of the juvenile justice system in India. Even before the enactment of the JJ Act, various provisions of the IPC also deal directly with juveniles' immunity from prosecution, especially Sections 82 and 83." In *Kakoo v. State of Himachal Pradesh*,[61] "the Apex Court considered Section 83 and 84 of the IPC, while reducing the sentence of the juvenile aged thirteen years, accused of raping a child aged two years, stating that minors cannot be regarded as adults. Thus, it is well-established law that the court should accept reformative and humane methods when dealing with juveniles. Thus, it is well-established law that the court should accept reformative and humane methods when dealing with juveniles." In *Raghbir v. State of Haryana*,[62] "whether the person below 16 years of age being guilty of the crime committed as per Section 302 IPC may gain from the Haryana Children's Act was the issue sought to be decided by the Apex Court. Noticing a prior judgment in" *Rohtas v. State of Haryana*[63] "the Supreme Court held that "proceedings against a child were not prohibited under the provisions of the Act."

In *Sheela Barse and Anr. v. Union of India*,[64] "the Apex Court emphasized the need for a uniform statute for the children all over the country, as the Children Acts have been passed but were not enforced in some of the States. The petition was against the incarceration of the children who were under the age of 16. It was recommended that the trial of a case related to juveniles be conducted by a juvenile court and, that too by a special Magistrate and the trial should be completed in a maximum period of three months. The recommendations of the Supreme Court in" *Sheela Barse'* s case[65] have led to the passing of the JJA in 1986. "Various other directions were also passed by the Supreme Court in this case which have not been complied with in true letter and spirit, therefore, as a follow up, the Supreme Court again made certain directions and observations in *Sheela Barse*" *(II) and others v. Union of India and others*[66] "regarding the effective implementation of the laws relating to juveniles to ensure social, economical, and psychological rehabilitation of the juveniles."

The participation of a youngster in the Delhi Gang Rape case has led to many debates and outrage amongst the whole nation. A demand was made for reducing the age of juveniles who commit heinous offenses like rape, murder, etc." On July

---

[60] *Id.*

[61] (1976) 2 SCC 215.

[62] 1982 SCR (1) 686.

[63] AIR 1979 SC 1839.

[64] 1986 SCC (3) 596.

[65] *Id.*

[66] (1986) 3 SCC 632.

17, 2013, seven writ petitions were dismissed by the Apex Court in *Salil Bali v. Union of India &Anr.*[67] "where the constitutionality of the JJA 2000 was challenged, demanding a reduction in the age of children from eighteen to sixteen. The Apex Court observed that though a juvenile in the age group of 16 to 18 years may develop criminal propensities but an effort must be made to reintegrate him into the main-stream society otherwise he will become a hardened criminal which is worst for the juvenile as well as for the whole nation. The Supreme Court declined to re-incarcerate the juvenile criminal in the Nirbhaya case saying that there was no law to keep him imprisoned any longer because he had already completed the entire three-year sentence for his involvement in the horrible crime. The court did declare, however, that the youngster might be made to undergo therapy without being confined to the special juvenile home, thereby giving the government verbal permission to tether him to an NGO, monitor him, and put him through a rehabilitation program. "Parents of Nirbhaya said that they were "greeted with disappointment at every door. I had hoped that the judges would see it as a unique case. The release is merely a motivator. It has given all those under the age of 18 a license to commit any crime, including rape, her sobbing mother, Asha Devi, lamented. A vacation bench of the Supreme Court dismissed an eleventh-hour case filed against the juvenile's release by the Chairman of the Delhi Commission for Women, in limine (without serving notice on the juvenile), saying, We share your concern, but our hands are bound by statute." It was said, "The law is clear on this subject. An adolescent can be held in a reform home for a maximum of three years. You (DCW) are asking us to view the law in such a way that the juvenile is held longer than the constitutionally mandated three years. We cannot strip away rights granted by the Constitution by the mechanism of interpretation. There is nothing in the legislation that allows him to be retained at this time. There is a specific clause that no juvenile's detention lasts three years." "Through Shri G.K. Kumar, Senior Advocate, and Shri Devadatt Kamat, Advocate, the DCW brought the court's attention to the reports of the Intelligence Bureau on the juvenile. A serious IB report on the juvenile's mental condition is available. It is said that he has become radicalized. It expresses grave concern that he will commit the crime again," Shri Kumar said. The effort to portray a dramatic scene in which the now-major juvenile, is capable of repeating the offense failed to persuade the Supreme Court to hear the DCW's matter because it was adamant about the legal sanction behind the interim order sought by the DCW, whose chairperson viz. Ms. Swati Maliwal was present in the court. DCW rushed to the court at the eleventh hour and tried to get the case scheduled for a hearing, with Nirbhaya's parents serving as a rallying point for protests against the juvenile's release. At the time of hearing, the DCW essentially criticized the Government of Delhi for failing to implement the reformative program at the home where the accused juvenile had been for 3 years." Shri G.K. Kumar said, "*The juvenile has not undergone any reform process for three years because no such program was in place at home.*" "The court was requested to appoint an expert body to assess his mental state and report back to the bench on the need for him to go through further change and rehabilitation." Since the hearing

---

[67] (2013) 7 SCC 705.

seemed to take the reverse direction from DCW, Additional Attorney General stood up and said that the Union administration endorsed the request to keep the young person strictly alert. The bench asked the Additional Solicitor General the same question: "How long will the juvenile be held at the reform home. The law specifies three years. If you wanted him to be held, you should have enacted legislation." "Additional Attorney General said that the required legislation was in the works. However, the court declined to hear DCW's plea, stating that the juvenile's recovery should continue without him being detained. The Apex Court and High Courts of the States play a vital role in interpreting new legislation." The judiciary plays a critical role in uplifting "juveniles in need of care and treatment" and the early disposition of "juveniles in conflict with the law." Lower Courts follow the pattern developed by the Apex Court and the High Courts.[68]

8 Conclusion and Suggestions

The Rehabilitation Management Committee set up under JJ Act said that the juvenile's mental health report was not available in most cases, which is a crucial part of the rehabilitation plan. An emotionally disturbed young person would need comprehensive and long-term mental health plan, including services like psychiatric assessment and therapy, counseling, day-to-day supervision, monitoring, life skills education, etc. The main failure is in the juvenile justice care homes and their working which allows the radicalization and exploitation of the juvenile rather than rehabilitation. A committee set up by the US center for Disease Control, reviewed the US juvenile transfer system and found that those transferred to adult jails became more hardened criminals than those who served in juvenile rehabilitation centers. Thus, in conclusion, it can be said that the act has various provisions to deal with the necessity of life. However, the recent amendment has been debated to strengthen the bureaucracy at the cost of civil society."[69]

In order to have full control of delinquencies, the effective implementation of the JJ Act is essential, with the full monitoring of the public as well as orientation with professionals and law enforcement institutions. Under the amended Act, adoption of a child is final once a court issues an adoption order. With this, the child becomes the lawful child of his adoptive parents, with all the rights, privileges, and responsibilities that are given to a biological child. The bill shifts the power to issue adoption orders from the court to the district magistrate, including the additional district magistrate. The question is whether it is appropriate for an administrative authority to issue adoption orders instead of a judicial body. Adoption of a child is a legal process which creates a permanent legal relationship between the child and adoptive parents. When

---

[68] Venudhar Routiya, *A Critical Study of Juvenile Justice System in India* (Dec. 13, 2023, 4.00 PM)http://www.serialsjournals.com/serialjournalmanager/pdf/1500032698.pdf.

[69] (Dec. 13, 2023, 4.00 PM) (https://plutusias.com/juvenile-justice-amendment-act-a-socio-economic-analysis/.

deciding on adoption, courts review documents, ensure necessary procedures have been complied with, and conduct an inquiry of the child and adoptive parents. This helps ensure that due consideration is given to the wishes of the child, and the adoption is for the welfare of the child. It may be argued that determining whether the adoption is in the best interests of the child requires judicial training and competence. The new bill is by all accounts progressive, the key changes brought to the Juvenile Laws reinforce the insurance and care of children including to ones who require assurance under the laws and to the individuals who struggle with the laws. It likewise streamlines the adoption system of the Juvenile to the gatherings. It seems like the encouraging bill brings straightforwardness to the well-being of the children. The new change is invited by the opposition parties too in the parliament which shows the significance of the genuinely necessary advance brought to the laws. It likewise appoints excellent capacity to the District Magistrate to screen the Juvenile Justice framework to eliminate any vagueness to its system and to convey better interest to the government assistance of Juvenile."

Nobody is born criminal from the womb of mother, but due to certain circumstances, misfortune, and adversity, as already mentioned, some children or adolescents are distracted and sidetracked. In order to set them right, most countries have adopted a reformatory approach but of late it is seen that this approach is not working well with these incorrigible and inveterate young offenders. In order to sort and unravel this, the laws and policies in the USA have changed as the time progressed. The practice of a liberal approach in the USA has presently shifted to tough reforms in some cases seeing the nature of crime committed by juveniles. What are we waiting in India for"? When so-called juveniles can commit heinous, nasty, ferocious crimes as already mentioned can they be seriously called as juveniles who are innocent. If we talk about Nirbhaya case, the question which keeps on haunting us and every time raises our eyebrows is can the so-called juvenile be really called innocent when it is a known fact that he was actively involved in such ferocious, nasty, and brutal act.

Presently, in India it is seen that much importance is given to age factor[70] of accused and when the person is below 18 years of age howsoever he might be guilty, he is sent to reformatory school for a period of three years and is let free, courtesy, Juvenile Justice (Care and Protection) Act, 2006. It does not make any difference that he had with full knowledge and acquaintance actively played a part in the crime, it does not make any difference that his co-accused are getting life imprisonment or

[70] In a number of cases, there has been no unanimity between the judges as to what is the date to determine the age of juvenile? In the case of Umesh Chandra v. State of Rajasthan 1982(2) SCC 202, a decision given by three judge bench of the Supreme Court, the court laid down that the Act is applicable on the child who at the date of occurrence is of particular age. The age on the date of trial is not to be determined. However, in Arnit Das v. State of Bihar (2000)5SCC488, the Court laid down that reckoning date is the date when the accused is produced before the court and not the date when the accused has committed the offence. Finally, in the case of Pratap Singh v. State of Jharkhand(AIR 2005 SC 2731), the court laid down that the relevant date to determine the age of juvenile would be the date on which the crime is committed and not the date on which the juvenile is produced.

maybe they are hanged. Is it justified? Does not the act committed by them clearly speaks of their intent? Recently, there has been issue regarding the age of juveniles whether it be 18 or should it be reduced to 16 years. The point here is should age factor be given that much importance?

Should not intention of the person play an important role in making the person culprit and culpable irrespective of the age, should person less than 18 years of age be considered as less culpable and less blameworthy than 18 years of age person when both have committed similar crime with similar intent? Should not the degree of atrocity be considered as important factor in making a person liable? All these and many more questions keep on cropping up and bring frown on our faces. Why it is forgotten that crime is crime, be it committed by adult or a juvenile. Why is it forgotten that heinous crimes like rape, etc., totally ravishes and shatters not only the woman but also her family and near ones throughout their lives and a person who is actually responsible for such barbaric act is let free after a meager punishment of three years. It is not understandable that is why our society is more sympathetic toward the person who had actually ruined, wrecked, and devastated the life of another person? As already said, the skimpy punishment of three years for such an atrocious act clearly endorses this. Isn't it high time now that parliamentarians and our society should also look from the angle of the girl who dies every day and night after such a crime is committed."

International Corporate Governance: A Tool to Overcome Legal, Regulatory, Ethical, and Cultural Challenges in Internationalization of Business

Rituraj Sinha, Jane Eyre Mathew, and Aditya Tomer

Abstract Multinational companies, often abbreviated as MNCs, are companies that run and conduct business in multiple countries. They are active and influential on a global scale, with operations, influence, or recognition in multiple countries or regions typically have subsidiaries, branches, or affiliates in various countries around the world. Multinational companies are a product of the globalization of business and the expansion of markets beyond national borders. This places a spotlight on various legal, regulatory, ethical, and cultural challenges in the effectiveness of corporate governance faced in the internationalization of business by these MNCs. We often label it as challenges in effective implementation of International Corporate Governance in MNCs. International Corporate Governance, with respect to MNCs, denote to the system of rules, practices, and processes by these companies are directed, controlled, and managed at the global level during the internationalization of their business. It focuses, primarily on maximizing shareholder value, promoting transparency, accountability, and ethical behavior by protecting the interest of various stakeholders of the company. Though the concept of International Corporate Governance is a complex and evolving issue, it becomes essential for invoking investor confidence, economic stability, and long-term success of the MNCs in an interconnected world. At the outset, it is pertinent to note that MNCs often face unique challenges and issues in establishing corporate governance standards in the internationalization of their business in different countries due to diverse stakeholders, diverse legal and regulatory frameworks, cultural and ethical differences, governance discrepancies, lack of transparency in various countries, political and economic stability, and diverse business strategy. The authors in this research have made an effort to identify the various challenges faced by the MNCs and attempted to provide

R. Sinha (✉)
School of Law, CHRIST (Deemed to be University), Delhi NCR Campus, Ghaziabad, India
e-mail: rituraj.sinha@christuniversity.in

J. E. Mathew · A. Tomer
Amity Law School, Noida, India
e-mail: jemathew@amity.edu

A. Tomer
e-mail: atomer@amity.edu

J. Aston et al. (eds.), *Comparative Law*, https://doi.org/10.1007/978-981-97-7815-7_17

suggestions to overcome such challenges with the aid of International Corporate Governance.

Keywords Multinational companies · Globalization · Transparency · Accountability · Ethical behavior

1 Introduction

Multinational companies (hereinafter referred as MNCs) find numerous legal, regulatory, ethical, and cultural challenges, once they widen their operations internationally, making it tough for them to adhere to corporate governance principles. They confront inequalities in the enforcement and supervision throughout several jurisdictions, placing challenges to the establishments of unvarying and effective corporate governance practices all around their global operations due to variety of factors including diverse stakeholders, disparate legal and regulatory frameworks, cultural distinctions, governance disparities, varying degrees of transparency across different countries, political and economic stability, and varied business strategies.[1] These challenges demand a complete understanding of the local laws and regulations and a sustainable study and analysis of all the contributing factors including proactive participation with the key stakeholders.[2] Therefore, in order to put the expected compliance steps in place and to counter these challenges, International Corporate Governance can play a vital role. International Corporate Governance is a set of values, guidelines, and procedures that guide how businesses are operated internationally. It ensures accountability, transparency, equity, and integrity in the operations of organizations, regardless of their location or type of business.[3] The notion of International Corporate Governance is essential for furthering investor confidence, asserting economic stability, and assuring the long-term success of MNCs. The authors in this research have made an effort to identify the challenges faced by the MNCs and made an effort to establish International Corporate Governance as a tool to handle such challenges in an interconnected world.

[1] Rahul Bedi and Darshan Desai, "Corporate Governance Bundles for Emerging Markets" (2014) Corporate Governance and Corporate Social Responsibility 3.

[2] K Roth, "The Use of the Multinational Corporation as a Research Context" (2003) 29(6) Journal of Management 883.

[3] CK Prahalad, "Globalization: The Intellectual and Managerial Challenges" (1990) 29(1) Human Resource Management 27.

2 Internationalization of Business and MNCs

During the era of privatization, liberalization, and globalization, becoming global with business has transformed into a basic strategic imperative for MNCs desiring to acquire a competitive edge and sustainable development. In the modern world, a company's operations and actions are expanded beyond the borders to explore for new market segments, problems, opportunities, and consumers. The attempt is to flourish operations to gain market share and footprint outside its own inland market for the users in multiple countries. It is termed as internationalization of business. It has become a necessity to company's development and success in the modern globalized economy, and thus, companies are seeking out more and more foreign resources and global markets. Technological developments, lower trade barriers, the possibility of more sales opportunities, and risk diversification have all contributed to this trend.[4] Internalization of business not merely focuses on the companies seeking horizontal integration on a worldwide scale, but also treated as critical strategy for countries addressing the sustainability of their development in various manufacturing and service sectors. In simple terms, it is primarily a broad strategy with concurrently intense valences, with diversification as the ultimate goal.

However, there are drawbacks to doing business internationally as well, including legal and regulatory barriers, ethical challenges, cultural disparities, and political and economic hazards.[5] There are number of factors in determining a proper strategy for the internationalization which can greatly enhance a MNCs' long-term success. Every MNCs must weigh the benefits and drawbacks very carefully before entering a foreign market. Taking your business globally is a great way to lower your risks and boost profits. It expands the customer base by providing MNCs the access to more promising markets. Expanding the client base abroad can also assist companies in funding the creation of new products. It allows them to grow or to take advantage of new opportunities through investment. It also helps companies to adjust to shifting consumer preferences and economic condition by establishing a presence in multiple regions. Therefore, it is significant for them to overcome various obstacles to entry, pertaining to a particular nation, domestic market, and their own organizational structure.[6]

When a company reaches to the level of saturation and has little or no potential in the domestic market, internationalization in distinct seasonality and economic cycles lower the risk of market saturation and help in stabilizing the revenues year-round. Companies make efforts to take market share before competitors in the same industry expand into the foreign region and grab the opportunity to strengthen the band image and visibility. However, significantly, the MNCs might be privy to unique market

[4] Michael A Hitt et al., "International Diversification: Antecedents, Outcomes, and Moderators" (2006) 32(6) Journal of Management 831.

[5] Philip M Rosenzweig and Janet L Shaner, "Internationalization Reconsidered: New Imperatives for Successful Growth" Advances in International Marketing 159.

[6] Vargas Hernandez JG and Alejandro OZ2, "Methodology and Strategies for Companies in the Process of Internationalization" (2016) 04(04) Journal of Global Economics.

know-how about overseas clients or prospects, markets, or market conditions that are not yet available to other competitors. Hence, it is considered as one of the main forces behind the global competitive economy today. Though it gives companies chances to expand and diversify, it poses difficulties because of trade disputes, entry barriers, and shifting governmental regulations.[7]

Internationalization of business is regarded as one of the fundamental constituents of MNCs' development and growth. They acquire plethora of opportunities to arouse and flourish in the global market with the internationalization of business.[8] As a result of gaining concern by the MNCs in the internationalization procedure of business, diverse models have been formulated in an effort to explain how businesses move into foreign markets. Consequently, these models, namely Uppsala Model, Born Global Model, Network Model & Eclectic Paradigm Model, furnish distinct model for preferring strategies and building decisions by keeping in consideration of ownership advantages, business networks, market distance, and transaction costs.[9] The noteworthy multifariousness that could exclusively be brought out and systematized with the assistance of models is reflected in the internationalization of business.

Since its evolution by Jan Johanson and Jaan Sture Vahlne in 1970s, the Uppsala Model has grown to rank amongst the most substantial theories of internationalization. The Uppsala Model underlines on the gradual internationalization of the business and based on the notion that business favors to internationalize gradually and are risk averse. It depicts how business increasingly stretch their global operations over time. The model advocates that business commence with modest, low-risk investment in well-known markets and progressively extend their participation and commitment as they acquire knowledge and experience.[10] Businesses become more at ease with the expanding internationally and are willing to take on bigger risks as they gain experience and understanding of foreign markets. On the other hand, Born Global Model, originated by Knight and Cavusgil, pertains to MNCs that aim to benefit a major competitive edge through resource usage and exportation of their products throughout borders from the beginning.[11] Companies pursuing it often approach foreign markets and eschew the gradual internationalization process that conventional Uppsala Model recommends. However, it opposes the traditional notion that internationalization is a step-by-step process. The companies are set to export as soon as they commence functioning and with the guidance of entrepreneur's visionary beliefs, enforce a strategy and an organizational culture that facilitates the

[7] Gordon Anderson, "Labour Law in a Globalising World" (2003) 66(4) The Modern Law Review 640.

[8] Vihang R Errunza and Lemma W Senbet, "The Effects of International Operations on the Market Value of the Firm: Theory and Evidence" (1981) 36(2) The Journal of Finance 401.

[9] Jan-Erik Vahlne, "Development of the Uppsala Model of Internationalization Process: From Internationalization to Evolution" (2020) 10(2) Global Strategy Journal 239.

[10] Jan-Erik Vahlne, Inge Ivarsson and Jan Johanson, "The Tortuous Road to Globalization for Volvo's Heavy Truck Business: Extending the Scope of the Uppsala Model" (2011) 20(1) International Business Review 1.

[11] Justin Paul and Alexander Rosado-Serrano, "Gradual Internationalization vs Born-Global/International New Venture Models" (2019) 36(6) International Marketing Review 830.

internationalization. They are chiefly driven by resources and capabilities like knowledge, networks, and financial capital and perception of treating world as boundless interconnected.

Presented by Johanson and Mattsson[12] in 1980s, Network Model emphasizes on internationalization of companies through creation, maintenance, and expansion of connections with network members on oversea markets. It highlights on the purpose that connections and cooperation make for in breaking into overseas markets, underlining the implication of business networks and relationships in the internationalization process. A MNCs can use the network to integrate with other international companies once it has successfully got into foreign markets. This model highlights the purpose that connections and cooperation play in altering overseas markets, emphasizing the implication of business networks and relationships in the internationalization process. However, very lately, the Eclectic Paradigm Model has demonstrated itself as a fundamental component of international business theory and has been the leading explanation for the emergence of multinational activity. Developed by John Dunning in 1979, the model comprises of three main components, i.e., ownership-specific advantages (O), location-specific advantages (L), and internalization advantages (I) and therefore as referred to as OLI framework.

As internationalization of business is a complicated procedure that calls for strategic vision, flexibility, and a deep comprehension of international dynamics, it is paramount to recognize the option to prefer any one of the above theories is intricate and demands punctilious evaluation of multiple aspects such as market analysis, risk evaluation, execution of effective corporate governance practices, and heedful consideration of legal, regulatory, and ethical challenges.

3 International Corporate Governance: An Overview

Corporate Governance is the framework of policies, procedures, and guidelines that control how an organization is run. It assures how decisions are arrived at and carried outside an organization and includes the interactions between different stakeholders, including shareholders, management, and board of directors.[13] A substantial amount of organizational interest has been piqued in corporate governance due to its seeming implication for the financial stability of both corporations and society at large. Consequently, assorted forums and institutions have been constituted in the recent past. They have proposed various norms and principles to create international framework through international cooperation for enhancing corporate governance with an international benchmark in companies internationalizing their business, especially

[12] Jan Johanson and Lars-Gunnar Mattsson, "Interorganizational Relations in Industrial Systems: A Network Approach Compared with the Transaction-Cost Approach" (1988) Strategies in global competition 194.

[13] Pengcheng Tang, Shuxiang Yang and Shuwang Yang, "How to Design Corporate Governance Structures to Enhance Corporate Social Responsibility in China's Mining State-Owned Enterprises?" (2020) 66 Resources Policy 101619.

MNCs. They must commit for effective corporate governance if they promise to be sustainable over the long run and maintain stakeholder's faith. They have to discover a balance between their responsibilities and financial performance.[14]

The year 1961 witnessed the establishment of Organization for Economic Co-operation and Development (OECD) as one of the first non-governmental organizations to undertake the task to set international standards for corporate governance. It serves as the primary international standard for good corporate governance for numerous jurisdictions with varied legal frameworks. The OECD Principles of Corporate Governance were originally published in 1999, got subsequently revised majorly in 2004, 2015, and 2023. The recent revision is named as 'G20/OECD Principles of Corporate Governance' of 2023. As a tool of reference for all over the world, the purpose of the recent revision was to assist policy makers of various jurisdictions in the assessment and enhancement of subsisting legal and regulatory framework on the enhancement of corporate governance. It is a comprehensive guide that delineates the essential principles and optimal practices for corporate governance.[15]

The revised principles deal with a number of matters such as the duties of the board, shareholder rights, disclosure, and transparency and the involvement of stakeholders in the decision-making process. These principles evoke six most important recommendations to be taken into consideration while drafting legal framework on the enhancement of corporate governance. Firstly, the framework should focus on the accessibility to capital, overall financial stability and performance, the sustainability, and resilience of corporations. It should be also consistent with the applicable rule of law, transparent, and enforceable. Secondly, framework should also assure judicious treatment to all shareholders together with minority and foreign investors and should also guard and promote the exercise of their rights. Thirdly, it ought to render reasonable incentives at every level of the investment and facilitate the operation of stock markets in a fashion that advances sound corporate governance. Fourthly, the framework should guarantee the prompt and precise disclosure of all pertinent information about the company, encompassing its financial status, operational efficiency, long-term viability, ownership, and governance. Fifthly, the company's strategic direction, the board's effectual oversight of management, and the board's accountability to the company and shareholders ought to be too guaranteed by the framework. Sixthly, the companies and their investors should be advocated by the corporate governance framework to construct choices and supervise their risks in a way that progresses the resilience and sustainability of the company.[16]

The object of these principles is not to substitute or override domestic legal and regulatory frameworks but to furnish direction to legislators, regulators, and market

[14] Siti Setyawati Kartika Sari and Raden Roro Widya Ningtyas Soeprajitno, "Healthy Environmental Parameters as the Identification of Mining Entities" (2021) 23(1) Jurnal Akuntansi dan Keuangan 33.

[15] A. Tarantino, "EU Efforts to Improve Internal Controls: OECD Principles" [2012] Manager's Guide to Compliance 91.

[16] "G20/OECD Principles of Corporate Governance 2023".

players of various jurisdictions on manners to toughen the subsisting legal and regulatory frameworks on corporate governance.[17] It also renders recommendations for stock exchanges, companies and other stakeholders who are called for in the process of making a healthy corporate governance. Accordingly, the global unanimity on the Principles of Corporate Governance urge investment, innovation, leads to the growth, financial stability, and productivity growth and enhance market confidence, financial market integrity, and economic efficiency in addition to raising economic dynamism. It bolsters market assurance of the investors and safeguard their interest which is significant in today's globalized market.

It was succeeded by the institution of the Global Corporate Governance Forum (GCGF) by the World Bank Group and OECD to converge and bring uniformity of Corporate Governance standards among diverse jurisdictions. The idea was to entice attention to the need of advancing corporate governance standards and to offer a perspective on enhancement of corporate governance practices and institutional frameworks in various countries. It operates with the objective of boosting responsibility, fairness, transparency, and an entrepreneurial intent and to cause reforms more visible in the local, regional, national, and global initiatives.[18] It furnishes a structure for global collaboration and generates opportunities for the planning and accomplishment of collaborative or individualized support initiatives to put through effective frameworks.

In 1995, International Corporate Governance Network (ICGN) was established with the objective of promoting effective standards of corporate governance worldwide by facilitating international dialog. It developed 'Global Governance Principles' first time in 2001 which got updated several times, latest being in 2021, to take into account changes in the world's best practices and advancements. These principles focus on the efficient governance control through fairness, accountability, responsibility, and transparency by outlining the respective duties of board of directors and shareholders and establishing a transparent communication among them.

The board of directors must act in the best interest of the shareholders for the long-term interests of the company. It stressed on clarity and balance in the board and their roles for the long-term success of the company and reiterates the importance of having a diversified composition of directors with necessary independence, competence, and experience to foster an objective decision-making process for the benefits of all. To a greater extent, the ICGN applauded the OECD Principles and considered them to be the fundamental cornerstone of a sound corporate governance.

Recently, the globalization of market has ushered in an era where the traditional concept of corporate governance has been challenged continuously to achieve a global standard on corporate governance. Therefore, to promote the best international standards pertinent to a country on corporate governance the Commonwealth Association of Corporate Governance was founded in 1998. It has developed certain

---

[17] Fianna Jesover and Grant Kirkpatrick, "The Revised OECD Principles of Corporate Governance and Their Relevance to Non-OECD Countries" (2005) 13(2) Corporate Governance 127.

[18] *Ibid.*

guidelines in 1999 focusing primarily on the role of board of directors. These principles set forth the requirements for the care and diligence duties that directors are expected to uphold and help them to decide whether their course of action complies or deviates from the established standards on corporate governance.

The board should exercise leadership, enterprise, integrity, and judgment in directing the corporation and make sure that a variety of skilled directors are appointed for an efficient procedure. It must ascertain the goals and values of the company and ways of achieving them and while assessing the existing policies, performance, and strategies. With a focus on the emerging and transition economies in the global market, which include a significant number of Commonwealth countries, these guidelines have been structured to complement the OECD Principles of Corporate Governance.

These international initiatives intend to enhance the knowledge of current corporate governance practices in a particular region and disseminates information about national and regional reforms at global level. They make it easier for investors and corporations to adopt a mindset that sees corporate governance as means of enhancing value. These initiatives help in the formulation of strategies for reforms and identification of areas of improvement in the legal and regulatory frameworks and thereby make it easier for a region to fully integrate itself with the current global trends of corporate governance. Therefore, at the outset, it looks pertinent that efforts on the enhancement of International Corporate Governance are crucial for the overall development, success, and stability of MNCs in a globalized business environment. It is the way forward for promoting transparency, accountability, and ethical business practices in MNCs.

4 Challenges for MNCs: Legal and Regulatory

Multinational companies face up with diversified legal and regulatory challenges in the field of corporate governance in today's globalized business environs.[19] These difficulties are aftermaths of the countless legal frameworks and regulatory policies that these MNCs essentially navigate. Every so often these encounters come along because of conflicting demands and unproven recommendations. They confront unparallel challenge to cling to the local corporate governance requirements and international standards and guidelines, while complying with diverse legal frameworks across multiple countries where they operate.[20] Although the corporate governance frameworks should turn more democratic in order to address the everchanging risk distribution and diminishing regulatory authority of national governments, the

---

[19] G.F. Davis, "The Responsibility Paradox (SSIR)," (c) 2007. <https://ssir.org/articles/entry/the_responsibility_paradox>

[20] Robert M Bushman, Joseph D Piotroski and Abbie J Smith, "What Determines Corporate Transparency?" (2004) 42(2) Journal of Accounting Research 207.

impact of nations' legal and regulatory framework on the competence of corporate governance mechanisms in MNCs is apparent.

MNCs call for interface with a range of stakeholders including local communities, shareholders, employees, and customers in order to perceive their demands and expectations and apply them into their governance procedures.[21] They have a huge task to balance the prerequisites of each jurisdiction while taking the needs of diverse stakeholders into account. They have to ascertain transparency and enough disclosure of financial and non-financial information across their global operations.[22] Consequently, it becomes important for them to set up systems for keeping their directors answerable and guaranteeing their independence, diversity, and skill.[23] It expects them to maintain clear policies and procedures to manage such situations and to handle any conflict of interest face by their directors.[24] To efficaciously monitor compliance with corporate governance standards and identify, assess, and mitigate risks across their geographical dispersed operations, MNCs are required to demonstrate vigorous frameworks for risk management and internal control systems.[25]

The primary legal and regulatory challenges faced by MNCs in corporate governance embrace navigating complex regulatory landscapes, establishing compliance programs, adapting governance practices to local laws, working with local experts, monitoring evolving regulations, conducting due diligence, putting internal control systems in place, ensuring compliances with laws pertaining to financial reporting, taxation, environmental sustainability, labor and employment, and competition.[26] These complications are recurrently induced by variations in national legal and regulatory framework, cultural norms, commercial procedures, and other applicable laws.[27]

To warrant effective piloting of these obstacles and to diminish the risk of non-compliance or legal disputes, MNCs often need to capitalize significant resources

[21] Justin Tan, "Multinational Corporations and Social Responsibility in Emerging Markets: Opportunities and Challenges for Research and Practice" (2009) 86(S2) Journal of Business Ethics 151.

[22] Igor Filatotchev, Annette Poulsen and R Greg Bell, "Corporate Governance of a Multinational Enterprise: Firm, Industry and Institutional Perspectives" (2019) 57 Journal of Corporate Finance 1.

[23] Ram Kumar Mishra and Shital Jhunjhunwala, "As Companies Go Global, Boards Must Follow" [2013] Diversity and the Effective Corporate Board 45.

[24] Paul F Buller and Glenn M McEvoy, "Creating and Sustaining Ethical Capability in the Multi-National Corporation" (1999) 34(4) Journal of World Business 326.

[25] Jo Rhodes et al., "A Framework for Stakeholder Engagement and Sustainable Development in MNCs" (2014) 5(1) Journal of Global Responsibility 82.

[26] Ronald J Gilson, "Globalizing Corporate Governance: Convergence of Form or Function" (2001) 49(2) The American Journal of Comparative Law 329.

[27] Andrew J Sherman, "Expanding Abroad: What Problems Will You Face?" (2007) 18(6) Journal of Corporate Accounting & Finance 21.

in legal expertise and compliance departments.[28] They are frequently required by these challenges to stay updated with the international laws and regulations, undergo consistent audits, and push transparent communication among stakeholders.[29] Defeating these challenges becomes significant as they make it unmanageable for MNCs to uphold uniform corporate governance standards throughout their international operations, which could exhibit them to legal risks, hurt to their reputations and deterioration in stakeholder trust.[30] Thus, to adeptly handle the legal and regulatory obstacles associated with corporate governance, MNCs must exercise strategic legal and regulatory risk management.

Compliance with relevant laws and regulations necessitates carrying out in-depth risk assessments, tapping in place sturdy compliance programs, and routinely updating governance policies and procedures.[31] MNCs are able to spot probable compliance gaps and move swiftly to close them by holding close eye on regulatory varies and carrying proactive monitoring.[32] Additionally, they ought to build up trusting bonds with regional legal authorities and advisors who are well-versed in the laws and regulations governing each jurisdiction. This would make it conceivable for MNCs to navigate local laws, get timely legal advice and make sure local regulatory requirements are met.[33] They must also give accountability and transparency topmost priority in their governance procedures. This can be accomplished by realizing robust internal control systems to cease fraud and misconduct, observing to international standards and reporting and unveiling financial information in a transparent fashion.[34] Additionally, they also need to indorse a strong culture of ethical behavior and respect for local laws and customs in order to deal with the challenges offered by cultural variances and differing legal and regulatory frameworks.[35]

---

[28] Anne Anderson and Parveen P Gupta, "A Cross-Country Comparison of Corporate Governance and Firm Performance: Do Financial Structure and the Legal System Matter?" (2009) 5(2) Journal of Contemporary Accounting & Economics 61.

[29] Sarianna M Lundan, "Human Rights Issues in Multinational Value Chains," Edward Elgar Publishing eBooks (September 30, 2013). <https://china.elgaronline.com/view/edcoll/9781848449664/9781848449664.00011.xml>

[30] George Cairns and Sharif As-Saber, "The Dark Side of MNCs" [2017] Multinational Corporations and Organization Theory: Post Millennium Perspectives 425.

[31] Harald Haelterman, "Breaking Silos of Legal and Regulatory Risks to Outperform Traditional Compliance Approaches" (2020) 28(1) European Journal on Criminal Policy and Research 19.

[32] Igor, *supra* note 22.

[33] Shital Jhunjhunwala and Sharvani B, "Corporate Governance Disclosure and Transparency Framework" (2011) 4(1) Indian Journal of Corporate Governance 62.

[34] SKB Asante, "The Concept of the Good Corporate Citizen in International Business" (1989) 4(1) ICSID Review 1.

[35] Rahul, *supra* note 1.

5 Challenges for MNCs: Ethical and Cultural

MNCs firms, apart from legal and regulatory challenge, also confront a variety of ethical and cultural issues in maintaining corporate governance standards in the host countries.[36] These difficulties comprise navigating various cultural norms and values, observing to international legal requirements and making definite that ethical business practices are followed at several business locations.[37] They engross themselves with an extensive range of stakeholders and conduct business across national borders, which brings with it both opportunities and challenges. For example, cultural differences may have an effect on organizational values and decision-making procedures.[38] Furthermore, they may find it problematic to uphold consistency and their values and principles across all business operations due to disparities in ethical standards and practices across national boundaries.[39] Balancing the interests and expectations of multiple stakeholders, handling cultural diversity inside the organization, founding a common code of conduct that is relevant across cultures, warranting transparency and accountability in decision-making processes, and encouraging responsible business practices across all business units and subsidiaries are some of the major ethical and cultural challenges that MNCs face in the execution of corporate governance standards.[40]

MNCs must create strong corporate structures that address the moral and cultural issues they encounter. These frameworks ought to have explicit rules and regulations that endure moral behavior, cultural sensitivity, and adherence to global norms. In addition, they should render avenues for staff members to voice any ethical problems they may have at work, as well as systems for keeping an eye on and administering these rules and regulations.[41] MNCs must judiciously balance the needs and interests of many stakeholders, including governments, local communities, employees, and shareholders, in order to encounter these challenges.[42] There is frequent pressure on them to upsurge shareholder value and profits, which can from time-to-time clash with moral obligations and the requirement to give social and environmental responsibility top priority. Therefore, these companies need to deliberate about how their actions

[36] Terence Jackson, "Cultural Values and Management Ethics: A 10-Nation Study" (2001) 54(10) Human Relations 1267.

[37] Allen Morrison, "Ethical Standards and Global Leadership" Advances in Global Leadership 165.

[38] Paul, *supra* note 24.

[39] Vahideh Rafiee and Jawahitha Sarabdeen, "Cultural Influence in the Practice of Corporate Governance in Emerging Markets" [2012] Communications of the IBIMA 1.

[40] Minwir Al-Shammari, "On the Corporate Cultures of Cross-cultural Organizations" (1994) 1(1) Cross Cultural Management: An International Journal 28.

[41] Archie B Carroll, "Managing Ethically with Global Stakeholders: A Present and Future Challenge" (2004) 18(2) Academy of Management Perspectives 114.

[42] John Friedman, "Corporate Responsibility: Effectively Addressing and Communicating Across Cultures" (2018) 9(2) European Journal of Risk Regulation 351.

might affect local communities in terms of human rights, labor laws, environmental sustainability, and corruption.[43]

MNCs must set up strong governance and ethical frameworks that go beyond simply complying rules and laws in order to deal these issues. From the boardroom to the frontline staff, they must inculcate a culture of moral behavior and corporate social responsibility throughout their organizations.[44] This puts in place accountable and transparent process for making decisions, encouraging inclusivity and diversity, maintaining open lines of communication, and routinely evaluating and tracking how their operations affect stakeholders and the environment.[45] MNCs need to actively interact with stakeholders and local communities to realize their specific requirements, values, and issues. They must ensure that their operations are carried out responsibly and sustainably by customizing their business practices and strategies in confirmation to local cultural norms and ethical standards.[46]

A comprehensive approach that reassures accountability, stakeholder engagement, and the amalgamation of local values and norms is obligatory to address ethical and cultural challenges in corporate governance for MNCs. It assists them minimize ethical dilemmas, navigate the intricacies of cross-cultural variances, and develop trust with stakeholders.[47] It is evident that there are a lot of ethical and cultural issues with corporate governance that MNCs must deal with. To ensure that business operations are conducted in a way that compliments varied cultural norms, upholds ethical standards, and protects the rights and interests of all stakeholders involved, these encounters impose careful consideration and proactive measures.

6 International Corporate Governance: A Timely Remedy

The set of values, guidelines, and procedures that direct how businesses are run internationally is known as International Corporate Governance. It pursues to guarantee accountability, transparency, equity, and integrity in the operations of organizations, regardless of their location or category of their business. Even though, it is apparent from the prior discussion that MNCs do face diverse legal, regulatory, ethical, and cultural challenges, International Corporate Governance extends them structure to efficaciously confront these issues and promise suitable stakeholder management through the preferment of accountability, transparency, and moral conduct across

[43] G J Rossouw, "The Ethics of Corporate Governance," ed GJ Rossouw (2009) 51(1) International Journal of Law and Management 43.

[44] Heli Wang et al., "Corporate Social Responsibility: An Overview and New Research Directions" (2016) 59(2) Academy of Management Journal 534.

[45] Justin *supra* note 21.

[46] Som Sekhar Bhattacharyya, "Development of International Corporate Social Responsibility Framework and Typology" (2019) 16(5) Social Responsibility Journal 719.

[47] Geert Hofstede, "Organising for Cultural Diversity" (1989) 7(4) European Management Journal 390.

the entire enterprise. It assists MNCs to bring into line their internal procedures with international standards, guaranteeing uniformity in risk assessment and management and decision-making process. It makes it easier for them to comply with local laws and regulations, which dilutes legal and reputational risks and guarantees compliance. With this, International Corporate Governance fosters an incessant cultural improvement by enabling MNCs to gain from the best practices and knowledge exchanged across national borders and companies.

International Corporate Governance supports MNCs to overcome their complications by advocating ethical behavior, accountability, and transparency, reducing the risks of doing business in multiple jurisdictions, building the company's sustainability and reputation, guaranteeing local laws and regulation compliance, facilitating the exchange of best practices and knowledge, easing effective stakeholders management and urging a culture of innovation and continuous improvement.[48] It assists MNCs in navigating intricate international markets, accommodating cultural disparities, and promoting efficient communication and cooperation among heterogenous teams. Apart from furnishing a framework for efficient risk management and financial supervision, it also guarantees a strong internal controls and procedures in place to prevent fraud and financial misconduct. Hence, International Corporate Governance is treated as a vital tool for the MNCs in ensuring ethical and sustainable business practices across borders.

While framing the International Corporate Governance standards, diverse legal and cultural frameworks set up in each country where MNCs carry on businesses should be borne in mind. By employing a customized approach, governance procedures can be made to conform with regional legal requirements and cultural norms while upholding international standards.[49] To reassure consistent moral behavior and decisions in the company, values of moral leadership and integrity through the formation of unambiguous moral standards and codes of conduct that are relevant to all employees globally must be fostered.[50] In order to affirm well-informed decision-making process, the board of directors must be diverse in gender, nationality, and work experience which can support governance with viewpoints and insights.[51]

International Corporate Governance helps in carrying on routine assessments to recognize and deal possible risks associated to operating in diverse markets.[52]

---

[48] Shamsher Mohamad and Zulkarnain Muhamad Sori, "Corporate Governance from a Global Perspective," Social Science Research Network (January 1, 2011). <https://papers.ssrn.com/sol3/papers.cfm?abstract_id=1817082>

[49] Erin Meyer, "When Culture Doesn't Translate," Harvard Business Review (November 27, 2019). <https://hbr.org/2015/10/when-culture-doesnt-translate>

[50] Jiatao Li and J Richard Harrison, "National Culture and the Composition and Leadership Structure of Boards of Directors" (2008) 16(5) Corporate Governance: An International Review 375.

[51] Phipps, L C P S T A. "Reconfigure Your Board to Boost Cooperative Advantage | MIT Sloan Management Review," MIT Sloan Management Review (February 16, 2021). <https://sloanreview.mit.edu/article/reconfigure-your-board-to-boost-cooperative-advantage/>

[52] "Future-Ready Boards," The Harvard Law School Forum on Corporate Governance (February 10, 2021). <https://corpgov.law.harvard.edu/2021/02/10/future-ready-boards/>

It generates avenues for interacting with local communities, workers, and clients from various cultural backgrounds to get their thoughts and gain insights that can channelize governance plans. By encouraging the culture of transparency, accountability, and ethical conduct, International Corporate Governance support the long-term viability of MNCs. It is one of the means for them to ameliorate their credibility and reputation in global marketplace. Increased stakeholder support and trust can ensue from this, which is indispensable for sustaining corporate operations across various jurisdictions.[53]

MNCs can demonstrate their commitments to ethical conduct, sustainability, and legal compliance on a worldwide basis by employing these best practices in International Corporate Governance.[54] By creating consistent standards across nations and regions, lowering the likelihood of legal and regulatory arbitrage, and guaranteeing justice and transparency in business operations, International Corporate Governance levels the playing field.[55] MNCs can efficaciously navigate cultural and ethical variances and adjust their business strategies to suit local market conditions with the support of International Corporate Governance. Hence, International Corporate Governance is a key tool to handle the challenges faced by MNCs in today's global business environment by promoting accountability, transparency, risk mitigation, ethical behavior, effective communication, cultural management, and alignment with societal, ethical, and sustainability goals.

7 Conclusion

MNCs that operate across multiple jurisdictions are getting more predominant as a result of globalization.[56] They must stick to various legal, regulatory, ethical, and cultural norms. In order to ensure that MNCs uphold their governance standards and adjust to various jurisdictional necessities in which they operate, International Corporate Governance is indispensable.[57] However, when measuring the effectiveness of International Corporate Governance, it is paramount to take into account the contextual variations and obstacles encountered by MNCs that operate across various jurisdictions.[58] The ability of International Corporate Governance

[53] David A Detomasi, "International Regimes: The Case of Western Corporate Governance" (2006) 8(2) International Studies Review 225.

[54] G F, *supra* note 19.

[55] Igor Filatotchev and Günter K Stahl, "Towards Transnational CSR" (2015) 44(2) Organizational Dynamics 121.

[56] Stijn Claessens and B Burcin Yurtoglu, "Corporate Governance in Emerging Markets: A Survey" (2013) 15 Emerging Markets Review 1.

[57] Andrew Delios, "Governance: The Next Frontier for Research on Multinational Firms" (2011) 48(2) Journal of Management Studies 456.

[58] Ruth V Aguilera and Gregory Jackson, "Comparative and International Corporate Governance" (2010) 4(1) Academy of Management Annals 485.

to encourage accountability, ethics, and transparency among MNCs can be used to estimate its efficaciousness and attain competitive advantage. MNCs can reduce risks, increase operational effectiveness, and boost overall performance by putting International Corporate Governance standards into practice.

Canute's Laws? Legislative Responses to the Surging Tide of Digital Sexual Privacy Violations

Phil Glover and Cecilia Anthony Das

Abstract Our discussions about digital technology are notable for their predictable pointlessness and the sense of stalemate underlying the tug of war between denunciation and defence. The problem of assessing the internet is compounded by the fact that, while no single thing we ever do online seems momentous, dire effects emerge from aggregates of our collective use. The internet is only for other people: permanent elsewhere. Our sense of what we each do at any given time is therefore—whether by method, design, or happenstance, disconnected and self-exempt from the knowledge that we are voting with our digits, that we contribute to what it all adds up to. To an unprecedented and dismaying extent, it really is true that no one is responsible for what is happening. (Everyone else is.) The ugliest effects in this way unfold from humdrum causes. Systems are the watchword of our age, our way of understanding aggregate responsibility for racism, ecocide, or economic disparity, so click baiting is now the single most powerful force at work shaping the world. Its effectiveness is borne of the small habits of our banality. The more we encourage each other to 'change the world', the less we can or do.

Keywords Deep fakes · Internet offending · Digital crime · Image abuse

---

P. Glover · C. A. Das (✉)
School of Business and Law, Edith Cowan University, Joondalup, WA, Australia
e-mail: cecilia.das@ecu.edu.au

P. Glover
e-mail: p.glover@ecu.edu.au

J. Aston et al. (eds.), *Comparative Law*, https://doi.org/10.1007/978-981-97-7815-7_18

1 Introduction—Our Digital Enabling Environment

The year 2024 marks twenty-eight years of humanity's entrenchment in Castell's 'network society'.[1] Of the world's population (almost 8 billion),[2] 5.35 billion (66%) have access to the internet, with that number expected to increase to 7.9 billion by 2029.[3] The same source evidences that Internet users are online for an average of 6.5 hours per day.[4] In what has become an extremely 'digitized' milieu, 75% of Gen Z globally are able to access the internet via digital technology, spending on average 2.5 hours per day more online than 'Gen X' and 'Boomers'.[5] The direction of travel for these statistics appears to be inevitably upward. Today, the initiation, continuation, and termination of intimate relationships have seamlessly transitioned to the digital domain, eliminating the imperative of physical presence.[6] As Barba-Kay has stated, digital technology forms a network in which each node is accessible to every other—the web of such nodes is possible to the extent that all input can be coded into standard signals. Electronic data render what we say and what we do not into a common code: 'information'. Every node can therefore be in touch with every other at the speed of light. Moreover, the system is able to transmit data at such volume as to allow us to easily exchange highly defined sounds, images and vide [thus creating] *a compelling, alternative reality*...

Laptops, tablets, smartphone, [and now wearable (even implantable) technology] and other smart devices have rendered the network's nodes portable and ubiquitous digital technology has continued to colonize more areas of our life. The more we carry our devices on our persons, the more completely are our devices identified with us as persons. The more digital sensors gather all kinds of information, the more the web can really claim to be worldwide. Finally, our digital devices are designed to connect with and anticipate human intention; they are 'smart'. This feature bears as much on the way in which algorithmic data analysis can gradually 'learn' to reflect and engage our preferences as it does on how immediately engaging digital devices are for anyone who picks them up. We have in hand the first world-changing technology made for ready use; unlike the printed page, the pulley, or the wheel, it is so intuitive, straightforward, and compelling as to be child's play, fun for every age. We only have to touch and see; *it is agreeable to all.*[7]

---

[1] Anton Barba-Kay, *A Web of Our Own Making: The Nature of Digital Formation* (Cambridge University Press, 2023) 2-3

[2] See generally Manuel Castells, *The Network Society* (Wiley Blackwell, 2nd ed, 2009)./

[3] Lexie Pelchen, 'Internet Usage Statistics in 2024' *ForbesHome* (Web Page, 1 March 2024) < https://www.forbes.com/home-improvement/internet/internet-statistics/#:%7E:text=There%20are%205.35%20billion%20internet%20users%20worldwide.&text=Out%20of%20the%20nearly%208,the%20internet%2C%20according%20to%20Statista>

[4] Ibid.

[5] Ibid

[6] Nicola Henry, Asher Flynn and Anastasia Powell, 'Technology-facilitated domestic and sexual violence: A review' (2020) 26 (15-16) *Violence against women* 1828, 1831.

[7] Barba-Kay (n 2) 6.

Users of digital service platforms can undoubtedly enjoy the ease, excitement, and possibilities offered by social media and dating apps enabled by 'Big Tech', principally Meta (Facebook), Alphabet (Google), Amazon, Apple, and Microsoft. However, as the 2020s progress, scholarly research, ably assisted by investigative journalism, is increasingly highlighting a plethora of deleterious side effects arising from our entrenchment in this digital reformation. Effects include but are not limited to burgeoning ideological extremism,[8] internet addiction,[9] loss of critical thinking skills,[10] anxiety and an inability to focus in the offline domain.[11] Jonathan Hadith has even asserted (to considerable critical acclaim) that 'the great rewiring of childhood' brought about by embedding children in indoor, introspective internet activities for protracted periods has caused 'an epidemic of mental illness'.[12] It seems that, despite the many positive outcomes of the digital reformation, clear and present dangers have emerged.

2 Non-consensual Distribution of 'Intimate' and/or 'Sexualised' Imagery in the Digital Domain—An Explainer

As the title suggests, this chapter engages with another emergent head on the digital society Hydra, namely the proliferating use of digital technology to *distribute* (here given the same interpretation as in the *Criminal Code* (WA))[13] 'intimate' or 'sexualized' imagery,[14] without consent of the person depicted in the relevant imagery.[15] Two initially seemingly related but readily distinguishable manifestations of this conduct are discernible.

[8] Dr Jonathon Kenyon, Dr Jens Binder and Dr Christopher Baker-Beall, 'Exploring the Role of the Internet in radicalisation and offending of convicted extremists, *Ministry of Justice Analytical Series* (UK Ministry of Justice,2021) https://assets.publishing.service.gov.uk/media/614088c2e90e070442fbdde2/exploring-role-internet-radicalisation.pdf

[9] Gaia Bernstein, *Unwired: Gaining Control Over Addictive Technologies* (Cambridge University Press, 2023).

[10] Nicholas Carr, *The Shallows: What the Internet Is Doing to Our Brains* (W.W Norton, 2011).

[11] Johann Hari, *Stolen Focus: Why You Can't Pay Attention* (Bloomsbury, 2022).

[12] Jonathan Haidt, *The Anxious Generation: How the Great Rewiring of Childhood is Causing an Epidemic of Mental Illness* (2024, Allen Lane).

[13] *Criminal Code* (WA), s221BC 'In this Chapter a person distributes an intimate image of a person by—(a) communicating, exhibiting, selling, sending, supplying, offering or transmitting the image to a person other than themselves or the person depicted in the image; or (b) making the image available for access by electronic or other means by a person other than themselves or the person depicted in the image; or (c) entering into an agreement or arrangement to do anything referred to in paragraph (a) or (b)'.

[14] We will argue that that the two mischiefs are different and should be separated in legislation.

[15] The consent relates to the distribution, thus removing the relevance of the question of whether the imagery was originally consensually obtained.

The first is the non-consensual distribution of *authentic* or *genuine* intimate or sexualized imagery, where 'authentic' refers to the fact that the imagery has not been altered or manipulated in any material way by either the image subject or the party recording the imagery prior to its distribution.[16] Legislative responses to this phenomenon are largely in place across the democratic world, including Australia,[17] and can be broadly described as 'intimate image' legislation.[18] This includes criminalizing the distribution of intimate imagery,[19] while also establishing civil proceedings regimes purporting to enable its removal upon complaint, supported by sanctions for failure to comply.[20] As will be shown, what we call 'sexualized imagery', wherein the depicted subject appears to participate in 'sexual acts', falls within a statutory subset of 'private acts', the totality of which forms 'intimate' imagery.

The second form of conduct involves the non-consensual creation and distribution of *inauthentic* (deep fake) imagery,[21] which Jacobsen and Simpson define broadly as 'photorealistic images, videos, or voice recordings that have been algorithmically generated or manipulated'.[22] The Australian government offers a similar definition.[23] As a metastasized malignant variant on the non-consensual misuse of *authentic* intimate imagery, deepfake pornography's highly problematic nature has been succinctly articulated by Abigail George (citing others).[24]

---

[16] The authors accept that there is a continuum of image-alteration by means of computer software but mean 'authentic' or 'genuine' to exclude image alteration wherein the image subject is depicted as involved in conduct they were not involved in when the original was recorded. Software enhancements such as filters or Photoshop would not, for present purposes, prevent imagery from being classed as genuine or authentic.

[17] For useful and comprehensive critical evaluation of the WA legislative response, see generally, Paris McNeil, 'Efficacy of Intimate Image Legislation in Western Australia', (2021) 5(1) *Western Australian Student Law Review* 1

[18] See *Criminal Code* (WA), ss 221BA-BF which constitute Chapter XXVA–'Intimate images', which dovetails with the Australian Commonwealth's response, the *Online Safety Act 2021*(Cth), which creates an E-Safety Commissioner who, *inter alia*, administers (at Part 6, ss 74-86) a complaints and objections system for non-consensual sharing of intimate images.

[19] *Criminal Code* (WA), s221BD(2) (2) A person commits a crime if—(a) the person distributes an intimate image of another person (the depicted person); and (b) the depicted person does not consent to the distribution.

[20] Online Safety Act 2021 (Cth), Div 3–Removal Notices

[21] A history of deepfakes appears in a prescient article by Federica Celli, 'Deepfakes are Coming: Does Australia Come Prepared' (2020) 17 (2) *Canberra Law Review* 193, 194

[22] Benjamin Jacobsen and Jill Simpson. 'The Tensions of Deepfakes', (2023) *Information, Communication & Society*,1.

[23] E-Safety Commissioner, 'Deepfake trends and challenges-position statement' *Australian Government E-Safety Commissioner* (Web Page, 23 January 2022) https://www.esafety.gov.au/industry/tech-trends-and-challenges/deepfakes

> 'A deepfake is a digital photo, video or sound file of a real person that has been edited to create an extremely realistic but false depiction of them doing or saying something that they did not actually do or say'.

[24] Abigail George, 'Defamation in the Time of Deepfakes', *SSRN* (Web Page, 7 February 2024)

The accuracy and accessibility of deepfake pornography have grown at an exponential rate with no signs of slowing. At least 244,625 videos of deepfake pornography circulate online[25] and the top six deepfake pornography websites receive over forty-six million visits per month.[26] Deepfake technology has evolved from requiring hundreds of facial images and advanced computer skills in 2017 to needing just one image, twenty-five minutes, and basic computer skills.[27] Sexual deepfake images can be made on user-friendly iPhone apps. In a few years, it will be possible to make realistic 3D sex avatars of any person without their consent.[28] Accordingly, while deep fakes initially primarily targeted women in the public sphere, private individuals are now the primary target, with the number of deepfake videos growing by 900 per cent annually.[29]

3 Deepfake Image Misuse

Jacobsen and Simpson highlight the reality that 'discussions around deepfake [focus on issues beyond gender discrimination/violence] including...political legitimacy, misinformation, transparency, integrity, and trust',[30] and as a credible threat to

< https://dx.doi.org/10.2139/ssrn.4719803>

25 Ibid, citing Matt Burgess, Deepfake Porn Is Out of Control, *Wired* (Web Page, 16 October 2023), <https://www.wired.com/story/deepfake-porn-is-out-of-control/>(noting that over 113,000 videos were uploaded in the first nine months of 2023 and more videos produced in 2023 than all other years combined).

26 Ibid, citing [John Doe Website Analytics] (data on file with author); see also Home Security Heroes, '2023 State of Deepfakes: Realities, Threats, and Impact' *Home Security Heroes* (Web Page, 2023), <https://www.homesecurityheroes.com/state-ofdeepfakes/> (finding the ten most popular platforms had over 300 million combined views in 2023).

27 Ibid.

28 Ibid, citing Danielle Keats Citron, *The Fight for Privacy: Protecting Dignity, Identity and Love in the Digital Age* (Penguin, 2022), 48.

29 Ibid, citing Matthew Miller, 'Deepfakes: Real Threat 3' *KPMG* (Web Page, 2023), https://kpmg.com/kpmgus/content/dam/kpmg/pdf/2023/deepfakes-real-threat.pdf

30 Jacobsen and Simpson (n 23) 2

stable government and national security.[31] Maddocks has even highlighted a relationship between political and pornographic deepfakes, finding they operate similarly to silence critical speech.[32]

Kindred observes how the 'indistinguishable from reality' nature of deepfake videos and photos means that criminals are using the technology for broader nefarious purposes including cybercrime; extortion; targeted attacks; misinformation; fraud; getting around authentication methods; threatening personal, professional, and company reputations and blackmail or 'sextortion'.[33] The author further highlights that, as the technology becomes more readily available, the public are starting to use it for other reasons, including relatively harmless reasons such as comedy.[34] The latter means that legislative responses to the deepfake mischief have taken longer to formulate, with several attempts failing at bill stage, not least because of the labyrinthine complexity of the image misuse problem, and the need to encompass broader concerns than gendered violence and prevent over-criminalization.

Responses to intimate/sexualized imagery distribution are further complicated by the fact that *consensual* distribution is widespread,[35] indeed 'part and parcel of our contemporary algorithmic culture'.[36] Consensual sexual communication is endemic, particularly amongst teenagers, who may not (particularly in light of Haidt *et al's* research on smartphone harms)[37] fully foresee its relevant harms. Adults are also part of this new digital reality, particularly those in intimate and often physically separate relationships.[38]

---

[31] Anonymous, 'The Evolution of Disinformation: A Deepfake Future'–Highlights from an unclassified joint workshop of the Academic Outreach and Stakeholder Engagement (AOSE) and Analysis and Exploitation of Information Sources, 24 May 2023, Ottawa, Canada. Chapter 3 examines 'Deepfakes: A real Threat to a Canadian Future'. https://www.canada.ca/en/security-intelligence-service/corporate/publications/the-evolution-of-disinformation-a-deepfake-future/table-of-contents.html; US National Security Agency/Central Security Service 'Contextualising Deepfake Threats to Organisations' *NSA* (Press Release, 12 September 2023) https://www.nsa.gov/Press-Room/Press-Releases-Statements/Press-Release-View/Article/3523329/nsa-us-federal-agencies-advise-on-deepfake-threats/

[32] Sophie Maddocks, "A Deepfake Porn Plot Intended to Silence Me": Exploring Continuities Between Pornographic and Political Deep Fakes', (2020) 7 (4) *Journal of Porn Studies* 415

[33] Micah Kindred, 'Deepfakes: The Effect on Women and Potential Protections' (2023) 91 (4) *University of Cincinnati Law Review* (Web Page) https://uclawreview.org/2023/08/02/deepfakes-the-effect-on-women-and-potential-protections/.

[34] Ibid.

[35] Nicola Henry, Asher Flynn and Anastasia Powell, 'Image-based Sexual Abuse: Victims and perpetrators' *Australian Institute of Criminology: Trends and Issues in Crime and Criminal Justice No 572* (Web Page, March 2019)

https://www.aic.gov.au/sites/default/files/2020-05/imagebased_sexual_abuse_victims_and_perpetrators.pdf

[36] Jacobsen and Simpson (n23) citing Ted Striphas, 'Algorithmic culture'. (2015) 18 (4-5) *European Journal of Cultural Studies* 395–412

[37] Haidt, *the Anxious Generation* (n13) Chapter 5 examines the 'four foundational harms:

[38] See, for example Nazanin Kafaee and Taylor Kohut, 'Online sexual experiences and relationship functioning in long distance relationships' (2021) 30 (1) *Canadian Journal of Human Sexuality* 15-25.

Consequently, as for complaints of non-consensual autonomy violations in the offline sphere, the 'wicked problems' of proving the absence of consent and complainant re-traumatization (particularly in criminal proceedings) arise, particularly in circumstances where the imagery was originally consensually shared with the alleged perpetrator. Indeed, as regard to actually detecting and attaching criminal responsibility to deepfake creators/distributors, the prolific use of end-to-end encryption (E2EE) and/or virtual private networks (VPN) is increasingly problematic.[39]

4 Feminist Conceptualizations of Image Misuse in the Digital Domain

Feminist discourse continues to ground image misuse (authentic and deepfake) as a *gendered* phenomenon, conducted principally against women.[40] While available statistics and much published research lends weight to this, it is not completely accurate and thus risks misdirecting policy responses or resource allocation.[41] Men and teenage boys experience the phenomenon too, and in largely unknown numbers.[42] Deepfake child pornography transcends gender.[43]

---

[39] Australian Federal Police, 'AFP Submission to the Parliamentary Joint Committee on Law Enforcement: Inquiry into the capability of law enforcement to respond to cybercrime' [175–183] available at https://www.aph.gov.au/Parliamentary_Business/Committees/Joint/Law_Enforcement/LECybercrime47/Submissions.

[40] See generally Kim Barker and Olga Jurasz, 'Sexual Violence in the Digital Age: A Criminal Law Conundrum?' (2021) 22 (5) *German Law Journal* 784-799

Professor Clare McGlynn, 'Deepfake porn: why we need to make it a crime to create it, not just share it' *The Conversation*, (Web Page, 9 April 2024) https://theconversation.com/deepfake-porn-why-we-need-to-make-it-a-crime-to-create-it-not-just-share-it-227177. Professor McGlynn is a leading law scholar in this field in the legal regulation of pornography, sexual violence and online abuse, particularly cyberflashing and image-based sexual abuse (taking, creating and sharing intimate images without consent)–see generally https://www.durham.ac.uk/staff/clare-mcglynn/

[41] It is unclear as to how many instances of intimate image misuse (authentic and deepfake) involve female perpetrators, (for example following the breakup of a female same-sex relationship or simply falling out)

[42] Henry, Flynn and Powell (statistics on victimisation) (n 36); Asia A Eaton, 'Sextortion: A Growing Crime Against Men' *Psychology Today* (Web Page, 20 December 2023)

https://www.psychologytoday.com/au/blog/power-women-relationships/202312/sextortion-a-crime-growing-against-men asserting, *inter alia*, that during the COVID-19 pandemic, men received higher rates of sextortion than women.

[43] Office of Public Affairs, US Department of Justice 'Recidivist Sex Offender Sentenced for Possessing Deepfake Child Sexual Abuse Material' *US Office of Public Affairs* (Press Release, 1 May 2024) https://www.justice.gov/opa/pr/recidivist-sex-offender-sentenced-possessing-deepfake-child-sexual-abuse-material

5 Intimate Image Misuse as Image-based *Sexual Abuse* (IBSA)

The feminist perspective builds upon early research (2017-a long time in this fast-evolving offending area) wherein Clare McGlynn, Erika Rackley and Ruth Houghton, citing Liz Kelly,[44] proposed that what was then colloquially termed 'revenge porn' (referring to the non-consensual creation/distribution of intimate images by a vengeful ex-partner or cyberbully) should actually 'be understood as just one form of a range of *gendered, sexualized forms of abuse* that have common characteristics forming…[a]…. 'continuum of image-based *sexual abuse'* (IBSA).[45] In a related article, Clare McGlynn justified the use of the phrase 'sexual abuse', opining that it 'immediately and accurately conveys the significant harms that may occur and reflects the experiences of victim-survivors'.[46] The potential harms to image subjects caused by the distribution of authentic or deepfake intimate or sexualized imagery depicting them without their consent are indisputable (despite their subjective nature), and space precludes revisiting the weight of scholarly evidence portraying their seriousness.[47] We respectfully suggest, however, that the deployment of the term for online non-invasive conduct (and it is *conduct* that grounds the criminal law) is at odds with medico-sociological interpretations of '*sexual* abuse'[48] and actually runs the risk the authors highlight of 'skewing the focus of legislative debates'.[49] The term also arguably (although, we accept, unintentionally) diminishes the unique physiological and psychological trauma experienced by complainants in physical-invasive 'abuser physically-present' sexual abuse. 'Abuse', whether or not anchored in a 'sexual' context, suggests an abuse of power, or of an imbalanced

[44] Clare McGlynn, Erika Rackley and Ruth Houghton, 'Beyond "Revenge Porn": The Continuum of Image-Based Sexual Abuse' (2017) *Feminist Legal Studies* 25

[45] Ibid (Emphasis added).

[46] Clare McGlynn and Erica Rackley, 'Image -Based Sexual Abuse' (2017) 37 (3) *Oxford Journal of Legal Studies* 534

[47] Clare McGlynn, Kelly Johnson, Anastasia Powell. Erika Rackley, Nicola Henry, Nicole Gavey and Asher Flynn, 'It's Torture for the Soul': The Harms of Image-Based Sexual Abuse' (2020) 30 (4) *Journal of Social and Legal Studies* 541-562

[48] The United Nations hold that [within the context of sexual exploitation and sexual abuse], 'Sexual abuse means the actual or threatened *physical intrusion of a sexual nature, whether by force or under unequal or coercive conditions* (emphasis added). United Nations Protocol on Allegations of Sexual Exploitation and Abuse Involving Implementing Partners (Web Page) https://www.un.org/preventing-sexual-exploitation-and-abuse/sites/www.un.org.preventing-sexual-exploitation-and-abuse/files/un_protocol_on_sea_allegations_involving_implementing_partners_en.pdf

The Australian Government Department of Social Services, in respect of *child* sexual abuse (although readily transferable to adult-to-adult power abuses, state that it 'may include (but is not limited to): sexual *touching* of any part of the body, either clothed or unclothed, preparing or encouraging a child to engage in sexual activity, sex of any kind with a child, persuading or forcing a child to engage in sexual activity, *sexual acts* done by an adult of any gender, to a child of any gender.' (emphasis added) Australian Government, 'Guides to Social Policy Law: National Redress Guide (Web Page, 20 March 2024) <https://guides.dss.gov.au/national-redress-guide/1/1/s/30>

[49] McGlynn and Rackley (n47) 534

Table 1 United Nations definition of violence against women

Arena	Includes
Family	Physical, sexual and psychological violence, including battering; sexual abuse of female children in the household; dowry-related violence; marital rape; female genital mutilation and other traditional practices harmful to women; non-spousal violence and violence related to exploitation.
Community	Physical, sexual and psychological violence, including rape; sexual abuse; sexual harassment and intimidation at work, in educational institutions, and elsewhere; trafficking in women and forced prostitution.
State	Physical, sexual and psychological violence perpetrated or condoned by the state, wherever it occurs.

power dynamic, or a desire to dominate, that is not *always* present in this type of offending, which encompasses parody and the undertaking of pranks.[50] This is the first reason we would advance for reframing non-consensual image distribution as a *sui generis* 'digital sexual privacy violation' which should be labelled and proceeded against as such, rather than image-based 'sexual abuse'.

6 Non-consensual Image Misuse as Technology-Facilitated *Sexual Violence* (TFSV)

The same authors (and others) have further asserted that IBSA exists on a continuum with other forms of *sexual violence*, describing a range of technology-facilitated abuse, including, but not limited to, cyberbullying, trolling, hate-based harassment, image-based sexual abuse, digital coercive control, or technology-facilitated coercive control.[51] This aligns with earlier work by Jordan Fairbairn, which sought to align violence in the offline theatre with conduct directed towards females online.[52] The tables below illustrate the definition of violence against women and girls (United Nations) as well as from other sources (Tables 1 and 2).

Accordingly, Fairbairn argues that since the definition of sexual violence explicitly includes psychological and verbal abuse, an unnecessary task to state that these transgressions can occur in cyberspace.[53] Thus, the origins of IBSA as technology-facilitated sexual violence are clearly discernible, particularly in the Ontario Sexual Violence Action Plan.

As an example of how the quality of feminist of scholarship, augmented by feminist-led advocacy in the area of violence against women and girls, has influenced

[50] See generally Graham Meikle, *Deepfakes* (Polity Press, 2023).

[51] Henry, Flynn and Powell (n5) 1831

[52] Jordan Fairbairn, 'Rape threats and revenge porn: Defining sexual violence in the digital age' in J. Bailey and V. Steeves (eds.) *E-Girls, E-Citizens: Putting Technology Theory, Policy, & Education into Dialogue with Girls' and Young Women's Voices.* (Ottawa: uOttawa Press, 2015) 229-251

[53] Ibid.

Table 2 Definitions of sexual violence from other sources

Source	Definition of sexual violence
World health organization (WHO)	Any sexual act, attempt to obtain a sexual act, unwanted sexual comments or advances, or acts to traffic, or otherwise directed against a person's sexuality using coercion by any person regardless of their relationship to the victim, in any setting, including but not limited to home and work
Centres for disease control and prevention (CDC)	Any sexual act that is perpetrated against someone's will. Sexual violence encompasses a range of offences, including a completed non-consensual sex act (i.e. rape), an attempted non-consensual sex act, abusive sexual contact (i.e. unwanted touching), and non-contact sexual abuse (e.g. threatened sexual violence, exhibitionism, verbal sexual harassment).
Ontario sexual violence action plan	Any violence, physical or psychological, carried out through sexual means or by targeting sexuality. This violence takes different forms, including sexual abuse, sexual assault, rape, incest, childhood sexual abuse and rape during armed conflict. It also includes sexual harassment, stalking, indecent or sexualized exposure, *degrading sexual imagery*, voyeurism, cyber harassment, trafficking and sexual exploitation

legislative responses, the Law Reform Commission of Western Australia (LRCWA), as part of its mammoth Project 113 Inquiry into reform of sexual offences that reported in May 2024, defined 'sexual violence' as referring, broadly to all *sexual activity* that occurs without consent, or which involves the sexual exploitation of vulnerable people…[irrespective of whether]…reported to the police, charged as a criminal offence or proceeded to trial. It also does not matter if the activity involved physical violence. We acknowledge that some people may find use of the term 'violence' strange, as they may associate it with the use of physical force. However, the term violence recognizes that *sexual acts which violate a person's autonomy* or exploit their vulnerabilities are inherently violent, even in the absence of force. We also note that the term sexual violence is commonly used by people who work in the area.[54]

The reference to 'sexual acts violating a person's autonomy' is interesting. We agree that enabling access to intimate or sexualized imagery (whether 'real' or deepfake) certainly *violates a person's autonomy* (their sexual autonomy, as a component part of their private sexual self), but we concur with the LRCWA that to constitute a 'sexual offence' any conduct by one person against another requires a non-consensual 'sexual act', being an act of a sexual nature'. As to what constitutes a 'sexual act', it might be assumed that the answer is objectively obvious, but the problems with a wholly objective assessment are highlighted by Camargo and Renzikowski,[55]

[54] Law Reform Commission Western Australia, *LRCWA Project 113 Discussion Paper 1* (Government of Western Australia, 2022) 2 (emphasis added).

[55] Beatriz Correa Camargo and Joachim Renzikowski, 'The Concept of an "Act of a Sexual Nature" in Criminal Law', (2021) 22 (5) *German Law Journal* 753, 754.

by reference to, amongst other Gordian cases, the controversial 'cultural defence' Supreme Court of Maine (US) decision in *State v Kargar.*[56] They similarly explore the limitations of a subjective assessment of conduct, noting that, if the sexual nature of an act can only be constituted by the intention of seeking sexual pleasure, many other courses of action would have to be excluded from the definition. However, there are courses of action that cannot be described as pursuits of sexual gratification, but are, or should be, recognized as sexual...[for example]...sexual violence in the context of armed conflicts...[where]...violence is perpetrated particularly against women and girls with the purpose 'to humiliate, dominate, instil fear in, disperse, and/or forcibly relocate civilian members of a community or ethnic group'...[citing United Nations Security Council Resolution 1820 (June 19, 2008). These cases show that *the recognition of an act as a violation of someone's sexual autonomy* cannot depend on how the perpetrator feels or on whether his or her actions have other purposes as well, in addition to sexual gratification.[57]

They conclude that, the evaluation of an act as a 'sexual' act is determined not only by objective cultural standards but also, at the same time, by the subjective intentions of the actor. However, we do not defend a purely subjective or even a subjective-objective approach as commonly understood because we do not reduce the relevant criterion to the purpose of sexual gratification. Rather, *a sexual act is an act of communication it is about the language of sexuality.* Following this, an act of a sexual nature as a legal term must always be understood in the framework of an objective-subjective perspective—just like communication in a certain language depends on the partners in the conversation understanding the meaning of the words used. Following this, the legal definition of a 'sexual act' conforms, to a large degree, with the general understanding of sexual behaviour. However, it is not identical with that because for criminal law, not all sexual behaviour is *per se* relevant, but only those acts that are defined by a certain offence type as a *gross violation of another person's sexual autonomy.*[58]

We return to the concepts of 'sexual privacy' and 'sexual autonomy' shortly but conclude that conduct enabling people to access intimate or sexualized imagery online by distributing it by means of digital technology without their consent is not, when viewed objectively and subjectively, a 'sexual act'. At its narrowest, the 'act'

---

[56] *State v. Kargar*, 679 A.2d 81, 83 (Me. 1996). The authors describe how Kargar (an Afghan refugee) was convicted for gross sexual assault against his 18-month-old son. The Criminal Code of the state of Maine defined 'an act of a sexual nature' as, *inter alia*, 'any act between two persons involving direct physical contact between the genitals of one and the mouth or anus of the other'. As per Afghan tradition, Kargar had kissed his son's penis several times, and this was witnessed by visitors to his house. Kargar himself had no doubt that the sexual abuse of children was a crime and that Islam prohibited sexual activity between an adult and a child. The Supreme Court of Maine accepted Kargar's 'cultural' defence of his conduct, and his witnesses, all relatively recent emigrants from Afghanistan, testified that kissing a son's penis is common in Afghanistan, it shows love for the child, and that it is the same whether the penis is kissed or entirely put into the mouth because there are no sexual feelings involved.

[57] Camargo and Renzikowski (n 56) 759.

[58] Camargo and Renzikowski (n 56) 767 (Emphasis added).

is the clicking of a mouse or keystroke, and at its broadest, the 'act' is the communication, by digital means, of the sensitive personal data constituting an intimate or sexualized depiction of a non-consenting subject.[59] As a matter of conceptual and objective logic, the egregious conduct described as IBSA or TFSV is simply not IBSA or TFSV. It appears that legislatures share our view.

As recently as 2019, the WA legislature, enacted the *Criminal Law Amendment (Intimate Images) Act*, the new Criminal Code Chapter it created (Chapter XXVA) meant its provisions were not added to Chapter XXXI—'Sexual Offences', perhaps an indication of Parliamentary hesitancy to classify the distribution of intimate imagery without consent alongside pre-digital sexual offences 'sexual assaults (penetrative and 'indecent'), sexual coercion, incest and sexual servitude. McNeil's examination of the principal Second Reading speeches extrapolates no mention in them of intimate image distribution as a 'sexual offence' or 'sexual abuse'.[60] Furthermore, the Terms of Reference for the Law Reform Commission of Western Australia's (LRCWA) recently completed 'Project 113- Sexual Offences' limited it to 'reviewing *Criminal Code* (WA), Chapter XXXI and sections 186, 191 and 192'.[61] The LRCWA specifically ruled out investigating 'any current offences other than those outlined…*even if they relate to sex*…[including]…pornography offences and *other image-based offences*'.[62]

The WA conceptualization contrasts with that in England and Wales, wherein the frequently controversial passage of the *Online Safety Act 2023* ultimately saw the enactment of amending provisions within 'Part 10 Communications Offences', wherein specific provisions required the insertion of offences of 'sharing or threatening to share intimate photograph or film' into the *Sexual Offences Act 2003*.[63] This followed blanket acceptance of the 2022 findings of Law Commission of England and Wales (LCE&W), which recommended a new tiered framework of offences which uses one consistent definition of an intimate image, covers the *full range of perpetrator motivations*, and applies protective measures for victims consistently. This framework comprises…A base offence of 'taking or sharing an intimate image without consent'...[m]ore serious offences of…'taking or sharing an intimate image without consent with the intention of causing the victim humiliation, alarm, or distress', 'taking or sharing an intimate image without consent with the intention that the image will be looked at for the purpose of obtaining sexual gratification... 'threatening to share an intimate image' and 'installing equipment in order to commit a taking offence'.[64]

---

[59] On the Australian criminal law view of what constitutes an 'act', see *Kaporonowski v The Queen* [1973] HCA 35; 133 CLR 209; 47 ALJR 472; 1 ALR 296 (973_

[60] McNeil (n18)

[61] Law Reform Commission of Western Australia, *Project 113 Sexual Offences: Discussion Paper 1* (n 55) 12.

[62] Ibid, 14, (emphasis added).

[63] *Sexual Offences Act 2003* (E&W), s66B

[64] Law Reform Commission of England and Wales, 'Taking, making and sharing intimate images without consent' *Law Reform Commission* (Web Page, undated), <https://lawcom.gov.uk/project/taking-making-and-sharing-intimate-images-without-consent/>

The LRCE&W defined 'intimate image' as an image that is either sexual, nude, partially nude, or of toileting. These types of images show something that is inherently personal, private and intimate.[65]

In their final report, the LRCE&W returned to the problematic term IBSA, stating that,

We are aware that the term 'image-based sexual abuse' is accepted terminology used to describe the sort of conduct with which this report is concerned. Much intimate image abuse has a sexual element; it can involve sexual images, have a sexual motive and victims report experiencing the abuse as sexual abuse. *Some forms, however, are not sexual*: an image of a teacher using a toilet shared amongst a class is not sexual, but it is intimate. We therefore chose to use the term 'intimate image abuse' in the consultation paper to reflect the range of behaviours and harms.[66]

7 The Devil in the Definitions

(1) An 'absurd' conflation of imagery?

The WA and England & Wales approaches have similarities, but also differences. As shown, the latter's legislature is comfortable embedding intimate image laws within sexual offences legislation, whereas WA distinguishes them in the Criminal Code. Both, however, and we argue absurdly, fail to extrapolate 'sexualized' imagery as a unique debasing category of imagery that, in addition to violating their right to privacy, violates their right to sexual privacy, the latter constituting, in our opinion, a significantly more egregious violation.[67] We find it strange that 'protection' of the identifiable 'sexual self'[68] from egregious violations of sexual privacy/autonomy[69] through the non-consensual distribution of imagery depicting them in 'sexual acts',[70] has ended up subsumed within broader statutory provisions addressing conduct with no sexual connotations in circumstances where the sexual self of a particular image subject may not even be identifiable.

In Western Australia, imagery is 'intimate' if it is, a still or moving image, in any form, that shows, in circumstances in which the person would reasonably expect

---

[65] Ibid.

[66] Law Reform Commission of England and Wales, *Intimate Image Abuse: A Final Report* (Law Com 407, HC 326) 4.

[67] Just as in data protection legislation, where 'sensitive' personal information receives greater protection in the relevant law–See *Privacy Act 1988* (Cth), Schedule 1 Australian Privacy Principles, APP 3

[68] Or sexual self-concept (SSC) (discussed later herein) Marilyn Ashley, Stephanie Drouin and Krystelle Shaughnessy, 'Measuring sexual self-concept: a methodological review', (2024) 15 (2) *Journal of Psychology & Sexuality*, 254.

[69] Nora Scheidegger, 'Balancing Sexual Autonomy, Responsibility, and the Right to Privacy: Principles for Criminalizing Sex By Deception' (2021) 22 German Law Journal 769,770 (sexual autonomy as right to be protected);

[70] Camargo and Renzikowski (n 56) 15.

to be afforded privacy—(i) the person's genital area or anal area, whether bare or covered by underwear; or (ii) in the case of a female person, or transgender person or intersex person identifying as female, the breasts of the person, whether bare or covered by underwear; or (iii) the person engaged *in a private act;* and (b) includes an image, in any form, that has been created or altered to appear to show any of the things mentioned in paragraph (a).[71]

McNeil's analysis arguably implicitly endorses this statutory construction, describing it as 'clear and comprehensive' and 'providing protection and recourse for a wider range of persons [than in other jurisdictions]'.[72] She further observes that the WA legislature has circumvented 'the need for a sexual element' in the definition 'by including the terms 'private act' and 'circumstances in which the person would reasonably expect to be afforded privacy'.[73]

However, a deeper dive into the WA definition reveals that a sexual element is present within Section 221BA. The actual Code definition is 'engaged in a private act', which is to be interpreted as the image subject being (a) in a state of undress; or (b) using the toilet, showering or bathing; or (c) *engaged in a sexual act.*[74] Strangely, no statutory guidance appears for 'sexual act' within Chapter XXVA, the term only appearing in the separate (and thus irrelevant) context of 'prescribed offences' against children under 16.[75] We have already highlighted that defining a sexual act is not as straightforward as might be first thought.

The definition thus encompasses imagery depicting an *identifiable subject* engaged in 'private acts' (including 'sexual acts', which we discuss later herein) with imagery depicting the genital, anal or breast areas of a subject who may or may not be identifiable. McNeil posits that 'as the non-consensual taking and distribution of non-sexual images can be just as harmful and distressing as those of a sexual nature, broadening the scope of 'intimate images' to capture non-sexual intimate images promotes the purpose of the legislation'.[76] We have already countered this argument. However, as she earlier highlights in the same paper, the primary purpose for the insertion of a new Chapter XXVA into the Criminal Code, 'was to protect victims of Image-based *Sexual Abuse* by providing recourse, including rectification orders (often requiring the images be removed, forfeited or destroyed), and to impose harsh penalties to deter this conduct.'[77] If the feminist position asserting intimate image abuse as sexual abuse is to stand, it surely means that sexualized imagery requires *distinct* legislative protection.

---

[71] *Criminal Code* (WA), s221BA (emphasis added).

[72] McNeil (n 18) 12-13.

[73] Ibid.

[74] *Criminal Code* (WA), s221BA, emphasis added.

[75] Ibid, s321A

[76] McNeil (n18) 14, citing Henry, Flynn and Powell, 'Responding to 'Revenge Pornography': Prevalence, Nature and Impacts' (Report to the Criminology Research Advisory Council, March 2019) 83.

[77] Ibid, by reference to *Criminal Code Act Amendment Act* 2019, Western Australia, Parliamentary Debates, Legislative Assembly, 14 August 2018, 4311 (Peter Katsambanis), emphasis added

The conflation of sexual and non-sexual imagery in England and Wales is arguably more surprising, given the LRCE&W acknowledgement that sexual imagery is distinguishable from intimate imagery.[78] We find it problematic that 'intimate image' laws lump 'intimate' imagery that captures genital/anal/cleavage shots (often without identifying a particular individual and arguably belonging in the 'voyeur' part of the offending continuum)[79] alongside imagery depicting a person engaging in a sexual act, where the internet audience can discern the identity of the image subject. We suggest that depictions of a person in objectively sexual acts belong in a more serious category of privacy infringement.

(2) Deepfakes and a 'private sexual material' conundrum

At the federal level in Australia, in a recent submission to the Federal Joint Committee on Law Enforcement, Australia's Commonwealth Director of Public Prosecutions (CDPP) advised it has received 'deepfake' referrals from investigative agencies citing cases where individuals have created media that depict victims in certain poses or saying or doing things, where those victims have not in fact said or done those things. For example, an individual might create a deepfake image or video that superimposes a victim's face on another body so as to depict the victim engaging in a sexual act, in circumstances where the victim was never in fact involved in that sexual act. The following observations were made with respect to the *Commonwealth Criminal Code*;[80]

The federal offences under ss 474.17 [using a carriage service to menace, harass or cause offence] and 474.17A [Aggravated offences involving private sexual material—using a carriage service to menace, harass or cause offence] ...may not capture this conduct. Section 474.17(1) [provides that it is] an offence for an individual to use a carriage service in a way that reasonable persons would regard as being, in all the circumstances, menacing, harassing or offensive. Section 474.17A(1)—[aggravates]—the 474.17(1) offence and provides that where the offence in s474.17(1) is committed in a way that involves the transmission, making available, publication, distribution, advertisement or promotion of *private sexual material*, the offender will be liable for the offence in s 474.17A(1) which is punishable by a maximum of five years' imprisonment. While an individual's transmitting of deepfakes using a carriage service may...[contravene]...s 474.17(1), the CDPP considers that such conduct is unlikely to constitute [the aggravated offence] That is, even if the deepfakes being transmitted depict a victim engaging in a sexual activity or purport to

[78] Law Reform Commission of England and Wales, 'Taking, making and sharing intimate images without consent' (n67).

[79] See Stuart P Green, *Criminalising Sex: A Unified Liberal Theory* (OUP, 2020) 196-228. Voyeurism does not require the capturing of imagery, but rather involves the generally covert observation of their subject (in the absence of that subject's consent) in some degree of physical proximity to them. Internet access is not a prerequisite. Similarly, 'downblousers' and 'upskirters' record their imagery by being physically present and proximate to their subject. While it can be argued that all such conduct envisages possession of intimate imagery in the absence of the depicted subject's consent, it is the digital distribution of the imagery to a potentially infinite recipient digital audience that distinguishes it.

[80] *Criminal Code Act 1995* (Cth) Division 474 'Telecommunications Offences'

depict the victim's sexual organ, anal region, or breast region [in alignment with non-AI intimate image violations] such conduct is unlikely to contravene s 474.17A(1). This is because …[such]…deepfakes will not constitute 'private sexual material' as defined in s 473.1. *The definition of 'private sexual material' in s 473.1 can be satisfied in two ways—first where the material depicts the victim engaging in a sexual pose or sexual activity in circumstances that reasonable persons would regard as giving rise to an expectation of privacy; and/or second where the material depicts the victim's sexual organ, anal region, or breast region, in circumstances that reasonable persons would regard as giving rise to an expectation of privacy.* The issue that arises is that, *as the victim was not involved in the creation of the fictional 'deepfake' version of themselves, it cannot be said that any expectation of privacy attaches to the depiction of the victim.* The consequence of the above is that where an individual engages in conduct relating to deepfakes using a carriage service, the most likely available Commonwealth offence will be that available under s 474.17(1) of the Criminal Code. The CDPP observes that the maximum penalty for an offence against s 474.17(1) is three years' imprisonment.[81]

Setting aside discussions of the propriety of the current penalties, the CDPP's view is perplexing, and, in our view, erroneous. It is surely ripe for statutory interpretation using a purposive approach. The view seems to articulate that, because what is depicted is an 'artificial' or 'distorted' or 'fake' depiction of the complainant's conduct, that conduct cannot be said to attract a reasonable expectation of privacy because the complainant *never did what is depicted*. The sentence surely requires to be read a whole. The statutory test requires a 'reasonable person' objective assessment of the *depiction* of a complainant (i.e. an assessment that asks, 'on the basis of what is depicted, is this fake depiction of our complainant a depiction of them engaging in sexual activity or exposing their private parts a depiction of them that, if they were *actually* doing it, they would reasonably expect privacy?). The answer is of course, yes.

By way of an example (with apologies to my co-author!) if, having never participated in group sex, or having been present in group sex, our images are superimposed onto a group sex-themed pornographic film and distributed online, the CDPP's position is that, because we were never really present, we can have no expectation of privacy, and the aggravated offence under s474.17A is not established. It is correct that we are *depicted* participating in a pornographic film that *we have not factually participated in*, but, as in broader 'intimate image-related offending', the gravamen of the conduct is the click of the mouse that enables the *violation of our sexual self-image*. This is what would ground our complaint.

Even if a judge were to find in line with the CDPP's view, the definitional issue seems readily resolvable by an amendment wherein the law (a) acknowledges that any complainant subject has the right to control (by means of consent) the uses to

---

[81] Commonwealth Director of Public Prosecutions (CDPP), *Submission by the Commonwealth Director of Public Prosecutions to the Parliamentary Joint Committee on Law Enforcement: The Capability of Law Enforcement to respond to cybercrime* (December 2023) 5-6 available at <https://www.aph.gov.au/Parliamentary_Business/Committees/Joint/Law_Enforcement/LECybercrime47/Submissions>.

which their images are put, including the right to seek criminal proceedings and/ or civil remedies for violation of sexual autonomy. Alternatively, the law could be amended to read that the fact that imagery depicting a complainant in intimate or sexualized activity is in reality 'fake' shall be disregarded in determining whether there has been a breach of the complainant's right to sexual privacy.

8 Recasting Deepfake Sexualized Imagery as a More Egregious *Sui Generis* Digital Sexual Privacy Violation

We have earlier highlighted the absurdity that legislative 'protection' (analogous with 'sensitive personal data protection') of the identifiable 'sexual self' in imagery from egregious violations of sexual privacy/autonomy through the non-consensual distribution of imagery depicting them in sexual acts, has ended up subsumed within broader statutory provisions addressing conduct with no sexual connotations in circumstances where the sexual self may not even be identifiable. We have also shown that conceptualizations of authentic/deepfake image misuse (at its broadest) do not fit into well-intended models of image-based *sexual abuse* or even technology-facilitated *sexual violence*. We do, however, unequivocally endorse feminist scholarship's view as to the harms of image misuse.

9 What is Meant by 'Sexual Self'?

Ashley, Drouin and Shaughnessy describe 'sexual self' or, more accurately, 'sexual self-concept (SSC) as 'the domain of self-concept focused on sexual aspects of the self'.[82] They outline how researchers 'have previously discovered that both heterosexual and sexual minoritized people's' SSC is linked to their psychosexual health outcomes, including sexual satisfaction, relationship satisfaction, general life satisfaction, anxiety, and depression'.[83]

Given feminist scholarship's powerful articulations of the potential harms wrought by non-consensual image misuse, it follows that such conduct may have serious repercussions for an individual's SSC. So, while the criminal 'act' is the communication of data that will be hosted on the internet, the outcome is a violation of the depicted subject's SSC. This conception withstands scrutiny, irrespective of the whether the images are authentic or deepfake.

---

[82] Ashley, Drouin and Shaughnessy (n 71) 254.

[83] Ibid.

10 What is Sexual Autonomy?

Valentiner, writing in 2021, makes a compelling, if not irrebuttable, case for sexual autonomy as a human right, by outlining a 'multidimensional approach to sexual autonomy' discernible through international human rights treaties, decisions of the European Court of Human Rights (ECtHR) in respect of the right to privacy outlined in Article 8 of the European Convention on Human Rights (ECHR), including a duty to protect sexual autonomy through criminal law, and soft law instruments. In examining, she cites the leading cases holding that 'sexual life is part of private life'.[84] She opines that the ECtHR includes not only privacy protection but also a right to personal autonomy and development, which in addition to imposing positive obligations on Member States to protect private (and thus sexual) life from third-party interference and fulfilling basic conditions for autonomy, includes protecting individuals from sexual violence and prevention through education. Given the extensive jurisprudence of the ECtHR holding that violations of data protection legislation are violations of the right to private and family life, home, and correspondence, it is not difficult to see that violations of rights to one's own image are violations of sexual privacy.

It is to compelling feminist scholarship that we revert in order to make our next argument for reframing image misuse laws to distinguish non-consensual sexualized imagery distribution as *sui generis*. McCaughey and Cermele observe that 'while feminist scholars have been concerned with technology-facilitated sexual violence, they have not addressed *digital privacy invasions as such,* even when they occur as part of technology-facilitated sexual violence'.[85] She further calls attention to *sexualized invasions of privacy* [arguing that] rape culture and surveillance culture have become mutually reinforcing'.[86] They ingeniously bring our research back into the TFSV domain by opining that TFSV 'encompasses a wide variety of intrusive acts in which some technological method is used to *invade someone's sexual privacy*,[87] citing Citron's definition of the latter, 'the social norms (behaviours, expectations, and decisions) that govern access to, and information about, individuals' intimate lives'.[88]

Our final argument builds on the previous scholarship asserting sexual imagery misuse as constituting a violation of sexual privacy by reference to the Declaration of Sexual Rights 2014 promulgated by the World Association for Sexual Health.[89] This

---

[84] Dana-Sophia Valentiner, 'The Human Right to Sexual Autonomy' (2021) 22 *German Law Journal* 703, 707-12.

[85] McCaughey, M., & Cermele, J. (2022). Violations of Sexual and Information Privacy: Understanding Dataraid in a (Cyber) Rape Culture. *Violence Against Women, 28*(15-16), 3955-3976. Emphasis added.

[86] Ibid.

[87] Ibid.

[88] Danielle Keats Citron, 'Sexual privacy' (2018-19) 128(7) *Yale Law Journal* 1870-1960.

[89] Valentiner (n87) 712. The authors were unable to locate this document via the link she provided, but see now Sofia Gruskin, Vithika Yadav, Anton Castellanos-Usigli, Gvantsa Khizanishvilli and

arguably under-cited source distils concepts of 'sexual agency', 'sexual autonomy', 'bodily integrity' and 'privacy 'into a 'right to sexual privacy' which we feel should form the conceptual core of future legislative responses to sexualized image misuse in the age of AI deepfakes. We feel that there is wealth of evidence and compelling argument supporting the optimal descriptor for the relevant conduct being grounded in 'privacy violation' as opposed to '*sexual* violence' or '*sexual* abuse'. Our choice is 'Digital Sexual Privacy Violation' (DSPV). We feel that a distinctly labelled criminal offence, distinct from 'intimate' image misuse, with appropriate penalties, is the most logical way to proceed. Labelling sends a strong message.

11 Conclusion—Recasting the Enabling of Access to Non-consensually Distributed Authentic/Deepfake Sexualized Imagery as Criminal Accessory Liability

Jaani Riordan opines that 'internet intermediaries may be criminally liable as accessories where they participate in criminal wrongdoing with the required mental element'.[90] This refers to the English common law conceptions of *actus reus* and *mens rea* (essentially intention or recklessness). Some Australian jurisdictions also follow this approach to criminal responsibility. In WA and Queensland criminal law, however, in the absence of express statutory provision, neither the motive underpinning particular conduct nor intention are relevant to determining criminal liability.[91] Those unfamiliar with this 'Griffith Code approach' can struggle to adapt to it, but all that is required is a conduct element coupled with the negation of a particular defence (e.g., mistake of fact) determines guilt.[92] We feel that the Griffith approach to intimate or sexualized image misuse is ideal when seeking draft proscribing provisions. The offence can be complete upon complaint that intimate and/or sexualized imagery depicting the complainant has been used in any way beyond any consent originally given. If a complainant asserts that such imagery is online (the proof of which is not difficult), the relevant defendant, if identified, has an evidential burden to prove, on the balance of probabilities, that the depicted complainant had, as a matter of fact, consented to the posting of the imagery online. There is thus no requirement to qualify the actus reus with a requirement that it be conducted to 'humiliate, alarm or distress' (or similar), as such a requirement unnecessarily introduces subjective questions of motive and intention, which are inappropriate steps to require a complainant to take in these circumstances. The fact of the online accessibility of the impugned imagery should be sufficient to prove a violation of the individual complainant.

Eszter Kismodi, 'Sexual health, sexual rights and sexual pleasure (2019) 27(1) *Journal of Sexual and Reproductive Health Matters*, 29-40

[90] Jaani Riordan, *The Liability of Internet Intermediaries* (Oxford University Press, 2016) 129-30

[91] *Criminal Code* (WA) s23 (1)-(2).

[92] Riordan (n 91) 129

Riordan observes, by reference to Section 8 of the *Accessories and Abettors Act* (UK), that 'criminal accessory liability is defined both by statutory and common law rules…[wherein] any accessory who 'shall aid, abet, counsel or procure the commission of any indictable offence...shall be liable to be tried, indicted and punished as a principal offender'. WA has a similar approach, which we have adapted to show how a digital service platform hosting non-consensually distributed sexualized imagery might be criminally liable.

When an offence is committed, each of the following persons is deemed to have taken part in committing the offence and to be guilty of the offence and may be charged with actually committing it, that is to say—(a) Every person who *actually does the act*… [i.e. distributes the relevant imagery]…or makes the omission which constitutes the offence; (b) *Every person who does or omits to do any act for the purpose of enabling or aiding another person to commit the offence*…[the digital platform 'host' arguably attracts criminal responsibility here]…; (c) Every person who aids another person in committing the offence; (d) any person who counsels or procures any other person to commit the offence.

What Riordan states next, though (again by reference to relevant UK law) resonates similarly for other jurisdictions.

The exact boundaries of secondary participation in crime are the subject of extensive case law, and readers are referred to a specialist work for detailed treatment. In broad terms, these connecting factors are in some ways wider than those of the civil law; for example, civil liability will not attach for merely assisting or aiding a civil wrong. They are also narrower: the accessory must know or believe that the primary acts will occur. In 2007, three new forms of criminal accessory liability were enacted [in the UK]: (1) intentionally encouraging or assisting an offence; (2) encouraging or assisting an offence, believing it will be committed; and (3) encouraging or assisting offences, believing one or more will be committed. *These offences are not limited to offline crimes and could, in theory, be applied to service providers who relevantly encourage or assist digital crimes…*[93]

We also feel that a dedicated tort, enabling redress in civil procedure, should also be legislated for. This could be used whether or not criminal proceedings are instituted. We feel that the gravamen of conduct whereby internet users are able to access sexualized images (we use sexualized as opposed to sexual to allow for the sexualization of non-sexual imagery by means of deepfake software) lies in its trauma-inducing *reputational* harm.[94] We appreciate that we are not the first to suggest this,[95] but the matter is becoming increasingly more pressing as the impugned conduct becomes entrenched. Of course, the inherent problem with AI deepfake sexualized imagery distribution lies in the inability in the majority of cases to trace a perpetrator.[96] So while E-Safety Commissioners and 'take-down' legislation have their place, the proliferation of AI sexualized deepfakes is going to continue to grow. Attaching

[93] Riordan (n 91) 130 (emphasis added).

[94] McGlynn *et al.* (n48).

[95] Abigail George (n25).

[96] CDPP (n82).

primary criminal and/or civil liability by detecting and bringing relevant proceedings will become ever more difficult. This is why we argue for attaching criminal/civil accessory liability to digital platform services, with meaningful penalties. Holding digital platform services strictly and criminally liable for enabling access to non-consensually obtained/created/acquired/distributed *sexual* imagery is not censorship. Carve-outs may be possible for parody, but a 'defence' of parody would mean the 'perpetrator' would have to come forward and discharge an evidential burden. This is only proper.

12 Turning the Tide?

It appears legislatures are recognizing that existing laws are somewhat Canute-like and have failed to stem the tide. Despite an initially hesitant reaction to sexualized imagery misuse, the UK,[97] EU[98] and certain US states[99] are now moving legislation to suppress the mischief. Some are modelling their responses on those already in place in England and Wales and Western Australia, others have recognized the defamatory implications of deepfake imagery. Time will tell which approach proves to be more effective in a rapidly evolving digital offending context.

[97] See Forensic Focus, 'UK Parliamentary Legislation Introduced against Deepfakes Forensic Focus (Web Page, 2nd May 2024) <https://www.forensicfocus.com/news/uk-parliamentary-legislation-introduced-against-deepfakes/>

[98] European Parliament legislative resolution of 24 April 2024 on the proposal for a directive of the European Parliament and of the Council on combating violence against women and domestic violence (COM(2022)0105–C9-0058/2022–2022/0066(COD))

https://www.europarl.europa.eu/doceo/document/TA-9-2024-04-24_EN.html#sdocta25

Proposed Article 5 states…Member States shall ensure that the following intentional conduct is punishable as a criminal offence:(a) making accessible to the public, by means of information and communication technologies ('ICT'), images, videos or similar material depicting sexually explicit activities or the intimate parts of a person, without that person's consent, where such conduct is likely to cause serious harm to that person; (b) producing, manipulating or altering and subsequently making accessible to the public, by means of ICT, images, videos or similar material making it appear as though a person is engaged in sexually explicit activities, without that person's consent, where such conduct is likely to cause serious harm to that person; (c) threatening to engage in the conduct referred to in point (a) or (b) in order to coerce a person to do, acquiesce to or refrain from a certain act.

[99] The US National Conference of State Legislatures (NCSL), 'Deceptive Audio or Visual Media ('Deepfakes') 2024 Legislation' (Web Page, 2024) https://www.ncsl.org/technology-and-communication/deceptive-audio-or-visual-media-deepfakes-2024-legislation 'At least 40 states have pending legislation in the 2024 legislative session [with] at least 20 bills…enacted'. A complete list of states is provided.

Simplifying Investments in Real Estate Through Real Estate Investment Trusts (REITs)

Anindhya Tiwari and Mayank Shrivastava

Abstract As a financial instrument, Real Estate Investment Trusts (REITs) have emerged as a recent addition to India's real estate market. This research paper explores the conceptual framework of REITs in India and provides an overview of the current scenario and the way ahead. The paper begins with an introduction to REITs and their importance in the sector concerning real estate in India. It then delves into the framework of regulations that govern REITs in India and highlights the key regulatory changes that have taken place over the years. The paper also provides a comprehensive analysis of the current status of REITs in India. This includes an overview of the current market size, the types of properties that are included in REIT portfolios, the major players in the Indian REIT market, and the challenges faced by these players. Finally, the paper discusses the way ahead for REITs in India. This includes an analysis of the potential growth opportunities for REITs, the steps that need to be taken to attract more investors to this sector, and the role that REITs can play in development of the Indian real estate sector. Comprehensively, this research paper intends to give valuable insights into the conceptual framework of REITs in India and offers practical recommendations to help stakeholders navigate the challenges and opportunities presented by this emerging market.

Keywords REIT · RE · Investment trusts; · SPVs · Derivative securities · SEBI

1 Introduction

The conceptual understanding stands as "*real estate refers to property consisting of land and the buildings, structures, and natural resources attached to it. This includes residential as well as commercial properties, such as houses, apartments, office buildings, retail spaces, and industrial properties.*" Real estate can also include undeveloped land, such as vacant lots or farms. The holding and use of real estate is governed by laws and regulations, and the real estate market involves the buying,

---

A. Tiwari (✉) · M. Shrivastava
Hidayatullah National Law University, Raipur, India
e-mail: anindhya.tiwari@hnlu.ac.in

J. Aston et al. (eds.), *Comparative Law*, https://doi.org/10.1007/978-981-97-7815-7_19

selling, and leasing of these properties. Real estate is assumed as a valuable investment because it tends to appreciate over time, and can generate income through rent or lease agreements.[1]

Real estate regulation in India is governed by the RERA Act, 2016.[2] This law was enacted to bring transparency and fairness to the concerned sector and to protect the interests of homebuyers and investors.

Under RERA, the developers have to get their projects registered with the appropriate state regulators and provide necessary information about the project, like its completion timeline, amenities, and pricing. They are also required to maintain a separate escrow account for each project, into which a minimum of 70% of the project's funds must be deposited. This is intended to ensure that developers use the funds for the specific project and that homebuyers' investments are protected.

RERA also establishes a mechanism for resolving disputes between homebuyers and developers and imposes penalties and fines for non-compliance with its provisions.

Further to RERA, concerned transactions in India are also subject to various other laws including the Transfer of Property Act,[3] Indian Stamp Act,[4] and Income Tax Act.[5] The Goods and Services Tax (GST) also applies to the sale of under-construction properties, while completed properties are subject to stamp duty and registration fee.

1.1 Real Estate Business Vis-À-Vis Investment

Here are some of the most common approaches to invest in concerned sector other than the REITs[6]:

1. Buying and holding properties:

A very common way to invest is to buy and hold properties. This involves purchasing a property, such as a house, apartment, or commercial building, and holding onto it for an extended period while collecting rental income and waiting for the property to appreciate.

2. Flipping houses:

---

[1] REAL ESTATE, CFI, https://corporatefinanceinstitute.com/resources/commercial-real-estate/real-estate/ (last visited May 07. 2023).

[2] "The Real Estate (Regulation and Development) Act, 2016, Act No. 16 of 2016, Acts of Parliament, 2016 (India)"

[3] "Transfer of Property Act, 1882, Act No. 4 of 1882, Acts of Parliament, 1882 (India)"

[4] "Indian Stamp Act, 1899, Act No. 2 of 1899, Acts of Parliament, 1899 (India)"

[5] "Income-Tax Act, 1961, Act No.43 of 1961, Acts of Parliament, 1961 (India)"

[6] FORBESADVISOR, FORBES, https://www.forbes.com/advisor/in/investing/how-to-invest-in-real-estate/ (last visited May 10, 2023).

Another popular way of investment is to buy a house property, fix it up, and sell it for a profit. This is known as flipping houses, and it can be a lucrative way to make money in real estate.

3. RE Mutual funds:

Mutual funds are investment vehicles that allocate funds into a collection of real estate assets. These funds are overseen by experienced investors, providing investors with the benefits of diversification and liquidity. Investors have the ability to purchase and sell shares within the fund, enhancing their flexibility in managing their investments.

4. Crowdfunding:

Crowdfunding is a process of investing in the sector by pooling your money with other investors to purchase a property. This can be done through an online platform, and it allows you to invest in real estate with a smaller amount of capital.

5. RE Syndication:

Syndication involves pooling together money from multiple investors to purchase a property. In this scenario, the investors have shared ownership over the property and share in the rental income and any appreciation in value. This type of investment is typically managed by a professional real estate investment company or sponsor.

2 Investment Trusts—Genesis

2.1 Introduction

It is a form of mutual fund that pools funds from various investors to invest in a diverse portfolio of assets, such as stocks, bonds, and other securities. They are frequently traded on the stock exchanges, Thus allowing investors to buy and sell the units on the open market.

Professional fund managers are responsible for making investment decisions on behalf of the shareholders of investment trusts. These managers aim to generate long-term financial growth for the participants of the trust by investing in a wide range of assets.

The investment decisions made by the fund managers are driven by the investment objectives and policies outlined in the trust's prospectus. One notable characteristic of investment trusts is that they are closed-ended, meaning that there is a fixed number of shares available in the trust. This sets them apart from open-ended funds like mutual funds, where the number of shares can fluctuate based on investor demand. The fixed number of shares in investment trusts can cause their prices to be influenced by supply and demand factors, resulting in them being traded at a premium or discounted value compared to the original net asset value (NAV) of the trust's underlying assets.

Investment trusts offer several advantages to investors, including access to a diverse portfolio of assets, professional management of investments, and the ability to trade shares on a stock exchange. However, they also come with certain risks, such as market risk, liquidity risk, and the possibility of shares being traded at a discount to the NAV. It is crucial for investors to carefully evaluate their investment objectives, risk tolerance, and other relevant factors before deciding to invest in an investment trust.

2.2 Regulation of Investment Trusts in India

Investment trusts are regulated by the SEBI which oversees the market related to securities in India and is responsible for regulating mutual funds[7] to protect investors' interests and maintain market integrity.[8]

SEBI has established a comprehensive regulatory framework that governs the establishment, operation, and management of investment trusts in India. This regulatory framework covers various aspects of investment trusts, including the registration process, disclosure requirements, investment restrictions, and pricing rules. The regulatory framework also sets out the role and responsibilities of various stakeholders involved in the investment trust ecosystem, such as trustees, asset management companies, custodians, and registrars.

SEBI has implemented various measures over the years ensuring the transparency and accountability of the same. For instance, SEBI has mandated investment trusts to disclose their portfolio holdings and investment strategies regularly. SEBI has also set up a system for rating investment trusts, which helps investors make informed investment decisions.

Overall, SEBI's regulatory framework has played a crucial role in the development of India's mutual fund industry, which has grown significantly over the years and has become an important source of funding for various sectors of the economy.

---

[7] "INVESTMENT TRUSTS, SEBI, https://www.sebi.gov.in/legal/regulations/feb-2023/securities-and-exchange-board-of-india-infrastructure-investment-trusts-regulations-2014-last-amended-on-february-14-2023-_68062.html (last visited May 10, 2023)"

[8] "Securities & Exchange Board of India".

3 RE Investment Trusts—REITs

3.1 Introduction

A REIT is a legal entity that gathers capital from various investors to invest in income-generating properties.[9] The trust then distributes the income generated from these properties to its investors as dividend. REITs are like mutual funds, in that they pool capital from multiple investors to purchase a diversified portfolio of properties, including office buildings, retail centers, apartments, hotels, and other types of commercial real estate.[10]

The mandatory requirements primarily include:

Ownership: REIT must own a substantial portion of its assets in real estate, cash, or public securities.
Income: REIT's major income must come from rent, interest on mortgages, or profits from the sale of real estate assets.
Distribution: A REIT must pay a substantial amount of its taxable income to shareholders as dividends.
Shareholders: A REIT must have shareholders and the control shall not be concentrated among a few shareholders, rather it should be diversified.[11]

There are several types, including[12]:

1. Equity REITs:

Equity REITs specialize in purchasing and operating real estate assets that generate income, such as office buildings, shopping centers, and residential properties. These REITs earn profits through leasing agreements with tenants and the appreciation of their property portfolios.

2. Mortgage REITs:

Mortgage Real Estate Investment Trusts (REITs) allocate their investments toward mortgages and various other real estate debt instruments. Their revenue is generated by the interest payments they receive from borrowers on the mortgages they possess. Additionally, such REITs may choose to invest in mortgage-backed securities and other forms of debt securities.

3. Hybrid REITs:

---

[9] "REITs, INVESTOR.GOV, https://www.investor.gov/introduction-investing/investing-basics/investment-products/real-estate-investment-trusts-reits (last visited May 10, 2023)"

[10] "REITs, SEBI, https://www.sebi.gov.in/legal/regulations/aug-2021/securities-and-exchange-board-of-india-real-estate-investment-trusts-regulations-2014-last-amended-on-august-03-2021-_38449.html (last visited May 10, 2023)"

[11] "Office of Investor Education and Advocacy, *Investor Bulletin REITs,* SEC, https://www.sec.gov/files/reits.pdf"

[12] "NAREIT, https://www.reit.com/what-reit/types-reits (last visited May 10, 2023)"

These REITs combine the strategies of equity REITs and mortgage REITs by investing in both real estate properties and mortgage securities. This allows them to diversify their portfolios and potentially earn income from both sources.

4. Retail REITs:

These REITs invest in retail properties, such as shopping centers and malls. They earn income through rent payments from tenants, and their performance is often tied to the strength of the retail industry.

5. Office REITs:

These REITs invest in office buildings and other commercial properties. They earn income through rent payments from tenants, and their performance is often tied to the strength of the commercial real estate market.

6. Residential REITs:

These REITs invest in residential properties, such as apartments and single-family homes. They earn income through rent payments from tenants, and their performance is often tied to the strength of the rental market.

7. Industrial REITs:

These REITs invest in industrial properties, such as warehouses and distribution centers. They earn income through rent payments from tenants, and their performance is often tied to the strength of the industrial real estate market.

8. Healthcare REITs:

These REITs invest in health care-related properties, such as hospitals, medical offices, and nursing homes. They earn income through rent payments from tenants, and their performance is often tied to the strength of the healthcare industry.

9. Infrastructure REITs:

These REITs invest in infrastructure-related properties, such as toll roads, airports, and communication towers. They earn income through rent payments from tenants, and their performance is often tied to the strength of the infrastructure market.

3.2 Advantages of REITs

REITs offer several benefits to investors, including[13]:

1. Diversification:

[13] "OUTLOOK, https://www.outlookindia.com/business/how-to-invest-in-reits-and-what-are-the-benefits-read-here-to-know-more-news-197535 (last visited May 11, 2023)"

Investing in REITs can lead to a diversified investor's portfolio. By investing in a REIT, an investor is gaining exposure to a diverse range of properties, sectors, and geographies. This can reduce chances of risk, as losses from one property or sector can be offset by gains from others.

2. Passive income:

REITs are legally obligated to distribute a minimum of 90% of their taxable income to shareholders in the form of dividends. Consequently, investors have the opportunity to generate passive income from their REIT investments, making it an appealing option for those in search of consistent cash flow.

3. Capital appreciation:

Along with providing a steady flow of income, REITs can also offer the potential for capital appreciation. As the value of the properties owned by the REIT increases, so too does the value of the shares in the REIT. This can allow investors to realize gains when they sell their shares.

4. Liquid investment:

REITs are listed on stock exchanges, which makes them an investment with high liquidity. Consequently, investors have the convenience of swiftly and effortlessly buying or selling shares in a REIT, without being bound by long-term obligations.

5. Professional management:

They are overseen by seasoned experts with a profound comprehension of the real estate market. This allows investors to leverage the knowledge and skills of these professionals, eliminating the necessity for them to possess their own expertise in real estate investment.

6. Tax benefits:

REITs can offer tax benefits to investors. They are not subject to corporate income tax because of the high dividend payout. Additionally, because REITs are classified as pass-through entities, investors only pay taxes on their share of the REIT's income, rather than on the REIT's entire income.

3.3 Conceptual Framework in India

In India, REITs are regulated by the Securities and Exchange Board of India (SEBI) under the SEBI (Real Estate Investment Trusts) Regulations, 2014.[14]

To be registered as a REIT in India, a trust should have a minimum net worth of 500 crore rupees and a minimum of two projects within its portfolio. Additionally, minimum 80% of the total value of assets of the trust must be invested in completed

[14] "Securities and Exchange Board of India (Real Estate Investment Trusts) Regulations, 2014"

and revenue-generating real estate properties. The remaining 20% can be invested in under-construction properties, mortgage-backed securities, and other permissible investments.[15]

REITs in India are required to distribute at least 90% of their income to investors as dividends and are also required to distribute dividends on a quarterly basis. The dividends received by investors are taxed as per their respective income tax slabs.[16]

Investors have the option to invest in REITs by participating in an initial public offering (IPO). In India, REITs are listed on stock exchanges, offering investors a chance to enter the real estate market without the complexities associated with owning physical properties.

These were introduced in 2014 to enable the public to invest in real estate assets.

REITs in India are required to adhere to SEBI regulations regarding governance and reporting, including regular disclosures and audits. The trustee and sponsor of the REIT are responsible for ensuring compliance with these regulations.

3.4 Regulatory Framework

SEBI (Securities and Exchange Board of India) issued regulations for Real Estate Investment Trusts (REITs) in India to provide a platform for retail investors to invest in the real estate market. Here is a summary of the SEBI (REIT) Regulations, 2014[17]:

1. Eligibility:

It must be a trust registered under the Indian Trusts Act, 1882, and have a minimum net worth of Rs. 500 Crores. The REIT should have at least two projects, the size of each project should not be less than Rs. 500 crores, and the combined value of all projects owned by the REIT must be at least Rs. 1,000 crores. Additionally, the trustee of the REIT must have a minimum net worth of Rs. 1 crore.

2. Investment:

A REIT shall invest at least 80% of its assets in completed and revenue-generating real estate properties. The remaining 20% can be invested in under-construction properties or other approved investments. These assets must be held for at least three years. However, investment in equity shares of a developer is not allowed.

---

[15] *"New REITs regulations by SEBI is a game changer: 7 ways how it can help fractional real estate investors"* https://economictimes.indiatimes.com/wealth/real-estate/new-reits-regulations-by-sebi-is-a-game-changer-7-ways-how-it-can-help-fractional-real-estate-investors/articleshow/108390813.cms?from=mdr (last visited June 23, 2023)"

[16] *"New REITs regulations by SEBI is a game changer: 7 ways how it can help fractional real estate investors"* https://economictimes.indiatimes.com/wealth/real-estate/new-reits-regulations-by-sebi-is-a-game-changer-7-ways-how-it-can-help-fractional-real-estate-investors/articleshow/108390813.cms?from=mdr (last visited June 23, 2023)"

[17] *"Sebi notifies small and medium REITs"* https://www.livemint.com/money/sebi-notifies-small-and-medium-reits-11709999868347.html (last visited June 02, 2023)"

3. Minimum offer size:

The minimum offer size for an initial public offering (IPO) of a REIT is Rs. 250 crore. The minimum subscription size for an investor is Rs. 1 lakh. However, investors must hold a minimum of 200 units of the REIT.

4. Listing:

A REIT must be listed on a recognized stock exchange within 12 days of the closure of the initial offer.

5. Distribution:

The REIT must distribute at least 90% of the net distributable cash flows to unit holders on a half-yearly basis. The remaining 10% can be retained as reserves for distribution in the following years.

6. Related party transactions:

A REIT is required to obtain approval from unit holders for related party transactions exceeding 5% of the REIT's total asset value.

7. Governance:

The REIT must have an independent trustee, a manager, and a principal valuer. The manager is responsible for the management of the REIT's assets. The REIT must have a minimum of three independent directors on its board. Additionally, the REIT must have a principal valuer to value its properties, and an asset management company (AMC) to manage its assets.

8. Leverage:

A REIT can borrow up to 49% of its total asset value. However, the total debt of the REIT cannot exceed 2.5 times its net worth.

3.5 Current Scenario

Real Estate Investment Trusts (REITs) have gained significant popularity among investors in India in recent years. These investment vehicles enable individuals to invest in real estate without the need to own property directly, by purchasing shares in a trust that manages income-generating real estate assets. One of the key reasons for the growing interest in REITs in India is the relatively low-risk nature of these investments. By law, REITs are mandated to distribute a major portion of their income as dividends to shareholders, providing investors with a steady income stream without the challenges of owning and overseeing physical real estate properties.

Additionally, REITs in India are regulated by the Securities and Exchange Board of India (SEBI), which provides investors with a level of transparency and oversight that is not typically available in the real estate market. This regulatory oversight helps to mitigate some of the risks associated with real estate investments, such as fraud, mismanagement, and market volatility.

Finally, the Indian government has introduced several tax incentives to encourage investment in REITs, such as tax exemptions on capital gains and dividend income. These incentives make REITs an attractive investment option for both domestic and foreign investors.

Overall, the trend toward REITs in India is likely to continue in the coming years, as more investors become aware of the benefits of investing in these vehicles. As the Indian real estate market continues to mature, REITs are likely to become an increasingly important part of the investment landscape, providing investors with a convenient and low-risk way to invest in one of the fastest-growing real estate markets in the world.

3.6 The Way Ahead

These investment vehicles have been introduced in India recently and are still in their early stages of development. Here are some suggestions to improve the situation of REITs in India:

1. Taxation:

The taxation policies for REITs need to be made more favorable to attract more investors. Currently, dividends received from REITs are taxed among the highest tax bracket. Tax exemptions for REITs can encourage more investment in this sector.

2. Regulations:

Regulations governing REITs need to be made more transparent and investor-friendly. The Securities and Exchange Board of India (SEBI) has already taken some steps to ease the regulations for REITs. More measures can be taken to make the process of investing in REITs easier and more accessible.

3. Increasing awareness:

More awareness needs to be created among investors about REITs. The benefits of investing in REITs, the risks involved, and the anticipated returns need to be communicated to potential investors. This can be done through various channels, such as social media, seminars, and workshops.

4. Diversification of REIT portfolios:

REITs need to diversify their portfolios to include different types of assets, such as commercial properties, residential properties, and warehouses. This can reduce the risk associated with investing in a single type of asset.

5. Investor education:

Investors need to be educated about the basics of REITs, such as how they work, the benefits, and the risks involved. This can be done through educational programs or workshops organized by SEBI or other financial institutions.

6. Improving liquidity:

REITs need to improve their liquidity by increasing the number of investors and the volume of trading. This can be achieved by improving investor confidence, increasing awareness, and creating a more efficient trading system.

By implementing these suggestions, the situation of REITs in India can be improved, which can ultimately lead to increased investment and growth in the real estate sector.

4 Global Comparative Study

Comparing Real Estate Investment Trusts (REITs) across various structured capital markets globally involves analyzing their regulatory frameworks, market performance, investor preferences, and other factors. Here is a comparative study focusing on some key markets:

4.1 USA

The SEC regulates REITs. They must distribute at least 90% of their taxable income to shareholders and meet other criteria to qualify as REITs. The U.S. REIT market is one of the largest globally, with a diverse range of REITs across various property types. REITs are popular among both institutional and individual investors due to their potential for stable income and portfolio diversification.[18]

4.2 Canada

Canadian REITs are regulated by the "*Canadian Securities Administrators (CSA) and the Toronto Stock Exchange (TSX).*" They must meet certain distribution and asset requirements to qualify as REITs for tax purposes. The Canadian REIT market has experienced steady growth, driven by demand for income-producing assets and favorable tax treatment. Canadian REITs invest in various property types, including commercial, residential, and industrial.[19]

---

[18] National Association of Real Estate Investment Trusts (NAREIT), U.S. Securities and Exchange Commission (SEC).

[19] Canadian REIT Association, Toronto Stock Exchange (TSX).

4.3 United Kingdom

In the UK, REITs are regulated by the Financial Conduct Authority (FCA). They must meet specific criteria related to asset diversification, income distribution, and governance. The UK REIT market has expanded rapidly since its introduction in 2007. UK REITs offer investors exposure to a wide variety of property types, like office, retail, and residential.[20]

4.4 Australia

Australian REITs are regulated by the "*Australian Securities and Investments Commission (ASIC) and the Australian Securities Exchange (ASX).*" They must distribute at least 90% of their taxable income to shareholders and meet other eligibility criteria. The Australian REIT market has grown significantly, supported by strong demand for commercial real estate assets. Australian REITs invest in office buildings, shopping centers, industrial properties, and other asset classes.[21]

4.5 Singapore

REITs in Singapore are regulated by the *"Monetary Authority of Singapore (MAS) and the Singapore Exchange (SGX)."* They must divide 9:10 of their taxable income and adhere to specific asset and income requirements. The Singapore REIT market is well established and offers investors exposure to diverse property sectors, including retail, office, industrial, and hospitality. Singapore REITs are popular among both domestic and international investors.[22]

4.6 Japan

REITs in Japan are regulated by the Financial Services Agency (FSA). They must meet certain criteria related to asset composition, income distribution, and leverage limits. The Japanese REIT market has grown steadily, driven by demand for income-producing assets and favorable regulatory reforms. Japanese REITs invest in various property types, including office buildings, residential complexes, and retail centers.[23]

[20] British Property Federation, Financial Conduct Authority (FCA).

[21] Property Council of Australia, Australian Securities and Investments Commission (ASIC).

[22] Monetary Authority of Singapore (MAS), Singapore Exchange (SGX).

[23] Japan Real Estate Investment Corporation Association, Financial Services Agency (FSA).

5 Conclusion

Overall, the SEBI (REIT) Regulations aim to provide a regulatory framework for REITs in India, allowing investors to invest in the real estate sector in a transparent and regulated manner. The SEBI (REIT) Regulations provide a framework for the establishment, operation, and listing of REITs in India. The regulations aim to provide retail investors with a regulated platform to invest in the real estate sector and provide liquidity to developers. The regulations ensure transparency, good governance, and investor protection.

Investors in India have the chance to engage in real estate assets through REITs, without the need to own the actual property. By offering tax advantages and regular income distribution, REITs can serve as a reliable and consistent source of earnings for investors. Opting for REITs allows investors to tap into the real estate market without the burdensome task of property management. Nevertheless, it is important to acknowledge that, like any investment, REITs carry certain risks. These risks include the possibility of fluctuations in real estate values, interest rates, and overall economic conditions. Therefore, it is crucial to conduct thorough research and analysis before making any investment decisions regarding REITs.

REITs around the globe follow similar trends of distributing major portions of income to the unit holders, and the same is followed by developing markets like India. The adoption of various policies throughout the world will surely make the overall regime more concrete.

In conclusion, the REIT framework in India has reached a long way since its beginning in 2014 and has the potential of being a significant way of channeling investment into the Indian real estate sector. Despite the challenges that have been faced by the industry, such as the COVID-19 pandemic and the regulatory framework, the REITs market has shown resilience and continued growth. Going forward, there is a need for further regulatory reforms and investor education to boost the REIT market and realize its full potential. With the right policies and measures in place, REITs can emerge as a viable investment option, providing liquidity, diversification, and long-term returns to investors, while also contributing to the growth and development of the Indian real estate sector.

Integrating Climate Change and Development: *Policy* and *Strategy* in the Coastal Zone Management of Bangladesh

Tanzim Afroz

Abstract The coastal zone of Bangladesh characterizes the intricate relationship between climate change and development, marked by both significant vulnerabilities and promising potential. Frequent natural disasters such as cyclones, floods, and riverbank erosion exacerbate the vulnerability of the region, positioning Bangladesh among the world's most climate-impacted nations, according to the latest Global Climate Risk Index. Despite these challenges, the coastal zone is rich in natural resources, including coastal fisheries, mangrove forests, and potential mineral deposits, which support both local livelihoods and economic growth. Additionally, the presence of export processing zones, harbors, airports, and tourism complexes highlights the region's substantial economic potential. By leveraging these resources, the coastal zone can significantly contribute to poverty reduction and the overall development of Bangladesh. Given the dual nature of its challenges and opportunities, an integrated climate development approach to coastal zone management is essential. This paper delves into the current coastal zone management framework in Bangladesh, examining key policy documents like the *Coastal Zone Policy* and the *Coastal Development Strategy*. These documents serve as the blueprint for harnessing the region's potential while mitigating the challenges posed by climate change and environmental degradation. However, a detailed analysis of these documents reveals a gap in their approach to integrating climate change and development considerations at the policy level. The study advocates for a more cohesive and synergistic approach that strategically weaves climate adaptation and mitigation measures into the fabric of development strategies, rather than treating them as parallel and disconnected efforts. This entails re-evaluating the policies to ensure that climate considerations are not mere add-ons but are fully integrated into the broader development narrative.

Keywords Climate change · Integrated approach · Climate development nexus · Policy

---

T. Afroz (✉)
School of Business and Law, Edith Cowan University, Joondalup, Australia
e-mail: t.afroz@ecu.edu.au

J. Aston et al. (eds.), *Comparative Law*, https://doi.org/10.1007/978-981-97-7815-7_20

1 Introduction

The coastal zone of Bangladesh offers a unique perspective on the interplay between climate change and development, characterized by both vulnerability and potential.[1] Over time, the zone has been recognized as a hotspot of vulnerability to climate change and sea level rise.[2] Researchers have identified several hydro-geological and socio-economic factors contributing to its vulnerability. These factors include: its geographical location in South Asia, its flat deltaic topography with very low elevation, its extreme climate variability governed by monsoons resulting in acute water distribution over space and time, its high population density, poverty incidence, and its majority of population being dependent on crop agriculture, which is highly influenced by climate variability and change.[3] These factors adversely affect the lives and livelihoods of the people living in this zone, and slow down the pace of social and economic developments in this region.

Over the last few decades, the coastal region of Bangladesh has faced the severe threat posed by climate change, with its initial impacts already evident. This area has become increasingly vulnerable to frequent natural disasters such as cyclones, floods, and storm surges, along with riverbank erosion. These adversities collectively position Bangladesh as one of the world's most vulnerable nations to climate change in the Global Climate Risk Index 2021.[4] Spanning 710 km in length and covering an area of 47,201 square kilometres,[5] nearly 32 percent of the country's total geographical area, the coastline of Bangladesh is a critical focal point. According to the Bangladesh Bureau of Statistics, in 2022, approximately 35 million people will live in the coastal area,[6] constituting a staggering 29 percent of the nation's population.[7] Government projections indicate that by 2050, one in every seven Bangladeshi citizens will be displaced by climate change, which equates to approximately 13.3 million people.[8] The populace residing along this 710 km low-lying coastal belt bears the brunt of

---

[1] Ministry of Water Resources, Government of the People's Republic of Bangladesh, *Coastal Zone Policy*, 2005, 1.

[2] Md Shariot-Ullah, 'Sea-Level Rise and Sustainable Shore Protection Strategies in the Low-Lying Delta: A Case Study of Bangladesh' (2024), 71 *Regional Studies in Marine Science*, 1, 2.

[3] Sanzida Murshed et al, 'Assessing Sensitivity to Climate-related Disasters in the Context of a Developing Country: Evidence from the Coastal Region of Bangladesh' (2023) 97 *International Journal of Disaster Risk Reduction*, 1, 2.

[4] David Eckstein, Vera Künzel and Laura Schäfer, *Global Climate Risk Index 2021, Who Suffers Most from Extreme Weather Events? Weather-Related Loss Events in 2019 and 2000–2019* (Briefing Paper, 2021), 13.

[5] Mosa Tania Alim Shampa et al., 'A Comprehensive Review on Sustainable Coastal Zone Management in Bangladesh: Present Status and the Way Forward' (2023) 9 *Heliyon*, 1, 1.

[6] Bangladesh Bureau of Statistics, Population & Housing Census 2022 (Preliminary Report, August 2022), vii.

[7] Hafez Ahmad, 'Bangladesh Coastal Zone Management Status and Future Trends' (2019) 22(1) *Journal of Coastal Zone Management*, 1.

[8] IOM UN Migration Bangladesh, *Bangladesh Redoubles Efforts to Include Migration and Human Mobility in Climate Change Discussions* (News-local, 25 October 2022).

these challenges. It is anticipated that this region will be among the hardest hit by climate change, necessitating urgent and tailored interventions at the policy level of the government.[9]

At the same time, the coastal region of Bangladesh presents distinctive development opportunities. It boasts a rich tapestry of ecosystems, such as coral reefs, mangroves, beaches, dunes, and wetlands.[10] This distinctive landscape is intersected by an extensive network of rivers, a dynamic estuarine system, and a vast drainage basin, rendering the coastal ecosystem a veritable treasure trove of natural resources and diverse flora and fauna.[11] The region hosts a plethora of natural resources, including coastal fisheries, mangrove forests, salt, onshore and offshore natural gas, and minerals. These resources not only support local livelihoods but also offer opportunities for commercial exploitation and export, thereby fostering economic growth and prosperity of the region. Moreover, the presence of the Export Processing Zones (EPZs), harbors, airports, land ports, tourism complexes, and opportunities for other industries further accentuates the region's economic potential.[12] By capitalizing on these opportunities, the coastal zone can play a pivotal role in poverty reduction and contribute significantly to the overall development of Bangladesh.

Given the unique characteristics of this coastal zone—its potentials and vulnerabilities—it is imperative for the government to adopt a climate development integrated approach in the coastal zone management. This approach should address the impacts of climate change to region while harnessing the full potential of its coastal resources to propel sustainable development forward, benefiting both present and future generations. In this context, this paper explores the country's coastal zone management framework in section II and evaluates different stages of the policy cycle of the integrated coastal zone management in section III. Sections IV and V of this paper critically evaluate and compare two key policy documents—the *Coastal Zone Policy* and the *Coastal Development Strategy*—crafted by the government of Bangladesh to guide the development and management of the coastal region. These documents serve as the blueprint for harnessing the region's potential while mitigating the challenges posed by climate change. A detailed analysis of these documents reveals a significant gap in their approach to integrating climate change and development considerations at the policy level. The study highlights the need for a more cohesive and synergistic approach that strategically weaves climate adaptation and mitigation measures into the fabric of development strategies, rather than treating them as

[9] Mahbuba Nasreen, Mohammed Moniruzzaman Khan and Khondoker Mokaddem Hossain, 'Introducing Coastal Region of Bangladesh' in Mahbuba Nasreen, Khondoker Mokaddem Hossain and Mohammed Moniruzzaman Khan (eds), *Coastal Disaster Risk Management in Bangladesh: Vulnerability and Resilience* (Routledge, 2023), 1, 4.

[10] Md. Giashuddin Miah et al, 'A Changing Coastal Ecosystem: Cox's Bazar in Southeastern Coastal Region of Bangladesh' (2022) 25 *Environment, Development and Sustainability*, 6141, 6142.

[11] Md. Shamsuddoha and Rezaul Karim Chowdhury, *Climate Change Impact and Disaster Vulnerabilities in the Coastal Areas of Bangladesh* (COAST Trust, 2007) 5.

[12] Md Giashuddin Miah, Md Rafqul Islam, and Joyashree Roy, 'A Changing Coastal Ecosystem: Cox's Bazar in Southeastern Coastal Region of Bangladesh' (2023), 25 *Environment, Development and Sustainability*, 6141, 6142.

parallel and disconnected efforts. This entails re-evaluating the policies to ensure that climate considerations are not mere add-ons but are fully integrated into the broader development narrative.

2 The Evolution of the Coastal Zone Management in Bangladesh

In examining possible mitigation and adaptation responses to climate change in the coastal management of Bangladesh, it is crucial to understand the underlying framework guiding these efforts. The endorsement by Bangladesh of coastal zone management, under the auspices of the UNEP sponsored South Asian Regional Seas Program,[13] is a follow-up of international developments after the United Nations Conference on Environment and Development (UNCED) in 1992. The coastal zone management in Bangladesh is a belated phenomenon in comparison with international developments. The country has mostly followed the diktat of its donors in instituting the program. As a result, initiatives came mostly from the external agents rather than from the evolution of coastal zone management in Bangladesh. Even so, the process has a history of its own, marked by certain landmark events.[14] According to Azad:

Such events and developments made policymakers aware of the coastal problems not only in terms of hazards and disasters, but also about people's vulnerability in terms of their livelihood, isolation of the area, extreme unequal distribution of assets, and non-accessibility to local resources.[15]

The following sections delve into the various approaches taken by policymakers in Bangladesh for coastal management. These analyses aim to provide a thorough understanding of the evolution of coastal zone management in Bangladesh and the challenges and opportunities that have shaped its development.

2.1 Reactive Approach for a Disaster-Prone Area

Development challenges in Bangladesh are formidable across the country, but the coastal zone has historically been neglected in government development policies. This region has often been labelled interchangeably as a disaster-prone area, risk zone, or high-risk zone[16] due to its susceptibility to natural disasters such as cyclones,

[13] Abul Kalam Azad, 'Integrated Coastal Zone Management: A Case for People's Management' (BIISS Papers No 20, Bangladesh Institute of International and Strategic Studies, December 2003) 66, 5.

[14] Ibid 67.

[15] Ibid 65.

[16] Ibid 67.

floods, and storm surges. As a result, the approach to managing this area has primarily been reactive. Azad notes, 'there was a rush to the affected zones immediately after the havoc, with aid and assistance from the donors for rehabilitating the local masses, supplying them with food and clothes etc.'.[17] This quote encapsulates the reactive nature of the response, which focused on immediate relief and rehabilitation following disasters rather than proactive planning and long-term development. This historical neglect and reactive approach underscore the need for a paradigm shift in coastal zone management.

2.2 Construction Approach to Protect the Area

The catastrophic cyclone and tidal surge of 1970 (during erstwhile East Pakistan) claimed nearly 150,000 lives.[18] This disaster profoundly impacted policy planners, and they adopted a construction approach[19] for protecting the coast from such natural hazards. Climate change is still not an issue to address at policy level in the coastal management. As part of the Coastal Embankment Project (CEP), funded mostly by external donors, approximately 4,800 km of embankments were constructed.[20] Since Bangladesh's liberation in 1971, an estimated US$72 million in grant assistance and US$700 million in loans have been invested in various construction initiatives for the coastal zone.[21]

The construction approach was sectoral in nature and largely managed by a single agency, the Bangladesh Water Development Board (BWDB).[22] For a long time, the problem of coastal areas was viewed primarily through the lens of physical protection. Consequently, efforts were focused on building embankments and cyclone shelters. This approach was limited in scope as it failed to address several critical issues, such as livelihood vulnerability, inequitable distribution of assets (such as land), or limited access to resources of the coastal communities.[23]

[17] Ibid 67.

[18] Ibid 67.

[19] DFID, 'Integrated Coastal Zone Management in Bangladesh: A Policy Review, Livelihood-Policy Relationships in South Asia' (Working Paper No 6, The UK Department for International Development) , 4.

[20] Azad, above n 13, 68.

[21] Ibid, 68.

[22] Ziaur Rahman, Integrated Coastal Zone Management Capacity in Bangladesh (Master of Defence Studies Thesis, National University of Bangladesh, 2006) R 1.

[23] Idid, 3.

2.3 Integrated Approach for a Unique Area

Beginning in the mid-1980s, policymakers in Bangladesh began to recognize the broader significance of coastal issues, and the necessity of integrating them into the national development process. This shift was largely driven by directives from international donors financing the country's development projects.[24] The Economic and Social Commission for Asia and Pacific (ESCAP) initiated the first effort to formulate a coastal management policy in Bangladesh, resulting in the 1988 report titled 'Coastal Environmental Management Plan for Bangladesh (CEMPBD)'. This report emphasized the importance of integrating socio-economic and environmental issues[25] marking a pivotal step toward an integrated approach.

Several other initiatives followed, aiming to introduce area-specific strategies for the coastal zone, including: the Off-Shore Islands Development Board (1977–1982), the Bangladesh National Conservation Strategy (1987), the UN/ESCAP-GoB Coastal Environment Management Plan for Bangladesh (1987), the Coastal Area Resources Development Plan (1988), the formation and activities of the Special Parliamentary Committee on Coastal Area Development (1988–1990), and national capacity building on ICZM initiative (1997).[26] These efforts signalled a gradual shift toward a new approach in coastal management, with policy planners beginning to adopt a broader perspective on coastal development.[27] Over the last decade, management objectives for the coastal zone have evolved from a prescriptive, sectoral approach reliant on plans, laws, and administrative measures[28] to a more holistic and unified one that addresses the coastal system as a whole.

In 1999, the World Bank, in collaboration with the Netherlands government and the World Food Programme, initiated efforts to advance to advance the Integrated Coastal Zone Management (ICZM) in Bangladesh. This initiative led to the establishment of the Programme Development Office for ICZM Planning (PDO-ICZMP) in 2000, tasked with preparing a comprehensive framework for ICZM in the country.[29] ICZM aims to structure all aspects of coastal management within the development process, reflecting the needs and interests of all stakeholders and addressing the zone's unique challenges.[30] The next section of the paper evaluates different stages of the policy cycle of coastal zone management in Bangladesh.

---

24 Azad, above n 13, 68.

25 DFID, above n 19, 5.

26 Ministry of Water Resources, above n 1, 2.

27 Azad, above n 13, 68.

28 DFID, above n 19, 7.

29 Rahman, above n 22, 14.

30 Susana Lincoln et al, 'Interaction of Climate Change and Marine Pollution in Southern India: Implications for Coastal Zone Management Practices and Policies' (2023) 902 Science of The Total Environment, 1, 12.

3 Conceptualizing the Policy Cycle of ICZM in Bangladesh

The process by which ICZM programs evolve is known as the ICZM policy cycle.[31] This cycle consists of five stages: (i) issue identification and assessment, (ii) program preparation, (iii) formal adoption and funding, (iv) implementation, and (v) evaluation. The European Commission similarly identifies these stages as information collection, planning, decision making, management, and monitoring of implementation'.[32]

The ICZM process in Bangladesh began with the approval of a government policy note titled 'Integrated Coastal Zone Management: Concept and Issues' in September 1999.[33] This policy note mentions the first four stages[34] of the ICZM policy cycle, omitting the evaluation stage. Below is a brief overview of these initial four stages:

(i) **Issue Identification:** Achieving consensus on the issues for the ICZM program in Bangladesh was challenging. The finalized issues included poverty reduction, the development of sustainable livelihoods, and the integration of the coastal zone into national processes.[35] The goal of ICZM was defined as 'to create conditions, in which the reduction of poverty, the development of sustainable livelihoods, and the integration of the coastal zone into national processes can take place.'[36] This indicates that ICZM in Bangladesh follows a people-centered approach,[37] and not the ecosystem approach. The ecosystem approach considers the entire ecosystems, including humans,[38] whereas ICZM in Bangladesh primarily focuses on humans. That is why its goal is to create the context within which the people and communities of the coastal zone can sustain and improve their livelihoods. Notably, addressing climate change, despite its significant impact on the coastal zone, is not explicitly included as a goal.

---

[31] Stephen Olsen, James Tobey and Meg Kerr, 'A Common Framework for Learning from ICM Experience' (1997) 37(2) *Ocean & Coastal Management* 155,160.

[32] European Commission, 'Towards a European Integrated Coastal Zone Management (ICZM) Strategy: General Principles and Policy Options' (1999) 16.

[33] Ministry of Water Resources, Government of the People's Republic of Bangladesh, 'Investment and Financing Strategy for Coastal Zone Development in Bangladesh'(Working Paper No WP037, Programme Development Office, Integrated Coastal Zone Management Plan Project, April 2005) 4.

[34] Ministry of Water Resources, Government of the People's Republic of Bangladesh, 'Integrated Coastal Zone Management: Concept and Issues' (Policy Note of Government of Bangladesh, 22 September 1999) 19.

[35] Ministry of Water Resources, above n 1, 3.

[36] Ibid.

[37] Water Resources Planning Organization, Government of the People's Republic of Bangladesh, 'Previous Initiatives and Base Conceptual Documents' (Working Paper No WP001, Program Development Office-Integrated Coastal Zone Management, May 2002)1.

[38] West Coast Ecosystem-based Managemnet Network, Community-Based Management of Coastal Ecosystems:Highlights and Lessons of Success from the West Coast Ecosystem-Based Management Network (May 2010) <http://www.westcoastebm.org/WestCoastEBMNetwork_EBMGuide_June 2010.pdf> 2.

(ii) **Program Preparation:** This stage involved a comprehensive process of multi-level consultation over two years, engaging sectoral line ministries and departments, local government agencies, and a diverse range of stakeholders.[39] The *Coastal Zone Policy* (the *Policy)* was finalized at a cabinet meeting on January 17, 2005. This document provides a framework for integrated management and development of coastal resources[40] establishing eight development objectives based on the issues identified in the first stage of the policy cycle. Section IV of this paper evaluates the extent to which the *Policy* reflects a climate development integrated approach, analysing how the *Policy* can be enhanced to better address the challenges posed by climate change.

(iii) **Formal Adoption and Funding:** To implement the *Coastal Zone Policy*, a *Coastal Development Strategy* (the *Strategy*) was adopted by the government in 2006.[41] This strategy outlines approaches for effectively translating policies into concrete actions. The eight development objectives of the *Policy* were expanded into nine strategic priorities in the *Strategy*. Section V of this paper assesses the extent to which this *Strategy* reflects the climate development integrated approach.

The *Coastal Development Strategy* identifies four sources of financing investments for coastal development: (a) the public sector investments; (b) assistance from multilateral institutions and donors; (c) direct foreign investment; and (d) investments by the private sector entrepreneurs.[42] The government is already involved in regular investments in the coastal zone. Donor agencies are providing financial and technical assistance to a series of coastal development projects.[43] The NGOs also make a significant contribution to the financing needs for small-scale investment.

(iv) **Implementation:** The *Coastal Development Strategy* serves as the primary mechanism for implementing the *Coastal Zone Policy*. Each of the nine strategic priorities outlined in the *Strategy* is translated into 2–5 investment projects, which are collectively organized into a Priority Investment Programme (PIP).[44] Section V of this paper provides a detailed description of these investment projects and evaluates to what extent they reflect the climate development integrated approach.

---

[39] Ministry of Water Resources, Above n 1, 4.

[40] Ibid, 3.

[41] Ministry of Water Resources, above n 1.

[42] Ibid 34.

[43] Ibid.

[44] Ibid, ii.

4 Climate Development Integrated Approach and the Coastal Zone Policy

The *Coastal Zone Policy*, formulated by the government of Bangladesh, provides comprehensive guidance for the management and development of the coastal zone. Its primary aim is to enable coastal people to pursue their lives and livelihoods in a secure and conducive environment.[45] This *Policy* is unique in its harmonized approach, transcending sectoral perspectives to foster coordination and cooperation among various ministries, departments, and agencies. It establishes a coordinated mechanism to ensure that all stakeholders work together effectively in the coastal zone.

The *Policy* sets forth the goal of ICZM and outlines eight development objectives, which are (i) economic growth; (ii) basic needs and opportunities for livelihoods; (iii) reduction of vulnerabilities; (iv) sustainable management of natural resources; (v) equitable distribution; (vi) empowerment of communities; (vii) women's development and gender equity; and (viii) conservation and enhancement of critical ecosystems.[46] Addressing climate change is neither a goal nor one of these eight development objectives. However, the intrinsic link between climate change and development in the coastal zone is undeniable. The impact of climate change can significantly hinder developmental efforts in crucial sectors, such as poverty reduction, agriculture, and health.[47] In fact, any development effort will be seriously hampered by the risks of climate change.[48] Therefore, the goals and development objectives of ICZM could be compromised if climate change is not adequately addressed and integrated into Bangladesh's coastal development policy.

While climate change is not explicitly stated as a goal or one of the objectives of ICZM in Bangladesh, it is implicitly addressed within two of the eight development objectives of the *Policy*: (a) the reduction of vulnerabilities and (b) the conservation and enhancement of critical ecosystems. Under the first one, the government acknowledges that the majority of households of the coastal zone are vulnerable to climate change,[49] and the second one includes the government's commitment to addressing climate change while conserving and enhancing critical ecosystems of the coastal zone.[50]

[45] Ministry of Water Resources, above n 1, 3.

[46] Ibid.

[47] Paramita Roy et al, 'Effects of Climate Change and Sea-level Rise on Coastal Habitat: Vulnerability Assessment, Adaptation Strategies and Policy Recommendations' (2023) 330 Journal of Environmental Management, 1, 2.

[48] Lin Sun et al, 'Coupled Impacts of Climate and Land Use Changes on Regional Ecosystem Services' (2023) 326 Journal of Environmental Management, 1, 2.

[49] Ministry of Water Resources, above n 1, sec 4.3.

[50] Ibid, sec 4.8.3.

Table 1 Response Strategies by the IPCC CZMS

	Retreat = effort to abandon vulnerable areas	Accommodate = effort to continue living in vulnerable areas by adjusting living and working habits	Protect = effort to continue use of vulnerable areas
Hard	Relocating threatened buildings	Building on pilings, adapting drainage, emergency flood shelters	Dikes, seawalls, groins, breakwaters, saltwater intrusion barriers
Soft	Land use restriction, set-back zones	New building codes, growing flood or salt-tolerant crops, early warning and evacuation systems, risk-based hazard insurance	Sand nourishments, dune building, wetland restoration or creation

Source Inspired by European Commission[55] but modified by the author

4.1 The Coastal Zone Policy and Adaptation Options to Climate Change

The United Nations Framework Convention on Climate Change (UNFCCC)[51] identifies two primary responses to climate change: (i) mitigation, which involves reducing greenhouse gas emissions and enhancing sinks and (ii) adaptation, which focuses on adjusting to the impacts of climate change.[52] The *Coastal Zone Policy* exclusively addresses adaptive response options, without exploring mitigation strategies to climate change. Sections 4.3 and 4.8.3 of this *Policy* outline adaptive measures for reducing vulnerabilities and conserving critical ecosystems in the face of climate change impacts in the coastal zone.[53] At the international level, the Coastal Zone Management Subgroup of the Intergovernmental Panel on Climate Change (IPCC CZMS) identified three possible adaptation strategies in response to rising sea levels: (i) planned retreat, (ii) accommodate, and (iii) protect[54] (see Table 1).

Sections 4.3.f and 4.8.3.c of the *Coastal Zone Policy* focus on the protective strategy, specifically emphasizing on hard or static structures. These sections highlight the importance of maintaining sea-dykes as a primary defence against storm

---

[51] *United Nations Framework Convention on Climate Change*, UN Doc 1771 UNTS 107 (21 March 1994, adopted 4 June 1992).

[52] Richard J T Klein et al., 'Inter-relationships between Adaptation and Mitigation' in Martin L Parry et al. (eds), *Climate Change 2007: Impacts, Adaptation and Vulnerability. Contribution of Working Group II to the Fourth Assessment Report of the Intergovernmental Panel on Climate Change* (Cambridge Univesity Press, 2007) 745, 748.

[53] Job Dronkers et al., *Strategies for Adaptation to Sea Level Rise*, Report of the Coastal Zone Management Subgroup (1990) ii.

[54] Ibid, 12.

[55] European Commission, The Economics of Climate Change Adaptation in EU Coastal Areas, Summary Report (2009) 13.

surges[56] and predicted sea level rise in the coastal area.[57] However, the *Policy* does not address other hard structure options such as seawalls, groins, breakwaters, saltwater intrusion barriers, and so on. The *Policy* is also silent about the soft or dynamic structures, like sand nourishment, dune building, wetland restoration, or creation (Table 1). Effective coastal management necessitates a combination of both hard and soft protection measures. No single solution can universally protect the coast from sea level rise and other climate change impacts.[58] Integrating diverse adaptive strategies will better equip the coastal zone to handle the varied challenges posed by climate change.

Several sections of the Policy highlight the second adaptive option, accommodation, as outlined in Table 1. Few notable examples include: safety measures by combining cyclone shelters, multi-purpose embankments, road systems, and a disaster warning system (Sect. 4.3.e); effective measures to enhance coping capacity of the poor during the period of disaster (Sect. 4.3.c); initiation of an insurance scheme for improving the poor's social security (Sect. 4.3.c); safety of livestock during the disaster and post-disaster period (Sect. 4.3.h); integration of a Comprehensive Disaster Management (CDM) Plan on aspects concerning the coastal zone (Sect. 4.3.b); small water reservoirs to capture tidal water in order to enhance minor irrigation in coastal areas (Sect. 4.4.b); rainwater harvesting and conservation (Sect. 4.4.c); development of salt-tolerant crop varieties (Sect. 4.4.5.d), etc. However, the Policy does not address the first adaptive option (planned retreat) as outlined in Table 1. It states, '[i]implementation of adaptive measures identified in relation to climate change for coastal zone and resources shall be gradually undertaken'.[59] This omission highlights a gap in the *Policy*'s approach to comprehensive climate adaptation, particularly concerning the strategic relocation from highly vulnerable areas.

4.2 The Coastal Zone Policy and Mitigation Options to Climate Change

The *Policy* is also silent on the mitigation aspect of climate change. Preventing the degradation of coastal ecosystems such as mangroves, seagrasses, and intertidal marshes could significantly contribute to global emission reduction. According to the United Nations Environment Programme (UNEP) blue carbon report,[60]halting the degradation of coastal ecosystems would achieve emission reductions equivalent to 1–2 times those of the entire global transport sector or at least 25% of the total

[56] Ministry of Water Resources, above n 1, sec 4.3.f.

[57] Ibid, sec 4.8.3.c.

[58] Dronkers et al, above n 53, 1.

[59] Ministry of Water Resources, above n 1, sec 4.8.3.c.

[60] Christain Nellemann et al. (eds), *Blue Carbon: The Role of Healthy Oceans in Binding Carbon* (2009) 19.

global carbon emission reductions needed. Additionally, this would provide benefits for biodiversity, food security, and livelihoods for coastal communities.

One of the eight development objectives of the *Policy* is to conserve and enhance critical ecosystems in the coastal zone. Bangladesh can contribute to climate change mitigation by conserving and enhancing its mangroves, seagrasses, and intertidal marshes in the coastal area. However, Sect. 4.4.4.b of the *Policy* encourages seagrass exploitation, which contradicts this concept. Despite this, several other sections in the *Policy* promote the conservation of coastal ecosystems. Section 4.8 advocates for necessary measures to conserve and develop mangrove and seagrass beds, along with other critical ecosystems identified by the Bangladesh National Conservation Strategy. Other sections relevant for this issue are as follows: conservation and development of the natural environment of Sundarban (Sect. 4.8.b); afforestation in the coastal areas, including newly accreted lands (Sects. 4.3.f and 4.4.7); conservation of forests (Sect. 4.4.7); social forestry (Sect. 4.4.7), etc.

While mitigation is not the primary objective of these sections of the *Policy*, they contribute to conserving and enhancing the blue carbon[61] sinks in the coastal area. Additionally, the *Policy* says that the government will honour all commitments as signatory to relevant international protocols and guidelines,[62] and harmonize the provisions of different national laws and enact new laws (if required) to protect and preserve the coastal ecosystems.[63] That means Bangladesh can explore the blue carbon response options under the UNFCCC, the national Land Use, Land Use Change, and Forestry (LULUCF), the Clean Development Mechanism (CDM), reducing emissions from deforestation and degradation (REDD), and the nationally appropriate mitigation actions (NAMA). Through these mechanisms, Bangladesh can adopt blue carbon response options effectively.

5 Climate Development Integrated Approach and the Coastal Development Strategy

The *Coastal Development Strategy* (the *Strategy*) is designed to implement the *Coastal Zone Policy* (the *Policy*), serving as a crucial link between the policy and concrete interventions.[64] The *Strategy* does not provide a single comprehensive framework for all development actions in the coastal zone.[65] Instead, as stated in the document, '[i]t describes about building a process to implement policies, not preparing a classic master plan.'[66] The *Strategy* sets priorities and targets based

[61] Blue carbon is a descriptive term that captures carbon stored and potentially lost from coastal and marine ecosystems.

[62] Ministry of Water Resources, above n 1, sec 4.8.1.f.

[63] Ibid, sec 4.8.1.g.

[64] Ministry of Water Resources, above n 1, i.

[65] Ibid.

[66] Ibid, 4.

on the *Policy* objectives. By following a selective approach, the *Strategy* aims to complement the ongoing but often fragmented activities of various government agencies, NGOs, and development partners.[67] The main objectives of the *Strategy* are as follows:

To select strategic priorities and actions in the implementation of the *Coastal Zone Policy* with emphasis on the creation of an institutional environment that will enable the government of Bangladesh to embark on a continuous and structured process of prioritization, development, and implementation of concerted interventions for the development of the coastal zone.[68]

The *Strategy* aims to transcend the traditional one-shot approach, fostering a continuous planning process for the government and development partners. By doing so, it addresses the dynamic and complex nature of coastal zone management, ensuring that development efforts are adaptive, coordinated, and sustainable.

The eight development objectives, described in the *Policy* in section IV of this paper, have been translated into nine strategic priorities in this document. These strategies are the following: (i) ensuring fresh and safe water availability; (ii) safety from man-made and natural hazards; (iii) optimizing use of coastal lands; (iv) promoting economic growth emphasizing non-farm rural employment; (v) sustainable management of natural resources, exploiting untapped and less explored opportunities; (vi) improving the livelihood conditions of people, especially women; (vii) environmental conservation; (viii) empowerment through knowledge management; and (ix) creating an enabling institutional environment.[69] The linkage between the Coastal Zone Policy objectives and the Coastal Development Strategy strategic priorities is shown in Table 2.

As mentioned in section IV, two of the eight development objectives of the Policy address climate change: (a) the reduction of the vulnerabilities and (b) the conservation and enhancement of the critical ecosystems. Table 2 indicates that the first development objective is reflected in eight strategic priorities, and the second one is reflected in six strategic priorities of the Strategy. This means that five strategic priorities encompass both development objectives of the Policy. These are as follows: (a) safety from man-made and natural hazards; (b) optimizing use of coastal lands; (c) environmental conservation; (d) empowerment through knowledge management; and (e) creating an enabling institutional environment. Three strategic priorities exclusively address the reduction of the vulnerabilities, and one solely focuses on the conservation and enhancement of the critical ecosystems (Table 2).

Sections V.A to V.I of this paper now evaluate the extent to which the nine strategic priorities of the *Strategy* consider climate change. The sections are organized as follows: first, the five strategies that address both development objectives; then, the three strategies that reflect the reduction of vulnerabilities objective; and lastly, the one strategy that deals exclusively with the conservation and enhancement of critical ecosystems objective of the *Policy.*

---

[67] Ibid.

[68] Ibid.

[69] Ministry of Water Resources, above n 1, 4.

Table 2 Linkage between development objectives and strategic priorities

The *Coastal Development Strategy* Strategic priorities	CZPo Objectives							
	Economic growth	Basic needs opportunities for Livelihoods	Reduction of vulnerabilities	Sustainable management of natural resources	Equitable distribution	Empowerment of communities	Women's development and gender equity	Conservation & Preservation of critical ecosystem
Ensuring fresh and safe water availability	■	■	■	■			■	
Safety from man-made and natural hazards	■	■	■					■
Optimizing use of coastal lands	■	■	■	■	■	■		■
Promoting economic growth emphasizing non-farm rural employment	■	■	■	■	■		■	
Sustainable management of natural resources		■		■	■			■
Improving livelihood conditions of people; especially women	■	■	■				■	
Environmental conservation			■	■				■
Empowerment through knowledge management	■	■	■	■	■	■	■	■
Creating an enabling institutional environment	■	■	■	■	■	■	■	■

Source Ministry of water resources[70]

[70] Ibid, 6.

5.1 Safety from Man-Made and Natural Hazards

This strategic priority reflects both the reduction of vulnerabilities and the conservation and enhancement of critical ecosystem objectives outlined in the *Policy*. Two investment projects have been suggested under this strategy. These are the following: (i) strengthening and rehabilitation of sea-dykes; and (ii) reduction of severe vulnerability in the coastal zone through multi-purpose cyclone shelters including coping mechanisms.[71] The first project focuses on the third adaptive measure of climate change—protection of the coast (Table 1). Under this project, sea-dykes are considered as the first line of defense against storm surges and possible sea level rise due to climate change. Given that the existing sea-dykes do not cover the entire coastline, the project includes construction of new sea-dykes where necessary, implementing a regular maintenance program, and conducting risk analysis of sea-dykes against the projected climate change scenario, etc.[72] Like the *Policy*, this strategy does not mention soft structure options and other hard structure options besides sea-dykes.

The next project for this Strategy primarily involves the second adaptive measure—accommodation (Table 1). It encompasses the construction of cyclone shelters, connecting roads, design and development of a cyclone monitoring system, the development of a database and an Interactive Information System (IIS), and public awareness and communication.[73]

5.2 Optimizing Use of Coastal Lands

This strategic priority also addresses both the reduction of vulnerabilities and the conservation and enhancement of critical ecosystem objectives of the *Policy*. Coastal land use is highly diverse, encompassing agriculture, forests, shrimp farms, natural fisheries, salt production, industrial and infra-structural developments, settlements, and tourism.[74] The Land Use, Land Use Change, and Forestry (LULUCF) has immense impacts on the global carbon cycle.[75] According to the IPCC's special report,[76] the LULUCF activities can either add or remove carbon dioxide (CO2) from the atmosphere, thereby influencing climate change. The United Nations Climate Change Secretariat defines LULUCF as '[a] greenhouse gas inventory

[71] Ibid, 16.

[72] Ibid.

[73] Ibid, 17.

[74] Ibid.

[75] Sun et al., above n 48.

[76] Robert T Watson et al (eds), Land Use, Land-Use Change, and Forestry: A Special Report of the Intergovernmental Panel on Climate Change (Cambridge University Press, 2000) 10.

sector that covers emissions and removals of greenhouse gases resulting from direct human-induced land use, land use change, and forestry activities.'[77]

Land use change in the coastal zone, such as converting mangrove forests into agricultural land or shrimp farms, contributes to CO2 atmospheric concentration, and thus to climate change. Bangladesh can leverage its coastal carbon sinks, particularly mangroves, under the LULUCF framework. However, the *Coastal Development Strategy* has overlooked this issue while addressing the strategic priority of optimizing coastal land use. Nonetheless, three out of four proposed investment projects under this priority may contribute to both climate change mitigation and adaptation: (i) development and settlement of accreted land; (ii) integrated management of coastal water infrastructures; (iii) coastal land zoning; and (iv) development of coastal agriculture in Bangladesh.

The first program states, '[n]ewly accreted land in the form of mud shall be utilized for planting mangrove plants, the existing mangrove forests shall be managed through a participatory way, and the degraded/depleted forests land shall be planted...'[78] The third program recognizes that the coastal ecosystems are degrading because of diversified uses of coastal land, and recommends coastal zoning.[79] Both of these projects can enhance coastal carbon sinks, thereby contributing to climate change mitigation. The fourth program promotes several adaptive measures like expansion of floating agriculture, the promotion and dissemination of a soil-less cultivation system, management practices for producing crops in saline soil, etc.[80]

5.3 *Environmental Conservation*

The coastal ecosystems, particularly mangroves, tidal salt marshes, and sea meadows, function as significant coastal carbon sinks, also known as the blue carbon sinks. These ecosystems play a crucial role in climate change mitigation under the UNFCCC framework.[81] The *Coastal Development Strategy* of Bangladesh places special emphasis on conserving these coastal ecosystems within this strategic priority without referring them as mitigation options to climate change. It recommends harmonizing the provisions of different existing laws and enacting new laws, where required, to protect and preserve the coastal ecosystems.[82]

This strategic priority acknowledges the rapid decline of mangroves in the coastal area due to insufficient enforcement of conservation laws. To address this, it calls for

---

[77] United Nations Framework Convention on Climate Change, Glossary of Climate Change Acronyms <http://unfccc.int/essential_background/glossary/items/3666.php#L>

[78] Ministry of Water Resources, above n 1, 18.

[79] Ibid.

[80] Ibid 19.

[81] International Partnership for Blue Carbon, Coastal Blue Carbon Ecosystems in International Frameworks and Conventions (Overview Report, October 2021).

[82] Ministry of Water Resources, above n 1, 25.

capacity building and strengthening the coast guard's role in enforcing these laws. Historically, the coast guard's services have not been actively utilized in managing the coastal environment. This strategic priority recommends a project entitled 'Strengthening of Coast Guard for Improvement of Coastal Safety and Security, Coordination with Other Law Enforcing Agencies'.[83] This project aims to identify critical ecosystems for targeted enforcement of conservation laws by the Coast Guard, addressing issues as sustainable harvesting of marine resources and forestry.[84] These initiatives promote the conservation of coastal ecosystems.

While the primary objective of the *Coastal Development Strategy* is not explicitly climate change mitigation, it inherently supports coastal carbon sinks, contributing to global mitigation efforts. Additionally, the strategy mentions that adaptive measures for the coastal zone, especially those outlined in the National Adaptation Plan of Action (NAPA)[85] will be gradually implemented. Similar to the 'Safety from Man-made and Natural Hazards' strategy, this one also emphasizes continuous maintenance of sea-dykes along the coastline as a first line of defense against predicted sea level rise.[86] However, there is scope for exploring other adaptive measures, as discussed in section IV.B of this paper, to further protect the coast.

5.4 Empowerment Through Knowledge Management

Knowledge management is not merely a technological solution but a conceptual framework.[87] It is the process of achieving organizational goals through a strategy-driven approach that motivates and facilitates knowledge workers to interpret data and information effectively, thereby giving it meaningful context.[88] This process typically involves four steps: gathering, organizing, refining, and disseminating. The gathering involves bringing data and information into the system, organizing involves associating items to subjects for easier access, refining involves adding value by identifying relationships and synthesizing information, and disseminating involves sharing knowledge with those who can use it.[89]

---

[83] Ibid, 25.

[84] Ibid.

[85] Ibid.

[86] Ibid, 25.

[87] Simona Arduini, Martina Manzo and Tommaso Beck, 'Corporate Reputation and Culture: The Link between Knowledge Management and Sustainability' (2024) 28 (4) Journal of Knowledge Management, 1021.

[88] Dev Raj Adhikari and Prakash Shrestha, 'Knowledge Management Initiatives for Achieving Sustainable Development Goal 4.7: Higher Education Institutions' Stakeholder Perspectives' (2023) 27(4) Journal of Knowledge Management, 1109.

[89] 'Climate Change Knowledge Management Strategy' in Knowledge Management & Capacity Development (Ministry of Environment and Mineral Resources, Governement of Kenya, 2012) .

Knowledge management and sharing are central to the climate development integrated approach.[90] Reliable and accessible climate and development knowledge are especially important for decision-makers and policy influencers.[91] In ICZM, knowledge production should be a collaborative effort among national-level policy makers, scientists, and coastal communities. Many coastal communities of Bangladesh have generated a significant amount of information and experience in climate change adaptation. They have adopted community-based indigenous coping techniques, such as raising the plinths of their homes, making structural adjustments, developing specific forms of housing for long-term adaptation, and developing floating gardens for growing vegetables.[92] The resilience of a few coastal communities has been enhanced through indigenous knowledge of how to survive a cyclone (through actions taken before, during, and after the cyclone).[93] These knowledge products need to be organized, refined, and disseminated among the coastal population at large.

Moreover, climate change science is constantly evolving, with new information and coping strategies continuously emerging at national, regional, and global levels.[94] Unfortunately, this updated knowledge often does not reach the coastal communities in Bangladesh. Additionally, there is a lack of appropriate institutional architecture for knowledge management in the coastal zone, and there is no national strategy on climate change knowledge management. In this context, it is commendable that the *Strategy* includes a strategic priority for empowering coastal communities through knowledge management. However, the projects suggested under this strategy are very general and do not specifically address climate change knowledge management.[95] Therefore, while the inclusion of this strategic priority is a positive step, there is a need for more focused and detailed projects that emphasize climate change knowledge management to fully empower coastal communities.

5.5 *Creating an Enabling Institutional Environment*

Institutionalization of ICZM requires the development of mechanisms for coordination and interaction between and among the various parties involved at national, regional, and local levels.[96] This strategy recommends eight projects, namely: (i)

---

[90] Climate & Development Knowledge Network, 'Knowledge Management and Stakeholder Engagement in Climate Change Adaptation' (Paper presented in UNFCCC NWP Workshop, Daees Salam, Tanzania, 21-23 March 2013) 6.

[91] Ibid.

[92] Asian Development Bank, 'People's Republic of Bangladesh: Climate Change Capacity Building and Knowledge Management' (Technical Assisstance Report, Project No 45065, Capacity Development Technical Assisstance, August 2011) 1.

[93] Ibid 2.

[94] Ibid.

[95] See Ministry of Water Resources, above n 1, 26-27.

[96] Ibid, 28.

operationalization of a Program Co-ordination Unit (PCU) at national level; (ii) operationalization of an institutional and coordination mechanism; (iii) capacity building and training; (iv) supporting initiatives by local government institutions, NGOs, and media in coastal management; (v) empowerment of women members /commissioners of local government institutions of the coastal zone; (vi) establishment of Information Technology (IT) supported model unions in sea facing *upazilas*; (vii) promotion of coastal community services through the establishment of community radio; and (viii) capacity building of the local government institutes for integrated coastal resource management.[97] If addressing climate change is set as one of the goals of ICZM in Bangladesh, this institutional environment can contribute a lot for better adoption of the climate development integrated approach in ICZM.

5.6 Ensuring Fresh and Safe Water Availability

This strategic priority aligns solely with the reduction of vulnerabilities objective outlined in the *Coastal Zone Policy*. One significant challenge contributing to the diminished inflow of fresh water in the coastal zone is the intrusion of saline water due to rising sea levels which is a direct implication of climate change in this zone. Similar to the *Coastal Zone Policy*, the *Coastal Development Strategy* advocates for the adoption of the second adaptive measure—accommodation—to address this issue (Table 1). It asks for the development and promotion of small-scale alternatives to fresh water supply systems, such as rainwater harvesting and pond sand filter techniques.[98]

The *Strategy* suggests four investment projects in this regard. These are as follows: (i) strengthening sanitation and safe water supply programs in arsenic and salinity affected areas; (ii) ground water management in the coastal zone of Bangladesh; (iii) integrated water resource management of the greater Noakhali; and (iv) integrated drainage improvement of the tidal influenced southwest region of Bangladesh.[99] One of the goals of the first project is to provide salinity-free water to the coastal people.[100] The second project also aims to control saline water intrusion, among other activities.[101]

---

[97] Ibid, 28-30.

[98] Ibid, 14.

[99] Ibid, 14-15.

[100] Ibid, 14.

[101] Ibid, 15.

5.7 *Promoting Economic Growth Emphasizing Non-Farm Rural Employment*

This strategic priority also aligns with the reduction of vulnerabilities objective. The rural non-farm sector encompasses a wide array of activities, including rural manufacturing, transportation, trade, and various services, along with employment opportunities in tourism.[102] This strategic priority suggests two projects: (i) enhancement of coastal livelihoods through enterprise development; and (ii) tourism development in the coastal zone for improvement of livelihoods and poverty reduction.[103]

The first program proposes initiatives such as floating agriculture and windmills. Floating agriculture, a traditional practice in the southwest region of the coastal zone for over two centuries, involves cultivating a variety of vegetables and spices. More than 20 different kinds of vegetables and five different types of spices are cultivated following floating agriculture.[104] This practice serves as an effective adaptive measure in the coastal region. Additionally, windmills offer potential contributions to climate change mitigation, given their low greenhouse gas emissions compared to conventional energy systems.[105]

5.8 *Improving Livelihood Conditions of People*

This strategic priority primarily addresses the reduction of vulnerabilities objective and does not directly relate to the conservation and enhancement of critical ecosystems outlined in the *Policy*. It proposes five projects: (i) enhancement of livelihoods in exposed coast areas; (ii) integrated development of remotely located islands; (iii) capacity building of female fish processors in Cox's Bazar district; (iv) comprehensive rehabilitation program for erosion victims of the coastal zone of Bangladesh; and (v) improvement of livestock services in the coastal zone.[106] While these projects do not explicitly mention their implications for climate change, recent literature emphasizes the interconnectedness between climate change and livelihoods.

Livelihoods have become a focal point in climate change adaptation strategies, as they are vulnerable to shifts in resource flows induced by climate change.[107] For

---

[102] Ibid.

[103] Ibid 20.

[104] Ibid 19.

[105] DavideAstiaso Garcia et al, 'Climate Change Mitigation by means of Sustainable Development of Energy, Water and Environment Systems' (2023) 17 Energy Conversion and Management: X, 1.

[106] See Ministry of Water Resources, above n 1, 23-24.

[107] The Task Force on Climate Change, 'Vulnerable Communities and Adaptation, Livelihoods and Climate Change: Combining Disaster Risk Reduction, Natural Resource Management and Climate Change Adaptation in a New Approach to the Reduction of Vulnerability and Poverty' (International Institute for Sustainable Development, International Union for Conservation of Nature and Natural Resources, and Stockholm Environment Institute, 2003) 8.

instance, sea level rise is expected to displace millions of people in low-lying coastal areas like southern Bangladesh,[108] impacting their ability to sustain themselves. Furthermore, climate-induced changes may diminish natural resources essential to coastal communities' livelihoods, such as coastal fisheries and mangroves.[109]

The emergence of the livelihood approach has spurred the integration of adaptation into broader development processes, known as climate-resilient development. The primary goals of climate-resilient development in coastal regions are to mitigate vulnerability to climate-induced changes and to support and improve the livelihoods of vulnerable coastal populations. While this strategic priority of the *Coastal Development Strategy* holds potential for contributing to climate change adaptation, its projects must be designed and implemented with climate resilience considerations in mind.

5.9 Sustainable Management of Natural Resources

This strategic priority aligns with the conservation and enhancement of the critical ecosystem objectives of the *Policy*. The *Strategy* focuses on the access of people to the sustainable use of coastal resources. However, it also takes into account that such access should not in any way adversely affect the coastal ecosystem. One of the projects recommended under this strategy is the introduction and expansion of solar, tidal, and wind energy in the remote coastal areas of the country.[110] These renewable energy initiatives not only contribute to mitigation efforts but also support low-emission development practices.

The analysis of the strategic priorities within the *Strategy* highlights its recognition and elaboration of concerns regarding climate change and its developmental impacts. While some strategic priorities effectively address the interplay between climate change and development and propose relevant responses in their investment projects, others may overlook their potential contribution to mitigation options, even if it emerges as a co-benefit. Additionally, there is room for improvement in exploring more adaptive options across several projects and promoting synergy between climate change adaptation and mitigation efforts.[111] Enhancing the complementarity between mitigation and adaptation within these projects could foster sustainable development outcomes. For instance, mitigation options could simultaneously reduce the vulnerability of coastal ecosystems and improve the socio-economic resilience of coastal communities. Similarly, integrating adaptation practices into project designs

[108] PallaviDeka, 'Changing Climate and New Migration Crisis in Bangladesh' in Amit Ranjan, Rajesh Kharat and PallaviDeka (eds) Environment, Climate Change and Migration in South Asia (Routledge India, 2023), 49.

[109] Ibid 14.

[110] Ministry of Water Resources, above n 1, 21.

[111] Gert Jan Nabuurs et al, 'Forestry' in Bert Metz et al (eds), Climate Change 2007: Mitigation of Climate Change. Contribution of Working Group III to the Fourth Assessment Report of the Intergovernmental Panel on Climate Change (Cambridge University Press, 2007) 541, 566.

would optimize investment utilization and enhance institutional capacities to address climate change risks effectively.[112]

6 Conclusion

The *Coastal Zone Policy* and the *Coastal Development Strategy* stand as foundational documents for the ICZM in Bangladesh, providing comprehensive guidelines for the development and conservation of coastal areas. While both documents acknowledge the challenges posed by climate change, their integration of climate considerations is still evolving, as indicated by their scores in relevant assessments. Recognizing the significance of addressing climate change in coastal management plans, there is a growing awareness of the need for greater integration of climate and development objectives within these documents.

According to the Sixth Assessment Report of the IPCC, the degree to which climate change is factored into coastal management plans serves as a crucial indicator of a nation's commitment to sustainability and integration.[113] While the *Policy* and the *Strategy* have incorporated some adaptive measures, there remains considerable scope for enhancing their integration of climate change mitigation and adaptation efforts. This includes not only addressing the direct impacts of climate change but also leveraging opportunities to conserve coastal ecosystems as carbon sinks, thereby contributing to global climate mitigation efforts.

An integrated approach to climate and development within coastal management frameworks is imperative for ensuring the long-term sustainability and resilience of coastal communities. By aligning policy responses with both mitigation and adaptation strategies, these documents can better address the multifaceted challenges posed by climate change in coastal areas. Furthermore, integrating climate considerations into the broader objectives of ICZM in Bangladesh will help ensure internal consistency across national policies and investment projects, fostering more effective and coordinated responses to climate-related risks.

Moving forward, it is essential to strengthen the legal and policy frameworks supporting ICZM in Bangladesh, ensuring that they reflect a robust climate development integrated approach. This will require ongoing efforts to update and refine existing policies, incorporating emerging knowledge and best practices in climate adaptation and mitigation. Ultimately, a well-defined legal framework, coupled with comprehensive policy guidelines, will be instrumental in guiding the sustainable management of Bangladesh's coastal areas and mitigating the adverse impacts of climate change on coastal communities.

---

[112] Ibid.

[113] Sarah R Cooly and David S Schoeman, 'Oceans and Coastal Ecosystems and Their Services' in Hans-Otto Portner et al, (eds) Climate Change 20222: Impacts, Adaptation and Vulnerability. Working Group II Contribution to the Sixth Assessment Report of the Intergovernmental Panel on Climate Change (Cambridge University Press, 2022), 379.

A Politico-Media Nexus in the Globalizing World: A Comparative Study on Compromised Agenda-Driven Media

Showkat Ahmad Wani and Dhriti Bole

Abstract The media landscape is experiencing seismic shifts in the wake of economic crises, with certain media entities, especially those embracing digital transformation and benefiting the deep-pocketed investors, managing to survive and thrive. Conversely, independent journalism, particularly beyond the Western world, faces acute financial challenges. In today's globalized world, the media significantly impacts how we receive and process information. Corporate media has an agenda that determines what information is shared with the public because there is a strong affinity between the media and political organizations. The book chapter offers an analysis of how governments strategically employ funding mechanisms to exert control over the media. It scrutinizes the trends whereby governments allocate financial resources to media outlets that align with their own interests and objectives, be they political, ideological, or commercial, while sidelining independent journalism. It has been reported through different studies that the political and media nexus is damaging the free press in a systematic way. The book chapter primarily focused on an in-depth analysis of provisions pertaining to press freedom in diverse jurisdictions. The book chapter further takes into account on how globally the political parties are controlling media, both directly and indirectly, to fulfill their agenda. In the context of India, the media's role as a potent instrument in shaping public opinion and fostering democracy is under scrutiny. Freedom of the press is the fulcrum upon which the scales of truth and accountability delicately balance, and the guardian of societal enlightenment. The constraints placed upon freedom of the press aren't confined to India alone; they extend to countries like China and Russia, where the majority of media outlets operate under governmental control. In stark contrast, the United Kingdom, lacking a formal written provision for press freedom, excels in upholding this fundamental liberty.

Keywords Press · Advertising · Constitution · Democracy

S. A. Wani (✉)
Assistant Professor, School of Law, Alliance University, Bengaluru, India
e-mail: showkatamu001@gmail.com

D. Bole
Disputes and Litigation, King Stubb and Kasiva, Bengaluru, India

J. Aston et al. (eds.), *Comparative Law*, https://doi.org/10.1007/978-981-97-7815-7_21

1 Introduction

The landscape of journalistic independence has undergone profound changes in recent times, shaped by contemporary electoral shifts and technological advancements. Today, mainstream media is perhaps the institution most responsible for keeping the leaders in power. The mainstream media are proxies of political parties particulary those who are in power. The influence of authorities on the press has evolved significantly in various nations, rendering pre-publication restrictions and prior authorization largely obsolete, albeit with some exceptions. Noteworthy transformations are evident in countries like Myanmar, where censors have relinquished the traditional markup of preparatory media editions, opting instead to subtly guide reporters on the stories to pursue. Even in nations with active governmental control over reporters, such as China and Vietnam, a burgeoning online space has emerged for the discussion of taboo topics and the amplification of opposition voices.

Another notable trend in politically turbulent regions over the past two decades is the growing collaboration between corporate entities operating media houses and government officials, posing a threat to the professional integrity of the media. Strong relationships between governmental authorities and the press are observed in countries such as Myanmar, Argentina, Bangkok, North Africa, Ankara, and across Europe. These connections may be forged through advertising, government sponsorship of media outlets, or affiliations between media owners and influential politicians. Regardless of the specific method, the common outcome is a media landscape that aligns with ruling powers, with absolute lack of independence. Scholars specializing in the press and mass media have long scrutinized issues related to ownership, financial control, government support, and various forms of political bias that shape news reporting. The "five filters" proposed by Edward S. Herman and Noam Chomsky in 1988 highlight factors such as corporate ownership, ideological influence, and source pressure as determinants of coverage.

Contemporary scholars are expanding upon these concepts, employing diverse terminology to deepen our understanding of the multifaceted factors that constrain or bias media exposure. Social scholar Alina Mungiu-Pippidi's concept of "media capture" stands out as particularly insightful, defining it as a situation where the media fails to achieve autonomy in manifesting their will or fulfilling their primary function of informing the public. Instead, they persist in an intermediate state, influenced by vested interests, not limited to the government, and used for purposes beyond journalism.

In the Republic of Venezuela, media organizations have undergone acquisition by commercial companies with ties to the authorities. The Erdogan administration in Turkey has exerted pressure on commercial groups to acquire struggling news organizations, while Silvio Berlusconi solidified his authority in Italy by leveraging his journalistic resources. For years, business and political leaders have wielded dominance over Thailand's media. This scenario presents a formidable challenge to the nation's system of separation of powers, as the press, rather than diligently performing its vital social duty of monitoring, is now owned by the very entities it should hold accountable—whether governmental, corporate, or community-based. This situation complicates citizens' ability to discern the true intentions of these influential entities and exacerbates societal inequality.

2 Media and Freedom

A wealth of research underscores the pivotal role of the press in contemporary society, particularly its capacity to unveil a spectrum of transgressions within both commercial and governmental spheres. Journalism stands as a linchpin for upholding a system of checks and balances in our nation, striving to ensure that government, corporations, and other entities align with public sentiments. The power of the press to address violations is constrained, relying on the belief that awareness alone can act as a deterrent and catalyze solutions. In a robust civil society, transparency and good governance remain indispensable. Examples such as the 2014 Luxembourg Files documentary exposing tax avoidance and the 2016 Panama Papers on offshore banking, released by the International Consortium of Investigative Journalists, highlight instances where journalists brought violations to light.[1]

Despite the acknowledged benefits of independent or democratic media, an ongoing debate surrounds the criteria for such outlets. Consideration should extend beyond legal and economic aspects to encompass the role and practices of the media. Freedom House factors in legal, political, and economic contexts when evaluating media freedom.[2]

Integral components of an independent press encompasses constitutional guarantees of press freedom and journalistic independence, the application of these rights, the absence of regulations hindering disclosure, the ability of news organizations to curate their content, autonomy from government surveillance and self-censorship, freedom from harassment and assault, protection against financial control by authorities and individual media ownership, independence from financial manipulation through advertising or subsidies, and clear ownership separation allowing consumers to assess news impartiality.[3]

Governments deploy four primary financial techniques to control the press sector: state-run press financing, state-run advertising, national incentives, and market-disruptive policies. The first three types essentially involve direct sponsorship, while the fourth category encompasses fiscal strategies aimed at shaping marketplace dynamics, undermining critical journalism, or supporting government-affiliated news organizations. The boundaries between these funding categories are often blurry.

[1] Dutton, W. H. (2009) 'The Fifth Estate Emerging through the Network of Networks', Prometheus: Critical Studies in Innovation, 27/1: 1.

[2] Economic and Political Weekly, The Media: Politics, Ethics and the Law, February 11, 2006.

[3] Jenifer Whitten-Woodring, "Watchdog or Lapdog? Media Freedom, Regime Type, and Government Respect for Human Rights", International Studies Quarterly, Sep., 2009, Vol. 53, No. 3 (Sep., 2009), pp. 595 625.

Examples of official funding include state marketing expenses, license fees collected from state-appointed entities, and state budget allocations, all distributed to media outlets through various agreements and contracts.

A particularly insidious form of government intervention in journalism is official branding, where authorities allocate funds to promote state-owned businesses' products and services. This practice, funded by resources from state-owned enterprises or official finances, essentially borrows favor with reporters and the press. Decisions not to advertise in certain news channels, especially smaller, independent ones, can jeopardize their survival, serving as a potent means of influencing the press. Government grants, within the realm of the media, represent perhaps the least transparent form of support.

Governments may choose to assist press organizations at their discretion, ostensibly in an effort to promote independent media and journalism's growth. However, this can be a covert means of rewarding the sympathetic press. The most intricate tactic employed by authorities to gain media influence is market manipulation, taking various forms such as legislation designed to financially cripple journalism organizations, orders protecting the financial interests of government-friendly press, or incentives to independent financiers in exchange for supporting news organizations aligned with the government.[4]

For years, concerns have been extensively documented regarding the unequal allocation of public advertising funds. State advertising funds are frequently channeled to support media organizations that either align with the government or refrain from criticizing state authority.[5] During approximately ten years of the global economic recession, government advertising has become an increasingly effective tool for controlling dissenting/opposing news organizations. By withholding government advertisements, the government can drive many media outlets, particularly small, independent ones, to extinction.[6] State advertising serves as a lifeline for numerous news organizations, especially when the state is one of the country's largest advertisers, and these organizations are grappling to survive.

3 Economic Capture

The term "capture" was initially coined in the context of financial incentives. Authorities had an incentive to take care of individuals they were overseeing since they often returned to work in the industries, they had previously regulated. However, over the years, scholars of politics and analysts have studied a broader range of acquisition

[4] Rasmus Kleis Nielsen and David A. L. Levy, "The Changing Business of Journalism and its Implications for Democracy", Reuters Institute for the Study of Journalism, Department of Politics and International Relations, University of Oxford,

[5] Baker, C. Edwin (2002) Media, Markets, and Democracy. Cambridge: Cambridge University Press.

[6] WAN (2009) World Press Trends 2009. Paris: World Association of Newspapers.

methods. One of the most significant concepts is the idea of regulatory capture, which suggests that through continuous interaction and connection, regulators can begin to operate similarly to the people they are supposed to regulate. Even politicians who consciously attempt not to let financial considerations influence them may be affected by this phenomenon. After years of working in financial institutions, these government officials start to identify with banking professionals.

The increasing emphasis on the universality of ideas, opinions, and behaviors is evident in contemporary macroeconomic research. As social beings, the people we interact with have a variety of influences on us. Some research even suggests that individuals who have worked in financial institutions tend to display more self-centered behavior when reminded of their previous roles as bankers.[7] Economic circumstances, in addition to social and legal regulations, can significantly impact the freedom of the press. While media ownership is often considered the primary factor limiting coverage, it's important to note that government sponsorship or influence over the media does not necessarily equate to control over media operations. For example, the British Broadcasting Corporation is funded by the government but remains "editorially independent".[8]

Despite the potential benefits of making journalism more profitable, there are legitimate concerns that this could lead to subpar reporting that neglects various perspectives as control becomes more consolidated and media conglomerates become closely linked. There are indeed valid concerns that reporters may self-censor when selecting stories to please their columnists and owners in order to avoid issues, although none have suggested that broadcasting investors could act as gatekeepers. In fact, a survey of reporters revealed that self-censorship is common in media organizations. Another issue related to ownership concerns the potential shift from quality journalism to profit generation as media outlets increasingly come under the ownership of global corporations. Since the "Penny Press Revolution" of the 1830s, it has been argued that economic considerations have influenced journalism in the United States.[9]

The first set of issues arises from the declining profitability of traditional media in the age of digitization, making them more of a plaything for the extremely wealthy. Additionally, the investigative journalism essential for the media to fulfill its watchdog role is not supported by the new financial models of the digital age. Many outlets lack the funding required for in-depth investigations. Furthermore, the value of "breaking" a story may diminish when it is quickly disseminated online through numerous other websites. Some essentially "free ride" off the initial research reports. As newspapers struggle to secure funding, the cost of conducting investigations has shifted to non-profits and charitable contributions that often have an "agenda."

[7] Wen, Yuxi (2021) "The Political and Economic Impact of Media Ownership Structures and Concentration on Global Communication," Butler Journal of Undergraduate Research: Vol. 7, Article 15. Retrieved from: https://digitalcommons.butler.edu/bjur/vol7/iss1/15.

[8] Cass R. Sunstein, "Government Control of Information", California Law Review, May, 1986, Vol. 74, No. 3, Symposium: New Perspectives in the Law of Defamation (May, 1986), pp. 889–921.

[9] Media systems, digital media and politics, Book Title: Social Theory after the Internet, Book Subtitle: Media, Technology, and Globalization, Ralph Schroeder, UCL Press.

However, there is less protection against capture when investigative reporting is absent.[10]

Media capture is different from traditional regulatory control only in terms of ownership. A regulator cannot be privately or publicly corrupted, despite the arguments of those who oppose the U.S. political finance system, which suggests that open purchases are not fundamentally different from closed ones. However, powerful individuals and businesses can and do purchase media. They do so not only as a financial investment but often to advance their ideological views or out of a sense of civic duty. Many individuals buy newspapers because they believe that the press has the power to shape their opinions, their worldview, and ultimately, their politics. Various motivations that the press must contend with have been extensively covered elsewhere, such as in Besley and Prat's "Handcuffs for the Grabbing Hand?" The 2006 article "Media Capture and Government Accountability" explores the pressures surrounding entry and advertising and how they can lead to de facto dominance of the media.

Media owners worry about sponsors and customers because they want to make money, regardless of whether they have non-monetary objectives. The financial industry gains control over the financial press in part because it is at risk of losing advertising and customers if it does not represent their interests. Similarly, media owners and journalists may behave as if they are being watched by the subjects of their coverage because they know that negative reports could result in denied access to information, putting their businesses at a competitive disadvantage. Acquisition and surveillance are ways in which authorities that do not support press freedom can still ensure that the media delivers the news and expresses their views without having to own the media. All they need to do is control the content that gets published. While self-censorship is practiced in many parts of the world, not only in relation to the government but also with regard to corporations, using the term "capture" to describe government–media relationships in such a context adds little to the discussion and offers no new insights into what is happening—in fact, it appears to further exacerbate the already intense relationship. Media organizations pull back, toning down what they say and forgoing certain investigations that their organization could have pursued due to the fear of losing viewers, advertising revenue (from the public or private sector), and access to critical information necessary for their survival.

4 Cognitive Capture

One of the most intriguing aspects of control is inattentional blindness, which is perhaps the subtlest and most challenging phenomenon to grasp. It relates to how journalists perceive and interpret global events, subsequently influencing how they convey information about reality. The potential for inattentional blindness among

[10] Timothy Besley, "Handcuffs for the Grabbing Hand? Media Capture and Government Accountability", American Economic Review, Vol. 96, No. 3, JUNE 2006.

journalists to lead to the cognitive capture of society is a compelling reason for the significance of this subject. The newsroom wields a significant influence over the collective opinions of the population, and when its portrayal of events is persuasive, it can lead to a willingness to embrace opinions that align with personal values. Contrary to the traditional idea of the press as the "fourth pillar of democracy," isolated from the broader public and tasked with safeguarding the essential checks and balances for democracy's smooth operation, it is deeply ingrained within society, often merely reflecting commonly held opinions.[11] This phenomenon can contribute to the echo chamber effect, reinforcing and amplifying pre-existing beliefs.

These assertions find ample support in the reporting of events leading up to the global economic meltdown of 2008. While figures like "Maria Bartiromo" became the leading proponents of the financial industry, it is astonishing how few journalists spoke out against the widespread deception, extortion, and various other oppressive practices within the finance sector. "Mike Hudson, Gretchen Morgenson, Peter Goodman, and Floyd Norris" stand out as a few of the American journalists who dared to pose tough questions about the situation. It is undeniably challenging to completely evade such manipulation. In theory, consumers can guard themselves against some of the more overt forms of control, especially those related to ownership. However, the subtler forms of manipulation are often the most damaging. People may read the front-page articles skeptically, but political manipulation is pervasive and often unintentional. Cognitive capture also undermines the press's ability to fulfill its public duty, as clearly revealed by the recession of 2008. In 2003, 71% of African nations had monopolistic authority over their media channels. In the region, government organizations dominated 81% of publications and 84% of media outlets. In the Middle East countries, governmental control of the press was equally prevalent, with authorities overseeing 50% of the publications. The African Media Development Project in 2015 made a comparable finding about substantial government control throughout the continent, particularly within the media sector. Authoritarian management and ownership systems, especially in nations with fragile checks and balances, tend to result in a range of adverse outcomes, including not just biased reporting but also adverse economic, political, and social consequences. In contrast, publicly funded news agencies in highly advanced democracies typically deliver exceptional journalism.

The changes implemented in different settings were intended to revitalize the media sector, with goals of liberalization, expansion, and the growth of civil society to foster a more diversified and democratic press.[12] Indeed, some nations made significant changes to their media policies during the rise of democratization. For example, in Kenya, the two phases of democratization—1992, when rebel groups

[11] Eyal Ophir, Clifford Nass, Anthony D. Wagner and Michael I. Posner, "Cognitive Control in Media Multitaskers", Proceedings of the National Academy of Sciences of the United States of America, Sep. 15, 2009, Vol. 106, No. 37 (Sep. 15, 2009), pp. 15,583–15,587.

[12] Joel Dresang, "Authoritarian Controls and News Media in the Philippines", ISEAS—Yusof Ishak Institute, Contemporary Southeast Asia, June 1985, Vol. 7, No. 1 (June 1985), pp. 34–47.

gained constitutional legitimacy, and 2002, when a dictator in office was removed—were associated with two corresponding phases of media liberalization in 1997 and 2006. Tanzania made a similar decision in the 1990s to privatize its press following the introduction of multi-party elections.

5 Corporate Capture

Due to press liberalization in India, corporations have gained substantial authority as they utilize marketing to support broadcasting and newspaper content. While the increase in advertising revenue during the nineteenth century in the West enabled media outlets to gain independence from government regulation, the contemporary advertising industry lacks financial stability. Instead, it compels press organizations to compete against each other for meager profits.[13] This is mainly due to the fact that advertisers now have a broader range of options for ad placement, along with increased leverage to negotiate lower rates or demand more favorable reach, thanks to the growth of the internet and traditional media. India's television advertising market is currently expanding at an annual rate of 35%, which is a result of a significant increase in the number of news outlets in operation and the increased hourly airtime dedicated to advertisements.

6 Trump/Facebook: A Winning Combination

"Trump is ubiquitous: he appears on our screens, in our newspapers, and on our news-feeds. He lingers on our devices, capturing our attention. Even those who dislike him tend to stay tuned when he speaks. Trump possesses a high entertainment factor, and many view him as funny, entertaining, or, at the very least, provocative. Journalists and politicians, particularly liberals and supporters of Hillary, often perceive Trump through the lens of a clown. The Daily News even made a recurring theme out of it".[14]

Many factors contributed to the unexpected victory of Republican nominee Trump in the 2016 US presidential election, but one of the most influential was Facebook's impact on the electoral landscape.[15] While a variety of elements, such as the Republican Party's shifting stance on racial supremacy, economic challenges, Hillary Clinton's perceived shortcomings, and the unforeseen interference by the

[13] Jiaxing You, Bohui Zhang and Le Zhang, "Who Captures the Power of the Pen?", The Review of Financial Studies, Oxford University Press, January 2018, Vol. 31, No. 1 (January 2018), pp. 43–96.

[14] InterMEDIA I January 2017 Vol 44 Issue 4, "How The Internet Got Donald Trump Elected", www.iicom.org

[15] The Guardian, *Revealed: 50 million Facebook profiles harvested for Cambridge Analytica in major data breach*, available at: https://www.theguardian.com/news/2018/mar/17/cambridge-analytica-facebook-influence-us-election (last visited on: Dec. 11, 2023).

FBI, played essential roles in Trump's triumph, Facebook played a pivotal role in disseminating information and shaping voter sentiments.[16] As the most robust and influential social media platform, Facebook has become the primary venue for political discourse and information exchange in the United States. With its extensive user base, broad audience, revenue, and influence, it has become the most prominent participant in the digital political arena. Facebook's influence extends beyond the results of the 2016 presidential election, serving as a testament to the platform's ability to disrupt established hierarchies and profoundly transform society.

It is evident that Facebook's failure or hesitance to address issues of disinformation and false content played a significant role in Trump's victory. While disinformation is not unique to Facebook, the platform's large user base and content distribution methods, reliant on the emotional appeal of shared content and the algorithmic response system of the news feed, have made it a fertile ground for dishonest purveyors of information. Such media outlets entice readers with sensationalized or entirely fabricated news to visit ad-laden pages rather than the social network itself. Stories such as claims that Hillary Clinton purchased illegal weapons or that the Pope endorsed Trump garnered substantial investments, votes, and views.[17] The headlines themselves became hot topics that garnered significant attention in both online and traditional media formats, often obviating the need for readers to delve into the articles' content.

Publishing false information was not solely motivated by financial gain; political bias and the intent to deceive prospective voters also played a role. However, the emphasis on engagement rather than a specific political agenda gave disinformation an irrational edge that typical political campaigns lack. Facebook's design, which prioritizes engaging content, facilitated the proliferation of misleading information.

Even with the best intentions, fact-checking sites like Snopes struggled to contend with sensational yet fabricated stories in Facebook's timeline due to the platform's structural design. As a result, disinformation thrived, capitalizing on communal opinions and psychological responses. With approximately 170 million daily users in North America, Facebook wields significant influence. It has become a primary source of information on current events for 44% of the US population.[18] Such prominence necessitates a level of social responsibility to ensure that disinformation does not deceive a wider population beyond just US voters. However, Facebook has shown an unwillingness or inability to acknowledge its role as perhaps the most effective disseminator of false information in history.

[16] CNN, "Fact check: Trump's self-serving comparison to Hillary Clinton's classified email scandal", available at: https://edition.cnn.com/2023/06/14/politics/fact-check-donald-trump-hillary-clinton-classified-documents/index.html (last visited on: Dec. 11, 2023).

[17] CNBC, "Read all about it: The biggest fake news stories of 2016", available at: https://www.cnbc.com/2016/12/30/read-all-about-it-the-biggest-fake-news-stories-of-2016.html (last visited on: Dec. 11, 2023).

[18] Social Media Today, "New Research Shows that 71% of Americans Now Get News Content via Social Platforms", available at: https://www.socialmediatoday.com/news/new-research-shows-that-71-of-americans-now-get-news-content-via-social-pl/593255/ (last visited on: Dec. 11, 2023).

The proliferation of false information is just one facet of the problem; another is the transformation of civic discourse. Facebook has disrupted the traditional flow of information, fostering the growth of communities and political organizations that might have struggled to thrive in a tightly regulated media landscape. Political mobilization has evolved due to the platform's capacity to unite like-minded individuals and enable them to self-organize independently of established political parties.

In the twentieth century, a few dominant news corporations controlled the communication landscape, limiting the range of ideological perspectives and favoring centrist, establishment-friendly policies. Facebook now provides both the medium and the readership that media organizations once held, along with the organizing capacity that political parties used to enjoy, challenging this established power dynamic. It allowed Trump to engage with and rally his supporters outside of established party structures. Facebook also served as a counterprogramming tool to counteract unfavorable press coverage.

Facebook's influence extends beyond the spread of false information; it transforms political discourse itself by altering influence ratios and expanding viewpoints. Each new medium introduced in the past century has disrupted existing structures of political power by broadening audiences and amplifying new voices. Facebook's involvement in elections represents a continuation of this trend, further reshaping American democracy.

7 India–Modi: The Ongoing Influence of Learning from the USA

The 2019 general election in India was a watershed moment, marking the country's inaugural truly digital election, with nearly half of the electorate having access to internet-based platforms, and one-third enjoying social media access.[19] This historic event not only reshaped the political landscape but also witnessed a transformative social shift between 2016 and 2019, garnering limited attention and research despite its profound implications.[20]

Approximately 50% of India's electorate gained access to information channels that were previously beyond reach in 2019, according to the Election Commission of India.[21] Google estimated that four hundred million Indians were regular internet users, with a notable annual increase of 40 million new users.[22] Notably,

[19] Nalin Mehta, "Digital Politics in India's 2019 General Elections", Economic and Political Weekly (Engage), Vol. 54, Issue No. 51, 28 Dec, 2019.

[20] Sheikh Tajammul-ul-Islam, "Is Indian Media Free from State Control? An Appraisal"; Pluto Journals, Policy Perspectives, Vol. 16, No. 2 (2019), pp. 27–40.

[21] Hindustan Times, *India adds 40 mn new internet users each year*, available at: https://www.hindustantimes.com/business-news/india-adds-40-mn-new-internet-users-each-year/story-BjLUWWwS5Jh5TDkydhz8VJ.html (last visited on: Dec. 13, 2023).

[22] *Ibid.*

non-metropolitan cities, contributed to nearly half of Google's search traffic.[23] This surge in internet users was driven by India's average monthly mobile data consumption per user exceeding 8 GB, aligning it with advanced economies.[24] By May 2019, over thirty percent of Indians had the ability to access Facebook, WhatsApp, and YouTube, a substantial increase from the 9% recorded in 2014, according to CSDS Lokniti.

The launch of the Jio phone network in September 2016 played a pivotal role in this era of affordable data access, fundamentally impacting Indian politics.[25] Prime Minister Narendra Modi, known for embracing online platforms over traditional press, adeptly developed an engaging and consistent campaign strategy. Initiatives such as Swacch Bharat (Clean India) and the Fit India Movement showcased his effective use of online platforms to advance political strategies, facilitate policy crowdsourcing, and enhance publicity.

Following Modi's remarkable victory in the 2014 general election, other Indian political figures began recognizing the transformative influence of social media on the political landscape. Amidst an extensive and transparent debate on the need to regulate online content, major social networking platforms such as Google, Facebook, WhatsApp, Twitter, ShareChat, and TikTok committed to a pioneering "Voluntary Code of Ethics" during the 2019 general election.[26] On March 20, 2019, the Internet and Mobile Association of India (IAMAI) submitted a rule to the Election Commission of India (ECI). Companies adhering to these codes of conduct actively participated in four significant initiatives, the first being to use awareness and interaction initiatives to increase public awareness of elections. To address undesirable posts reported to the Election Commission of India under various election regulations, including Sect. 126 of the Representation of People Act, 1951, several objectives were established.[27] Firstly, the aim is to establish a high-priority dedicated complaint resolution route. Secondly, digital firms pledged to respond to breaches of the 48-h no-campaigning and silent period for candidates within three hours of being reported. Thirdly, in compliance with the Supreme Court's directive, political ads on their platforms must have pre-approval from the government's media certification and monitoring bodies. Lastly, there is a commitment to openly examine sponsored

---

[23] Inc42, *Internet In India 2019: Equal Split Of Internet Users In Rural And Urban Areas*, available at: https://inc42.com/buzz/internet-in-india-2019-equal-split-of-internet-users-in-rural-and-urban-areas/%23%3A%7E%3Atext%3DThe%20report%20also%20finds%20that,to%20internet%20usage%20in%20India (last visited on: Dec. 13, 2023).

[24] Nalin Mehta, "Digital Politics in India's 2019 General Elections", Economic and Political Weekly (Engage), Vol. 54, Issue No. 51, 28 Dec, 2019.

[25] Quartz, *Reliance Jio's cheap data turned India's internet dreams into reality*, available at: https://qz.com/india/2055771/reliance-jios-cheap-data-turned-indias-internet-dreams-into-reality (last visited on: Dec. 13, 2023).

[26] Press Information Bureau, *"Voluntary Code of Ethics" by Social Media Platforms to be observed in the General Election to the Haryana & Maharashtra Legislative Assemblies and all future elections*, available at: https://pib.gov.in/PressReleaseIframePage.aspx?PRID%3D1586297%23%3A%7E%3Atext%3DIAMAI%20has%20assured%20the%20Commission,for%20the%20General%20Elections%202019 (last visited on: Dec. 13, 2023).

[27] Section 126 of the Representation of People Act, 1951.

campaigns and clearly identify and declare them as such. Despite these initiatives, outcomes have been inconsistent.

Concerning public awareness initiatives, Facebook introduced campaigns like "Share You Voted" and "Candidate Connect," while Google News ran the "Poll-Check" campaign to educate reporters on information presentation, fact verification, and authentication.[28] In terms of removing offensive content, the ECI reported that 909 posts were removed by technological networks during the election season. ShareChat removed 31 posts, Twitter removed 220 tweets, and Facebook removed 650 posts.[29] A few WhatsApp users had their access suspended after the ECI reported five clips on YouTube. While these actions were deemed appropriate, the numbers are relatively small given the vast volume of content on social media.[30]

Regarding campaign spending disclosure, Facebook and Google initiated Ads Disclosure programs, revealing the quantity, source, and cost of endorsements. Both platforms reported gross campaign internet marketing revenue of over Rs. 53 crore from February to May 2019.[31] Facebook's ad portfolio included more personalized commercials, but the funds allocated to each platform were comparable. The BJP topped internet campaign investment on both platforms, and other parties quickly adopted some of the BJP's strategies.[32] Leading up to the 2019 elections, Rahul Gandhi and the Congress party, despite facing limitations in their social media strategy, made significant progress in utilizing social media for political gains. Rahul Gandhi successfully (re)branded himself as a serious national-level political contender through regular, humorous, and strategic engagement with audiences on social media.

In terms of political advertising on Google, the BJP accounted for 41.4% (Rs 12.19 crore), the Congress at 10% (Rs 3 crore), and the DMK of Tamil Nadu at 13.6% (Rs 4 crore).[33] Despite the BJP's dominance in campaign investment, the Congress made substantial strides in leveraging social media for political advantage, showcasing Rahul Gandhi's successful (re)branding efforts as a national-level political contender.

On the flip side, the Bharatiya Janata Party (BJP) outpaced its rivals in terms of electoral marketing on Facebook and Google. The BJP secured the top spot-on Google with 41.4% of political advertisements, with the Congress trailing in the third position at 10%. On Facebook, the Congress lagged significantly in second

---

[28] Meta, *Preparing for Upcoming Indian Elections*, available at: https://about.fb.com/news/2019/04/preparing-for-indian-elections/ (last visited on: Dec. 13, 2023).

[29] ANI, *647 cases of paid news registered during LS polls: ECI*, available at: https://www.aninews.in/news/national/general-news/647-cases-of-paid-news-registered-during-ls-polls-eci20190519200301/

[30] Joyojeet Pal, "Twitter in the 2019 Indian General Election: Trends of Use Across States and Parties", Economic and Political Weekly (Engage), Vol 54, Issue 51.

[31] The Hindu, *BJP tops political advertisement spend on Facebook, Google in Feb-May*, https://www.thehindu.com/elections/lok-sabha-2019/political-advertisements-spend-on-facebook-google-tops-53-crore/article27177595.ece (last visited on: Dec. 13, 2023).

[32] Charis Papaevangelou. Funding intermediaries: Google and Facebook's strategy to capture journalism. Digital Journalism, 2023, pp.1–22.

[33] *Supra* Note 20.

place with 6.1% of political advertisements, while the BJP led with 14.7%.[34] The likelihood of political parties investing more in online channels is high, considering the involvement of different branches and supportive categories, even though the disclosed political marketing expenditure is minimal.

Determining political advertising on online platforms proves challenging due to a significant portion of funding originating from allied or supportive organizations, offering a plausible defense. Disclosed expenditures by parties likely represent only a fraction of more extensive online political mobilization efforts. The complex nature of online campaigning and spending is evident in the substantial amount of marketing funds, despite authorized and pre-declared political advertisements on platforms like Facebook, originating from distinct but affiliated organizations supporting the BJP.

While Narendra Modi was the central figure, official BJP social media handles shared content from various BJP leaders, contributing to a higher volume of content compared to Congress handles. The operational message discipline also played a role, with key Congress members refraining from reposting Rahul Gandhi's "Chowkidar Chor hai" statement on their accounts, unlike BJP ministers who shared every post from Modi. Throughout the campaign, Rahul Gandhi did not share any communications from Priyanka Gandhi, appointed as the representative for eastern Uttar Pradesh.

Although web-based campaigns can be potent tools, their effectiveness is contingent on the organizations they aim to promote. The disparity between the Congress's Shakti program and the trajectory of the NaMo app is illustrative of this. By March 2019, the NaMo app had generated over Rs 5 crores in product sales and had been installed over ten million times on both Android and iOS operating systems.[35] Beyond functioning as an exclusive Twitter-like ecosystem for user-generated content, the NaMo app, previewed on Jio phones, served as a vital two-way mechanism for conducting interviews and gathering data.

The Congress's Shakti application, reportedly enlisting 60 lakh members, served as a strategic review instrument for party officials to engage with local employees, influencing decisions on key matters such as Rafale and the Chowkidar Chor Hai campaign.[36] However, the app faced allegations of widespread "bonus registrations," "fake users," and "BJP infiltration" post-voting. There is contention that the electoral

---

[34] India Today, BJP tops political advertisers chart on Google, rival Congress ranked sixth, available at: https://www.indiatoday.in/elections/lok-sabha-2019/story/google-political-advertiser-bjp-congress-ysr-1493589-2019-04-04 (last visited on: Dec. 13, 2023).

[35] The Economic Times, *Branded Narendra Modi merchandise worth Rs 5 crore sold in three months from PM's personal mobile app*, available at: https://economictimes.indiatimes.com/news/politics-and-nation/branded-narendra-modi-merchandise-worth-rs-5-crore-sold-in-three-months-from-pms-personal-mobile-application/articleshow/67457405.cms?from=mdr (last visited on: Dec. 13, 2023).

[36] The Economic Times, Congress app gives 'Shakti' to party workers, available at: https://economictimes.indiatimes.com/news/elections/lok-sabha/india/congress-app-gives-shakti-to-party-workers/articleshow/68474760.cms?from=mdr (last visited on: Dec. 13, 2023).

result was dictated more by "media logic" than "political logic," with the BJP's effective press operation playing a significant role.[37]

Irrespective of the interpretation of the 2019 elections, it is undeniable that these political endeavors marked a turning point in India's progression toward an affordable, digital society. While digital platforms are just beginning to address content violations and enhance transparency in political finance through self-regulation, there is still much work to be done. Nevertheless, a notable beginning has been made. Social media has empowered individuals previously excluded from politics based on their location and demographics, fostering inclusiveness in Indian politics. Technology has facilitated unprecedented levels of public participation and a diversity of opinions.

The 2019 national election also stands out for its record low in open discourse, widespread dissemination of false information, and systematic disregard for ethical standards in political communication.[38] The advent of technological advances is exacerbating the already complex issue of morality in political communication. These innovations are eroding traditional moral boundaries among all political participants, including politicians, journalists, the mass media, and the audience.

The lead-up to the 2019 general elections witnessed a prominent aspect: the emergence of contentious and divisive material, with both the Congress and the BJP emphasizing communal aspects in their campaigns. Social media, providing a platform for populist ideologies, has allowed political discourse to adopt a combative and personal character. This has led to the proliferation of slanderous remarks and extremist views, particularly in unregulated online forums, indigenous dialects, and private WhatsApp group chats.

Social media's role in allowing populist ideologies to adopt an aggressive and personal tone has contributed to the spread of slanderous remarks and extremist views, particularly in unregulated online forums and private WhatsApp group chats. It has been observed that both parties and their proxies disseminated a significant amount of false material, presenting a considerable challenge for fact-checking organizations and vigilant individuals attempting to verify each instance and uncover the truth. While low-class speech and unethical debate, including insults and fake news, have always been present, social media has exacerbated these issues. Participants have lamented the decline in the nation's political discourse, where disinformation, insults, and slander have become commonplace even among experienced and prominent political figures.

The routine nature of such political speech in the age of social media is undeniably problematic, given that these messages are amplified, spread, and duplicated across audiences with little critical digital literacy. These alarming patterns raise fresh concerns about the morality of political communication in the modern era and the

---

[37] '*Rahul Gandhi Apology for "Chowkidar Chor Hai" Claim Accepted, He's Warned,*' NDTV, https://www.ndtv.com/india-news/rahul-gandhi-let-off-in-contempt-case-over-rafale-case-remarks-supreme-court-says-needs-to-be-more-c-2132256 (last visited on: Dec. 13, 2023).

[38] Quartz, Technology could torpedo India's first WhatsApp election, available at: https://qz.com/india/1563318/indias-2019-election-is-threatened-by-fake-news-on-whatsapp (last visited on: Dec. 13, 2023).

shared responsibility of institutions, businesses, the media, and individuals to prevent unethical political speech. Surprisingly, each of these players has an underlying role in the spread of this issue. To halt routinely unethical communication and its negative impacts via social media, collaborative efforts with academia, civil society, and ethicists are essential.

National security and harmony are two critical areas where immoral use of digital platforms can have severe consequences, as demonstrated by the surge in false information following the terrorist attack in Pulwama in February 2019. After the attack on Indian paramilitary forces in Kashmir, fact-checkers observed the dangers of deceptive posts proliferating on the internet, reaching a new high in false news dissemination. The rapid spread of false information following Pulwama had numerous security ramifications, nearly leading India and Pakistan into war due to heightened emotions, dramatic reporting, and political sloganeering fueled by the distribution of false information.

Modi's authorization of airstrikes on purported terror camps in Balakot, Pakistan, after the Pulwama attack, triggered a series of retaliatory measures between the two nations. The situation only de-escalated when Pakistan released Indian Air Force pilot Abhinandan Varthaman. The outbreak of unprecedented hostilities between India and Pakistan, heavily influenced by social media, false information, and public opinion, had security ramifications for the entire region. Social media played a significant role in shaping public perception and contributing to the BJP's electoral success through the politicization of Pulwama.[39]

Following the Pulwama incident and the Balakot airstrike, there was a concerning trend in which well-known individuals, common people, and media outlets disseminated graphic photos of carnage, fueling rumors, and stirring controversy. Whether intentional or not, incorrect and misleading social media messages regarding Pulwama exacerbated communal tensions and jingoistic nationalism in an already divisive election campaign. Social media was used to demonize Muslims and Kashmiris, leading to incidents of violence, terrorization, and harassment in certain regions of the nation.

Press reports indicate that numerous hate tactics were orchestrated through Facebook groups and WhatsApp groups during this period.[40] The branding and bullying of less extreme viewpoints or those opposing the government's activities as "anti-national" constituted another harmful factor. The term gained popularity, especially among followers of the Hindu right wing, who used it to label as traitors those with differing opinions and to subject them to online harassment and abuse. The spread of fake news and rumors surrounding Pulwama and Balakot falls into a category of rumors known as wedge-driving rumors, capable of causing social unrest and having a lasting impact on communities.

---

[39] *Ibid.*

[40] The Hindu, Karnataka assembly whatsapp group admins step in to restrict political messages fake news, available at: https://www.thehindu.com/elections/karnataka-assembly/whatsapp-group-admins-step-in-to-restrict-political-messages-fake-news/article66684587.ece (last visited on: Dec. 13, 2023).

8 Around the Globe

8.1 Brazil

In 2016, the early closure of Dilma Rousseff's subsequent administration following impeachment hearings, referred to by some political observers as a parliamentary dictatorship, was an unexpected outcome for Brazil, a country thought to be more stable than most in South America.[41] Brazil received recognition for establishing an intricate transparency network encompassing all three branches of administration, the press, community organizations, and the prosecutors' office. Notably, it has been seen as a positive development in the Brazilian news media toward greater independence and analytical practices. However, a particularly intriguing aspect of the coup is the active participation of transparency organizations and, crucially, the dominant press. The latter developed an intense bias against Partido dos Trabalhadores authorities and portrayed their actions as an imminent danger to the rule of law.[42]

8.2 South Africa

During the apartheid regime in South Africa, the government-owned South African Broadcasting Corporation (SABC) served as the government's marketing limb, and documents supporting the struggle for freedom were severely concealed, subjecting journalists to state tyranny. Independent media relied on foreign funding from organizations supporting the anti-apartheid cause, a reliance that has decreased since the democratic transition in 1994. However, the current ANC government maintains strict oversight of SABC.[43] Despite the availability of independently sponsored press in both Afrikaans and English, over ninety percent of South Africans remain reliant on SABC, particularly in the countryside where competing and unbiased media are unavailable.

The ANC government has introduced new anti-terrorism regulations, akin to apartheid-era laws, raising criticism that the SABC functions as an arm of the ANC, similar to its role under apartheid thirty years ago. SABC primarily depends on advertisement revenue (80 percent of revenue) and a smaller amount of public funding,

---

41 Teun A van Dijk, "How Globo media manipulated the impeachment of Brazilian President Dilma Rousseff", Sage Journal, 2017, Vol. 11(2) 199–229.

42 Vilaca, Luiz and Morucci, Marco and Paniagua, Victoria, Anti Political Class Bias in Corruption Sentencing (January 20, 2023). Available at.
SSRN: https://ssrn.com/abstract=4332033 or http://dx.doi.org/10.2139/ssrn.4332033.

43 Anita Franklin and Roy Love, "Whose News? Control of the Media in Africa", Review of African Political Economy, Dec., 1998, Vol. 25, No. 78, Whose News? Control of the Media in Africa (Dec., 1998), pp. 545–55.

making it susceptible to governmental and commercial control.[44] The economic vulnerability of news organizations, coupled with drops in banner prices, makes them more likely to be taken over by business supporters. The media industry has consolidated post-dictatorship, leading to the closure or mergers of smaller media operations that relied on foreign assistance. In 2013, the largest newspaper company, Independent News and Media, was taken over by ANC associate Sekunjalo Investments, resulting in resignations from employees.

The Gupta family, close associates of President Jacob Zuma, launched a new national daily newspaper and a 24-h TV station with pro-ANC editorial positions.[45] The Gupta case exemplifies the intersectionality of plutocratic capture, corporate capture, and state power in South Africa.

9 Government Funding and Media Capture: A Call for Transparency

Government-funded media outlets, such as the BBC, ABC, and Yle, are globally praised for their unbiased, accurate coverage. However, in many countries, especially those in Eastern Europe or with highly politicized environments, governments have used funding to "capture" and manipulate the media to serve their objectives, particularly after unsuccessful democratic revolutions.[46] Some nations, like Brazil and Peru, have witnessed civil society demand greater transparency in government funding expenditures. Solutions-based, policy-focused advocacy becomes crucial in such environments to support autonomous journalism.[47]

Ironically, the government's control tool—money—could also break state media monopolies. Redirecting public funds to more media groups could revitalize independent journalism globally. This necessitates a significant shift in government practices and coordinated civil society advocacy. Governments must review regulations, ensuring openness and fair distribution of public funds in the media, despite their resistance to public disclosure. Civil society organizations and media exposure play a vital role in this advocacy, expanding discussions to include citizens concerned about tax allocation.

---

[44] D.W. Akademie, The rise and fall of public broadcasting in South Africa, available at: https://akademie.dw.com/en/the-rise-and-fall-of-public-broadcasting-in-south-africa/a-19206060 (last visited on: Dec. 15, 2023).

[45] The World, New South Africa TV network pushes pro-gov 't 'sunshine journalism', available at: https://theworld.org/stories/2013-09-09/new-south-africa-tv-network-pushes-pro-govt-sunshine-journalism (last visited on: Dec. 15, 2023).

[46] Journalism, 'Fake News' & Disinformation Handbook for Journalism Education and Training, UNESCO Series on Journalism Education available at: https://en.unesco.org/sites/default/files/journalism_fake_news_disinformation_print_friendly_0.pdf (last visited on: Dec. 15, 2023).

[47] Antoine Heuty, "The Role of Transparency and Civil Society in Managing Commodities for Inclusive Growth and Development", IMF elibrary, available at: https://www.elibrary.imf.org/display/book/9781616353797/ch018.xml.

To effect real change, three factors are essential:

1. Disclosure System:

Establish a public information system disclosing all government support for media, ensuring comprehensive expenditure reports are released.

2. Transparency in Funding Allocation:

Ensure transparency in discussions and fund allocation processes, allowing representative organizations a role in decision-making.

3. Engagement with Civil Society:

Engage civil society and the press industry significantly when developing or updating media regulations and promoting journalism initiatives, as public financing for reporting needs to be collaborative and reflective of the people's interests.

In an era where unbiased reporting is essential, public funding, built on transparency and citizen engagement, emerges as a sustainable solution for journalism initiatives.

10 Conclusion

The dynamic landscape of new media keeps evolving in new and perhaps unexpected ways that have major ramifications for democratic politics and government. The way political leaders communicate, how elections are contested, how government institutions, function, and how citizens engage have all been profoundly impacted by new media. New political media are modes of communication that enable the creation, publication, and exchange of political information via platforms and networks that allow for interaction and collaboration. The impact of new media on democratic governance and political activities is far-reaching. They have fundamentally transformed how government institutions, function and political leaders interact. They have altered the political media system and reshaped journalists' roles. They have reshaped the way elections are contested and citizens participate in politics.

When a society loses its free press, the foundational pillars supporting it inevitably crumble. The dominance of corporate media in conjunction with a dictatorial and totalitarian regime becomes glaringly evident. The strength of a thriving democracy lies in the autonomy of its media, yet the current state of the Indian media suggests a troubling allegiance to the ruling powers. Rather than serving as a watchdog, it has transformed into a supportive entity, actively participating in the propagation of divisive narratives and exacerbating the already charged political climate. Regrettably, the Indian media now functions as an instrument for political parties to manipulate public opinion. Breaking away from this perilous trajectory won't happen overnight, but it poses a genuine risk of perpetuating a destructive cycle.

In recent years, the media has been seen working in a political direction. There has been a growing concern about media promoting political agendas instead of reporting objectively without any bias. Such reporting by media outlets, known as "agenda-driven media," has serious ramifications on constitutional democracy. The media has lost its credibility in information dissemination. The corporate-driven media prioritize their interests, thereby making nexus with political parties to spread their agenda by using media as a tool. Agenda-driven media has multiple faces that work as per the directions they are receiving from their political bosses, like misinformation, selective reporting on certain issues, creating a skewed narrative that misrepresents the truth, reporting on unverified or false information, and sensationalism.

The media plays a vital role in shaping or changing public opinion about important issues. The transparency and accountability of media organizations need to be addressed so that the general public can restore trust in the media. Journalistic integrity must require several measures to promote transparency in funding and other interest relationships with corporate entities. The essence of democracy depends upon how accountability mechanisms are working to hold media watchdogs accountable for their reporting. This will encourage the general public to make prudent decisions about the credibility and reliability of news sources. Furthermore, there is a dire need to develop and enforce ethical standards to ensure media reporting is fair and balanced without any partiality. Such enforced standards are essential for promoting a healthy and vibrant democracy. To tackle this problem, there is an urgency to strengthen the regulatory framework governing media to prevent media entities from being influenced by political or corporate interests. It is desirable to make specific legislation that may play a positive role in ensuring freedom of speech and the press. By doing so, the general public becomes more discerning consumers of media and reduces the influence of agenda-driven media. By implementing these strategies, it is possible to uphold the integrity of journalism, safeguard democracy, and create a more informed and engaged citizenry.

Study on Anti-defection Law and Inner-Party Democracy with Specific Reference to India and the United Kingdom

B. Muthu Kumar

Abstract The inner-party democracy has become a buzz word not because of the recent election in the Indian National Congress to elect its president but due to the elections in the British Conservative Party to choose their leader after ousting Mr. Boris Johnson, the then Prime Minister of the United Kingdom. The Representation of the People Act, 1951, did not insist on internal elections, and there is no punishment for not conducting periodical elections by the political parties as per their party constitutional norms. The question here is 'can we adopt the U.K. model of inner-party elections?' or 'Do we need a unique system of party elections?' The Indian Constitution miserably failed to mention the party system and its functional aspects at the commencement of the Constitution, although we adopt party-led democracy. Unlike Britain, the members of a political party owe great allegiance and gratitude not only to their party leader but also to the heirs of their leader. The members never attempt to voice their dissent against their leader due to the threat of the anti-defection law, and it is difficult to expect them to criticize their own party leaders or party's policies during the inner-party elections. This article focuses on the political defections in India and how it is controlled through (mis)use of anti-defection law, in comparison with the major parliamentary democracies, particularly U.K. The analysis extends to the feasibility of adopting inner-party democracy with the reformed disqualification procedure of members under X Schedule of the Constitution as suggested by the Indian Supreme Court. This paper argues that the X Schedule in the Indian Constitution has been watered down and made almost ineffective due to selective approach of its use on defections by the speaker, and the ill-intended law acts as a stumbling blog to promote the inner-party democracy. It is suggested that the retention of anti-defection laws will not allow inner-party democracy to blossom in India.

Keywords Anti-defection law · Inner-party elections · Party system · Parliamentary democracy · Representation of Peoples Act · Parliamentary system

---

B. Muthu Kumar (✉)
Government Law College, Ramanathapuram, India
e-mail: drbmuthukumar@gmail.com

J. Aston et al. (eds.), *Comparative Law*, https://doi.org/10.1007/978-981-97-7815-7_22

1 Introduction

The success of a parliamentary democracy is influenced by the healthy party system, as the latter is a *sine qua non* for participative democracy.[1] We adopted the Westminster type of parliamentary system with representative democracy, and the survival of political parties is indispensable as the majority of the elected representatives belong to an organized political party.[2] Unfortunately, the nomenclature 'political party' has not been thought of by our founding fathers and did not find a place in our Basic Law. The Constitution (52nd Amendment) Act, 1985, gave a constitutional recognition to 'party system' through the introduction of anti-defection laws.[3] It is also significant to state that there is no comprehensive legislation dealing with the formation, function, and regulation of political parties in India. However, the Representation of Peoples Act, 1951, mandates the political parties to adhere to certain norms and requirements which are vital for the smooth conduct of a transparent electoral process, and failure of which results in derecognition and deregistration. Besides the legislative provisions, there are certain essential practices followed by them, such as organizing the party with administrative hierarchies in a democratic way and adhering to the model code of conduct as accepted through consensus during the elections.

However, the cases are piling up before the courts relating to the internal issues of different political parties and the courts are finding it difficult to resolve the factional rivalry as the anti-defection laws are interpreted without evolving any authoritative precedents to resolve the internal commotion of a political party. The most contemporary factional rivalry was the battle between Uddhav Thackeray and Shri. Eknath Shinde, the Maharashtra Chief Minister over 'who heads the 'real' Shiv sena?' and factional rivalry between Shri. Ajith Pawar, the Deputy Chief Minister of the Nationalist Congress Party (NCP), and the founder President of NCP, Shri. Sharad Pawar over 'who heads the 'real' NCP?'.[4] Similarly, Shri. Y.S. Jagan Mohan Reddy, the Chief Minister of Andhra Pradesh and the President of Yuvajana Shramika Rythu Congress Party (YSRCP), who has been elected as a party president for lifetime and this conduct obviously meant that the inner-party elections are never encouraged in India.[5] The Election Commission of India (ECI) in its guidelines requires the political parties to conduct inner-party elections for every 5 years to renew their leadership.[6] Nevertheless, it is just a guideline which needs to be followed at the time

---

[1] V. Sudhish Pai, Constitutional Supremacy: A Revisit—Essays On Constitutionalism, Rule of Law And Constitutional Adjudication 211 (2019).

[2] Kanhiya Lal Omar v. R.K. Trivedi, AIR 1986 SC 111.

[3] The X Schedule of the Indian Constitution and consequent amendments in Articles 102 and 191 of the Indian Constitution.

[4] Krishnadas Rajagopal, *SC to hear on Oct.13 Sharad Pawar camp's plea against Speaker*, THE HINDU (MADURAI), Oct. 10, 2023 at 8.

[5] Staff Reporter, *Andhra Pradesh CM Jagan unanimously elected as lifetime President of the YSR Congress*, THE HINDU (GUNTUR), July 09, 2022 at 5.

[6] The ECI issued guidelines requesting to conduct the inner party democracy at the time of registration of political party under Sect. 29A of the Representation of the People Act, 1951.

of application for recognition of political party and not a statutory obligation, and the ECI has no power to enforce it as it lacks the penal provisions,[7] and the Supreme Court categorically observed in the case of *Indian National Congress (I) v. Institute of Social Welfare*[8] that the ECI cannot derecognize a political party for breaching any undertakings made at the time of registration of the political party, which includes conducting internal elections. Thus, the absence of inner-party democracy, galore of hereditary politics, and factional rivalry after the demise of charismatic leader of the party costs leads to murky politics and affects the healthy competitive development politics both at the Centre and the state.

With this background, the author has brought to the light the significance of inner-party democracy and how a leader is chosen in a political party in the U.K. party system with the recent instance of Boris Johnson's exit as leader of the Conservation Party and election of Liz Truss with that of election of the President of All India Congress Committee (AICC) in India, and moreover, the paper brought the challenges in ensuring the inner-party democracy in India as the anti-defection law acts as a stumbling block. Hence, the author did a comparative study of anti-defection law in other major parliamentary democracies specifically focusing on U.K. and attempted to make reforms in X Schedule so as to ensure inner-party democracy, at least in major political parties that has a substantial vote bank.

2 Internal Democracy V. Dynastic Politics

Intra-party democracy is significant for the functioning and legitimacy of every political democratic system in which the political parties compete for power.[9] The National Commission to Review the Working of the Constitution (NCRWC) has categorically mentioned in its report that the 'inner-party democracy' is one of the immediate concerns in the structural and organizational reforms of the political party.[10] Of late, Congress M.P. Manish Tewari has introduced a private member's Bill in the Lok Sabha to regulate the operations of political parties by the ECI, so as to comply the directions of the ECI in conducting internal elections.[11] There are advantages and disadvantages in dynastic politics but the latter outweigh the former. The political inclusion in dynastic politics is miserably low as only few in the high echelons of society, either in terms of caste or sex or age occupy high positions in the party

---

[7] Editorial, *Internal democracy,* THE HINDU (MADURAI), Sep. 23, 2022 at 10.

[8] (2002) 5 SCC 685.

[9] Scarrow S.E, Political Parties and Democracy in Theoretical And Practical Perspectives: Implementing Intra-Party Democracy 3 (Washington: National Democratic Institute for International Affairs, 2005).

[10] NCRWC, Electoral Processes and Political Parties, para 4.14 on High Cost of Elections and Abuse of Money Power in Ministry of Law and Justice, *available at:* http://lawmin.nic.in/ncrwc/finalreport/v1ch4.htm.

[11] The Hindu Bureau, *Bill seeks EC role in parties' internal polling,* The Hindu (Madurai), Dec. 12, 2022 at 9.

through hereditary. The women and young people even from the affluent or forward society find it difficult to get into the politics.[12] In such circumstances, it is difficult to expect the downtrodden and disadvantaged people to enter into the political fray and the non-inclusion of substantial number of women representatives in the Parliament left the reservation for women in the legislature in limbo for many years. Furthermore, the non-representation of different communities in the higher post in the party eventually led to the mushrooming of caste-based political parties. Although the dynastic politics is a contentious issue during every election to target any political party which is intertwined with family politics, it has become a norm as people tend to tolerate it. The only way to reduce the dynastic politics is to conduct an intra-party election for every post periodically. Concerning the significance of inner-party elections, Shri. S.L. Shakhdher, the former Chief Election Commissioner, has remarked that 'Political parties make strong demands for the conduct of free and fair elections to legislative bodies, but choose to ignore the application of the same principles when it comes to the functioning of their own party'.[13] Invariably, the dynastic politics and autocratic authoritative leadership is found both in the national and regional parties, and unfortunately, the contemporary politics is increasingly witnessing the dynastic politics due to the mushrooming of many regional parties as India adopts federal and multi-party system.[14]

It is unsurprising about dynastic politics, as the data around the globe reveals that the members of the same family have been elected to the highest offices. Countries, such as U.S., Japan, Pakistan, Sri Lanka, the Philippines, Indonesia, and India, can be cited as an example for perpetual dynasticism.[15] On the other side, one person elect themselves as party supremo and appoint other party functionaries to meet out the conditions of the Election Commission without adhering to democratic ideals. There are numerous instances, where one person reigned the party till their death not allowing any election or conducting sham election to retain their leadership. In 2011, Ms. Mamata Banerjee was elected as Chairperson for Trinamool Congress; similarly, in 2014, AIADMK declared Ms. J. Jayalalithaa as permanent General Secretary, whereas Shri. Lalu Prasad declared himself as the President of RJD and reformed the office-bearers of the party.[16] This is the scenario happening in all the states, and the national parties are not an exception to it. The Indian National Congress has conducted the internal election to elect its President only in the year 2022, almost 22 years since its previous election held in the year 2000 after Election Commission of India (ECI) reminded several times with a deadline. The 137-year-old Congress

---

[12] Kanchan Chandra, *Democratic Dynasties—State, Party, and Family in Contemporary Indian Politics, in* Democratic Dynasties—State, Party, and Family in Contemporary Politics 51–52 (Kanchan Chandra).

[13] Bhanu Dhamija, *In Democratic India, why do we still have autocratic parties?* April 25, 2017, https://www.thequint.com/voices/blogs/no-inner-party-democracy-internal-elections-in-india#read-more.

[14] *Ibid.*

[15] Tish Sanghera, *BJP no less dynastic than Congress, Lok Sabha Data Shows*, March 29, 2019, https://www.indiaspend.com/bjp-no-less-dynastic-than-congress-lok-sabha-data-show/.

[16] Bhanu, *Supra* note 13.

Party had conducted elections only six times to choose its President, i.e., 1939, 1950, 1977, 1997, and 2000.[17] The Communist Party of India (Marxist), a non-believer of democratic principles, has chosen Shri. Somnath Chatterjee as the longest serving dynast.

The data analyzed by the researchers at Harvard University of the United States and the University of Mannheim of Germany through IndiaSpend revealed that the Bharatiya Janata Party (BJP) succumbs to dynastic politics similar to the INC, particularly in the lower rung of the party, where MLAs and MPs are from the same family. The data also revealed that 40 percent of the members were elected from the same constituency, invariably from different political parties, following their father, mother, or spouse, and accounted for nearly 40–50 years of successive generations in power in almost 10 consecutive durations of the Lok Sabha.[18] Further, in an interview with Kanchan Chandra,[19] Professor of Politics of New York University had revealed that the Indian political dynasties, which multiplied at a consistent rate in the last three Lok Sabha elections, i.e., 20% of all MPs in 2004, 30% in 2009, and around 22% in 2014, were dynasts and further remarked that there is an upper-caste bias in the Indian Politics as the biggest political parties, such as BJP and INC, are subjugated by the upper castes and support most upper-caste dynasties.[20]

3 Why Dynastic Politics—is it Inevitable in India?

The Indian electoral arena has a multitude political parties with different ideologies and structures both nationally and regionally. The ideologies are mainly based on religion or caste. Moreover, there is a deep interrelationship between caste-based and dynastic politics in every state. The caste-based political parties are dominated by the founder and their family as they are 'charismatic' personalities. The regional parties are predominantly patronage-based parties rather than power-dispersed parties.[21] The caste leader who helm the political party is considered as a matinee idol for the whole community as he is able to take the community's representation in getting reservation benefits or to raise voice against the Government for the community's interest. For instance, the Pattali Makkal Katchi (PMK) in Tamil Nadu is acting as a crusader of

[17] Outlook Web Desk, *A Look Back at History of Congress Presidential Elections as Party Awaits New Chief*, Oct. 16, 2022, https://www.outlookindia.com/national/congress-president-elections-history-of-six-congress-elections-news-230287, (last visited on Jan. 12, 2023).

[18] Sanghera, *Supra* note 15.

[19] Kanchan, *Supra* note 12.

[20] Ajaz Ashraf, Interview with Kanchan Chandra: The wide appeal of the BJP, Congress ends up benefitting upper-caste dynasties by default, March 25, 2019, *available at:* https://scroll.in/article/917320/interview-the-wide-appeal-of-the-bjp-congress-ends-up-benefiting-upper-caste-dynasties-by-default (last visited on Jan. 17, 2023).

[21] Vivek Mishra and Ambar Ghosh, *Dissecting the Evasiveness of Inner Party Democracy*, Liberal Studies Journal (June 30, 2019), *available at,* https://www.neliti.com/publications/321962/dissecting-the-evasiveness-of-inner-party-democracy-in-india (last visited on Oct. 18, 2023).

vanniyar community and able to get 10.5% reservation for the vanniyar community alone carving out of 20% in MBC criteria consisting of almost 41 communities in the State of Tamil Nadu by influencing the AIADMK regime in 2021, although it failed the constitutional test in the Hon'ble Supreme Court of India.[22]

The founding members and their kith and kin create a brand name not only to the party but also to themselves through mass media, eventually becoming a notable face to contest in elections and garner votes as the electorate are lured easily.[23] The empirical analysis of Francesca R. Jensenius found two obvious reasons for the dynastic politics in India; firstly, the economic and educational status of electorates did not play any role in electing candidates from political families as it is integral part of Indian Politics. The Indian traditional family system is unlike feudalism in the West and accepts the succession of family members through hereditary, which not only includes in the occupation, profession, or family business but also in public life. Secondly, the members of dynastic politics almost belong to royal families, who are sensitive to public sufferings rather than being with elite people. They act as a campaigner for the eradication of poverty and set an ideology to uplift social and educational status of the community people.[24]

On the other hand, the party and people look forward to the family dynast to take the ruins of the party if the party suffers due to lack of leadership and cohesion among the party members. For instance, the INC was rescued initially by Smt. Indira Gandhi after the demise of Pandit. Nehru as the latter did not declare the former as his political heir. Similarly, after the assassination of Smt. Indira Gandhi, the leadership of INC was unwillingly taken by Shri. Rajiv Gandhi and the heirship continues even to Smt. Sonia Gandhi, although she was not in active politics for almost eight years. A similar trend happened even in Tamil Nadu after the demise of Shri. M.G. Ramachandran, where Smt. Janaki Ammal has been brought as a political heir by a faction of AIADMK but it did not last long as the party lost in the election in the year 1989 and she withdrew from the politics and merged her party with Ms. J. Jayalalithaa's faction. Thus, there are numerous instances, where the people and party members have strong belief and confidence in the family dynasty as they carry their leader's legacy and act as a formidable competitors to their opposition parties.

The other major reason is the institutional weakness. The dominant members of the party who form the dynasty will make the party weak through centralization. The centralized tendency of the party leader, with the influence of power, will make him and his family members wealthier and to expand his family business both legally and illegally. The dominance of the dynastic leader will make the other members weak and meek, eventually surviving at the mercy of the leader. They never question the

---

[22] Pattali Makkal Katchi v. A. Mayileruperumal, (2023) 7 SCC 481.

[23] Nikhil Rampal, *Sunny Deol Join Politics: But do actors really perform well in Lok Sabha?* India Today, (March 26, 2019) *available at,* http://www.indiatoday.in/elections/lok-sabha-2019/story/actors-turned-politicians-flop-show-16th-lok-sabha-1487187-2019-03-26 (last visited on Oct. 16, 2023).

[24] Francesca R. Jensenius, *A sign of backwardness? Where dynastic leaders are elected in India, in* DEMOCRATIC Dynasties—State, Party, and Family in Contemporary Politics 102 (Kanchan Chandra).

leadership and be loyal to his command, not only to enjoy the pleasure of the post and power but to further the development of his dynastic politics in the region, where the member is powerful. Furthermore, if any member act against the leadership interests on dynastic politics or if they show any dissent on the decision of the leadership, he may be expelled from the party or get disqualified on the ground of anti-defection. On the contrary, a leader of the party may allow its members to follow dynastic politics in apprehension that they may split the party or defect with substantial members.[25] Thus, these are the ways and means that the dynastic politics is thriving and has become the norm in the Indian political arena.

4 Does Anti-defection Law is Obverse to Intra-Party Democracy?

It is a fact that dynastic politics is everywhere around the globe with varied reasons, even in the flourishing democracies of western countries. There are certain attempts made by the Law Commission of India to implement the intra-party democracy. The Fifteenth Law Commission headed by Shri. Justice B.P. Jeevan Reddy had submitted a report (170th report) on 'Reform of the Electoral Laws', wherein they briefly stated about the 'necessity for providing law relating to internal democracy within political parties'[26] and similarly, the Twentieth Law Commission headed by Shri. Justice A.P. Shah has submitted a report (255th report) titled 'Electoral Reforms',[27] under which chapter III has been devoted for the analyzation of 'Regulation of Political Parties and Inner-Party Democracy' particularly in comparative perspective. Thus, with the light of the above reports, it is pertinent to analyze the significance of internal democracy of parties with specific reference to anti-defection law.

5 Anti-defection Laws and its Requirement in Representative Democracy

The anti-defection law has been introduced in India to maintain discipline among the party cadres and to shun political defections and consequently the fall of governments. The law was contemplated by both the Congress and Janata Party in 1970s itself but could not materialize until it brought into force through the Constitution (52nd

[25] Kanchan, *Supra* note 12, at 38.

[26] Law Commission of India, Report on Reform of the Electoral Laws, 170, May 1999, *available at,* https://cdnbbsr.s3waas.gov.in/s3ca0daec69b5adc880fb464895726dbdf/uploads/2022/08/2,022,082,424.pdf.

[27] Law Commission of India, Report on Electoral Reforms, 255 (March 2015) *available at:* https://cdnbbsr.s3waas.gov.in/s3ca0daec69b5adc880fb464895726dbdf/uploads/2022/08/2022081635.pdf.

Amendment) Act, 1985, by the Rajiv Gandhi Congress Government, although it faced criticisms that it may undermine the democratic principles.[28] The anti-defection law contains three important features, such as:

a) It prescribes the grounds of disqualification for a member of the Parliament or State Legislative Assembly belonging to a political party under para (2) of the X Schedule under two modes: (1) voluntarily giving up of membership under whose symbol that the member has been elected; and (2) acting contrary to the direction of the party whip either to vote or abstain from voting in a particular way. Actually, the former mode has brought many litigations before the Court to determine 'what is voluntarily giving up of membership?' as the latter is forthright in determining the defections.[29]
b) It permits the legislators to defect as a separate group without facing disqualifications; however, it was criticized vehemently for permitting defections based on a group while disallowing the individual defections and considering them as illegal.[30] The bulk defections were removed through the amendment in 2003, wherein it discouraged the decision taken by the 1/3rd of the legislative members of the party to split from the parent party, thus making the anti-defection provisions very strict.[31] The Parliament tightened the anti-defection laws by imposing certain detrimental effect to the members who faced disqualification under the anti-defection laws. The Constitution (91st Amendment) Act, 2003, inserted a new clause under Articles 75 and 164 stipulating that a disqualified member is not entitled to be appointed as a Minister from the date of disqualification to the term of the expiry of the house or till (s)he is re-elected after contesting any election, whichever is earlier. Similarly, Article 361B has been added to bar the disqualified member from enjoying any rewarding political post from the date of disqualification to the term of expiry of the house or till (s)he is re-elected after contesting any election, whichever is earlier. However, these provisions have created no change in curbing the unprincipled defections of the legislators.
c) Presently, the only exemption under the Tenth Schedule is the merging of the parties with the consent of a 2/3rd majority of the legislative members of the original political party, as laid down under para 4 to avoid disqualification and not splitting up the party. The recent split of shiv sena leads to challenging questions in this provision, such as 'who is the original political party and whether the 2/3rd legislative members can be viewed as a dissident of a political party or an original political party?' Of late, the Goa Bench of the Bombay High Court in

---

[28] Darsan Guruvayurappan, *Rethinking Defection: An Analysis of Anti-defection Laws in India*, Parliamentary Affiars, 1.

[29] K. Venkataramanan, *Has the anti-defection law failed in India?* The Hindu (Madurai), June 26, 2022 at 14.

[30] V.S. Rama Devi and S.K. Mendiratta, How India Votes: Election Laws, Practice and Procedure 1167 (2014).

[31] The Constitution (91st Amendment) Act, 2003.

the case of *Girish Chodankar v. The Speaker, Goa State Legislative Assembly*[32] held that the merger of 2/3rd legislative members of a political party is deemed to be the merger of the original party. Ironically, the 2/3rd legislative members belong to Goa Pradesh Congress Committee (GPCC) which is a state unit of the Indian National Congress (INC). Thus, can we assume from the judgment of the High Court that the legal fiction 'deemed merger' of a political party (INC) with that of the BJP although there is no actual merger? However, the Constitution Bench of the Supreme Court in the case of *Subhash Desai v. Principal Secretary, Governor of Maharashtra and Others*[33] held that the speaker shall recognize the whip and the leader of the shiv sena party after conducting an inquiry based on the principle that there is a link between the legislative party and political party. The legislative party would have obtained votes based on the general good faith of the people in its political party. The members after being elected from the legislative party cannot suddenly cede away from the political party to which they belong to.

d) It mandates the chairperson of the house to decide on the defection and disqualification of a defected member. The role of the chairperson in deciding the petition of disqualification of members on the grounds of anti-defection law is a perennial problem for the constitutional courts to adjudicate, as the chairperson(s) still show their loyalty and affinity to the party attached with and eventually, the decision tends to unfair, partial, and influenced. It is evident from the practices of the chairperson(s) that their decisions are either in 'hot haste' without following the principles of natural justice or at a 'snail's pace' in order to please the ruling helm.

The NCRWC proposed that the ECI should be vested with the power to decide the disqualification on the ground of defection instead of the chairperson of a house.[34] However, the Law Commission of India, in its 255th report, recommended that the President and the Governor should decide the question of disqualification on the grounds mandated under X Schedule for the members of the Parliament and the State Legislatures, respectively, based on the opinion of the ECI, which is similar to the Office of Profit.[35] The strict anti-defection law, although ambitious, failed in its objective as defections continue unabated; nonetheless, the laws are used as a counterproductive as defected legislators are able to retain their constituency with a different party ticket in the bye-election besides earning personal gains. The instances are many and one such was the nineteen legislators out of twenty-two were re-elected from the BJP ticket in March 2020 after they defected from the Congress in the State of Madhya Pradesh. The research conducted by the National Elections Studies through Lokniti-CSDS found that the large majority of Indian voters vote for the party and

[32] The Hon'ble High Court of Bombay (Panaji Bench) Writ Petition No. 1228 of 2021 dated February 24, 2022.

[33] Writ Petition (C) No. 493 of 2022 dated May 11, 2023; 2023 SCC Online SC 607.

[34] NCRWC, *Supra* note 10, para 4.18.

[35] LCR 255th Report, *Supra* note 27.

not for the candidate.[36] Thus, defection does matter only to political parties and not for the Indian voters.

The critics of the anti-defection law observe that it acts as an antithesis to representative democracy as it makes a legislator—a mere agent of a party and not a delegate representing their constituency. The legislators sail along with the party's agenda and policies, eventually defending the Bills emanates from the party leadership although it affects the people of their constituency.[37] Moreover, the anti-defection laws are used to enslave the legislative members from expressing their opinions freely both on the party agenda and governmental policies. It is pertinent to mention that the X Schedule is not born perfect, which is evident from the statement made by the former Prime Minister—Shri. Rajiv Gandhi, 'There are lots of grey areas in the Bill... There will be shortcomings in this Bill but as we see and identify those shortcomings, we will try to overcome them'.[38] This statement is vividly true as the challenges of anti-defection law is growing exponentially due to different factual matrixes and the spirit of the law shows that the objective to sustain the stability of the government is a failed phenomenon, and it is a high time to reexamine the law to make an accountable government rather than a stable government, which is essential in a representative democracy.

6 The Essence of Time: Judicial Intervention *Vis-À-Vis* Anti-Defection Law

The Chairperson, i.e., the Speaker of the House, in the capacity of a tribunal, has the authority to decide on the petition relating to the disqualification of members under the Tenth Schedule. The Constitution has reposed much confidence on the Office of the Speaker to perform his constitutional role in a neutral and unbiased manner and allows the speaker to resign from their political party once they adorn the position of a Speaker in the House. However, till date, no speaker has resigned from the party in which they are affiliated with. The requirement of impartiality is the basic tenets of a speaker which is being followed as a Constitutional Convention.[39] The Speaker has to observe this convention to glorify the spirit of the Constitution either as a paramount constitutional duty or due to apprehension of judicial intervention.[40] Nonetheless, many past instances reveal that the Speaker neither concerned about his constitutional obligation nor bothered about the judicial intervention as his

[36] Sanjay Kumar, *Why is defection a non-issue for voters?* The Hindu (Madurai), July 4, 2022 at 7.

[37] M.R. Madhavan, *The absurdity of the anti-defection law*, The Hindu (Madurai), February 26, 2021 at 6.

[38] P.D.T. Achary, *Do not weaken the anti-defection law*, The Hindu (Madurai), July 01, 2022 at 10.

[39] Harsimran Kalra, *Decisional Analysis and the Role of the Speaker,* 1 The Hindu Centre for Politics and Public Policy (2013), available at, (accessed 10 July 2020.

[40] Matthew Laban, *More Westminster than Westminster? The Office of Speaker across the Commonwealth* 20 (2) The Journal of Legislative Studies 143 (2014).

actions were in tune with the ruling dispensation. A judicial intervention is warranted when the Speaker's decision not only suffers from jurisdictional errors, such as mala fides, perversity, violation of constitutional mandate, and non-compliance with the principles of natural justice,[41] but also fails to exercise the jurisdiction on time.[42]

Furthermore, it is also inevitable for the judiciary to answer certain complex constitutional questions that arose due to innovative methods founded by our elected representatives to circumvent the anti-defection law. In *Shrimanth Balasaheb Patil v. Karnataka Legislative Assembly*,[43] the Supreme Court held that the Speaker has no option but to accept the resignation of a member when it is tendered voluntarily. The Court also held that the Speaker shall not disqualify any member for any duration except as mentioned under Articles 75(1-B), 164(1-B) & 361B of the Constitution or till the end of the legislative term. Of late, the Constitution Bench of the Supreme Court[44] held that the Governor shall act in lieu of Article 174 *sans* the aid and advice of Council of Ministers, if the Speaker and the Government attempt to defeat a no-confidence motion by adjourning the House to prevent voting and not recommending the Governor to convene the session. Further, the Court referred a question to the Constitution Bench of 7 Judges that 'Whether the Speaker can decide the disqualification petition of members under Tenth Schedule when a no-confidence motion is pending against him?' as in the *Nabam Rebia & Bamang Felix v. Deputy Speaker, Arunachal Pradesh Legislative Assembly*,[45] the Court held that the Speaker shall not decide the disqualification of members till the no-confidence motion against the Speaker is disposed of. Initially, the Supreme Court took a stance in the case of *Kihoto Hollohan v. Zachillhu*[46] that the judicial review over speaker's decision is available only after the Speaker's determination on disqualification petitions and not at an intermediary stage of the proceedings. Nevertheless, the above-said Constitution Bench reasoning has been diluted in many cases to do complete justice to the party aggrieved.

The Supreme Court has invoked Article 142 in the case of *Keisham Meghachandra Singh v. Hon'ble Speaker Manipur Legislative Assembly and Others*,[47] wherein 13 disqualification petitions were filed before the Hon'ble Speaker of the Manipur Legislative Assembly in April 2017. However, no stone was left unturned till the appellant approached the Supreme Court in 2020. The Supreme Court has granted one month time through its Order dated January 21, 2020,[48] but the Hon'ble Speaker has not relented, which eventually forced the Supreme Court to pass interim Order by invoking its extra ordinary power to dispense complete justice in the extra ordinary

[41] Kihoto Hollohan v. Zachillhu, 1992 Supp (2) SCC 651.

[42] Rajendra Singh Rana v. Swami Prasad Maurya, (2007) 4 SCC 270.

[43] (2020) 2 SCC 595.

[44] Subhash, *Supra* note 36.

[45] (2016) 8 SCC 1.

[46] 1992 Supp (2) SCC 651.

[47] Miscellaneous Application No. 820/2020 in Civil Appeal No. 547/2020 dated March 18, 2020.

[48] Keisham Meghachandra Singh v. The Hon'ble Speaker, Manipur Legislative Assembly & Others, Civil Appeal No. 547/2020.

circumstances of the case, restraining respondent 3, Shri. Thounaojam Shyamkumar from entering the Manipur Legislative Assembly and relieving him from the cabinet minister. In consequent to the interim Order, the Hon'ble Speaker, Shri. Y. Khemchand Singh, has sprung into action and disqualified him for defection on March 20, 2020.[49] Similarly, the Supreme Court has fixed a deadline to Maharashtra Assembly Speaker to decide 34 disqualification petitions in 'sena v. sena' dispute by December 31, 2023, and nine in Ajith Pawar faction of NCP by January 31, 2024, after rendering many opportunities.[50] Nevertheless, it is to be mentioned that in July 2021, the Supreme Court refrained from making any guidelines to fix time limits for both the speakers of the Parliament and the State Legislative Assemblies to decide the disqualification petitions against the MPs and MLAs under the X Schedule.[51] Thus, the Court now and then is applying the purposeful interpretation to make the anti-defection law workable amidst the clutter created by our honorable legislative members to make it unworkable.

7 Anti-defection Laws and Intra-Party Democracy—Experiences in Other Jurisdictions

The inaction of the speaker based on their political loyalties and unabated defections, with delaying tactics either through procedural infirmities or raising a question of law for judicial determination, makes the anti-defection law, a mockery of legislation. There are different voices for and against the anti-defection law and its implementation in India. Some suggest that the anti-defection law should be strengthened, and some believe that it enslaves members to their party line, denying freedom of expression. In these circumstances, it is inevitable to compare with the foreign jurisdictions on maintaining the stability of the Government by curbing the unethical political defections and to strengthen the representative democracy through the encouragement of internal democracy. There are certain developed democracies, such as U.S., Japan, Canada, Australia, and New Zealand, which allow their members to freely vote in accordance with their best judgment on governmental policies not at the cost of their legislative membership.[52] It is significant to mention that the working of representative democracy in U.S. *vis-à-vis* liberty of members in casting their votes without any legal obligations. Of late, seven members of republican party voted in the Senate to impeach its own party man and leader, Mr. Donald Trump—the former President of

[49] Live Law News Network, *After SC Intervention, Manipur Assembly Speaker Disqualifies MLA Th Shyamkumar for Defection,* March 28, 2020, *available at,* https://www.livelaw.in/top-stories/manipur-assembly-speaker-disqualifies-mla-th-shyamkumar-for-defection-154455?infinitescroll=1.

[50] Krishnadas Rajagopal, *SC puts Maharashtra Speaker on deadline over defection pleas,* The Hindu (Madurai), Oct. 31, 2023, at 1 & 8.

[51] Legal Correspondent, *Cannot fix time limit in defection pleas, says SC,* The Hindu (Madurai), July 2, 2021, at 1.

[52] Christopher J. Kam, Party Discipline and Parliamentary Politics 1–15 (2009).

the United States.[53] Likewise, there are many democracies which provide complete freedom to the legislative members although they face challenges of political defections and toppling the Government. In this context, it is worth to mention the work of G.C. Malhotra titled 'Anti-defection law in India and the Commonwealth'[54] The work comprises 65 countries including the commonwealth nations and their experiences of political defection and the law relating to it.[55] The author has confined only with the U.K. system as the Westminster model of Parliamentary system is considered as the mother of all Parliaments, wherein India, a commonwealth nation, follow suit the British Parliamentary conventions. At the Constituent Assembly, Dr. B.R. Ambedkar has differentiated between the presidential and parliamentary form of government, as the former had higher stability but lower accountability by citing the election and removal of U.S. President, whereas the latter ensures greater accountability as the Government is answerable on daily basis, nonetheless, less stability as it can be toppled when they are reduced as a minority in the House of the People. The constitutional framers adopted the parliamentary model to make the Government accountable rather than stable.[56]

In the U.K., switching over the party is not uncommon, and they are called 'cross benchers', which is a great concern only to the political party, and the functioning of the House of Commons is never affected. At times, the defection cost the government to lose its majority. For instance, in May 1976, the Labour Party has lost its majority due to defection of a member besides the defeat in the bye-elections.[57] The legislators of both the houses of the U.K. cannot be deprived of their seats even if they defect or expelled from the party, nevertheless, the only control that the party can exercise over its members are denying the cabinet post or expel from the party for defection.[58] The members enjoy their legislative seat either as an independent member or newly attached political party.[59]

The British model of inner elections in choosing their prime minister is yet another example that India can adopt. The recent ousting of the British Conservative Party, Mr. Boris Johnson shows the importance of elected representatives in choosing their leader and the leader's inability to maintain the confidence of their own partymen. The strong reason behind the member's independence was that they are not chosen by the party leadership but rather selected by the party of the local constituency to contest the election. However, in India, it is a reverse phenomenon, where party leader selects the candidates based on their loyalty to the leader. The U.K. constitutional system

[53] Chakshu Roy, The Anti-Defection Law That Does Not Aid Stability, *The India Forum*, Oct. 5, 2022, *available at:* https://prsindia.org/articles-by-prs-team/the-anti-defection-law-that-does-not-aid-stability (last visited on Jan. 28, 2023).

[54] G.C. Malhotra, Anti-Defection Law in India and the Commonwealth (2005). The book has been published for the Lok Sabha Secretariat under Rule 182 of the Rules of Procedure and Conduct of Business in Lok Sabha.

[55] *Ibid.*, at 91.

[56] Madhavan, *Supra* note 37.

[57] Malhotra, *Supra* note 54, at 68.

[58] Darsan, *Supra* note 28, at 2.

[59] Malhotra, *Supra* note 54, at 69.

is the oldest as well as evolving. The practice of choosing a leader from the elected representatives has taken its origin when individual conservative MPs wrote to the 1922 committee expressing their dissatisfaction on their leader and to initiate a no-confidence motion to preserve the party's electoral advances through new headship. A system which evolved since 1922 is a norm now, which enables a ruling party to seek an alternate leadership through a fresh mandate in the Parliamentary party by mobilizing the numerical strength of 15% of the party's M.P. against the performance of the incumbent leadership.[60] The U.K. practice not only strengthens the internal and representative democracy but also avoids the despotic persons holding high positions both in the party and the government. Thus, the Indian legal system has to undergo certain modifications to adopt the practices of the U.K.

8 The Way Forward

The inner-party democracy is indirectly proportional to dynastic politics in India. It is evident from the above discussion that the inner-party democracy is a myth as long as we follow dynastic politics. Firstly, the existing legal regime, i.e., anti-defection laws, is impeding the elected members from expressing their opinions in a free and transparent manner, as they may lose the faith of party leadership, ultimately depriving them of the coveted party post or ministerial berth in the cabinet. The Courts are acting as a watchdog of the anti-defection law, instead of the speaker, who adorns a political color contrary to the constitutional trust expecting him as a neutral person.[61] The opposition parties banking on the judiciary to enforce the anti-defection law for each and every defection not only entangles the Court in a factional rivalry of a political party but also put the Court in great embarrassment when their orders are not respected by the Speaker of the House. It is saddening to observe that the people's acceptance of the unprincipled defection of their representative and their re-election from the same constituency under different party ticket, which they hail it as 'Chanakya Neethi'. Any attempt to strengthen the anti-defection law is a sheer waste of time, instead it can be scrapped as it miserably failed to curb the menace of unethical political defections. The stability of the government is a political problem, which is not appropriate to address it through legal means. The party members can be kept intact either by the party ideology or ensuring guaranteed positions based on their skills and achievements, which shall be accomplished only through democratic means, i.e., conduct of periodical internal elections. The empowerment of legislators begins when they take part in the transparent decision-making process within the party through a fair and open internal election, which alone ensures a stable government curbing the defections. The Constitution is silent on the electoral conduct of the political parties in India, unlike in Germany, Spain, and Portugal, wherein they have

---

[60] Shourya Dasgupta, *No inner-party democracy,* The Hindu (Madurai), July 20, 2022 at 8.

[61] S. Y. Quraishi, *When defection is a mere detour for an MLA*, The Hindu (Madurai), Jan. 3, 2020, at 8.

provided constitutional regulations on party actions, including their philosophy and ideology. Similarly, there is no comprehensive legislation to deal with the internal elections. Thus, it is high time for the Parliament to enact a specific legislation for regulating the party activities including its ideology and aim of political association. The new Act should contain a transparent procedure in conducting internal elections only for Registered Recognised Political Parties (RRPP) since the internal elections for all political parties including the Registered Unrecognized Political Parties (RUPP) is beyond reality. The internal elections should be conducted to select the party office-bearers to the taluk and district levels by the party itself. However, the office-bearers selected at the state level should be monitored by the State Election Commission. The non-compliance of statutory obligations should lead to penalty, and the same may increase each day, ultimately leading to the derecognition of party and symbol for continued violations. The periodic internal elections will control the dynastic politics and check the criminalization of politics, which will eventually strengthen the party system and representative democracy in our country.

Application of Artificial Intelligence in the Healthcare Sector: A Critical Analysis

Rajesh Kumar, Kanchal Gupta, and Rupendra Singh

Abstract Artificial intelligence (AI) is the term used to describe the creation of computer systems that are capable of tasks that normally require human intelligence. The tasks encompassed in this domain are acquiring knowledge, logical thinking, finding solutions to problems, interpreting sensory information, and comprehending language. The incorporation of artificial intelligence (AI) into several industries offers numerous benefits, fundamentally transforming the framework of contemporary commercial operations. AI systems have the capability to mechanize monotonous and laborious jobs, enabling firms to optimize procedures, diminish operational expenses, and augment overall efficiency. Predictive analytics, a component of artificial intelligence (AI), enables enterprises to make more informed decisions by forecasting trends, anticipating maintenance requirements, and optimizing resource allocation. The integration of artificial intelligence (AI) in the healthcare sector, although offering significant advantages, presents a series of legal obstacles that require meticulous examination. AI is utilized in health care for diagnostic purposes, creating individualized treatment programs and facilitating drug discovery. Artificial intelligence (AI) and robotics are currently employed in both surgical and clinical environments to assist healthcare professionals and improve patient care. Hospitals and clinics are currently utilizing robots for a broader spectrum of duties in order to minimize the risk of exposure to viruses amidst the COVID-19 epidemic. On the other side, the implementation of technology in health care pertains to the confidentiality challenges and protection of patient data. The extensive quantities of confidential patient data handled by AI systems prompt concerns regarding adherence to data protection regulations, such as the Health Insurance Portability and Accountability Act (HIPAA) in the United States or the General Data Protection

R. Kumar · K. Gupta
School of Law, UPES, Dehradun, India
e-mail: rajesh.k@ddn.upes.ac.in

K. Gupta
e-mail: kgupta@ddn.upes.ac.in

R. Singh (✉)
Amity Law School, Noida, India
e-mail: rsingh22@amity.edu

J. Aston et al. (eds.), *Comparative Law*, https://doi.org/10.1007/978-981-97-7815-7_23

Regulation (GDPR) in the European Union. Fixing liabilities for the accountability of errors in diagnosing patients and malfunctions of AI-based medical devices is the most critical challenge for the global legal system. The absence of standardized legal frameworks for AI in health care exacerbates the situation, as current legislation may not adequately include the distinct issues presented by new technologies. This study examines the current legislation and regulations pertaining to artificial intelligence in the European Union (EU) and the United States (US). The absence of comprehensive AI legislation in India has created a significant gap, giving rise to worries about the ethical, legal, and societal consequences of AI implementation. In light of this, the researchers, after analyzing the current legal position of India and comparing it with the European Union (EU) and the United States (US). After this, the researchers proposed the good practices that India need to adopt and incorporate in the existing legal framework.

Keywords Artificial Intelligence · Ethics · Health care · Robotics · Regulation · EU · US · India

1 Introduction

Healthcare systems globally encounter substantial obstacles in attaining the "quadruple purpose" for health care: enhancing population health, improving patient care experience, enhancing caregiver experience, and reducing the escalating cost of care.[1,2] Aging populations, an increase in the prevalence of chronic illnesses, and rising healthcare expenses worldwide present a challenge for regulators, payers, providers, and governments to innovate and change healthcare delivery methods. Furthermore, due to the worldwide pandemic, healthcare systems are now facing the challenge of delivering effective, high-quality treatment and transforming care on a large scale by utilizing real-world data insights in patient care.

Utilizing technology and artificial intelligence (AI) in health care can help tackle supply and demand concerns. The growing accessibility of diverse types of data, such as genomics, economic, demographic, clinical, and phenotypic, combined with advancements in mobile technology, the Internet of Things (IoT), computing capabilities, and data security, indicates a significant shift toward the integration of health care and technology. This convergence is expected to revolutionize healthcare delivery models through AI-enhanced healthcare systems.

The healthcare industry is in the midst of a transformation. The causes of this revolution are rising total healthcare costs and a growing lack of healthcare experts. As a

---

[1] Donald M. Berwick, Thomas W. Nolan and John Whittington, "The triple aim: care, health, and cost," 27 *Health affairs (Project Hope)* 759–69 (2008).

[2] Thomas Bodenheimer and Christine Sinsky, "From triple to quadruple aim: care of the patient requires care of the provider," 12 *Annals of family medicine* 573–6 (2014).

result, the healthcare industry is looking to implement new information technology-based solutions and processes that can cut costs and provide solutions to these rising difficulties.

Healthcare systems around the world face huge issues, including a lack of access, high costs, waste, and an older population. Pandemics like the coronavirus (COVID-19) put a strain on healthcare systems, resulting in a lack of protective equipment, insufficient or erroneous diagnostic tests, overworked physicians, and a lack of information exchange, to mention a few consequences.[3,4] More crucially, a healthcare catastrophe like COVID-19 or the development of the human immunodeficiency virus (HIV) in the 1980s exposes the stark reality of our healthcare systems' flaws. As healthcare crises exacerbate current difficulties, we can reinvent and actualize systems of care and back-office health systems, such as inequitable healthcare access, that there are not enough on-demand healthcare services, high costs, and a lack of price transparency.[5] Technological breakthroughs are being adopted slowly. Burnout among healthcare practitioners is a result of physicians' incapacity to keep up with the latest breakthroughs in medicine due to the large amount of data to be assimilated.

This paper is organized as follows. Section 2 discusses the literature review part. Section 3 elaborates on the methodology. Section 4 presents bibliometric analysis and content analysis part. Section 5 describes the global market of artificial intelligence and awareness. Section 6 presents the concept of AI and its application. Section 7 presents different challenges after implementing AI in healthcare sector. Section 8 concludes the chapter.

1.1 Background of the Study

Recently, AI techniques have sent vast waves across health care, even fueling an active discussion of whether AI doctors will eventually replace human physicians in the future. We believe that human physicians will not be replaced by machines in the foreseeable future, but AI can definitely assist physicians to make better clinical decisions or even replace human judgment in certain functional areas of health care (e.g., radiology). The increasing availability of healthcare data and rapid development of big data analytic methods has made possible the recent successful applications of AI in health care. Guided by relevant clinical questions, powerful AI techniques can

[3] Neil Greenberg et al., "Managing mental health challenges faced by healthcare workers during covid-19 pandemic," 368 *BMJ (Clinical research ed.)* (2020).

[4] Androula Pavli, Maria Theodoridou and Helena C. Maltezou, "Post-COVID Syndrome: Incidence, Clinical Spectrum, and Challenges for Primary Healthcare Professionals," 52 *Archives of medical research* 575–81 (2021).

[5] Winnie T. Maphumulo and Busisiwe R. Bhengu, "Challenges of quality improvement in the healthcare of South Africa post-apartheid: A critical review," 42 *Curationis* (2019).

unlock clinically relevant information hidden in the massive amount of data, which in turn can assist clinical decision-making.[6]

2 Literature Review

Artificial intellect (AI) is the replication of human intellect in machines, such as computers or robots, that are designed to imitate cognitive abilities like learning and problem-solving often associated with human minds. Artificial intelligence, machine learning, and deep learning are currently trendy terms that are widely used. Machine learning involves algorithms designed for tasks like regression, grouping, etc., which must be trained using data. Increasing the amount of data you/user feed into your algorithm enhances its performance. Deep learning is a nascent branch of artificial intelligence that relies on artificial neural networks. Deep learning algorithms necessitate data to acquire the ability to accomplish problems.

As AI-based technologies become more interwoven into daily life, utilizing them will be essential for every enterprise.[7,8] Despite the significant advancements of deep learning in addressing AI challenges over the years, companies must take into account the computational expenses associated with training algorithms on large datasets.[9]

AI-based technologies are being integrated into our daily lives.[10] For instance, the AI speaker "Aria," introduced by SK Telecom from South Korea, is a sophisticated voice-controlled device. Aria has the capability to place emergency calls in scenarios where the user is unable to utilize other devices due to accidents, physical disabilities, or specific circumstances. When an elderly individual falls and requests assistance from Aria, she contacts the care center, assigned family member for emergencies, or ADT Caps, a security platform offering machine security, personal guards, and security services in South Korea. If the center confirms an emergency, it will notify 119, the emergency call number in South Korea. This assistance has already led to the rescue of several elderly individuals who reside by themselves. Aria can also serve as a culinary assistant. When the customer requests assistance with a salmon recipe by saying, "Aria, please help me with a salmon recipe," Aria will provide detailed guidance through each stage of the dish. Aria can also help with personal budget management. Aria may recommend the most suitable credit card based on interest

[6] Travis B. Murdoch and Allan S. Detsky, "The inevitable application of big data to health care," 309 *JAMA* 1351–2 (2013).

[7] Don Hee Lee, "Strategies for technology-driven service encounters for patient experience satisfaction in hospitals," 137 *Technological Forecasting and Social Change* 118–27 (2018).

[8] Don Hee Lee, "Effects of key value co-creation elements in the healthcare system: focusing on technology applications," 13 *Service Business* 389–417 (2019).

[9] Yann Lecun, Yoshua Bengio and Geoffrey Hinton, "Deep learning," 521 *Nature 2015 521:7553* 436–44 (2015).

[10] Sang M. Lee and Seongbae Lim, "LIVING INNOVATION: From Value Creation to the Greater Good" *Living Innovation: From Value Creation to the Greater Good* 1–148 (2018).

rates and yearly fees when prompted by the user. Additionally, Aria can remind the user of upcoming credit card payment due dates for a specific month.

As AI-based technologies become more interwoven into daily life, utilizing these technologies will be essential for every enterprise.[11,12] Consumers in the digital age are increasingly seeking unique, personalized, and prompt services from smart mobile apps and gadgets, while still prioritizing security and flexibility. It is crucial to examine real-world examples of how healthcare organizations are currently using AI for patient care and operational management. This analysis should also consider the necessary regulations, responsibilities, and support systems required for advanced AI applications, such as ethics, training programs, and consulting services.

3 Review Methodology

Bibliometric analysis and systematic literature review (SLR) are used in the comprehensive review investigation. Scientific data can be examined using bibliometric analysis, a widely used and rigorous method. An important methodology in fields like public policy research and the health sciences, on the other hand, is structural logic regression. The researcher used materials obtained from Springer, PubMed, Web of Science, IEEE, and Scopus to conduct the search. The results were presented in a logical order.

For the literature review process and selection of relevant papers for completing this study, the author used VOSviewer Software.[13] VOSviewer helped in finding the most cited papers, top authors related to the area of the work, and the contribution of countries in the immediate field of work.

From 2010 through 2022, the published research spans twelve years. For further analysis, the databases were filtered by kind of publication (review, research, and journal-published), as well as excluding items that were already published. On average, there are 8264 publications produced in the fields of health care, legal, and technical growth (Scopus database).

The authors chose three important keywords for their research: Artificial intelligence, "health care," and "legal challenges." The database returned around 15,706 items when those keywords were entered into the search engine. VOSviewer was used by the researcher to reduce the scope of the investigation and locate the most relevant documents. VOSviewer returned 2000 results after using and importing all of the papers. The author has utilized these 2000 publications in his research because they have received a lot of citations.

---

[11] Sang M. Lee, DonHee Lee and Youn Sung Kim, "The quality management ecosystem for predictive maintenance in the Industry 4.0 era," 5 *International Journal of Quality Innovation 2019 5:1* 1–11 (2019).

[12] Don Hee Lee, "Strategies for technology-driven service encounters for patient experience satisfaction in hospitals," 137 *Technological Forecasting and Social Change* 118–27 (2018).

[13] "VOSviewer—Visualizing scientific landscapes,"*available at*: https://www.vosviewer.com/ (last visited March 16, 2024).

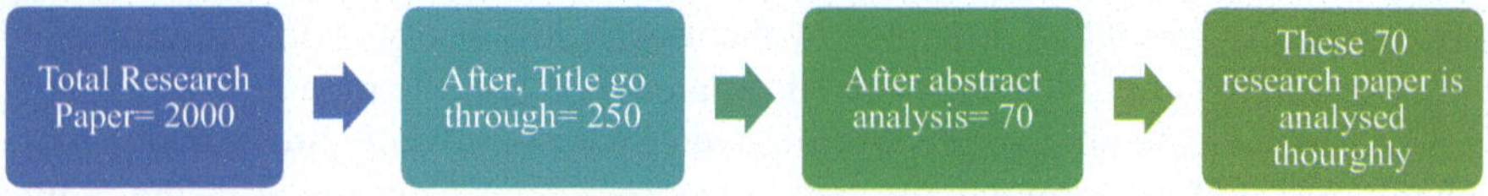

Fig. 1 Screening process

Figure 1 shows the author's four-step screening process after reaching 70 papers that have been thoroughly evaluated and on the basis of which the author finished his research.

4 The Bibliometric Analysis

4.1 The Data

As a whole, China has the world's most active healthcare system. To set a standard for other countries in the healthcare industry, it has been taking steps to improve the healthcare system and make it more advanced. Today, the top 10 countries' contributions to healthcare sector growth and development are extraordinary. Fourth place goes to India, whose work has been quoted and referenced 349 times in Table 1

In addition, the collaborative work between India's contribution to the research of the healthcare sector and that of other nations is 21, indicating that India is attempting to adopt the best practices essential for the development of the healthcare industry.

This cluster demonstrates how assiduously the Indian healthcare industry is attempting to adopt the new trends, and artificial intelligence plays a very important role in giving a new shape in the healthcare sector (Fig. 2). Numerous technologies are currently being utilized like deep learning, machine learning, telemedicine, that

Table 1 Work done by countries

Country	Citations	Link strength
United States	53,275	705
United Kingdom	24,920	601
China	23,007	325
India	19,642	349
Australia	11,665	290
Italy	9832	291
South Korea	8004	145
Canada	7911	249
Saudi Arabia	5794	220
Singapore	5658	194

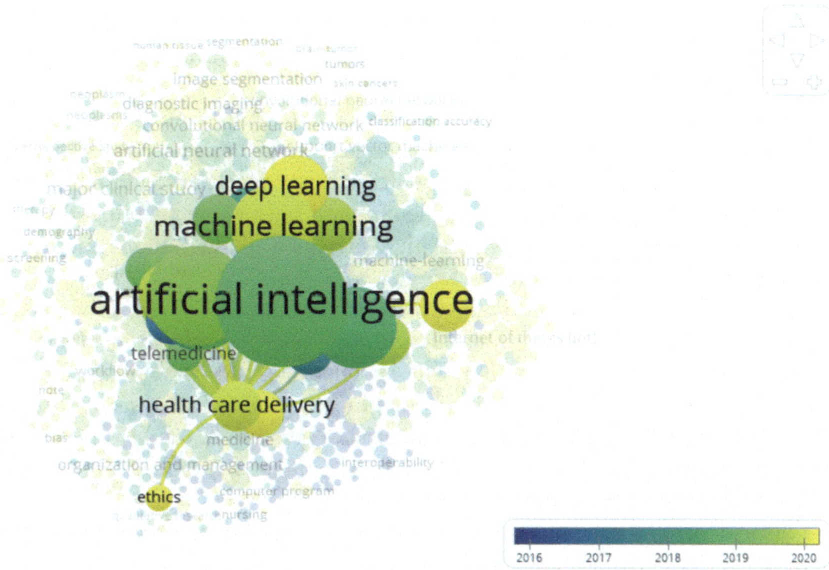

Fig. 2 Healthcare working with artificial intelligence

are applied for the expansion of the healthcare industry. The artificial intelligence is the most widely recognized and utilized technology to better the healthcare system. The IT industry focuses mostly on artificial intelligence technology deployment in order to provide numerous apps and devices for usage in the healthcare industry. The link strength and frequency indicate that other technologies readily embrace AI for fusion and creating healthcare applications (Fig. 2).

4.2 Content Analysis

Top 70 cited papers from the bibliometric analysis were used and reviewed to understand the research that has been done in the implementation of artificial intelligence in the health care. AI technology is utilized by the majority of healthcare devices, including smart diagnostic systems, patient trackers, smart watches, badges, and other healthcare gadgets. Artificial intelligence is referred to as AI. The industry is expanding, and there is a high demand for AI workers. Explore AI further and envision the future.[14] AI plays a significant role in advancing the healthcare industry and making it easier to enhance patient care and improve the working environment. It enables doctors and patients to connect electronically for information exchange and treatment facilitation. To comprehend the operation of IoT and its application

[14] "AI in Health Care: Applications, Benefits, and Examples," *Coursera*, 2023*available at*: https://www.coursera.org/articles/ai-in-health-care (last visited March 16, 2024).

in health care, it is necessary to comprehend its application. As the healthcare landscape evolves, it is necessary to identify the various issues faced by the present legal framework.

Smartwatches can display the wearer's heart rate, pulse, number of steps, and many other metrics. These gadgets are equipped with wireless sensors that permit connectivity in order to provide users with access to recorded data in real time to tremors and disease symptoms. Embedded motion sensors can be utilized to track a variety of data ranging from body activities, such as walking patterns and heart rate to tremors and disease symptoms.

The sensors capture all the data, which is subsequently saved, processed, and sorted systematically using various algorithms. Later, based on the doctor's and patient's requests, this information will be retrieved and disseminated properly. This data covers all patient-related information required for analysis and treatment by medical professionals. There are numerous types of wearables utilized in the healthcare industry. Patches are one of the most popular wearables in hospitals.

For the past few years, patches have been widely used since they are inexpensive, disposable, and easy to dispose of. Fabric and flexible devices are other names for these devices. Among the many disposable flexible patches available are the BioStamp, the iRhythm, the BP monitor, the UV sensor, and the electro pad. Patches like these can be used to remotely collect data on a variety of conditions, including cancer, heart disease, and type 2 diabetes. All of the wearables come equipped with sensors that can measure glucose levels, heart rates, electrocardiograms, and other biomarkers related to cancer, diabetes, and heart disease. Patients' identification numbers are collected and stored separately, which is this technology's most essential feature. In the cloud database, the acquired data will be deposited.

5 Market of AI: Globally

The artificial intelligence (AI) market is anticipated to grow rapidly over the next ten years, according to Next Move Strategy Consulting. The value is predicted to increase from about 100 billion U.S. dollars to almost two trillion U.S. dollars by 2030, a 20-fold growth. The AI market encompasses a wide range of industries. Various industries, such as supply chains, marketing, product development, research, and analysis, will incorporate artificial intelligence into their commercial operations. Chatbots, image-generating AI, and mobile applications are significant trends that will enhance AI in the upcoming years.

5.1 Generative AI a Growing Market

The publication of ChatGPT 3.0 in 2022 sparked a renewed interest in the potential of generative artificial intelligence. One can gain insight into this trend by comparing the

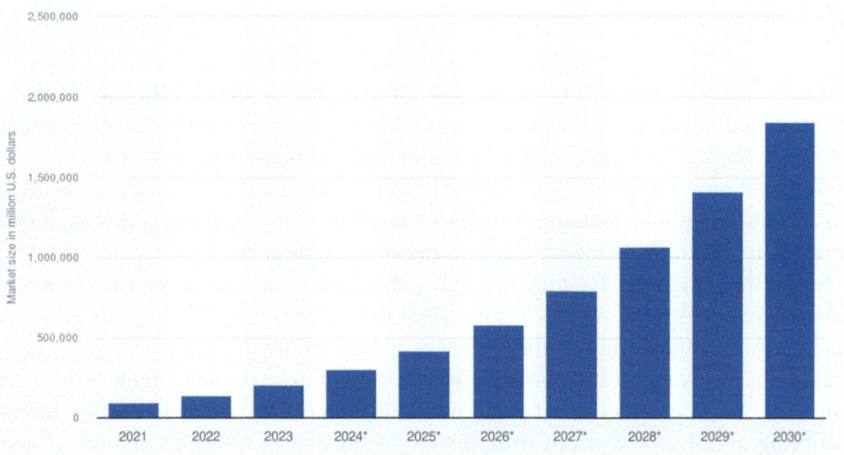

Fig. 3 Artificial intelligence (AI) market size worldwide in 2021 with a forecast until 2030 (in million U.S. dollars)[15]

level of interest in generative AI on Google, which has been significantly increasing from 2022 to 2023. Anticipate a sustained interest in this area as ChatGPT and other entities work toward enhancing chatbot versions and developing more advanced generative AI programs.

5.2 *Growing Awareness in Academia*

Artificial intelligence is a rapidly evolving topic, requiring academics to stay updated on fast-paced technical advancements. Most specialized PhDs in North America often work in the industrial sector, while less than half choose to work in academia. Traditional academic writing about AI has been consistently outdated since the academic approach is time-consuming. An alteration in this pattern is noticeable as an increasing number of publications on the subject are being released (Fig. 3).

6 AI in Health Care

The increasing adoption of artificial intelligence is leading to a growing variety of applications across different industries. AI provides a number of benefits to the field of health care, the professionals working within it, and the patients that interact with it every day. Some medical artificial intelligence applications used in the healthcare sector include the ones listed below:

---

[15] "Artificial Intelligence market size 2030," *Statista*, 2023*available at*: https://www.statista.com/statistics/1365145/artificial-intelligence-market-size/ (last visited March 16, 2024).

6.1 *AI for Drug Discovery*

Artificial intelligence offers numerous advantages to the healthcare sector, its workers, and the patients they serve on a daily basis.[16] AI drug discovery enhances efficiency and reduces repetitive work in the AI and healthcare industries.[17]

Several therapies created by leading biopharmaceutical companies are available. Pfizer is utilizing IBM Watson, an artificial intelligence system that relies on machine learning, to aid in the discovery of immuno-oncology drugs.[18]

Sanofi has engaged Exscientia's AI platform for the discovery of medications for metabolic diseases, while Roche subsidiary Genentech is using an AI system from GNS Healthcare in Cambridge, Massachusetts, to aid in the search for cancer treatments. Many major biopharmaceutical companies have such alliances or internal programs. If the proponents of these methods are correct, AI and machine learning will bring about a new era of drug development that is faster, more cost-efficient, and more successful. The majority of specialists predict that these tools will become increasingly vital in the future, despite some skepticism. Scientists face obstacles and opportunities as a result of this transition, particularly when integrating the approaches with automation.[19]

6.2 *AI for Clinical Trials*

A clinical trial is a procedure in which newly developed treatments are given to individuals to assess their effectiveness. This has necessitated a significant allocation of time and financial resources. The success rate is somewhat limited. Automating clinical trials has proved advantageous for artificial intelligence and the healthcare sector. Artificial intelligence and health care can expedite data monitoring processes that are typically lengthy. Moreover, AI-assisted clinical studies handle vast amounts of data and produce very accurate outcomes. Below are some common artificial intelligence applications in health care, specifically for clinical trials:

---

[16] Óscar Díaz, James A. R. Dalton and Jesús Giraldo, "Artificial Intelligence: A Novel Approach for Drug Discovery," 40 *Trends in pharmacological sciences* 550–1 (2019).

[17] H. C. Stephen Chan et al., "Advancing Drug Discovery via Artificial Intelligence," 40 *Trends in pharmacological sciences* 592–604 (2019).

[18] Debleena Paul et al., "Artificial intelligence in drug discovery and development," 26 *Drug discovery today* 80–93 (2021).

[19] H. C. Stephen Chan et al., "Advancing Drug Discovery via Artificial Intelligence," 40 *Trends in pharmacological sciences* 592–604 (2019).

Intelligent Clinical Trials

Traditional clinical trials that adhere to a linear and sequential process are still the most dependable way to confirm the efficacy and safety of new drugs. The traditional process of distinct and specific phases in randomized controlled trials (RCTs) was initially developed for evaluating widely available drugs and has undergone little change in recent times. Artificial intelligence can shorten clinical trial duration and enhance productivity and outcomes in clinical development. This is the third study in a series that explores the impact of artificial intelligence on the biopharmaceutical value chain. Biopharmaceutical businesses have been increasingly utilizing scientific and research data from many sources in recent years, referred to as real-world data (RWD). They frequently did not possess the essential skills and tools to efficiently make use of this data. Using predictive artificial intelligence models and advanced analytics on real-world data (RWD) can help researchers obtain profound insights into diseases, discover appropriate patients and key investigators, and enable creative clinical trial designs.[20]

When paired with a robust digital framework, AI algorithms can be utilized to clean, gather, code, store, and manage clinical trial data. Enhanced electronic data capture (EDC) can minimize human error in data collecting and facilitate seamless system integration.[21]

Clinical Trial Cooperation and Model Sharing

Researchers from several disciplines are collaborating closely to support the response to COVID-19 in an exceptional demonstration of scientific cooperation. For AI tools to have a worldwide influence, it is crucial to utilize scalable methods for exchanging data, models, and code, while also customizing applications to local settings and promoting international collaboration.[22] AI applications require data. There are many data-sharing activities for COVID-19 at global, national, and local levels across different application scales. Multiple resources, including genetic sequences, genomic studies, protein structures, patient clinical data, medical imaging, event data, epidemiological information, movement data, social media comments, news headlines, and scientific literature, are available. Excessive fragmentation of data-sharing activities might impede progress by limiting enhancements to specific projects and groups. Enhancing the progress and dissemination of new applications could be accomplished by adopting scalable approaches for sharing data, models, and code. Currently, sharing worldwide, transparent, thorough, standardized, and confirmable

[20] Marcus Woo, "An AI boost for clinical trials," 573 *Nature* S100–2 (2019).

[21] Irene Mayorga-Ruiz et al., "The Role of AI in Clinical Trials" *Artificial Intelligence in Medical Imaging* 231–43 (2019).

[22] Miguel Luengo-Oroz et al., "Artificial intelligence cooperation to support the global response to COVID-19," 2 *Nature Machine Intelligence* 295–7 (2020).

information can facilitate connecting and promoting collaboration among various communities and locations.[23,24]

Collaborative research involving multiple stakeholders and artificial intelligence collaborations that cross international borders can speed up the sharing of information and the enhancement of capabilities in national health systems.[25] The Epidemic Intelligence from Open Sources (EIOS) network uses open-source data to detect, verify, and evaluate public health risks and threats early.[26] The healthcare intelligence network comprises countries, international organizations, and research institutes collaborating to assess and share information on outbreak occurrences promptly, emphasizing cooperation over rivalry in early identification. Epidemiologists propose that implementing global standards and database interoperability can facilitate efficient coordinated responses and decision-making on several levels, including global, national, and local. It is crucial to analyze the epidemiological characteristics, risk factors, health system resources, public health measures, environmental factors, and societal implications of COVID-19 as the pandemic progresses.[27]

Currently, there are few platforms that exchange trained AI models for purposes other than data sharing. Challenges encompass specific computational, design, and infrastructural needs, insufficient documentation, verification, and interpretability obstacles, and legal issues related to secrecy and intellectual property. Sharing pre-trained and approved AI models could speed up the process of applying solutions to different situations. Versatile algorithms include those capable of diagnosing illnesses from photographs, predicting medical outcomes, identifying and filtering misinformation on social media based on spreading patterns, and extracting knowledge graphs from massive databases of academic papers.[28,29,30]

AI in healthcare influences patient outcomes. Medical AI businesses create a system that provides comprehensive assistance to patients. Clinical intelligence analyzes patients' medical information to offer insights that can enhance their quality of life. Here are several crucial clinical intelligence systems that improve patient care:

---

[23] Stefanie Lip, Shyam Visweswaran and Sandosh Padmanabhan, "Transforming Clinical Trials with Artificial Intelligence" *Artificial Intelligence* 297–306 (2020).

[24] Miguel Luengo-Oroz et al., "Artificial intelligence cooperation to support the global response to COVID-19," 2 *Nature Machine Intelligence* 295–7 (2020).

[25] Mohammed Yousef Shaheen, "AI in Healthcare: medical and socio-economic benefits and challenges" *SSRN Electronic Journal* (2021).

[26] G. Sucharitha and Deshoju Vemana Chary, "Predicting the Effect of Covid-19 by using Artificial Intelligence: A Case Study" *Materials today. Proceedings* (2021).

[27] *Ibid.*

[28] Miguel Luengo-Oroz et al., "Artificial intelligence cooperation to support the global response to COVID-19," 2 *Nature Machine Intelligence* 295–7 (2020).

[29] "Adoption of machine learning for medical diagnosis,"*available at*: https://www.researchgate.net/publication/354841623_Adoption_of_machine_learning_for_medical_diagnosis (last visited March 16, 2024).

[30] Hanaa Fatoum et al., "Blockchain Integration With Digital Technology and the Future of Health Care Ecosystems: Systematic Review," 23 *Journal of Medical Internet Research* e19846 (2021).

Maternal Care

A potential approach to identify high-risk mothers and reduce maternal mortality and postpartum problems is as follows:

- Utilizing electronic health data and artificial intelligence (AI) to predict the likelihood of pregnant women experiencing difficulties after childbirth.
- Using digital technology to improve patient access to both regular and high-intensity healthcare services during pregnancy. High-risk obstetric women who give birth at low-acuity clinics are more likely to incur significant maternal morbidity than those who deliver at higher-acuity clinics with better resources and more experienced professionals.

Healthcare Robotics

Medical robots assist patients as well as medical personnel. Exoskeleton robots have the potential to assist paralyzed patients in walking and regaining autonomy.[31] An intelligent prosthesis exemplifies technology in action. Bionic limbs are enhanced with sensors that increase their responsiveness and precision beyond those of natural body parts. Bionic skin can be applied to them and linked to the user's muscles. Robots can aid in rehabilitation and medical operations. Cyberdyne's Hybrid Assistive Limb (HAL) exoskeleton is designed to assist patients in rehabilitation from lower limb abnormalities resulting from illnesses, such as spinal cord injuries and strokes. The device uses sensors on the skin to precisely detect electrical signals in the patient's body and adjust the joint accordingly.[32]

Genetics AI Data-Driven Medicine

Consumers are more involved in their medical care, leveraging genome sequencing and data from fitness trackers to personalize their health management. Extensive data is being collected and linked to generate a more precise prediction of our health or medical status. Utilizing data in medicine can improve the precision and adaptability of identifying genetic illnesses and support tailored medical treatments.[33]

---

[31] Shi, D., Zhang, W., Zhang, W., & Ding, X. (2019). A review on lower limb rehabilitation exoskeleton robots. Chinese Journal of Mechanical Engineering, 32(1), 1–11.

[32] Oliver Cruciger et al., "Impact of locomotion training with a neurologic controlled hybrid assistive limb (HAL) exoskeleton on neuropathic pain and health related quality of life (HRQoL) in chronic SCI: a case study (.)," 11 *Disability and rehabilitation. Assistive technology* 529–34 (2016).

[33] Patrik Hummel and Matthias Braun, "Just data? Solidarity and justice in data-driven medicine," 16 *Life Sciences, Society and Policy* (2020).

AI-Powered Stethoscope

One major advantage is that, unlike traditional stethoscopes, the readings may be taken even in noisy environments, allowing for a more accurate diagnosis. Anyone can retrieve the records and forward them to the doctor without needing training to use the digital device.[34] This also decreases their susceptibility to contracting COVID-19 and enables the provision of enhanced medical care in distant areas and for individuals with chronic conditions. Artificial intelligence (AI) and machine learning allow computers to recognize patterns of illness and deviations in vast clinical data. The blood flowing through healthy arteries is distinct from the blood surrounding a blood clot in the blood vessels; hence, the same principle applies here.[35]

7 Issues and Challenges

To enhance the accuracy of AI-applied diagnostic systems, the market should create specialized systems for each field using machine learning algorithms. These systems should be trained on a diverse dataset that includes ethnic and cultural patient information.[36] AI systems can enhance their intelligence by incorporating additional learning instances provided by healthcare researchers and practitioners. The effects of medical AI systems can be viewed as both idealistic and pessimistic, similar to the introduction of any new technology. The utopian perspective offers numerous opportunities to enhance disease treatment, improve care quality and patient experience, promote patient involvement in treatment, decrease medical errors and healthcare expenses, and enhance the managerial efficiency of healthcare providers.[37] The dystopian viewpoint introduces numerous formidable obstacles. Utilizing patient data for analytics might heighten cybersecurity vulnerabilities related to privacy, security, accountability for medical errors, and even job loss.[38] We think that the issues associated

---

[34] "SmartScope: An AI-Powered Digital Auscultation Device To Detect Cardiopulmonary Diseases,"*available at*: https://www.researchgate.net/publication/353248105_SmartScope_An_AI-Powered_Digital_Auscultation_Device_To_Detect_Cardiopulmonary_Diseases (last visited March 16, 2024).

[35] "Applications of Artificial Intelligence (AI) in healthcare: A review,"*available at*: https://www.researchgate.net/publication/354841638_Applications_of_Artificial_Intelligence_AI_in_health care_A_review (last visited March 16, 2024).

[36] "Reflecting the Past, Shaping the Future: Making AI Work for International Development," *USAIDavailable at*: https://www.usaid.gov/digital-development/machine-learning/AI-ML-in-dev elopment (last visited March 16, 2024).

[37] Seong No Yoon and Don Hee Lee, "Artificial intelligence and robots in healthcare: What are the success factors for technology-based service encounters?," 12 *International Journal of Healthcare Management* 218–25 (2019).

[38] Seong No Yoon and Don Hee Lee, "Artificial intelligence and robots in healthcare: What are the success factors for technology-based service encounters?," 12 *International Journal of Healthcare Management* 218–25 (2019).

with the introduction of technology and AI systems in the healthcare industry need to be carefully analyzed to ensure their effective and widespread application.

AI applications present new prospects for enhancing people's daily lives, but they also introduce issues that need to be adequately addressed. The issues in the healthcare sector are particularly formidable due to their potential impact on human lives. Several difficulties requiring prudent management include the following.

7.1 Accountability of the System Use

Following a glitch in a Tesla Model's autonomous car resulting in a fatality on May 7, 2016, the primary issue was determining accountability for the incident. Who is accountable if medical personnel utilize AI technologies for patient care and an accident or mistake happens? AI programs function using a specific set of machine learning algorithms created by individuals. Hospital administrators, in collaboration with technological specialists, consultants, and medical staff, chose to acquire the system due to its versatile application capabilities. The hospital's medical personnel implemented the system to deliver necessary care services to a patient. Should the accountability for the issue lie with the system design firm, hospital, or medical staff? Answering this question is challenging due to the technological, managerial, and ethical complexities involved.

Despite the rapid advancement and widespread applications of AI-related technologies, there has been less research on the ethical implications of AI. Dr. Stephen Hawking noted that the rapid advancement of AI and clever robots is bringing humanity close to a point where human influence may become uncontrollable. He proposed the creation of a new international regulatory body to oversee the utilization of artificial intelligence.[39] Lupton[40] stressed the importance of cultivating moral and ethical conduct in AI to have a beneficial impact on society. AI-based technologies/systems in numerous industries are expected to significantly grow in the future and should be built to align their performance with human social norms and values. Accountability for any adverse effects of AI applications in the evolving healthcare sector should be determined by societal agreements. AI Division One key feature that sets the healthcare sector apart from other service businesses is the tendency for patients to trust medical workers without reservation. The phenomenon can be attributed to the placebo effect, where a patient's trust in a doctor's therapy and belief in the cure of their ailment lead to a medical response.[41] Physician–patient

[39] "Stephen Hawking warns artificial intelligence could end mankind," *BBC News*, 2014*available at*: https://www.bbc.com/news/technology-30290540 (last visited March 16, 2024).

[40] Michael Lupton, "Some ethical and legal consequences of the application of artificial intelligence in the field of medicine," 18 *Trends in Medicine* (2018).

[41] Ted J. Kaptchuk and Franklin G. Miller, "Placebo Effects in Medicine," 373 *The New England journal of medicine* 8–9 (2015).

trust is crucial since it enhances the efficacy of treatment. When an AI-based technology/system acts as a doctor, the patient will engage in a care delivery process that involves forming a connection with an artificial system instead of a human doctor. The success of this new relationship between an AI-enabled technology/system and the patient hinges on trust.[42] Individuals without familiarity with digital technology, particularly AI, may struggle to trust an AI system. To address this potential split, the doctor should reassure the patient about how the system will improve their care.

7.2 *Cybersecurity for Privacy and Security*

Privacy concerns emerge due to the extensive data collection and sharing involved with AI technologies/systems that rely on large datasets.[43,44] Sharing and regulating disease-related data across multiple databases is challenging due to the presence of personal information in patient records.[45] Companies creating software must follow confidentiality regulations, which can hinder AI progress. AI technology makes judgments based on accumulated data through machine learning, without considering particular patient situations, leading to ethical, moral, and legal concerns. It is essential to consider the regulations and standards that AI technology must adhere to, including ethics, laws, and personal values that govern human conduct in society.

7.3 *Loss of Managerial Control*

In the digital era, numerous sectors are no longer operating as separate entities. The healthcare sector is no different. Historically, the healthcare industry was viewed as a location where patients received medical treatment from doctors and nurses. Today, good health results from healthy lifestyle behaviors, such as a nutritious diet, consistent physical activity, and daily wellness practices, together with access to high-quality medical care. Preventive medicine has become crucial, leading to a blending of healthy lifestyle practices, medical interventions, and technological advancements.[46] Artificial intelligence has the ability to exceed limitations related to time and space. The old idea of a closed healthcare system is now obsolete. For instance, many smartphone applications, such as Robot Maria, Alexa, and AI speaker

---

[42] Michael Lupton, "Some ethical and legal consequences of the application of artificial intelligence in the field of medicine," 18 *Trends in Medicine* (2018).

[43] Kaveh Safavi, "How AI Can Change the Future of Health Care" *Harvard Business Review*, 2019.

[44] Michael J. Rigby, "Ethical dimensions of using artificial intelligence in health care," 21 *AMA Journal of Ethics* 121–4 (2019).

[45] Sajal K. Das, Krishna Kant and Nan Zhang, "Handbook on Securing Cyber-Physical Critical Infrastructure" *Handbook on Securing Cyber-Physical Critical Infrastructure* (2012).

[46] "AI to Save Healthcare Sector US$52 Billion in 2021," 2018.

Aria, can aid in the amalgamation of diverse facets of individuals' well-being. AI systems remotely monitor, diagnose, treat, and manage patients in their homes.

AI technologies are widely used in health care, leading care providers to rely more on consultants, specialists, and experts in ICT, convergence, and human resource management. Thus, care services now involve collaboration among numerous external and internal experts. The traditional bureaucratic governance system is not suitable for modern hospitals. During the process, hospital administrators may perceive a decrease in managerial authority. This is a novel kind of governance that functions as a dynamic living system, linking all systems, devices, and individuals to deliver optimal patient care.[47]

7.4 *Job Loss, Training/Education Needs, and the Pain of Transformation*

Amazon has revealed plans to provide training classes on new technologies to 100,000 employees by 2025 in order to prepare them for more advanced roles in the AI future. Amazon's worldwide consumer CEO, Jeff Wilke, noted that advancements in technology provide employees with the chance to progress in their careers and benefit from these improvements.[48] The Health Innovation Big Data Center at Asan Medical Center in Seoul, Korea, has just started educational programs for aspiring AI specialists to create and market AI algorithms.[49]

Many people think that radiography, a medical profession, will become obsolete in the future as artificial intelligence might potentially assess diagnostic medical images more precisely than humans. Some think that implementing AI will enable radiologists to offer more specialized diagnostic services to patients.[50,51]

AI-related technologies will undoubtedly render several repetitious jobs redundant. Although certain positions may be eliminated, several new jobs will emerge to facilitate the integration of AI-driven systems and gadgets. Ultimately, AI is anticipated to enhance relationships between healthcare providers and patients by compensating for AI's limitations. Medical school curricula should efficiently include AI-related instruction and technology. Furthermore, the development of more precise AI applications is necessary due to the constraints faced by medical AI from outdated

---

[47] Sang M. Lee and Seongbae Lim, "LIVING INNOVATION: From Value Creation to the Greater Good" *Living Innovation: From Value Creation to the Greater Good* 1–148 (2018).

[48] "Amazon to spend $700 million to train 100,000 workers for digital age," 2019.

[49] "Medical World News."

[50] Filippo Pesapane, Marina Codari and Francesco Sardanelli, "Artificial intelligence in medical imaging: threat or opportunity? Radiologists again at the forefront of innovation in medicine," 2 *European radiology experimental* (2018).

[51] Thomas H. Davenport Davenport, "AI Will Change Radiology, but It Won't Replace Radiologists" (2018).

patient datasets. Medical staff participation is essential at the onset of AI development. To resolve this issue, it is essential to cultivate a skilled professional workforce capable of quickly responding in the consumer-focused healthcare industry by offering various educational opportunities on cutting-edge technology, like utilizing AI to work alongside medical personnel. We propose incorporating new curriculums, such as technological innovation and application, human–machine convergence, data analytics courses, human–machine interchange, cyber ethics, and responsibility into the medical school curriculum to generate new employment opportunities.

8 Legislation for AI: United States (US) and Europe (EU) Legislation

8.1 Role of HIPPA Security to Respond to Artificial Intelligence:

Artificial intelligence (AI), also known as augmented intelligence in health care, utilizes mathematical modeling with established algorithms trained on specific datasets to assist clinical providers and patients in the practice of medicine.[52]

One prevalent misunderstanding concerning AI in medicine is the idea that AI would "replace" physicians and other healthcare practitioners in the field of medicine. The optimal application of AI in health care will enhance medical decision-making. It is crucial because clinical decision support technologies decrease medical errors and aid in diagnosis[53] and develop treatment plans, and offer prompts for optimal practice advice and reminders for preventative care.[54]

AI in health care supports doctors by delivering fast information on the patient's present status, laboratory, and imaging results to uncover care deficiencies in a data-intensive environment. Putting all that information in the clinician's hands helps predict future ailments and diseases, allowing for early alarms through predictive analytics.[55] AI is utilized in wearable devices and remote patient monitoring, such as continuous glucose monitoring,[56] real-time insulin pump modifications, smart implanted devices, pacemakers, defibrillators, and deep brain stimulators.

---

[52] Elliott Crigger et al., "Trustworthy Augmented Intelligence in Health Care," 46 *Journal of Medical Systems* 1–11 (2022).

[53] Lina F. Soualmia et al., "Health Data, Information, and Knowledge Sharing for Addressing the COVID-19," 30 *Yearbook of medical informatics* 4–7 (2021).

[54] Thomas Grote and Philipp Berens, "On the ethics of algorithmic decision-making in healthcare," 46 *Journal of Medical Ethics* 205–11 (2020).

[55] A. V. L. N. Sujith et al., "Systematic review of smart health monitoring using deep learning and Artificial intelligence," 2 *Neuroscience Informatics* 100028 (2022).

[56] Martina Vettoretti et al., "Advanced Diabetes Management Using Artificial Intelligence and Continuous Glucose Monitoring Sensors," 20 *Sensors 2020, Vol. 20, Page 3870* 3870 (2020).

Research shows that errors related to health care are a concern in the industry. Research published in the Irish Journal of Medical Science in 2022 reviewed how AI[57] in health care presents significant opportunities to improve quality and safety using big data analytics, rendered for various special applications in health care. The benefits of AI include having more accurate and efficient diagnoses.

Radiologists can utilize AI for imaging analysis to enhance efficiency and accuracy, which may help alleviate workforce productivity challenges. AI can assist in providing patient-oriented information, including scheduling appointments, accessing lab and imaging data, and communicating with healthcare practitioners. Enhancing contact with doctors boosts patient satisfaction. Providers can utilize advanced language models like ChatGPT to generate an initial answer for patient communication.

Data analytics is essential for specific surgical robotics and can enhance the safety and efficiency of surgeries. This enables surgeons to conduct more intricate or accurate procedures, resulting in improved patient outcomes. Consumer wearables that monitor health data can utilize AI technology to analyze extensive data, aiding healthcare experts in interpreting its importance. This information can then be discussed with patients during in-person or virtual appointments.

An article published in 2020 in the JAMA Journal of Ethics examined various significant danger implications associated with artificial intelligence in health care.[58] System problems present a significant risk due to the increased storage or reception of data, perhaps leading to system shutdowns. Moreover, employing AI may extend the downtime duration because of the large volume of data that needs to be recovered. Continuous monitoring and improvements are necessary due to the growing complexity of privacy measures.

Data repurposing involves utilizing de-identified medical data for AI training, posing a high danger of unwanted access to private information. This specific scenario necessitates obtaining explicit agreement from the patient, which is not typically included in the routine consent required upon hospital admission for treatment, procedures, billing, and insurance under the Health Insurance Portability and Accountability Act of 1996 (HIPAA) Privacy Rule. This would involve obtaining a specialized informed consent from patients for the utilization of patient health information (PHI) in research and artificial intelligence (AI) applications. HIPAA laws do not cover Protected Health Information (PHI) if it has been de-identified for a specific purpose.

Data Security and Ethical Implications

HIPAA offers regulations for protecting the confidentiality and security of medical data. It also governs the way healthcare providers and related parties manage and

---

[57] Sri Venkat Gunturi Subrahmanya et al., "The role of data science in healthcare advancements: applications, benefits, and future prospects," 191 *Irish journal of medical science* 1473–83 (2022).

[58] John Banja, "Peer-Reviewed How Might Artificial Intelligence Applications Impact Risk Management?" *AMA Journal of Ethics* (2020).

utilize patient data. The Health Information Technology for Economical and Clinical Health Act (HITECH) of 2009 and the Omnibus Rule of 2013 provide further protections for PHI through accompanying regulations.

The HIPAA Security Rule mandates physical, technical, and administrative precautions, including restricted office access, computer logins, encryption, tight policies, procedures, and training. The HIPAA Privacy Rule governs the handling and sharing of Protected Health Information (PHI).

The relationship between HIPAA and AI relies on extensive data, which includes PHI regulated by HIPAA. Organizations must enhance data security, mitigate cyber-attacks, and be vigilant for potential vulnerabilities[59] in administrative, technical, and physical safeguards. As technology advances, it is crucial to revise HIPAA standards to accommodate the growing significance of AI in health care. Proposed HIPAA updates aim to enhance consumer understanding and transparency by clarifying language in the Notification of Privacy Practices regarding the use of patient data. Other updates include encrypting data during transmission and securely transferring PHI to reduce the vulnerability to cyber-attacks, as well as restricting third-party vendor access.

Expanding the definition of a covered entity and revising security and privacy responsibility can enhance consumer safeguards. Organizational policies and procedures need to be revised to cover artificial intelligence applications for administrative and medical-support tasks,[60] and employee HIPAA training should incorporate artificial intelligence capabilities.

Any conversation about utilizing AI in health care and maintaining HIPAA security must include ethical considerations. Ensuring patient safety is of utmost importance, and non-maleficence involves safeguarding patients from harm. AI regulations often lag behind the rapid progress and advancements in the field[61] as AI shows no signs of slowing down.

AI uses extensive datasets to produce precise diagnoses, but these databases can contain explicit or implicit bias. Evaluating and managing this bias will be essential to ensuring fairness in health care. Cybersecurity issues can result in HIPAA breaches. The extensive datasets required for AI and machine learning are susceptible to hacking and cyber-attacks. Data breaches can potentially disclose extensive amounts of data, such as information spanning a patient's whole life, including distinct genetic tendencies and particularly safeguarded groups.

---

[59] Chenxi Dong et al., "Characterizing browser-based medical imaging AI with serverless edge computing: towards addressing clinical data security constraints," 12469 *Proceedings of SPIE–the International Society for Optical Engineering* 5 (2023).

[60] Javad Pool, Saeed Akhlaghpour and Farhad Fatehi, "Health Data Privacy in the COVID-19 Pandemic Context: Discourses on HIPAA," 279 *Studies in Health Technology and Informatics* 70–7 (2021).

[61] Shania Kennedy, "FDA Releases Guidance on AI-Driven Clinical Decision Support Tools" (2022).

The issues of data ownership and breach culpability under AI have not been definitively resolved.[62] De-identification is an inefficient privacy approach for research. Patients have been effectively re-identified in datasets compliant with HIPAA rules.[63] This compromises patient confidentiality. Who would be accountable? Data pools might extend across national and international boundaries; however, privacy regulations vary between different governments. As HIPAA is a federal legislation in the US, developers must ensure compliance with international regulations, as prosecution and compensation may not apply outside the country.

Priority is given to high-quality treatment, as errors in health care can lead to severe repercussions. IBM Watson for Oncology, an AI-based system, was found to provide treatment suggestions that were deemed "unsafe and incorrect"[64] during pre-clinical testing. Other ethical considerations include provider liability; some AI functions have been shown to provide more accurate diagnoses than humans. Thus, is there an obligation to use it if it is more effective? If it is used, then who is liable if AI and the provider disagree. What if harm is incurred?

Providers must describe procedures clearly, although they may struggle to adequately clarify the AI functions due to their technological complexity. Conversely, some consumers may lack digital literacy and fail to comprehend the consequences and risks associated with AI. AI developers may lack comprehension of the reasoning behind their conclusions or diagnoses. Furthermore, suppliers may not be able to confirm the accuracy of AI recommendations[65] as modern computing can hide techniques, and thus, the technology is opaque to scrutiny.

If AI/machine learning is utilized, the supplier bears the final responsibility.[66] What happens if the patient concludes that there is an excessive amount of risk? There are chances that patients will revoke their consent, and how may their data be removed from datasets used in algorithms? User agreements with health apps, social media, and chatbots powered by AI are not required to comply with HIPAA regulations.[67] So, there is much to consider and future research that is needed.

---

[62] Sara Gerke, Timo Minssen and Glenn Cohen, "Ethical and legal challenges of artificial intelligence-driven healthcare" *Artificial Intelligence in Healthcare* 295–336 (2020).

[63] Luc Rocher, Julien M. Hendrickx and Yves Alexandre de Montjoye, "Estimating the success of re-identifications in incomplete datasets using generative models," 10 *Nature communications* (2019).

[64] Sara Gerke, Timo Minssen and Glenn Cohen, "Ethical and legal challenges of artificial intelligence-driven healthcare" *Artificial Intelligence in Healthcare* 295–336 (2020).

[65] Nithesh Naik et al., "Legal and Ethical Consideration in Artificial Intelligence in Healthcare: Who Takes Responsibility?," 9 *Frontiers in Surgery* 862322 (2022).

[66] X. Du-Harpur et al., "What is AI? Applications of artificial intelligence to dermatology," 183 *The British journal of dermatology* 423–30 (2020).

[67] Katharina M. Busl et al., "Use of Social Media in Health Care-Opportunities, Challenges, and Ethical Considerations: A Position Statement of the American Academy of Neurology," 97 *Neurology* 585–94 (2021).

AI Drives HIPAA Changes

What modifications are required for HIPAA security, considering operational and ethical factors? It is essential to conduct proactive vulnerability assessments, fortify security measures, and implement stronger encryption and anonymization protocols. Enhancing access management can stem from adhering to the principles of "need to know" and "minimum necessary" criteria. The Department of Health and Human Services (HHS) supports improved care coordination and emphasizes the need of sharing relevant information. By doing this, the scope of necessary knowledge and the quantity of information sent can be expanded. Engaging in this practice can lead to improved care coordination while maintaining the confidentiality of Protected Health Information (PHI).

The Notice of Privacy Practices may include information under the consumer rights section regarding the utilization of artificial intelligence for managing patient health information. The HIPAA Security Rule, 45CFR164.304, discusses how technical safeguards can utilize artificial intelligence to identify subtleties and irregularities in data usage. Additionally, according to 45CFR164.312(d), it is necessary to establish how to incorporate artificial intelligence into discussions concerning individual or entity authentication (45CFR164).

Another approach is for the government to develop a policy on artificial intelligence. The FDA can take the lead as it has concluded that supervision is essential to ensure the safety of patients and their Protected Health Information (PHI). In 2019, the FDA issued a proposal outlining the regulation of AI technologies in medical devices. The FDA completed its "Artificial Intelligence/Machine Learning (AI/ML)-Based Software as a Medical Device (SaMD) Action Plan" in January 2021.[68] Under this framework, AI applications can be iteratively upgraded while still being adequately monitored for patient safety and privacy.

Hank.ai is an AI firm that specializes in developing software and APIs for healthcare business operations like document indexing, data entry, medical coding, and auditing, while ensuring HIPAA security measures are in place.

Hank.ai's goal is to assist humans by removing repetitive and labor intensive manual jobs. The platform utilizes natural language processing, computer vision, machine learning, neural networks, and autonomous computer programming. It enhances current workflows while learning at the same time, helping clients enhance the efficiency, accuracy, and charge capture of medical coders, clinical documentation specialists, and insurance auditors.

The Hank.ai platform's accuracy surpasses human-only data entry by utilizing a vast dataset to effectively identify, extract, and organize data from challenging sources, such as hard-to-read papers, handwritten forms, PDFs, photos, emails, and other formats. This can decrease the occurrence of expensive mistakes, the time needed to file insurance claims, and the frequency of claim rejection.

Darktrace is another instance of AI technology being used to enhance HIPAA security. Darktrace records each keystroke made within the business to create a

[68] "Introducing QuerySurge AI," *QuerySurge*.

comprehensive dataset of typical behavior. The platform, like Hank.ai, is centered around aggregating data into extensive datasets. Darktrace can detect abnormal assault patterns. When a breach is identified, the threat can be promptly reduced in real time, rather than retroactively. This is another defense strategy to comply with the technological security standards outlined in HIPAA.

Artificial intelligence in cybersecurity is a prominent subject of conversation in the healthcare sector. The HHS Office for Civil Rights (OCR) oversees a database that is open to the public and contains information on breaches that impact a minimum of 500 individuals.[69] The healthcare sector had the highest reported cost and frequency of data breaches, with a 51% increase in breaches[70] since 2019, and a 10 percent increase in cost from 2020 to 2021.

Machine learning intrusion detection systems offer potential in safeguarding healthcare companies by emphasizing four primary components:

- Ensure the confidentiality of secure communications from outside monitoring
- Authentication features to protect against unauthorized access
- Integrity and accuracy of care data
- Access controls, whereby only specific authorized entities can access the data, are critical.

Hybrid intelligent intrusion detection technologies are behind all four of these[71] (HIIDS) used in the detection and prevention of cyber-attacks.

To optimize privacy and security compliance with AI models, it is essential to incorporate privacy-preserving strategies[72] when safeguarding PHI. Examples include cryptographic techniques, which utilize mathematical concepts and algorithms to encrypt messages for enhanced security; differential privacy, a mathematical model that involves adding random or noisy data to sensitive information to protect individual contributions; and federated learning, a secure method for training AI models that safeguards data privacy. This method enables the extraction of valuable information to aid in creating new AI programs.

AI tools can be a great asset for healthcare firms to achieve their HIPAA security and privacy compliance standards. Specialized AI technology designed for security and privacy in health care can enhance security and reduce human effort by automating compliance processes, therefore improving HIPAA compliance.

---

[69] "Health Information Privacy," *available at*: https://www.hhs.gov/hipaa/index.html (last visited March 18, 2024).

[70] George A. Gellert et al., "Zero Trust and the future of cybersecurity in healthcare delivery organizations," 12 *Journal of Hospital Administration* 1 (2023).

[71] Sohail Saif et al., "HIIDS: Hybrid intelligent intrusion detection system empowered with machine learning and metaheuristic algorithms for application in IoT based healthcare" *Microprocessors and Microsystems* 104622 (2022).

[72] Ursula Hübner et al., "Technology Informatics Guiding Education Reform—TIGER," 57 *Methods of Information in Medicine* e30–42 (2018).

8.2 *Role of European Agency is Regularizing AI Medical Devices*

AI risks can be characterized and classified according to the severity of the harm they may induce, as well as to the probability and frequency of the harm induced. Currently, the applicable regulations for medical AI tools in the EU are the 2017/745 Medical Devices Regulation (MDR) and the 2017/746 In Vitro Diagnostic Medical Devices Regulation (IVDR), which were passed in 2017. However, because they were derived at a time when AI was at an early stage in its development, many aspects specific to AI are not considered, such as the continuous learning of AI models or the identification of algorithmic biases.

In 2021, the European Commission released a much-anticipated proposal for an AI law aimed at standardizing the regulations for AI technologies throughout Europe. The top category includes AI tools that go against EU ideals and hence should be banned. The intermediate category, representing high-risk AI including medical AI technologies, may be authorized if the tools meet certain standards and commitments for effective risk management, such as having human control and doing post-market monitoring.

The European Commission's proposal for AI regulation is broad and does not include the unique characteristics and hazards of AI in the healthcare sector, unlike the MDR and IVDR laws. The European Commission proposal maintains some shortcomings of the MDR and IVDR, including the absence of tools to deal with the evolving nature and ongoing learning of medical AI systems.

Risk Minimization Through Risk Self-assessment

Stakeholders have proposed a formal self-assessment method for identifying risks in AI, which includes specific checklists and questions. The European Commission's independent High Level Expert Group on Artificial Intelligence (AI HLEG) released a trustworthy AI evaluation checklist named ALTAI. The checklist is organized into seven areas: (1) human agency and oversight; (2) technical robustness and safety; (3) privacy and data governance; (4) transparency; (5) diversity, non-discrimination, and fairness; (6) environmental and societal well-being; and (7) accountability.

The ALTAI model is broad and does not specifically focus on AI in health care. A network of European Commission supported research initiatives, along with worldwide inter-disciplinary experts, has recently developed consensus standards for trustworthy AI in medicine. The guidelines named FUTURE-AI are structured around six principles (fairness, universality, traceability, usability, robustness, and explainability) and include specific recommendations and a self-assessment checklist. They are designed to assist AI designers, developers, evaluators, and regulators in creating reliable and ethical AI solutions for medicine and health care.

Risk Identification Through Comprehensive, Multifaceted Clinical Evaluation of AI Solutions

Although it is essential to identify and reduce dangers in medical AI through thorough evaluation studies, current scientific research primarily concentrates on assessing the accuracy and resilience of AI tools in controlled laboratory environments. Medical AI's clinical safety, effectiveness, fairness, non-discrimination, transparency, traceability, privacy, and security are more difficult to assess in controlled settings and have not been as well explored in the scientific literature.

A comprehensive and multifaceted review methodology is required for upcoming AI technologies in health care. Optimal methods to improve clinical assessment and implementation consist of the following: (i) employing standard definitions of clinical tasks (e.g., disease definition) to enable objective community-driven evaluations; (ii) defining performance elements beyond accuracy, such as for fairness, usability, explainability, and transparency; (iii) subdividing the evaluation process into stages of increasing complexity (i.e., to assess feasibility, then capability, effectiveness, and durability); (iv) promoting external evaluations by independent third-party evaluators; and (v) employing standardized guidelines for reporting the AI evaluation results to increase reproducibility, transparency, and trust.

Despite the substantial investments made by the EU in AI in recent years, disparities still exist among various European countries. The AI divide is due to variations in research programs, technological capabilities, and varied amounts of funding from the public and commercial sectors. There are significant differences in the advancement and utilization of artificial intelligence (AI) among European Union (EU) countries, especially in the field of medical AI. In this scenario, the EU can serve as a central coordinating body to develop a comprehensive policy aimed at narrowing the disparities in medical AI technology between European nations. The policy should outline specific measures to enhance the technological, research, and industrial capabilities of rising EU nations in the AI healthcare sector.

EU Member States, especially those in eastern Europe, might create specialized programs to enhance support for upcoming AI applications in health care. The European Commission could establish coordination and support programs for actions carried out in this sector by various Member States to assist in implementing shared guidelines and practices. Infrastructure projects should be developed exclusively for EU nations with restricted research infrastructures and data accessibility. Current education-focused programs like the Marie-Curie training networks should be improved to boost training capabilities and human resources in medical artificial intelligence.

AI Act 2023

High-risk artificial intelligences must adhere to the regulations outlined in Chapter II of the AI Act, which introduces increased complexity. There are discrepancies in the language and definitions between the AI Act and the MDR and IVDR. Identical terminologies are employed, although the interpretations differ. Secondly, certain restrictions outlined in the AI Act for high-risk devices conflict with those in other

EU legislation. The standards outlined in Article 10 ("Data and data governance") and Article 12 ("Record-keeping") are very challenging, if not unattainable, for medical device manufacturers to fulfill. Manufacturers are prohibited from retaining patient-specific data since it would violate privacy laws like the General Data Protection Regulation (Regulation (EU) 2016/679, GDPR). Device manufacturers lack access to patient data utilized in clinical studies to prove clinical advantages, safety, and efficiency. The maker must be able to identify the specific individuals involved in the verification results.

The AI Act mandates that training, validation, and testing datasets must be pertinent, inclusive, accurate, and comprehensive. Device manufacturers must comply with the GDPR. They may find it challenging to verify the accuracy and completeness of data that they are not allowed to access due to the GDPR and member states' healthcare regulations.

Similar issues arise for clinical investigations and compliance with the AI Act. Creating comprehensive clinical datasets for devices designed for uncommon diseases can be a time-consuming process that spans several years. Devices with AI components cannot be sold in the EU until the necessary data is acquired and confirmed, as outlined in the present draft of the AI Act. This could restrict therapy choices for patients.

9 Conclusion

Rapidly evolving technologies are the main instruments for executing and merging value-generating concepts. Organizations must embrace and utilize AI and similar technologies as a necessary trend to gain a competitive edge, rather than an optional decision. Artificial intelligence (AI) is increasingly being used in health care as it becomes more common in contemporary business and daily activities. The healthcare sector is particularly vulnerable to the innovative possibilities of AI because of the transformative characteristics of health care. AI applications are transforming care delivery by impacting diagnosis, treatment, and patients' lifestyles, which are essential for their well-being. Some sources suggest that artificial intelligence can match or exceed human performance in certain health-related tasks, like identifying illnesses. However, the complete replacement of humans by AI in various medical roles is expected to take a considerable amount of time. This study analyzed the diffusion of AI technology in health care and the new opportunities and difficulties it has presented. Effectively addressing these opportunities and challenges demands the combined intelligence and determination of all healthcare sector players.

Exploring the Landscape of AI-Generated Output: Challenges and Regulatory Insights

Nikos Koutras

Abstract The concept of artificial intelligence (AI) was initially introduced in the 1940s, when some philosophers and mathematicians tried to describe human thinking as the mechanical manipulation of symbols. The term "artificial intelligence" was coined in 1956, at a workshop held at Dartmouth College, where some of the pioneers of AI research gathered to discuss the possibility and challenges of creating machines as intelligent as humans. The need for regulation of AI has been voiced by experts and advocates in responsible AI, AI ethics, consumer protection, and cybersecurity since at least the 1960s. However, the regulation of AI is still an emerging issue in many jurisdictions, and there is no consensus on what, when, and how the uses and applications of AI should be regulated. Some of the challenges and controversies of regulating AI include the definition and scope of AI, the ethical and social implications of AI, the balance between innovation and regulation, the accountability and transparency of AI systems, and the global coordination and cooperation of AI governance. The chapter promotes the adoption of proactive strategies in response to the rapid development of AI technology, emphasizing the importance of a well-rounded strategy that recognizes both the constraints and potential of AI systems. In conclusion, the chapter argues for a transition toward conducting ethical evaluations after the deployment phase, with a focus on the significance of retrospective legislation to tackle any negative consequences.

Keywords Artificial intelligence · Generated output · Regulations · Challenges

N. Koutras (✉)
Curtin Law School, Curtin University, Perth, WA, Australia
e-mail: nikos.koutras@curtin.edu.au

J. Aston et al. (eds.), *Comparative Law*, https://doi.org/10.1007/978-981-97-7815-7_24

1 Introduction

The term "artificial intelligence" (AI) was first coined in 1956 by computer scientist John McCarthy at a summer conference at Dartmouth College in the US.[1] Further, the term AI reflects the purposes of producing machines feasible to perform activities and tasks that normally require human intelligence (e.g., reasoning, learning, problem solving).[2] It should be mentioned that vital methodological issues of AI are of paramount importance in the context of philosophy since ancient times.[3] The literature argues that early AI researchers were influenced by several ideas from philosophy, psychology, and mathematics.[4] One of the earliest examples of AI is the "Turing test," developed by Alan Turing in 1950 and demonstrates a way that determines whether a machine can exhibit human-like intelligence by engaging in a conversation with a human evaluator.[5]

Since its inception in 1956, AI has evolved significantly.[6] In the 1950s and 1960s, AI researchers focused on creating programs that could perform tasks that required human intelligence, such as playing chess, proving mathematical theorems, and understanding natural language.[7] Some of the notable achievements of this period include the Logic Theorist,[8] the first AI program that could prove mathematical theorems; the General Problem Solver,[9] a program that could solve a wide range

[1] David Mulpeter, 'The Genesis and Emergence of Web 3.0: A Study in the Integration of Artificial Intelligence and the Semantic Web in Knowledge Creation' [2009] *Dissertations* <https://arrow.tudublin.ie/scschcomdis/23> ('The Genesis and Emergence of Web 3.0').

[2] Gias Ahammed, 'Who Invented Artificial Intelligence? | History of Ai—Nothing but AI' (November 2022) <https://nothingbutai.com/who-invented-artificial-intelligence/> ('Who Invented Artificial Intelligence?').

[3] William Bechtel and Mitchell Herschbach, 'Philosophy of the Cognitive Sciences' in *Philosophies of the Sciences* (John Wiley & Sons, Ltd., 2010) 237 <https://onlinelibrary.wiley.com/doi/abs/10.1002/9781444315578.ch10>.

[4] Mariusz Flasiński, 'History of Artificial Intelligence' in Mariusz Flasiński (ed), *Introduction to Artificial Intelligence* (Springer International Publishing, 2016) 3 <https://doi.org/10.1007/978-3-319-40022-8_1>.

[5] BBC, 'What Is AI? What Does Artificial Intelligence Do?', *BBC Newsround* (online, 8 August 2019) <https://www.bbc.com/newsround/49274918> ('What Is AI?').

[6] Peter Bock, 'The Emergence of Artificial Intelligence: Learning to Learn' (1985) 6(3) *AI Magazine* 180 ('The Emergence of Artificial Intelligence').

[7] Luciana Lazzeretti et al., 'The Emergence of Artificial Intelligence in the Regional Sciences: A Literature Review' (2023) 31(7) *European Planning Studies* 1304 ('The Emergence of Artificial Intelligence in the Regional Sciences').

[8] AA Zinov'ev, *Foundations of the Logical Theory of Scientific Knowledge (Complex Logic)* (Springer Science & Business Media, 2012).

[9] Shunryu Colin Garvey, 'The "General Problem Solver" Does Not Exist: Mortimer Taube and the Art of AI Criticism' (2021) 43(1) *IEEE Annals of the History of Computing* 60, 68 ('The "General Problem Solver" Does Not Exist').

of problems using heuristic search; and ELIZA,[10] a program that could simulate a psychotherapist by using pattern matching and natural language processing.

Between 70s and 80s, AI researchers shifted their attention to creating systems that could represent and manipulate knowledge, rather than just perform calculations.[11] These systems, known as expert systems, could emulate the reasoning and decision-making of human experts in specific domains, such as medicine, engineering, and law.[12] Some of the notable achievements of this period include MYCIN,[13] an expert system that could diagnose and treat bacterial infections; DENDRAL,[14] an expert system that could identify the structure of organic molecules; and Cyc, an ambitious project that aimed to create a general knowledge base that could support common sense reasoning.[15]

In the late 1980s and 1990s, AI researchers faced several challenges and limitations of the symbolic and rule-based approaches that dominated the field.[16] These challenges included the difficulty of acquiring and maintaining large amounts of knowledge, the brittleness and inflexibility of the systems, and the lack of learning and adaptation capabilities.[17] To overcome these challenges, AI researchers explored alternative approaches that were inspired by biological and cognitive processes, such as neural networks, evolutionary algorithms, fuzzy logic, and artificial life. Some of

---

[10] Heung-yeung Shum, Xiao-dong He and Di Li, 'From Eliza to XiaoIce: Challenges and Opportunities with Social Chatbots' (2018) 19(1) *Frontiers of Information Technology & Electronic Engineering* 10 ('From Eliza to XiaoIce'); Joseph Weizenbaum, 'ELIZA—a Computer Program for the Study of Natural Language Communication between Man and Machine' (1983) 26(1) *Communications of the ACM* 23.

[11] Martin Schmitt, 'Socialist AI? Societal Use, Economic Implementation, and the Tensions of Applied Computer Science in Late Socialist GDR' (2023) 45(3) *IEEE Annals of the History of Computing* 66, 70 ('Socialist AI?').

[12] William P Wagner, 'Trends in Expert System Development: A Longitudinal Content Analysis of over Thirty Years of Expert System Case Studies' (2017) 76 *Expert Systems with Applications* 85, 91 ('Trends in Expert System Development').

[13] Milan Daniel, Petr Hájek and Phuong Hoang Nguyen, 'CADIAG-2 and MYCIN-like Systems' (1997) 9(3) *Artificial Intelligence in Medicine* 241; Edward H Shortliffe et al., 'Computer-Based Consultations in Clinical Therapeutics: Explanation and Rule Acquisition Capabilities of the MYCIN System' (1975) 8(4) *Computers and Biomedical Research* 303, 312 ('Computer-Based Consultations in Clinical Therapeutics').

[14] Ghaliya AlFarsi et al., 'Heuristic and Meta Dendral Systems: A Review' in *2021 22nd International Arab Conference on Information Technology (ACIT)* (2021) 1 <https://ieeexplore.ieee.org/abstract/document/9677414> ('Heuristic and Meta Dendral Systems'); Edward A Feigenbaum and Bruce G Buchanan, 'DENDRAL and Meta-DENDRAL: Roots of Knowledge Systems and Expert System Applications' <https://direct.mit.edu/books/edited-volume/4349/chapter/182192/DENDRAL-and-Meta-DENDRAL-roots-of-knowledge> ('DENDRAL and Meta-DENDRAL').

[15] Douglas Foxvog, 'Cyc' in Roberto Poli, Michael Healy and Achilles Kameas (eds), *Theory and Applications of Ontology: Computer Applications* (Springer Netherlands, 2010) 259 <https://doi.org/10.1007/978-90-481-8847-5_12>.

[16] Paul Lin and Tom Hazelbaker, 'Meeting the Challenge of Artificial Intelligence: What CPAs Need to Know' (2019) 89(6) *The CPA Journal*.

[17] Caiming Zhang and Yang Lu, 'Study on Artificial Intelligence: The State of the Art and Future Prospects' (2021) 23 *Journal of Industrial Information Integration* 100224 ('Study on Artificial Intelligence').

the notable achievements of this period include the development of backpropagation, a learning algorithm that enabled neural networks to learn complex functions,[18] the creation of genetic algorithms, a search technique that mimicked natural selection and evolution; and the emergence of artificial neural networks, a paradigm that simulated the behavior and learning of biological neurons.[19]

In the 2000s and 2010s, AI researchers witnessed a resurgence and a revolution of the field, thanks to the availability of large amounts of data, the advancement of computing power, and the improvement of machine learning algorithms. These factors enabled AI systems to achieve remarkable performance and surpass human capabilities in various tasks, such as image recognition, speech recognition, natural language processing, and game playing. Some of the notable achievements of this period include the development of deep learning, a technique that enabled neural networks to learn from multiple layers of abstraction; the creation of *AlphaGo*,[20] a program that defeated the world champion of *Go*,[21] a complex board game; and the emergence of *GPT-3*, a language model that could generate coherent and diverse texts from natural language prompts.[22]

The regulation of AI is the development of public sector policies and laws for promoting and regulating AI, which is related to the broader regulation of algorithms. The need for regulation of AI has been voiced by experts and advocates in responsible AI, AI ethics, consumer protection, and cybersecurity since at least the 1960s. However, the necessity to introduce a regulatory framework to manage potential implications that stem from AI-generated outcomes remains a challenge for many jurisdictions, and there is no consensus on what, when, and how the uses and applications of AI should be regulated.[23] Potentially, a key obstacle in the concerned regulation lies in determining the precise meaning and extent of AI. The ongoing inquiry for a universally acknowledged definition for the concept of AI poses challenges in developing a comprehensive regulatory framework that can effectively

---

[18] Kaizhu Huang et al. (eds), *Deep Learning: Fundamentals, Theory and Applications*, vol 2 (Springer International Publishing, 2019) <http://link.springer.com/10.1007/978-3-030-06073-2> ('*Deep Learning*').

[19] Kory Becker and Justin Gottschlich, 'AI Programmer: Autonomously Creating Software Programs Using Genetic Algorithms' in *Proceedings of the Genetic and Evolutionary Computation Conference Companion* (Association for Computing Machinery, 2021) 1513 <https://dl.acm.org/doi/10.1145/3449726.3463125> ('AI Programmer').

[20] Scott R. Granter, Andrew H. Beck and David J. Papke Jr., 'AlphaGo, Deep Learning, and the Future of the Human Microscopist' (2017) 141(5) *Archives of Pathology & Laboratory Medicine* 619.

[21] Jim X. Chen, 'The Evolution of Computing: AlphaGo' (2016) 18(4) *Computing in Science & Engineering* 4 ('The Evolution of Computing').

[22] Kris McGuffie and Alex Newhouse, 'The Radicalization Risks of GPT-3 and Advanced Neural Language Models' (No arXiv:2009.06807, arXiv, 14 September 2020) <http://arxiv.org/abs/2009.06807>.

[23] Nathalie A. Smuha, 'From a "Race to AI" to a "Race to AI Regulation": Regulatory Competition for Artificial Intelligence' (2021) 13(1) *Law, Innovation and Technology* 57 ('From a "Race to AI" to a "Race to AI Regulation"').

include the wide range of its capabilities and applications.[24] Further, ethical, and social ramifications of AI can pose substantial difficulties. What is more, AI systems have the potential to continue or worsen biases that exist in the data they are trained on, resulting in outcomes that are unjust or discriminatory. Moreover, implementation of AI in critical sectors including criminal justice, health care, and employment gives rise to apprehensions over privacy, consent, and the possibility of abuse.

Regarding the international character of this technology, it is crucial to have worldwide coordination and cooperation in the context of the associated with AI technology (e.g., systems, software, generated outcomes, etc.) governance.[25] Creating shared rules and frameworks for efficient governance of this technology can facilitate coordination among regulators and be implemented in manners beneficial for the humanity.[26] The following section pursues to provide the emerging field of AI regulatory frameworks that have been undertaken, around the globe up to date.

2 The Landscape of AI Regulation

2.1 European Institutions: Initiatives

In 2017, the European Council called for a sense of urgency to address emerging trends including issues, such as AI, while at the same time ensuring a high level of data protection, digital rights, and ethical standards.[27] In its 2019 *Conclusions on the coordinated plan on the development and use of AI*, the Council further highlighted the importance of ensuring that European citizens' rights are fully respected and called for a review of the existing relevant legislation to make it fit for purpose for the new opportunities and challenges raised by AI.[28]

The European Council has also called for a clear determination of the AI applications that should be considered high risk. The most recent Conclusions from 21 October 2020 further called for addressing the opacity, complexity, bias, a certain degree of unpredictability, and partially autonomous behavior of certain AI systems,

[24] Jeffrey T. Hancock, Mor Naaman and Karen Levy, 'AI-Mediated Communication: Definition, Research Agenda, and Ethical Considerations' (2020) 25(1) *Journal of Computer-Mediated Communication* 89 ('AI-Mediated Communication').

[25] Pekka Ala-Pietilä and Nathalie A Smuha, 'A Framework for Global Cooperation on Artificial Intelligence and Its Governance' in Bertrand Braunschweig and Malik Ghallab (eds), *Reflections on Artificial Intelligence for Humanity* (Springer International Publishing, 2021) 237 <https://doi.org/10.1007/978-3-030-69128-8_15>.

[26] Schmitt (n 11).

[27] Gonçalo Carriço, 'The EU and Artificial Intelligence: A Human-Centred Perspective' (2018) 17(1) *European View* 29 ('The EU and Artificial Intelligence').

[28] European Council, 'European Coordinated Plan on Artificial Intelligence' <https://www.consilium.europa.eu/en/press/press-releases/2019/02/18/european-coordinated-plan-on-artificial-intelligence/>.

to ensure their compatibility with fundamental rights and to facilitate the enforcement of legal rules.[29]

The European Parliament has also undertaken a considerable amount of work in AI.[30] In October 2020, it adopted several resolutions related to AI, including on ethics, liability, and copyright. In 2021, those were followed by resolutions on AI in criminal matters and in education, culture, and the audio-visual sector. The European Parliament resolution on a *Framework of ethical aspects of artificial intelligence, robotics and related technologies* specifically recommends to the Commission to propose legislative action to harness the opportunities and benefits of AI, but also to ensure protection of ethical principles.[31] The resolution includes a text of the legislative proposal for a regulation on ethical principles for the development, deployment and use of AI, robotics, and related technologies.[32]

On one hand, it is comprehensive and future-proof in its fundamental regulatory choices, including the principle-based requirements that AI systems should comply with. On the other hand, it puts in place a proportionate regulatory system centered on a well-defined risk-based regulatory approach that does not create unnecessary restrictions to trade, whereby legal intervention is tailored to those concrete situations where there is a justified cause for concern or where such concern can reasonably be anticipated soon. At the same time, the legal framework includes flexible mechanisms that enable it to be dynamically adapted as the technology evolves and new concerning situations emerge.

The proposal sets harmonized rules for the development, placement on the market, and use of AI systems in the Union following a proportionate risk-based approach. It proposes a single future-proof definition of AI. Certain particularly harmful AI practices are prohibited as contravening Union values, while specific restrictions and safeguards are proposed in relation to certain uses of remote biometric identification systems for the purpose of law enforcement. The proposal lays down a solid risk methodology to define "high-risk" AI systems that pose significant risks to the health and safety or fundamental rights of persons. Those AI systems will have to comply with a set of horizontal mandatory requirements for trustworthy AI and follow conformity assessment procedures before those systems can be placed on the Union market. Predictable, proportionate, and clear obligations are also placed

---

[29] European Council, 'Artificial Intelligence: Presidency Issues Conclusions on Ensuring Respect for Fundamental Rights' <https://www.consilium.europa.eu/en/press/press-releases/2020/10/21/artificial-intelligence-presidency-issues-conclusions-on-ensuring-respect-for-fundamental-rights/>.

[30] Endre Rudi, 'Responsiveness to a Digital Age: Voting on Artificial Intelligence in the European Parliament' (Master thesis, The University of Bergen, 2022) <https://bora.uib.no/bora-xmlui/handle/11250/3012956> ('Responsiveness to a Digital Age').

[31] Martin Ebers et al., 'The European Commission's Proposal for an Artificial Intelligence Act—A Critical Assessment by Members of the Robotics and AI Law Society (RAILS)' (2021) 4(4) *J* 589, 595.

[32] European Parliament, 'Framework of Ethical Aspects of Artificial Intelligence, Robotics and Related Technologies' <https://www.europarl.europa.eu/doceo/document/TA-9-2020-0275_EN.html>.

on providers and users of those systems to ensure safety and respect of existing legislation protecting fundamental rights throughout the whole AI systems' lifecycle.

For some specific AI systems, only minimum transparency obligations are proposed, when chatbots or "deep fakes" are used. Yet, the literature shows that the European Union's approach is also adopted from a few common law jurisdictions, such as the United Kingdom and United States.[33]

3 Challenges in AI Regulation: The DABUS Cases

3.1 United Kingdom

In the UK, a case involving DABUS was heard by the High Court of Justice in 2020, which ruled that an AI system cannot be named as an inventor in a patent application, as the *Patents Act* 1977 requires an inventor to be a natural person.[34] The court also rejected the argument that the owner of DABUS, Dr Thaler, could be the inventor by default, as he did not make any intellectual contribution to the invention.[35] The decision was appealed to the Court of Appeal, which upheld the High Court's ruling in 2021. The case is now pending before the Supreme Court.

It should be noted that the UK has been working on a regulatory framework to address the challenges posed by AI-generated outputs. In Spring 2023, the UK Government published its policy paper on *A pro-innovation approach to AI regulation*.[36] The policy paper focuses on the context in which AI is deployed and sets out five cross-cutting principles[37] that will underpin the UK's AI regulatory approach.

The government does not initially intend to introduce new legislation to avoid placing undue burdens on businesses. Instead, it will issue its five principles to the UK's regulators on a non-statutory basis and ask them over the next 12 months to deliver guidance on how these will apply to AI technologies. The UK Government is also confirming its commitment to establish a regulatory sandbox for AI to bring

[33] Corinne Cath et al., 'Artificial Intelligence and the "Good Society": The US, EU, and UK Approach' (2018) 24(2) *Science and Engineering Ethics* 505, 519 ('Artificial Intelligence and the "Good Society"').

[34] *The Patents Act 1977 (Cth)* 102, 7(1).

[35] *Thaler v Comptroller-General of Patents, Designs and Trademarks* (The Supreme Court, Term Michaelmas, 2021).

[36] Chris Reed and Keri Grieman, 'Response to the UK White Paper: A pro-Innovation Approach to AI Regulation' (SSRN Scholarly Paper No. 4478556, 14 June 2023) <https://papers.ssrn.com/abstract=4478556> ('Response to the UK White Paper').

[37] (i) Safety, security, and robustness: AI systems in the UK need to have been trained and built on robust data; (ii) appropriate transparency and explainability: operationality of AI systems should be explainable to their users; (iii) fairness: individuals' legal rights should not be undermined from the AI; (iv) accountability and governance: AI systems must have appropriate oversight over the way it is used and clear lines of accountability; (v) contestability and redress: availability of avenues for redress if an AI system causes harm. See also.

together regulators to support innovators directly. It is therefore evident that the human factor and human's contribution should play a vital role in the process of policy development.[38]

It is worth noting that unlike most other countries, UK legislation provides copyright protection to a work generated by a computer in circumstances where there is no human author.[39] The law provides that such works will be owned by a human or corporate person, but the computer program or AI itself can never be the author or owner of the IP.[40]

This regulatory framework is still evolving, and the UK Government has expressed a commitment to engaging internationally to support interoperability across different regulatory regimes.[41] Therefore, while the framework is taking shape, it is not yet fully settled and is expected to adapt as AI technologies continue to evolve.

3.2 United States

In the US, a case involving DABUS was decided by the US Patent and Trademark Office (USPTO) in 2020, which also denied the patent application on the grounds that an inventor must be a human being under US patent law. The USPTO cited the legislative history and the case law that support the interpretation that the term "inventor" refers to an individual or a group of individuals, not a machine. The decision was appealed to the US Court of Appeals for the Federal Circuit, which affirmed the USPTO's ruling in 2021.[42]

---

[38] Adam D. Thierer, 'Flexible, Pro-Innovation Governance Strategies for Artificial Intelligence' (SSRN Scholarly Paper No. 4423897, 20 April 2023) <https://papers.ssrn.com/abstract=4423897>.

[39] Stanley Lai, *Copyright Protection of Computer Software in the United Kingdom* (Bloomsbury Publishing, 2000); Andreas Rahmatian, 'Originality in UK Copyright Law: The Old "Skill and Labour" Doctrine Under Pressure' (2013) 44(1) *IIC—International Review of Intellectual Property and Competition Law* 4 ('Originality in UK Copyright Law').

[40] Dr. Pratap Devarapalli, 'Machine Learning to Machine Owning: Redefining the Copyright Ownership from the Perspective of Australian, US, UK and EU Law' (SSRN Scholarly Paper No. 3293518, 1 November 2018) <https://papers.ssrn.com/abstract=3293518> ('Machine Learning to Machine Owning'); Jane C Ginsburg, 'The Concept of Authorship in Comparative Copyright Law Annual Center for Intellectual Property Law & (and) Information Technology (CIPLIT) Symposium: The Many Faces of Authorship:Legal and Interdisciplinary Perspectives—Featuring Professor Jane C. Ginsburg as the Fifth Annual Niro Distinguished Intellectual Property Lecturer' (2002) 52(4) *DePaul Law Review* 1063 ('The Concept of Authorship in Comparative Copyright Law Annual Center for Intellectual Property Law & (and) Information Technology (CIPLIT) Symposium').

[41] Racheal Adams, 'The Evolution of Intellectual Property Rights in the Digital Age' (2023) 3(2) *Journal of Modern Law and Policy* 52; Simone Schroff, 'The Evolution of Copyright Policies (1880–2010): A Comparison between Germany, the UK, the US and the International Level' (doctoral, University of East Anglia. School of Law, 2014) <https://ueaeprints.uea.ac.uk/id/eprint/49708/> ('The Evolution of Copyright Policies (1880–2010)').

[42] Ryan Abbott, Rita Matulionyte and Paul Nolan, 'A Brief Analysis of DABUS, Artificial Intelligence, and the Future of Patent Law' [2021] (125) *Intellectual Property Forum: Journal of the Intellectual and Industrial Property Society of Australia and New Zealand* 10.

The literature shows that in the US governmental bodies and national stakeholders have been actively working on a regulatory framework to address the challenges posed by AI-generated outputs. The first example to consider is the *AI Disclosure Act of 2023*.[43] This act requires all material generated by AI technology to include a disclaimer based on which it is explicitly addressed that the generated output has been created from the related AI system and this sentence applies to videos, photos, text, audio, and any other AI-generated material.[44] This information would include the purpose of the AI system, the data that the AI system is trained on, and the algorithms that the AI system uses including potential risks and benefits that stem from these uses, accordingly.

The bill would also create a new agency within the Federal Trade Commission (FTC) to oversee the implementation of the law. This bill is important because it would increase transparency and accountability in the use of AI. By requiring companies to disclose information about their use of AI, the bill would help consumers to understand how AI is being used and to make informed decisions about whether to use AI-powered products and services. Yet, it is still early to say whether the *AI Disclosure Act of 2023* will become law. However, the bill has generated a lot of interest and debate, and it is likely to continue to be a topic of discussion in the coming months. Further, the concerned bill demonstrates that US government representatives have been greatly influenced from the Chief Executive Officer's (CEO) of OpenAI request, when few months before (i.e., March 2023) he called for US to regulate AI as it could cause harm to the world.[45]

There are scholars who argue that regulating AI technology will be one of the central challenges confronting Congress in the years and decades to come.[46] The abovementioned bill is seen as a step toward addressing the threat of "mass disinformation, dislocation, and destruction" potentially posed by AI. Yet, there are concerns addressed concerning the Act. For example, Lilian Edwards, who specializes in Internet law at Newcastle University, UK, warns that the AI Act should not be over-analyzed at this point as it will keep evolving before it passes.[47] In addition, the Act treats violations of its generative AI disclosure requirement as "unfair or deceptive acts or practices" under the terms of the *Federal Trade Commission Act (FTCA)*.[48,49]

---

[43] Ritchie Torres, AI Disclosure Act 2023 2023 (D-NY).

[44] Ibid 2(a).

[45] Aslıhan Ünal and İzzet Kılınç, 'The Feasibility of Artificial Intelligence Performing as CEO: The Vizier-Shah Theory' (2021) 23(6) *foresight* 698, 717 ('The Feasibility of Artificial Intelligence Performing as CEO').

[46] Yogesh K. Dwivedi et al., 'Artificial Intelligence (AI): Multidisciplinary Perspectives on Emerging Challenges, Opportunities, and Agenda for Research, Practice and Policy' (2021) 57 *International Journal of Information Management* 101,994 ['Artificial Intelligence (AI)'].

[47] Lilian Edwards and Charlotte Waelde, *Law and the Internet* (Bloomsbury Publishing, 2009).

[48] Róisín Áine Costello, 'Law, Policy and the Internet, by Lilian Edwards' (2019) 27(2) *International Journal of Law and Information Technology* 204, 205; Edwards and Waelde (n 47).

[49] Those using generative AI without this disclaimer would violate section 18(a)(1)(B) of the Federal Trade Commission Act (15 U.S.C. 57a(a)(1)(B)), which prohibits unfair or deceptive acts. Accordingly, the Federal Trade Commission would enforce the Act, meaning that entities suspected of

This means that enforcement of the bill is designated to the FTC, which could potentially pose challenges given the FTC's current enforcement orientation. Further concerns exist with respect to the potential impact of the Act on innovation.[50] As it has been mentioned before, the bill requires all material generated by artificial intelligence technology to include a disclaimer stating that the generated output has been produced from the associated AI system. This requirement could potentially impact the development and deployment of AI technologies.[51] Even though the *AI Disclosure Act of 2023* has been considered as a step that has the potential to contribute to regulating AI systems, the literature shows that disclosing statements and guidelines related to AI-generated output has not been seen as the sole and efficient solution.[52]

4 Primary Thoughts

The above discussion illustrates that the regulatory framework concerning patent protection is not well equipped to deal with the emerging phenomenon of AI inventorship.[53] In addition, scholars argue that that there is a variety of perspectives and arguments on whether an AI system can be considered as an inventor (or not), and if so, who should then be entitled to rights that stem from the AI-generated inventions.[54]

It follows that there are challenges and uncertainties that stem from the use of AI systems to generate inventions and other creative outputs.[55] The traditional notion of inventorship assumes that only human beings can have the necessary creativity, intelligence, and intention to invent. However, AI systems are increasingly capable of generating novel and useful ideas without human intervention or guidance. This

non-compliance would be subject to the same penalties, privileges, and immunities as under the Federal Trade Commission Act.

[50] Fadi Shehab Shiyyab et al., 'The Impact of Artificial Intelligence Disclosure on Financial Performance' (2023) 11(3) *International Journal of Financial Studies* 115.

[51] Bruce D. Sokler et al., 'New AI Disclosure Bill and AI Strategic Plan Update—AI: The Washington Report' <https://www.mintz.com/insights-center/viewpoints/2191/2023-06-12-new-ai-disclosure-bill-and-ai-strategic-plan-update-ai>.

[52] Enrique Bonsón and Michaela Bednárová, 'Artificial Intelligence Disclosures in Sustainability Reports: Towards an Artificial Intelligence Reporting Framework' in Vikas Kumar et al. (eds), *Digital Transformation in Industry* (Springer International Publishing, 2022) 391 ('Artificial Intelligence Disclosures in Sustainability Reports').

[53] Donrich Thaldar and Meshandren Naidoo, 'AI Inventorship: The Right Decision?' (2021) 117(11–12) *South African Journal of Science* 1, 2 ('AI Inventorship').

[54] Matthew Horton and Austin Kim, 'Inventorship: Why AI Is Not Smart Enough Yet US: AI Patents' (2020) 286 *Managing Intellectual Property* 19, 22 ('Inventorship').

[55] Madeleine de Cock Buning, 'Artificial Intelligence and the Creative Industry: New Challenges for the EU Paradigm for Art and Technology by Autonomous Creation' in *Research Handbook on the Law of Artificial Intelligence* (Edward Elgar Publishing, 2018) 511 <https://www.elgaronline.com/edcollchap/edcoll/9781786439048/9781786439048.00032.xml> ('Artificial Intelligence and the Creative Industry').

raises the question of whether an AI system can meet the legal requirements of inventorship, such as the inventive step or non-obviousness, and whether it can have the moral or legal rights and responsibilities of an inventor.

In general, contemporary regulatory systems for patent protection around the world provide that the inventor or the person who derives the right from the inventor is entitled to apply for and own a patent. However, there is not yet addressed a patent provision or any other regulatory framework to delineate the person who derives the rights from the inventor when an AI system generates an invention. Some possible candidates are the AI system itself, the owner or operator of the AI system, the developer or programmer of the AI system, the provider of the data or inputs for the AI system, or the user or beneficiary of the AI system. Each of these candidates may have different claims and interests in the AI-generated inventions and may face different legal and ethical issues. Thus, the importance of human factors in this respect is slightly blurred.

It should be mentioned that due to different legal traditions, principles, and interpretations the theoretical framework of discussion around the necessity to efficiently deal and regulate AI-generated output varies.[56] Hence, it is reasonable for different approaches and standards to be undertaken toward an efficient dealing with AI inventorship and AI-generated inventions.[57] This may create inconsistencies and uncertainties for the patent applicants, the patent offices, the courts, and the public. It may also affect the international recognition and protection of AI-generated inventions, and the global innovation and competition in the AI field. Therefore, there is a need for a harmonized and consistent approach to address the intellectual property issues posed by AI inventorship and AI-generated inventions. Such an approach should consider the following aspects:

The vital objective of the patent system per se is to encourage innovation and the spread of technology by providing inventors with exclusive rights to their innovations for a certain period.[58] The exclusivity of this arrangement offers a substantial motivation for individuals and corporations to allocate resources toward research and development, hence cultivating an environment conducive to innovation. As a condition for obtaining these rights, inventors should publicly reveal their inventions, therefore adding to the shared body of knowledge and facilitating additional progress.[59]

---

[56] Pak-Hang Wong, 'Cultural Differences as Excuses? Human Rights and Cultural Values in Global Ethics and Governance of AI' (2020) 33(4) *Philosophy & Technology* 705 ('Cultural Differences as Excuses?').

[57] Söğüt Atilla, 'Dealing with AI-Generated Works: Lessons from the CDPA Section 9(3)' (2024) 19(1) *Journal of Intellectual Property Law & Practice* 43, 49 ('Dealing with AI-Generated Works').

[58] Li Jiang, 'Alienation from the Objectives of the Patent System: How to Remedy the Situation of Biotechnology Patent' (2019) 25(3) *Science and Engineering Ethics* 791 ('Alienation from the Objectives of the Patent System').

[59] Laura Pedraza-Farina and Ryan Whalen, 'The Ghost in the Patent System: An Empirical Study of Patent Law's Elusive "Skilled Artisan"' (2022) 108(1) *Iowa Law Review* 247 ('The Ghost in the Patent System').

We should also consider, additional to its economic and technological goals, the patent system embodies the societal principles of fairness, justice, and human dignity.[60] It guarantees that inventors receive equitable compensation for their contributions, the benefits of new technology are dispersed equally, and the associated process upholds the inherent dignity of parties involved.[61] Hence, any strategy, policy, and regulatory framework anticipated to be introduced for addressing AI inventorship and AI-generated inventions should align with these benefits and social values. It follows that equitable consideration of the interests and rights of several stakeholders, including inventors, owners, users, and the public, should be also undertaken.[62]

Albeit the social nature of patent system, the emergence of AI inventorship poses challenges for the patent system. Deciding who deserves credit for AI-generated inventions, whether it is the AI developers, the end users, or the AI itself, necessitates a thoughtful examination of principles of fairness and justice. Issues of personhood are also raised reasonably and determine another challenge to encounter.[63] Therefore, it is crucial to modify, for example, disclosure regulations as the one addressed in the *AI Disclosure Act 2023* [i.e., addressed in s2(a)], to enable the public to understand and then we will be able to contribute to the development of AI-generated outcomes. Consequently, the involvement of human factor is going to be increased which seems "absent" and concerns a few scholars.[64] As far as the patent system is concerned, this is also vital for upholding the capacity to distribute inventions that enrich our knowledge background.[65]

Expanding upon this basis, it is crucial to acknowledge that AI systems are neither uniform nor unchanging; they differ greatly in their categories, purposes, and degrees of self-governance, intellect, and inventiveness. Hence, it is imperative to consider these varied qualities and capacities when discussing about AI inventorship and AI-generated outcomes. It is essential to differentiate between various levels and methods of AI participation to properly assign credit and maintain fairness and justice in the patent system and always considering human factor's involvement, respectively.

---

[60] Andrew C. Michaels, 'Benefits of the Invention and Social Value in Patent Law' (2021) 29(3) *George Mason Law Review* 827.

[61] Aiting Xu et al., 'Accelerated Green Patent Examination and Innovation Benefits: An Analysis of Private Economic Value and Public Environmental Benefits' (2024) 200 *Technological Forecasting and Social Change* 123105 ('Accelerated Green Patent Examination and Innovation Benefits').

[62] Pat Roberts, Joseph Herkert and Jennifer Kuzma, 'Responsible Innovation in Biotechnology: Stakeholder Attitudes and Implications for Research Policy', ed Alastair Iles and Philip Macnaghten (2020) 8 *Elementa: Science of the Anthropocene* 47 ('Responsible Innovation in Biotechnology'); Deli Yang, 'Patent Litigation Strategy and Its Effects on the Firm' (2019) 21(4) *International Journal of Management Reviews* 427.

[63] John-Stewart Gordon, 'Artificial Moral and Legal Personhood' (2021) 36(2) *AI & SOCIETY* 457.

[64] Monika Westphal et al., 'Decision Control and Explanations in Human-AI Collaboration: Improving User Perceptions and Compliance' (2023) 144 *Computers in Human Behavior* 107714 ('Decision Control and Explanations in Human-AI Collaboration').

[65] Nobuya Fukugawa, 'Knowledge Creation and Dissemination by Kosetsushi in Sectoral Innovation Systems: Insights from Patent Data' (2016) 109(3) *Scientometrics* 2303 ('Knowledge Creation and Dissemination by Kosetsushi in Sectoral Innovation Systems').

In conclusion, the evolving nature of AI technology requires careful adjustments to the patent system. To ensure the promotion of innovation and technology dissemination while maintaining fairness, justice, and human dignity, it is important for those who rule and govern to give a more dynamic scheme to the patent system by considering the abovementioned elements that characterize the AI technology AI systems and provide effective mechanisms for check and balances.

Legal Impact of the Sharing Economy on Commercial Real Estate

Abhinav Tomer, Rupendra Singh, and Nuha Rahman

Abstract The research paper examines the significant influence of the sharing economy on commercial real estate, emphasizing the legal, regulatory, and operational challenges it poses. It highlights how platforms like Airbnb and Uber have revolutionized consumer behavior, fostering new trends, such as co-working spaces, short-term rentals, and pop-up stores. These trends present both opportunities and challenges for property owners, landlords, and regulators. The paper discusses the necessity for clear legal frameworks to address issues related to liability, insurance, and zoning. It also explores the implications of the sharing economy on traditional leasing models, emphasizing the need for effective communication and innovative strategies to resolve conflicts. Furthermore, it analyzes the Indian context, highlighting the country's digital transformation and its potential as a testing ground for new technologies. The paper underscores the importance of regulatory clarity and proactive legal measures to sustain the growth of the sharing economy, ensuring it aligns with safety and quality standards. Overall, the study provides a comprehensive overview of the dynamic interplay between the sharing economy and commercial real estate, offering insights into future regulatory and operational directions.

Keywords Sharing economy · Commercial real estate · Co-working spaces · Short-term rentals · Pop-up stores · Legal frameworks

1 Introduction

The platform (or sharing) economy business model is defined by Katz[1] as having "(A) an online intermediary that (B) acts as a market for P2P services and (C) facilitates exchanges by lowering transaction costs." India stands at the precipice of an era marked by the convergence of its natural riches, a burgeoning middle-class

[1] Vanessa Katz, *Regulating the sharing economy*, 30(385), BTLJ 1063 (2015).

A. Tomer (✉) · R. Singh · N. Rahman
Amity Law School Noida, Noida, India
e-mail: atomer2@amity.edu

J. Aston et al. (eds.), *Comparative Law*, https://doi.org/10.1007/978-981-97-7815-7_25

population, and a rapid embrace of digital technologies. As the country gears up to claim the title of "the youngest nation," its ideal social and economic landscape lays the foundation for a flourishing access and sharing economy.[2] Bolstered by the status of being the second-largest smartphone market globally, with Internet users projected to double by 2025, India presents a fertile ground for the expansion of sharing platforms.[3]

A survey conducted by The Boston Consulting Group revealed a staggering 83% of respondents in India expressing a desire to engage with access and sharing platforms, indicating a strong appetite for collaborative consumption.[4] Recognizing this momentum, it is imperative for India to proactively address the regulatory challenges that accompany the unfolding opportunities in the access and sharing economy. The country, with its scale and a relatively smaller average transaction size, provides an ideal environment for testing and refining new technologies at scale.

One notable example is Facebook's strategic decision to test its WhatsApp payments platform in India before launching it in higher-risk markets like the EU and the United States. This underscores India's role as a testing ground for innovations, benefiting from the vast user base and dynamic market conditions. Moreover, India has the potential to lead in the development of trust networks, leveraging new technologies. The suggestion to actively partner with Indian companies focusing on consensus algorithms and distributed ledger technologies demonstrates a commitment to fostering homegrown talent and contributing to the global technological ecosystem.

Despite India's recent jump in the "ease of doing business" rankings, moving from 130th to 63rd place,[5] there is still work to be done in terms of regulatory clarity. Access and sharing economy companies find themselves navigating a gray zone, highlighting the need for a robust legal framework. As the current government seeks to leverage political capital and embrace change, it becomes crucial to formulate and revise laws that not only encourage innovation but also facilitate the sustained growth of the access and sharing economy.

The rise of sharing economy platforms, exemplified by giants like Uber and Poshmark, has ignited a paradigm shift in consumer behavior. Seeking flexibility and cost-effectiveness, consumers are not only redefining their daily solutions but are also reshaping the landscape of commercial real estate. This transformation extends beyond traditional sectors, impacting office spaces and creating a ripple effect in various dimensions.

---

[2] United Nations, *Achieving sustainable development and promoting development cooperation*, 23 (2008), https://www.un.org/en/ecosoc/docs/pdfs/fina_08-45773.pdf.

[3] PIB, *Summary of the Economic Survey 2022–23*, 22 (2022), https://static.pib.gov.in/WriteReadData/userfiles/file/EconomicSurvey2023Q44O.pdf.

[4] Vikash Jain et al., *Unlocking the potential of the Gig Economy in India*, BCG, 111 (2020), https://media-publications.bcg.com/India-Gig-Economy-Report.pdf.

[5] Yogima Seth Sharma, "*India jumps to 63rd position in world banks doing business 2020 report*", ET, October 24, 2019.

1.1 Rise of Co-working Spaces

The sharing economy has given birth to the phenomenon of co-working spaces, revolutionizing the office space market. These platforms facilitate easy access to co-working spaces, offering memberships that grant users entry to multiple locations. This convenience caters to the needs of frequent travelers and those who crave a dynamic work environment. Beyond convenience, these platforms enhance their value propositions by collaborating with other sharing economy services like Uber and Airbnb, providing users with enticing discounts and perks.

1.2 Short-Term Rentals

Platforms, such as Airbnb, have spurred property owners to explore short-term rentals in commercial spaces.[6] The sharing economy has intensified competition in this market, compelling companies to differentiate their offerings to attract tenants. This shift is not only about competition but also reflects a changing mindset among tenants who prefer flexibility over long-term commitments. Some organizations are now opting for short-term rentals as they align better with the dynamic nature of their operations.

1.3 Pop-Up Stores: Temporary Ventures in Commercial Real Estate

The concept of pop-up shops is yet another manifestation of the sharing economy's impact on commercial real estate. These temporary retail spaces, used for short periods, have become a favored strategy for established and emerging businesses looking to experiment with new products or markets. Property owners stand to benefit from the revenue generated by pop-up shops and the increased foot traffic they attract to their properties.

1.4 New Opportunities for Property Owners

The sharing economy has opened novel avenues for property owners to monetize underutilized spaces creatively. A vacant parking lot transforms into an event venue

---

[6] Von Briel, D. and Dolnicar, S. (2021) The evolution of Airbnb regulations, in S. Dolnicar (Ed.) *Airbnb before, during and after COVID-19*, University of Queensland.

on weekends, and a rooftop terrace becomes a space for yoga classes or other activities.[7] This trend reflects property owners' innovative approaches to maximizing revenue by capitalizing on the diverse uses their spaces can offer.

1.5 Impact on Traditional Leasing Models

While the sharing economy brings forth numerous opportunities, it has also triggered concerns about its impact on traditional leasing models. Landlords, wary of potential security issues, liabilities, and disruptions to other tenants, may hesitate to embrace co-working spaces, short-term rentals, and pop-up shops. Effective communication between tenants and landlords becomes essential to navigate potential conflicts and find common ground that aligns with the evolving dynamics of the sharing economy.

As stakeholders navigate this evolving landscape, effective communication, innovative strategies, and a willingness to adapt will be key to harnessing the full potential of the sharing economy in the realm of commercial real estate.

1.6 How Does Property Law Apply to the Sharing Economy?

Property law plays a crucial role in navigating the complexities of the sharing economy, focusing on the legal intricacies surrounding the ownership and use of shared property. A question of law arises while regulating this economic model under Rental agreements, Town planning Act, Building Codes, etc., RERA (Regulation and Development) Act 2016, poses a complex situation to bind models like Airbnb under the ambit of law. In this context, the legal landscape encompasses the rights and responsibilities of individuals engaged in sharing their property, with particular emphasis on liability, insurance, and taxation. In 2017, the Delhi High Court considered a case involving the legality of short-term rentals and emphasized the need for clear regulations to govern the sharing economy, including platforms like Airbnb. A significant challenge arises concerning liability, as property owners who share their assets may find themselves accountable for damages resulting from the property's use.

For instance, if a homeowner rents their residence on Airbnb and a guest causes damage, the property owner may be legally responsible for covering repair costs. Another pivotal concern is insurance, as conventional policies may not extend coverage to property shared within the sharing economy. This necessitates individuals engaging in property sharing to explore specialized insurance options, ensuring

[7] Delhi Urban Art Commission, *The Enabling of safe public spaces in India,* DELHI URBAN ART COMMISSION (2018), https://duac.org.in/Upload/City%20Level%20Studies/Vision%20of%20Delhi/653209398198444.pdf.

adequate protection against potential liabilities. In essence, the application of property law to the sharing economy underscores the need for clear legal frameworks addressing liability and insurance issues in this evolving and dynamic economic landscape.

1.7 Legal and Safety Concerns in the Sharing Economy: A Comprehensive Overview Rights of Ownership

In the sharing economy, questions surrounding the rights of ownership are pivotal. Platforms like BetrSpot, allowing the sale of seats and queue spots, raise intricate issues. While transactions may transfer occupancy, venues argue that such items are non-assignable licenses and cannot be sold. Drawing parallels to the early challenges faced by peer-to-peer file-sharing systems, where copyright violations led to shutdowns, current ventures demand a nuanced consideration of ownership concerns.

1.8 Liability Limits

Liability poses a significant challenge in the sharing economy, exemplified by scenarios where users incur injuries while utilizing shared resources. Take the instance of a skier renting equipment from GearCommons and subsequently getting injured. The company's liability becomes a gray area, with users arguing negligent screening and companies emphasizing their role as intermediaries protected by the Communications Decency Act, 1996. Negotiating liability limits is a critical aspect for companies operating in the sharing economy, given the unique challenges posed by their digital presence.

1.9 Zoning Problems

Zoning regulations add another layer of complexity, especially when residential properties are used for short-term rentals in areas exclusively zoned for residential dwellings. The evolving demographics and changes in work patterns necessitate a fresh perspective on zoning codes that may not always accommodate flexible uses. The rise of micro-houses and shifts in housing availability underscore the urgency for reevaluating zoning laws to align with the evolving needs of a dynamic urban population.

1.10 Permitting and Licensing

The ambiguity surrounding permitting and licensing requirements further complicates the sharing economy's legal landscape. While common sense may dictate different requirements for a pop-up event versus a traditional business, the overlap of sharing economy platforms with heavily regulated industries, such as restaurants and hotels, raises uncertainties. Determining whether a sharing model necessitates the same licenses and permits as traditional operations remains a challenge, highlighting the need for clearer regulatory frameworks in this evolving economic landscape. As the sharing economy continues to reshape industries, addressing these legal and safety concerns is imperative for sustainable growth and user trust.

2 The Famous Co-working Model

In the vibrant landscape of India, the co-working industry is experiencing exponential growth while operating within the contours of diverse local regulations. Compliance with land-use permissions, labor laws, and strict adherence to safety and health regulations are paramount considerations for co-working spaces in the subcontinent.

The sector's adaptability is evident as Indian co-working spaces tailor internal policies to align with local cultural nuances and legal requisites, contributing to the global spectrum of regulatory diversity within the co-working sector. A crucial aspect is bridging the sector with government initiatives to ensure that innovation and technology lead to reduced legal conflicts and more amicable dispute resolutions.

Two prevalent business models, the Ownership Model and Landlord Partnership, shape the co-working landscape in India.[8] However, despite being subject to various statutes, such as the Indian Contract Act, 1872, Transfer of Property Act, 1882, and the Information Technology Act, 2000, there is currently no specific legislation exclusively governing legal issues in this burgeoning business sector.

Key legal due diligence requirements for co-working space companies include a thorough verification of legal title, incorporation of vital legal clauses in leasehold agreements, ensuring conformity with sanctioned plans for existing structures, and procuring all necessary licenses for commercial operation. Co-working entities must be incorporated under the appropriate legal structure, be it a partnership firm, LLP, or a company, with compliance requirements varying for each entity type.

Legal diligence and strict compliance with existing laws are imperative for the seamless operation of co-working spaces. As legal arenas evolve, strategies must be devised to navigate emerging laws, such as the Digital Data Protection Act, 2023, and cross-border regulations related to data, technology transfer, and cybersecurity,

[8] Edward Yates et al., *From coworking to competing? Business models and strategies of UK coworking spaces beyond the COVID-19 pandemic*, 8, COMPETITION & CHANGE, 123-143 (2023).

ensuring effective conflict mitigation. The dynamism of the co-working industry in India demands a forward-looking legal approach to foster innovation and sustainable growth.

3 Practice of Sharing Economy in India and United States of America

3.1 Indian Emerging Sharing Economy

The emergence and proliferation of the sharing economy in India have been greatly facilitated by the government's push toward digitization, leading to the rapid expansion of digital businesses across various sectors. This trend has particularly benefited startups, which are continually registering and offering new products and services through digital platforms, thus contributing to the growth of the sharing economy.[9] However, despite its potential benefits, the sharing economy in India faces regulatory challenges, particularly in sectors, such as transportation and accommodation.[10]

One notable development in the transportation sector is the Indian government's efforts to amend the Motor Vehicles Act to regulate cab aggregators like Ola and Uber more effectively. The existing provisions of the Act are deemed insufficient to oversee the operations of these aggregators, prompting the authorities to consider new legislation that includes provisions for driver verification, GPS installation, and other safety measures. Similarly, in the accommodation sector, while platforms like Airbnb and Oyo Rooms have gained popularity, concerns persist regarding the quality of service and safety standards offered by smaller room aggregators.[11] Issues, such as misinformation, lack of transparency, and unauthorized accommodations, pose significant challenges, necessitating appropriate government regulations to address them.

Moreover, the growth of the sharing economy in India is reflected in the increasing acceptance of innovative business models in sectors, such as transport, hospitality, and co-working spaces. Uber, Airbnb, and Oyo Rooms have emerged as key players, leveraging technology to connect service providers with consumers. For instance, Airbnb, founded in 2008, has expanded globally, offering accommodations in 190 countries, while Oyo Rooms, a homegrown startup, has focused on providing

[9] PWC Hungary, *Sharing or paring? Growing of the sharing economy* (2013), https://www.pwc.com/hu/en/kiadvanyok/assets/pdf/sharing-economy-en.pdf.

[10] V.A. Platnikov & Y.A. Anisimova, *The Sharing Economy: Concept, Features and Development*, RUSSIAN PRESIDENTIAL ACADEMY OF NATIONAL ECONOMY, Issue 1,42,44 (2023).

[11] Sakshi Shairwal, *Regulation for Ola & Uber under Motor Vehicle Act- An understanding*, LEXOLOGY (2022).

affordable yet quality accommodations, backed by substantial funding and expansion plans.[12] Similarly, Uber has revolutionized the transportation sector with its ride-sharing services, exemplifying the potential of the sharing economy model in India.

The Indian government's Startup India initiative, launched in 2016, aims to foster an ecosystem conducive to innovation and entrepreneurship, thereby driving economic growth and employment opportunities.[13] However, a critical analysis of the initiative reveals certain shortcomings, particularly in terms of intellectual property protection and collaboration platforms for startups. While measures, such as the Startup Intellectual Property Protection (SIPP) scheme, aim to facilitate IP registration for startups, the emphasis on IP production overlooks the role of startups as consumers of intellectual property.[14] Additionally, initiatives for fostering collaboration and infrastructure development lack inclusivity, raising questions about accessibility and equitable opportunities for all stakeholders.

Furthermore, the growth of the sharing economy in India has significant implications for employment, with the gig economy witnessing a surge in gig jobs. Platforms like Ola, Uber, Swiggy, and Zomato offer flexible work opportunities, particularly for unemployed youth seeking low-cost, low-investment labor options. However, the classification of workers as "partners" or "mini-entrepreneurs" by these platforms raises concerns about accountability and social security.[15] The lack of comprehensive social security, coupled with stagnant real incomes and rising living costs, has driven many individuals, especially young people, toward platform-based gig work as a means of survival.

Hence, while the sharing economy holds immense potential for driving economic growth and innovation in India, regulatory challenges, and labor issues must be addressed to ensure sustainable development and inclusive growth. Effective regulation, collaborative initiatives, and equitable opportunities are essential for harnessing the full potential of the sharing economy while safeguarding the interests of all stakeholders.[16]

---

[12] Simon Mundy & Shannon Bond, *Airbnb invests $100 Mn in Indian Hotel Startuo OYO*, FT, April 1 (2019).

[13] SUPERSCOUT, https://superscout.co/hub/new-delhi (last visited Mar. 21, 2024).

[14] IP India, *Scheme for Facilitating Start-Ups Intellectual Property Protection (SIPP)* (2023), https://ipindia.gov.in/writereaddata/Portal/News/885_1_approved_SIPP_scheme.pdf.

[15] Niti Aayog, *India's booming gig & Platform economy* (2022), https://www.niti.gov.in/sites/default/files/2022-06/Policy_Brief_India%27s_Booming_Gig_and_Platform_Economy_27062022.pdf.

[16] Fourier Agency Inc., *Navigating Insurance Issues in the sharing economy* (2023), https://www.fourrieragency.com/blog/navigating-insurance-issues-in-the-sharing-economy.aspx.

3.2 *Sharing Economy in USA*

In the United States, the emergence of the sharing economy has presented both opportunities and challenges, particularly in the realm of taxation and regulation. While sharing economy services have transformed traditional industries and provided flexible opportunities for workers, they have also raised questions regarding compliance with tax laws and regulatory frameworks. Shu-Yi Oei and Diane Ring have observed that while sharing economy services pose enforcement challenges, they generally do not challenge the fundamental concepts of tax law. This consensus is evident in various reports, including those from the OECD, the EU Commission, and the FTC.[17]

Regarding taxation, there is a growing recognition that platform-based services should contribute to public revenue and be subject to the same taxes as other services.[18] The EU Commission's communication emphasizes the need for sharing economy services to comply with taxation regulations, while the FTC staff report acknowledges the consensus that platforms like Airbnb should be subject to local hotel taxes.[19] However, there is disagreement over the adequacy of tax collection efforts by these platforms, highlighting the need for clearer guidelines and enforcement mechanisms.

One of the defining features of sharing economy platforms in the US is their flexibility, particularly for contractors. These platforms, often referred to as "digital matching firms," leverage technology and user ratings to provide self-employed workers with flexible schedules. The number of independent contractors working via such firms has skyrocketed in recent years, reflecting the significant growth and valuation of companies like Uber. While these platforms offer flexibility and lower costs for consumers, they also raise concerns about worker rights and regulatory compliance.

The low entry barrier for workers in the sharing economy, particularly in sectors like transportation, has led to demographic shifts and changes in employment patterns. Compared to traditional taxi drivers, Uber drivers are generally younger and better educated, reflecting the appeal of flexible gig work among certain demographics.[20] However, there are disparities in earnings and access to benefits, raising questions about the long-term sustainability of gig work as a primary source of income.[21]

---

[17] Aqib Aslam & Alpa Shah, *Taxation and Peer-to-Peer Economy*, IMF, Digital Revolutions in Public Finance (2017).

[18] Vito Tanzi, Howell Zee, *Tax Policies for developing countries*, IMF, 27 (2018).

[19] Isabel Teixera Nadkarni, *Sharing economy: Parliament for clear EU guidelines* (2017), https://www.europarl.europa.eu/news/en/press-room/20170609IPR77014/sharing-economy-parliament-calls-for-clear-eu-guidelines.

[20] *Id* at 8.

[21] ILO et al., *Providing adequate and sustainable social protection for workers in the gig and platform economy* (2021), https://www.ilo.org/wcmsp5/groups/public/dgreports/documents/publication/wcms_867535.pdf.

Regulatory challenges abound in the sharing economy, with platforms often operating in a gray area between existing laws and regulations. The rapid expansion of companies like Uber and Airbnb has prompted legal battles and debates over issues, such as worker classification, safety regulations, and liability. While some argue that existing regulations are burdensome and anti-competitive, others call for greater oversight and accountability to protect consumers and workers.

In the realm of housing, the blurring of boundaries between home-sharing and traditional accommodation has raised legal and regulatory questions.[22] Cities like New York and San Francisco have implemented regulations to address issues, such as zoning laws, occupancy taxes, and registration requirements for home-sharing platforms. Legal battles, such as the lawsuit between Airbnb and the city of San Francisco,[23] highlight the complex legal landscape surrounding the sharing economy.

Overall, the sharing economy in the United States presents both opportunities and challenges for policymakers, businesses, and workers. While it has the potential to drive innovation, create jobs, and lower costs for consumers, it also raises concerns about taxation, regulation, and worker rights. Achieving a balance between fostering innovation and ensuring compliance with existing laws will be crucial in shaping the future of the sharing economy in the US.

4 How Can Property Law Be Improved to Better Support the Sharing Economy?

As the sharing economy becomes an integral part of modern business, adapting property law is crucial to foster its growth. An effective approach involves crafting specialized legal frameworks tailored to the unique dynamics of the sharing economy. These frameworks should address key facets, such as liability, insurance, and taxation, offering a clear and comprehensive legal structure for individuals engaged in sharing their property. Encouraging collaboration among regulators, industry stakeholders, and consumers is equally paramount. This collaborative effort can identify and navigate legal challenges in a manner that ensures fairness and equity for all parties involved. The transformative potential of the sharing economy extends to reshaping how we live and work. To fully unlock this potential, property law must evolve, creating frameworks that not only accommodate but actively support the sharing economy. By embracing collaboration, addressing legal challenges, and enhancing frameworks around liability and insurance, property law can play a pivotal role in nurturing the continued growth and success of the sharing economy in the years ahead.

---

[22] Badger, E., *Airbnb is about to start collecting hotel taxes in more major cities, including Washington* (2015).

[23] Maria Denzio, *San Francisco, Airbnb settle dispute over short-term rental law*, COURT HOUSE NEWS SERVICE (2017).

5 Conclusion

The evolution of laws and legal practices within the sharing economy reflects a dynamic global shift toward a more decentralized and interconnected economic landscape. As nations grapple with the challenges and opportunities presented by this emerging paradigm, it becomes evident that the legal frameworks must adapt to ensure equitable and efficient regulation. Across various jurisdictions, including India, the proliferation of digital platforms and peer-to-peer transactions has reshaped traditional notions of commerce, necessitating a comprehensive reevaluation of regulatory structures.

In India, a nation poised to harness the potential of the sharing economy amidst its burgeoning middle class and increasing smartphone penetration, the imperative for clear and adaptable legal frameworks is paramount. While the government has taken significant strides in improving the ease of doing business, there remains a pressing need to provide clarity and guidance for participants in the access and sharing economy. Ambiguities within the current regulatory landscape can impede growth and innovation, hindering the sector's ability to realize its full potential.

Moreover, as the sharing economy continues to expand into diverse sectors, such as hospitality, transportation, and health care, the need for specialized regulatory frameworks becomes increasingly apparent. While traditional industries may be resistant to change, the emergence of digital platforms offering healthcare services underscores the transformative potential of the sharing economy across all facets of society.

One of the key challenges faced by regulators is striking a balance between fostering innovation and protecting consumers' rights and interests. The rapid pace of technological advancement often outpaces the development of regulatory frameworks, leading to uncertainty and potential legal loopholes. Collaborative efforts between industry stakeholders, tech pioneers, and policymakers are essential to navigate these complexities and ensure that regulations remain relevant and effective in safeguarding the interests of all parties involved.

Furthermore, the sharing economy presents unique opportunities for developing trust networks and leveraging new technologies to enhance transparency and accountability. By embracing 12 innovative solutions, such as blockchain and decentralized platforms, India can position itself as a leader in fostering a resilient and inclusive sharing economy ecosystem.

In conclusion, the evolution of laws and legal practices within the sharing economy reflects a paradigm shift toward a more decentralized and interconnected economic model. As India and other nations navigate this transformative landscape, it is imperative to prioritize the development of clear, adaptable, and equitable regulatory frameworks. By fostering collaboration between industry stakeholders and policymakers and embracing innovative technologies, India can harness the full potential of the sharing economy to drive economic growth and societal development in the years to come.

The manufacturer's authorised representative in the EU is Springer Nature Customer Service Centre GmbH, Europaplatz 3, 69115 Heidelberg, Germany. If you have any concerns regarding our products, please contact ProductSafety@springernature.com

Printed and bound by CPI Group (UK) Ltd, Croydon, CR0 4YY
01/10/2026
02225858-0017